"The authors provide a masterful synthesis of the teaching of the Messiah in the Old Testament, the context of Judaism, and in the New Testament. By intentionally addressing the contextual, canonical, messianic, and christological readings of all the key texts, and asserting how these grew and developed in their interpretation into the Christian era, these three scholars, each with expertise in expounding the message of the relevant texts, provide the reader with a clear path for understanding the fulfillment of the messianic expectation in Jesus Christ as more than just a collection of diverse prophecies. The work demonstrates the messianic message as woven through the text of Scripture and finding unique fulfillment in Jesus of Nazareth. This is the most useful work to date on the subject."

—Richard S. Hess,
Earl S. Kalland Professor of Old Testament and Semitic Languages,
Denver Seminary

"Many lay readers of Scripture and scholars have been waiting for a book like this, which sets a new standard and establishes a new method for exploring themes in biblical theology. The authors systematically examine the written evidence for the growth of the messianic hope in Israel, exploring in order the witness of the First Testament, Jewish writings from the second temple period, and the New Testament. Resisting the impulse to impose later visions of the Messiah upon earlier texts, they have offered a fair and balanced picture of a gradually revealed but vibrant and persistent thread of biblical belief. Thoroughly researched, logically organized, and lavishly illustrated, this volume represents the finest full length treatment of the subject available."

—Daniel Block,
Gunther H. Knoedler Professor of Old Testament,
Wheaton College

"I like the authors' distinction between a text's original, contextual meaning and the canonical significance ultimately given to it, and their progression from Old Testament to New via second temple Jewish literature."

—Leslie C. Allen,
Senior Professor of Old Testament,
Fuller Theological Seminary

"Bateman, Bock, and Johnston have definitely filled a gaping hole in this crucial area with their new work and done so artfully while specializing in their respective fields—Old Testament, second temple literature, and New Testament. It is about time we have a detailed discussion on this important area from evangelical scholars bridging this whole time period. Their discussions are nuanced and carefully worded, avoiding many pitfalls of either extremes and yet providing a very readable and clear work. Especially helpful is their progressive development in which they have highlighted crucial themes related to the Messiah throughout the biblical and non-canonical works. Whether one agrees or disagrees with all of their conclusions, there is no doubt that they have provided a workable, clear foundation in this area that will spawn many lively discussions into the future."

—Paul D. Wegner,
Professor of Old Testament,
Golden Gate Baptist Theological Seminary

JESUS
THE
MESSIAH

Tracing the Promises, Expectations, and Coming of Israel's King

HERBERT W. BATEMAN IV
DARRELL L. BOCK
GORDON H. JOHNSTON

Jesus the Messiah: Tracing the Promises, Expectations, and Coming of Israel's King

© 2012 by Herbert W. Bateman IV, Darrell L. Bock, and Gordon H. Johnston

Published by Kregel Publications, a division of Kregel, Inc., P.O. Box 2607, Grand Rapids, MI 49501.

This is available in digital format at www. kregel.com.

All scripture quotations, unless otherwise indicated, are taken from the NET Bible® copyright ©1996-2006 by Biblical Studies Press, L.L.C. www.bible.org All rights reserved.

Maps are from the *Kregel Bible Atlas* by Tim Dowley, copyright © 2003 Angus Hudson Ltd./ Tim Dowley & Peter Wyart trading as Three's Company. Used by permission.

Library of Congress Cataloging-in-Publication Data

Bateman, Herbert W., 1955-
   Jesus the Messiah : tracing the promises, expectations, and coming of Israel's King / Herbert W. Bateman IV, Darrell L. Bock, Gordon H. Johnston.
     p. cm.
    Includes indexes.
   1. Jesus Christ—Person and offices. I. Bock, Darrell L. II. Johnston, Gordon H., 1959– III. Title.
   BT203.B38 2010
   232'.8—dc22

            2010028702

ISBN 978-0-8254-2109-9

Printed in the United States of America
12 13 14 15 16 / 5 4 3 2 1

To
Sally Bock,
Danielle Johnston,
and Cindy Bateman
Thank you, ladies

CONTENTS

ACKNOWLEDGMENTS

It was a pleasure to accept Herb Bateman's invitation to contribute to this volume. The collaboration is special for me because I was a professor to both Herb and Gordon. Our families have grown up together. In fact, Gordon and I attend the same church even today. The ideas we write about reflect decades of discussion between us all. They represent a way of putting the messianic puzzle together that makes sense out of what we have in the Testaments from both a historical and canonical point of view. Our hope is that this piecing together of the puzzle proves helpful to our readers.

Special thanks goes to the students and faculty I have had over the years on the use of the Old Testament in the New, including Don Glenn, Ken Barker, and Eugene Merrill, who taught me Hebrew and Old Testament. Howard Marshall, Harold Hoehner, and Martin Hengel have been the greater influences in my reading of the New Testament, while Elliott Johnson has been another wonderful conversation partner in all of this.

My deepest appreciation goes to my wife, Sally, who has had to endure many "conversations" on topics that look back centuries in history. Her faithfulness has been most appreciated, as has her understanding and support.

—Darrell L. Bock

In some publications, an author's acknowledgement is perfunctory; in my case, it is certainly sincere. Many scholars have shaped my thoughts on messianic prophecy and interpretation, but I want to acknowledge the profound impact of three of my former teachers/mentors at Dallas Theological Seminary: Professors Donald R. Glenn, Robert B. Chisholm Jr., and Darrell L. Bock.

It has been a delight to write this book with Darrell and Herb. Years ago Darrell first opened my eyes to the dynamics of messianic prophecy and interpretation in his doctoral course, "Christological Interpretation of the Old Testament," which he team taught with Don Glenn. Thus, this project represents something of the completion of a circle. Herb and I shared many great times together as doctoral students, then as junior professors getting started in our respective institutions. All three of us have shared many moments of laughter over the years. It has been a delight to work on a project with two good friends; they have sharpened my thinking throughout this project.

Words cannot express my appreciation to Danielle for her constant encouragement and more than occasional urging to finish already! Our three children—Bergen, Grey, Heath—are the joy of our lives, and the reason grappling with the Messiah is so important. May they continue to love Jesus and walk with him all the days of their lives!

—Gordon Johnston

Of all the books I have published, I am most excited about *Jesus the Messiah: Tracing the Promises, Expectations, and Coming of Israel's King.* First, the book includes work by two men with whom I have had a relationship with for well over twenty years, Gordon H. Johnston and Darrell L. Bock. Although it has taken since May 2001 to complete this project, we've enjoyed the process of writing, dialoguing, and promoting the work at conferences and colloquiums. (I must admit, however, we often asked ourselves which would come first: the completion of this book about Jesus the Messiah or the second coming of Jesus the Messiah.)

Second, it is always an honor to work with my mentor, Darrell Bock. Moving beyond my dissertation, *Jewish and Apostolic Hermeneutics: How the Old Testament Is Used in Hebrews 1:5–13* (1993), the second project we worked on together was *Three Central Issues in Contemporary Dispensationalism: A Comparison of Traditional and Progressive Views* (1999). In many respects, this book is a broader and yet further development of a hermeneutical approach presented in both of those two works. I owe a great debt of gratitude to Darrell as well as Don Glenn who first introduced me to this hermeneutical field of study as well as those who introduced and further refined my understanding of the history and literature of the second temple period: Gordon Ceperly (Philadelphia Biblical University), Hal Roning (Jerusalem University College in Israel), Harold Hoehner (Dallas Theological Seminary), and James VanderKam (Notre Dame).

Special thanks must go Jim Weaver and the Kregel staff who are always a delight to work with and deserving of many thanks. However, my deepest gratitude is reserved for my wife of over thirty years. She is forever committed to and supportive of the ministries I accept. Such support includes writing projects like this one that always appear to demand more of us than is initially expected. Thank you, Cindy, for the patience, support, and encouragement you extended to me so that this book might reach the press.

—Herbert W. Bateman IV

ABBREVIATIONS

Ancient Near Eastern Sources

AEL	Miriam Lichteim, *Ancient Egyptian Literature*, 3 volumes (Berkeley: University of California Press, 1973–80).
ANET 3	James B. Pritchard, ed., *Ancient Near Eastern Texts Relating to the Old Testament*, Third Edition. Princeton: Princeton University Press, 1969.
AR	Adolf Erman, *Die ägyptische religion*, Handbücher der Königlichen museen zu Berlin. Berlin: G. Reimer, 1905.
ARE	James Henry Breasted, *Ancient Records of Egypt: Historical Documents*, Volume II: The Eighteenth Dynasty. New York: Russell & Russell, 1906.
COS	W.W. Hallo and K. Lawson Younger, Jr., eds., *The Context of Scripture, Volume 1: Canonical Compositions from the Biblical World*. Leiden/Boston: E.J. Brill, 2003.
SAA 9	Simo Parpola, *Assyrian Prophecies*, State Archives of Assyria 9 (Helsinki: Helsinki University Press, 1997.
TAPE	William J. Murnane, *Texts from the Amarna Period in Egypt*, Writings from the Ancient World, Volume 5. Atlanta: Scholars Press, 1995.

Apocrypha and Pseudepigrapha Sources

1 Esdr	First Esdras
2 Esdr	Second Esdras
Tob	Tobit
Bel	Bel and the Dragon
Jdt	Judith
Wis	Wisdom of Solomon
Sir	Wisdom of Jesus the Son of Sirach (Ecclesiasticus)
1 Macc	First Maccabees
2 Macc	Second Maccabees
3 Macc	Third Maccabees
4 Macc	Fourth Maccabees
Barn.	*Epistle of Barnabas*
Ep. Arist.	*Epistle of Aristeas*
Jub.	*Jubilees*
Odes Sol.	*Odes of Solomon*

1En.	*1 Enoch (Ethiopic Apocalypse)*	
Poly *Hist*	Polybius *History*	
Pss. Sol.	*Psalms of Solomon*	
Sib. Or.	*Sibylline Oracles*	
T. Adam	*Testament of Adam*	
T. Ash.	*Testament of Asher*	
T. Gad	*Testament of Gad*	
T. Iss.	*Testament of Issachar*	
T. Jud.	*Testament of Judah*	
T. Levi	*Testament of Levi*	
T. Naph.	*Testament of Naphtali*	
T. Reu.	*Testament of Reuben*	
T. 12 Patr.	*Testaments of the Twelve Patriarchs*	
T. Sol.	*Testament of Solomon*	

Qumran Sources

CD	*Damascus Document*	
1QM	*1QWar Scroll*	
1Q28	1QS	*1QRule of the Community*
1Q28a	1QSa	*1QRule of the Congregation*
1Q28b	1QSb	*1QRule of Blessings*
1Q30		
4Q161	4QpIsaa	*4QIsaiah Peshera*
4Q171		
4Q174	4QFlor	*4QFlorilegium*
4Q175	4QTest	*4QTestimonia*
4Q246	4QpsDan ar	*4QAramaic Apocalypse*
4Q252	4Q*comm*Gena	*4QCommentary on Genesis A*
4Q266	4QDa	*4QDamascus Documenta*
4Q285	4QSM	*4QSefer ha-Milhamah*
4Q287		
4Q369	4QPEnosh	*4QPrayer of Enosh*
4Q375		
4Q376	4QapocrMosesb	*4QApocryphon of Mosesb*
3Q377		
4Q382	*4QParaphrase of the Kings*	
4Q423	*4QInstructiong*	
4Q458	*4QNarrative A*	
4Q496	4QMf	*4QWar Scrollf*
4Q521	*4QMessianic Apocalypse*	
11Q13	11Q*Melch*	*11QMelchizedek*

Josephus

Ant	*Antiquities*
Ap	*Against Apion*
War	*Jewish Wars*

Periodical

AUSS	*Andrews University Seminary Studies*
BBR	*Bulletin and Biblical Research*
BibTo	*Bible Today*
Bib	*Biblica*
BI	*Biblical Illustrator*
BSac	*Bibliotheca Sacra*
BT	*The Bible Translator*
BZ	*Biblische Zeitschrift*
BZAW	*Beihefte zur Zeitschrift für die alttestamentliche Wissenschaft*
CTJ	*Calvin Theological Journal*
CBQ	*Catholic Biblical Quarterly*
CJP	*Cambridge Journal of Philology*
ConJ	*Concordia Journal*
CurBS	*Currents in Biblical Research*
DBSJ	*Detroit Baptist Seminary Journal*
DSD	*Dead Sea Discoveries*
ErIsr	*Eretz Israel*
ETL	*Ephemerides theologicae lovanieness*
ExAud	*Ex Auditu*
GTJ	*Grace Theological Journal*
GOTR	*Greek Orthodox Theological Review*
HTR	*Harvard Theological Review*
HvTSt	*Hervormde Teologiese Stud*
Int	*Interpretation*
JBQ	*Jewish Bible Quarterly*
JAOS	*Journal of the American Oriental Society*
JATS	*Journal of the Adventist Theological Society*
JBL	*Journal of Biblical Literature*
JETS	*Journal of the Evangelical Theological Society*
JhebS	*The Journal of Hebrew Scriptures*
JJS	*Journal of Jewish Studies*
JNSL	*Journal of Northwest Semitic Languages*
JSNT:Sup	*Journal for the Study of the New Testament: Supplement Series*
JSOT	*Journal for the Study of the Old Testament*
JSP	*Journal for the Study of the Pseudepigrapha*
NovT	*Novum Testamentum*
NTS	*New Testament Studies*

OTE	*Old Testament Essays*
Or	*Orientalia*
PEQ	*Palestine Exploration Quarterly*
PQ	*Philological Quarterly*
PRSt	*Perspectives in Religious Studies*
RevQ	*Revue de Qumran*
RTR	*Reformed Theological Review*
SJOT	*Scandinavian Journal of the Old Testament*
SR	*Studies in Religion*
SWJT	*Southwestern Journal of Theology*
STRev	*Sewanee Theological Review*
TJ	*Trinity Journal*
TynBull	*Tyndale Bulletin*
UF	*Ugarit Forschungen*
VT	*Vetus Testamentum*
WTJ	*Westminster Theological Journal*
ZAW	*Zeitschrift für die alttestamentliche Wissenschaft*
ZNW	*Zeitschrift für die Neutestamentliche Wissenschaft*

Reference

ABD	*Anchor Bible Dictionary.* Edited by D.N. Feedman. 6 vols. New York, 1992.
BAGD	Walter Bauer, William F. Arndt, F. Wilbur Gingrich, and Frederick W. Danker. *A Greek–English Lexicon of the New Testament and Other Early Christian Literature.* Second Edition. Chicago and London: University of Chicago Press, 1979.
BDAG	Walter Bauer, Frederick W. Danker, William F. Arndt, and F. Wilbur Gingrich. *A Greek–English Lexicon of the New Testament and Other Early Christian Literature.* Third Edition. Chicago and London: University of Chicago Press, 2000.
BDB	Brown, Francis and S. R. Driver, and Charles A. Briggs, *The New Brown-Driver-Briggs-Gesenius Hebrew and English Lexicon.* Original publication: Oxford: Clarendon Press, 1907; reprint; Peabody: Hendrickson, 1996.
DJD	*Dictionary of Jesus and the Gospels.* Edited by J. B. Green and S. McKnight. Downers Grove, 1997.
EncDSS	*Encyclopaedia of the Dead Sea Scrolls.* Edited by L. H. Schiffman and J. C. VanderKam. 2 vols. New York, 2000.
EncJud	*Encyclopaedia Judaica.* 16 vols. Jerusalem, 1972.

| *HALOT* | Koehler, Ludwig; Walter Baumgartner, Johann Jakob Stamm. *The Hebrew and Aramaic Lexicon of the Old Testament.* 2 Volumes (Leiden/Boston: E.J. Brill, 2002). |
| *ISBE* | *The International Standard Biblical Encyclopaedia.* Ed. by G. W. Bromiley. 4 vols. Grand Rapids, 1979–1988. |

Series

AB	Anchor Bible
ANTC	Abingdon New Testament Commentaries
BECNT	Baker Exegetical Commentary on the New Testament
CBC	Cornerstone Biblical Commentary
CBQMS	Catholic Biblical Quarterly Monograph Series
DJD	Discoveries in the Judean Desert
EKKNT	Evangetisches Handbuch zum Altern Testament
EUS	European University Studies
HDR	Harvard Dissertations in Religion
ICC	The International Critical Commentary
IVPNT	IVP New Testament Commentaries (IVP)
NCB	New Century Bible Commentary
NIBCNT	New International Biblical Commentary on the New Testament
NICNT	New International Commentary on the New Testament
NICOT	New International Commentary on the Old Testament
NIDNTT	*New International Dictionary of the New Testament Theology*
NIDOTTE	*New International Dictionary of the Old Testament Theology*
NIGTC	New International Greek Testament Commentary
NTL	New Testament Library
SBLD	Society of Biblical Literature Dissertation Series
SNTSMS	Society for New Testament Studies Monograph Series
TDOT	*Theological Dictionary of the Old Testament*
TWOT	*Theological Wordstudy of the Old Testament*
WBC	Word Biblical Commentary
WUNT	Wissenschaftliche Untersuchungen zum Neuen Testament

Translations

ESV	English Standard Version
KJV	King James Version
LXX	Septuagint
MT	Masoretic Text
NASB	New American Standard Bible
NCV	New Century Version
NET	New English Translation
NIB	New Interpreter's Bible
NIRV	The New International Reader's Version (NIrV)

NIV	The New International Version
NLT	New Living Translation
NRSV	New Revised Standard Version
REB	Revised English Bible
RSV	Revised Standard Version
TEV	Today's English Version
TNIV	Today's New International Version

General

BCE	Before the Common Era (equivalent to B.C.)
CE	Common Era (equivalent to A.D.)
NT	New Testament
OT	Old Testament

INTRODUCTION

Herbert W. Bateman IV

Without question, Jesus is an unsurpassed, certainly an unequaled figure in human history. Belief in his life, death, and resurrection has transformed and even redirected world empires, cultures, and people. No one person has ever affected the world and its history like Jesus. And though the principle sources of information regarding Jesus' life and teachings are the Gospels (Matthew, Mark, Luke and John), Jesus has been the subject of personal and public letters, sermons and lectures, pamphlets and books, skits and plays, documentaries and movies. Identification with him can bring both positive and negative responses. Jesus can be both endearing and repelling. Thus Jesus has been and continues to be a worthy person to ponder. *Jesus the Messiah: Tracing the Promises, Expectations, and Coming of Israel's King* is yet another presentation about Jesus, more specifically a consideration about his messiahship. Who is Jesus, the Messiah?

Naturally our book about the messianic Jesus is not *totally* unique. Visit the religious section of a large bookstore or search online, and you will see an array of books about Jesus. Surprisingly, every book seems to have a different slant on Jesus. Some, for instance, do not consider Jesus' claim of Messiah and even minimize his Jewishness. They view him primarily through Greco-Roman lenses. For example, John Dominic Crossan creates a portrait of Jesus that envisions him as a Mediterranean Jewish peasant and cynic who lived like other itinerate cynics roaming the Greco-Roman world.[1] Jesus is, according to Crossan and a few others, a radical individual who advocates the avoidance of worldly entanglements and defies social conventions. His connection with his Jewish roots is clearly diminished.

---

1. John Dominic Crossan, *The Historical Jesus: The Life of a Mediterranean Jewish Peasant* (San Francisco: Harper Collins, Edinburgh: T & T Clark, 1991). For other works and advocates of this view, see Appendix A.

Others acknowledge Jesus' Jewishness but appear to ignore or reject his role as Messiah. He is a Jewish but non-messianic figure whose sole interest is social or religious reform. On the one hand, Theissen, Horsley, and Kaylor emphasize Jesus as a Jewish social reformer. On the other hand, Sanders Vermes, and Borg portray him as a religious reformer. Thus Jesus is some sort of Jewish reformer, yet non-messianic. Although his Jewishness is recognized, his claim of "Messiah" is minimized.

JESUS: A JEWISH NON-MESSIANIC REFORMER	
Social Reformer	**Major Proponent with a Selected Work**
Jesus: radical charismatic itinerant preacher of social reform	Gerd Theissen: *The Shadow of the Galilean* (1987)
Jesus: peasant prophet for radical social change.	Richard A. Horsley: *Jesus and the Spiral of Violence* (1987)
Jesus: political prophet for social reform	R. David Kaylor: *Jesus the Prophet* (1994)
Religious Reformer	**Major Proponent with a Selected Work**
Jesus: prophet of a Jewish eschatological restoration	E. P. Sanders: *The Historical Figure of Jesus* (1993)
Jesus: charismatic Jew	Geza Vermes: *The Religion of Jesus and the World of Judaism* (1984)
Jesus: charismatic, healer, sage, and prophet for social change	Marcus Borg: *Meeting Jesus Again for the First Time* (1994)

Still others portray Jesus as a Jewish Messiah, and yet ponder his messiahship. Numerous authors fall into this category. On the one hand, some stress that Jesus is a messianic prophet. Allison, Casey, Ehrman, and Meier portray Jesus as a prophet who speaks primarily about the future millennium or kingdom. Yet Fiorenza and Witherington spotlight Jesus as a messianic sage, a teaching messiah who speaks on many issues. On the other hand, Wright prefers to speak of Jesus as a Jewish Messiah of restoration. He is the one who will lead the nation of Israel out of exile. Others like Bockmuehl, de Jonge, and Stuhlmacher underscore various aspects of his messianic Sonship, namely whether that Sonship is Davidic, human, or divine.

JESUS: A JEWISH MESSIAH FIGURE[2]	
Messianic Prophet	**Major Proponent with a Selected Work**
Jesus: the millennium prophet	Dale C. Allison: *Jesus of Nazareth: Millenarian Prophet* (1991)
Jesus: eschatological or apocalyptic prophet	Maurice Casey: From *Jewish Prophet to Gentile God* (1991) Bart D. Ehrman: *Jesus: Apocalyptic Prophet of the New Millennium* (2001)
Jesus: eschatological prophet who ushers in the kingdom of God	John P. Meier: *A Marginal Jew: Rethinking the Historical Jesus*, 3 vols (1991, 1994, 1998, 2001)
Messianic Sage	**Major Proponent with a Selected Work**
Jesus: egalitarian sage	Elisabeth Schüssler Fiorenza: *Jesus: Miriam's Child, Sophia's Prophet Critical Issues in Feminist Christology* (1994)
Jesus: prophetic and eschatological sage	Ben Witherington III: *Jesus the Sage: The Pilgrimage of Wisdom* (1994)
Messianic Restorer	**Major Proponent with a Selected Work**
Jesus: eschatological Messiah who leads Israel out of exile	N.T. Wright, *Jesus and the Victory of God* (1996)
Messianic Son	**Major Proponent with a Selected Work**
Jesus: serving son of David	Marcus de Jonge: *Jesus, the Servant Messiah* (1991)
Jesus: martyred Son of Man	Markus Bockmuehl: *This Jesus: Martyr, Lord, Messiah* (1994)
Jesus: divine Son of Man	Peter Stuhlmacher: *Jesus of Nazareth—Christ of Faith* (1993)

---

2. For an overview and bibliography for each view, see Appendix A: "Contemporary Snapshots of Jesus."

Naturally, many of the proposed portraits about Jesus as a Jewish messiah have merit; some do not. While some strive to distance Jesus from his Jewish roots, others recognize and embrace those roots. Those who minimize Jesus' connection with his Jewishness and his cultural connection of his messiahship via the First Testament have limited value. For instance, some may claim that the identity of Jesus, his messiahship, and the nature of his redemptive work, was God's well-hidden mystery from ages past and only first clearly revealed in Jesus by his death, resurrection, and ascension. Jesus, it is pointed out, confided *only* to his inner circle that his true identity and nature of his mission was a divine secret—concealed from others, but revealed to them. Some lay inappropriate stress on Paul's assertion that the true nature of Jesus and his messianic mission was a divine mystery hidden from all ages past and only revealed by the death, resurrection, and ascension of Jesus. These sorts of claims not only underestimate, they also fail to fully appreciate a connection with the First Testament and thereby negate the element of progression in the revelation evident in the First Testament prophecies about the "messiah." Consequently many of these scholars underscore the capacity and creative work of human authors of Scripture and downplay and perhaps even disregard God's overarching involvement in redemptive history. We, however, do not.

Although this book neither critiques nor contributes *directly* to the selection of books listed above, we do ponder the same question: Who is Jesus, the Messiah? So in that sense there is some connection to the works introduced above. However, the scope of investigation in *Jesus the Messiah: Tracing the Promises, Expectations, and Coming of Israel's King* is much broader in that it traces God's promise of messiah as first presented in the Hebrew Scriptures, then reflected upon during the *latter portion* of the second temple period (often referred to as the "Intertestamental Period"), and finally fulfilled in the coming of Jesus.

FOUNDATIONS OF OUR APPROACH

Jesus the Messiah: Tracing the Promises, Expectations, and Coming of Israel's King offers contextual-canonical, messianic, and christological developments of God's promise of "messiah" within the larger framework and unfolding of Jewish history in canonical and extra-biblical literature. Naturally, the foundation upon which we build is with what Christians today call "the Old Testament." The books of "the Old Testament" were part of what was regarded by many Jews in Jesus' time as the sacred writings of their community. Our appeal to a canonical reading here, however, is distinct from its usual meaning today, which *assumes* a reading with the New Testament present. Consequently, when the books of the New Testament were being written, a New Testament as a collection of writings did not yet exist.[3] So

---

3. The earliest extant collection of the New Testament is p46 (200 CE), which includes most of Paul's writings and the book of Hebrews. The first extant manuscript to include

when someone asks, what Scriptures were read by those who wrote in the first century? The answer would be the Hebrew writings of the Jews. Their canonical and inspired works were the Hebrew Scriptures, what we Christians today call the Old Testament.

So in this book, *as a historical matter*, the term canonical refers to a reading that uses the sacred books of the Old Testament or Hebrew Scriptures, whether being read in the first century or even during the period when the First Testament was being completed. This is an important distinction to grasp because for us it is here in Hebrew Scriptures that any canonical reading, even in the broader sense used today of both Testaments, starts. In other words, when a person from the first century or earlier saw any of these theologically respected books depicting the promise of Israel and their hope, we will ask this question: how were passages of promise read in light of the whole while at the same time taking into account developments of promise within that First Testament? This is precisely how we will use the term canonical while also recognizing that today the canon Christians acknowledge contains a Second Testament (our New Testament) that completes the messianic picture. Thus, a significant point of our book is to argue how this portrait of messiah presented in both Testaments is gradually unfolded, yielding a *more* complete canonical portrait.

We must first ask the right questions and then respond to them. How did the First Testament portray the promise of messiah? Was the portrait of the messiah in the individual texts as *explicit* and clear to the original readers as it became later in the Psalms and the prophets or as a part of Jesus' work? Or was the full messianic potential of many passages more *implicit*, especially in the earliest passages, while the full legitimate Messianic meaning of these passages only became more explicit as more elements of this promise was revealed in later passages and subsequent Jewish history, whether from the First Testament or as a result of Jesus' own revelatory work? Does the First Testament reveal christological clarity at the moment each text was introduced?

Our complete answer to these questions is, yes, *eventually* a clear portrait emerges, but each inspired text is but a piece of a much larger puzzle where the entire portrait gains clarity as the other inspired pieces are assembled, granting more clarity to what initially was often only *implicitly visible* within a given literary piece. The promise was in the original wording, as we hope to

---

all 27 books of the New Testament is Sinaiticus (4 CE). It was Marcion (*ca.* 140 CE), the heretic, who compiled the very first "canonical" collection of New Testament works, which he limited to ten of Paul's writings and Luke's Gospel. Muratorian Canon (*ca.* 160–180) contains all 27 books of the New Testament. The point is simply this: when people were wrestling with Jesus as Messiah, the only "canonical" Testament they had was the Hebrew Scriptures. So, *we must be willing to travel back to a time in history* when the Old Testament canon of Scripture had yet to be *formally fixed* and the theological developments we find in the New Testament concerning God's Kingdom and God's Messiah were *not yet fully realized*.

show, but it also became gradually connected to other texts of promise and pattern as they were revealed reflecting back on the earlier text and giving it more context and clarity. Scripture assembles its doctrine as God inspires human authors to write it. God does not disclose everything at once, especially at the start. Seeing Scripture reveal itself progressively and with more detail and clarity is something the church has consistently affirmed. Thus, we seek to set forth one methodological model for how that progressive unfolding works and to show God's intentionality behind it. For the sake of illustration, the progress of messianic revelation is like pieces of a puzzle, a messianic puzzle of promise.

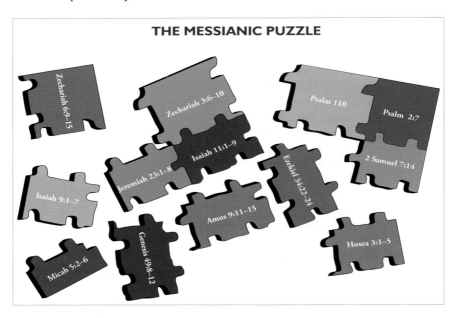

THE MESSIANIC PUZZLE

God provided pieces of the messianic puzzle very early in Jewish history. In the book of Genesis, God expressed it as a hope to Abraham, with links to ideas of the seed that go back to Adam, expressed initially in general terms. (For a focused treatment on Genesis 3:15, see the special appendix on this specific text.)[4] That same promise was given specifics in 2 Samuel when God

---

4. The christocentric interpretation of Genesis 3:15, known as the *Proto-Evangelion* enjoys a long tradition among Christian interpreters. Yet it tends to be understood in one of two ways: (1) it is the first hint of the gospel, as the seed of the woman will be victorious over the forces of evil the Serpent represents, namely, Satan; (2) there is no real hint of the gospel in the text. Whereas the first sees the most direct messianic fulfillment, the second merely introduces the conflict and the curse as a result of Eve's disobedience and thereby sees no real messianism nor messianic implication in the text. Because of these diverse perspectives, we will deal with the passage in the appendix.

provided assurances to David about his descendants. Unfortunately, these sacred writings (The Old Testament) close with no one on David's throne due to Nebuchadnezzar's invasion of Judah in 586 BCE when David's dynasty is dismantled.[5] Yet the prophets gave glimmers of hope for its restoration (e.g., Amos, Micah, Jeremiah, Ezekiel, Zechariah). This revelation progressed in the early sacred texts as the book of Daniel made clear. One day a human figure (the Son of Man) came with divine authority to establish God's kingdom and vindicate God's saints, completing the initial canonical picture of the hope of a deliverance for God's people (Daniel 2, 7, 9). Who exactly this figure was, where he fit, and how he connected to other pictures of deliverance opened up a discussion along with a host of views in Judaism that through our survey of the extra-biblical Jewish literature we shall show fueled the first century conversation about messianic hope.[6] Unlike those who underestimate or perhaps even reject the significance of Hebrew Scriptures for understanding Jesus the Messiah, our starting point *is* the Hebrew Scriptures because the sacred writings of the First Testament supply the essential pieces needed for joining and fitting together the scriptural puzzle about Messiah.

During the latter part of the second temple period (*circa* 100 BCE), people collected, pondered, and pieced together this messianic puzzle. Although some people appear indifferent (e.g., Ben Sirach and Josephus), others reflect on the scriptural puzzle and attempt to fit the pieces together (e.g., Qumran community). Gradually more and more scriptural pieces were linked together, in a variety of configurations, some of which the early Christians used and others which they rejected. The confusion these opinions introduced, as well as some of the helpful connections they saw in the Jewish sacred texts, are part of the early Christian conversation about Messiah and why Jesus handles the category of Messiah with as much care as he does. So by the time of Jesus, key elements were in place to make a unity of it all, something Jesus and the early church presented as a grand fusion of what God had said in Scripture and accomplished in Jesus. Jesus' teaching, life, death, resurrection, and ascension, therefore, complete the messianic puzzle.[7] Yet having

---

5. Some may question our use of BC–AD. or BCE–CE. We have opted to use the latter. The nomenclature began to change in the eighties and now BCE–CE tends to be the common practice in nearly all current biblical and second temple studies.

6. Why use the term "extra–biblical Jewish literature"? I prefer "second temple documents" but it lacks the needed separation from the Second Testament canonical works. So after some consideration, the description "extra–biblical" best communicates that later second temple texts of what is often called the intertestamental period are not read as inspired texts. Nevertheless, they contribute to the messianic ideas that are in play during Jesus' lifetime and during the time his followers write. Yet another good options used by Evans: "noncanonical." Craig A. Evans, *Noncanonical Writings and New Testament Interpretation* (Peabody: Hendrickson, 1992, 2nd printing 1995).

7. Darrell L. Bock first used the puzzle metaphor in "A Progressive Dispensational Hermeneutic" in *Three Central Issues in Contemporary Dispensationalism: A Comparison of Traditional and Progressive Views* (ed. Herbert W. Bateman IV; Grand Rapids: Kregel,

demonstrated that the foundation of our approach begins with the Hebrew Scriptures and thereby considers continuity with the Second Testament we might ask: How does our approach differ from other approaches that also begin with the Old Testament?

DIFFERENTIATING OUR APPROACH

Granted, our starting point is not unlike other approaches that acknowledge the value of Hebrew Scriptures (Old Testament) when discussing Messiah. Yet there is a difference. Many people today unfortunately fail to grapple with the human journey of discovery about "Messiah." Many preachers who preach sermons about Jesus as the Messiah often *over* emphasize their theological system with limited or even no consideration of any progress of revelation in human history. Others may read the text historically, often looking exclusively to the long-term reality. But in their quest for a *singular* historical-contextual meaning throughout all of Scripture, they argue that what a First Testament human author said about Messiah *equals* that which is stated about Jesus the Messiah in the Second Testament.[8] They tend to suggest that Jesus and the apostles assert that the Hebrew Scriptures testify *directly* and (or more importantly) *exclusively* about him. In their mind, the evangelists and epistolarists believe Moses foretold *only* the death of Jesus the Messiah; David foresaw *only* the resurrection of Jesus the Messiah; Isaiah predicted *only* Jesus' ascension into glory; and that Abraham heard *only* the Gospel to the Gentiles preached to him.[9] Thus, they stress the work of the

---

1999): 85–101; *idem.* "Single Meaning, Multiple Contexts and Referents" in *Three Views on the New Testament use of the Old Testament* Kenneth Berding and Jonathan Lunde, editors (Grand Rapids: Zondervan, 2007), 105–151.

8. See Walter C. Kaiser Jr., "The Single Intent of Scripture," in *Evangelical Roots: A Tribute to Wilbur Smith* (ed. Kenneth S. Kantzer; Nashville: Nelson, 1978), 123–41; *idem. The Uses of the Old Testament in the New* (Chicago: Moody, 1985); *idem.* "Single Meaning, Unified Referents," in *Three Views on the New Testament use of the Old Testament* (ed. Kenneth Berding and Jonathan Lunde; Grand Rapids: Zondervan, 2007), 45–89. Elliott E. Johnson, "A Traditional Dispensational Hermeneutic" in *Three Central Issues in Contemporary Dispensationalism,* 63–76. John H. Sailhamer, *Introduction to Old Testament Theology: A Canonical Approach* (Grand Rapids: Zondervan, 1995). For another discussion about Sailhamer see footnote #9 below.

9. As Fee and Stuart note, "The primary difficulty for most modern readers of the Prophets stems from an inaccurate prior understanding of the word 'prophecy.' For most people this word means what appears as the first definition in most dictionaries: 'Foretelling or prediction of what is to come.' It often happens, therefore, that many Christians refer to the prophetic books *only* for predictions about the coming of Jesus and/or certain features of the new-covenant age—as though prediction of events far distant from their own day was the main concern of the prophets. In fact, using the prophets in this way is highly selective. Consider the following statistics: Less than 2 percent of Old Testament prophecy is messianic. Less than 5 percent specifically describes the New Covenant age. Less than 1 percent concerns events yet to come." Gordon D. Fee and Douglas Stuart, *How to the Bible Book by Book: A Guided Tour* (Grand Rapids: Zondervan, 1993), 165–66.

divine author and thereby over emphasize an *unambiguous continuity* between the Testaments. The idea is that most or all of these texts need to be direct prophecies to work for Jesus being the messianic fulfillment in the way the Second Testament describes. Thus the argument is this: Jesus the Messiah is explicitly present very early on in a model that more often than not argues for direct prophecy in many specific First Testament texts, often exclusively directed at Jesus. There is but one single, *unambiguous* meaning concerning Messiah and that all authors, human and divine, are unified as to who that referent is. Clearly, they argue, he is Jesus.[10]

We, however, will offer a slightly different approach. Granted, there is most certainly a link, but we will argue, just *not a completely exclusive one*. One of our goals is to argue that these texts do not need to be *only* direct prophecies for them to reveal a messianic connections and fulfillment in Jesus. Such an *explicit-exclusive reading* of the First Testament tends to ignore the complexities of Jewish history as well as God's revelation and its progress. Such an explicit reading deprives us of historical information that ultimately helps us grasp what was going on in the lives of the Jewish people and what God's revelation told them about their present and future. While a traditional approach argues for *explicit predictions* about Jesus, we suggest that while the wording is *ultimately* messianic, it is often more implicitly stated and becomes clearer *only* as the entirety of God's portrait of messiah is eventually and fully disclosed, both by how the First Testament concludes and by what Jesus himself does to pull all the messianic pieces together.[11] What we mean to convey is

---

10. For a presentation and evaluation of four Evangelical approaches about the use of the First Testament in the Second Testament see Darrell L. Bock, "Evangelicals and the Use of the Old Testament in the New: Part 1." *BSac* 142 (July–September 1985): 209–23; "Evangelicals and the Use of the Old Testament in the New: Part 2." *BSac* 142 (October–December 1985): 206–19.
11. See Wolter H. Rose, "Messiah," in *Dictionary of the Old Testament: Pentateuch* (ed. T. Desmond Alexander and David W. Baker Downers Grove: InterVarsity Press, 2003),

simply this: *not all prophecy is exclusively pointing to Jesus,* just ultimately. Such a reading alerts us to the noteworthy reality of the dynamic nature of *pattern* and *prophecy* in Scripture, its progressive nature of revelation, and its various longitudinal trajectories across human history. Reading First Testament texts as though they are exclusively about Jesus ignores the prefiguring portraits that are also significant pieces of the puzzle that have to be both recognized and appreciated as we look from this side of Jesus' resurrection and exaltation.

Another way to say this is that we arrive at the same conclusion as these more traditional readings in terms of their being fulfillments in Jesus, but we take a different route to get there. The method we propose honors the clues in the original texts and aspects of their original meaning for the near historical context into which they were written. In essence, we have chosen to pause, ponder, and present God's gradual disclosure of his kingdom program preserved in God's inspired Scripture and written by people living in the midst of and wrestling with divinely directed historical events. Thus we adopt a threefold reading strategy of Scripture that is first contextual–canonical, then messianic, and finally christological.

DEFINING OUR APPROACH

As noted above, our commitment is to neither under estimate nor over emphasize the connection between the two Testaments. In order to follow through with that desire, we evaluate the text, using three criteria: first contextual–canonical, then messianic, and finally christological. So what does this all mean? With contextual-canonical, we express how the earliest testament in part and whole generated such promises in the context of the progress of revelation. By messianic, we conclude how these messianic options were being contemplated by Jews through messianic reflection as we enter the time of Jesus. The choice of messianic here does not imply that there was no messianic hope coming out of the First Testament because it is the messianic and eschatological hope of that Testament that is generating the various views. Nor will we say that all these Jewish options are of equal value. Some of them were a part of the early Christian discussion and others were rejected by them. With christological, we consider how Jesus and the earliest church put all of this together into a coherent portrait that they also saw as revelatory about the promise as they entered into the debate over the various options, affirming some elements, rejecting others, and adding fresh emphases of their own. The burden of this book is the demonstration of this threefold reading

---

565–568. Sydney Greidanus, in *Preaching Christ from the Old Testament* (Eerdmans 1999, 276), suggests seven different ways of preaching Christ from the Old Testament: "redemptive–historical progression, promise–fulfillment, typology, analogy, longitudinal themes, Second Testament references, and contrast." Rather than simply referring to "messianic prophecies" in general, it is helpful to point out that there are numerous ways in which the Old Testament paves the way for the recognition of Jesus as Israel's deliverer, hope, and messiah.

strategy as fundamental for making sense of Jesus' and the early church's messianic claim.

In the *promises* of Israel's king (part one), we address the contextual-canonical reading of the First Testament.[12] In a contextual reading, the interpreter seeks to understand the First Testament passage in its original historical setting. This is an important first and often neglected step when discussing God's promise of Messiah in the Hebrews Scriptures. Here, we are especially concentrating on what the original human author meant and understood in his original historical setting. Furthermore, we focus on the exegetical meaning of a passage within its immediate theological and literary context. Thus, we read the passage as an ancient Hebrew in the light of his historical background, antecedent theology, and literary context. While at the same time, we also pay attention to how the wording of God's promises have *potential* for development long term.

In a canonical reading the interpreter takes into account the progress of revelation. Although any passage has a particular referential meaning in its original context, many biblical themes are not static but dynamic in the gradual historical unfolding of Scripture. In the progress of biblical revelation, God develops theological themes across time and in history. In other words, in a canonical reading we consider our passage from the perspective of a wider context—the final canonical form of the Hebrew Scriptures.

The focus on the First Testament as a whole and the unfolding of its messianic portrait will help to set up both what was discussed in the latter part of the second temple period (beginning *circa* 167 BCE) and what Jesus does with all of these options as he assessed them both pro and con. Initial statements made by human authors allow the principle of God's design and activity to be appealed to again at a later historical moment. Patterns of application of God's promise become clearer as salvation history unfolds in the sacred texts and as the patterns earlier texts described reappear. Some prophets had the strong sense that whatever was happening to kingship in their time (and not all of it was good by any means), that would not stop God from accomplishing what he had promised. They knew in the eschaton there would be a decisive deliverance. Later, when we read the same passages, we attempt

---

12. Due to similar terminology, some might erroneously link Johnston's approach with John H. Sailhamer. However Sailhamer merges contextual and canonical into single reading and thereby argues for a fully developed messianic eschatology. Johnston, however, does not. Johnston clearly distinguishes the original contextual meaning from the later canonical significance (e.g., Brevard Childs). Thus Johnston does not merge the two into a single reading. Furthermore Sailhamer articulates his view in an article entitled "Hosea 11:1 and Matthew 2:15" (*WTJ* 63 (2001): 87-96), but Dan McCartney and Peter Enns believe Sailhamer has misread Brevard Childs and that he is incorrect in arguing that (1) Hosea 11:1 is explicitly messianic, (2) the Pentateuch contains a fully developed messianic eschatology, and (3) Matthew limited himself to a strict grammatical-historical exegesis of Hosea. See "Matthew and Hosea: A Response to John Sailhamer," *WTJ* 63 (2001): 97–105.

to do so as though we were a Jew living during the early second temple (post-exilic) period (e.g., Genesis in light of the Psalms and Prophets, not just as a book on its own). Thus, we strive to draw on the understanding of themes, messianic themes, as they stood at the time of a later Jewish reading in Israel's history.

In the *expectations* of Israel's king (part two), we focus attention on reflections about messianic promise evident in later extra-biblical but Jewish writings. Jewish interpreters read, explain, piece together, and apply sacred texts within a later second temple context (*circa* 167 BCE–70 CE). This involves interpretive, theological, and hermeneutical reflections that emerge during or as a result of major historical events: the rebuilding of the second temple (515 BCE), the desecration and rededication of the second temple (167, 164 BCE), the rise and fall of the Hasmonean dynasty that ruled Israel (143–63 BCE), etc. Although there remains a mysterious element about God's messianic promise, namely what and who was to come, *some* Jewish interpreters occasionally get it right in that they put some aspects of the messianic portrait together in helpful ways. They understood that First Testament trajectories could be interpreted as *ultimately* pointing to an eschatological Messiah.

Extra-biblical Jewish literature, composed during the intertestamental period, along with their numerous interpretations and reflections on theological themes in the sacred Hebrew writings, heighten the continuity and discontinuity between the Testaments. At times, open ended prophecies in the sacred texts are elaborated in extra-biblical materials, sometimes consistently producing a unified portrait—other times making a unity hard to find. And though extra-biblical Jewish literature authored around the time of Jesus are not Scripture nor inspired texts, they do inform us of early Jewish theological beliefs and expectations as well as provide us with examples of hermeneutical approaches to the First Testament that support those belief systems about various eschatological messiah figures.[13]

In the *coming* of Israel's king (part three), we concentrate on christological readings of the First Testament. In a christological approach, we look at the messianic portrait again, but as a Christian bringing scriptural hope together with the light of the ministry, death, resurrection and ascension of Jesus the Messiah. In some cases, passages are reused in ways that make their full force clear. In many cases the messianic understanding is assumed as present by revelation and vindicated by God so that the portrait is developed with a fullness and clarity that it had lacked, but now can be seen to have been there all along. In other words, we widen our context again—to Jesus and his inauguration of the new covenant. Here we discover both continuity

---

13. Herbert W. Bateman IV, "Second Temple Exegetical Practices: Extra-biblical Examples of Exegesis Compared with Those in the Book of Hebrews" in the Dead Sea Scrolls issue of *SWTJ* 53 (Fall 2010): 26–54.

and discontinuity with the variety of elements in early Jewish hope and with second temple Judaism. Pieces of the First Testament disclose the messianic identity and activity in Jesus' mission. Some of these elements were reflected upon and anticipated during the second temple period, but reaffirmed, unified, and fulfilled in the Second Testament.

So it should not come as a surprise that second temple interpretive approaches to the First Testament are often reflected in the Second Testament. Both second temple Jews and first century Christians were trying to make sense of what God had said. This is certainly the case in Hebrews 1:5–13 where the author links seven First Testament passages together to present Jesus as God's divine Davidic son.[14] We may also say that apostolic readings of the First Testament often connected new covenant truth into old covenant texts, making a revelatory step through the Spirit that brought together what had not yet been assembled into a coherent portrait. In doing so they complete a unified picture of the earlier pieces. Sometimes the picture is completed in unanticipated ways but never the less in ways that show a single hope is at work. This is why we find Second Testament writers sometimes engaged in literal, contextual exegesis (*peshat*), but other times in what some argue wrongly is christological eisegesis (*midrash*). This is not, however, eisegesis because the text is being handled appropriately in light of additional revelation, namely, an inclusion of the original fullness of the First Testament along with what took place in Jesus utilizing a larger historical and revelatory context. The difference is simply this: they are not dealing with exegesis of a specific book in its initial context alone, but rather performing exegesis across a collection of books, seeing God's Word as still active, alive and speaking to the new historical setting.[15] Furthermore, they are dealing with more than an individual verse. Instead they are dealing with theological concepts that appear throughout Hebrew Scriptures and reflected upon and written about during the latter part of second temple period. Unlike traditional readings that argue for an explicit exegesis of specific passages in a singular context, we contend for a unified reading involving canonical considerations of themes, reflections of which extend into the time of Jesus.

---

14. Herbert W. Bateman IV, "Two First Century Messianic Uses of the Old Testament: Hebrews 1:5–13 and 4QFlorilegium 1:1–19," *JETS* 38 (1995): 11–27; *idem.*, "Psalm 45:6–7 and Its Christological Contributions to Hebrews," *TJ* 22NS (2001): 3–21.

15. For other Second Testament examples see Steve Moyise, *The Old Testament in the New: An Introduction*, Continuum Biblical Studies Series (New York: Continuum, 2001); Richard N. Longenecker, *Biblical Exegesis in the Apostolic Period* (Grand Rapids: Eerdmans, 1st ed., 1975; 2nd ed., 1999); Craig A. Evans, "The Function of the Old Testament in the New" in *Introducing New Testament Introduction* (ed. Scott McKnight; Grand Rapids: Baker, 1989); E. Earle Ellis, *Paul's Use of the Old Testament* (Grand Rapids: Eerdmans, 1957).

RELEVANCE OF OUR APPROACH

Needless to say, all three backgrounds (contextual-canonical introductions, messianic reflections, and christological conclusions of God's promise of "messiah") are relevant to understanding how these texts ultimately are read and are part of the historical process by which these passages came to be affirmed as about Jesus. Neither approach trumps the other; *all three work in concert* but in distinct ways. The First Testament set the stage for the discussion, by introducing and presenting the promise, giving us many of its key revelatory elements. The time of messianic reflections was really a period of contemplating messianic options. It wrestled to make sense of all elements of these promises and put them together with varying degree of success and failure. This period showed the variety of ways the Jewish audience of the first century might have contemplated the topic and what options a messianic discussion of the first century needed to address. With the time of christological reading, Jesus and his followers renewed the revelatory activity missing since the early Testament and put the material together into a unit that also added additional features and emphases to the portrait. Thus, we emphasize equally a contextual-canonical, messianic, and christological reading of the text. That means, we neither under estimate Jesus' connection with his Jewishness and/ or his cultural understandings of "messiah" derived from the First Testament, nor do we simply make the conceptual connection of "Messiah" in the Old and New Testaments a mostly exclusive link. Herein lies the uniqueness of *Jesus the Messiah: Tracing the Promises, Expectations, and Coming of Israel's King*: we present a median approach to *discovering* who Jesus the Messiah is, and how Jesus himself, in the progress of revelation, fits together the pieces of God's messianic puzzle.

Although initially key elements about "messiah" were often present only *as the culminating part of a more comprehensive discussion* in the First Testament, some promises were seen more clearly by later interpreters as more revelation appeared. In addition, some later reflections and presentations of various elements of the end times and the messianic portraits generated during the second temple period were often valuable. As historical events unfolded, a look back on earlier texts of Hebrew Scripture provided fresh elements that could make more explicit what had been only implicit initially. With the coming of Jesus, the fulfillment of these promises became unified and clear. Authors of the Second Testament, influenced by their historical milieu, Jesus, and the Holy Spirit, proclaimed these fulfillments. Consequently, the Second Testament does not say *less* than the First Testament did, but it certainly tells us more about God's promise of "Messiah." Yet God knew where these passages and patterns were going. As he revealed pieces of the messianic puzzle throughout history, God was well aware of how they would fit together. Our approach, therefore, represents a Threefold Hermeneutical Reading Strategy (periods of promise, expectations, coming). It takes into consideration First

Testament canonical texts and appropriate ancient Near Eastern material, second temple history, and Jewish literature of the period as well as involving Jesus and the Apostles.[16] The following chart visually presents our methodological approach.

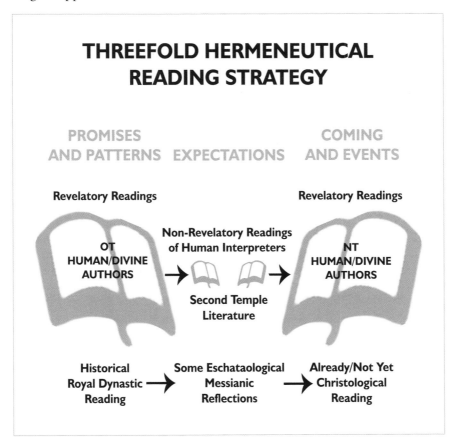

THREEFOLD HERMENEUTICAL READING STRATEGY

PROMISES AND PATTERNS   EXPECTATIONS   COMING AND EVENTS

Revelatory Readings

OT HUMAN/DIVINE AUTHORS

Non-Revelatory Readings of Human Interpreters

Second Temple Literature

Revelatory Readings

NT HUMAN/DIVINE AUTHORS

Historical Royal Dynastic Reading → Some Eschataological Messianic Reflections → Already/Not Yet Christological Reading

OUR THREEFOLD APPROACH

We begin with an equal emphasis concerning the human author and the divine author. We focus on kingship because the anointed deliverer is tied to a kingdom and the rule of a king. To be sure, other topics, such as salvation and the eschaton also can and do have messianic meaning. However, the bulk of

---

16. This approach was initially described as "Jewish Background and Apostolic School" in "Dispensationalism Yesterday and Today," in *Three Central Issues in Contemporary Dispensationalism*, 40–42.

the key features about Messiah surface in claims tied to kingship and kingdom. We intentionally restrict ourselves in this manner because to expand the consideration into additional areas risks making our study far too large. So, we purposely concentrate on kingship and covenant texts. (This also helps to explain why Genesis 3:15 is treated as an appendix).[17] What we find interesting is this: when we get to the time of Jesus and the early Christians, these other themes are often folded into the backdrop of kingship and Messiah, so not much is lost in our keeping this kingship as our primary focus. In our approach, dual authorships and their respective perspectives are important. On the one hand, the *human authors of Scripture record and disclose information about God within a context of human history.* The human authors have limited understanding of how God's ultimate goal will be played out (1 Peter 1:10–12; cp. Eph. 3:5–7). Thus when they discuss the issue of "messiah," they are not privy to nor are they presented with God's complete picture but merely pieces of it.

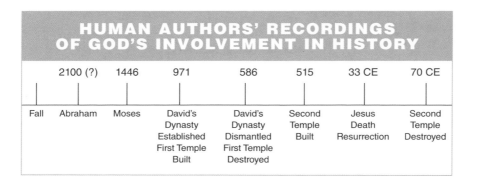

HUMAN AUTHORS' RECORDINGS OF GOD'S INVOLVEMENT IN HISTORY

2100 (?)	1446	971	586	515	33 CE	70 CE
Fall	Abraham	Moses	David's Dynasty Established First Temple Built	David's Dynasty Dismantled First Temple Destroyed	Second Temple Built	Jesus Death Resurrection	Second Temple Destroyed

On the other hand, the divine author knows the beginning and end of the story. But like any good author, *God gradually, progressively, reveals his messianic picture and builds upon it one piece* (i.e., one revelatory message) *at a time,* until Jesus and the Holy Spirit comes and fits the puzzle pieces together. Thus God not only makes a promise, he progressively builds upon that promise, expanding and giving new information about it throughout the unfolding of Jewish history until it is eventually fulfilled through Jesus.

Therefore we trace God's progress of revelation through the writings of human authors, what God has told them, what they wrote, and what they understood. We do not collapse all of redemptive history into a single statement about Jesus the Messiah that does not appreciate the progressive nature of God's revelation. There is a relationship and connection to the concept of

---

17. See footnote 4 in this chapter.

Messiah in sacred scriptures while there is also development as Jewish history unfolds and God provides more and more pieces of his messianic puzzle. Thus methods for determining the multiple human authors' histories about a Messiah (i.e., historical-exegetical) as well as methods for coming to grips with the divine author's revelation about Messiah (i.e., theological-canonical) are embraced and employed throughout this work.

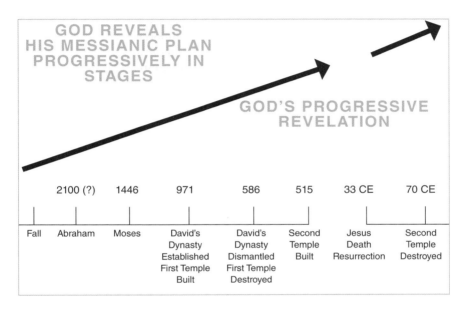

Part One: Promises of Israel's King
Johnston addresses the contextual and canonical introductory dimensions that are foundational for the Davidic dynasty of Israel. The contextual dimension focuses on the original historical exegetical meaning of key passages. The canonical dimensions identify trajectories that inner biblical development in later First Testament passages unpack. Contextual analysis indicates First Testament promises of royal dynasty and victory are clear—yet open enough to allow for later development of a diversity of eschatological messianic roles and expectations. Canonical analysis reveals how the ancient dynastic promises come to be interpreted. This canonical usage also provides the segue for the development of various forms of eschatological messianism evident in second temple literature and in the early church.

Part Two: Expectations of Israel's King
Bateman takes the second step in our threefold hermeneutic (contextual-canonical introductions, messianic reflections, and christological conclusions).

The move is made from historical, royal, dynastic promises of the First Testament to various portraits of eschatological messianic expectations evident in second temple literature. The discussion in this section is twofold. First, it identifies obstacles that hinder our ability to trace the history of ideas about eschatological messianism during this period: our limited resources, our blurred vision, and our lack of second temple historical and social sensitivities (ch. 8). Second, it isolates and illustrates from second temple literature epithets typically employed for speaking of expected messianic figures: "Messiah" (ch. 9), "Prince," "Branch" (ch. 10), and "Son" (ch. 11). Bateman identifies how a variety of messianic expectations arose from a combination of two factors: (1) the openness of First Testament promises and hopes concerning the restoration of David's dynasty as well as (2) the socio-historical dissatisfactions with current Judean leadership (e.g., Hasmonean dynasty).

Part Three: Coming of Israel's King
Bock explains how the Second Testament builds upon and unifies the First Testament promise of messiah, adopts First Testament concepts about the messiah, and presents the First Testament idea of messiah due in part to first century reflections of the messiah figure revealed in Jesus and God's authentication of him. In this section, Bock works backwards from the epistles toward the gospels. This route is taken because (1) most of the texts he chooses, especially the ones he works with first, are not debated as to their messianic affirmation, in contrast to the texts in the promise section covering the First Testament and some of the texts to be treated in the gospels; (2) the gospels are complicated, working with two time frames (that of the Jesus event and the time frame of the evangelist); and (3) by working backwards we can retrace the development of the argument starting from the least debated texts. In this way, we can work back to the origins of the messianic concept in the activity of Jesus, something debated among Second Testament scholars, but something that can be contended for in part as a result of carefully studying what emerged in the later confession of the church. Thus, Bock intentionally alters his approach and thereby does not take a chronological tact in treating this material.

Here, he discusses the "already–not yet" developments in the fulfillments of what Messiah Jesus does, as Jesus presents a Messiah in two comings (suffering and then glory). He also shows how this portrait is presented gradually in the Synoptic Gospels, emphasizing four mysteries that both make the presentation possible and unify the portrait. In two chapters, "Jesus the Messiah in the Gospels" and "Jesus the Messiah in Acts and the Early Church," Bock first identifies how the kingdom of Jesus the Messiah grows. It is *not large all at once* but grows from small to large. Second, he shows that the major opponent is Satan, not political structures as such. Third, Gentiles will be present in a way equal to Jews and yet in a way that connects the covenant promise.

Finally, and most crucially for Jesus' *ultimate* messianic identity, is how he ties together the kingdom, his role, and identity with the figure of the son of man. This results in a unique combination of divine-human authority for the delivering figure than had been seen previously in Judaism. So we see how Jesus represented the concept of Messiah, or the core figure of the new era in ways that nuanced the older presentation by bringing certain distinct images more closely together.

Thus the Second Testament presents a coherent portrait of messiah, which addresses Jewish background and yet goes its own way due to the teachings of Jesus and the revelatory work of God and the Holy Spirit through Jesus. It is this combination of features that produces our hermeneutical proposal, which helps to draw on the key historical elements of Jewish background and the period of Jesus and the early church. The concluding chapter will provide a synthesis of the study, revealing the coherence of the canonical portrait in its historical context as a hermeneutical way to understand how God authenticated Jesus.

OUR AUDIENCE

Jesus the Messiah: Tracing the Promises, Expectations, and Coming of Israel's King is not intended to be an overly technical work. And though it addresses issues of interpretation, it is written for anyone seriously versed in Scripture. More specifically, it is written for all those who wrestle with how the messianic portrait and claims of Scripture for Jesus work within human history and divine revelation. It is intended to help those who fail to see any connection between promise in the First Testament and fulfillment in the Second Testament about messiah, as well as to nudge others to consider moving beyond the notion that all First Testament readings about "messiah" were fixed and only spoke directly about Jesus. Thus, we neither minimize or maximize the connection with the First Testament and/or first century Jewish cultural understanding of Messiah, but rather offer an approach somewhere in between the two.

Our book is not solely an historical sketching of facts; it is not solely a theological treatise; nor is it solely a literary appraisal of the Bible. It is, however, a work that wrestles with all three: history, theology, and literature. How has our God revealed his kingdom program to us in progressive stages? What exactly does God reveal and when does he reveal it over long periods of time via God's unfolding of world historical events that affect directly the Jewish people through whom God works out his kingdom program? How much of God's kingdom program do those inspired human authors know completely when they composed their unique contributions to Holy Scriptures? Ultimately, how is the first-century Jew any different from us today? Whereas they had one Testament to reflect upon, we have two. We twenty-first-century followers of Jesus, the one through whom God's kingdom program has been initiated, have far more revelation than people of the first century, but do we have all the pieces of the messianic puzzle necessary to determine the consummation of God's kingdom program yet to come through the second coming of his anointed one, Jesus? Today, we may have a *more* complete canonical portrait, but we still do not have all the pieces of God's messianic puzzle. That's because ultimately *God wants us to trust him* for the time when he will complete his kingdom program.

Therefore it is our hope that readers will better comprehend and even more importantly appreciate the dynamics of messianic prophecy and fulfillment. These dynamics show that God not only made promises, he also progressively built upon those initial promises and eventually fulfilled them through Jesus, the inaugurator of God's kingdom program. And yet, the consummation of that kingdom is still to come. Scripture, early Christian preaching, and history point to Jesus as God's Messiah, Israel's king, who rules over and is worshiped by Jew and Gentile alike.

CHAPTER ONE

MESSIANIC TRAJECTORIES IN GENESIS AND NUMBERS

As one reads through the entire Bible from Genesis to Revelation, it becomes clearer at some point that God's redemptive plan for all eternity has always centered around and pointed to the coming of the Son of God. However, the person and work of the Messiah in the First Testament has always been the subject of much discussion. Most people reading the texts sense that there is much information regarding these passages on hope and promise, some of which cause the reader to pause about all that is being said. As we consider the foundational Messianic trajectories in the First Testament, we must explore the wording and scope of the earliest oracles in addressing issues in the near and far contexts. From that understanding we can celebrate the clarity with which the divinely inspired oracles ultimately pointed to, and spoke of the promised Messiah. Thus our discussion of the Hebrew Scriptures will unfold slowly in tracing this historical progress of revelation that ultimately leads to the final culminating revelation of God's program in the person of Jesus the Messiah. We will highlight key features even in the earliest oracles, which are recognized as ultimately prophetic about the Messiah from the very beginning.

MESSIANIC TRAJECTORIES IN GOD'S PROMISES TO THE PATRIARCHS

The book of Genesis is a book of beginnings: the beginning of creation (1–2), the beginning of sin (3), the beginning of king (5–11), and yes, the beginning of God's redemptive program. The earliest revelation of God's redemptive program through an explicitly *royal* figure finds its genesis in his repeated covenant promise to the patriarchs that from them would emerge "kings" (Gen. 17:6, 16; 35:11). This is not to deny that earlier passages in the book of Genesis, such as Genesis 3:15, did not originally contain an implicit Messianic potential whose full meaning and significance would be more clearly unpacked with the progress of revelation. Rather, it simply affirms that divine promises about God's redemptive program for Israel and the nations that would be mediated through a throne had not yet been made explicitly clear. A more comprehensive discussion of all the aspects associated with the culmination of God's redemptive program would need to take as its point of departure earlier passages in Genesis 1–11; namely, all the themes tied to the restoration of the rule of God in . This would add a host of texts and themes, making our study too large. So our discussion focuses on the First Testament foundation of the eschatological Messiah as a decidedly *regal* figure; clearly, the most central feature of this larger idea. The clearest starting point of the trajectory of royal promises leading to the eschatological Messiah as universal King was launched in God's promises to the patriarchs beginning in Genesis 12. These promises rotate around the term "seed," which has both corporate and individual features pointing to key individuals in the promise as well as to a line of descendants. Appreciating these features and how the promises unfold is important to grasping all that was promised.

God's Promise of a Plurality of Kings
When God called Abraham to leave Ur, he promised him fertile land, numerous offspring and incomparable blessing (12:1–3). As time went on, God progressively developed each element of promise. Chief among these was the promise of offspring—an immediate son (15:4; 17:19–21; 18:10, 13–14), future descendants (12:7; 13:15–16; 15:5, 13–16, 18–21; 17:4–6; 18:17–19; 21:12; 22:17; 26:4, 24; 28:14; 35:11), as well as a royal ("kings," 17:6, 16; 35:11) who one day would rule over the nation in the land that God had promised the patriarchs.

The plurality of this royal promise was emphasized in each of the three occasions in which God revealed the initial phase of his royal program (Gen. 17:6, 16; 35:11). The rest of Scripture shows this culminating in the individual eschatological Messiah. In each case, God's promise of future "kings" was linked with his promise of a multitude of descendants that would form the burgeoning nation over whom these kings would rule in the promised land of Canaan. Thus, the initial historical fulfillment of God's covenant promises to the patriarchs would center around earthly kings. They would rule over the nation in the promised land as the channel of God's blessing to the nations (cf. Psalm 72:17 which links the benevolent rule of the Davidic king with God's foundational promise to Abraham in Genesis 12:3 that all nations would be blessed through his seed).

Although Scripture as a whole reveals God's eternal plan of redemption ultimately centered around the Messiah, God did not fully reveal to the patriarchs how his plan of redemption, like the pieces of a puzzle, would fit together. At the time of Genesis, God only revealed how the initial phase of his program would unfold through a line of historic earthly kings descending from the patriarchs and ruling over the historic nation in the land of Canaan. More about this in Genesis 49:8-12 (see below).

God's Promise of Singular Seed

Although God initially spoke of the inaugural phase of his redemptive program being mediated through the blessed rule of the future "kings" of Israel, he also repeatedly promised to the patriarchs a coming "seed" (Gen. 12:7; 13:15, 16; 15; 15:5, 13, 18; 16:10; 17:7, 8, 9, 10, 12, 19; 21:12; 22:17, 18; 24:7, 60; 26:3, 4, 24; 28:4, 13, 14; 32:12; 35:12; 48:4, 19).

The singular form of the term "seed" (זֶרַע) is crucial to a proper interpretation of the initial as well as the ultimate manner in which God's promise would be fulfilled. This Hebrew word belongs to a unique class of terms that always appear in singular form but refers to more than one category, depending on how the term is used or intended: (1) singular of number: singular descendant (e.g., Gen. 4:25, referring to Seth); and (2) collective singular: multiple descendants (e.g., Gen. 9:9, referring to Noah's future descendants). In some cases, however, we must acknowledge the possibility of the presence of *double entendre* (a word capable of conveying two distinct meanings). The term may refer to both multiple descendants as well as a specific single descendant at one and the same time (e.g., 2 Sam. 7:12, applied to Solomon as the initial descendant of David to sit upon his throne, as well as his future royal descendants, but also culminating in the final descendant of David, that is, the Messiah).

In Genesis, the term "seed" was sometimes explicitly used to refer to the future multiple descendants of the patriarchs. For example, the collective sense is clear in promises to multiply Abraham's seed and to make his seed as innumerable as stars in the sky and sand on the seashore (Gen. 13:16; 15:5; 16:10; 22:17; 26:4, 24; 28:14; 32:12 [13]). In these cases, we are justified in understanding "seed" in terms of "descendants" (plural).[1] In the light of such clear collective uses, it is possible to explain the otherwise unqualified uses (12:7; 13:15; 15:18; 22:18; 24:7, 60; 26:3; 28:4, 13; 35:12; 48:4) in this sense as well, in the light of the principle of contextual interpretation.

However, the principle of contextual interpretation also must include the overall context of Scripture as a whole, allowing for an ultimate messianic referent. It is legitimate to recognize that the otherwise unqualified uses of the term also could be understood as allowing for an individual sense as well. For example, this is clearly the case in which "seed" refers to an individual son

---

1. This is also the case in which the term appears in reference to circumcision on the eighth day of Abraham's seed, which is explained as every future physical male descendant of Abraham (Gen. 17:7–10, 12; cf. 17:13–14, 23–27; 21:4; Exod. 12:48; Lev. 12:3). In one case, the term clearly refers to the Hebrews during their sojourn in Egypt: "Know for certain that your seed will be strangers in a foreign country, where they will be enslaved and oppressed for four hundred years" (Gen. 15:13; cf. Exod. 12:40).

of a patriarch, who as a descendant, would become the first of many future descendants of that patriarch (e.g., Gen. 15:3; 17:7; 21:2, 13; Josh. 24:3; cf. Gen. 38:8). Of course, as Paul makes clear, God's promise of seed to Abraham would find its ultimate culmination in the Messiah as his descendant *par excellence*, the One through whom God's covenant program would reach its decisive fulfillment.[2]

In the light of this wide range of meanings for "seed," it is easy to understand how it could embody an original to multiple applications and referents at one and the same time. The singular and collective meaning of God's promise of "seed" is not a matter of "either/or" but rather "both/end." On the one hand, God's promise of seed found its initial fulfillment in the birth of Isaac and the subsequent promulgation of the descendants of Abraham, Isaac,and Jacob (e.g., Deut. 1:8, 10; 4:37; 10:15; 34:4; Josh. 24:3; Neh. 9:7–8). On the other hand, the promise of seed also finds its ultimate fulfillment in the Messiah (see note 2). Hence, when promising seed to the patriarchs, God had both near as well as far fulfillments in view. God inaugurated the fulfillment of his promise through Isaac, continued the subsequent historic fulfillment through multiple descendants in subsequent generations of Israelites, and brought about its climatic fulfillment in the Messiah. All of these were wrapped up in the original promise.

MESSIANIC TRAJECTORIES IN JACOB'S TESTAMENT (GENESIS 49:8–12)

As Genesis unfolds, its narrative strategy leads the reader to wonder how God would begin to fulfill his promise of a royal dynasty of "kings" (Gen. 17:6, 11; 35:11). After all, the narrator piques the reader's interest by closing the Isaac narrative with a genealogy of his son Esau, highlighting the first Edomite kings who reigned before any king ruled over Israel (Gen. 36:31–43). So as the reader turns to the closing section of the book in Genesis 37–50, he is poised to learn how God would begin to initially fulfill his promise to establish a dynasty of kings for Israel as well.

Viewed in this light, Genesis 37–50 reaches its climax in Jacob's oracle of a coming ruler from the tribe of Judah in 49:8–12. Since God promised that "kings" would emerge from Abraham's descendants, the reader has been conditioned to view Jacob's oracle as a prediction of the future rise of the royal dynasty promised to Abraham. However, by divine design this enigmatically worded oracle speaks not only of the rise of the first historical king from the

---

2. Paul explained that God's promise of "seed" (singular) also included and ultimately pointed to Messiah (Gal. 3:16; cf. 3:19). At the same time, Paul did not exclude the collective sense, since he included believing Jews and Gentiles in the seed of Abraham in the light of the inclusion of both peoples in the new covenant community (Gal. 3:29; 4:4).

tribe of Judah (David), but also the ultimate eschatological King (Jesus, who is the Christ).

The Future of Jacob's Sons as the Tribes of Israel

In a deathbed speech, Jacob bestowed paternal blessings on his sons (49:1–28). Often dubbed the blessing of Jacob, it is more aptly called Jacob's testament, since his last words include curses (vv. 3–7), blessings (vv. 8–12, 22–27), and neutral predictions (vv. 13–21). As the epilogue reveals, Jacob's pronouncements set the destiny of the tribes that would descend from his sons: "These are the twelve tribes of Israel" (v. 28). For example, the blessing on his son Dan concerned his future tribe: "Dan will judge his people as *one of the tribes of Israel*" (v. 16).

The individual pronouncements in Jacob's testament envisioned the coming era of the conquest and settlement before the individual tribal distinctions began to wane in the monarchy period. This is suggested by the reduced status of the tribe of Reuben (vv. 3–4), the scattering of the tribes of Simeon and Levi (vv. 5–7), the location of land allotments of the tribes of Zebulun (v. 13) and Issachar (vv. 14–15), and the preeminence of the tribes of Judah (vv. 8–12) and Joseph/Ephraim (vv. 22–26). Since these oracles found some initial fulfillment in the conquest and settlement period, it is difficult—if not impossible—to argue that Jacob's blessing of Judah (vv. 8–12) was an exclusive direct prophecy of the eschatological Messiah. Rather, it initially conceived the role the tribe of Judah would play in the conquest and settlement of Canaan to fulfill God's ancient promise. Yet this oracle was divinely inspired in such a way that it also contained a messianic potential, whose full meaning would eventually become more clear as Scripture continued to unfold. The rule that came to Judah would reside there until God brought the full blessing he had promised to Abraham and his seed in Genesis 12.

The Future as Both Near and Far

The prologue emphasized that Jacob spoke of the future: "I will tell what will happen to you in the future" (v. 1). The expression "in the future" (lit. "in the backside of days") may refer to the near historical as well as distant eschatological future. Elsewhere in the Pentateuch, it refers to the near future (Deut. 4:30; 31:29), as well as distant future (Num. 24:14). In the Prophets, it is a technical expression for the eschatological future (Isa. 2:2; Mic. 4:1; Ezek. 38:16; Dan. 2:28; 10:14). Here in Genesis, it may refer to the initial historical dimension of Jacob's words, which foresaw the near future when the twelve tribes of Israel would begin to settle in the land of Canaan leading up to the early monarchy. Yet the words can also refer to a distant, future dimension of the eschatological days of the Messiah. There is an inherent openness in the expression, allowing it to convey both a historical and eschatological meaning. Thus, Jacob's declaration, "The scepter will not depart from Judah

. . . until he comes to whom it belongs" (49:10), not only pointed to the initial historical fulfillment in the coming of the first historical king of Judah (David), but also the ultimate eschatological fulfillment in the coming of the ultimate King of Judah (Messiah). The expression allows for a "both/and" fulfillment.

Literary Structure of Jacob's Testament

Jacob's blessings are arranged in the birth order of Jacob's sons (29:32–30:24; 35:18), but according to their mothers: the six sons of Leah are addressed first and the two sons of Rachel last, sandwiching the four sons of Zilpah and Bilhah, the two handmaidens of Leah and Rachel, respectively. The literary structure of the oracle is arranged in an ABBA chiasm: LEAH, Bilhah-Zilpah, Zilpah-Bilhah, RACHEL. Each group is addressed in descending birth order with two slight variations. The order of Leah's sons Zebulun and Issachar is reversed (30:17–20), possibly because the destiny of the former would be better than the latter (49:13, 14–15). The order of the four sons of the two handmaidens differs from their birth order (30:5–13), perhaps for the sake of chiastic structure or to reflect their geographical locations in the land from south to north: Dan (Josh. 19:40–48), Gad (Num. 32:33–36), Asher (Josh. 19:24–31), Naphtali (Josh. 19:32–39).

JACOB'S PRONOUNCEMENTS ON THE TWELVE SONS/TRIBES OF ISRAEL (GENESIS 49:3–27)		
Six Sons of Leah, Jacob's First Wife	Four Sons of Zilpah and Bilhah, Handmaids of Leah and Rachel	Two Sons of Rachel, Jacob's Second Wife
Reuben (Gen. 49:3–4)	Dan (Gen. 49:16–18)	Joseph (Gen. 49:22–26)
Simeon (Gen. 49:4–7)	Gad (Gen. 49:19)	Benjamin (Gen. 49:27)
Levi (Gen. 49:4–7)	Asher (Gen. 49:20)	
Judah (Gen. 49:8–12)	Naphtali (Gen. 49:21)	
Zebulun (Gen. 49:13)		
Issachar (Gen. 49:14–15)		

Since the order of Jacob's pronouncements is largely based on birth, the blessings of Judah and Joseph do not stand out in the literary structure. Nevertheless, Judah and Joseph are singled out from the others. Judah and Joseph receive the longest, and preeminent blessings. No fewer than ten of the twenty-five verses in the oracle are devoted to the two. While five verses are devoted to each Judah and Joseph, no other tribe merits more than two or three verses, most receiving only one. This mirrors chapters 37–50, where Joseph is destined to rule over his brothers and given preferential treatment by Jacob (37:3–4, 5–11, 34–35; 48:1–22), while Judah emerges as the leader among Jacob's other sons (37:26–27; 38:1–26; 43:3–10; 44:14–34; 46:28).

The preeminence of Judah and Joseph in Jacob's oracle foreshadows the leadership of the two tribes in the early history of Israel (cf. Josh. 18:5). In predicting the "scepter" would not depart from Judah (49:10) and designating Joseph "prince" over his brothers (49:26), Jacob foresaw the rise of the two prominent tribes of the north and south (cf. Pss. 60:7[9]; 108:8[9]). However, as Jacob's testament intimates and the rest of Scriptures explicates, the tribe from which both the initial conquering king and ultimate conquering King would arise was Judah. Therefore, our discussion of Messianic trajectories will focus on Jacob's blessing on Judah.

Contextual Reading of Genesis 49:8–12

In verses 8–12, Jacob pronounced the destiny of Judah/Judahites during the coming conquest and settlement period. He foresaw that the Judahites would exercise leadership until the tribal confederation would become a charter nation. He also foresaw a coming king who would arise from the tribe of Judah to subjugate all nations and reign over an ideal future period of virtual paradisiacal prosperity, effectively restoring the original fertility of Genesis 1–2. Here is the place where kingship and restoration of what was lost in Eden come together.

Judah Would Gain Ascendancy (49:8)

After denouncing his three oldest sons (Reuben, Simeon, Levi) in verses 2–7, Jacob at long last addressed one whom he could praise. Although Judah was not without his faults (37:26–27; 38:1–30), his willingness to sacrifice himself in the end (44:18–34) won a twofold blessing. Jacob pronounced that Judah would ascend over his brothers: "Your brothers will praise you . . . your father's sons will bow down before you" (v. 8a, c). Jacob also foresaw Judah's conquest of the Canaanites in the future conquest: "Your hand will be on the nape of your enemies" (v. 8b). Seizing one's fleeing enemy by the nape of the neck is a symbol of military conquest (Exod. 23:27; 1 Sam. 18:7; 2 Sam. 22:41). The term "enemies" occurs twice elsewhere in Genesis in God's promise that Abraham's descendants would take possession of the land by conquering the Canaanites: "Your descendants will conquer the strongholds of their enemies" (22:17; 24:60).

Jacob's prophecy found initial historical fulfillment in several stages. This began with the leading role that Judah played from the departure of Israel from Egypt through the conquest and settlement periods. In the wilderness, Judah was by far the largest tribe (Num. 23:3–4; 10:14) and led the Israelite march. Moses blessed Judah with great power for the conquest (Deut. 33:7–11), and Judah was the first tribe to whom land was allotted by Joshua (Josh. 15:1). Yahweh designated Judah to take the lead in the conquest of Canaan (Judg. 1:2–4) and the civil war with Benjamin (20:18). In the final unfolding of the initial historical fulfillment, Judah exercised hegemony over all tribes in David's enthronement over all Israel (2 Sam. 5:1–5). Yet these initial phases of historical fulfillment did not exhaust all that would be wrapped up in the fulfillment.[3]

The Lion of Judah Would Conquer His Enemies (49:9)
In verse 9, Jacob depicted Judah as a raging lion, which has devoured its prey. Lion imagery often depicts victorious warriors and/or conquering kings (2 Sam. 1:23; 1 Chron. 12:8; Pss. 57:4; 58:6; 91:13; Isa. 5:29; 15:9; Ezek. 32:2; Jer. 2:15; 4:7; 50:17; Hos. 5:14–15; 13:7–8; Nah. 2:11–13). The lion image (verse 9) created a segue between the predictions of Judah's leadership in the conquest period (verse 8), the following prophecy of Judah's tribal leadership (verse 10a), and the prediction of the coming ruler (verse 10b).

Judah Would Exercise Tribal Leadership (49:10a)
Verse 10a predicted Judah exercising tribal authority and leadership. Jacob envisioned the tribe as a mighty warrior/ruler wielding traditional weapons of war and emblems of authority. The first instrument mentioned is a term (שֵׁבֶט) with a wide range of meanings: (1) "club," used by a warrior to strike his foe in battle; (2) "rod," used by a father to strike a rebellious son in corporeal discipline; (3) "flail," used by a harvester to beat out grain; (4) "staff," used by a shepherd to strike or guide sheep; and (5) "scepter," used by a king as emblem of authority.[4] The context of verse 10 suggests a warrior's club as weapon of war or a king's scepter as emblem of royal authority. Quite possibly both are implied by metonymy of cause for effect: the mighty warrior

---

3. As we know now, God had more in mind than simply the kingship of David, as the Davidic covenant and all the prophecies associated with the future of Davidic kingship would make clear. The prophecy finds ultimate fulfillment in the Messiah who is not only identified as descending from the Judah (Heb. 7:14), but also pictured as "the Lion of the tribe of Judah" (Rev. 5:5). Both Second Testament statements are clear links to Genesis 49:8–12, highlighting the robust messianic meaning and ultimate significance of Jacob's oracle.

4. The term שֶׁבֶט has a fivefold range of meanings: (1) "club" of warrior to strike foe (Num. 24:17; Judg. 5:14; 2 Sam. 18:14; 23:21; 1 Chron. 11:23; Isa. 9:4; 10:5, 15, 24; 14:5); (2) "rod" of father or master to strike rebellious son or servant (Exod. 21:20; 2 Sam. 7:14; Pss. 2:9; 89:32[33]; Job 9:34; 21:9; 37:13; Prov. 10:13; 13:24; 22:8, 15; 23:13–14; 26:3; 29:15; Lam. 3:1; Isa. 11:4; 14:29; 30:31; Ezek. 21:10, 13; Mic. 5:1); (3) "flail" of harvester to beat grain (Isa. 28:27); (4) "staff" of shepherd to strike sheep (Ps. 23:4; Ezek. 20:37; Mic. 7:14); (5) "scepter" of king as emblem of royal authority (Ps. 45:6[7]; Isa. 14:5; Ezek. 19:11, 14; Amos 1:5, 8; Zech. 10:11).

wields his weapon victoriously and so also holds his scepter as he exercises kingship. It is unnecessary to force an interpretive decision between the two; in the ancient world the mighty warrior and powerful king were often one and the same.

The parallel term (מְחֹקֵק) also has a range of meanings: (1) "club, mace," used by a warrior as a weapon, and (2) "staff," used as a tribal chieftain's emblem of authority.[5] In the only other passage in which the parallel terms in verse 10a occur together (Judg. 5:14), they depict tribal chieftains wielding weapons in battle, conveying both tribal leadership and military might:

> The survivors of the mighty ones came down;
> > the Lord's people came down as warriors.
> They came down from Ephraim, who uprooted Amalek,
> > they follow after you, Benjamin, with your warriors.
> Commanders (מְחֹקְקִים) came to battle from Makir,
> > those wielding the staff (שֵׁבֶט) of an officer came from Zebulun.
> Issachar's leaders were with Deborah,
> > the men of Issachar supported Barak,
> > > into the valley they were sent under Barak's command
> > > > (Judg. 5:13–15c)

The evidence suggests that verse 10a pictures the tribe of Judah as a mighty warrior victoriously wielding a weapon of war, but also as a powerful ruler holding an emblem of his political and military authority, which he mustered as a result of military victory.

The initial historical fulfillment of this prediction was inaugurated in the events at the invasion of Canaan and in the early settlement period in which the tribe of Judah played a leading role. Yet Jacob's testament concerned not only the near future but also the distant future; the former foreshadowed the latter in terms of pattern prediction. The ultimate eschatological fulfillment will be inaugurated when the tribe of Judah, embodied by the Messiah Jesus who is called the Lion of the Tribe of Judah (Rev. 5:5), brings about ultimate victory over cosmic enemies and establishes his eternal kingdom. The dual nature of this prophecy allows both. The pattern introduces a feature we shall see often in this kind of fulfillment. What happens in a limited way in the initial presence of the pattern will happen more comprehensively, and in an escalated manner in its ultimate realization. In this case we move from earthly victory to cosmic triumph.

---

5. The term מְחֹקֵק has two basic meanings: (1) "mace, club," as a warrior's weapon (Pss. 60:7[9]; 108:8[9]); and (2) "staff," as an emblem of a tribal chieftain's authority (Num. 21:18; cf. Deut. 33:21; Judg. 5:9, 14; Isa. 33:22).

A Ruler Would Come from Judah (49:10b)

Verse 10b is traditionally interpreted as a prediction of a ruler who would arise from the tribe of Judah to become king over the Israelite tribes as well as conquered nations. Yet this is one of the most cryptic lines of Hebrew poetry in Scripture. The interpretive challenge centers around the term (שִׁילֹה) (traditionally translated "Shiloh" cf. KJV, NKJV, ASV, NASB, NCV), which is textually uncertain, syntactically debated, morphologically unusual, and semantically ambiguous.

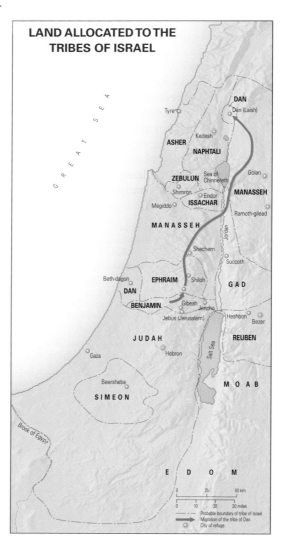

Depending on how one takes this one term, verse 10b may be nuanced in six ways: (1) "until he comes *to Shiloh*," (2) "until *Shiloh* comes," (3) "until *a ruler* comes," (4) "until *his ruler* comes," (5) "until *to him tribute* comes," or (6) "until he comes *to whom it* [= the scepter] *belongs*." It seems the best way to render verse 10 is thus: "The scepter will not depart from Judah or the ruler's staff from between his feet, until he comes to whom it belongs; even the obedience of the nations will be his" (cf. RSV, NIV, TNIV, NLT, cf. NET, NIRV, HCSB).[6] Understood this way, verse 10b pictures an unidentified figure arising upon the scene of history to whom

---

6. For discussion of the interpretive options and exegetical issues of Genesis 49:10b, see Raymond de Hoop, *Genesis 49 in its Literary and Historical Context*, Oudtestamentische Studiën, Deel XXIX (Leiden/Boston: Brill, 1999), 122–39.

the weapons of military victory and the emblems of royal authority belong. He will triumph over his foes as a mighty warrior and then assume his rule as king over the nations who will be subject to him.

Initial Historical Fulfillment in David's Rise to Kingship.
Considered from the perspective of its initial historical fulfillment, it is likely that verse 10 predicted the leading role the tribe of Judah would play in the conquest and early settlement period running up to the rise of the early Israelite monarchy when the surrounding nations were originally subjugated by David, the nation's first king from Judah (cf. 2 Sam. 8:1–14; 1 Chron. 14:17; 18:11). Several factors suggest this. First, later inner-biblical interpretation understood Genesis 49:10 as finding initial historical fulfillment in the Israelite monarchy in general (Num. 24:9, 17–19; Ezek. 19:1–14; 21:32),[7] and the kingship of David in particular (1 Chron. 5:1–2).[8] Second, the historical events predicted in Jacob's oracle about his other sons seem to have been realized (at least initially) during the conquest and settlement period, as well as Israel's early monarchy.[9] Third, the strategy of the patriarchal

---

7. For Numbers 24:9 and verses 17–19, in terms of its initial historical meaning/fulfillment, as well as its ultimate messianic meaning/fulfillment, see the next section of this chapter, "Messianic Trajectories in Balaam's Oracles."

8. First Chronicles 5:1–2 provides inner-biblical evidence of how Genesis 49:10 was understood in the postexilic era. This passage is a parenthetical comment in the genealogical lists of the twelve tribes (1 Chron. 2–9). The Chronicler explains that Jacob withdrew the firstborn's right from Reuben for his indiscretion and transferred it to Joseph—despite the fact that Judah was the strongest tribe and that a leader would descend from him: "Now Reuben was the firstborn, but when he defiled his father's bed, his rights as firstborn were given to the sons of Joseph, the son of Israel. So Reuben is not listed as firstborn in the genealogical records. Although Judah was the strongest among his brothers and a leader would descend from him, the right of the firstborn belonged to Joseph" (1 Chron. 5:1b–2). The Chronicler's comment about Judah alludes to two elements of Jacob's blessing in Genesis 49:8–12. First, his statement, "Judah was strongest of his brothers," reflects Jacob's depiction of Judah as a mighty lion before whom siblings and foes bow in submission (Gen. 49:8–9). Second, the statement, "a ruler (נָגִיד) would descend from him," alludes to Jacob's declaration, "the scepter will not depart from Judah . . . until a ruler (שִׁילֹה) comes" (Gen. 49:10). The Chronicler's choice of the term "ruler" (נָגִיד), equivalent to "king" (מֶלֶךְ), is a patent reference to king David, elsewhere designated the "ruler" *par excellence* (1 Sam. 13:14; 25:30; 2 Sam. 5:2; 6:21; 7:8; 1 Chron. 11:2; 17:7; 28:4). Thus, the Chronicler understood Genesis 49:10 as predicting David's kingship (cf. 1 Chron. 3:1–24).

9. This is clear in Jacob's predictions of the reduction of the status of Reuben (vv. 3–4), as well as the scattering of Simon and Levi (vv. 5–7): (1) The demotion of Reuben began in the wilderness era in its subordination to Judah in the order of march (Num. 2:16). By the second census, the population of Reuben already had dropped considerably (Num. 26:7; cf. Deut. 33:6). After settling in Gilead (Num. 32:1–42; 34:14; Deut. 3:12–17; 4:43; 29:8; Josh. 12:6; 13:8–23), Reuben became disconnected from the tribes west of the Jordan (Josh. 22:1–34) and no longer participated in national life (Judg. 5:15–16).

narratives (Gen. 12–50) has been pointing toward the initial historical fulfill-ment of God's promise to establish the descendants of Abraham as a nation in the land of Canaan under the sway of a royal dynasty of kings through whom the nations would be blessed. Understanding Genesis 49:10 as pointing to the initial historical fulfillment of the royal aspects of God's promises to the patriarchs rounds off the overarching narrative plot, as the story of the patri-archs reaches its conclusion in the next chapter. Yet it is crucial to emphasize that this initial historical fulfillment did not exhaust the original meaning and divinely intended prophetic significance of verse 10. Although this kind of initial historical fulfillment in David's rule means Genesis 49:10 was not an exclusive, direct messianic prophecy, this does not rule out its equally robust nature as ultimately being a messianic prophecy. In the divinely designed pat-tern comes the culminating messianic connection. As it was initially, so it will be in the end; only more so.

Ultimate Eschatological Fulfillment in Messiah's Kingship.
Considered from the perspective of its decisive eschatological fulfillment, it is likely that verse 10b also predicted the coming of the Messiah on the scene of human history. The Second Testament linkage of Genesis 49:8–9 (opening lines of the oracle) with the messianic moniker "the Lion of Judah" (Rev. 5:5) assures us that Genesis 49:10–12 (closing lines) also was certainly divinely in-spired as prophetic of the Messiah, albeit in a final decisive sense. Understood in this sense, Jacob foresaw not simply David as Judah's first king in the initial historical stage of implementation of God's program of redemption, but also the Messiah Jesus as Judah's final and ultimate King through whom God's plan of the ages would reach its climactic culmination. As God had promised Abraham, Jacob declared that through this institution, victory would come through the seed and through this tribe.

Jacob's oracle identified the tribal origin of the ultimate King as Judah (cf. Mic. 5:2[1]), where he is described as hailing from Bethlehem, (the ancestral home of David). He is also pictured as both Warrior and King, two roles which find elaboration in apocalyptic visions of the eschatological coming

---

Reuben was subordinated under Judah in David's administrative structure (1 Chron. 26:32). From this point, the Reubenites fade out of national history. (2) The decline of Simeon began in the wilderness when the tribe was reduced by two-thirds (Num. 1:23; 26:14). Neither the Blessing of Moses (Deut. 33) nor Song of Deborah (Judg. 5) mention Simeon—a sign of its decline. In the settlement, Simeon was allocated a mere enclave in Judah (Josh. 19:1–9; 15:32–42). Eventually, Judah swallowed up Simeon. Simeon even-tually lost its status as a tribal entity and its territory long remained unsettled (1 Chron. 4:38–42; 2 Chron. 15:9, 34:6). (3) The decline of Levi began when Moses withheld ter-ritorial allotment and dispersed the tribe among forty-eight cities scattered throughout Israel (Num. 35:1–8; Josh. 14:4; 21:41–42). Moses foresaw this would mean the Levites would be among the economically depressed social classes within Israel (Deut. 12:12; 14:27–29).

of Messiah (e.g., Rev. 19:11–16). Rather than simply functioning as a synecdoche of part for the whole (as it would be understood in terms of its initial historical fulfillment in the reign of David), the prediction, "the obedience of the nations will be his" (verse 10b) conveys its most robust sense as a declaration of his universal dominion (e.g., Pss. 2:8–10; 72:8–11; 89:25–27 [26–28]; 110:1–2, 5–6; Isa. 9:7 [6]; Mic. 5:4–6 [3–5]).

It is also important to note that Jacob spoke in terms of a single individual. Admittedly, the singular figure in verses 8–10 could be understood in a collective sense for the Davidic kings as a whole who traced their descent from Judah. Yet the divinely inspired portrayal of a singular figure certainly points to David as the initial historical king of Judah, but also particularly to the Messiah as the final and ultimate king of Judah. This is also supported by the literary portrait of the nations being in subjugation to this king in a manner presented as seemingly without end. Likewise, the idyllic portrait of this king in seemingly paradisiacal terms in verses 11–12 is reminiscent of the image of the garden paradise in Genesis 2, which was lost in the fall. In fact, it might be suggested that the imagery in verses 11–12, taken in its most literal sense, point to a restoration of the paradise which was lost in the fall.

Blessing and Prosperity in the Promised Land (11–12)
Using extravagant imagery, Jacob envisioned the coming initial settlement of Canaan as an era of virtual paradisiacal prosperity. To convey the fullness of blessing, he pictured an idealized individual enjoying the land's bounty: "He will bind his donkey to the vine, his foal of an ass to the choicest vine; he will wash his garments in wine, his robes in the blood of grapes; his eyes will be red from wine, his teeth white from milk." This highlights the superabundance of the land in three ways. First, grapevines would be so plentiful that a viticulturalist could tether his beast to his choicest vine without caring that the animal would ruin the plant. Second, wine would be so abundant it could be used for mundane tasks such as washing clothing. Third, wine and milk would be imbibed in such quantities that his eyes and teeth would be discolored by consumption. This harmonizes with later descriptions of Canaan as a land flowing with milk and honey. This effectively rounds off the future expectation of the patriarchs by picturing Judah and her king in the promised land enjoying the covenant blessings lavished by Yahweh.

Our discussion of verse 10 introduced the "both/and" approach to this passage as finding fulfillment not only initially in the days of David, but also ultimately in the days of the Messiah. It is easy to understand therefore how the extravagant imagery in verses 11–12 naturally lends itself to being prophetic of the eschatological kingdom of the Messiah. While the fulfillment of the promise of the land flowing with milk and honey would be inaugurated with Joshua and later enjoyed more fully by David, God's restoration of his creation blessing of the land of Canaan as well as the world as a whole will transpire in the eschatological kingdom of Messiah (cf. Isa. 11:6–9; 65:17–25; Amos 9:13–15). Indeed, the lush imagery of abundant agricultural fertility is reminiscent of the bounty of the garden of God that was lost in the fall but to be restored in the age of redemption (cf. Rev. 21–22).

Finally, mention of the purebred donkey of the ideal figure in verse 11 also has clear royal connotations. Although it might strike a modern reader as odd, the purebred donkey was the stereotypical mount of royalty in the ancient Near East. A poetic text from Mari suggested it was more appropriate for a king to ride a donkey than a horse: "My lord should not ride a horse, let my lord ride in a chariot or a mule, and he will thereby honor his royal head." The purebred ass also was the preferred mount of premonarchial chieftains (Judg. 5:10; 10:4; 12:14; 21:19–21; 1 Sam. 3:22) and monarchial era royalty (2 Sam. 13:29; 16:1–2; 18:9; 19:26[27]; 1 Kings 1:33, 38, 44). Furthermore, in the literature of Mari and Ugarit, the donkey was the animal on which a deity may ride. Zechariah likely picked up on this royal imagery in Genesis 49:11 in his portrait of the Divine Warrior making his royal entrance into Jerusalem as its coming King mounted on a purebred donkey (Zech. 9:9), having subjugated all nations (Zech. 9:1–8). This motif resurfaces one final and climactic time at the triumphal entry of Jesus into Jerusalem where he is mounted on a purebred donkey as a patent intimation of his royalty as well as his deity (Matt. 21:5).[10] As we shall see, this kind of intertextual linking is a common literary technique, which later biblical passages employ to unpack the full messianic potential of earlier biblical passages.

Canonical Reading of Genesis 49:8–12

Although Genesis 49:8–12 found initial historical fulfillment in the rise of kingship from the tribe of Judah through David's ascent, this did not exhaust the oracle's ultimate messianic potential whose fuller meaning and significance was equally inspired. Several later passages provide expositions that reuse the imagery and develop the central themes of Genesis 49:8–12. The inner-biblical exposition of Jacob's blessing of Judah is instructive, developing a trajectory that follows the ebb and flow of redemptive history. The visions of Balaam, for example, expand upon Jacob's portrait of Judah as a mighty lion (Num. 24:9, cf. Gen. 49:8–9) and expectation of a coming victorious king (Num. 24:7, 17–19, cf. Gen. 49:10). The seer's depiction of a "scepter"

---

10. In making these series of allusions in linking Genesis 49:11 to Zechariah 9:9 to Matthew 21:5, the referent is complex. Nevertheless, the inner-biblical development of this royal motif clearly leads the reader to associate the coming king of Judah (Gen. 49:10–12) with the Divine Warrior (Zech. 9:9) who is ultimately identified as Jesus the Messiah (Matt. 21:5). These intertextual links demonstrate that Zechariah (and likely Matthew, although his point of departure was the Zechariah passage) understood Genesis 49:8–12 as ultimately messianic.

arising from Judah recalls Jacob's prediction of the "scepter" not departing from Judah until a ruler would come upon the scene (Gen. 49:10–12). Allusions to Genesis 49:8–12 in several royal psalms suggest this expectation was realized in the reign of David and the founding of his dynasty (Pss. 2:9; 45:6; 60:7[9]; 108:8[9]; 110:2, 6). In Ezekiel 19, however, the patriarchal blessing is reversed and turned into a prophetic curse due to royal sin: the mighty lion of the royal house of Judah is captured and carried away into exile (vv. 1–9, contra 49:8–9), his vines plucked up (vv. 10–14a, contra 49:11–12) and the royal scepter taken away (v. 14b, contra 49:10). Ezekiel 21:32 may feature an even more dramatic reversal: the blessing of a coming ruler (David) in Genesis 49:10 is turned into a curse (i.e., the coming of another king, Nebuchadnezzar), who would terminate the monarchy and inaugurate an era of judgment. But this would not be the end of the prophecy's life cycle. In the postexilic era, God breathed new life into the old oracle. Zechariah 9:9–10 clarified Jacob's prediction of the coming king from Judah by placing it into a clear eschatological context as a prophetic vision of the coming of the ultimate King (Yahweh). The eschatological realization of Genesis 49:8–12 was facilitated by the prose frame of Jacob's testament, in which the formula, "in future days" (49:1), which carried clear eschatological connotations (i.e., "in the last days") in the time of Zechariah.

Several crucial hermeneutical principles, which are relevant to messianic prophecy and interpretation, emerge from the inner-biblical development of Genesis 49:8–12. First, progressive revelation of an early prophetic oracle by later writers expounds its original meaning and may expand its original scope. Second, although ancient Hebrew oracles were irrevocable in their final fulfillment, they also were implicitly contingent in any given period on the faithfulness of the recipients from generation to generation. God could and did discipline the nation and the line from time to time in ways that sometimes looked as if the promise might be placed in jeopardy. Yet the nature of the promise and God's grace meant that any discipline for unfaithfulness was temporary. The promise made would be a promise completed. So third, even if a particular generation forfeited the promised blessing due to its sin, God remained faithful to his eternal purpose and could renew ancient promises in future generations. Fourth, later inner-biblical use of ancient oracles may involve interim developments that temporarily take the original language and motifs in new directions, yet without jeopardizing the originally intended ultimate future fulfillment. Finally, ancient Hebrew royal/messianic prophecy was not always static but dynamic in its inner-biblical development in the progress of revelation from the initial fulfillment in the historical monarchy to ultimate fulfillment in the eschatological Messiah. This means these texts often had stages of realization and fulfillment as opposed to simply being about the end result. Our study throughout this book is designed to show this dimension in some detail. Seeing the patterns and appreciating how God built the portrait actually adds depth and appreciation for where the story ends up, as well as explaining how the individual texts work.

MESSIANIC TRAJECTORIES IN BALAAM'S VISIONS (NUMBERS 24)

The next major stage in our revelatory trajectory appears in the visions of Balaam. Hired by Balak king of Moab to curse the Israelites as they passed through his land, the Aramean prophet was faithful to the God who spoke through him. To the chagrin of Balak, he blessed Israel (23:7–10, 18–24; 24:3–9, 15–19) but cursed Moab (24:20, 21–22, 23–24). In two of his four prophecies, Balaam foresaw the coming of a mighty king from Israel who would conquer the Transjordanian nations (24:3–9, 14–19). In one vision, he identifies the coming figure as Israel's "king" (24:7). In the other, he describes him as a rising "star" and conquering "scepter" (24:17).

Numbers 24:3–9 and 14–19 are similar to Jacob's blessing of Judah (Gen. 49:8–12) since both envision a "scepter" smiting the enemies of Israel (Gen. 49:10; Num. 24:17). Yet there are differences. Jacob described this coming "scepter" as a mighty warrior who would conquer his foes (Gen. 49:8–10) then prosper as a viticulturalist in the land of Canaan (49:11–12). Balaam envisioned the coming "scepter" in royal terms only; he would conquer the Transjordanian nations and then rule them as king (Num. 24:17–19; cf. 24:7). Whereas Jacob's oracle found its initial historical fulfillment in the Israelite subjugation of the land of Canaan led by the tribe of Judah during the conquest and settlement period leading up to the rise of David to kingship, the initial historical fulfillment of Balaam's visions came to pass in the hegemony of the fledgling Israelite monarchy under its early kings, whether Saul or David. In both cases, however, the ultimate future fulfillment will come to pass in the eschatological triumph of the Messiah over his enemies and his resultant enthronement as the universal King over all nations.

Contextual Reading of Numbers 24:3–9

Perched atop Mount Peor (24:1–2), Balaam delivered his third oracle from the God who opened his eyes and spoke in his ears (24:3–4). As he beheld the Israelite encampment sprawled out and filling the valley below, Balaam saw a portent of things to come (24:5). The Israelites would be like valleys spreading out in all directions, thriving like gardens, watered by streams of water, and standing sturdy like cedars planted beside a river (24:6). Israel would be like a well-watered land; its descendants would multiply like flowing water to become a fledgling kingdom under a great king (24:7). Blessed by the God who rescued them out of Egypt, the Israelites would trample hostile nations like a virile bull and devour its prey like a ravenous lion (24:8–9).

As Balaam saw it, following the conquest (24:5–7a, 8–9), a king would emerge to rule over his kingdom (24:7b). Given the historical context, the initial historical fulfillment can only refer to the establishment of the Israelite monarchy. The seer foresaw that Israel's king would trump Agag the king of Amalek: "his [=Israel's] king will be greater than Agag, and his kingdom will be elevated." The rise of Israel would spell the demise of Amalek, the traditional archenemy of Israel (Exod. 17:8–16; Deut. 25:17–19), as well as all other nations (24:7–8, cf. 17–19, 20).

Balaam's vision was initially fulfilled in the early days of the fledgling monarchy in the reigns of Saul and David. Although the judges temporarily delivered Israel from Amalekite oppression,[11] the decisive subjugation of Amalek was a divine commission reserved for Israel's first king (1 Sam. 14:48). When God commanded Saul to exterminate the Amalekites (1 Sam. 15:1–3), he smote the Amalekite army (1 Sam. 14:48) but spared king Agag (1 Sam. 15:2–8, 18–20), disobeying God (1 Sam. 28:18). It was left to David to decisively defeat and subjugate Amalek (1 Sam. 30:18; 2 Sam. 1:1; 8:12; 1 Chron. 18:11). Saul inaugurated fulfillment of Balaam's oracle, but his failure to obey God resulted in the premature demise of his kingdom and transfer of his throne to David, who brought this prophecy to actual fulfillment. In fact, the chronicler's notice, "His kingdom was elevated" (1 Chron. 14:2; cf. 2 Sam. 5:12), is reminiscent of Balaam's oracle, "His kingdom will be elevated" (Num. 24:7). Yet the historical kingship of Saul and David did not exhaust the prophecy that envisioned the total triumph of the king of Israel over all his enemies. The reigns of Saul and David were therefore a pattern of the reign of One greater to come who would triumph over all hostile nations after the pattern of Amalek.

Contextual Meaning of Numbers 24:14–19

In his fourth vision (24:14–16), Balaam foresaw the coming of the mighty Israelite king who would establish his rule and conquer the Transjordanian nations of Moab, Ammon, and Edom (24:17–19). In verse 14, Balaam introduced his oracle to Balak with an explanation: "Let me tell you what this people (=Israel) will do to your people (=Moab) in the future." The phrase "in the future" (lit. "in the backside of the days") typically refers to some decisive change at an indeterminate future point. The precise point, however, is linguistically open as it may refer to the near or distance future; the context always determinative. In the Pentateuch, this expression refers to a time in the relatively near future (Deut. 4:30; 31:29), but also in a "both/and"

---

11. The oppression experienced by the Israelites at the hands of the Amalekites is ancient. The Amalekites were one of the many descendents of Esau (Gen. 36). In fact Amalek was the grandson of Esau (Gen. 36:11, 12; cf. 1 Chron. 1:36). Although linked with the land of Edom (Gen. 36:16), they were nomadic or semi-nomadic people who roamed the regions of the Sinai and Negev (Num. 13:29, 1 Sam. 15:7). Conflict between the Amalekites and Israelites is first noted in Exodus 17:8–13 but continues throughout the period of the Judges (Judg. 3:13; 5:14; 6:3, 33; 7:12; 10:12).

sense to refer to the near historical future as well as far eschatological future (Gen. 49:1). In the Classical Prophets, it is used almost exclusively in a more technical sense for the eschatological future (Isa. 2:2; Mic. 4:1; Ezek. 38:16; Dan. 2:28; 10:14). We have already seen that royal/messianic prophecy often features some kind of *double entendre*, which is likely the case here. In other words, Balaam's vision dealt with both the historical future as well as the eschatological future.

Balaam's vision opens with a mysterious figure arising in the indefinite future: "I see him, but not now; I behold him, but not near" (v. 17a). It was unclear to Balaam precisely when this mysterious figure would come upon the scene, but it would not be in the immediate future. Whether he would arise in a few generations, after many centuries, or both in a pattern was unclear to him. What he did know was that when he came, victory would come.

Balaam pictured him in decidedly royal terms: "a star will march forth from Jacob, a scepter will arise from Israel" (v. 17b). Stars were viewed as ruling the night (Gen. 1:16; Ps. 136:9) and associated with the heavenly throne (Isa. 14:13), thus the astral metaphor was a royal image (Isa. 14:12). Yet this royal star does not rise on the horizon, but marches forth to battle; the verb "will come" (דָּרַךְ) is often used of a warrior: "march forth" (Amos 4:13; Mic. 5:5–6 [4–5]).

The image of royal warrior is reinforced by referring to a royal object of antiquity and its twofold range of meanings: (1) "scepter," metonymic for a king's rule (Judg. 5:14; Ezek. 19:11, 14; Amos 1:5, 8; Zech. 10:11; Ps. 45:6), and (2) "war club," wielded by royal warriors (Isa. 10:15; 14:5; Mic. 5:1; Pss. 2:9; 125:3). The term represents two kinds of royal objects wielded by ancient Near Eastern rulers: the long slender ornamented ceremonial staff whose function was symbolic, and the shorter heavy mace, which had military function. Since verse 18 envisions this royal warrior shattering the skulls of his foes in battle, the war club is probably in view.

Verse 19 merges the royal and martial imagery: "He will rule from Jacob and destroy survivors of Ar." The verb "to rule" may refer to military subjugation of one's foreign enemies (Lev. 26:17; Isa. 14:12); political control of other nations (1 Kings 4:24; Ezek. 29:15; Ps. 68:27); or political control due to military subjugation (Pss. 72:8; 110:2; Isa. 14:6; Neh. 9:28). The coming Israelite king would defeat his enemies then execute all who had survived the battle.

In verses 17–19, Balaam identified three peoples whom the coming Israelite king would conquer: the Moabites, Edomites, and Canaanites. In the case of Moab and Edom, this would be retribution for the opposition of Moab and Edom against Israel during its trek through the Transjordan. Previously, Moses predicted God would subdue the nations of Transjordan (Moab, Edom) and Cisjordan (Canaan, Philistia) (Exod. 15:15). However, Israel failed to conquer Moab and Edom due to its apostasy at Baal-Peor (Num. 25:1–16). Worse yet, Israel was subjugated to Moab as punishment for departing from Yahweh (Judg. 3:12–30; cf. 1 Sam. 12:9). Eventually, Saul defeated Moab and Edom (1 Sam. 14:47), while David annexed them into his empire. David later annexed Moab and Edom (2 Sam. 8:2, 12, 14; cf. Pss. 60:8[10]; 108:9[10]). So Balaam's vision of the subjugation of Moab and Edom found its initial historical realization in the reigns of Israel's first two kings, Saul and David. Yet this would not exhaust its fulfillment since these nations did not remain subject to the Israelite kings. Balaam pictured a total and lasting triumph.

Considered from its initial historical fulfillment, Numbers 24:17–19 envisioned the rise of the early Israelite monarchy and its conquest of surrounding nations in the tenth century BCE. Although Saul inaugurated the historical fulfillment of Balaam's vision, victory over these enemies was not brought to pass until David's reign. Balaam's prophecy of the coming "star" and "scepter" was initially fulfilled by David, who struck down the Moabites and Edomites, and subjugated the other peoples (2 Sam. 8:2, 6; 13–14; 1 Kings 11:15–16; 1 Chron. 18:12–13).

This initial historical fulfillment in the time of David did not, however, constitute the complete fulfillment of Balaam's vision. The Moabite prophet had envisioned total triumph over Moab and Edom with no survivors left. While David initially fulfilled Balaam's expectation when he conquered Moab and Edom, their subjugation was not permanent. During the divided monarchy, Edom freed itself from Judah (2 Kings 8:20–22). Moab also broke free (2 Kings 1:1; 3:4–5) and even successfully invaded Israel (2 Kings 13:20) and Judah (2 Kings 24:2; 2 Chron. 20:1; cf. Ps. 83:1–8). Although David subjugated Moab and Edom, Moab was never permanently subjugated to Israel. So it is clear that David did not fully subjugate the Edomites, for at many points in Israel's history they rose up against her (1 Kings 11:14; 2 Kings 8:20, 14:7; 2 Chron. 28:17). Therefore, Balaam's vision of the total triumph of Israel's king over Moab and Edom was not fully fulfilled in the history of the monarchy. As later biblical writers would make clear, this total victory ultimately would be wrought by the eschatological Messiah (see below).

Canonical Reading of Numbers 24:9, 17–19

Later passages develop several themes in Balaam's vision of the rise of the early monarchy and the coming of its king. The inner-biblical exposition of Numbers 24:9, 17–19 supports our thesis that Balaam initially foresaw the reign of David, the first illustrious king of Israel. The inner-biblical exposition also traces the rising and falling fortunes of the Davidic empire, not only celebrating the fulfillment of Balaam's prophecies in the reign of David, but their tragic undoing during the subsequent reigns of his wicked descendants. This means that Balaam's oracle was still looking for final resolution.

We have already mentioned that Balaam's vision of the Israelite king's total victory over Moab and Edom was not fully fulfilled historically. The pre-exilic prophets revived the ancient oracles of Moses (Exod. 15:15) and Balaam (Num. 24:17–19), announcing that Israel and its future king would permanently subjugate or totally destroy Moab and Edom. In some cases, the prophets had Moab specifically in mind, but in other cases, Moab stood as an

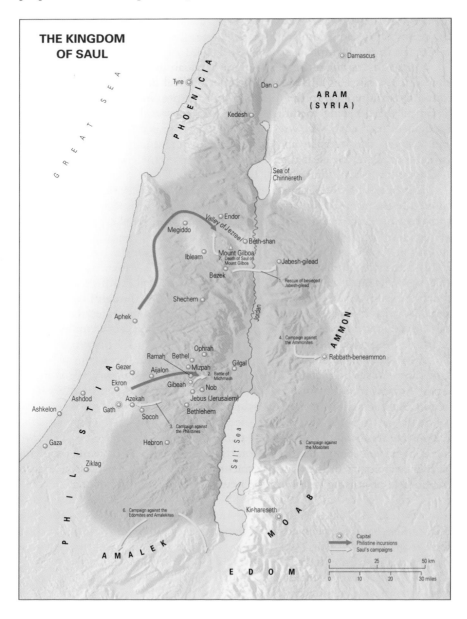

archetype for all hostile Gentile nations (Isa. 11:14; 15:1–9; 16:2–14; 25:10; Jer. 9:26; 48:1–47; Ezek. 25:8–11; Amos 2:1–3; Zeph. 2:8–11). The prophets likewise pictured the future destruction of Edom, sometimes focusing on the specific nation itself, but other times as an archetype for all nations as well (Isa. 34:5–8; 63:1; Jer. 49:7–22; Ezek. 25:12–14; 32:29; 35:15; 36:5; Joel 3:19; Amos 1:6–11; 9:11–12; Obad. 1:8; Mal. 1:4). In several cases, the total defeat of Moab and Edom is directly linked to the eschatological triumph of the Messiah. For example, Isaiah 11:10–16 and 16:2–14 alluded to Numbers 24:17–19, linking the ultimate conquest of Moab to the future ideal Davidic king (Isa. 11:10; 16:5). This kind of inner-biblical development of Balaam's vision draws attention to the total triumph the prophet had pictured as well as ultimately pointing to the eschatological intervention of Messiah as the Divine Warrior who will wreak utter havoc on all of God's enemies, triumphing as well over sin and death itself. Thus, in the progress of divine revelation, it became clear that God had more in mind from the very beginning than simply the first king of Israel.

The language and imagery of Balaam's visions are picked up in later biblical texts that develop the royal themes and develop them in ways that even more clearly bring out their initial Davidic as well as ultimate messianic connotations. For example, Psalms 72 and 110, two royal coronation psalms, both reflect the distinctive vocabulary and royal themes of Numbers 24:17–19. First, the language of Numbers 24:17, "He will rule from Jacob," is echoed in Psalm 72:8, "May he rule from sea to sea, from the Euphrates to the ends of the earth," and in Psalm 110:2, "May the LORD extend your dominion from Zion, so that you may rule in the midst of your enemies." Whereas Balaam predicted that Israel's future king one day would extend his rule over other nations, the royal coronation psalms invoked God to bless the newly enthroned king so that his rule would extend over other nations. But while Balaam foresaw that the coming king would rule over the Transjordanian nations of Moab and Edom, Psalm 72 extended this expectation over all nations. Second, Psalm 110 echoes the language of conquest from Balaam's fourth vision. The prediction, "He will shatter the skulls of Moab, the heads of all the sons of Sheth" (Num. 24:17), is echoed in Psalm 110:6, "He will shatter their heads on the vast battlefield." Balaam's prophecy of military victory of the coming Israelite king came to be expressed as a divine oracle promising victory to the newly enthroned Davidic king.

CONCLUSION

The earliest future royal expectations of ancient Israel appear in God's promises to the patriarchs of "kings" (Gen. 17:6, 16; 35:11), Jacob's oracle of a coming king to inherit Judah's "scepter" (Gen. 49:8–12), and Balaam's vision about a coming "scepter" and rising "star" (Num. 24:14–19). Although not exclusively and directly prophetic of the eschatological Messiah, they were ultimately prophetic about the One to come, culminating in him. Each promise ultimately pointed to a day when God would provide ideal kingship for his people through the eschatological Messiah, who himself would bring victory and peace to the world.

MESSIANIC TRAJECTORIES IN GOD'S COVENANT PROMISE TO DAVID

David was the second king of Israel and finished what Saul was unable to accomplish. During his forty-year reign (1010–970 BCE), he united the tribes, defeated Israel's enemies, and extended Israel's borders. Although David began his reign in Hebron, he eventually shifted his seat of power to the captured city of Jebus, a Jebusite city, and renamed the city Jerusalem (2 Sam. 5:1–10). This move helped unify the tribes of Israel into a united kingdom. By defeating the Philistines, he made Israel safe from her enemies. Finally, he subdued the peoples of Aram, Ammon, Edom, and Moab and thereby extended Israel's borders. And despite his numerous faults, he was a man after God's heart and one whom God greatly honored with a special promise.

Perhaps the most significant element in the progressive revelation of eschatological messianism in Hebrew Scripture was God's promise to David of an everlasting throne. Although the Davidic covenant was not exclusively prophetic about the Messiah and his eschatological kingdom, the promise finds its ultimate future fulfillment in the eternal kingdom of David's son through the reign of the eschatological Messiah. To be sure, the historical dimension of the kingdom was inaugurated with the reign of David, continued with his son Solomon, and perpetuated from one generation of Davidic king after another up to the Babylonian exile. Yet the Hebrew prophets made clear that God's promise to establish an eternal kingdom and to secure an eternal throne for David's son would be fulfilled in the ultimate son of David, namely, Jesus who came to be called the Messiah.

NATHAN'S ORACLE IN 2 SAMUEL 7:8–16

Original Setting of Nathan's Oracle
The initial purpose of Nathan's oracle was to fulfill David's desire to build a temple for Yahweh. In the ancient Near East, kings typically built temples

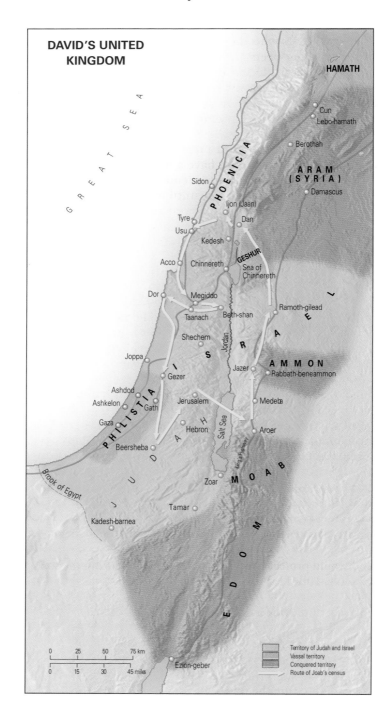

DAVID'S UNITED KINGDOM

HAMATH

Cun
Lebo-hamath

Berothah

ARAM
(SYRIA)

Damascus

Sidon

PHOENICIA

Ijon (Jaan)

Tyre
Usu

Dan

Kedesh

GESHUR

Acco

Chinnereth

Sea of
Chinnereth

Dor

Megiddo

Taanach

Beth-shan

Ramoth-gilead

Shechem

Jordan

ISRAEL

Joppa

Gezer

Jazer

AMMON

Rabbath-beneammon

Ashdod

PHILISTIA

Ashkelon

Gath

Jerusalem

Medeba

Gaza

Salt Sea

Hebron

Aroer

Beersheba

JUDAH

King's Highway

Brook of Egypt

Zoar

MOAB

Tamar

Kadesh-barnea

EDOM

GREAT SEA

0   25   50   75 km
0   15   30   45 miles

Territory of Judah and Israel
Vassal territory
Conquered territory
Route of Joab's census

Ezion-geber

for their patron deities who they believed empowered them to win military victories. Having been blessed by Yahweh with many military triumphs (cf. 2 Sam. 5–6), David desired to honor God in this traditional manner (2 Sam. 7:1–3). Yahweh responded favorably to his offer, but he withheld this privilege from David. He would not allow David to build the temple (2 Sam. 7:4–7); he promised to provide him a royal heir, who would build the temple (2 Sam. 7:8–16).However, God also promised more. Not only would a son build a temple for God, but God would give David a house, a rule that would have a unique relationship to God. In that house would come a rest from enemies. Here is a promise of peace that would drive the hope of the line until it was realized in full. Pictured in the son who built the temple, this hope continued to live with the nation. This promise and its expectation drove the development of messianic hope and ultimately landed in the work of a son to come who would bring total deliverance.

Literary Structure of Nathan's Oracle
Nathan's oracle consisted of two stanzas (vv. 8–11a, 11b–16), each introduced by a divine speech formula: "This is what Yahweh of hosts says" (v. 8a), "Yahweh declares to you" (v. 11b). In the first stanza, Yahweh promised to grant security to Israel in its land from their enemies, by magnifying David's reign (vv. 8–11a). In the second, Yahweh promised David a secure throne to ensure the future transfer of his kingdom to his son, who would build the temple. This relationship to God, established with the heir, would be characteristic of the dynasty to which God was committing himself. The hope of peace from enemies became a hope of the people of God for a complete deliverance. We may summarize God's promises to David as follows:

- God would make David a prominent king (v. 9b)

- God would firmly establish Israel in the land during the son's reign (v. 10a)

- God would protect Israel from enemy attack during the son's reign (vv. 10b–11a)

- God would provide a dynasty for David (v. 11b)

- God would secure the succession of David's son on his throne (v. 12a)

- God would secure the rule of his son over his kingdom (v. 12b)

- God would protect his son so that he could build the temple (v. 13)

- God would elevate his son into a father-son relationship (v. 14)

- God would discipline his son, but would not revoke his kingship (vv. 14b–15)

- God would establish David to ensure dynastic succession to his son (v. 16)

GOD'S PROMISE OF HOUSE, THRONE, AND KINGDOM

The basic features of the Davidic covenant are developed in the repetition of three key terms: "house," "throne," and "kingdom." Although each has a distinct meaning, they share the same semantic domain, depicting various features of a king's reign over his dominion. In order to fully appreciate God's promise we must understand the contextual meaning of these terms.

House. The term "house" occurs fifteen times. In six cases, it refers to a building: David's palace (vv. 1–2), Yahweh's temple (vv. 5–7, 13). Nine times it is figurative for David's dynasty (vv. 11, 16, 18, 19, 25, 26, 27, 29). Whereas David wished to build a house (temple) for Yahweh, God would build a house (dynasty) for David and place one of his sons upon his throne to build the house (temple) for Yahweh. When the term "house" is used in a royal sense, it may refer to the

> **Nathan's Prophecy to David (2 Samuel 7)**
>
> Although David desired to build a temple for Yahweh, Nathan received a divine oracle rejecting David's proposal. After recounting David's divine selection as leader over Israel and his successful campaigns against Israel's enemies, Nathan announced to David God's plan to establish David's house by promising (1) military success, (2) enduring dynasty, (3) unique father–son relation with David's son, and (4) future construction of the desired Temple by David's son.

individual reign of the current king (2 Sam. 3:1, 6, 8, 10; 12:8; 1 Kings 2:24) or the royal dynasty of its founder and his future heirs (1 Sam. 20:16; 1 Kings 12:19, 26; 13:2; 14:8; 17:21; Isa. 7:2, 13; Jer. 21:12; 2 Chron. 21:7). David understood the term in this broader sense, since he responded by asking God to fulfill his promise throughout all future generations (2 Sam. 7:29).

Throne. The term "throne" occurs twice in Nathan's oracle (vv. 13, 16). God promised to establish the throne of David (v. 16) and his son (v. 13). Like the royal scepter, the throne was a symbol in the ancient world for royal power. So closely associated was this symbol with royal power that "throne" is often figurative for a king's authority (Gen. 41:40; Neh. 3:7), dominion (2 Sam. 3:10; 1 Kings 8:20; Hag. 2:20) and dynasty (1 Kings 2:33, 45).

Kingdom. The term "kingdom" occurs thrice. In each case, Yahweh promised to establish the rule of David and his son: "I will establish his kingdom"

(v. 12); "I will establish the throne of his kingdom" (v. 13); "Your (David's) kingdom will be established" (v. 16). This term connotes that power and authority of a king reigning over a particular domain. The promised kingdom was initially inaugurated with David and his first son Solomon, but it will be ultimately fulfilled with the final son of David, namely, the eschatological Messiah. The initial historical realm of the kingdom of David and Solomon was the united kingdom of the twelve tribes of Israel and Judah. The ultimate eschatological realm of the kingdom of the Messiah will be nothing less than all nations of the earth. They will be under his power and authority.

THE SON OF DAVID TO BUILD THE TEMPLE OF YAHWEH

In Nathan's oracle, God promised to establish one of David's sons on a throne that would be secure perpetually and that this son would build the temple. Technically speaking, Nathan's oracle originally promised the kingdom and throne would be given to two individuals: David and his son. The symmetrical structure (see below) moves from promises concerning David (v. 11) to promises concerning his son (vv. 12, 13b–15) back to promises concerning David (v. 16), and the center highlights God's provision of a son for David who would build the temple (v. 13a):

A		I will give you rest from your enemies (11a)	David
		I will build a "house" for you (11b)	David
	B	I will raise up your seed, who will come from your belly (12a)	David's Son
		I will establish his kingdom (12b)	David's Son
	C	He will build a house for my name (13a)	God's temple
	B	I will establish the throne of his kingdom (13b)	David's Son
		I will become his father, he will become my son…(14–15)	David's Son
A		Your house and your kingdom will be established (16a)	David
		Your throne will be established (16b)	David

It is important to observe that the precise identity of David's son in Nathan's oracle is not identified. Considered in terms of its initial historical fulfillment, the biblical narrator reports that it was Solomon who ascended David's throne and built the temple (1 Kings 8:12–26). However, considered in terms of its ultimate eschatological fulfillment, the subsequent Hebrew prophets declare that it would be the Messiah who would sit on David's throne forever and inherit his kingdom (Isa. 9:6; 11:1, 10). The openness of the term "son" allows for a both/and rather than either/or approach to fulfillment.

Nathan's oracle envisioned as one aspect an initial historical fulfillment in one of the biological sons of David. Verse 12 describes the ascent of one of David's sons to the throne near the time of his own death: "When the time comes for you to die, I will raise up your offspring, who will come from your own loins, to succeed you, and I will establish his kingdom." Although the term "offspring" occasionally functions as a collective for future generations, here it functions in an individual sense referring to an individual son (v. 12).

The expression "your offspring" often refers to one's biological son. Moreover, the Chronicler restates the original wording in Nathan's oracle, "Your offspring, *who will come from your own loins*" (2 Sam. 7:12), in more explicit terms, "Your offspring, *who will be one of your own sons*" (1 Chron. 17:11). Finally, in his prayer of dedication of the temple, Solomon quotes this line in Nathan's oracle. Identifying himself as the son whom God promised to David, he declared that this aspect of the dynastic promise had come to fulfillment on that very day (1 Kings 8:15–24). Once again, Solomon was not *explicitly* in view when Nathan's oracle was delivered because Solomon had not yet been born, and because David had several sons. So it was not a foregone conclusion from the beginning that this son would be Solomon.

Since the identity of David's son was not explicitly identified in Nathan's oracle, the openness of the promise of a "son" allowed not only for an initial historical fulfillment through Solomon the first son of David to inherit his throne, but also for future eschatological fulfillment through the Messiah as David's ultimate son. God's promise that David's son would build the temple was initially fulfilled by Solomon in the physical temple that he constructed in Jerusalem (1 Kings 8:12–26), but will be decisively fulfilled by Messiah in a greater eschatological temple that he would build (Zech. 6:14–15). God's promise of rescue from enemies, initially realized in Solomon, had its more comprehensive, pattern fulfillment in the Messiah Jesus (Luke 1:71–75). Whereas the past reign of Solomon inaugurated the eternal throne and kingdom granted to David, the future eschatological reign of the Messiah would bring this eternal promise to ultimate fruition. So the terms "son" and "temple" feature a significant linguistic openness by divine design to allow for an initial fulfillment of God's promise in Solomon and the ultimate fulfillment in the Messiah. It is not a matter of either/or but both/and.

> **Solomon's Temple**
>
> Solomon, at God's command, laid the corner stone to build Israel's first temple ca. 966 BCE. Seven years later, Solomon dedicated the temple to the Lord saying, "The Lord God of Israel is worthy of praise because he has fulfilled what he promised my father David" (1 Kings 8:15).

INITIAL AND ULTIMATE FULFILLMENT

Initial Fulfillment of God's Promise
Once Solomon ascended the throne and succeeded in building the temple,

he declared that God had fulfilled his promise to David (1 Kings 8:15–21). While Solomon employed fulfillment language in his dedicatory prayer, the completion of the temple did not exhaust God's purposes in establishing the dynasty. God commissioned the Davidic king to function henceforth as the royal patron and sponsor of the temple, as well as a protector of the people. As long as the temple stood on Mount Zion, the Davidic king would sit on the dynastic throne to protect this sacred space from foreign enemies and to provide offerings for the Levitical priests to place on the altar on behalf of the nation. Completion of the temple did not bring God's purposes for the house of David to an end; rather, it inaugurated the new ongoing sacral role that future generations of Davidic kings would play (cf. Ps. 110:4). Henceforth, the Davidic king would not simply function as the political and military leader of Israel, but as its sacral leader and official patron of the temple of Yahweh. Moreover, the security of the House of David and the temple on Mount Zion would become permanently linked from this point forward (cf. Ps. 132:11–18).

Future Eschatological Fulfillment

When considered in the light of the larger context of Scripture as a whole, it becomes clear that God's covenant promise to David laid the theological foundation for the everlasting kingdom of the eschatological Messiah. When Mount Zion was destroyed in 586 BCE by the Babylonians, the temple razed ,and the Davidic dynasty dismantled, God promised that he would one day renew his ancient promise to David. God would raise up another "Son" of David who would be greater than Solomon. He would inherit the throne of David and rule over an eternal kingdom; however, rather than passing on his rule to a successor, he would reign forever. Furthermore, this greater "Son" of David would build an eschatological temple after the pattern of Solomon's temple, yet it would it be more glorious than Solomon's historical temple. For its building would signal the age of redemption and the invitation for all peoples to worship God.

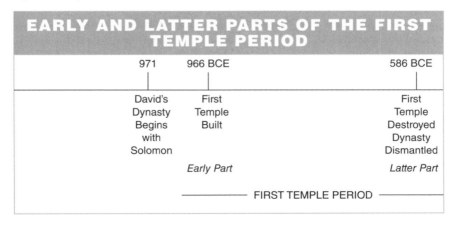

EARLY AND LATTER PARTS OF THE FIRST TEMPLE PERIOD

971	966 BCE		586 BCE
David's Dynasty Begins with Solomon	First Temple Built		First Temple Destroyed Dynasty Dismantled
	Early Part		*Latter Part*
		FIRST TEMPLE PERIOD	

FROM SON OF DAVID TO SONS OF DAVID

On the surface it may seem that God's promise was limited in scope to David and his son (Solomon). However, this kind of overly literal approach overlooks the deeper significance of the speech, which was implied as part of its original cultural script. No one establishes a dynasty with the intent of limiting it to two generations. God guaranteed the first two generations of the dynasty in order to secure the successful building of the temple and to provide a legitimate foundation for the continuation of the dynasty in future generations. The lack of any direct mention of future generations beyond David and his son (Solomon) does not rule out God's further intentions. Subsequent revelation made explicit what was originally implicit in Nathan's oracle. God intended to perpetuate David's dynasty throughout future generations. This was originally implicit in Nathan's oracle, but only made explicit in subsequent passages. This is an important factor to keep in mind when we later consider the future eschatological and messianic potential of God's promise. Although Nathan's oracle was not exclusive, direct prophecy of the eschatological Messiah, subsequent revelation reveals that God ultimately had in mind the eschatological Messiah and his eternal kingdom.

On the surface, it might seem that God's promise applied to the reign of only two individuals—David and his son. After all, the expression, "(one's) kingdom," is used elsewhere of the reign of individual kings (Jer. 26:1; 27:1; 28:1; Hos. 1:4; 1 Chron. 29:30). Also, the expression, "establish (his) kingdom," is used elsewhere of God providing a secure reign for an individual king throughout the course of his lifetime (2 Chron. 17:5). Yet it is unreasonable to limit the extent of God's promise to David to two generations. The kingdom of any king was typically inherited by his royal heirs (2 Chron. 21:4). Moreover, subsequent passages make clear that Yahweh would establish David's kingdom by providing an enduring dynasty of royal heirs upon his throne from one generation to the next in uninterrupted succession—provided they obey God (1 Kings 9:5; 2 Chron. 13:8).

Although future generations are not directly mentioned in Nathan's oracle, this promise set the stage for a perpetual regal line, given the nature of dynasties. Subsequent passages make explicit what is implicit in Nathan's oracle, namely, God intended to extend David's throne for all generations—provided they obeyed. However, when the disobedience of his heirs did place the dynastic throne in jeopardy, God promised to restore his throne through a second "David." So the line was both preserved in a promise that would ultimately be realized and yet held accountable for sin in any generation. God was patient in the face of regal disobedience, as the biblical history of Israel indicates. God's judgment was slow to come; but come it did. When divine discipline did arrive, the Davidic line was called back to faithfulness in the period of the exile. The hope of the line would be in one who would be a faithful king.

FROM PERPETUAL HISTORICAL KINGDOM
TO ETERNAL ESCHATOLOGICAL KINGDOM

God promised David and his son a kingdom that would endure "forever" (vv. 13, 16). Subsequent statements by David and Solomon reveal that both understood God as promising a dynasty that would endure through a perpetual succession of royal descendants on the throne from one generation to the next (1 Kings 2:45; 2 Sam. 22:15//Ps. 18:50[51]). Abijah, king of Judah and a Davidic descendant, also understood God's promise to David of an everlasting kingdom in terms of a perpetual dynasty of Davidic heirs ruling over Israel in succession from one generation to the next (2 Chron. 13:5).

Certainly the historical reigns of David and Solomon themselves did not endure for all eternity. Their throne was "eternal" in the sense that they inaugurated a dynasty of royal heirs who perpetuated their rule one generation after another. The psalmist seems to reflect this understanding of the promise in dynastic terms: "I will place one of your own sons upon your throne. If your sons keep my covenant and the rules I teach them, then their sons will also sit on your throne forever" (Ps. 132:11–12).

Although it is foreign to the thinking of a modern reader, kings in the ancient world viewed their own reign as eternal if their rule inaugurated a perpetual dynasty of royal heirs who would continue their rule from one generation to the next. For example, the royal enthronement inscription of Shulgi king of Sumer (2094–2047 BCE) recounts an oracle in which the god Enlil is said to have established the royal dynasty. According to this inscription, Enlil chose Shulgi's father as king to establish an enduring dynasty and called him to build the Ekur temple: "A faithful man will build the Ekur temple to earn a lasting name; the son of that faithful man will long hold the scepter, their throne will never be overthrown!" (*COS* 1.172). This dynastic oracle is similar to Nathan's oracle promising David an heir to build the temple of Yahweh and an everlasting throne.

God's promise to David of an eternal kingdom certainly entailed the historical aspect of a perpetual dynasty inheriting his throne from one generation to the next, but it is clear from the Hebrew prophets that God also had more in mind in Nathan's oracle than a perpetual dynasty. The divinely designed wording in God's promise of an eternal kingdom also envisioned a future eschatological aspect. Thus, Nathan's oracle went beyond the historical-cultural patterns of the ancient world. The dynastic oracle of Shulgi certainly did not envision an eschatological king to come, but announced the inauguration of an enduring dynasty, which would be given the royal scepter and called to function as royal patron of the temple to be built. To be sure, Nathan's oracle promised David an enduring dynasty and a royal heir who would build the temple. Yet for all its similarities, Scripture makes clear that God's promise to David involved much more than traditional ancient Near Eastern royal expectations! For as we have already seen, God's promise to David of an everlasting kingdom was not only predictive of the historical dynasty, but also prophetic for the eternal kingdom of the Messiah.

NATURE OF THE DAVIDIC COVENANT

Up until this point, we have discussed the Davidic covenant in terms of its features related to messianic prophecy. Now, we will consider the Davidic covenant in terms of its features related to messianic *history*. By this we mean that the historical unfolding of the nature of the Davidic covenant created certain historical dynamics that would eventually lead to the explicit prophetic declarations that the solution to the problems with the historical dynasty could only be resolved through the coming of the future eschatological Messiah. To appreciate how this worked, we must focus on the promissory and obligatory features of the Davidic covenant.

The Davidic covenant featured two main elements, namely, divine promise and human obligation. In Nathan's original oracle God promised an eternal kingdom to David, but in subsequent passages God made clear that the perpetual unbroken succession of individual kings from one generation to the next depended on the king's faithfulness. Nevertheless, it is crucial to recognize that God's grace and mercy more than counterbalanced human failure by the Davidic dynasty as a whole. The ultimate future eschatological fulfillment of God's covenant program is guaranteed in the end as a result of God's faithfulness to his promise to David and his irrevocable commitment to bring his covenant promise to ultimate fruition in the Messiah.

Promissory Nature of God's Original Promise
Second Samuel 7 developed three central promises, none of which were

explicitly conditioned by obedience: (1) God would secure the throne of David and his son (Solomon) in a context of peace; (2) God would provide David an heir (Solomon) who would build the temple; and (3) God would provide a perpetual dynasty for David. The lack of explicit moral obligations in Nathan's oracle emphasizes the fundamental promissory nature of God's original promise. This is important to understand since subsequent passages will indicate that God's covenant also entailed implicit obligations. Yet the overarching principle would not be human obligation but divine promise. This suggests that God was irrevocably committed to bring his covenant promises to ultimate fulfillment. In the face of eventual human failure, God's grace and faithfulness would prevail. The promise would stand.

All the same, the theme of obedience was not altogether absent from the oracle. Yahweh declared that he would discipline any sin on the part of David's offspring (2 Sam. 7:14–15). The mention of divine discipline here implied the resultant repentance of the son. The obligation of obedience to God is therefore implicit in Nathan's oracle. This implicit obligation to obey will be made explicit in subsequent passages dealing with the covenant. But for now it was God's promise that was being emphasized to make the point that the fulfillment was assured.

Subsequent Passages Feature Promise and Obligation

Although Nathan's oracle did not contain any explicit moral obligations, subsequent passages made clear that God required David's sons to be faithful to him for the initial historical fulfillment of these promises: (1) fulfillment of God's promise to provide a secure throne for David and Solomon was dependent on obedience (1 Chron. 28:7); (2) fulfillment of the promise that Solomon would succeed in building the temple required his faithfulness (1 Kings 6:11–13; 1 Chron. 22:11–13; 28:4–10); and (3) fulfillment of God's promise of the historical perpetuity of the dynasty in any particular generation was conditioned on obedience of each generation of royal descendants (1 Kings 2:3–4; 3:14; 6:11–13; 8:25–26; 9:4–5; 11:38; 2 Chron. 6:16; 7:17–18). Thus, subsequent passages dealing with the covenant explain that the initial historical fulfillment of each of the promises would demand faithfulness on the part of David's sons. What was originally implicit in Nathan's oracle was made explicit in subsequent passages.

It should not come as a complete surprise to discover that other versions of the dynastic oracle make the demand of obedience explicit. For example, when David rehearsed Yahweh's covenant promise to Solomon, he made the moral obligation to obey explicit (1 Kings 2:1–4). Psalm 132:11–12 likewise echoed the wording of 2 Samuel 7:12 but made explicit two features that were implicit in Nathan's oracle: (1) From an historical perspective, God's promise to inaugurate an eternal kingdom for David meant the historical dynasty would begin with one son (Solomon), but continue with many future descendants; but (2) the unbroken succession of this historical dynasty in any one generation to the next would be conditioned on the obedience of each generation of royal heirs.

The nature of the qualification "in any generation" is important. To be sure, God would keep the promise of the covenant in the end; the ultimacy of the promise was irrevocable in that sense. Nevertheless, God would hold the son accountable, rooted in the call to obey and the warning about using the rod for discipline. In the end, however, such discipline was temporary.

The biblical historian stressed that dynastic perpetuity in any particular generation was contingent on whether or not the Davidic kings obeyed Yahweh. The biblical narrator stressed that God evaluated each king according to the standard of David's faithfulness to Yahweh. Although several kings followed the faithful example of David, the majority failed.

The apostasy of Solomon and evil of Rehoboam led to the division of the kingdom in fulfillment of God's promise to discipline David's son when he sinned (2 Sam. 7:14). The persistent sin of subsequent generations of royal heirs eventually led to the temporary suspension of the historical Davidic kingdom. God sent an occupant of David's throne into exile at the hand of Nebuchadnezzar king of Babylon in fulfillment of God's threat of exile (1 Kings 9:5–9), but left the door open for its restoration in the future (cf. Jer. 33:17).

GOD'S FAITHFULNESS TO HIS COVENANT PROMISE AND IRREVOCABLE COMMITMENT TO FULFILL HIS PURPOSES

Although security of the royal throne in any particular generation had been conditioned on obedience, the Davidic dynasty was the object of divine grace and mercy. Human failure was more than counterbalanced by God's faithfulness to his covenant promise to David. Moreover, God was irrevocably committed to the future eschatological fulfillment of his covenant program, so he repeatedly demonstrated his patience, grace, and mercy.

On no fewer than five separate occasions, the evil of individual Davidic kings could have doomed the dynasty to exile, but Yahweh refrained from judgment out of his great mercy and commitment to David.[1] In 1 Kings 15:3–5, for example, the biblical historian explains that the evil of Abijah, grandson of Solomon, was so great that God did not send the dynasty into exile out of respect for David's exceptional faithfulness: "Nevertheless for the sake of David . . . God did this because David had done what was right in the eyes of Yahweh, and had not disregarded any of his commands during his lifetime" (1 Kings 15:4, 5).

---

1. In two cases, God's esteem for the exceptional loyalty of David counterbalanced the evil of the current Davidic king, effectively staying the wrath of God (Solomon: 1 Kings 11:31–36; Abijah: 15:3–5). In three other cases, Yahweh demonstrated forbearance out of his commitment to preserve David's dynasty and to shield Zion as his dwelling place (Ahab: 2 Kings 8:18–19//2 Chron. 21:6–7; Manasseh: 2 Kings 19:34//Isa. 37:35; Hezekiah: 2 Kings 20:6).

DAVID AND SOLOMON'S SUCCESSORS*

Davidic Kings of Judah (931–586)	Kings of Northern Israel (931–722)
Rehoboam (931–913)	Jeroboam (931–910)
Abijah (913–911)	Nadab (910–909)
Asa (911–870)	Baasha (909–886)
	Elah (886–885)
	Zimri (885)
	Omri (885–874)
Jehoshaphat (873–848)*	
	Ahab (874–853)
Jehoram (848–841)	Ahaziah (853–852)
	Jeoram (852–841)
Ahaziah (841)	
Athaliah (841–835)	Jehu (841–814)
Joash (835–796)	
	Jehoahaz (814–798)
Amaziah (796–767)	Jehoash (798–782)
	Jeroboam II (793–753)
Uzziah (790–740)*	Zechariah (753–752)
	Shallum (752)
Jotham (750–735)*	Menahem (752–742)
Ahaz (744–715)*	Pekah (752–732)
	Hoshea (732–722)
Hezekiah (729–686)*	ASSYRIAN CONQUEST
Manasseh (696–642)*	
Amon (642–640)	
Josiah (640–609)	
Jehoiahaz (609)	
Jehoiakim (609–597)	In 609, Assyrians are defeated at Carchamesh by Babylon
Zedekiah (597–586)	
BABYLONIAN CONQUEST	

* As it was with ancient Near Eastern kings, it was not unusual for expectant heirs to co-rule with their fathers. For example Belshazzar coruled with his father Nabonidus over Babylon. See Jean-Jacques Galassner's "Chronicle of Nabonidus (556–539)" in *Mesopotamian Chronicles*, Writings from the Ancient World (Atlanta: Society of Biblical Literature, 2004), 232–239. Solomon co-ruled with his father David beginning in 973 BCE until David relinquished his kingship to Solomon and eventually died in 971 BCE. In a similar manner Jehoshaphat, Uzziah, Jotham, Ahaz (4 yrs.), and Manasseh co-ruled (note the *) with their fathers before assuming sole kingship over Judah. For coregency and reign of kings, see Eugene H. Merrill, *Kingdom of Priests: A History of Old Testament Israel* (Grand Rapids: Baker, 1987).

Many passages emphasize God's faithfulness to his covenant promise and irrevocable commitment to fulfill the ultimate purpose of his covenant program. For example, despite the gross wickedness of Jehoram, God spared the dynasty because of his covenant promise to David (2 Kings 8:18–19//2 Chron. 21:6–7). Likewise, since Jehoram had failed to fulfill the stipulations of obedience, on which perpetuity of the dynastic throne for his generation was conditioned, God could have sent the Davidic dynastic into exile in his day.[2] Yet human failure was more than counterbalanced by God's commitment to his promise to perpetuate David's dynasty from one generation to the next: "[Jehoram] did evil in the eyes of Yahweh, but Yahweh did not destroy the house of David, because of the covenant he had made with David, since he promised to give him and his sons a perpetual dynasty" (2 Chron. 21:6–7).

As Jeremiah noted, the persistent evil of the dynasty eventually exhausted God's patience with the last four generations of Davidic kings (Jer. 15:1, 6; 21:1–23:2). God announced that none of the descendants of Jehoiakim (608–598 BCE) or Jehoiachin (598–597 BCE) would succeed in sitting upon David's throne (Jer. 22:30; 36:30). Yet judgment would not be God's last word. God also promised to one day raise up a second David, who would sit upon David's throne and restore his kingdom to its former glory (Jer. 23:5–6; 30:9; Ezek. 34:23–24; 37:24–25; Hos. 3:5).

When Judah was in exile and the Davidic throne unoccupied, God reassured his people that he one day would restore one of David's descendants to the throne to fulfill his promise: "David will never lack a man to sit on his throne" (Jer. 33:17). As the progress of revelation makes clear, this promise would be fulfilled in the eschatological Messiah Jesus who would ascend the throne to reign forever (Acts 2:31). So the temporary suspension of the Davidic throne at the Babylonian exile demonstrated that the perpetuity of Davidic rule for any particular generation was conditioned on obedience. However, God's promise to restore the throne of the disciplined dynasty through the coming of the future new David also demonstrated the profound faithfulness of God to his covenant promises and his irrevocable commitment to fulfill his eschatological program through the future reign of the Messiah.

FROM THE HISTORICAL DYNASTY TO THE ESCHATOLOGICAL MESSIAH

Scripture repeatedly emphasizes that the fundamental duty of the Davidic dynasty was to demonstrate moral righteousness and to uphold social justice.[3] Some of David's royal descendants lived up to this calling (2 Sam. 8:15; Jer. 22:15), but most failed to rule in righteousness and justice (Jer. 13:13; 22:13;

---

2. Cf. 2 Samuel 23:1–7; 1 Kings 2:3–4; 3:14; 6:11–13; 8:25–26; 9:4–5; 11:38; Jeremiah 17:27–29; 22:1–9; Psalm 132:11–12; 2 Chronicles 6:16; 7:17–18.

3. 2 Samuel 23:3; 1 Kings 10:9; Psalms 72:1–2; 122:5; Jeremiah 21:12; 22:3; Ezekiel 45:9.

cf. 21:1–23:2). Nevertheless, the matchless grace of God would provide one to come who would fulfill these dynastic duties. Moral righteousness and social justice, effectively fulfilling the moral conditions of the Davidic covenant, would characterize this second "David."[4] God would intervene to provide what was naturally lacking from the house of David. Divine grace and commitment to David would counterbalance the dynasty's failure to fulfill its obligation.

The historical realities of the division of David's kingdom in 931 BCE and the subsequent dismantling of David's throne in 586 BCE led to a theological crisis. How would Yahweh fulfill his promise of an everlasting Davidic kingdom, when the House of David had been removed from the throne and cast into exile as punishment for persistent rebellion? The prophets revealed that God one day would raise up a second "David" who would restore the Davidic kingdom to its former glory and inaugurate an everlasting kingdom characterized by righteousness. If God had established David's kingdom in the past, he could reestablish his throne through a second "David," through whom he would fulfill his promise of an everlasting kingdom (e.g., Isa. 9:7[6]; 11:1, 10; Ezek. 34:23–24; 37:24–25; cf. Hos. 3:5; Jer. 30:9; 33:17). So while Nathan's oracle was not exclusive prophecy of the eternal eschatological kingdom, it was ultimately prophetic of the eschatological kingdom and the Messiah as the ultimate son of David.

Canonical Development of the Davidic Covenant

Our contextual analysis of 2 Samuel 7 suggests the Davidic covenant was not exclusively prophetic of the future eternal Kingdom or the eschatological Messiah. Nevertheless, it was ultimately prophetic of the Messiah and his future kingdom. In it was the pattern of the presence of God and peace that one day would be fully realized in the One to come. As subsequent passages explained, God also had promised David the covenant Nathan revealed, an everlasting dynasty composed of a succession of royal descendants sitting upon his throne for perpetuity. As the prophets revealed, the suspension of the dynastic throne by the Babylonian exile did not represent the abolition of God's covenant-promise to David. There would be a greater Son who would bring peace, just as Nathan had described. God would restore David's throne. Although the House of David initially failed to fulfill its duty to obey Torah, the prophets believed Yahweh would somehow honor his promise to David of an everlasting throne.

God revealed to the prophets that one day he would restore David's throne and inaugurate an eternal kingdom. Since the individual prophets were only given one or two pieces of the puzzle, each of them envisioned an aspect of this future restoration. Rather than providing a single unified profile, the prophets paint complementary portraits of the future, each with

---

4. Isaiah 9:7[6]]; 16:5; 32:1; Jeremiah 23:5; 33:15; Ezekiel 37:24; Zechariah 9:9; cf. Isaiah 42:1, 4.

its own contribution to the whole portrait. Their portraits of the restoration resembled a kaleidoscope of images in the process of being brought into a crisp, finely tuned picture as revelation progressed.

CONCLUSION

God's original promise to David ensured the successful building of the temple and provided a son as part of a house God has given for David. God had promised a son who would bring peace. Yet the extent and permanence of the dynasty was secure as long as David's heirs obeyed God and ruled the nation in moral righteousness and social justice. With the historical failure of the dynasty to obey Yahweh, the Davidic throne was temporarily dismantled and the royal house was sent into Babylonian exile. Yet judgment was not God's last word. The exilic and postexilic prophets envisioned a day when God would raise up a greater heir of David who would restore his kingdom. God would keep the irrevocable covenant promise to David revealed through Nathan. This greater Son of David would not only rule over the eschatological kingdom, but he would build the eschatological temple whose glory would surpass that of Solomon's temple. That greater Son would also bring the peace God had promised his people.

CHAPTER THREE

MESSIANIC TRAJECTORIES IN THE ROYAL PSALMS

Crucial features of Israel's royal Davidic ideology were enshrined in six royal psalms. Each developed themes dealing with the historical reign of the Davidic king in the pre-exilic period, laying the foundation for eschatological messianism. Psalms 89 and 132 focus on the God's eternal promise to David. Psalms 72 and 45, written on the occasions of the king's enthronement and marriage, respectively, celebrate God's promise of the universal rule of the Davidic king. Psalms 2 and 110 celebrate the enthronement of the newly anointed Davidic king.

SIX ROYAL PSALMS		
Psalms 2 and 110	Psalms 72 and 45	Psalms 89 and 132
Prophetic Oracles Recited during the Royal Enthronement of the Newly Anointed Davidic King	Portraits of Idealized Davidic King Whose Dominion Expands As He Rules in Righteousness and Justice	Prayers of Lament Addressing the Promissory and Obligatory Aspects of the Dynastic Promise

MESSIANIC TRAJECTORIES IN PSALM 2

Psalm 2 is a royal coronation hymn celebrating the ascension of a newly enthroned Davidic king.[1] It probably was originally composed to celebrate the enthronement of David or Solomon. Psalm 2 may have been recited whenever any new Davidic heir ascended to the throne as part of the royal protocol

---

1. John W. Hilber, *Cultic Prophecy in the Psalms*, BZAW 352 (Berlin/New York: Walter de Gruyter, 2005), 89–105.

in the traditional coronation ceremony. So it was only natural that it also anticipated the enthronement of the eschatological Messiah. The progress of revelation would make it clear that God also had the Messiah in view.

Contextual Reading of Psalm 2

The psalm contains four stanzas: (1) the psalmist describes foreign vassals plotting to rebel against the new king (vv. 1–3); (2) Yahweh mocks the recalcitrant nations and asserts his support of his anointed king (vv. 4–6); (3) the king rehearses Yahweh's declaration that he was his royal "son," whom he would empower to conquer the nations as his inheritance (vv. 7–9); (4) the psalmist exhorts the assembly to pledge loyalty to the king and submit to him (vv. 10–12).

Prophetic Nature of Psalm 2

Psalm 2 features elements typical of prophetic speech: revelation of divine anger against foreign nations (vv. 1–3), revelation of heavenly scene and divine declaration (vv. 4–6), recitation of divine oracle (v. 6–9), and prophetic description of consequences of rebellion (vv. 10–12). Considered from a purely contextual and historical point of view, Psalm 2 initially functioned as an oracle of legitimization during a royal enthronement ceremony of the historical Davidic king. Yet interpreted in its most literal sense, the prophetic features are only fully fulfilled in the reign of the Messiah in the future eschatological kingdom. So it is best to adopt a "both/and" rather than "either/or" approach to its prophetic nature. The enthronement of each historical Davidic king foreshadowed the future eschatological coronation of the ultimate Davidic king.

Ancient Israelite Royal Enthronement Protocol

Psalm 2 reflects ancient Israelite royal enthronement customs, which unfolded in two phases. The king first was anointed at the sanctuary where a prophet uttered an oracle of divine legitimization (1 Kings 1:39; 2 Kings 11:14). Then the entourage proceeded to the palace, where the newly anointed king ascended the throne and the assembly—the royal court and representatives of foreign vassals—swore allegiance (1 Kings 1:40, 46; 2 Kings 11:19).

Features of this royal coronation ritual appear in Psalm 2: the king was anointed (v. 2); he was installed on the throne (v. 6); his enthronement was legitimized by an oracle declaring him to be the divinely chosen king (v. 7); he was empowered with royal symbolic acts (v. 9); and his reign was divinely blessed by a prophetic assurance of future success (vv. 8–10).

Historical-Cultural Features of Psalm 2

Several other features of Psalm 2 also reflect its original historical-cultural setting. For example, verse 9 pictures the newly enthroned king squelching recalcitrant vassals in a dramatic way: "You will break them with an iron scepter; you will smash them in pieces like a potter's vessel." This kind of imagery was frequent in the ancient world. For example, Egyptian kings would often write the names of their vassals on pieces of ceramic pottery, then smash the pottery with their scepter to illustrate how they would destroy rebels. Mesopotamian texts also feature this motif, e.g., "Sargon shattered the lands like pottery and bridled the four corners of the earth."

Psalm 2 also describes the ceremonial enthronement of the Davidic king in terms that were at home with the traditional royal protocol of the ancient world. The following chart, for example, highlights several features that Psalm 2 shared in common with an ancient Near Eastern text describing the coronation ceremony of the Assyrian king Ashurbanipal.[2]

ANCIENT NEAR EASTERN CORONATIONS COMPARED	
Coronation of Assyrian King (SAA 9)	Coronation of Davidic King (Psalm 2)
divine speech formula (line 2)	prophet quotes rebellious vassals (verses 1–3)
promise of enthronement (lines 3–7)	introduction of divine speech (verses 4–5)
vassals speak of allegiance (lines 8–11)	performance of enthronement (verses 6–7a)
promise of world dominion (lines 12–17)	affirmation of royal sonship (verse 7b)
affirmation of royal sonship (lines 18–23)	promise of world dominion (verses 8–9)
protection of new king (reverse line 12)	destruction of rebellious vassals (verses 10–12)

This comparison does not suggest Psalm 2 was dependent on an ancient Near Eastern text. Our point is simply that the protocol of the ceremonial enthronement of the historical Davidic king reflected its original historical-cultural context. The ancient Israelite kings ascended the throne and were coronated with all the pomp and circumstance of any other king in the ancient world. If ancient Near Eastern nations celebrated the coronation of their king, how much more fitting was it for Israel to celebrate the coronation of its king! Yet there were also crucial differences. First, the prophetic oracle

---

2. See Hilber, *Cultic Prophecy in the Psalms*, 92-93.

of legitimization for Israel's kings was uttered, not by cult prophets of foreign gods but by true prophets of Yahweh, the one true God. Second, the prophetic oracle legitimatizing the enthronement of the historical Davidic king was also a portend of things to come. So Psalm 2 ultimately points to the enthronement of the eschatological Messiah.

Davidic King as the LORD's "Anointed"

In verse 2, the psalmist refers to the newly enthroned king as "His Anointed" (מְשִׁיחוֹ). The term "anointed one" (מָשִׁיחַ) designated various divinely chosen figures whom God empowered to fulfill a specific task: (1) priests (Lev. 4:3, 5, 16; 6:15; Num. 3:3); (2) kings (1 Sam. 2:10, 35; 12:3, 5; 16:6; 24:7, 11; 26:9, 11, 16, 23; 2 Sam. 1:14, 16, 21; 19:22; 23:1; Pss. 2:2; 18:51; 20:7; 28:8; 84:10; 89:39, 52; 132:10, 17; Lam. 4:20; 2 Chron. 6:42; Isa. 45:1); and (3) patriarchs (Ps. 105:15; 1 Chron. 16:22; cf. Gen. 20:7; 23:6). Although "anointed one" was not originally a technical term for the eschatological Messiah, it eventually took on this nuance in the progress of revelation[3] and was used in this more technical sense in second temple period literature.

When designating a royal figure, it could (1) designate a particular individual chosen by God as king, e.g., Saul (1 Sam. 12:3; 24:6, 10; 26:9, 11, 16, 23; 2 Sam. 1:14, 16), David (1 Sam. 16:6; 2 Sam. 19:21; 23:1), Solomon (2 Chron. 6:42) and even Cyrus (Isa. 45:1); (2) function in a generic sense to designate any divinely chosen king (1 Sam. 2:35); or (3) refer to the Davidic kings as a whole, as parallel plural terms suggest, e.g., "He is faithful to *his anointed one*, to *David and his descendants* [plural] forever" (Ps. 18:50); "your anointed ones" (2 Chron. 6:42). In Psalm 2:2, the royal title, "His Anointed One," recalls Samuel's anointing of David (1 Sam. 16:13). As Psalm 2 was reused throughout the monarchial period in the royal enthronement of each new Davidic king, the title "anointed one" functioned in a generic sense, referring to any king in the line of David. However, in the progress of revelation, the title includes the eschatological Messiah ("the Anointed One") who also is a Davidic son. The elasticity of its application and the lack of a specific referent in Psalm 2 itself created a divinely designed openness. This allowed

---

3. Many suggest the expression מָשִׁיחַ נָגִיד "anointed prince" (Dan. 9:25) and the anarthrous term מָשִׁיחַ "anointed one" (Dan. 9:26) are two cases in which this term explicitly refers to the eschatological Messiah. For detailed discussion of this approach, see Sir Robert Anderson, *The Coming Prince* (reprint, Grand Rapids: Kregel, 1957), 88–105, 119–29; Harold W. Hoehner, *Chronological Aspects of the Life of Christ* (reprint, Grand Rapids: Zondervan, 2010), 115–40. Others suggest the former predicted the arrival of Joshua the first postexilic high priest in 538 BCE, while the latter predicted the assassination of Onias III the last legitimate high priest in 171 BCE (cf. 2 Macc 4:34–38). For this approach, see John J. Collins, *Daniel*, Hermeneia (Minneapolis: Augsburg Fortress Press, 1993), 166–70. Since this debate involves questions of eschatological systems, a full discussion is beyond the scope of our book.

Psalm 2 to refer to the original historical Davidic king being enthroned, as well as to all subsequent historical Davidic kings, but also to the eschatological Messiah. The text ultimately points to the eschatological king because the hope was that the king coronated might be all the text affirmed.

The Davidic King as the "Son" of God

Verse 7 recounts the divine oracle which designated the Davidic king as God's royal son on the day of his enthronement: "I will tell you what the Lord decreed; he said to me, 'You are my son! This very day I have become your father!'" (NET). The English translation of the Hebrew literally means "I have begotten you" (יְלִדְתִּיךָ from יָלַד). This Hebrew term depicts a father procreating a son (Gen. 4:18; Prov. 23:22) or a mother giving birth (Ps. 7:14[15]; Job 38:29). Used figuratively, it depicts God procreating Israel by delivering the Hebrews from Egypt, then birthing the nation at Sinai: "You have neglected the Rock who fathered you (יְלָדְךָ), and forgotten the God who gave you birth (מְחֹלְלֶךָ)" (Deut. 32:18). In a similar way, verse 7 metaphorically pictured God fathering the Davidic king on the day of his enthronement, that is, designating him as divinely chosen king.

The depiction of the Davidic king as metaphorically "begotten" by God on the day of his enthronement is not to be confused with the ubiquitous ancient Near Eastern convention in which the king was conceived as seminally begotten by his patron deity in his mother's womb. For example, a Sumerian royal coronation hymn depicted Shulgi as begotten by Enlil, thus the divinely chosen heir destined for the throne (COS 1.172). Assyrian enthronement inscriptions metaphorically portray the king as begotten in the womb by his patron deity, securing his eventual ascent to the throne (SAA 9:XL). Ugaritic poetry pictured king Keret as begotten by El, and so a semidivine being: "A son of El is Keret, an offspring of the Kindly One and a holy being. Shall then a god die? Shall an offspring of the Kindly One not live?" (KTU 1.16). Egyptian royal mythology went so far as to claim that the pharaoh was not only seminally begotten by Horus, but the very incarnation of Horus during his earthly life as universal ruler of the world, only to become the incarnation of Osiris in death as universal ruler of the underworld.

By dramatic contrast, Israel refused to view her kings as semidivine beings begotten in the womb by deity, but as truly mortals seminally begotten by a human father (e.g., 2 Sam. 7:12, "I will raise up your offspring after you, who shall come forth from your own loins," cf. 1 Chron. 17:11; Pss. 45:16[17]; 89:30[31]; 132:11). The image of God fathering the Davidic king was figurative of his designation of the Davidic scion as divinely appointed king and legitimate heir to the throne. This echoes Nathan's dynastic oracle proclaiming that David's son would enjoy an enduring father/son relationship with God: "I will become his father, and he will become my son: when he commits iniquity, I will discipline him . . . but my lovingkindness will never depart from him" (2 Sam. 7:14–15). In contrast to Saul whose dynasty God rejected due to continual sin, God would never reject David's dynasty but lovingly discipline the king to ensure his obedience and repentance when he would inevitably falter. This father/son motif also recalls God's promise to David himself: "He [=David] shall cry to Me, 'You are my Father, my God, and the Rock who protects me!' I will appoint him [=David] as my firstborn son, the most exalted of the kings of the earth" (Ps. 89:26–27[27–28]). As in Psalm 89:26–27, Psalm 2:7–10 links God's designation of the Davidic king as his designated "son" with the promise of future inheritance of all nations.

Interpreted from an initial historical contextual perspective, verse 7 most naturally would have been interpreted in a metaphorical sense, identifying the contemporary Davidic king as the divinely chosen ruler. Yet the language is open enough, when taken in its most literal sense, to allow for an elevated meaning. Its linguistic character allowed for an elevated messianic potential, albeit in the sense of escalated messianic pattern prophecy or typology. The Second Testament proclaims that this fuller sense (*sensus plenior*) and ultimate messianic reference (vis-à-vis *references plenior*) was divinely designed within the text's wording. Simply because the ancient Israelites did not grasp this full messianic potential does not mean it was not there all along. It was a messianic mystery, awaiting the full realization of the language and the incarnation of Jesus, especially his resurrection and ascension, for this heightened sense to be fully recognized for the first time.

Universal Dominion of the Davidic King

Verses 8–11 express the prophet's confidence of the king's universal dominion over "all the nations." Interpreted from a purely historical-contextual perspective, this may be understood as a prediction of the Davidic king's conquest of all surrounding nations. In fulfillment of this prediction, David did, in fact, subjugate all nations surrounding Israel (Edom, Moab, Ammon, Philistia, Amalek), described as the conquest of "all the nations" (1 Chron. 14:17; 18:11).

Considered from an historical-cultural perspective, verses 8–11 could be interpreted as reflecting the common literary convention of royal hymns of the ancient world in which the new king's rule was described in seemingly universal terms. For example, Egyptian royal coronation inscriptions depicted the newly enthroned king as having a universal rule. The coronation hymn of Horemheb features the declaration of his universal rule, despite the reality that Egypt had recently lost control of its traditional enemies: "[Amon] embraced his beauty crowned with the royal helmet, to assign to him the circuit of the sun; the Nine Bows (=Egypt's traditional enemies) are beneath his feet" (*ARE* 3.18; *TAPE* 232). Likewise, Assyrian coronation hymns contain prayers that the new king exercise universal dominion. The coronation hymn of Ashurbanipal reads, "May Shamash, king of heaven and earth, raise you [Ashurbanipal] to shepherd the four corners!" (*COS* 1.142). Assyrian coronation oracles also declare that the king would one day exercise universal dominion. Assur is said to have promised universal dominion to newly crowned Esarhaddon: "Listen, O Assyrians! The king will vanquish his foe. Your king will put his enemy under his foot, from sunset to sunrise, from sunrise to sunset!" (*SAA* 9:23).

Perhaps Psalm 2 expressed the Israelite version of the royal court's expectation that Yahweh's divinely chosen king would one day exercise universal dominion. If foreign kings could express such optimism, it should come as no surprise that the anointed king of the one true God would express no less confidence. Yet Psalm 2 supersedes such stereotypical convention since it was more than political propaganda, but was genuine divinely inspired prophecy.

Psalm 2 predicted nothing less than that Yahweh's universal kingship would manifest itself in the earthly rule of his Davidic coregent. In a partial inaugural fulfillment of the oracle, God elevated David's kingdom (2 Sam. 5:12), causing him to defeat "all his foes" (2 Sam. 7:9; 22:1). Noting that David subjugated the surrounding nations (Philistia, Aram, Moab, Ammon, Edom, Amalek), the biblical narrator reported that he conquered "all the nations" surrounding Israel (2 Sam. 5:17–25; 8:1–15; 12:26–31). However, David also foresaw that his historical victory of these nations was a portend of the ultimate destiny of his dynasty. For after God had given him victory over "all" his foreign foes (2 Sam. 22:1), David expressed confidence that his dynasty eventually would conquer "all nations" to manifest God's kingship (2 Sam. 22:2–51). As the rest of Scripture would eventually make clear, this future universal subjugation of all nations to the Davidic king will occur through the agency of the future eschatological Messiah. So by divine design the ambiguity of the poetic imagery allowed verses 8–10 to explicitly predict the historical elevation of David's dynasty over the surrounding nations, as well to implicitly foreshadow a greater future hope of the universal reign of the eschatological Messiah.

Exhortation to Submit to the Newly Enthroned Davidic King
Verses 11–12 threaten the destruction of the Davidic king's enemies. The psalmist exhorted the assembled representatives of the royal court and foreign vassals to pay homage to the newly enthroned Davidic king, lest he destroy them. When read from a purely historical contextual perspective, this likely reflected traditional ancient Israelite court style. A similar motif occurs in ancient Near Eastern coronation inscriptions. For example, the Egyptian royal coronation inscription of Hatshepsut exhorts the court to pay homage to the new king under penalty of death (*ARE* 3.98). The Assyrian coronation ritual of Ashurbanipal demands loyalty of the court and assembled vassals, threatening destruction of his foes (*SAA* 11.4–7).

While verses 11–12 may have initially reflected traditional Israelite court style, the rest of Scripture makes clear that God ultimately had more in mind than conventional royal rhetoric. The language was divinely designed to open the door for the hope of a greater king to come who would fulfill these expectations in an elevated sense. Understood in this heightened sense, the warning is nothing less than prophetic of the destruction of the evil in the final judgment at the inauguration of the Messiah's eschatological rule. Since Yahweh is the universal ruler of all nations, verses 11–12 mean that God one day will subjugate all nations to the Davidic throne as the earthly instrument of his own rule. If this would not happen during the imminent future, it must happen in the eschatological future.

Canonical Reading of Psalm 2

We have already hinted at several features in Psalm 2 that would eventually lead to a more robust canonical reading. And there are many ways that we can get at the fuller canonical significance of this royal coronation psalm. One way is simply to consider its placement in the book of Psalms. When the earliest canonical form of the book of Psalms was compiled in the second temple period, this coronation psalm was given prominent position. Although several others were composed much earlier (e.g., Moses wrote Psalm 90), early Jewish editors saw fit to open the collection with this psalm. In the traditional order of the Hebrew Psalter (dating to ca. 100 CE), it follows only Psalm 1; hence we know it today as Psalm 2. However, in some earlier Hebrew versions, it actually opened the Psalter. For instance, in the Dead Sea Scrolls, predating the later Masoretic version, the Psalter opened with this very psalm. In other words, our Psalm 2 was their Psalm 1. Sometime after the fall of Jerusalem and for reasons we do not completely understand, the canonical order of the Psalter opened with what we now know as Psalm 1, our psalm becoming what we now know as Psalm 2.

It is quite remarkable that this psalm—composed in the preexilic period to celebrate the coronation of the current Davidic king—would play such a prominent role in the worship of the second temple community. After all, ever since Nebuchadnezzar destroyed Jerusalem, razed the temple, and carried Jehoiachin and Zedekiah into Babylonian exile, the Davidic throne had been unoccupied. It remained so even after the exiles returned, the priesthood was restored, and the temple rebuilt. In fact, as long as Yehud remained under foreign dominion—and according to Daniel 9:24, this would be much longer than the seventy-year exile itself—the royal line was blocked from reclaiming the throne to resume Davidic rule over an independent nation.

In the light of these new historical realities of the postexilic and second temple periods, Psalm 2 came to address new realities as it portrayed the hope of the Davidic promise. No longer did it celebrate the coronation of a current Davidic king. It came to express the future expectation of the restoration of David's dynasty after the people were restored to the land, with the priesthood reconsecrated and temple rebuilt (Jer. 33:14–26; Zech. 3:1–10; 6:12–15; cf.

Hag. 2:20–23). After all, the prophets predicted that a new David would one day arise. Yet as it became clear with the passing of time that the Davidic dynasty would not take the throne anytime soon, this hope became focused on the eschatological future and the Messiah. Psalm 2 appropriately expressed the hope of the second temple community for the ultimate "Anointed One," who would ascend David's throne to inaugurate the eschatological kingdom.

When read in the light of the biblical canon as a whole, Psalm 2 functions typologically. The past enthronement of the historical Davidic king foreshadowed the future enthronement of the eschatological Messiah. What was predicated to historical Davidic kings in a hyperbolic sense would be literally true of the eschatological King: the Messiah really would rule all nations. While the historical Davidic king was the metaphorical covenant "son" of God (cf. 2 Sam. 7:14), the eschatological Messiah would be the greater Son of God in a heightened sense. The text meant all of this from the beginning as the pattern pointed to the eventual fullness of fulfillment.

MESSIANIC TRAJECTORIES IN PSALM 45

Psalm 45 makes an important contribution to the progressive unfolding of royal Davidic ideology leading to eschatological messianism. Although this psalm initially referred to an historical Davidic king, it also provided the foundation for a later robust messianic hope.

Contextual Reading

Psalm 45 was a originally composed as a royal wedding psalm, dedicated to the Davidic king on the occasion of his marriage to a foreign bride. The king's marriage was celebrated since their union gave the nation hope that the dynasty would be perpetuated by royal heirs to the throne (cf. verses 16–17). The superscription calls it a "love song," reminiscent of the Song of Songs, a collection of love poems celebrating a royal courtship and wedding (e.g., Song 3:6–11).

The psalm contains four stanzas: (1) the poet addressed the royal groom (vv. 1–9); (2) the poet addressed the bride (vv. 10–12); (3) the poet described the beautiful bride (vv. 13–15); (4) the poet blessed the king with assurance of royal heirs who would one day inherit his throne (vv. 16–17). It pictured the Davidic king at his finest—enjoying God's blessing since he rules in righteousness and justice; admires the beauty of his foreign bride and offers her encouragement; and celebrates the royal union in anticipation of royal offspring.

It is important to recognize that the identity of the Davidic king and of his foreign bride is not explicitly stated. Mention of a foreign bride immediately calls to mind one of the foreign brides of Solomon, perhaps the renown and oft-mentioned daughter of Pharaoh, whom he especially loved (1 Kings 11:1; 2 Chron. 8:11). However, Solomon was not the only king to marry a foreign bride. While Psalm 45 might have been composed to celebrate the occasion of one particular historical king, it was likely reused on the occasion of subsequent royal marriages. Such a reuse of this psalm throughout the history of the dynasty provided the theological and hermeneutical segue for the decisive connection of this psalm to the ultimate Davidic king.

Idealization of the Royal Groom/Davidic King (vv. 1–9)
The opening lines extol the royal groom as the ideal man—the epitome of masculinity: "You are the most handsome of all men!" (v. 2a). Such praise reflects the literary conventions of Hebrew love poetry (cf. Song 1:16; 2:3; 5:10–16; cf. 1:12–14; 5:13). The royal groom is also the ideal king—the epitome of royalty. The poet mixed historical reality with rhetorical hyperbole. The poet recalls that God anointed the king—whether ritually at his coronation or ceremonially on the day of his wedding—and lavished his blessings on his reign (vv. 2b, 7) since he ruled on behalf of righteousness and justice (vv. 4, 7). As a reward, God promised one day to subjugate all nations under his feet (v. 5; cf. Pss. 2:8–12; 18:47; 110:3, 6–7).

This ideal praise soars in verse 6, where the Davidic king is addressed as—or associated with—deity and an unending rule. It is ironic that the Hebrew syntax is so ambiguous that it may be rendered variously: "Your throne, O God, endures forever" (KJV, NKJV, ASV, NRSV, NASB, NIV, TNIV, NLT, NCV, NET, HCSB), "Your divine throne is forever and ever" (RSV, HCSB margin), "Your throne is [like] God's throne—eternal" (NEB); "Your throne is the [throne] of God—it is forever" (NIRV, NRSV margin, HCSB margin), "Your throne, [given] of God, is forever" (JPS).

The Christian reader intuitively sees the full messianic potential of verse 6 as ultimately speaking of the Messiah as God incarnate. However, verse 6 initially addressed the historical Davidic king at the time of his royal wedding to a foreign bride. So in what way could the poet legitimately address him as "God"? The regal authority of the Davidic king was based on the divinely bestowed throne, which was one aspect of God's promise to David (2 Sam. 7:13, 16). This divinely bestowed throne points to a divine king, whom the Davidic king represents. This is suggested by four features which are clearly addressed elsewhere in the Hebrew Scriptures.

First, those God appointed to represent him were called "God" (אֱלֹהִים) in a representative sense. God appointed Moses as his spokesman to Aaron and Pharaoh: "He will speak for you to the people; he will be your mouth, you will be [like] God (אֱלֹהִים) to him" (Exod. 4:16); "I have made you [like] God (אֱלֹהִים) to Pharaoh, your brother Aaron will be your prophet" (Exod. 7:1). Moses instructed Aaron what to say and commanded Pharaoh what to do with divine authority.

Second, the term *elohim* (אֱלֹהִים) designates a wide range of referents besides Yahweh the only true God: (1) angelic beings: "You have made man a little lower than the angels (*elohim*, אֱלֹהִים)" (Ps. 8:5[6], LXX; also Ps. 82:1; 138:1); (2) ghosts such as Samuel's spirit rising from the dead: "I see [one like] a god (*elohim*, אֱלֹהִים) coming up out of the earth!" (1 Sam. 28:13); (3) divinely appointed human judges: "His master will bring him to the judges (*elohim*, אֱלֹהִים)" (Exod. 21:6; also Exod. 22:8[7], 9[8]; 28[27]); and (4) divinely appointed human rulers: "He (God) chose new leaders (*elohim*, אֱלֹהִים), then fighters appeared in the gates" (Judg. 5:8).

Third, the royal psalms portray the Davidic king as God's earthly vice-regent (Pss. 2:6–12; 72:17; 89:21–27; 110:1–2). David's throne was seen as God's throne: "He chose Solomon to sit on the throne of the kingdom of the LORD over Israel" (1 Chron. 28:5). In the Chronicler's account, David's kingdom is viewed as God's kingdom: "your kingdom" (2 Sam. 7:16) is glossed "my kingdom" (1 Chron. 17:14). Since the Davidic king was called to rule on behalf of Yahweh, his rule was to be the earthly representative of God's throne and kingdom.[4]

Fourth, like Psalm 45:6, Isaiah 9 bestows robust royal titles on the Davidic king as the earthly representative of God: "Wonderful Counselor, Mighty God, Everlasting Father, Prince of Peace" (v. 6[7]). We will examine these titles more fully in chapter 5. For now, it is important to note that since the Davidic king represents God's rule on earth, Psalm 45 declares that it is he who wages battle on behalf of justice and righteousness in the name of Yahweh (vv. 3–5).[5]

Although the historical Davidic kings were pictured as the earthly representative of God's rule on earth, they were not equated with God or identified as God himself. Although human rulers whom God appointed as his vice-regents could be designated by the term *elohim* (אֱלֹהִים), the kings of Israel recognized that they were, in fact, not God (2 Kings 5:7). In contrast to ancient Near Eastern kings who often identified themselves as gods, Moses

---

4. Scripture pictures all earthly rulers in general, but the Davidic king in particular, as called to function as his divinely appointed representative on earth in several ways. Human kings wield divinely appointed authority (Rom. 13:1–4). Scripture often compares the command of the king to the command of God—both are absolute (Prov. 24:21; Eccl. 8:2–5). The earthly king was called to demonstrate his love for the nation by ruling in righteousness and justice (1 Kings 10:9; Ps. 72:1–2), as God loves by ruling in righteousness and justice (Ps. 89:14[15]). Likewise, Psalm 45:6–7 compares David's throne with God's throne. As long as the Davidic kings would rule in moral righteousness and social justice, the dynastic throne would endure (1 Kings 2:3; 6:12; 9:4; 10:9; Ps. 132:11–12). When they failed to uphold the same, the dynastic throne was placed in jeopardy (Jer. 21:12; 22:3, 13, 15).

5. The study note on Psalm 45:6, written by Robert B. Chisholm Jr., in the NET Bible reads: "Ancient Near Eastern art and literature picture gods training kings for battle, bestowing special weapons and intervening in battle. According to Egyptian propaganda, the Hittites described Rameses II as follows: 'No man is he who is among us, It is Seth great-of-strength, Baal in person; Not deeds of man are these his doings, They are of one who is unique' (*AEL*, 2:67). Psalm 45:6 and Isaiah 9:6 probably envision a similar kind of response when friends and foes alike look at the Davidic king in full battle regalia. When the king's enemies oppose him on the battlefield, they are, as it were, fighting against God himself."

prohibited the kings of Israel from exalting themselves over their fellow Israelites (Deut. 17:20).

Nevertheless, taken in its most robust literal sense, the words of the psalmist do in fact address the ultimate Davidic king as God. Indeed, the Second Testament would later proclaim that this is ultimately nothing less than prophetic of the Messiah as God incarnate (Heb. 1:8).[6] God's actions in Jesus and the words of the text come together to show the pattern of what God was doing in Davidic kingship.

Hence, we conclude that the expression of verse 6 was divinely designed to describe the historical Davidic king as God's human representative and to lay the Scriptural foundation for the later, fuller revelation of the ultimate Davidic king as God incarnate. It was not an explicit, direct prophecy of Messiah's deity, but the divinely designed wording of verse 6 allowed for the pattern of a proclamation of Messiah's deity as seen through the incarnation and ascension of Jesus.

Encouragement to the Foreign Bride (vv. 10–12)

In verse 9b, the poet shifted his attention to the stunning beauty of the royal bride and, in verses 10–12, directly addressed her.[7] Recognizing she might be homesick for her homeland and family, he encouraged her to take courage and enter into her marriage with joy.[8] The poet noted that the king was enthralled with her beauty (v. 11a) and that she received lavish wedding gifts from foreign rulers wanting to curry her favor (v. 12). He reminded her that she was obligated to bring pleasure to her husband who had absolute authority over her as king (v. 11b).

Description of the Foreign Bride's Beauty (vv. 13–15)

In verses 13–15, the poet described the bridal procession. He admired the stunning beauty of the bride in her wedding dress, decked out in pearls with

---

6. For a discussion of Psalm 45 in Hebrews 1, see Herbert W. Bateman IV, "Psalm 45:6–7 and Its Christological Contributions to Hebrews," *TJ* 22NS (2001): 3–21.

7. The term "royal bride" refers to a queen/royal consort. The term is an Akkadian loanword, meaning "queen, royal consort." The related Aramaic term is used of queens or consorts of the foreign kings (Dan. 5:2–3, 23; Neh. 2:6).

8. In the ancient Near East, kings often married the daughter of foreign kings for various reasons. In some cases, political alliances between two neighboring nations were sealed through intermarriage between royal households (*COS* 1.102). So it should come as no surprise that various Hebrew kings married daughters of foreign rulers for various reasons—some legitimate, others illegitimate. David married Maacah daughter of Talmai king of Geshur (1 Chron. 3:2 other examples: 1 Kings 3:1; 7:8; 9:24; 16:31). Solomon's marriages to foreign wives led to his religious apostasy and Ahab's marriage to Jezebel led to the importation of Baal worship into Israel; yet David's marriage to Maacah is not condemned and Psalm 45 celebrates an historical Davidic king's marriage to a foreign princess.

brocade, trimmed with gold (v. 13). Then he described how she was escorted to the king, her maidens bubbling with joy (vv. 14–15).

Anticipation of Royal Heirs to the Throne (vv. 16–17)
In verses 16–17, the poet addressed the royal groom. He anticipated that this royal union would produce sons who would become princes throughout the land and future successors to the dynastic throne (v. 16). Mention of future heirs to the Davidic throne makes clear that Psalm 45 was not directly messianic. After all, this royal marriage was to produce physical offspring, that is, sons who would rule in Israel to perpetuate the dynastic throne: "Your sons will carry on the dynasty of your ancestors; you will make them princes throughout the land" (v. 16, NET). The psalm pictured the king as a mortal ruler whose marriage would sire his successors.

The hereditary nature of the historical Davidic throne through procreation suggests the kind of perpetuity the psalmist had in mind was the continuation of his throne through heirs. Psalm 132:11–12 likewise promised that David's throne would endure perpetually *in terms of any generation*—if his descendants (plural) would obey God. Psalm 89:29–37 promised that David's throne would endure as long as the sun and moon—not that David himself would sit on the throne forever. God would perpetuate his dynasty with royal descendants—assuming they would obey God.

Finally, the king's reputation would be praised through coming years and among all nations from one generation to another (v. 17). Considered from a purely historical contextual perspective, this meant that the king's name would live on in his royal line. Yet the elasticity of the terminology in verse 17 does not preclude an even more robust messianic sense, albeit one that likely was not explicit at the time. The language allows that the perpetual universal praise of the Davidic king would be realized through an eternal reign over an unending kingdom.

Canonical Reading of Psalm 45
Although Psalm 45 was not originally direct prophecy of the eschatological Messiah, it laid the hope for eschatological messianic expectations. The dismantling of David's throne in 586 BCE threatened to turn this psalm into little more than a romantic relic of the past. Yet the inclusion of this royal wedding poem in the Psalter, whose final form was settled much later—long after the Davidic throne was excavated and so long after the last royal wedding—reveals that hope of future royal nuptials continued to live in the hearts of the postexilic community.

Read from the viewpoint of its canonical setting, Psalm 45 celebrated not only an historical royal wedding, but also expresses the future expectation of the divinely restored Davidic dynasty—and with it the joy of future royal nuptials. Of course, when the dynasty was not restored during the second temple era, this future expectation pointed to eschatological messianism. With the theological move to a decisive eschatological Messiah, the faithful came to realize that Psalm 45 should be understood as typological of the eschatological Messiah.

MESSIANIC TRAJECTORIES IN PSALM 89

Psalm 89 contrasts the eternal heavenly kingship of Yahweh and his promise to David of an everlasting earthly reign with the historical reality of a recent crisis, when God's commitment to David's dynasty and his own rule over chaos was called into question. Although its precise date of composition is debated, the psalm clearly was written after some catastrophe threatened David's dynasty. Options include: (1) siege of Jerusalem in 927 BCE by Shishak king of Egypt; (2) siege of Jerusalem in 735–34 BCE by the Syro-Ephraimite coalition to remove Ahaz from the throne; (3) tragic death of Josiah the last godly Davidic king in 609 BCE; (4) exile of Jehoiachin the last Davidic king in 597 BCE; or (5) destruction of Jerusalem by Nebuchadnezzar in 586 BCE.

Psalm 89 grapples with the tension between God's promise to David of an enduring dynasty and elevation of his throne over all earthly kings (cf. 2 Sam. 7:10–16) versus his apparent recent rejection of the Davidic king and casting of his crown to the dust under his foes. The psalmist laments the contrast between God's promise to exalt the Davidic king and uphold his dynasty perpetually with the historical reality of its recent demise. He not only asks God how long this state of affairs will persist, but challenges him to keep his promise by restoring David's throne. In effect, the psalmist expresses confidence that the current rejection of the current Davidic king and his subjugation to kings of foreign nations was only temporary. God one day would not only restore the throne, but elevate a future Davidic descendant to rule over all nations of the earth.

Contextual Reading of Psalm 89

Psalm 89 opens with features of a thanksgiving song, but it closes as a lament. It consists of four stanzas: (1) praise of God's kingship which endures for eternity and is exalted above all heavenly beings (vv. 2–18); (2) recollection of God's election and anointing of David to kingship and promise to exalt him over all earthly kings (vv. 19–27); (3) rehearsal of God's promise to David of an everlasting dynasty (vv. 28–37); and (4) complaint of God's recent seeming rejection of the current Davidic king and his subjugation to foreign nations (vv. 38–51).

God's Heavenly Kingship: Represented by David's Earthly Kingship (vv. 1–18)

The opening lines praise God's kingship. Qualities ascribed to God's heavenly eternal kingship (vv. 5–18) are mirrored by David's earthly enduring kingship (vv. 19–27). Just as Yahweh is the most exalted ruler in heaven (vv. 6–9),

God appointed the Davidic king as the most exalted ruler on earth (v. 27). Just as Yahweh exercises sovereign control over the raging waters of chaos (vv. 9–10), God will elevate the Davidic king over the rivers and sea (v. 25). Just as Yahweh's throne is established by his steadfast faithfulness (v. 14), the Davidic throne is maintained by the same (v. 25). Thus, Yahweh's kingship was the basis of and paradigm for Davidic kingship, since the Davidic king was the earthly representative of Yahweh's kingship. God's eternal heavenly kingship is unassailable, so the kingship of David's dynasty was secure.

God's Election and Elevation of the Davidic King (vv. 19–27)
The second stanza details God's election and elevation of David. In verses 19–20, the psalmist rehearses God's election and anointing of David as king. While the Egyptians claimed their king was incarnate deity having been divinely begotten in the womb, the psalmist notes that David simply was "found" by God among the Israelites as one whose heart was inclined toward him. In verses 21–23, he recalls that God promised to elevate David by giving him victory in battle. In verses 24–27, he recounts God's promise to elevate David over all earthly kings by designating him as his own royal "son" and "firstborn," that is, the most exalted king of earth.

The most significant feature for our purposes is God's promise to elevate David's rule over all nations (vv. 24–25) and to designate the king as his royal "son" whom he would appoint as his "firstborn" as the most exalted king of earth (vv. 26–27). The expression "firstborn" was a title of socio-political primacy, not chronological priority.[9] The Davidic king would enjoy the highest rank among all earthly kings. This designation effectively guaranteed that the Davidic king one day would rule all nations. In the face of the current catastrophe in which the king had been subjugated to his foes, this promise provided an anchor for the future hope that God would not only restore the throne but elevate the Davidic king as universal ruler. So this title conveys an implicit future eschatological destiny for David's dynasty. With the progress of revelation, it would become clear that this hope would only be realized in the eschatological Messiah. How God would do this, when he would do it, and through whom he would do it were yet a mystery.

God's Promise to David of an Enduring Dynastic Throne (vv. 28–37)
The third stanza rehearses Nathan's dynastic oracle promising David an enduring throne (2 Sam. 7:10–16). The psalmist develops three themes: (1) God's promise to establish David's throne and continue his dynasty from one generation to the next for perpetuity (vv. 28–29); (2) God's irrevocable covenant promise to maintain David's dynasty, even if his descendants disobey God—but assuming discipline would bring them to repentance (vv. 30–34);

---

9. *NIDOTTE* 1144; *TDOT* 2:121–27; *TWOT* 244.

and (3) God's oath to perpetuate David's dynastic throne for all eternity (vv. 35–37).

God's Temporary Rejection of the Davidic King (vv. 38–52)

The last stanza laments the stark contrast between God's promise to elevate David's throne and perpetuate his dynasty with the harsh realities of the historical plight of the most recent contemporary Davidic ruler. The king had been defeated in battle; his crown trampled in the dust by his foes; his throne cast to the ground and his own life cut short; the fortified walls of Jerusalem had been breached and the city itself laid in ruins (vv. 38–45). This shocking state of affairs led the psalmist to call into question Yahweh's faithfulness to his covenant promise to David, and to plea that Yahweh restore the Davidic throne in keeping with his vow (vv. 45–52).

Canonical Reading of Psalm 89

While Psalm 89 originally was not exclusively messianic, it laid a foundation for the hope of the future restoration of the Davidic dynasty to its former position, as well as the elevation of the Davidic king over all rulers. It is difficult not to sense an eschatological element in the realization of this expectation. Although it might appear that the psalmist had in view an unbroken succession of royal heirs in view (vv. 28–29), subsequent revelation shows that the wording referred to a dynastic line that eventually would lead to the ultimate realization of the hope God had promised though a specific individual. With the dismantling of the Davidic throne at the Babylonian exile in 586 BCE and the non-restoration of the Davidic line in the postexilic period, some of the faithful eventually began to understand that God would one day fulfill this only through the eschatological Messiah.

However, since Psalm 89 ends on an ambiguous note, some scholars question whether the canonical position of Psalm 89 reflects this kind of eschatological messianic hope. For example, Wilson suggests Psalms 2–72 (Books I–II) reflect a positive view and optimistic expectation of the future of the Davidic monarchy, but Psalms 73–89 (Book III) represent a theological revision of this hope in the light of the harsh realities of the exile and non-restoration of the Davidic throne in the postexilic period.[10] Psalm 89 represents a theological reevaluation of the optimism of the future of the dynasty reflected in Books I–II. Psalm 89 views God's promise to David as a theological relic of the past—a covenant that God revoked. Book III closes with the demise of the Davidic monarchy and the uncertainty of what this means for Israel's future. Wilson suggests Psalms 90–106 (Book IV) provide

---

10. Gerald Wilson, *The Editing of the Hebrew Psalter*, SBLD 76 (Chico: Scholars Press, 1985), 212–15; idem, "The Use of Royal Psalms at the 'Seams' of the Hebrew Psalter," *JSOT* 35 (1986): 85–94.

a theological reorientation for the future expectation of the post-monarchial community. Book IV develops four themes that offset the loss of the monarchy: (1) Yahweh is the eternal king; (2) Yahweh was a refuge for his people long before the Davidic monarchy; (3) Yahweh will continue to be a refuge for his people apart from the Davidic monarchy; and (4) Yahweh will bless those who are faithful to him.

Yet one wonders whether the author of Psalm 89 would have shared Wilson's approach. After all, the psalmist did not conclude from the harsh realities of the current crisis that God had revoked his promise to David; he pled with God to show himself faithful to the covenant that he had said was inviolable. Rather than concluding that God had revoked his covenant, Psalm 89 protests that God demonstrate his covenant faithfulness and restore the Davidic king to power.

According to Childs, however, the location of Psalm 89 at the close of Book III does not represent God's revocation of his covenant promise to David, but evidence of a transition from traditional dynastic expectations to a future eschatological messianic hope. While the royal psalms originally expressed a royal dynastic ideology, this canonical reorientation functioned as "a witness to the messianic hope which looked forward for the consummation of God's kingship through his Anointed One."[11] In effect, the psalmist's plea came to express the postexilic community's prayer for the coming of Messiah, the One through whom God would restore the throne of David and establish an eternal kingdom to fulfill his ancient promise. When the psalmist's lament remained unanswered during the second temple era, the non-restoration of the Davidic dynasty eventually led to the future expectation of eschatological messianism. Rather than sounding the death knell of the Davidic throne, Psalm 89 provided a future hope of a new work of God—the divine provision of a Second David. As the Second Testament eventually would make clear, this kind of eschatological reading of Psalm 89 should not be attributed to the whims of the believing community, but was divinely designed as to create a robust messianic hope.

MESSIANIC TRAJECTORIES IN PSALM 110

Psalm 110 is a royal enthronement psalm. It reflects ancient Israelite royal enthronement ritual, since the newly anointed Davidic scion is invited by God to sit on the royal throne at his "right hand" (v. 1). The new king is called "lord" (v. 1), and designated "priest" after the pattern of Melchizedek, the ancient king-priest of Zion (v. 4). The new Davidic king is also promised universal dominion by God's enablement (vv. 2–3, 5–7). The scope of the

---

11. Brevard S. Childs, *Introduction to the Old Testament as Scripture* (Philadelphia: Fortress Press, 1979), 517.

language and extent of the hope appropriately led to a messianic reading that focused on the totality of his ultimate exaltation.

Contextual Reading of Psalm 110

Psalm 110 contains two stanzas (vv. 1–3, 4–7). The first focuses on the royal aspects of Davidic kingship, the second its priestly aspects. Each opens with a quotation formula: "Yahweh says to my lord: 'Sit down at my right hand …'" (v. 1); "Yahweh vows and will not revoke it: 'You are a priest forever …'" (v. 4). The psalm seems to be a poetic adaptation of a prophetic oracle delivered on the occasion of the royal enthronement of the new historical Davidic king.[12]

The Davidic King Designated as Lord

Verse 1 introduces God's address to the Davidic king who is identified with an elevated title: "the LORD said to my Lord" (KJV, NKJV, NASB, NLT, NCV, HCSB, ESV); "the LORD said to my lord" (RSV, NRSV, NIV, TNIV, GNT, JPS); "the LORD's oracle to my master" (NET). The speaker is identified as God by the divine name "Yahweh" (Heb. יְהוָה), traditionally rendered "the LORD." The Davidic addressee is identified by the title ʾădōnî (Heb. אֲדֹנִי), which translations alternately render "my Lord" or "my lord/master." It is important to recognize that the vocalization of the Davidic king's title as ʾădōnî in verse 1 is different from the vocalization of God's divine title as ʾădōnāy (Heb. אֲדֹנָי) in verse 5. While the latter always refers to God in Hebrew Scripture, the former never refers to God but always to a human lord (e.g., king, master, father, husband, etc.). Thus, verse 1 recounts an oracle in which God addressed the psalmist's human lord rather than his divine Lord. In other words, the divine LORD was addressing the psalmist's human lord.

Nevertheless, it is important to recognize that the original Hebrew was unvocalized and that the inspired consonantal text originally would have allowed the more robust vocalization in verse 1. However, the traditional vocalization certainly reflects the scribal avoidance of just such a divine interpretation of the title in verse 1, since it would have represented a serious theological conflict with the absolute monotheism of orthodox Judaism. Considered from a purely linguistic point of view, the original inspired consonantal text allowed the possibility that Yahweh was addressing the psalmist's divine Lord. Considered in the light of the theological boundaries of orthodox Judaism, such an interpretation would have been blasphemous. Nevertheless, the vagueness was there in the Hebrew text and is a part of its potential meaning. It was this very kind of ambiguity which Jesus would one day highlight and expound. Not simply hinting at this in subtle ways, Jesus would boldly challenge the traditional boundaries, explicitly identifying himself as incarnate

---

12. Hilber, *Cultic Prophecy in the Psalms*, 76–88.

Son of God and divine Lord, arguing that God's actions in exaltation would vindicate Jesus in order to indicate who the Messiah truly was.

Returning to the initial historical contextual meaning of verse 1, we also must consider the identity of the psalmist who referred to the historical Davidic king being addressed by God as "my lord." There are four options: (1) a prophet delivered an oracle to the new king (David or Solomon), but spoke as a subordinate to the king who was his human lord; (2) a prophet spoke for king David to address the new king Solomon who was about to ascend the throne; (3) David spoke prophetically and delivered an oracle to Solomon, who now was David's lord as newly anointed king; or (4) David recited an oracle composed by a prophet, but referred to himself by the fixed royal title "my lord."[13] Perhaps as a parallel phenomenon, Hittite kings often referred to themselves in royal inscriptions with the fixed royal title, "my majesty" (^{d}UTU-*ši*).[14] Even in the modern world, it is not uncommon for British citizens to address the monarch of England as "your royal majesty," albeit a royal idiom cast in the secondperson rather than first person, as in verse 1.

So it is possible that an unnamed prophet composed this psalm, recounting Yahweh's address to David on the day of his enthronement in Jerusalem. Since David would have been the prophet's human lord at the time when he took the throne, it would have been appropriate for him to refer to king David as "my lord." In fact, the prophet Nathan customarily addressed David as "my lord, the king" (1 Kings 1:24, 27), as was the custom of all David's subjects.[15]

It is also possible that David composed this psalm, functioning as a prophet (cf. 2 Sam. 23:1–3), recounting God's address to Solomon at the time of his enthronement in Jerusalem. It will be remembered that in the last days of his life David played the key role in securing Solomon's succession against Adonijah's attempt to usurp the throne (1 Kings 1:1–53). Perhaps Psalm 110 even played an important role in validating Solomon's kingship as divinely ordained. Regardless of authorship, David is the speaker and author of the Psalm from the perspective of the verse's declaration. That is key to all that follows. As David relinquished the throne to his son, it would have been appropriate for him to refer to Solomon as "my lord" on that occasion. In fact, it was customary for all Solomon's subjects to refer to him as "my

---

13. Eugene H. Merrill, "Royal Priesthood: An Old Testament Messianic Motif," *BSac* 150 (Jan–Mar 1993): 50–61; Herbert W. Bateman IV, "The Use of Psalm 110:1 in the New Testament," *BSac* 149 (Oct–Dec 1992): 438–53.

14. For multiple examples, see Gary Beckman, *Hittite Diplomatic Texts*, 2nd ed. (SBL Writings from the Ancient World Series, vol. 7; Atlanta: Scholars Press, 1999), 33–44, 54–59, 69–77, 95–98, 104–17.

15. For example, 2 Samuel 3:21; 4:8; 9:11; 13:32, 33; 14:9, 12, 15, 17, 18, 19, 20, 22; 15:15, 21; 16:4, 9; 18:28, 31, 32; 19:19, 26, 27; 24:3, 21, 22; 1 Kings 1:13, 17, 18, 20, 21, 31, 36, 37.

lord" once he ascended the throne (e.g., 1 Kings 2:38; 3:17, 26). Granted, it was unusual for one who was the king and founder of a dynasty to refer to a descendant as his lord. Yet the unusual nature of this setting is why Jesus later raises the question about this passage and ultimately, he was right to raise the question and contemplate its significance. Nevertheless, this did not mean that David had not originally addressed his son Solomon.

Despite our attempts to identify the most likely candidate for the initial referent, it is crucial to recognize that the addressee is not explicitly identified. This linguistic openness vexes any interpreter who wants to uncover the historical setting and original contextual meaning of Psalm 110. We must resist the temptation to fill in the interpretive gaps where God intentionally left openness. By divine design, Psalm 110 studiously avoids explicit identification of the original Davidic king being addressed in order to open itself up for reuse on the occasion of the future enthronement of subsequent Davidic kings. This likely accounts for the archival preservation of the psalm from one generation to the next. Moreover, this divinely inspired vagueness meant that it contained a robust messianic potential since any oracle addressing one Davidic king about the perpetual dynastic throne also would apply to the ultimate Davidic king in an elevated sense. Second Testament assertions that God spoke to the Messiah in Psalm 110:1 is theologically and hermeneutically valid (Matt. 22:44; Mark 12:36; Luke 20:42; Acts 2:34; Heb. 1:13).[16] Since Messiah is the ultimate Davidic king, God's address to the original Davidic king applied equally—if not ultimately—to him in a generic sense (vis-à-vis *references plenior*).[17]

The Davidic King Sits at God's Right Hand

In verse 1b, God invites the newly anointed Davidic king to ascend the royal throne: "Sit at my right hand!" Since God is pictured sitting on a heavenly throne, it is easy to understand how this is decisively prophetic of the Messiah ascending into heaven. Indeed, this ultimate messianic sense was eventually revealed with the ascension of Jesus into heaven. However, when this psalm was originally written, it likely also had some relevance to the historical Davidic king on the occasion of his own ascension to the royal throne in Jerusalem.

The image of the Davidic king being invited to sit upon the throne at God's right hand was not necessarily limited to a literal ascension into heaven. The image of God's right hand was often metaphorical for God's power or

---

16. For a similar hermeneutical application of the inspired words of David to the Messiah as the ultimate David, see the use of Psalm 40:7–9 in Hebrews 10:5–9.

17. This hermeneutical move also explains how Jesus could extend the invitation to sit down at God's right hand to his followers (Rev. 3:21) in the light of the blessing of co-inheritance in the mystery of the new covenant (Eph. 3:1–6).

favor. In fact, David is often pictured as ruling by God's right hand (Pss. 16:11; 17:7; 18:35[36]; 20:6[7]; 63:8[9]; 108:6[7]; 138:7; 139:10). Furthermore, since the royal palace was located to the south of the temple on Mount Zion, both structures facing east, the throne of the king was geographically located to the east of temple, where God was enthroned. Psalm 110:1 metaphorically pictures the historical Davidic king sitting at God's right hand, so to speak, as he sat on the earthly throne in Jerusalem. In Israelite royal ideology, David's earthly throne represented God's heavenly throne. The Davidic king administered God's rule on earth. David's rule was the manifestation of God's rule. By divine design, this set up the pattern for the more complete realization of the text's meaning that was still to come.

This theological concept occurs elsewhere. For example, the Chronicler reframes the wording of Nathan's oracle to picture the kingdom promised to David as the kingdom of God: "your kingdom" (2 Sam. 7:16) is interpreted as "my kingdom" (1 Chron. 17:14). The psalmist pictures the throne of the Davidic king as nothing less than God's throne, and its occupant as nothing less than the human representative of God's rule (Ps. 45:6–7[7–8]). In ancient Israelite royal ideology, the human Davidic king was the divinely chosen coregent who was called to represent God's moral rule on earth (Pss. 2:7–8; 89:27[28]). So when viewed in its initial historical context, God invited the historical Davidic king in verse 1 to ascend the earthly throne in Jerusalem that was both metaphorically and geographically at his "right hand."

The concept of a deity inviting a new king to sit upon his throne at the time of his original coronation appears in ancient Near Eastern literature as well. For example, in an Assyrian royal inscription, the Assyrian deity invites Ashurbanipal (669–627 BCE) to take his throne as newly coronated king: "Sit down!" (SAA 11.4–7). If ancient Near Eastern kings could claim that their gods installed them upon their earthly throne, should it come as a surprise that the Israelite king would be pictured as every bit their equal if not their superior in this regard? In any case, the main point of God's invitation to the new Davidic king was to legitimate his rule as being divinely chosen and installed on the earthly throne of Zion.

When viewed in its initial historical-cultural contextual sense, we may identify the locus on which the Davidic king was invited to sit as the earthly throne in the Jerusalem palace. Yet the language of verse 1 is actually more open than this. Taken in its most literal sense, it allows for a literal ascension of the Davidic king to sit on a heavenly throne. While no historical Davidic king ever ascended into heaven on the day of his coronation, the language allowed for just this sense. Such a literal sense would not have been ruled impossible in ancient Israel. After all, God summoned three servants into heaven at their deaths: Enoch, Moses, and Elijah. Moreover, Zechariah witnessed a prophetic vision in which he saw Jeshua standing before God's throne in heaven being installed as high priest of the earthly temple (Zech.

3:1–10). So it is possible to even take verse 1 as a prophetic vision in which the new Davidic king was invited by God to ascend into heaven where he was installed as divinely chosen ruler of the earthly kingdom.[18] In fact, when Jesus said that God would do this, he was invoking the full force of this text.

The Davidic King Is Promised Universal Dominion

One of the themes of Psalm 110 is the universal rule of the newly enthroned Davidic king. God promised to subjugate the foreign foes to Davidic rule: "Sit at my right hand until I make your enemies your footstool" (v. 1b). The psalmist was confident God would empower the king to conquer his foes and embolden his warriors to fight courageously (vv. 2–3, 5–7).

Considered from its initial historical context, this prediction was partially fulfilled in an inaugural sense in God's elevation of David (2 Sam. 5:12) empowering him to conquer the surrounding nations (2 Sam. 5:12), including "all his enemies" (2 Sam. 7:9; 22:1) and "all the nations" surrounding Israel (2 Sam. 5:17–25; 8:1–15; 12:26–31). Yet since God himself is the universal heavenly ruler of all earthly nations, he promised to gradually bring about the universal dominion of the dynasty as individual kings ruled in moral righteousness and social justice, while trusting and obeying Yahweh (Pss. 2:8–10; 18:29–50[30–51]; 20:1–9[2–10]; 45:3–5[4–6]; 72:8–11; 89:22–27[23–28]). Ultimately, this promise was rooted in Nathan's dynastic oracle, in which God promised to subdue all David's enemies (2 Sam. 7:10–11//1 Chron. 17:10).

The motif of the newly enthroned king subjugating his foes under his feet was a common convention in ancient Near Eastern royal coronation inscriptions. Assyrian royal enthronement oracles typically proclaim the new king would exercise seemingly universal rule. The Assyrian gods promised to subdue the nations under the feet of the newly enthroned king. For example, Ishtar informs Esarhaddon the newly enthroned king: "O Esarhaddon, king of Assyria! I will seize your enemies and trample them under my foot!" (SAA 2.1.10–12). In another Assyrian royal enthronement inscription, the deity assures the new king: "Ninurta shall go at the right and left side of [ ] shall put his enemies under his foot!" In another inscription, we read, "Listen, O Assyrians! The king has vanquished his foe. Your king has put his enemy under his foot, from sunset to sunrise and from sunrise to sunset!" (SAA 3.2.27–34). Furthermore, in an Assyrian enthronement oracle the deity not only is said to have promised to subjugate the foes of the newly coronated king, but also is pictured inviting the royal scion to sit on his royal throne:

---

18. In the royal coronation inscription of Thutmose III (1504–1450 BCE), an Egyptian prophet delivered an oracle designating Thutmose III as the new king, who claimed the gates of heavens were opened in a vision, whereupon he was transported into heaven, where he was divinely crowned as the new earthly king (ARE 2.55–68).

"I will vanquish the enemy of Ashurbanipal. Sit down! I will put the lands in order!" (*SAA* 11.4–7).

Certainly, this motif in Psalm 110 is more than royal convention. As genuine spokesman of the one true living God, the prophet's prediction will one day be fulfilled in its most literal sense. Taken in its most robust sense, the theme of the universal dominion of the Davidic king ultimately points to the Messiah. Only in the future eschatological victory of the Messiah over all his enemies, including even sin and death itself, would the wording of the psalm find their fullest fulfillment. Nevertheless, the presence of this convention in the ancient world, as well as the hyperbolic depictions of David ruling "all the nations," helps the Christian reader understand how the pattern of fulfillment works in terms of an initial and an ultimate realization, rather than speculate about what the ancient Israelite audience might or might not have understood.

The Davidic King Designated as Royal Priest

While the Davidite is enthroned as king in verse 1, he is designated as royal priest in verse 4: "You are a priest forever according to the order of Melchizedek." Like Melchizedek, the ancient king-priest of Jerusalem (Gen. 14:18), the Davidic king would exercise royal as well as priestly functions. David clearly functioned in some kind of priestly capacity. David transported the Ark to Jerusalem, offered up sacrifices en route, wore a priestly ephod, and bestowed priestly blessings (2 Sam. 6:13–18; 1 Chron. 15:27). David and Solomon both offered sacrifices (2 Sam. 24:18–25; 1 Chron. 21:18–28; 1 Kings 3:2–4; 8:5, 54, 62–63). David arranged for the building and administration of the temple (1 Chron. 22–29). Finally, the royal sons of David and heirs to his throne are explicitly called "priests" (2 Sam. 8:18). To be sure, the Davidic kings and royal heirs were not priests in the sense of the Levites, but king-priests in the pattern of Melchizedek.

Reference to Melchizedek, the Amorite king-priest of Salem, suggests that the way the Davidic kings functioned as royal priests may be understood in the light of the model of the sacral kingship of Melchizedek. While some kings in the ancient Near East were no more than patrons who sponsored a particular temple, many participated in the cult to such a degree that they were designated as royal priests in the form of sacral kingship.

Although many ancient Near Eastern rulers functioned in some priestly capacity, there was a clear distinction between the traditional role of cultic priest and the royal role of sacral kingship. We may distinguish between the administrative royal priest and the functional cultic priests. In the ancient Near East, the functional priests had roles similar to the Israelite Levitical priests; they were solely responsible for the cultic service at the temple in offering of sacrifices and given access to the temple precincts. The king-priest had an administrative role; he was responsible for the organization and administration of the state worship. The king's role did not include performing services in the temple, but did involve organizing the priesthood, arranging for the construction of temples and financing sacrifices offered on behalf of the throne and state.

Sumerian King-Priest. The Sumerian concept of sacral kingship is reflected in the royal coronation hymn of Shulgi (2094–2047 BCE) (*COS* 1.172). The first section recounts an oracle in which the god Enlil established the royal dynasty: he chose Shulgi's father as king to establish an everlasting dynasty and called him to build the Ekur temple (lines 1–14). In the second section, Shulgi is depicted as divinely begotten in the temple at the time of his royal enthronement (lines 15–20). In the third section, Enlil proclaims Shulgi as divinely chosen king, the presiding official places royal emblems in his hands, then Shulgi sits on his throne and lifts his head heavenward to acknowledge Enlil (lines 21–27). In the closing section, Shulgi is designated "high priest" and "king of the (cultic) festival," and offers sacrifices to Enlil and Ninlil (lines 28–30).

Assyrian King-Priest. The Assyrian sacral kingship is reflected in several coronation inscriptions. For example, Shalmaneser II (1031–1020 BCE) is designated royal "priest" in his royal coronation inscription (*AR* 1.107, 346). Esarhaddon (681–669 BCE) claims the gods chose him as king-priest to restore their temples, and that he was placed on the throne because, "Ishtar, who loves my priesthood, stood by my side" (*SAA* 9: LXXIII). Shamash-shumu-ukin (667–648 BCE) claims he was chosen by the gods as a king-priest: "Erua called my name for the priesthood of the people in the womb of the mother . . . and called me to restore the forgotten cultic practices."

Eternal Nature of the Royal Priesthood of the Davidic King

In verse 4, the David king is designated a royal priest for *perpetuity*: "You are a priest *forever* according to the order of Melchizedek." Since the historical Davidic king initially addressed in verse 4 was mortal, mention of "the order of Melchizedek" could suggest a perpetual dynasty in which this office would pass from one generation to another. Just as the sacral kingship of Melchizedek, the ancient Amorite king-priest of Jerusalem, passed to his royal sons, the sacral kingship of David, who conquered Jerusalem, would pass to his royal heirs. The Davidic king would function as a sacral king throughout his reign; then his successor would inherit the office (cf. 2 Sam. 8:18). The hereditary nature of his perpetual office finds parallel in Ezekiel's vision of the future prince, patron, and sponsor of the restored temple, whose sacral office likewise would be inherited by his descendants (Ezek. 45:7–9; 46:16–18).

Considered in its initial historical context, the pronoun "you" was likely understood as synecdoche of part for the whole, the individual king standing in a generic sense for the dynasty. In a similar way, promising Jacob that his future descendants would eventually spread out throughout the entire land of Canaan, God said, "Your descendants will be numerous as the dust of earth; you (singular!) will spread to the west, east, north and south" (Gen. 28:14). However, as is the pattern in these fulfillment texts, the realization of the pattern pushes the language to its fullest extent. What initially might have seemed only to be a dynastic line also may legitimately include an ultimate son who is a king-priest eternally in the most literal sense of the term.

Canonical Reading of Psalm 110

This royal psalm was not originally composed for the cultic worship of ancient Israel, but to celebrate the enthronement of the current Davidic king. So it is remarkable that when the final canonical form of the Psalter was compiled sometime in the postexilic/second temple era, this royal psalm would be included in the worship hymnal of the community. As in the case of Psalm 2, the dismantling of the Davidic throne in 586 BCE and its vacancy throughout the restoration period led to a new appreciation of its meaning. During the postexilic period, it gave voice to the expectation that the royal dynasty would be restored to the throne soon after the return of the people, reconsecration of the priesthood, and rebuilding of the temple (Jer. 33:14–26; Zech. 3:1–10; 6:9–15; cf. Hag. 2:20–23). When the restoration of Davidic kingship did not immediately materialize, the faithful came to understand correctly that Psalm 110 ultimately pointed to the future Messiah, who would ascend God's right hand to usher in the eschatological kingdom.

The location of Psalm 110 in the final canonical form of the Psalter provides a future reorientation, which looks for an ideal Davidic king to come. Psalm 110 is strategically nestled between two short collections: Psalms 107–109, which open Book V (Psalms 107–150), and Psalms 111–113, which are Hallelujah hymns. When read in its new canonical context in the light of the historical realities of the postexilic period, the faithful came to see that Psalm 110 carried an eschatological messianic significance that transcended its original historical meaning.

Psalms 103–106, which close Book IV (Psalms 90–106), provide an historical/narrative orientation that starts with creation and moves forward to the Babylonian exile. Psalms 103 and 104 celebrate God's past mighty deeds at creation, while Psalms 105 and 106 rehearse his past acts in Israel's history, from his promise to Abraham and covenant at Sinai through the punishment of Babylonian exile. Book IV closes with the prayer of the Babylonian exiles: "Deliver us, O Yahweh our God! Gather us from the nations! Then we will give thanks to your holy name and boast about your praiseworthy deeds! Yahweh the God of Israel deserves praise in the future and forevermore! Let the people say, 'We agree! Praise Yahweh!'" (Ps. 106:47–48).

Psalms 107–109, which open Book V, continue on this redemptive-historical trajectory, giving appropriate voice to the postexilic community's prayer for full restoration. Psalm 107 opens with a call to praise befitting those redeemed from Babylonian exile: "Give thanks to Yahweh, for he is good, his loyal love endures forever! Let those delivered by Yahweh speak out, those whom he delivered from the power of the enemy and gathered from foreign lands—from east and west, north and south!" (Ps. 107:1–3). Psalms 108 and 109, attributed to David, were reused to voice appropriate lament by the postexilic community of God's apparent rejection of his royal scepter (Ps. 108) and David himself (Ps. 109), which both came to stand as symbols of Davidic kingship. Yet both end with future expectation: "By God's power we will conquer; he will tramp down our enemies" (Ps. 108:13); "I will thank Yahweh . . . because he stands at the right hand of the needy to deliver him from those who threaten his life" (Ps. 109:30–31).

Following hard on the heels of the hymns opening Book V, Psalm 110 voiced the postexilic community's expectation of the coming Davidic king, who would sit at God's right hand. In fact, the expression, "right hand," forms a link between the closing line of Psalm 109 and the opening line of Psalm 110. Despite the fact that God had temporarily rejected him, David was confident that God was *standing* at his "right hand" (Ps. 109:31). As if in future fulfillment of this expectation, the very next line in the Psalter pictures God inviting the new David to *sit* at his "right hand" (Ps. 110:1). Whereas Psalm 109 was read generically as the temporary rejection of the Davidic dynasty at the exile, Psalm 110 effectively predicted the future restoration of the Davidic throne and God's invitation to the new David to sit at his right hand.

This kind of canonical reading began to unpack the full messianic potential that was embedded in Psalm 110 by divine design. This also led to the flowering of eschatological messianism in second temple period literature. As Bateman will show, some texts relate the coming Davidic king whom God invites to sit down at his right hand (Ps. 110:1) with the One like the Son of Man who approaches the throne of the Most High to receive the kingdom (Dan. 7:13–14). Juxtaposition of these two figures—one Davidic and one heavenly—anticipated the more startling typological fulfillment in the heavenly ascension of Jesus to the right hand of God.

MESSIANIC TRAJECTORIES IN PSALM 132

Psalm 132 treats an important element in royal Davidic ideology: the relation between the promissory and obligatory features of God's dynastic promise to David as the twofold basis for the perpetuation of his dynasty. Psalm 132 viewed this issue from a preexilic perspective, when the Davidic throne was still occupied, but facing adversity. While not originally composed as exclusive messianic prophecy, Psalm 132 laid a foundation for eschatological messianism, which appropriately began to be understood once David's throne was vacant as a result of the Babylonian exile.

Contextual Reading of Psalm 132

This psalm is composed of two sections: a prayer uttered by or on behalf of the current Davidic king in response to some kind of historical crisis (vv. 1–10); and divine response in the form of two oracles of reassurance (vv. 11–18). The first oracle focuses on God's election of David: God irrevocably vowed to establish David's throne for perpetuity—conditioned on the obedience of his successors (vv. 11–12). The second focuses on God's election of Zion: God chose Zion as his perpetual dwelling place and would bless the faithful inhabitants of Jerusalem and uphold the royal household (vv. 13–18). The relationship between the twin themes of God's election of David and his election of Zion is crucial to the overall message of the psalm.

Human Petition: Davidic Dynasty in Crisis (vv. 1–10)
In verses 1–10, the psalmist petitions Yahweh to protect the dynasty of David and the city of Jerusalem. He grounds his appeal on the exceptional loyalty of David who worked tirelessly to find a suitable dwelling place for the ark of the covenant. The section concludes with the appeal: *"For the sake of David, your servant, do not turn your face away from your anointed [king]!"* Just as God sometimes spared entire populations on account of the exceptional loyalty of certain individuals (Gen. 18:26, 29, 31, 32; 26:24; 1 Sam. 12:22), the psalmist pleads that God spare Zion and the current Davidic ruler on account of the past loyalty of David. The notion of God sparing Jerusalem and the dynasty from judgment out of respect for the past loyalty of David is repeated elsewhere (e.g., 1 Kings 11:34; 15:5; 2 Kings 8:19; 19:34; 20:6; 2 Chron. 21:7).

This petition may reflect some crisis that threatened the safety of Zion and security of David's dynasty. Indeed, Solomon had prayed at the time of the dedication of the temple that God not reject the Davidic line in times of national crisis and calamity. Solomon's prayer, "O LORD God, *do not reject your anointed ones! Remember* the promises to *your servant David!*" (2 Chron. 6:42), echoes in the opening and closing lines of the psalm: "O LORD, *remember* David … For the sake of *your servant David, do not reject your anointed one!*" (Ps. 132:1, 10).

Divine Response: Reaffirmation of God's Promises (vv. 11–18)
In verses 11–18, the psalmist received a response to his prayer in the form of the recitation of two oracles dealing with the twin themes of God's election of David and Zion (cf. Ps. 78:68–70). The first reaffirmed the continuing validity of God's promise to David of an enduring dynasty (vss. 11–12). The second reasserted his election of Zion as his permanent dwelling place (vss. 13–18). However, the perpetuity of David's dynasty and security of Zion were not guaranteed irrespective of the conduct of the Davidites and Jerusalemites. In any given generation, the perpetuity of David's throne was conditioned

on the obedience of his heirs: "If your sons keep my covenant and the rules I teach them, their sons will also sit on your throne perpetually" (v. 12). Likewise, God's protection of Zion was implicitly linked to the faithfulness of its people: "I will protect her priests and *her godly people* will shout exuberantly" (v. 16). Of course, given the fact that there were numerous generations of disobedient kings and people whose sin did not result in immediate exile, it is clear that the fundamental overriding principle was God's promise to David of an everlasting throne and vow to dwell in Zion perpetually.

God's Eternal Covenant Promise to David (vv. 11–12). In the first oracle, Yahweh gave reassurance that he would not reject the house of David but would perpetuate his dynasty throughout future generations—if his descendants would obey God. This oracle holds two features of the Davidic covenant in tension. On the one hand, God's dynastic promise to David was an unbreakable covenant which he would not annul: "The LORD swore to David a sure oath from which he will not turn back." God irrevocably promised that one of David's sons (Solomon) would inherit his throne to perpetuate his dynasty: "One of the sons of your own body I will set on your throne" (v. 11b). God also made clear that an unbroken succession of the historical dynasty in future generations beyond David and Solomon was contingent on the obedience of their royal heirs: "If your sons keep my covenant . . . , their sons also shall sit on your throne forever" (v. 12). The contingent nature of the promise was a double-edged sword. On the one hand, it vouchsafed *an unbroken succession* in the dynasty—provided that his royal scions obeyed. On the other hand, it threatened the temporary interruption of dynastic perpetuity if David's successors failed to follow his example. Verse 12 warns of a temporary end to the dynasty if his heirs rebelled. Obedience by David's successors would be rewarded with an enduring dynasty, but disobedience would place the royal house in temporary jeopardy (Jer. 17:19–27; 22:1–5). *In the end God would keep the ultimate promise, but God would do so through a faithful king, Jesus.*

God's Eternal Election of Zion (vv. 13–18). The second oracle provided a more secure basis for the ongoing endurance of the dynasty—even in the face of royal sin. Since David's throne resided in Zion, it was perpetually secure due to God's election of Zion as his permanent dwelling place and promise to shield the city from her foes. The inviolability of Zion as the eternal dwelling of the Most High was the ultimate basis of dynastic security. Thus Psalm 132:13–18 joins the royal ideology of the Davidic covenant with the historical Zion tradition, celebrating the inviolability of Jerusalem—the dwelling place of the Most High—from its foes (e.g., Pss. 46, 48). The Davidic king was unconquerable since God enthroned him on Zion (Ps. 2:1–6) and would protect him there (Ps. 132:17–18). The twin themes of God's election of

David and Zion are interwoven in verse 17: "There [Zion] I will make David strong; I have determined that my chosen king's dynasty will continue." God's protection of the dynasty was vouchsafed by his commitment to his temple in Zion (vv. 13–18), but also conditioned on the obedience of the royal house (vv. 11–12). Nevertheless, the psalmist understood that God was irrevocably committed to fulfill his covenant promise to dwell in Zion eternally and to perpetually secure a Davidic king upon the throne in Jerusalem.

Inner-Biblical Development of Psalm 132
Unfortunately, such celebrations of the inviolability of Zion eventually was twisted into the popular misconception that God's protection was guaranteed regardless of the moral condition of its people. Jeremiah denounced the people's false confidence that Zion was inviolable simply because of God's presence (Jer. 7:2, 4, 14; 26:6, 9; 27:16; 28:16). Since their unrepentant sin had irrevocably defiled the temple (Jer. 11:15; 23:11), God would destroy the temple (Jer. 7:14; 26:12; 27:18, 21; 39:8; cf. 50:28; 51:11; 52:13, 17, 20).

Since Psalms 2 and 132 founded the security of the dynasty on its location on Mount Zion, a popular misconception also arose that the Davidic throne was likewise inviolable. Micah denounced the royal dynasty's mistaken belief in its absolute inviolability: God would protect Zion only if her citizens obeyed the covenant. Jeremiah refuted the misguided assumption that David's throne was absolutely secure: the royal house was accountable to God and would be removed from the throne as punishment for sin (Jer. 17:19–27; 21:11–14; 22:1–5). In the end this line would be preserved and God's promises would be realized, as the concluding assurance of Psalm 132 emphasized. Ultimately, this was a work of God's grace rooted in his covenant promise to David and later assurances found in this very psalm.

Canonical Reading of Psalm 132
Originally composed during a time of crisis in the preexilic period, Psalm 132 seems to reflect an historical situation when the security of Zion was threatened and the occupant of the throne of David was in danger. In the midst of this crisis, the psalmist reassured the occupants of the royal house and inhabitants of Jerusalem that the house of David and the house of the LORD would remain secure in any given generation—provided the Davidites obeyed God's commands and Jerusalemites remained faithful worshippers. Unfortunately, the sad history of Jerusalem tells us that the royal family and the people of Jerusalem eventually departed from Yahweh. When repeated prophetic invitations to repent went unheeded, God eventually sent the royal household along with the people into exile in Babylon, and destroyed Jerusalem along with his defiled dwelling-place. Rather than calling into question his election of David and Zion, the judgment underscored its conditional nature for any given generation. Thus, the fall of Jerusalem in 586 BCE was not due to the

failure of God's promise, but the moral failure of the inhabitants of Zion and wickedness of the post-Josianic Davidic kings. Yet the ultimate promise remained, as did the hope. Despite human sin and dynastic failure, God remained irrevocably committed to the ultimate fulfillment of his covenant program in the eschatological Messiah.

During the postexilic period, Psalm 132 came to be reused as one of the Ascent Psalms (Pss. 120–134) to celebrate the revitalization of God's presence in the second temple. The rebuilt temple only confirmed God's election of Zion as his permanent dwelling place—not withstanding the seventy-year interim for divine discipline. As for God's conditional promise of the perpetuity of David's dynasty (vv. 10–12), the postexilic community came to understand that Psalm 132 offered the hope of the future restoration of the Davidic dynasty, because God also promised to work through David's line and bring the promise to full realization. Whereas during the preexilic period, the psalm initially discussed God's conditional promise of the continuation of the dynasty, the postexilic community saw in it the potential for dynastic restoration. Since God had restored Zion, it offered hope for the future restoration of the Davidic throne.

Although the psalm was not originally understood in an exclusively messianic sense, the faithful eventually realized that its generic language and longitudinal themes carried implicit, divinely inspired messianic potential. Four features in Psalm 132 lent themselves to providing the foundation for the hope of eschatological messianism in the second temple period. First, the title "anointed one" occurs twice in the psalm (vv. 10, 17). This title is used in a technical sense of the eschatological Messiah in second temple literature. Looking back to the regal texts of eschatological hope in the Hebrew Scripture, second temple literature read many of these texts in this light. Second, the promise, "I will cause to sprout up a horn for David" (v. 17), which initially discussed a perpetual historical dynasty, came to be correctly interpreted messianically during the second temple period (e.g., Jer. 23:5; 33:15; Zech. 6:12; cf. Isa. 58:8). Third, the promise of an enduring dynasty from one generation to another (v. 12) came to be interpreted eschatologically. Fourth, the psalmist initially described God's promise of an enduring dynasty in terms of a perpetual succession of one generation after another of obedient Davidic descendants: "If your *sons* keep my covenant and the rules I teach *them*, then *their sons* will also sit on your throne forever." However, during the second temple period it soon became clear that there was little hope that the house of David would repent or remain perpetually loyal to Yahweh. As a result, some Jewish interpreters correctly shifted their attention from the conditional dynastic promise of verse 12 to the explicitly irrevocable promise to David in verse 11, "The LORD swore to David a sure oath from which he will not turn back: 'I will place one of your own sons upon your throne'." In time, this irrevocable oath to David came to be appropriately understood as ultimately pointing to one ultimate Davidic descendant, Messiah Jesus, who would rule for all eternity in his own person (Acts 2:30).

CONCLUSION

The royal psalms provide crucial insight into the royal Davidic ideology of ancient Israel. While originally describing various features of the historical Davidic dynasty or celebrating the royal enthronement of the current Davidic king, they made a significant contribution to the foundation for eschatological messianism. Although not direct prophecy about Jesus, they are explicitly applicable to subsequent Davidic kings. Viewed from a broader canonical perspective, the royal psalms gave voice to the royal expectation of the second temple community about God's future restoration of the Davidic kingdom and placement of one of David's sons on his throne once again. This king would have an authority closely related to God and his rule, a seat at God's side, even sharing the name and authority of God, leading into justice, righteousness, and peace. This future hope finds fulfillment in the current reign of Jesus, as well as in his future eschatological kingdom. But before moving to the Second Testament there are several prophets that anticipate the collapse of David's dynasty and yet express a hope of restoration.

CHAPTER FOUR

MESSIANIC TRAJECTORIES IN AMOS, HOSEA, AND MICAH

We now turn to the contribution of the Hebrew prophets to ancient Israel's messianic hope. The preexilic prophets stood at the crossroads between the early promises of an enduring Davidic dynasty over an historical kingdom and later eschatological expectations of a second David over an eschatological kingdom. Thanks to the sin and folly of Solomon and Rehoboam, the once united Davidic kingdom had been fractured into two rival monarchies. The prophets Hosea, Amos, and Micah responded to this tragic situation by predicting that the once united kingdom would be restored under an ideal new "David," who would usher in a new golden age.

Some interpret these predictions in a solely eschatological sense as direct prophecies of the Messiah and his eschatological kingdom, still awaiting future fulfillment.[1] Others take them in a purely historical sense as expectations of the dynasty's historical restoration, but which originally did not look beyond the near future to the distant future of the Messiah.[2] We adopt a more nuanced approach. The prophets responded to the calamities that had befallen the Davidic kingdom in their day by predicting its future restoration through the use of idealized imagery, typological patterns, conventional terminology, and open-ended language whose fulfillment would only be fully realized in the eschatological Messiah and his kingdom.

MESSIANIC TRAJECTORIES IN AMOS 9:11–15

Amos ministered during the reigns of Uzziah of Judah (767–740 BCE) and Jeroboam II of Israel (782–753 BCE). According to 1:2, he prophesied two

---

1. For example, Walter C. Kaiser, Jr., *The Messiah in the Old Testament* (Grand Rapids: Zondervan, 1995), 151–54.
2. For example, Joachim Becker, *Messianic Expectation in the Old Testament* (Philadelphia: Fortress Press, 1980), 58.

years before an earthquake struck Israel, which archaeologists date around 760 BCE.[3] Thus, he foresaw Judah's resurgence under Uzziah, but also predicted the destruction of Samaria and exile of the northern kingdom.[4] Amos opened his book with a series of oracles of doom against the surrounding nations (1:3–2:5), climaxing with an oracle of doom against Israel (2:5–16). Yahweh was about to destroy Samaria and send the inhabitants of the northern kingdom of Israel into exile (3:1–9:10). In stark contrast, God would spare Judah as well as repair the house of David and extend its rule over all nations (9:11–12), ushering in a future golden age of unprecedented blessings (9:13–15).

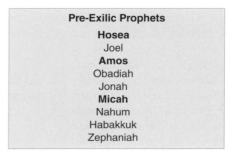

Pre-Exilic Prophets

Hosea
Joel
Amos
Obadiah
Jonah
Micah
Nahum
Habakkuk
Zephaniah

Contextual Reading of Amos 9:11–15

Amos' contribution to messianic prophecy appears in 9:11–15. This salvation oracle consists of two stanzas, each introduced by an opening temporal formula: "In that day . . ." (v. 11), "Behold, days are coming . . . !" (v. 13). The first foresaw the renaissance of the house of David and Yahweh's rule over all nations (vv. 11–12). The second portrayed the domestic peace, unprecedented prosperity, and perpetual security of that coming age (vv. 13–15).

Future Renaissance of David's House (vv. 11–12)

This oracle opens with the expression, "in that day" (v. 11a). This expression may refer to the remote or imminent future. Elsewhere in Amos, the slogans "in that day," "the day of Yahweh," and "days are coming," refer to the doom that befell Israel from 745–722 BCE.[5] The immediate context links the imminent judgment of Israel (vv. 1–10) and future revival of Judah (vv. 11–15). The closing declaration, "Yahweh is about to do this" (v. 12b), suggests this oracle was to be initially fulfilled in the imminent future. Yet while this oracle was fulfilled in some kind of "already" sense under king Uzziah (see below),

---

3. Yigael Yadin, *Hazor: The Rediscovery of a Great Citadel of the Bible* (London: Weidenfeld & Nicholson, 1975), 150; Philip King, *Amos, Hosea, Micah—An Archaeological Commentary* (Philadelphia: Westminster Press, 1988), 21.

4. For a chronological placement of Amos among the kings and fall of northern Israel, see page 53.

5. The phrases "in that day," "the day of Yahweh," and "days are coming" occur in Amos 3:14; 4:2; 5:18, 20; 8:3, 9, 11, 13; cf. 6:3. They speak of immediate judgment of northern Israel and revival in Judah.

the idealized imagery and universal tenor of the prophecy also demand a "not yet" fulfillment in the eschatological rule of the Messiah.

God Would Raise Up David's Fallen House (v. 11a). Amos described the object of God's restoration as "hut of David," an ironic play on the conventional idiom "house of David." The term "hut" (סֻכָּה), picturing a somewhat temporary structure, highlighted the precarious nature of David's house in the days of Amos, and even may have anticipated the collapse of the dynasty two centuries later when Jerusalem was destroyed and the last Davidic king was taken into exile.

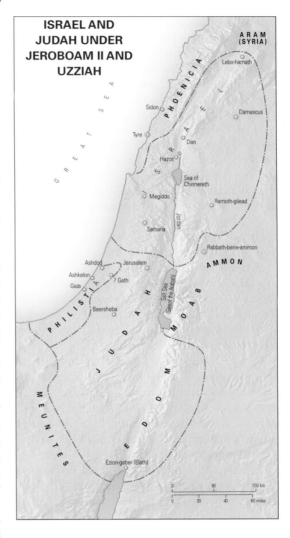

To whom or what did Amos refer by this image of the "hut of David"? The precise referent is ambiguous since it occurs only here in the Hebrew Scriptures. Yet it is certainly somehow related to the somewhat equivalent expression, "house of David." When used in a royal sense, the term "house" elsewhere refers to a variety of referents: (1) a royal dynasty as a whole (1 Sam. 20:16; 1 Kings 12:19, 26; 13:2; 14:8; 17:21; Isa. 7:2, 13; Jer. 21:12; 2 Chron. 21:7), particularly the royal dynasty of David (2 Sam. 7:11, 16, 18, 19, 25, 26, 27, 29); and (2) the reign of an individual dynastic king (2 Sam. 3:1, 6, 8, 10; 12:8; 1 Kings 2:24). Precisely who or what God intended is open in terms of the language, when considered strictly within contextual parameters.

Amos described David's once powerful house as having fallen or in process of falling and tottering on the brink of collapse in his own day. Following Solomon's reign, the united kingdom was divided into rival dynasties of north and south. During the next two centuries, Judah suffered setbacks at the hand of Israel. More recently, Amaziah king of Judah (796–767 BCE) was defeated in battle and taken prisoner by Joash king of Israel (798–782 BCE), who breached the wall of Jerusalem, conquered the city and captured the royal family (2 Kings 14:11–13//2 Chron. 25:20–23). Eventually Amaziah returned to Jerusalem, but only to be assassinated by his countrymen (2 Kings 14:19//2 Chron. 25:27), his young son Uzziah being placed on his throne (2 Kings 14:21//2 Chron. 26:21). David's house was at an all-time low.

Sometime after Uzziah's enthronement (767 BCE), Amos prophesied (ca. 760 BCE) that God would raise up David's house. In partial historical fulfillment, Uzziah restored David's kingdom to its former glory and proved to be one of Judah's most successful kings. Yet the restoration was short-lived. Just two centuries later, the Davidic house collapsed when Jerusalem was destroyed and her last king taken into exile. Since Amos predicted a permanent restoration, he must have looked beyond the temporary revival of the dynasty in the days of Uzziah to the ultimate elevation of David's house in the eschaton.

God Would Repair David's House (v. 11b). Amos depicted the restoration of David's house with three architectural metaphors: "I will repair their breaches, I will raise up his ruins, and I will rebuild her . . ." Two features of this architectural image are important to note. First, Amos pictured the walls of Samaria capital of Israel being breached by the Assyrians and her citizens forced out of the fallen city into exile: "You shall go out through the breaches" (4:3). In contrast, Amos pictured David's house as restored by God: "I will repair its breaches" (9:11).

Second, the motif of God repairing the "breaches" of David's house is an example of the historically contextualized imagery. Just a few decades before, Joash king of Israel conquered Jerusalem, making a six-hundred-foot breach in the city wall (2 Kings 14:13//2 Chron. 25:23). Sometime later in the lifetime of Amos, Uzziah repaired the physical breaches in the walls of Jerusalem (2 Chron. 26:9) as well as the political breaches in the dynasty's power (2 Chron. 26:6–8, 11–15). There is little question that the image of God repairing the "breaches" of the falling house of David was inspired by one of these two events. However, it is unclear whether Amos uttered this prophecy before or after Uzziah's repair of the breaches in the city walls. If this oracle followed this project, perhaps the present physical repairs of Jerusalem in the reign of Uzziah inspired Amos to look beyond this to the future spiritual repair of Jerusalem in the future reign of Messiah. If he delivered this oracle beforehand, perhaps Amos simply foresaw the restoration of Jerusalem, picturing it in generic terms and ambiguous imagery that provided a pattern in the imminent physical repair of the walls of Jerusalem under Uzziah, which foreshadowed a greater spiritual repair of the citizens of Jerusalem and David's house under Messiah in the more distant future. Ultimately, the timing of this oracle is not as relevant as the fact that Amos looked beyond the present in one way or another to the eschatological future.

God Would Restore David's House (v. 11c). Amos also predicted God would restore David's house to the former glory of its illustrious founder: "I will rebuild it as in days of old." The expression, "as in days of old," refers not to eternity past, but the historical past in general (Deut. 32:7; Isa. 63:9, 11; Mic. 7:14; Mal. 3:4) and the days of David in particular (Mic. 5:2[1]). In other words, v. 11 pictures the restoration of David's house as a revival of the former golden age of the historical rule of David. Yet it is clear from vv. 12–15 that this future work of God would supersede anything previously experienced. Although based on God's former work in the days of David, it would be a radically new work of God. The future fulfillment would be based on the pattern of the former glory of the historical idealized reign of David, but the future glory of the ideal eschatological rule of the new David would supersede the former pattern. Amos anticipated both continuity and discontinuity. He did not simply predict restoration of the historical dynasty in the imminent future; rather, he foresaw something greater: the future eschatological kingdom of Messiah over a completely victorious Davidic kingdom.

David's House Would Triumph (v. 12a). As in verse 11, Amos pictured the restoration of David's house after the pattern of its illustrious founder. The rise of David's kingdom had been marked by his conquest of Edom and occupation of its land (2 Sam. 8:11–12, 14–16; 1 Chron. 18:11–14). During the reign of Jehoram (848–841 BCE), however, Edom freed itself from Davidic control (2 Kings 8:20//2 Chron. 21:8). Judah resubjugated Edom when Amaziah (796–767 BCE) defeated ten thousand Edomite warriors in the Valley of Salt and captured Sela (2 Kings 14:7; 2 Chron. 25:10–12). Shortly after this, Edom once again broke free when Amaziah was defeated in battle by Jehoash king of Israel. However, during the reign of Uzziah, David's house reasserted partial control of Edom, bringing Eloth back under Judah's wing (2 Kings 14:22//2 Chron. 26:2).

While possibly inspired by these recent events, Amos was not simply speaking of Uzziah's partial reassertion of Davidic control of a single Edomite city. He presented a pattern linking the first David to the new David. His wording recalled David's renown conquest of Edom, which marked the initial rise of his kingdom. So crushing was his victory that no Edomite warrior survived (1 Kings 11:15–16). Amos predicted David's house would conquer Edom once again, yet this time capturing not executing the survivors: "they will capture the survivors in Edom." The coming triumph would not simply reprise David's triumph, but trump it.

In verse 12, Amos envisioned God engineering this triumph through a plural agency: "they will capture . . ." The precise identity of this plural group is fraught with ambiguity due to the absence of a clearly identified antecedent. Since the main agent in verse 11 is David's house (lit. "the fallen hut of David"), it seems reasonable that this is the implied antecedent. Yet it is not clear how the plural "they" should be understood in relation to the singular "hut of David." Some interpreters assume the plural refers to a plurality of Davidites, that is, a lineage of royal heirs sitting on David's throne in succession one generation after another.[6] According to this view, Amos envisioned not an *individual* Messiah ruling for eternity in his own person in the eschatological future, but a *plurality* of Davidites ruling in succession in the historical future.[7] Others suggest the plural refers to a plurality of Judahites, that is, the inhabitants of Jerusalem and people of Judah who would experience the future national blessings described in vv. 13–15. They also help capture those gained in victory. According to this view, Amos envisioned a *plurality* of Judahites flourishing under the rule of an ideal *individual* Davidic king through whom God would restore the glory of David's house. If viewed only in the light of the immediate context of vv. 11–12, it initially seems difficult to determine with any certainty precisely which option Amos envisioned. In fact, the juxtaposition of the singular and plural terms allows both for an initial historical fulfillment in the imminent restoration of David's house through a plurality of godly historical Davidic kings starting with Uzziah, as well as the ultimate future fulfillment of a plurality of godly Judahites under the eschatological Messiah. This kind of dual realization is exactly how pattern fulfillment works. It means a choice need not be made between the near and far realization. One is built into the divine design of the other.

David's House Would Exercise Universal Rule (v. 12b). At the founding of his kingdom, David conquered the surrounding nations (Edom, Moab, Ammon, Philistia, Amalek), which the biblical historians identified by synecdoche as "all the nations" (2 Sam. 8:11–12; 1 Chron. 14:17; 18:11). Amos predicted the resurgent house of David likewise would conquer "all the nations"

---

6. For example, see 2 Samuel 7:13; 1 Kings 2:4; 8:25; 9:5; Jeremiah 17:25; 22:2, 4; Psalms 89:4[5], 29[30], 36[37]; 132:11–12; 2 Chronicles 6:16; 7:18; cf. Psalm 18:50[51]; 2 Chronicles 6:42.

7. For example, Antti Laato, *A Star Is Rising: Historical Development of the Old Testament Royal Ideology and the Rise of the Jewish Messianic Expectations* (Atlanta: Scholars Press, 1997), 109–15; Kenneth Pomykala, *The Davidic Dynasty Tradition in Early Judaism: Its History and Significance for Messianism* (Atlanta: Scholars Press, 1995); J. J. M. Roberts, "The Old Testament Contribution to Messianic Expectations," in *The Messiah* (ed. James Charlesworth; Minneapolis: Fortress Press, 1992), 39–51.

(v. 12b). During the days of Amos, Uzziah reconquered David's former vassals, restoring the past glory of the dynasty (2 Chron. 26:6–8). Yet Amos predicted more than the mere restoration of David's former glory. The restored house would not simply conquer David's former vassals, but would exercise universal rule as the overall eschatological tenor of vv. 11–15 suggests. The triumph would not simply be partial and temporary, but total and eternal.

Amos identifies the subjects of this universal rule as "all the nations whom I will claim for Myself." The Hebrew expression (lit. "all the nations over whom my name will be called") is an idiomatic claim of ownership (Isa. 63:19; Jer. 7:10; Dan. 9:18). It reflects the ancient custom of renaming a city in honor of its conqueror.[8] Thus, Jerusalem was renamed the "City of David" in honor of its famous conqueror (2 Sam. 5:7, 9), his realm known as the "Kingdom of David." In typological escalation of this pattern, Amos foresaw a greater day when all nations would effectively be renamed in honor of its future Ruler, better known as the "Kingdom of Yahweh."

Unprecedented Blessings of the Coming Kingdom (vv. 13–15)
In the second stanza, Amos predicted unprecedented agricultural and domestic blessings. Quite possibly, his vision was inspired by the agricultural boon in his own day. As a man who "loved the soil," Uzziah launched a program of agricultural expansion resulting in viticultural fertility of unprecedented proportions in the nation's history (2 Chron. 26:10). In escalation of this pattern, Amos foresaw an even greater day of blessing in the future kingdom (vv. 13–15).

Verse 13a pictures the blessings of the future kingdom in terms echoing Leviticus 26:3–5, in which Moses depicted the blessings available to ancient Israel as reward for obedience in terms of agricultural abundance. The image drew on Israel's two agricultural cycles: the plowing and harvesting of grain, and planting and pressing of grapes. Amos envisioned grain harvests so bountiful it would take all summer to finish: when plowmen arrive to prepare the soil for planting, harvesters would still be working the fields. The yield of vineyards would be equally great-those who work the winepress would not be done when the next planting season arrives.

Verse 13b pictures the eschatological blessings in even more extravagant terms: "the mountains shall drip with fresh wine and all the hills will melt." After harvesting the vines, the ancient Israelites placed grapes in a winepress to squeeze out the juice. The grape juice was then placed in storage jars to ferment over time into wine. Both vineyard and winepress were located on top of a hill; the vats where the grape juice fermented were located below. Drawing

---

8. For example, when Joab was about to conquer Ammon, he sent word to David, "Besiege the city and capture it, otherwise I will capture the city and *it will be named for me* (lit., my name will be called over it)" (2 Sam. 12:28).

on these ordinary practices of his own day, Amos pictured God's future blessings in extraordinary terms. The vineyard would yield so many grapes, the
juice would overflow the winepress, then turn into wine cascading down the
hillside with such abundance as to erode the soil on the way. Whether we
understand this literally or metaphorically, it clearly pictures God's eschatological blessings in terms that exceeded anything Israel had ever experienced.
It is the heightening of a pattern.

Canonical Reading of Amos 9:11–15

In this oracle God revealed clear eschatological dimensions of the future
of the house of David. While Nathan's oracle of an everlasting throne and
kingdom was implicitly rather than explicitly eschatological, the oracle still
promised rest that resolves itself eschatologically. Amos explicitly located
restoration of the glory of David's house in the eschatological future. Yet
while his oracle explicitly described the eschatological kingdom, it was only
implicitly or indirectly messianic rather than explicit, direct prophecy of the
Messiah. Lack of mention of an individual Davidic king precludes classifying
this as direct, explicit messianic prophecy. After all, Amos refers to the house
of David, an open expression that demands at least one Davidic king but
could allow for an entire line (e.g., Ps. 132:11–12). So although Amos added
a significant piece to the puzzle, he did not explicitly set out all the pieces.
A certain mystery still remained in God's revelation of his future program
for the house of David. With the progress of revelation, God would provide
more pieces of the puzzle, allowing for a more precise canonical reading
of Amos 9:11–15 that properly placed this early oracle in the light of the
entire First Testament canon. In the light of subsequent prophecies by later
prophets, it would become more and more clear that the future restoration
of the house of David would be effected through an *individual* ideal Davidic
king. For example, Hosea 1:11 and 3:1–5, as well as Micah 4–5 would frame
the future in terms of the coming of an *individual* ideal new David.

MESSIANIC TRAJECTORIES IN HOSEA 1:11 AND 3:1–5

Hosea prophesied to the northern kingdom Israel in the eighth century. His
career began when Jeroboam II ruled Israel (782–753 BCE) and Uzziah was king
of Judah (767–740 BCE); continued through the reigns of Jotham (750–735
BCE) and Ahaz (735–715 BCE); and ended in the days of Hezekiah (715–686
BCE).[9] He witnessed the subjugation of Israel to Assyria in 734–732, as well as
the destruction of Samaria and deportation of her citizens in 722 BCE.[10]

---

9. For a chronological placement of Hosea among the kings and fall of northern Israel, see
   page 71.
10. Glassner's "From Nabonassar to Samas-suma-ukin (745–668)" in *Mesopotamian
    Chronicles*, 195.

The literary structure of the book of Hosea features five cycles, moving from judgment to deliverance (1:2–2:1; 2:2–3:5; 4:1–6:3; 6:4–11:11; 11:12–14:9). The first two cycles close with oracles of deliverance (1:10–2:1; 3:1–5), each featuring royal Davidic themes (1:11; 3:4–5). These two oracles lay the foundation for the eschatological Messiah.

Contextual Reading of Hosea 1:11

Hosea's first mention of Davidic kingship occurs in an oracle of restoration (1:10–2:1) following an oracle of judgment (1:2–9). God illustrated his fractured covenant relationship with Israel in an object lesson of Hosea's broken marriage with Gomer. In the three episodes of the birth and naming of Hosea's children, the Lord symbolically denounced the sins of the northern kingdom and announced his imminent judgment (1:2–5, 6–7, 8–9). God directed him to name his first son "Jezreel," denouncing Jehu's bloodshed at Jezreel and announcing he would defeat and destroy Israel in the Jezreel Valley (1:4–5). This was fulfilled in 722 BCE with the destruction of Samaria, located at the edge of the Jezreel Valley. God instructed Hosea to name his second child "No Pity," since he would not have pity on Israel, but would show pity to Judah (1:6–7). This was fulfilled when God destroyed Israel in 722 BCE, but spared Judah. God named Hosea's third child "Not My People," saying, "You are not my people and I am not your God" (1:8–9). Like a divorce decree ("You are not my wife and I am not your husband"), God terminated his covenant with Israel, reversing the original pledge at Sinai. This was fulfilled when Sargon II deported the inhabitants of Israel in 722 BCE. However, Hosea's oracle did not end with doom, for he also foresaw a future day of deliverance. God would reunite Israel and Judah under an ideal new David (1:10–2:1) and make a new covenant effectively restoring his people (2:2–23). Hosea linked God's future provision of the new David with inauguration of the new covenant.

First, Hosea predicted God one day would restore the Israelite exiles, reuniting them with the Judahites whom he had spared: "The Judahites and the Israelites will be gathered together" (1:11a). In the immediate context, this reunification is pictured as a restoration of the northern tribes from the Assyrian deportation of 722 BCE. However, in the broader context of the book as a whole, Hosea warned Judah to not imitate the example of Israel, threatening a similar fate if it also turned away (4:15; 5:5, 10–14; 6:4, 10–11; 8:14; 10:11; 12:2). The fact that Judah did suffer a similar fate in the Babylonian exile of 586 BCE did not put this prediction of the reunification of the northern and southern kingdoms in jeopardy. Rather, when God sent Judah into exile, it made clear that restoration of the united kingdom under the new David would be fulfilled in a future great second exodus in which God would restore his people (cf. Jer. 30–33).

Second, God would restore Davidic kingship over reunited Israel/Judah: "they will appoint one head over themselves" (1:11b). The term "head" is a technical term that refers to the king. The term "head" is synonymous with "king" (1 Sam. 15:17; 2 Sam. 22:44; Isa. 7:1, 8, 9, 16; Mic. 2:13; Hab. 3:13; Ps. 18:43[44]; cf. 60:7[9]; 108:8[9]) and "prince" (Ezek. 38:2, 3; 39:1). The expression "one head" effectively pictured a reversal of the divided monarchy currently ruled by two different kings (cf. Ezek. 34:23; 37:22, 24). Just as David founded the original united monarchy, Hosea thus envisioned a new David over a restored united kingdom.

Third, Hosea associated the rule of the new David and reunification of the nation with a future second exodus (1:11c). The motif of the second exodus is conveyed by the expression "they will go up from the land" (1:11c), used elsewhere of Israel departing from Egypt (Gen. 45:25; Exod. 1:10; Isa. 11:16; Hos. 2:15). God would reverse the Assyrian deportation, bringing the northern exiles back into the land of Israel where he would plant them forever (2:24–25).

The second exodus was a recurrent theme in the preexilic and exilic prophets alike. Although the deportees of Judah would one day return from exile in Babylon, there is no record of the deportees of Israel ever returning from deportation to Assyria. Thus, we may conclude that the second exodus imagery here ultimately points to the greater deliverance that Messiah would one day effect, which is often pictured in terms of a second exodus in the Second Testament.

Contextual Reading of Hosea 3:1–5

Hosea's second Davidic oracle occurs in 3:1–5. Once again, God illustrated his covenant relation with Israel by the object lesson of Hosea's marriage with Gomer (1:2–3:5). As an object lesson of Israel's unfaithfulness to her divine husband, God instructed Hosea to marry a woman who would prove unfaithful (1:2–3). Her repeated adultery illustrated Israel's persistent idolatry. Hosea's declaration of divorce, "She is not my wife, and I am not her husband" (2:2), illustrated Yahweh's termination of covenant with Israel, "You are not my people, and I am not your God" (1:9). However, Hosea expected God's punishment would bring Israel to repentance (2:1–13). He would make a new covenant in which Israel would perpetually be faithful to him by rejecting other gods (2:14–21). Just as Hosea sent Gomer out of his home, the Lord would exile Israel (3:4); however, when Israel would repent, he would restore her (3:5; cf. 2:14–21).

Hosea viewed the Assyrian exile (cf. 8:13; 9:3, 6, 15, 17; 10:6; 11:5; 12:9) as a time of rehabilitation when Israel would be deprived of the political and cultic perversions that led it astray: "The Israelites will live many days without king or prince, without sacrifice or cultic pillar, without ephod or teraphim" (3:4). Hosea also foresaw a day when Israel would repent and God would return Israel from Assyrian deportation and restore Davidic kingship over a reunited nation: "Afterward the Israelites will return and seek the Lord their God and David their king; they will submit to the Lord in fear and receive his blessings in days to come" (3:5).

The expression "David their king" should not be misunderstood in a woodenly literal sense as predicting the bodily resurrection of David the long deceased king. Rather, it functions as a typological moniker standing for a new David, that is, a future king who would embody all the ideals of the illustrious founder of the historical dynasty (cf. Ezek. 34:23–24; 37:24–25). Subsequent prophets would make clear that this future ideal king would not be David, but one who would rule over David's kingdom and inherit his throne as his ultimate descendant (e.g., Isa. 9:7; 16:5; 22:22; Jer. 23:5; 30:9). By designating this coming ideal king as "David," Hosea was speaking in terms of a pattern. Although he knew this coming king would exemplify the moral ideals of David and restore the past golden age of the united kingdom, this typological name also kept the ultimate identity of the new David as God incarnate a divinely hidden mystery. The Second Testament explained that when prophesying about the Messiah, the prophets of the Hebrew Scriptures neither understood his ultimate identity nor the precise time of his coming (1 Pet. 1:10–12).

Hosea did not specify the precise time frame between Israel's exile and loss of kingship (3:4) and her return and restoration of Davidic kingship (3:5). Rather, he predicted the restoration would occur "afterwards" and "in the future days." While the term "afterwards" (אַחַר) has a broad range of meanings, it almost always refers to a period within one's lifetime, but may refer to the distant future. The idiom "in future days" (בְּאַחֲרִית הַיָּמִים) may refer to the imminent future (Deut. 31:29; Jer. 23:20; 30:24), distant future (Gen. 49:1; Num. 24:14; Deut. 4:30; Jer. 48:47; 49:39; Dan. 10:14), or eschatological future (Isa. 2:2; Mic. 4:1; Ezek. 38:16). The open nature of these expressions reflects the fact that God did not reveal the precise time to the prophets as to when the restoration of Israel and provision of the new David would occur (cf. 1 Pet. 1:10–12).

Canonical Reading of Hosea 1:11 and 3:1–5

Hosea 1:11 and 3:1–5 clearly predicted the restoration of Israel and Judah as a reunited monarchy under the sway of an ideal new David. Yet it was unclear at the time whether this restoration would occur sometime in the imminent future when Judah was still secure in its own land. Yet while Judah had been faithful in his day (11:12), Hosea warned it to not imitate the example of Israel, threatening a similar fate if it also turned away (4:15; 5:5, 10–14; 6:4, 10–11; 8:14; 10:11; 12:2). When Judah later did fall into apostasy, God punished her by destroying Jerusalem, dismantling the Davidic dynasty and sending the people into exile. After seventy years in Babylonian exile, God restored a remnant but the full restoration of Israel and Judah as a reunited and independent kingdom would await the eschatological future. Therefore, when read in the light of the entire First Testament canon, we recognize that God would fulfill Hosea's prophecies only in the eschatological future. So the progress of revelation made clear that Hosea 1:11 and 3:4–5 provided not simply a future Davidic hope but a future eschatological messianic expectation. We view these two oracles of the future new David as implicit or indirect prophecy of the eschatological Messiah, setting up a typological pattern fulfillment, a second exodus. To be sure, Hosea added several significant pieces to the puzzle, but he himself did not have all the pieces. We can only appreciate the full messianic potential of Hosea's oracles in the light of subsequent progressive revelation that would fill in the gaps. One of the most significant contributions to the growing picture was provided in Micah 4–5.

MESSIANIC TRAJECTORIES IN MICAH

The prophetic career of Micah spans the reigns of Jotham (750–735 BCE), Ahaz (735–715 BCE), and Hezekiah (715–686 BCE). These were the worst of times and the best of times. Micah not only witnessed Samaria's destruction and deportation of her citizens but foresaw this calamity (1:5–7) and predicted an identical fate would befall Jerusalem (1:8–16). As a prophet to the southern kingdom, he prophesied that Judah would be conquered by a foreign army (2:4), Jerusalem besieged (4:11; 5:1), Temple Mount turned into an uninhabitable ruin (3:12), the people driven into exile (4:6–7, 10) and the Davidic king removed from the throne (4:9; 5:1). Yet judgment would not be God's last word. Once his people returned to him in genuine repentance (6:6–16), Yahweh would bring about a dramatic reversal (7:8–20). He would regather a remnant from among the nations (2:12–13; 4:6–7); give birth to a "new Judah" under a "new David" (5:2–6); restore the dominion of David's kingdom to its former glory (4:8; 5:7–9); purge the nations of their idolatrous practices and imperialistic aggressions (5:10–15); and usher in a new golden age characterized by the universal worship of Yahweh (4:1–5).

The book of Micah is arranged in three cycles, each opening with judgment and closing with deliverance (1:2–2:13; 3:1–5:15; 6:1–7:20). The oracles of doom announced the coming destruction of unrepentant Israel/Samaria and Judah/Jerusalem (1:2–2:11; 3:1–12; 6:1–7:7). The oracles of hope foresaw the future day of deliverance when God would restore his people, once they would return to him in genuine repentance (2:12–13; 4:1–5:15; 7:8–20).

Doom and Coming Destruction	1:2–2:11	3:1–12	6:1–7:7
Hope and Future Restoration	2:12–13	4:1–5:15	7:8–20

The three sets of oracles of deliverance paint different parts of the same picture. The first oracle highlights the role of Yahweh (2:12–13). The second introduces the human agent God would use to bring about deliverance:

the new "David" (5:2–6). The third emphasizes that restoration would be offered on the basis of divine faithfulness, but contingent on repentance (7:8–20).

Contextual Reading of Micah 5:2–6

Micah's prophecy of a new David in 5:2–6 occurs in his second cycle of oracles, which opens with woe (3:1–12) but closes with welfare of the community (4:1–5:15). To properly interpret and fully appreciate the original meaning of this prophecy, we must consider it in the light of this surrounding context.

Prediction of Zion's Imminent Destruction (3:1–12)

In this oracle of doom, Micah indicted Zion of social evil and announced God was about to destroy the city and send its inhabitants into exile. In his climactic conclusion, he declared that Mount Zion would become an uninhabitable waste (3:12). On the surface, this oracle seemed to be unconditional; it lacked a call to repentance and contained no conditional offer of forgiveness. Furthermore, God would ignore any last-minute pleas by the unrepentant for mercy (3:4).

Inherent Contingency of Micah's Oracle

Micah 3:12 represents a classic example of the inherent contingency of Hebrew prophecy (e.g., Jer. 18:1–10). In partial fulfillment of Micah's prediction, Sennacherib king of Assyria invaded Judah and besieged Jerusalem, threatening to destroy it in 701 BCE. However, God spared Jerusalem in response to the intercession of king Hezekiah and Isaiah (2 Kings 18:13–19:36; Isa. 36:1–37:37; 2 Chron. 32:1–23). According to Jeremiah 26:17–19, God had threatened to destroy Jerusalem, but graciously spared it when Hezekiah entreated him. In the end, God is committed to completing the promise. Any discipline in the divine program for Israel does not remove his irrevocable commitment to bring about the ultimate eschatological fulfillment of his covenant promise. This point is crucial in light of how the rest of Micah's prophecy proceeds.

Initial Reactualization of Micah's Oracle in Exile

Micah 3:12 also represents an example of the life of prophecy. Although God relented from judgment in 701 BCE, this deliverance did not unconditionally guarantee the perpetual security of Zion for the future. The potential would always exist for God to apply Micah's oracle of doom if the City of Zion and house of David returned to their evil ways. In fact, when Manasseh (686–642 BCE) led Jerusalem into apostasy (2 Kings 21:1–9 // 2 Chron. 33:1–9), God again announced that he would destroy Zion as he destroyed Samaria (2 Kings 21:10–15). This oracle mirrored Micah's earlier prediction that Jerusalem would suffer the same fate as Samaria (1:1, 5–9), effectively resurrecting his original oracle of doom.

In partial fulfillment of this oracle of doom, Yahweh sovereignly brought the Assyrian army against Jerusalem and sent Manasseh as prisoner into exile in Babylon (2 Chron. 33:10–11). Nevertheless, the Lord did not destroy Jerusalem and send her inhabitants into exile in those days, as he had threatened in 2 Kings 21:10–15. The Chronicler explains that God's punishment led the king to humble himself and plea for mercy; God relented from his threat to destroy Zion at that time and eventually restored a repentant Manasseh to the throne (2 Chron. 33:12–13).[11]

The evil of Amon (642–640 BCE) rekindled divine anger (2 Kings 21:19–26; 2 Chron. 33:21–25), but the penitence of Josiah (640–609 BCE) moved Yahweh to delay judgment for one generation (2 Kings 22:14–20; 2 Chron. 34:14–28). Since all four post-Josianic kings were evil, Jerusalem was helpless in the face of divine wrath, which had been boiling for more than a century. In fulfillment of Micah 3:12, Nebuchadnezzar king of Babylon destroyed Jerusalem and turned the Temple Mount in an uninhabitable ruin in 586 BCE (2 Kings 25:1–12; 2 Chron. 36:15–21).

Hermeneutical Impact on Micah's Oracle of Restoration

The original openness and subsequent application of Micah 3:12 have profound impact on our understanding of Micah's oracle of hope in 4:1–5:15. There is a pattern of divine activity in the short term that sets up an indication of a long-term realization. Jeremiah 26:17–19 informs us that Micah originally threatened that God would destroy Jerusalem at the hand of Sennacherib in the days of Hezekiah. However, the prophet also predicted in 4:1–5:15 that God one day would bring about a dramatic reversal of this prospect. According to 5:2–6 [MT 1–5], God would raise up a new "David," who would bring victory over enemies whoever they were (Micah 5:3 [2]). He even hypothetically pictured this figure (or ones like him, "seven shepherd rulers and eight commanders") as mustering a mighty army of Judahite warriors to destroy the Assyrian army and bring about the fall of the Assyrian empire (Note the hypothetical nature of Micah 5:5, "If Assyria *should* try and invade . . ."). Of course, this specific hypothetically posited event never did take place, but it did picture the victory. By the time Jerusalem was destroyed in 586 BCE and the exiles returned to Jerusalem in 538 BCE, the Assyrian empire had long since disappeared from the scene. In picture of the fulfillment of Micah 5:5–6, the Assyrian empire fell in 612–609 BCE. Its destruction, however, was orchestrated not by a Judahite army under the command of a new David, but by a coalition of Babylonian,

---

11. Second Chronicles 33:12 says, "When Manasseh prayed to the LORD, the LORD responded to him . . ." Although no one knows for sure what exactly Manasseh prayed, the *Prayer of Manasseh* in the *Apocrypha* captures a humble repentant approach to God who responds compassionately to and forgives those who repent.

Median, and Scythian warriors under Nabopolassar the king of Babylon.[12] So this cannot be the fulfillment of Micah. It must come later in a pattern like the earlier declaration of victory of the Davidite who defeats enemies. In 4:1–5:15 Micah was looking through a mirror indirectly and speaking of a mystery to be revealed in the progress of revelation (1 Cor. 13:12), foreseeing a coming deliverance that would supersede the historical realities of the seventh century BCE. To be sure, he spoke of the coming historical deliverance of Zion in the imminent future, but also of a greater deliverance to come. Later Jewish readers correctly saw this text in terms of this long-term hope, since the Jewish leaders told Herod and the magi that Messiah would be born in Bethlehem (Matt. 2:1–6).

Future Deliverance of Jerusalem (4:1–5:1)
Although Micah announced the coming doom of Jerusalem in 3:1–12, judgment would not be Yahweh's last word. In 4:1–5:15, the prophet predicted the return of a repentant remnant from exile, the restoration of the former glory of Judah's kingdom through an ideal Davidic king, and the resurgent dynasty's conquest of their Assyrian oppressors. The symmetrical arrangement of the oracles in 4:1–5:15 highlights its thematic unity and literary cohesion:

A Yahweh's universal reign over repentant nations (4:1–5)
  B Yahweh will strengthen remnant (4:6–7a)
    C Restoration of former dominion of Zion (4:7b–8)
      D Removal of Davidic king and Zion in labor (4:9–10)
        E Siege of Zion and affliction of her king (4:11)
          F God's hidden plan for Zion and the nations (4:12–13)
        E' Siege of Zion and affliction of her king (5:1)
      D' Return of Davidic king and rebirth of Judah (5:2–3)
    C' Restoration of dominion of Davidic kingdom (5:4–6)
  B' Yahweh will strengthen the remnant (5:7–9)
A' Yahweh's universal judgment of apostate nations (5:10–15)

Micah began by envisioning a future golden age of the LORD's universal reign over the nations, marked by the cessation of war and worship of the God of Israel (4:1–8). Likewise, he ended with the LORD's judgment of the nations that would usher in this future period of peace (5:7–15). Bracketed within the eschatological visions were oracles of doom dealing with the coming siege of Jerusalem and the exile of her king and people (4:9–11; 5:1), as well as oracles of hope dealing with the deliverance of Jerusalem and the coming of

---

12. Jean-Jacques Glassner, "Chronicle of the First Years of Nabopolassar (626–623)" in *Mesopotamian Chronicles*. Writings from the Ancient World (Atlanta: Society of Biblical Literature, 2004), 218–29.

the ideal Davidic king (4:12–13; 5:2–6). The movement back and forth from the eschatological reign of God (4:1–5 and 5:10–15) to the historical plight of Zion and the Davidic throne (4:6–5:9) would provide a crucial segue for the already/not yet fulfillment of Micah's prediction of the coming ideal new David in 5:2–6.

The symmetrical arrangement of the oracles in 4:1–5:15 obscures the chronological order of events that the prophet foresaw. The oracles move from later events backward to the earliest event at the center, then forward to the later events. If we rearrange the oracles into normal chronological order, a clearer picture emerges that makes better sense to the modern reader:

1. God will gather hostile nations against Zion to inaugurate his hidden plan (4:12–13)
2. Zion will suffer siege and her king will be afflicted by an invading foreign army (4:11//5:1)
3. Davidic kingship will be temporarily removed, but eventually restored (4:9–10//5:2–3)
4. The former dominion of Zion and Davidic kingship will be restored (4:7b–8//5:4–6)
5. The exiles will become a mighty remnant where they are scattered in exile (4:6–7a//5:7–9)
6. Yahweh will reign over the nations and put an end to warfare (4:1–5//5:10–15)

To understand the original meaning of Micah's royal prophecies (4:9–5:6), we must examine them in the light of their original literary context, bracketed within 4:1–10 and 5:7–15.

Siege of Zion and Suffering of Her King (4:11//5:1)
The parallel oracles in Micah 4:11 and 5:1 envisioned Jerusalem under siege. Micah did not identify the foreign enemy surrounding Jerusalem, but the reference to Assyria in 5:5–6 (envisioning a yet future invasion of Judah by Assyria) suggests the siege by Sennacherib in 701 BCE (2 Kings 19:32; 2 Chron. 32:10). According to Jeremiah 26:17–19, God had threatened to destroy Jerusalem at the hands of Sennacherib; however, Yahweh relented and spared the city, thanks to the intercession of Hezekiah (2 Kings 19:1–36; Isa. 37:1–37; 2 Chron. 32:20–22).

In 4:11b, Micah personified Zion as a maiden standing defenseless before her assailants who intend to strip her naked (MT preserves תֶּחֱנָף, "let her be profaned," LXX reflects תֶּחְשֹׁף, "let her be stripped"), then look upon her in mockery. This dramatic image pictured the humiliation of being sent into exile (Isa. 20:4; Jer. 13:26; 49:10). Micah resumed this theme in 5:1a, where he portrayed Zion as a defenseless maiden surrounded by enemy warriors about to rape her. Speaking on behalf of the people, he lamented, "We are besieged!"

In 5:1b, the prophet pictured a foreign ruler smiting Zion's king across the face with his own scepter. Since the scepter was the traditional emblem of royalty and kingship, this insulting act conveyed the king's loss of his throne and his subjugation to foreign rule. It also represented a reversal of traditional Davidic expectations since the royal scepter, which Jacob predicted would never depart from Judah (Gen. 49:10), is now wielded by a foreign ruler and used as the instrument of the Davidic king's punishment rather than as the emblem of his royal power.

Return of "David" and Rebirth of Judah (4:9–10//5:2–3)

Micah 4:9–10 and 5:2–3 share twin themes but by way of reversal. Micah 4:9a lamented removal of Davidic kingship from Jerusalem, while 5:2 celebrated its return. Micah 4:9b–10 personified Zion as a woman groaning in the pain of labor, expressing the grief of her citizens being taken into exile. Micah 5:3 resumed this image, picturing Zion as a woman in travail of labor until he gives birth to a new Jerusalem—the brothers of the new David of 5:2. Micah linked the coming of the new David and birth of the new Jerusalem by birth imagery, since the declaration, "O Bethlehem Ephrathah . . . from you shall come forth a ruler over Israel" (5:2), plays on a common birth motif (Gen. 17:6, "from you shall come forth kings").

According to 4:10 and 5:2, Zion would suffer the travail of childbirth until her former citizens would return from exile. Mention of Babylon in 4:10 ("You will leave the city and live in the open field; you will go to Babylon but from there you will be rescued") suggests to some interpreters that Micah envisioned Nebuchadnezzar's destruction of Jerusalem in 586 BCE, when he sent her inhabitants in exile to Babylon.[13] However, since Micah prophesied during the reign of Hezekiah, it could be that he had in mind Sennacherib's siege in 701 BCE, when the Assyrian king threatened to destroy the city and send her citizens into exile (2 Kings 18:32). According to Jeremiah 26:17–19, God had threatened to destroy Jerusalem at the hand of Sennacherib in the days of Hezekiah, but later spared her in response to Hezekiah's intercession. According to the biblical historians, a common practice of the Assyrian kings was to send exiles and prisoners to Babylon, which was under their control in those days.[14] Just as Micah 3:12 was an oracle threatening the destruction

---

13. The reality of Jerusalem's destruction at the hands of the Babylonians in 586 BCE is well documented in Scripture. Here are just a sampling of references: 2 Kings 25:7; 2 Chronicles 36:20; cf. 1 Chronicles 9:1; Ezra 2:1; 5:12.

14. Moving beyond Scriptural support (2 Kings 17:24, 30; 2 Chron. 33:11), ancient Mesopotamian records confirm that Assyrian kings fought constantly to maintain their controlling dominance over Babylon. For example, Tiglath-Pileser III (745–727 BCE), Shalmaneser V (727–722 BCE), Sargon II (721–705 BCE), and Sennacherib (704–681

of Jerusalem at the hand of Sennacherib, Micah 4:10 was also an oracle looking to a prospect that Sennacherib would send the people of Jerusalem to Babylon in exile—a threat the Assyrian king made (2 Kings 18:32). Yet when God answered Hezekiah's prayer, he not only relented from the destruction of Zion threatened in 3:12, but from the exile of her citizens in 4:10. God eventually fulfilled both oracles of doom a century later in the annihilation of Jerusalem and exile of her people by Nebuchadnezzar in 586 BCE. However, this represented a reapplication of the principle in Micah's prophecies. Hence, it is not necessary to attribute mention of Babylon in 4:10 to a later exilic editor, nor even to a later redaction by Micah himself, as if he followed Isaiah in predicting the Babylonian exile (2 Kings 20:17–18).

The final cycle of oracles in the book envision the future restoration emerging not from Babylon, but from everywhere: "In that day people will come to you from Assyria . . . Egypt, Euphrates . . . and seacoasts" (7:12). Micah portrayed the future restoration in terms of the remnant returning from Assyria, accompanied by repentant Assyrians turning to Yahweh (cf. Isa. 19:23–25), as well as from elsewhere. This more universal restoration points to the eschaton.

The Return of David (5:2). Micah depicted the coming king in riddle-like fashion as a second David, as the references to Bethlehem and his ancestral origins suggest. Other prophets picture him as an ideal descendant of David, or bestow on him the archetypal name "David."[15] Micah portrays him as a veritable David *redivivus*—not a second coming or resurrection of the historical founder of Zion's royal dynasty, but the moral embodiment of David, the ideal king.

Micah contrasted the present humiliation of Jerusalem with the future glory of Bethlehem through whom the future deliverance would come. Jerusalem's loss of her historical Davidic king would be reversed by Bethlehem's provision of the ideal Davidic king. The association of the coming ruler with Bethlehem, the cradle of David, is reminiscent of God's election of David, the smallest of the sons of Jesse, as anointed king (1 Sam. 16:1–13). Mention of Bethlehem—David's home town—represents a new beginning for David's house. God would bypass Jerusalem, the seat of the current Davidic king, to return to the portal through which David stepped

---

BCE) are all able to keep Babylon in check (Glassner, *Mesopotamian Chronicles,* Writings from the Ancient World [Atlanta: Society of Biblical Literature, 2004], 173–76, 195–98). More about these Assyrian kings and affect on God's people will be discussed in chapter five, "Messianic Trajectories in Isaiah."

15. Later prophets like Isaiah and Jeremiah picture the coming Davidic king as an ideal descendant of David (Isa. 11:1, 10; Jer. 23:5; 33:15). Some, as we have seen in Hosea and prophets like Isaiah and Jeremiah anticipate a King using the archetypal name "David." (Hos. 3:5; Jer. 30:9; Ezek. 34:23–24; 37:24–25).

onto the stage of redemptive-history centuries before.[16] Isaiah expressed the same concept of a new beginning for the house of David: "A shoot shall come out from the stump of Jesse" (Isa. 11:1).

The association of the coming king with Bethlehem (5:1a) and reference to his ancient origins (5:1b) are clear allusions to David. These motifs represent a new beginning for the Davidic dynasty, suggesting that the Babylonian exile constituted temporary suspension not permanent removal of David's throne. The house of David had violated its covenant obligations (Ps. 132:11–12), but God's covenant promises would never fail (2 Sam. 7:10–16; 1 Chron. 17; Ps. 89). God would rise up a new David through whom the promises would be fulfilled.

Micah's description of Messiah coming from Bethlehem emphasizes the figure as a symbol of God's promise to reestablish the Davidic dynasty. The expression, "From you will come forth one who will rule over Israel" (5:2), identified the king's dynastic origin. The idiom "come forth from" (יֵצֵא, "to come forth" + מִן, "from") often identifies a king's origin in various ways: (1) his ancestral origin: "kings will come forth from you" (Gen. 17:6; cf. Gen. 35:11); (2) his national origin: "one of their own people will become their leader; their ruler will come forth from their own midst" (Jer. 30:21; cf. Zech. 10:4); (3) his original social position: "He came forth from debt-prison to the throne; he was born poor in his own kingdom" (Eccl. 4:14); or (4) his city of origin: "From you [= Nineveh] has come forth one who devises wicked schemes" (Nah. 1:11). Micah 5:2b suggests his *ancestral* city of origin. Since he would be from the lineage of David, his ancestral roots would be from Bethlehem, the village of David: "From you a king will come forth who will rule over Israel on my behalf, one whose [ancestral] origins are in the distant past." Many interpreters view verse 2 as a prediction of the city of origin of the birth of the Davidic king. Indeed, the expression, "He shall come forth" (יֵצֵא) may refer to the biological birth of a son (Gen. 25:26; 46:26; Job 1:21; Hos. 9:13). Yet when used of a royal figure, it may also depict a royal scion ascending to the throne (2 Kings 11:12; 2 Chron. 23:11). This double entendre would allow for a later Christological typological interpretation.

Some interpret the term, "antiquity" (עוֹלָם), as an explicit revelation of the eternal preexistence of Jesus the Messiah. Thus they translate the term as "everlasting" (KJV) or "eternity" (NASB). Although this is a legitimate Christological extension, the original historical contextual sense of the term simply meant "distant past" (NRSV), "ancient times" (NIV) or "the old days" (NET) referring to the ancient past in earlier periods of human history.[17] The preceding oracle used a temporal expression to depict restoration of Davidic

---

16. See 1 Samuel 16:1, 4, 18; 17:12, 15, 58; cf. Genesis 35:19; 48:7; Ruth 1:1–2; 4:11.

17. This term, עוֹלָם, was discussed in chapter 2 while addressing the duration of the Davidic dynasty (p. 65).

kingship: "Your former dominion will be restored" (4:8). The accompanying expression, "from antiquity" or "ancient times" (מִקֶּדֶם) often refers to earlier periods in history (e.g., Pss. 74:12; 77:5, 11; 78:2; 143:5; Prov. 8:23; Isa. 45:21; 46:10; Mic. 7:20; Hab. 1:12; Lam. 1:7; 2:17). The phrase "from the ancient days" (מִימֵי עוֹלָם) occurs five other times in the Hebrew Scriptures, always referring to early periods in Israel's history.[18] So 5:2, certainly refers to the past golden age of David's kingship, when Yahweh inaugurated his covenant relationship with David and originally established the Davidic dynasty (2 Sam. 7). Nonetheless, the term can also go further back in a pattern fulfillment as implicit meaning, since pattern escalates and builds off of pushing original language to its fullest extent.

The Rebirth of the Nation (5:3). In verse 2, Micah used a birth metaphor to depict the coming of the new David: "O Bethlehem Ephrathah . . . from you will come forth a ruler" (cf. Gen. 17:6, "from you will come forth kings"). Verse 3 picks up this image, picturing Israel as a woman travailing in labor until she could give birth to the rest of his brothers. As in 4:9–10, Micah used the imagery of a woman suffering in labor to picture the travail of Zion losing her king and citizens in the exile. Verse 3 resumes the image, depicting the restoration of kingship and return of the exiles as the time when Zion finally gives birth to a new Jerusalem and finds relief from her suffering in the coming age of restoration.

Micah described the interregnum as a time during which "He will give them until the time when the woman in labor gives birth" (v. 3a). The expression, "He will give them" (יִתְּנֵם), has been interpreted in various ways. Most understand this as a reference to God sending the nation into exile: God will hand the people of Israel over to their enemies. Others take this as a description of God setting up an interregnum: God will put them ("his brothers") over the sons of Israel until the woman gives birth to the wonder child. Either way, verse 3 explains the delay in the appearance of this ideal king, and coordinates it with the end of the time of foreign oppression and the return of the Israelites who live outside Judah.

At the onset of the new age, Israel and Judah would be regathered and reunited under one ruler—the new David: "the rest of his brothers will return to/with the people of Israel" (v. 3b). The brothers of the coming king refer to fellow Judahites, who would join the Israelites to form a reunited kingdom. Reunification of Israel and Judah was the hope of both preexilic and exilic

---

18. Moses called Israel to remember the ancient days, namely past generations (Deut. 32:7). Isaiah wants his audience to remember the Exodus (63:9, 11). Amos remembers the days concerning David's dynasty (9:11). Later in Micah there is the call to remember the good old days when people once lived and prospered in the northern region of Israel (7:14). Finally there is a call to remember those days when gifts given to God were pleasing to him (Mal. 3:4).

prophets (Hos. 1:11; 3:5; Isa. 11:12–13; Jer. 31:2–6, 15–20; Ezek. 37). This laid the foundation for the pattern fulfillment to come, a regathered nation as the domain of the coming king's rule.

Restoration of the Davidic Empire (4:7b–8//5:4–6)
In 4:7b–8 and 5:4–6, Micah predicted that Yahweh would transform the currently weak nation into a mighty empire under the rule of an ideal "shepherd" who would embody the characteristics of David, the dynasty's illustrious founder. Both 4:8 and 5:4 are linked by the common motif of God's protection of his flock. In the former, Zion is addressed, "O watchtower of the flock," comparing the military protection that the fortified city of Jerusalem provided her citizens to the watchtower in the field from which a shepherd could keep watch over his sheep. In 5:4, Micah resumed the image of the new David, picturing the ideal king as a shepherd providing secure pasture for God's flock and protecting them in the power of Yahweh (2 Sam. 5:2; Ps. 78:71–72): "He shall stand and shepherd his flock in the strength of Yahweh . . . and they shall dwell secure" (5:4). Verses 5–6 identified in more concrete terms the predators from whom this ideal shepherd could protect God's flock: the Assyrians. This mention of the Assyrians was archetypal. They picture the kind of enemy from which God's protection would come.

In 5:5–6, Micah pictured the future time of deliverance in concrete terms that represented a dramatic reversal of the current plight in his own day. Having witnessed the invasion of Judah and siege of Jerusalem by Sennacherib in 701 BCE, the prophet envisioned the coming deliverance as reversing all this. Speaking hypothetically on behalf of his own countrymen, Micah proclaimed that if Assyria might try this again, things certainly would turn out differently: "Suppose the Assyrians try to invade our land or set foot upon our soil: we will send against them seven rulers—make that eight commanders!" (5:5).[19] So Assyria is a trope for the enemy looking to the current enemy as

---

19. Our approach to vv. 5b–6 [MT 4b–5] takes the imperfect/prefixed conjugation verbs in terms of a future hypothetical (irrealis) rather than future indicative sense. Therefore, we prefer the rendering, "*Should* the Assyrians try to invade our land and *should* they attempt to set foot in our fortresses, we *would* send against them seven shepherd-rulers, make that eight commanders." Of course, it could be objected that the Assyrians did, in fact, invade Judah another time, not during the reign of the godly king Hezekiah but the reign of the evil king Manasseh. God brought the Assyrian army to Jerusalem to seize Manasseh and carry him away to Babylon (2 Chron. 33:10–11). Sometime later, of course, Manasseh repented and God restored him to the throne in Jerusalem (2 Chron. 33:12–13). However, it is important to keep in mind that the Assyrians did not invade Judah to capture Manasseh and remove him into exile in quite the same way that they invaded Judah in the days of Hezekiah and Micah, when they destroyed forty-six fortress cities then besieged Jerusalem with the intent of destroying it. Furthermore, we are explicitly told that God raised up the Assyrian army in this situation in order to discipline Manasseh (2 Chron. 33:10–11), a divine act that accomplished its goal since Manasseh repented (2 Chron.

the example. Not only would the Judahite warriors turn back the Assyrian army at their border, they in turn would chase the retreating Assyrian army back to its own land, which they would conquer: "They will rule the land of Assyria with the sword, the land of Nimrod with a drawn sword!" (5:6a). Micah closed this oracle by emphasizing that this triumph would only be possible due to the intervention of Judah's coming king, whose arrival on the field of battle would turn the tide to bring about victory: "Our king will rescue us from the Assyrians, when they attempt to invade our land, and try to set foot in our territory" (5:6b).

The events which Micah witnessed in 701 BCE undoubtedly served as a pattern for his vision of future deliverance. Micah saw a foreshadowing of things to come in God's destruction of the Assyrian army encamped around Zion, Sennacherib's retreat to his own land, and his subsequent assassination by one of his own sons at the edge of the sword (2 Kings 19:35–37). The army of God then was the result of the intercession of the Israelite king, and the response of God was an army that Sennacherib had not counted on. Just as Yahweh had come to the rescue when Sennacherib invaded Judah and besieged Zion in 701 BCE (2 Kings 19:21–35), the future Davidic king would come to the rescue in the future (Mic. 5:6b). Just as Sennacherib had retreated to Nineveh (2 Kings 19:36), the warriors under the coming Davidic king would turn back the Assyrian army (or the enemies) at the border of the land of Judah (Mic. 5:5). Just as Sennacherib had been assassinated in his land at the edge of the sword (2 Kings 19:37), the coming Davidic king would rule over the land of Assyria with a sword (Mic. 5:6a). There is a thematic correspondence between God's past rescue of Zion from Sennacherib and the future deliverance of God's people through the coming Davidic king. We should understand this correspondence typologically. The prophecy envisioned the coming deliverance in terms of the destruction of the Assyrian empire as a type of victory over enemies.

The record of history also suggests Micah was speaking archetypically. If we view 5:5–6 in the light of history, it is clear that Assyria is an archetype, defeated by God and then later by the Babylonians. The Dead Sea Scrolls will view the Kittim and Rome in the same way centuries later.

33:12–13). So this does qualify as an exception to Micah's prediction (5:5b–6 [4b–5]). Of course, God himself also had threatened to destroy Jerusalem at the time of Hezekiah (Mic. 3:12). In fact, God would have done so if Hezekiah had not repented (2 Kings 18–19; Isa. 38–39; cf. Isa. 10). Nevertheless, the situation with Manasseh was different from the situation with Hezekiah in 701 BCE. Whereas the Assyrians had intended to destroy Jerusalem at the time of Hezekiah, they only intended to remove Manasseh from the throne. Thus, while the plural Judahites (who figure in Micah 5 by the repeated use of the first plural pronoun 'we') were threatened by Assyria in 701 BCE, the plural Judahites were not threatened by Assyria at the time of Manasseh, since it was only Manasseh himself who was the object of God's anger.

Since it was the historical archenemy of Israel/Judah, the prophets often use Assyria as an archetype of the hostile Gentile nations. For example, centuries after Assyria had been destroyed, Zechariah pictures the eschatological destruction of all hostile Gentile nations in terms of God's destruction of Assyria (Zech. 10:11). Isaiah, however, depicts the eschatological conversion of once-hostile Gentile nations in terms of the future conversion of Assyria, which would share equal status with Israel and Egypt as the people of God in the coming age (Isa. 19:23–25). These two dramatically different fates predicted by Isaiah and Zechariah for Assyria—salvation in the former, destruction in the latter—vividly illustrates its function as an archetype for the different fate awaiting repentant versus unrepentant nations or peoples.

Micah foresaw a day when God's people would no longer be afflicted by hostile empires such as Assyria, the archetypical enemy of Israel. Speaking in terms that were meaningful to his contemporaries, he portrayed the future in a way that would have been most relevant to them. Micah's prophecy was an example of the contextualization of Hebrew prophecy that also sets up a pattern fulfillment. The transcendent message of vv. 5b–6a appears in the heart of the oracle: "they will dwell in peace, for he will be exalted to the ends of the earth, and he will give us peace . . ." The universal scope of this predictions means that it ultimately looks to the eschaton.

Deliverance and Triumph of the Exiles (4:6–7//5:7–9)

As Micah saw it, the new David's conquest would be just the beginning of a new age of imperialism modeled on the military triumphs of David. Micah 5:7–9 pictures God orchestrating an uprising by the Jewish survivors among the nations in exile, empowering them to defeat their enemies. The prophet pictured this future triumph of the remnant with two dramatic images. The first pictures the victory of the remnant as entirely due to the sovereign work of God. Like the dew God sends and the rain falling on the grass by the command of God, the remnant would descend on their enemies in victory by the power of God. The second metaphor pictures the remnant vanquishing their foreign enemies like a vicious lion mauling its prey.

Eruption of the Kingdom of God (4:1–5//5:10–15)

Looking beyond the current moral crisis in Jerusalem and imminent judgment of the Temple Mount (3:1–12), Micah foresaw a day when Zion would be characterized by obedience to God's law and the Temple Mount exalted as the throne of Yahweh's universal reign (4:1–5). Although God was about to bring a foreign nation to destroy Jerusalem in the current period (3:12), in the future all nations would stream to restored Zion to learn his laws and to submit their disputes to his judgment. The new era would be marked by universal worship and obedience to Yahweh, resulting in the cessation of war and onset of worldwide peace. With no need to worry about enemy invasion, nations would devote their energies to more peaceful and productive activities. To bring about the first step in making his future vision an historical reality, Micah 4:5 exhorts his contemporary Jerusalemites to forsake foreign gods and to be loyal to Yahweh their God.

Micah's vision of this coming age highlights the universal reign of God, and points to an era involving a future Davidic king. Some interpreters suggest the Davidic dynasty violated God's law so grievously that its rule was terminated and Yahweh alone would rule in the eschatological kingdom. This is hard to reconcile with 5:2–6, where Micah envisions a future ideal David ruling over all nations as the representative of Yahweh. Rather than pitting 4:1–5 against 5:2–6, we should read each in the light of the other. Yahweh would exercise his theocratic kingship in the age of redemption through an ideal human king, depicted as a David *redivivus*.

It is likely the glorious events following Yahweh's deliverance of Zion from Sennacherib prompted Micah's vision of this future age: "The LORD delivered Hezekiah and the inhabitants of Jerusalem from the hand of Sennacherib king of Assyria and from the hand of all his enemies; and he gave them rest on every side. Many nations brought gifts to the LORD to Jerusalem and precious things to Hezekiah king of Judah, so that he was exalted in the sight of all nations from that time onward" (2 Chron. 32:22–23). There are several striking parallels between Micah's vision of the future ideal age and the Chronicler's account of historical events following 701. First, both Micah and the Chronicler portray an ideal Davidic king, who is exalted in the sight of all nations. Second, both describe the Lord's deliverance of Jerusalem from all her enemies. Third, the prophet and historian alike depict the nations streaming to Jerusalem to worship Yahweh and to honor the Davidic king as his human representative. Yet 4:1–5 supersedes any reasonable expectations for the historical reign of any mortal king. Thus, Micah's vision of the eschatological kingdom is an example of contextualization. God revealed the future glories of the coming new covenant age to him through the categories of old covenant structures with which he was most familiar. In effect, God revealed the unknown in the light of the known pointing to a fulfillment in pattern to come.

Canonical Reading of Micah 5:2–6

Micah's prophecy of the new David in 5:2–6 represents an example of the necessity of supplementing contextual exegesis with a canonical approach. Embedded as it is within his predictions of Zion's imminent doom (3:1–12) and future deliverance (4:1–5:15), this oracle highlights the dynamic nature of Hebrew prophecy and the sometimes surprising way in which prophetic expectations were fulfilled in divinely designed patterns of redemptive activity. Furthermore, Micah 5:2–6 offers crucial insight into the future royal Davidic expectations of the late eighth and early seventh centuries, particularly during the days of Hezekiah (715–686 BCE).

Micah's oracles of Zion's doom provide a parade example of the implicitly mirroring nature of prophecy, the potential for short-term events picturing how the long-term realization takes place. As noted above, God initially threatened that Zion could be destroyed in the days of Hezekiah, her people driven into exile and the Davidic king removed from the throne. Thanks to the efficacy of the intercession of Hezekiah, Jerusalem was spared from the hand of Sennacherib in 701 BCE. Nevertheless, when the people returned to their wicked ways and David's dynasty forfeited its right to the throne, God returned to the principles of Micah's oracle of Zion's doom. Nebuchadnezzar's destruction of Jerusalem, exile of her people, and removal of the Davidic dynasty from the throne brought Micah's ancient threat about the impact of disobedience to fulfillment, albeit in an essential generic and limited sense.

The fulfillment of Micah's oracles of Zion's future deliverance would take a different turn. In 3:1–5:15, the prophet predicted Yahweh would regather a remnant from all nations, restore the former dominion of his people under a new "David," who would muster a mighty army to destroy the archenemy of his people (depicted as the trope Assyria), then mediate the universal reign of Yahweh over all nations. In partial fulfillment of these idealistic expectations, a remnant returned from Babylon in 538 BCE, and the worship of Yahweh was restored under Zerubbabel, the Persian-appointed Davidic governor of Yehud, who along with Joshua the high priest orchestrated the rebuilding of the temple. However, the historical realities of the postexilic community fell short of the idealistic expectations that Micah envisioned for the age of restoration after the exile. This indicates that God had something more in mind all along.

Micah foresaw the coming deliverance as through a bifocal lens, the imminent and distant future merging into one indistinguishable image. The Assyrians besieged Zion and threatened to remove Hezekiah in his day, so it is easy to understand why he described the future deliverance in terms of a coming David, who destroys Assyria, a picture of the enemy overcome. What we come to see is that Assyria is a picture of the nations, just as the new David is not historical David, but one to come who is like him. Thus, this prophecy is entirely typological.

When this new David did not immediately emerge on the scene following the return of the exiles, interpreters of the second temple period began to appreciate that the original wording of these expectations were related to the eschatological future. If God did not fulfill Micah's prophecy in the postexilic era, he would do so in the eschatological future. When read from a canonical perspective, Micah 5:2–6 can be seen as divinely prophetic of the ultimate Davidic king. Our contextual exegesis suggests it was not exclusively messianic, but our canonical reading reveals it is nevertheless ultimately messianic. Embedded within Micah 4:1–5:15, the eschatological tenor of 4:1–5 and 5:10–15 suggests that 5:2–6 is one of the first examples of an eschatologically oriented prophecy of one to come. We recognize that God had the Messiah in mind all along.

This kind of messianic understanding is reflected in the Aramaic Targum reinterpretation of Micah 5:1, where the term "ruler" is replaced by "Messiah." While Micah distinguished the suffering Davidic king in 5:1 from the new David in 5:2–6, the Targum conflated the two into one person. This kind of typological escalation and reinterpretation reminds us of Luke 24:46 where Jesus explained that Messiah must suffer first then be exalted.

CONCLUSION

The prophets Amos, Hosea, and Micah each expressed a future expectation of One who was to come. Each foresaw a coming day when Yahweh would deliver his people and restore the kingdom through a divinely chosen servant. Since they each had a different piece of the same puzzle, each envisioned the One to come somewhat differently. Amos looked to a restoration of the Davidic house, as did Hosea speaking of national hope in Hosea 11. Micah saw a king tied to Bethlehem with origins from of old with nations coming to her king. These prophets share many features in common, but reveal diversity in future expectations. Since each had only one or two pieces of God's messianic puzzle, none had a crystal-clear understanding of how the whole picture fit together. Nevertheless, they represent a significant transitional stage in the historical progress of revelation. Although their future expectation was based on the traditional royal paradigm of the Davidic covenant, they revealed new insights into the future restoration of David's kingdom in the coming golden age.

MESSIANIC TRAJECTORIES IN ISAIAH

Isaiah's ministry took place during the days of Uzziah (767–740 BCE), Jotham (750–735 BCE), Ahaz (735–715 BCE), and Hezekiah (715–686 BCE). In fact, he was a contemporary of Amos, Hosea, and Micah. Unlike Amos and Hosea, who spoke to the people in northern Israel, Isaiah's energies were directed to the people of Judah. Furthermore, unlike Amos and Hosea, Isaiah composed many more oracles addressing the royal Davidic ideology of Israel and made predictions of a coming golden age when David's kingdom would be restored to its former glory. Isaiah foresaw both a future ideal Davidic king and an ideal time of deliverance and comprehensive peace. In keeping with the prophets of his day, Isaiah delivered oracles in terms meaningful to his contemporary audience, though many of his predictions did not come to realization during the preexilic period. Rather, they laid the foundation for the eschatological messianic hope of the postexilic and second temple period. Our discussion, however, steps back into history, to a time when Assyria not Babylon threatened Judah. It was a preexilic period when Isaiah spoke of an ideal Davidic king in three dynastic oracles (9:1–7, 11:1–9, 11:10–16), then predicted an ideal Servant who first would suffer and then be exalted by the Lord (42:1–9; 49:1–13; 50:4–11; 52:13–53:12).

MESSIANIC TRAJECTORIES IN ISAIAH 9:1–7

Isaiah 9:1–7 is an oracle of the nation's deliverance under an idealized Davidic king who fulfills the ancient promises to David. Some interpret this as an exclusive direct prophecy about the Messiah and his eschatological kingdom,[1] while others see this in an exclusive historical sense expressing Isaiah's original

---

1. For example, J. A. Motyer, *Isaiah: An Introduction and Commentary* (Downers Grove: InterVarsity, 1999), 98–105; Walter C. Kaiser Jr., *The Messiah in the Old Testament* (Grand Rapids: Zondervan, 1995), 162–64; John N. Oswalt, *Isaiah 1–39* (Grand

hope that Hezekiah would deliver Israel from Assyria and restore the united Davidic kingdom.[2] We avoid this false dichotomy. Reading the passage contextually as well as canonically allows us to see how Isaiah 9:1–7 might have been uttered at the celebration of the birth and enthronement of Hezekiah, but ultimately spoke of an ideal Davidic king to come who was greater than Hezekiah, that is, a powerful and victorious eschatological Messiah ruling over an unending kingdom in complete peace.

Contextual Reading

Isaiah 9:1–7 was originally composed as an oracle of national deliverance. It consists of three parts: prediction of deliverance from foreign subjugation (vv. 1–2), description of a stunning military victory over foreign oppressors (vv. 3–5), and the announcement of the birth and/or enthronement of an ideal royal son, who would be divinely empowered to restore the glory of David's kingdom and inaugurate a rule of peace (vv. 6–7).

Deliverance from Foreign Subjugation (9:1–2)

The northern kingdom recently suffered hardship, but Isaiah predicted a bright future for the nation. Whereas he portrayed judgment of the northern kingdom in 8:16–22 as a time of gloom, the coming deliverance in 9:1–2 would be seen as a light shining on a dark land.[3] Although Isaiah did not here explicitly identify the light, the rest of his oracle suggests it is the ideal Davidic king of verses 6–7. While this royal scion does not come into focus until verses 6–7, his presence is implied in verses 1–2. The predicted deliverance would be wrought by his agency, since he would bring the light of

---

Rapids: Eerdmans, 1986), 242–48; Edward J. Young, *The Book of Isaiah* (Grand Rapids: Eerdmans, 1965), 322–46.

2. For example, Joseph Blenkinsopp, *Isaiah: A New Translation with Introduction and Commentary* (New York: Doubleday, 2000), 242–51; Hans Wildberger, *Isaiah: A Commentary* (Minneapolis: Fortress Press, 1991), 384–410; Marvin A. Sweeney, *Isaiah 1–39: With an Introduction to Prophetic Literature* (Grand Rapids: Eerdmans, 1996), 180–87; John D. W. Watts, *Isaiah 1–33, WBC* (Waco: Word Books, 1985), 130–39; Otto Kaiser, *Isaiah 1–12: A Commentary* (Philadelphia: Westminster Press, 1983), 204–18; D. P. Cole, "Archaeology and the Messiah Oracles of Isaiah 9 and 11," in *Scripture and Other Artifacts* (Louisville: Westminster John Knox Press, 1994), 53–69.

3. The introductory כִּי functions adversatively to denote a strong contrast between v. 23a with the verses, which precede it: "But there will be no gloom for her who was in anguish . . . " (e.g., GKC 500 §163a–b; R. J. Williams, *Hebrew Syntax*, 73 §449; cf. Gen. 2:17; 17:15; 24:4; 37:55; 48:18; etc.). This usage of כִּי is well attested (Isa. 3:1; 7:13; 10:7; 14:1; 23:18; 28:27; 29:23; 30:5, 16; 32:22; 52:12; 62:4, 9). Thus, v. 23 contrasts two periods: a time of gloom and darkness (punishment) followed by a time of joy and light (deliverance). See R. B. Y. Scott, *The Book of Isaiah*, 230; R. E. Clements, *Isaiah 1–39*, 104; J. Ridderbos, *Isaiah*, 94; Watts, *Isaiah 1–33*, 129; Oswalt, *Isaiah*, 239; Paul D. Wegner, *An Examination of Kingship and Messianic Expectation in Isaiah 1–35* (Lewiston, NY: Mellen Biblical Press, 1992), 150.

deliverance (vv. 1–2) and drive foreign oppressors from the land (vv. 3–5). Thus, the ideal Davidic king, *the light*, would deliver the nation from its oppressors, namely *foreigners who are responsible for a period of darkness over the land*. But who were these foreign oppressors?

The initial historical meaning of the prediction of coming deliverance in Isaiah 9:1–2 is only properly understood in the light of the preceding oracle of doom in 8:16–22. The prophet foresaw a time of punishment befalling the northern kingdom, depicted as days of darkness when the people would be sent into exile (this chastisement is fittingly called a time of darkness for Israel's sin was its spiritual/moral darkness, v. 20). Isaiah envisioned the last days of Israel, when Assyria subjugated Galilee in 734–732 BCE, then destroyed Samaria and deported her citizens in 722 BCE. Similar predictions of judgment are evident in Hosea and Amos. Isaiah, however, made it clear the darkness of judgment would not shroud the land forever. Isaiah 9:1–7 introduced a contrast between the past gloom of 8:16–22 and coming light of deliverance that would dispel the darkness. Isaiah expected to see the end of the darkness and the dawn of the light in his own day: "I will wait patiently for Yahweh, who has rejected the family of Jacob" (8:16).

The contrast between the recent discipline and coming deliverance is emphasized by the expressions, "in the former time" and "the latter time." The literary context and historical setting of verses 1–2 suggest this former time of chastisement began in 734–732 BCE with the partial annexation of the northern kingdom by the Assyrian king Tiglath-Pileser III.[4] The overall context of 8:16–9:7 suggests the latter time of deliverance was to begin in the prophet's own lifetime (cf. "I will wait for Yahweh," 8:16). The prophet predicted the coming golden age would begin immediately and continue indefinitely: "from now and forevermore" (v. 7).

The geographical terms in verse 1 might suggest that Isaiah expected to see an aspect of deliverance in his own day. In verse 1, he referred to these northern regions by their traditional tribal names: "the land of Zebulun and

---

4. Tiglath-Pileser III reigned over the Neo-Assyrian empire from 745–727 BCE. He kept rebellion in check throughout his kingdom, particularly Babylon. During one of his campaigns in Northern Syria, Menahem, king of northern Israel, offers tribute to him (2 Kings 15:17–20). Ahaz, king of Judah, would later woo Tiglath-Pileser to serve as an ally and war against Pekah, king of northern Israel (2 Kings 16:5–14). At that time, Tiglath-Pileser annexed a portion of northern Israel (*ANET*, 282–284; Jean-Jacques Glassner, "Assyria Chronicles" in *Mesopotamian Chronicles*. Writings from the Ancient World [Atlanta: Society of Biblical Literature, 2004], 173–76). For more on the literary context, see Albrecht Alt, "Jesaja 8,23-9,6: Befreiungsnacht und Kronungstag," *Kleine Schriftcn Vtr Geschichte des Volkes Israels* (Münich: Kaiser, 1953), 2/2:206-25; M. B. Crook, "A Suggested Occasion for Isaiah 9.2–7 and 11.1–9," *JBL* 48 (1949): 213–24; R. A. Carson, "The Anti-Assyrian Character of the Oracle in Is. IX:1–6," *VT* 24 (1974): 130–35; Antti Laato, *Who Is Immanuel?* (Winona Lake: Eisenbrauns, 1986), 192-94.

Naphtali."[5] However, when announcing deliverance from foreign oppression, verse 2 shifts to the names after they were reorganized into Assyrian provinces by Tiglath-Pileser III in 734–732: "the way of the sea," the provincial region of the Mediterranean coast whose capital was Dor; "the other side of the Jordan," the province of Gilead in Transjordan; "the Galilee of the Gentiles," the west side of the Sea of Galilee with its capital at Meggido.[6] These geographical terms indicate Isaiah was predicting the imminent deliverance of the northern kingdom from its subjugation to Assyria in the eighth century.

Thus, part of what Isaiah envisioned was the imminent restoration of the nation. The fact that this deliverance did not materialize during his lifetime does not diminish the genuineness of his prophecy. This specificity likely reflects the historical-cultural context in which this broader generic prediction of ultimate deliverance originally was given. Its fulfillment was tied to the Davidic king, who was to function as the agent of deliverance, depending on Yahweh to accomplish this victory and its timing (cf. 9:7b). Thus, the promise and its hope lived on because of the linguistic openness in which Isaiah wrote the promise.

Stunning Victory over Foreign Oppressors (9:3–5)
Whereas verses 1–2 figuratively pictured coming deliverance as light dispelling darkness from the land, verses 3–5 put it in concrete terms of a military victory liberating Israel from a foreign army oppressing its land. Since Isaiah 8:16–9:2 envisioned the subjugation of Israel in 734–722 BCE by the Assyrians, 9:3–5 doubtless predicted military deliverance from these foreign oppressors.[7] In a similar manner, Micah 5:5–6 also pictured an ideal Davidic king driving the Assyrian invaders out of the land of Judah.

Several features indicate Isaiah had Assyria initially in mind.[8] First, the term for warrior's "boot" (v. 4) is an Assyrian loan word (סְאוֹן, *HALOT* 738). The "yoke" image (v. 3) is drawn from the language of Assyrian statecraft, which depicted foreign vassals as oxen pulling a yoke (*ANET*³ 286–88, 291,

---

5. Zebulun and Naphtali are tribal names for the regions of the Galilee. The two terms are often used as synecdoches of part for the Galilee region as a whole.

6. In 734 BCE, Tiglath-pileser III annexed the Mediterranean coastal region and changed its name to *Du'ru* after its capital city Dor. In 732 BCE, Jezreel and Galilee were included in the area *Magidŏ* with Megiddo as its capital. At the same time, the area east of the Jordan (formerly Gilead) became known as the province of *Gal'azu*. For the correlation of these three Assyrian provinces with the traditional regions of Zebulun and Naphtali, see Y. Aharoni and M. Avi-Yonah, *The Macmillan Bible Atlas* (revised edition; New York: Macmillan, 1979), 95; Clements, *Isaiah 1–39*, 104–6; A. F. Rainey, "Toponymic Problems [cont.]," *Tel Aviv* 8 (1981), 146.

7. R. A. Carson, "The Anti-Assyrian Character of the Oracle in Is. IX:1–6," *VT* 24 (1974):130–35; Laato, *Who Is Immanuel?* 192–94.

8. Wegner, *Kingship*, 177-78n. 8.

295–97).[9] Elsewhere Isaiah explicitly identified Assyria as the tyrant whose "yoke" God would break (10:27; 14:25). Much of the vocabulary in Isaiah 9:3–5 is identical to 10:24–27 and 14:24–27, both predicting God's judgment on Assyria.[10]

Second, verse 4 compared deliverance of the northern kingdom from foreign oppressors to Gideon's liberation of the northern tribes from Midian.[11] Isaiah made this comparison explicit elsewhere: "Do not fear *the Assyrians* . . . Yahweh will beat them with a whip as when he smote Midian at the rock of Oreb" (10:24, 26). Since this deliverance was linked to the new king of verses 6–7, he was the implied agent of victory in verses 3–5. Isaiah pictured the new David as a second Gideon. Just as Gideon conquered by divine intervention, God would conquer the Assyrians (v. 4b, "*You* will shatter") through his divinely empowered king (cf. v. 6b).

Announcement of an Ideal Davidic King (9:6–7)

The highlight of Isaiah's oracle is his description of an ideal Davidic king. Not formally introduced until now, this ideal ruler is the implied agent of deliverance in verses 1–5. This passage contains four parts: (1) celebration of the birth of the royal son (v. 6a); (2) declaration of the royal tutelary to be bestowed on the king at his enthronement (v. 6b); (3) prediction of the dominion, prosperity, peace, morality, and perpetuity expected to characterize his reign (v. 7a); and (4) expression of confidence that God would fulfill these prophetic expectations (v. 7b).

The passage follows the typical pattern of prophetic birth announcements.[12] Such oracles feature three elements: (1) *prediction* of the imminent birth of a son: "You will give birth to a son"; (2) *declaration* of his symbolic name: "You will call his name . . ."; and (3) *prophecy* concerning his destiny: "He will . . ."[13] Yet in its present form, verses 6–7 constitute a thanksgiving hymn celebrating the recent birth of the royal son.[14] Isaiah may have com-

---

9. For example, Sargon II depicted his subjugation of his western vassals thus: "I besieged and conquered the cities ... I declared them Assyrian vassals and they pulled the straps of my yoke" (*ANET*³ 286).

10. Wegner, *Kingship*, footnote 425, writes, "This passage appears to describe the hope of a coming deliverer, not in vague futuristic terms, but rather in the immediate future and in the context of the Assyrian crisis."

11. J. P. J. Olivier, "The Day of Midian and Isaiah 9:3b," *JNSL* 9 (1981): 143.

12. Wegner, *Kingship*, 181 n. 238. Examples of prophetic birth announcements are evident in Genesis 16:11–12; 17:19; Judges 13:3–5; Isaiah 7:14–17; Luke 1:13–17, 31–33; cf. Isaiah 8:1–4.

13. *Prediction*: Genesis 16:11; 17:19; Judges 13:5; Isaiah 7:14; Luke 1:13, 31. *Declaration*: Genesis 16:11; 17:19; Isaiah 7:14; Luke 1:13, 31. *Prophecy*: Genesis 16:12; Judges 13:5; Isaiah 7:15; Luke 1:15–17, 32–33.

14. S. Mowinckel, *He That Cometh*, 102; Laato, *Who Is Immanuel?* 176–78; Griphus Gakuru, *An Inner-Biblical Exegetical Study of the Davidic Covenant and the Dynastic Oracle*, Mellen

posed this in imitation of a prophetic birth announcement (cf. Isa. 8:1–4), or reworked an earlier oracle predicting the birth of the new king to celebrate its recent fulfillment. If we assume the latter, by the time he composed verses 6–7, the first half of his earlier oracle was fulfilled, but not the second. The new king had been born ("a son *has been born* to us"), but had not yet taken the throne ("He *will rule* on David's throne") nor fulfilled the prophet's idealistic expectations ("He *will establish and uphold* justice and righteousness"). Of course, actual fulfillment of his calling would be contingent on his loyalty to Yahweh (cf. 7b).

Emphasizing that verses 1–5 reflect the Assyrian crisis of 745–722 BCE, critical scholars argue that verses 6–7 were written about Hezekiah (ca. 729–686 BCE) and were not messianic prophecy.[15] Rabbinic scholars make the same claim, allowing them to argue that the royal tutelaries in verse 6 were simply figurative of Hezekiah and therefore did not predict the deity of the Messiah. There are problems with this approach. While it appropriately emphasizes the historical background of verses 1–5, it creates an unnecessary either/or approach to the interpretation of both verses 1–5 and 6–7. It is better to understand verses 1–5 and 6–7 in terms of a both/and pattern. The initial historical background of verses 1–5 was indeed the Assyrian crisis and an expression of hope about a Davidic king. Yet since Hezekiah did not bring about the deliverance, we must view him as merely foreshadowing a future ideal Davidic king whose birth, enthronement, and reign would bring about the ultimate deliverance of God's people. To be sure, it is quite possible that Isaiah delivered this oracle at the time of Hezekiah's enthronement. However, the fact that the identity of this ideal king is not explicitly revealed means that it is illegitimate to limit its application to Hezekiah. In fact, since God did not explicitly reveal the identity of this king, it is conceivable that even Isaiah himself did not know whether God was speaking of Hezekiah, a pattern of deliverance or one greater than Hezekiah to come. What God clearly revealed was that the birth and enthronement of this ideal Davidic king would signal the deliverance of God's people. Since the reign of Hezekiah hardly fulfilled Isaiah's descriptions in verses 6–7, the prophecy must have looked beyond Hezekiah for a greater ideal Davidic king to come, likely with Hezekiah as a type of what was to come. Understood in this way, the prophecy can only find its fullest fulfillment in the eschatological Messiah. In fact, when taken in the most literal sense, the royal titles (verse 6b) and poetic description of the reign of this ideal

---

Biblical Press Series, vol. 58 (Lewiston, NY: The Edwin Mellen Press, 2000), § 6.2.3.2; Wegner, *Kingship*, 176; G. von Rad, "The Royal Ritual in Judah," in *The Problem of the Hexateuch and Other Essays* (London: Oliver & Boyd, 1966) 222–31; Alt, "Jesaja 8,23—9,6," 2.219.

15. For example, Alt, "Jesaja 8,23–9,6," 2.206–25; M. B. Crook, "A Suggested Occasion for Isaiah 9.2–7 and 11.1–9," *JBL* 48 (1949): 213–24; von Rad, "Royal Ritual," 222–31.

Davidic king (verse 7) implicitly point to the deity and eternality of the future Messiah.[16]

Birth of the Royal Son (9:6a)

Isaiah 9:6a describes the birth of the new heir to David's throne. While the basic sense of the verse is clear, the precise time frame of the birth was open. The Hebrew may be translated one of three ways: (1) It may recall a *recent past* birth: "to us a child *has been born*, to us a son *has been given*." (2) It may celebrate a *present* birth: "to us a child *is born*, to us a son *is given*."[17] (3) It may predict a *future* birth: "to us a child *will be born*, to us a son *will be given*."[18] This syntactical openness was divinely inspired to allow for an original historical referent (Hezekiah), as well as a subsequent future typological referent (Jesus the Messiah).[19]

The declaration, "a child *is born*!" is conventional (Jer. 20:15; Ruth 4:17), but the parallel, "a son *is given*!" is theologically loaded. The implied agent is God, the passive form highlighting divine benevolence in the gift of this son (Gen. 30:6, 48:9; Isa. 8:18; 1 Kings 5:7; 1 Chron. 28:5). While the term "child" is conventional, the parallel "son" may carry the technical sense of heir to the throne (Pss. 72:1; 89:30; 132:12). In royal Davidic ideology, the king enjoyed a father/son relation with God (2 Sam. 7:14–16//1 Chron. 17:13–14; Ps. 89:26–27). In a similar way, Psalm 2:7 pictured the historical Davidic king as metaphorically "begotten" by God on the day of his formal enthronement. In other words, on the day of his enthronement as king, each historical Davidic king entered into a metaphorical "father/son" relationship with God.

---

16. Scott R. A. Starbuck, *Court Oracles in the Psalms: The So-Called Royal Psalms in Their Ancient Near Eastern Context*, SBL Dissertation Monographs 172 (Atlanta: Scholars Press, 1995), 168–178; Antti Laato, *Josiah and David Redivivus: The Historical Josiah and the Messianic Expectations of Exilic and Postexilic Times*, ConBOTT 33 (Stockholm: Almqvist & Wiksell, 1992), 69–80.

17. The closest parallels are announcements celebrating the birth of a son: "A man brought news to my father: '*A son is born to you!*'" (Jer. 20:15); "The village women proclaimed, "*A son is born to Naomi!*'" (Ruth 4:17).

18. The construction in each of the parallel lines may refer to a past, present, or future birth. In v. 6a, the perfect of the verb "give" + noun "son" or "child" + indirect object "to [someone]," may recall a past birth (1 Kings 3:6, "You have given a son to him"), celebrate a present birth (Gen. 30:6, "God gives a son to me!") or predict a future birth (Gen. 17:16, "I will give a son to her"). Likewise in v. 6b, the perfect of the verb "bear" + noun "son" or "child" + indirect object "to [someone]," may recall a recent birth (Gen. 21:7, "I have borne a son to him"), celebrate a present birth (Jer. 20:15, "A son is borne to you!" Ruth 4:17, "A son is born to Naomi!") or predict a future birth (Gen. 16:11; Judg. 13:3, 5, 7, "You shall bear a son").

19. H. G. M. Williamson, *Variations on a Theme: King, Messiah, and Servant in the Book of Isaiah*. The Didsbury Lectures 1997 (Carlisle, UK: Paternoster Press, 1998), 30–46; G. L. Klein, "The Prophetic Perfect," *JNSL* 16 (1990): 45–60.

Royal Tutelary of the New King (9:6b)

Names chosen for people were important. The birth of a son was often celebrated by proclamation of his name, carrying some kind of symbolic meaning: "He called his name . . . ." For instance, women from Naomi's neighborhood named her grandson, "they named him Obed."[20] Prophetic birth announcements of the imminent birth of a son often featured instruction about the child's name, conveying a special symbolic meaning: "Call his name . . ." For example, God told Hosea to name his three children Jezreel (as a sign of the forthcoming divine punishment), Lo-Ruhamah (meaning "No Pity"), and Lo-Ammi (meaning "Not My People"). In a similar manner, kings were given names at their coronation as the newborn ruler of a nation. During the time of Isaiah, royal titles were an important part of a coronation of a new king. In Isaiah 9:6b, the prophet followed this pattern in publicly proclaiming the symbolic name of the newborn king: "His name shall be called . . . ."[21] Thus the new king's name would consist of four theophoric royal titles: "His name shall be called, 'Wonderful Counselor, Mighty God, Everlasting Father, Prince of Peace'" (RSV). Isaiah gave a long double name to his own son, "Maher Shalal, Hash Baz," meaning, "Quick to the plunder, Hurry to the spoil" (Isa. 8:1).[22]

Many features of the ancient Israelite royal enthronement ritual find parallels in typical ancient Near Eastern practice.[23] In fact, it is possible that

---

20. Similar examples abound in the Genesis: Adam and Eve's naming of Seth (4:25; 5:3), Lamech's naming of Noah (4:29), Abraham's naming of Ishmael and later Isaac (16:15; 21:3), Lot's older daughter names Moab and his younger daughter names Ben-Ammi (19:37, 38), Rebekeh's naming of Esau and Jacob (25:25, 26), Leah's naming of Reuben, Simeon, Levi, Judah, Issachar (29:32, 33, 34, 35; 30:18), Rachel's naming of Reuben and Ben-Oni and renamed by Judah, Benjamin (30:8, 35:18), and Tamar's naming of Perez and Zerah (38:29, 30).

21. Due to ambiguity of Hebrew syntax, v. 6b can be rendered legitimately in four different ways. (1) The first three names refer to God who bestows the last name on the royal son: "The Wonderful Counselor, Mighty God, Everlasting Father will call his name, 'Prince of Peace'." (2) The first two names refer to God and the last two are royal names given to the son: "The Wonderful Counselor, the Mighty God calls his name: 'Everlasting Father, Prince of Peace'." (3 God bestows two parallel sets of theophoric names on the son: "His name will be called: 'The Mighty God is planning grace,' 'the Eternal Father is a peaceful ruler'." (4) God bestows four regal names on the son: "His name will be called, 'Wonderful Counselor, Mighty God, Everlasting Father, Prince of Peace'." The latter is the traditional approach and adopted here for complicated reasons about which we will spare the reader.

22. The length of these multiple names paled in comparison with the fourfold name Tiglath-Pileser III gave to the gates of Calah: "Gates of Justice, Which Give the Correct Judgment for the Ruler of the Four Quarters, Which Offer the Yield of the Mountains and the Seas, Which Admit the Produce of Mankind before the King their Master." John H. Walton, *The IVP Bible Background Commentary: Old Testament* (ed. John H. Walton, Victor H. Matthews, and Mark W. Chavalas; Downers Grove: InterVarsity, 2000), 597.

23. Since the practice of bestowing multiple throne names on the new king was widespread in the ancient Near East, it is not necessary to suggest that the royal titulary in v. 6b reflects

Isaiah's fourfold name given to this newborn king may reflect the typical ancient Near Eastern practice whereby a new king at his enthronement received a name that supplemented the king's personal name given at birth.[24] The typical ancient Near Eastern king had five names: his birth name and fourfold royal title. The following examples of royal tutelary from Egypt, Sumer, and Ugarit demonstrate the meaning and significance of these types of titles.

Egyptian Royal Tutelary. For over twenty-five centuries (ca. 2510–330 BCE), each Egyptian king received a royal tutelary on the day of his enthronement. Consisting of four throne names, taken at his accession, plus his personal name, given at birth, the fivefold tutelary was treated as a single name. Two titles depicted him as the physical embodiment/representative of Horus, two declared his control of all Egypt, and one restated his birth name while also identifying him as the royal son of the god Re.[25]

In royal enthronement inscriptions, declaration of a newly enthroned king's royal tutelary followed a fixed literary structure: (1) oracular introduction, "Let his tutelary/name be called . . ." (2) identification of the fivefold tutelary, (3) concluding wish-formula, ". . . may he live forever." The middle element, the royal tutelary, also followed a fixed order and form, consisting of (1) *Horus name*: presented the king as earthly embodiment of Horus, the prototype and patron god of Egyptian kings; (2) *Nebti name:* declared him ruler of Upper and Lower Egypt, as the embodiment of Nekhbet and Wadjet; (3) *Golden Horus name:* expressed the wish for his immortality as the embodiment of the eternal god Horus, and depicted by gold, thought to last for eternity; (4) *Throne name:* king's official name, preceded by the title, 'King of Upper and Lower Egypt,' and containing the name of the god Re; (5) *Birth name:* personal birth name (used by modern historians, e.g., Ramesses II),

---

one particular source of influence. However, scholars often compare the fourfold titulary in v. 6b with the fivefold royal titulary bestowed on Egyptian kings of the Middle and New Kingdom periods. In Egyptian royal coronation inscriptions, four titles were given to the king on the day of his enthronement, the fifth title (personal name) having been previously bestowed at his birth. See K. A. Kitchen, *Ancient Orient and Old Testament* (Downers Grove: InterVarsity, 1966), 109n. 86.

24. Jedidiah was renamed Solomon (2 Sam. 12:24, 25); Azariah called Uzziah (2 Kings 15:1; 2 Chron. 26:1–2); Shallum called Jehoahaz (2 Kings 23:30, 31, 34; Jer. 22:11); Eliakim renamed Jehoiakim (2 Kings 23:34); Mattaniah renamed Zedekiah (2 Kings 24:17). In Assyrian royal literature, Tiglath-Pileser III is known as Pulu; Shalmaneser V is called Ululai. In Hittite literature, Urkhi-Tesep is called Mursili III; Sharrikushukh of Carchemish is known as Piyassilis. See T. N. D. Mettinger, *Solomonic State Officials: A Study of the Civil Government Officials of the Israelite Monarchy*, Coniectanea Bib, Old Testament Series 5 (Lund: C. W. K. Gleerup, 1971); M. Crook, "A Suggested Occasion for Isaiah 9:2–7 and 11:1–9," *JBL* 68 (1949): 213–24.

25. James Henry Breasted, *ARE*, vol. 2: The Eighteenth Dynasty (New York: Russell & Russell, Inc., 1906): 24–25.

usually preceded by the title, 'Son of Re,' to depict the king as physically begotten by his human parents, but mythologically begotten by Re.[26]

Sumerian Royal Tutelary. Conventional fivefold royal tutelaries also appear in Sumerian royal enthronement inscriptions. For instance, the "lasting name," bestowed on Shulgi on the day of his enthronement, consisted of four royal titles, which he took on taking the throne, in addition to his personal name, given at birth. Thus we read in his enthronement inscription: "Shulgi, he of the lasting name: 'the shepherd of prosperity, the king of the festival, the mighty one, the seed engendered by a faithful man' . . ." (*COS* 1.172, lines 29–30). The first title, "shepherd of prosperity," conveyed his calling to exercise a benevolent rule, which was to provide prosperity to his people. The notion of sacral kingship was seen in the second title, "king of the festival." The third title, "the mighty one," depicted Shulgi as a victorious warrior, divinely empowered by the gods. The fourth title, "the seed engendered by a faithful man," asserted his legitimate claim to the throne as the physical offspring of his father, who was the divinely chosen founder of the royal dynasty. Thus the four titles pictured Shulgi as the ideal king.

Ugaritic Royal Tutelary. In the Ugaritic royal enthronement inscription of Niqmaddu, we find a sixfold royal tutelary. It consists of his personal name given at birth, followed by five titles bestowed upon his ascension: "Niqmepa the son of Niqmaddu, King of Ugarit, Legitimate Lord, Governor of the House, King of the Gate, King Who Builds."[27] The first three asserted his position as the newly enthroned king. The last two expressed his divine commission to render justice at the city gate and to build temples to his patron god who had chosen him as king.

Moving beyond the three examples above, many foreign kings adopted a royal protocol practice. For instance, Cambyses king of Persia employed an Egyptian priest to compose a suitable throne name. Greek kings from the Ptolemaic dynasty adopted Egyptian royal titularies.

So it should come as no surprise that Isaiah adopted the convention of the royal tutelary to depict the new Davidic king as the equal—if not the

---

26. For example, the royal titulary for Horemheb reads: "Let *his titulary* be like the majesty of Re: *Horus*: 'Mighty Bull, Ready in Plans,' *Favorite of Two Goddesses*: 'Great in Marvels in Karnak,' *Golden Horus*: 'Satisfied with Truth, Creator of the Two Lands,' *King of Upper and Lower Egypt*: 'Zeserkheprure, Setepnere,' *Son of Re*: 'Mernamon, Harmhab,' may he be given life!" Similarly for Thutmose I, "Make my titulary as follows: *Horus*: 'Mighty Bull, Beloved of Maat,' *Favorite of Two Goddesses*: 'Shining in the Serpent-diadem, Great in Strength,' *Golden Horus*: 'Goodly in Years, Making Hearts Live,' *King of Upper and Lower Egypt*: 'Okheperkere,' *Son of Re*: 'Thutmose,' living forever and ever!" See James Henry Breasted, *ARE*, vol. 2: The Eighteenth Dynasty (New York: Russell & Russell, Inc., 1906): §§ 131–166, §§ 215–242, §§ 841–844; William J. Murnane, *TAPE*, Writings from the Ancient World, vol. 5 (Atlanta: Scholars Press, 1995): § 106, § 107A.

27. KTU 7.63 1–7 = PRU II XVI—XVII. See John Gray, "Sacral Kingship in Ugarit," *Ugaritica* 6 (1969): 289–91.

superior—to any ancient Near Eastern ruler. And the omission of this Davidic king's birth name in this tutelary suggests that Isaiah realized that Hezekiah was not this ideal Davidic king. The precise identity of this ideal Davidic king would remain a mystery, of course, until the coming of Messiah Jesus.

Four Royal Titles of the Ideal King (9:6b)

Isaiah provides four royal titles for his ideal king. The first, *"Wonderful Counselor"* (יוֹעֵץ). This royal title depicted the Davidic king as an extraordinary military strategist.[28] The related expression, "wonderful in counsel," refers to supernatural guidance given to humans (28:29).[29] This title pictured the king as divinely equipped to conquer his foes, thanks to supernatural guidance God would provide (cf. Isa. 11:2, lit., "spirit of counsel and might," means "a spirit that provides ability to execute plans," NET).[30]

While carrying divine connotations, it did not necessarily suggest to the original historical audience that the historical Davidic king was God. Nevertheless it was open enough in wording to allow for subsequent hermeneutical escalation and legitimate messianic connection. Therefore, this royal title is a classic example of a divinely inspired pattern fulfillment, having one connotation in its initial reference to Hezekiah and heightened meaning in its climactic reference to Messiah Jesus.

Isaiah's second title is *"Mighty God"* (אֵל גִּבּוֹר). The original meaning and significance of this title is debated, since it may be translated five ways: "God [is] mighty," "God [is] a warrior," "divine warrior," "mighty warrior," or "mighty God." The ambiguity stems from several factors. First, God is frequently described as a warrior (גִּבּוֹר; Isa. 42:13; Jer. 20:11; Ps. 24:8). Second, the term frequently translated as "God" (אֵל) may mean "mighty one," which may refer to God (Isa. 5:6), a human king (Job 41:17; Ezek. 31:11; 32:21), or an angelic being (Pss. 29:1; 82:1; 89:7).[31]

---

28. Robert B. Chisholm Jr., "A Theology of Isaiah," in *A Biblical Theology of the Old Testament* (ed. Roy B. Zuck; Chicago: Moody Press, 1991), 312–13.

29. See H. B. Huffmon, *Amorite Personal Names in the Mari Texts: A Structural and Lexical Study* (Baltimore: Johns Hopkins Press, 1965), 254; M. D. Coogan, *West Semitic Personal Names in the Murasu Documents*, HSM 7 (Missoula: Scholars Press, 1976), 81.

30. Many ancient Near Eastern kings bore similar royal titles. For example, in Egyptian royal inscriptions, we find: "Ready in Plans," "Great in Marvels" (Horemhab); "Great in Wonders" (Amenmes); "Lord of Wonders" (Ramesses II); "Working Many Wonders" (Seti I, Ramesses II, Seti II). In the royal enthronement inscription of Ramesses, the god Ptah is said to have declared: "I will cause to befall your great wonders, and every good thing to happen to you, for the Two Lands under you are in acclamation" (*ARE* 3.180).

31. A parallel title occurs in an inscription from Medinet Habu, in which Ramesses III bears the royal epithet, "Divine Warrior," depicting him as supernaturally empowered in battle as the human representative of Re. Another inscription celebrates the military prowess of Ramesses II as the earthly embodiment of Seth and Baal, the celebrated war-gods in Egyptian and Canaanite mythology, respectively: "No man is he who is among us! It is

The king spoken of in Isaiah was clearly human ("a child has been born . . ."). This phrase, however, reappears in Isaiah 10:21, where it clearly refers to God (vv. 20–21, "they will rely on Yahweh . . . they will return to the Mighty God"). Therefore, this royal title has built within it a word play. It should be nuanced in the light of Psalm 45:6–7, in which an historical Davidic king, who was celebrating his wedding to a princess, was addressed as "God" as Yahweh's earthly representative.[32] Although the initial historical Davidic king was not God, he functionally represented God and bore divine ruling authority over the people of Israel.[33] Thus, we might render this title "Mighty *like* God" or perhaps "*Uniquely Mighty One.*" However, what was metaphorically true of the initial historical Davidic king would be literally true of the Messiah. While the historical Davidic king would merely function as the royal representative of God, the Messiah would be none other than God himself. This reflects the escalation in pattern fulfillment.[34]

Isaiah's third title is *"Everlasting Father"* (אֲבִיעַד). This title may be translated "eternal father" (KJV) or "everlasting father" (NASB, NRSV, NIV, NET). The diplomatic language of ancient Near Eastern royal inscriptions often pictured the king as a father, highlighting his benevolent protection and gracious provision of his people.[35] So, it was not unusual to speak of a royal figure as father. Furthermore, the term "everlasting" may refer to kings who rule their whole life (Isa. 47:7; Prov. 29:14). God promised David's dynasty would endure forever (Pss. 89:29; 132:12), so the Davidic kings' reigns were often depicted as everlasting (1 Kings 1:31; Pss. 21:4–6; 61:6–7; 72:5, 17). Thus, this child spoken of by Isaiah was to be a royal figure, who would act like a father and whose ruling authority would last his entire lifetime and extend

---

Seth great-of-strength, Baal in person! Not deeds of man are these his doings! They are of one who is unique!" (*AEL* 2.67).

32. A similar occurrence exists in Exodus 7:1 where God says to Moses: "See, I have made you God (אֱלֹהִים) to Pharaoh, and your brother Aaron will be your prophet." Except for KJV, most English translations recognize that Moses appeared *like* a God to Pharaoh and rightly insert the comparative, *like* (NIV, NRSV, NET) or *as* (NRSB).

33. John H. Hayes *and Stuart A. Irvine,* Isaiah, The Eighth-Century Prophet: His Times and His Preaching (Nashville: Abingdon, 1987), 181-82. See also my discussion of Psalm 45 in chapter 3, pp. 81-85.

34. Of course, this ultimate messianic sense, would not become clear until the incarnation of the Son of God. Even then the absolute monotheism of Israel caused many, but not all, to resist the startling claim of Jesus to be God incarnate, as those who rejected him accused him of blasphemy. Yet the deity of the Messiah as the ultimate Davidic king had been revealed as early as Isaiah 9:6–7. This understanding would be reinforced by God's actions in incarnation within Jesus' ministry and in the significance of the resurrection, pointing to the correspondence with a full sense of Isaiah's wording.

35. For example, Azitawadda of Adana said he was like "a father and a mother" to his people; Kilamuwa of Samal boasted, "To some I was a father; to some I was a mother" (*ANET* 3 499–500).

within the dynasty.[36] Yet in the typological escalation, the Christian may see in this title the eternality of Messiah Jesus.

Isaiah's concluding title is *"Prince of Peace"* (שַׂר־שָׁלוֹם). This title emphasizes that the king would be the agent of the nation's military security and domestic peace. In the context of verses 1–5, this would be won by defeating the foreign army occupying the land. As a second David, he would reprise the military success of his illustrious forefather, to whom God promised success in battle, ensuring national security (2 Sam. 7:10). As this title suggests, the new king would fulfill the dynastic duty of providing peace (Ps. 72:3, 7).[37]

When viewed from an historical perspective, these four royal titles pictured the historical Davidic king functioning as the earthly representative of Yahweh. As human coregent of God's rule on earth, he would exercise the divine will and demonstrate divine authority.[38] However, when considered in the light of the incarnation of the Son of God and his resurrection from the dead and ascension into heaven and in light of the scope of the promise of the victory in Isaiah's text, it is also clear that these four titles should be seen as climatically prophetic of the Messiah.

His Secure Throne and Perpetual Kingdom (9:7)

While Isaiah's oracle opened with the northern regions suffering under the oppression of the Assyrian Empire, it closed with the restoration of the former glory of David's kingdom. As a second David, the new king would sit on the throne of its illustrious founder and fulfill God's promise of an everlasting kingdom. Fulfilling the dynastic duty to establish moral righteousness and uphold social justice, he would inaugurate a rule of perpetual peace and security. Reflecting the traditional language and stereotypical imagery of 2 Samuel 7:12–16, where Nathan promised David an everlasting kingdom and dynasty, Isaiah depicted his reign as lasting forever.

---

36. Of course, the Christian reader in retrospect recognizes that the Messiah as the incarnate Son of God is himself preexistent and eternal in his own person. However, the title "Everlasting Father" should not be confused as a direct reference to God the Father as the first person of the Trinity. The term "father" must be understood as the Hebrew idiom of a benevolent ruler who acts like a father figure to his people. Thus, what was metaphorically true of the historical Davidic king such as Hezekiah is now seen to be literally true of the Messiah. Again pattern and escalation are at work here within the language of the text.

37. A parallel to this royal title occurs at the conclusion of a royal inscription of Ramesses II, "by the command of this your son, who is upon your throne, lord of gods and of men, sovereign celebrating the jubilees like when you bear the two sistrums, son of the white crown, heir of the red crown, possessing the Two Lands in peace, Rameses II, given life forever and ever." Breasted, *Ancient Records of Egypt*, 3.182.

38. This harmonizes with the royal ideology of the Chronicler who also viewed the Davidic kingdom as the kingdom of Yahweh, since the human king represented Yahweh on earth: "I will put him in permanent charge of my house and my kingdom" (1 Chron. 17:14; cp. Ps. 45:6–7).

Royal enthronement inscriptions and hymns of the ancient Near East also frequently featured the motif of an eternally secure throne.[39] Egyptian royal titularies typically close with the theme of the new king's rule enduring forever. Whereas the declaration of the royal titulary for Horemhab concluded with "Horemhab . . . may he live forever!"; Thutmose I concluded with "Thutmose . . . living forever and ever!" Similarly, the coronation hymn of the Assyrian King Ashurbanipal closes thus, "May his rule be renewed and may they establish his royal throne forever! May they bless him and guard his reign daily, monthly and yearly . . . Give our lord, Ashurbanipal, long days, copious years, great strength and a long reign—years of abundance!" (*COS* 1.143).[40] In an example of *ex eventu* prophecy, the rule of the Babylonian king Nebuchadnezzar II was "predicted" as universal in scope and eternal in duration: "After him (Nebuchadnezzar I) his son (Nebuchadnezzar II) will arise as king in Uruk and rule the entire world. He will exercise authority and kingship in Uruk, and his dynasty will stand forever. The kings of Uruk will exercise authority like gods." Thus the motif of everlasting throne as a literary trope for the king's longevity and secure reign was common among royal inscriptions.

Considered from an initial historical contextual orientation, Isaiah's prediction was likely understood simply as an example of conventional royal hyperbole, celebrating the inauguration of the new king in robust terms. Such extravagant court style was widespread throughout the ancient Near East. Yet further revelation reveals that God had more in mind with this wording. Although Isaiah 9:7 was originally true in a hyperbolic sense of the human Davidic king and his historical kingdom, we understand that it is literally true of the eschatological Messiah and his kingdom along the pattern of escalated realization in the decisive fulfillment of the pattern. The fact that several passages we have noted are read ultimately in this escalated manner points to its likelihood.

Isaiah described a period of comprehensive peace mediated by a royal figure who fully represents God. Viewed from an initial historical contextual perspective, this portrait fit traditional royal ideology and court rhetoric. However, viewed from the vantage of a broader canonical perspective, Isaiah provided a significant contribution to the foundation of what would eventually point to the eschatological Messiah.

---

39. For example, S. A. Kaufman, "Prediction, Prophecy, and Apocalypse in the Light of New Akkadian Texts," *Proceedings of the Sixth World Congress of Jewish Studies 1973* (ed. A. Shinan; Jerusalem: World Union of Jewish Studies, 1977), 1.221–28.

40. We find a similar wish in the enthronement hymn of Tukulti-Ninurta I: "May Assur and Ninlil, the lords of your crown, set your crown on your head for a hundred years!" (*COS* 1.140). The enthronement ritual celebrating the inauguration of the reign of Sargon II closed thus, "Decree for him as his fate a life of long days! Make firm the foundation of his throne, prolong his reign!" (*COS* 1.141).

Canonical Reading

Non-conservative interpreters often point to Isaiah 9:1–7, which voiced Isaiah's idealistic expectations of Hezekiah, as a parade example of the failure of prophecy. This is an overly narrow hermeneutic. To be sure, while God rescued Zion from Sennacherib in 701 BCE, the liberation of Israel from Assyria and glorious restoration of David's kingdom did not materialize in Hezekiah. However, the openness of Isaiah's oracle about an ideal king allowed for a subsequent referent. When Hezekiah made political alliances with Egypt and Babylon for protection from Assyria, Isaiah proclaimed that he had doomed— not saved—the nation. Hezekiah had failed, but the hope of Isaiah lived on. In a prophecy of judgment, Isaiah announced that Jerusalem would not be delivered from Assyria, but destroyed by Babylon and sent into exile (Isa. 39:1–8 // 2 Kings 12:12–19). But that was not the end of the story. After the second temple was built (515 BCE), and the Davidic throne was not restored, later Jewish interpreters began to appreciate that God was speaking of an eschatological future. This gave the hermeneutical segue for emergence of eschatological messianic readings in second temple literature. Seeing in Jesus the ultimate agent of God's delivering light, the Second Testament unpacked its Christological potential (Matt. 4:12–17; cf. Luke 1:79; John 1:5; 3:19–21; 8:12; 12:46). With that connection and realization, Christians also have seen in the royal titles of Isaiah 9:6 language suggestive of the deity of the Messiah. So when 9:1–7 is read in the light of the book of Isaiah as a whole, the fulfillment of his predictions— enthronement of new David, national deliverance, restoration of the kingdom, reign of perpetual peace—is pushed into the future, into a new age.[41] This is also true for Isaiah 11:1–9.

MESSIANIC TRAJECTORIES IN ISAIAH 11:1–9

Isaiah 11:1–9 envisions an ideal royal descendant of David's family tree. As the virtual embodiment of the dynasty's illustrious forefather and equipped to rule with the same energizing spirit, his rule would usher in an idyllic age of domestic peace and national security. Through his agency, God would restore the former glory of David's united kingdom, regathering a remnant of the exiles of the northern kingdom of Israel and bringing David's former vassals under his sway.

It is easy to see how this may be read as an exclusive direct prophecy about Jesus the Messiah and his eschatological rule due to what we *now* know from the Second Testament. Yet read contextually, it initially focused on Isaiah's idealized hope of the resurgence of Davidic kingship under Hezekiah, engendered by Yahweh's deliverance of Jerusalem in 701 BCE.[42] Rather than forcing

---

41. R. E. Clements, "The Messianic Hope in the Old Testament," *JSOT* 43 (1989): 3–19.
42. Willem Beuken, "The Emergence of the Shoot of Jesse (Isaiah 11:1–16): An Eschatological or a New Event?" *CTJ* 39 (2004): 88–108; Moshe Weinfeld, "The Roots of the Messianic

a false dichotomy between the two but insisting on the legitimacy of both, we will show how the initial contextual/canonical meaning of this passages also provides the segue for its ultimate Messianic/Christological meaning that will in God's progress of revelation be found in Jesus.[43]

Contextual Reading

Isaiah 11:1–9 may be classified as an oracle of restoration. It envisioned a coming royal "shoot," whose rule of justice and righteousness would usher in an idyllic age of peace. The oracle consists of three parts: prediction of the coming branch (v. 1); description of the ideal Davidic king (vv. 2–5); and portrait of his idyllic reign (vv. 6–9).

The initial meaning of this oracle can be appreciated fully only in the light of its literary context. The chart below suggests Isaiah 10–11 forms a symmetrical literary unit. The coming ideal Davidic king who would rule in righteousness (11:1–16) stands in stark contrast with the evil kings of those days: Uzziah, Jotham, Ahaz (10:1–4). The ultimate evil occurred when Ahaz made an alliance with Tiglath-Pileser III against northern Israel, which resulted in a portion of northern Israel being annexed by the Assyrians (2 Kings 16:5–14). Thus Isaiah pronounced a series of indictments, judgments, and expectations.

> A indictment of the unjust kings of Judah: Uzziah, Jotham, Ahaz
> (10:1–4)
> > B judgment of Assyria and Sennacherib's assault on Jerusalem
> > (10:5–11)
> > > C king of Assyria will be judged after God punishes Jerusalem
> > > (10:12–19)
> > > C' remnant will return to the Lord after God judges king of Assyria
> > > (10:20–23)
> > B' judgment of Assyria and Sennacherib's assault on Jerusalem
> > (10:24–34)
> A' provision of the ideal king for Judah and his rule of justice
> (11:1–9)

The first oracle announced coming judgment on Judah's unjust kings: Uzziah, Jotham, Ahaz (10:1–4). The second oracle envisioned the invasion of Judah in 701 BCE by the Assyrian king Sennacherib (cf. Isa. 36:1–10//2 Kings 18:13–26//2 Chron. 32), the agent of God's punishment (10:5–34).[44] Yet judgment would not be God's final word. The arrogant Assyrians would

Idea," in *Mythology and Mythologies* (Helsinki: University of Helsinki Press, 2001), 279–87.

43. Joseph Wimmer, "Isaiah's Messianism," *BibTo* 35 (1997): 216–21; D. P. Cole, "Archaeology and the Messiah Oracles of Isaiah 9 and 11," in *Scripture and Other Artifacts* (Louisville: Westminster John Knox Press, 1994), 53–69.

44. For the Assyrian account of this campaign and siege of Jerusalem, see *ANET* 287–88.

come under judgment (10:5–19, 24–34), and a faithful remnant of repentant Judahites/Jerusalemites would return to Yahweh (10:20–23). This return would be orchestrated by an ideal king, whose just and righteous rule would reverse the practices of his evil predecessors, restoring the glory of the Davidic kingdom (11:1–9). Thus, Isaiah 11:1–9 pictures a reversal of the crisis of 701 BCE.

Prediction of the Coming Royal "Branch" (11:1)

Verse 1 pictures the new king in arboreal images, representing the family tree of David: a new leafy branch growing out of a tree stock. In fact, the new shoot sprouts up from the roots of an established plant. The terms "shoot" (חֹטֶר), "stock" (גֵּזַע), and "branch" (נֵצֶר) each convey royal connotations.[45] The Hebrew word "shoot" (חֹטֶר) is related to Phoenician "scepter" (חטר). The term "branch" (נֵצֶר) is metaphorical of a royal scion as heir to the dynastic throne (Dan. 11:7). The related term "crown" (נֵזֶר) designates the royal emblem (Prov. 27:24) and Davidic diadem (Pss. 89:39[40]; 132:18; cf. 2 Sam. 1:10; 2 Kings 11:12).

Depiction of the new Davidic king as a branch of the stock of Jesse is not unique to Isaiah. Similar royal conventions exist among other ancient Near Eastern royal courts.[46] More pointedly, the royal title, "branch of [someone] of ancient stock," supports a new king's claim as legitimate heir to the throne, and pictures him as the one in whom the past glory of the dynasty's illustrious founder would be restored. For some, these royal inscriptions in Isaiah 11:1 are interpreted as an exclusive direct eschatological prophecy about the Messiah. For others, they are an exclusive depiction of the current king, Hezekiah, as an ideal monarch, whose roots reached back to the founding of the dynasty.[47] But once again this need not be an either/or approach to the interpretation and thereby we avoid this false dichotomy. Reading the passage as a both/and pattern and recognizing it speaks of hope out of the Davidic line without naming a specific king allows us to see how Isaiah 11:1–11 may have been uttered in association with Hezekiah, but ultimately speaks of an ideal Davidic king to come who was greater than Hezekiah.

---

45. Used literally, "shoot" (חֹטֶר) refers to a leafy branch as new growth of a tree. The term "stock" (גֵּזַע) may refer to the stem of a plant (Isa. 40:24) or tree stump (Job 14:8). The term "branch" (נֵצֶר) is a leafy bud representing new growth (Isa. 14:19; 60:21), sprouting from the root-stock of a plant (Ezek. 17:6–7, 9) or tree (Jer. 17:8).

46. The Assyrian king Tiglath-Pileser III is called "the precious branch of Baltil," and Sargon II is called "the precious branch of Assur of royal lineage and ancient stock." The Babylonian king Nebuchadnezzar I is "offspring of Enmeduranki, king of Sippar, a branch of Nippur of ancient stock."

47. Some suggest the prophecy of the second David as Josiah, e.g., Marvin Sweeney, "Jesse's New Shoot in Isaiah 11: A Josianic Reading of the Prophet Isaiah," in *Sanders Festschrift* (Sheffield: Sheffield Academic Press, 1996), 103–18; Antti Laato, *Josiah and David Redivivus: The Historical Josiah and the Messianic Expectations of Exilic and Postexilic Times*, ConBOTT 33 (Stockholm: Almqvist & Wiksell, 1992).

The arboreal image of Jesse's ideal shoot (11:1) must be read in the light of the controlling motif of the Divine Forester and thick forest in 10:5–34. Wielding Assyria as his ax, God would hew down the forest of Judah and hack down David's family tree, leaving a mere stump (10:12–19, 33–34), yet preserving a remnant (10:20–27). This judgment of 701 BCE would be reversed by God's nurture of an ideal tender shoot and root of Jesse (11:1, 10), whose reign would usher in an idyllic age of peace and security (11:1–16). The linking of 10:5–34 and 11:1–16 suggests an historical setting for the resurgence of David's dynasty under Hezekiah as an initial realization of the promise.

The image of a shoot coming forth from Jesse's root is reminiscent of Isaiah's promise to Hezekiah when Sennacherib besieged Zion, "The surviving remnant of the house of Judah will take root and bear fruit, for out of Jerusalem will come forth a remnant" (Isa. 37:31–32 // 2 Kings 19:30–31). Given the prophecy of the Assyrian king's invasion of Judah and siege of Jerusalem in 10:5–34, the prophecy may have initially applied to Hezekiah But due to the openness of Isaiah's prophecy, the potential for a future eschatological *shoot* who would be the agent of deliverance of the remnant of God's people and restoration of David's dynasty is also apparent.

Description of the Ideal Davidic King (11:2–5)
Verse 2 depicted the king as equipped with the same energizing spirit God put on Saul and David.[48] Isaiah described the enablement God provided special servants to fulfill divinely appointed tasks (Exod. 31:3; 35:31; Num. 11:25–26). Reminiscent of the pouring out of God's spirit on David at his anointing (1 Sam. 16:13), Isaiah portrayed the new king as a second David.

The basic duty of the house of David was to promote moral righteousness and uphold social justice (Pss. 72:1–4; 122:5; Isa. 16:5; Jer. 22:15). David and Solomon lived up to this ideal (2 Kings 8:15; 1 Kings 3:28); their royal descendants generally failed (Jer. 21:12; 22:3, 13, 15, 16). Isaiah indicted the unjust Davidic kings of his day (Uzziah, Jotham, Ahaz) of failing to protect the poor and punish the wicked (Isa. 10:1–4), but envisioned the coming royal scion as an ideal Davidic king whose reign would be characterized by moral righteousness and social justice (Isa. 9:3–5; 16:5; 32:1; cf. 42:1, 3–4; Jer. 23:5; 33:15; Ezek. 37:24)

Idyllic Portrait of His Reign of Peace (11:6–9)
Whereas the unjust practices of the house of David (Uzziah, Jotham, Ahaz) (10:1–4) had placed Jerusalem in jeopardy in 701 BCE (10:5–34), the coming

---

48. God clearly equips both King Saul (1 Sam. 10:10; 11:6; 16:14; 19:23) and King David (1 Sam. 16:13; 2 Sam. 23:2; cf. Ps. 51:11[14]) with an energizing spirit. Isaiah expects the same energizing spirit to empower the Davidic King who will drive the Assyrians from the land.

king's reign of righteousness (9:1–5) would grant national security for Zion (11:6–9). In a series of portraits drawn from nature, Isaiah envisioned fundamental changes in the current order: "the lion will lay down with the lamb" (cf. 65:25).[49] This picture of idyllic peace and harmony did not originally envision a miraculous transformation of the animal kingdom in the eschatological kingdom. The image of peace between hunter and hunted (vv. 6–8) is an extended metaphor of an equally dramatic change: foreign armies would no longer invade Judah or assault Zion (v. 9). Since God's spirit would rest on the coming king enabling him to promote righteousness and justice (vv. 1–5), Zion would be safe from the likes of Sennacherib—as long the house of David followed this path.[50] The new David, whoever he was, would bring real peace. Considered from an initial historical point of view, Isaiah envisioned a social-religious change with the royal anointing or birth of the new king, Hezekiah, to reign over and rid Judah of foreign oppressors. What Hezekiah did in part, the eschatological Messiah would do in full.

Canonical Reading

Critical scholars generally assume the image of the royal branch sprouting from the stock of Jesse in Isaiah 11:1 presupposes the collapse of the dynasty in 586 BCE, when the Babylonian king Nebuchadnezzar II destroyed Jerusalem, razed the temple and carried off the last Davidic king into Babylonian exile. According to this approach, a later editor composed 11:1–9 in the exilic or postexilic periods. Thus it expresses the exilic community's hope of the restoration of the dynasty in the near future in the person of the next Davidic king (Zerubbabel?), or—once that hope eventually waned—the postexilic community's eschatological expectation of the full-fledged inauguration of the eschatological kingdom in the last Davidic king (the Messiah).

However, the image of the new Davidic king as a shoot from the ancient stock of Jesse does not demand a late date of composition, nor evacuation of the royal throne in 586 BCE. As noted above, the arboreal imagery of Isaiah 11:1 continues the controlling motif of the Divine Forester in 10:5–34, where the Assyrian king is the agent of God as the ax wielded against Judah and the

---

49. As parallels in ancient Near Eastern literature hint, Isaiah's image of wolf lying down with lamb originally envisioned peace. For instance, the Enmerkar Epic pictures a past golden age when nations lived in harmony before the rise of warfare between empires as a time in hoary antiquity when no carnivores stalked the earth: "A time when there was no serpent, when there was no scorpion; a time when there was no hyena, when there was no lion; a time when there was neither fear nor terror." A similar image occurs in a Sumerian royal inscription which predicts the reign of a new king would usher in an age of national security and domestic peace, portrayed as harmony in the animal kingdom: "In Dilmun the lion will not kill, the wolf will not snatch the lamb ..."

50. See Edward Lipinski, "Straw in the Neo-Assyrian Period," in *Built on Solid Rock: Studies in Honor of Ebbe Egede Knudsen* (Oslo: Novus, 1997), 187–95.

sinful Davidic dynasty in Jerusalem (cf. 10:1–4). Thus, 11:1–16 is set against the historical events of 701 BCE, when Sennacherib invaded Judah, besieged Zion and threatened to terminate the dynasty. However, Isaiah foresaw that after God had cut the family tree of David's dynasty down to size (10:33–34), he would nurture a tender shoot from whom an ideal ruler would emerge, who would function as his agent to restore a righteous remnant (11:1–16).

Isaiah had voiced great expectations for Hezekiah, ideals engendered by his loyalty to Yahweh in 701 BCE, which brought about the destruction of the Assyrian army and deliverance of Zion (Isa. 37:1–38 // 2 Kings 19:1–37). Yet when read in the light of the final form of the book of Isaiah, 11:1–9 points to an ideal ruler to come beyond the Babylonian exile. Perhaps God's deliverance of Zion from Sennacherib prompted Isaiah to look beyond the immediate circumstances of 701 BCE into the eschatological future, when the Davidic throne would be occupied by one greater than Hezekiah—the one we now know as the eschatological Messiah and further reinforced in Isaiah 11:10–16.

MESSIANIC TRAJECTORIES IN ISAIAH 11:10–16

This oracle of restoration functions as a parallel passage to Isaiah 11:1–9, featuring a coming ideal Davidic king. It consists of three parts: prediction of the restoration of the exiles of Israel and Judah (vv. 10–12); reunification of the two once hostile nations into one mighty nation, which would conquer the nations (vv. 13–14); and typological portrait of a second exodus in which a remnant would be regathered from the Assyrian and Babylonian exiles (vv. 15-16).

Contextual Reading

Isaiah envisioned the coming king playing a central role in restoring David's once mighty united kingdom. Like a banner signaling the rallying point for troops scattered on a battlefield, he would regather the northern exiles scattered among the nations to form a potent army (vv. 10–12). Negotiating peace between Judah and Israel, he would command their united forces, giving the signal to attack the surrounding nations (vv. 13–14a). Under his leadership, the united nation would enjoy a renaissance of the past glory of the Davidic Empire since David's former vassals (Philistia, Moab, Ammon, Edom) would be subjugated once again (v. 14b). Using the archetypal motif of the past deliverance of the Hebrews from Egypt, Isaiah predicts a future second exodus of the remnant (vv. 15–16).

Second Exodus Typology

The second exodus typology in verses 15–16 often leads critical scholars to attribute this passage to a later editor when the inhabitants of Judah and Jerusalem were in Babylonian exile. They suggest the prediction of a new David in verses 10 and 12 presuppose the fall of David's throne in 586 BCE. However, mention of Assyria as the location of the exiles of the northern kingdom (vv. 11, 16) suggests 11:10–16 is set against the Assyrian deportation in the eighth century not the Babylonian exile in the sixth century. Granted, verse 12 predicts the restoration of Israelite and Judahite exiles. Yet this does not demand a sixth century date of composition by a later editor. Having seen Samaria's deportation to Assyria in 722 BCE, Isaiah predicted that Hezekiah's alliance with the Babylonian king Merodach-Baladan would doom Jerusalem to a similar fate in a future Babylonian exile (Isa. 39:1–8 // 2 Kings 20:12–19). It is legitimate to attribute this passage to Isaiah, but date it late in the reign of Hezekiah after Isaiah not only predicted the yet future Babylonian exile, but also the restoration of the Babylonian exiles in a glorious second exodus.

The Coming "Root" of Jesse

While Isaiah 11:1 depicts a "shoot of Jesse's root," 11:10 refers to a coming "root of Jesse." This subtle distinction in these two sets of royal titles might envision two distinct Davidic figures—one near, one far. While he probably composed 11:10–16 sometime during the reign of Hezekiah, Isaiah prophesied about a future king modeled after David, showing a pattern motif embedded in Isaiah's picture.

Hezekiah's successful break from Assyria and resistance of Sennacherib (2 Kings 18–19) prompted Isaiah's vision of the greater Hezekiah's complete liberation from Assyria (vv. 10–12, 15–16). Perhaps inspired by his success in reunification of northern survivors with southern faithful in worshiping Yahweh (2 Chron. 30:1–27, esp. v. 12, "God moved the people to unite"), Isaiah envisioned complete reversal of traditional hostility between Israel and Judah through the greater Hezekiah to come: "Ephraim's jealousy shall end and Judah's hostility will cease" (v. 13). Hezekiah's imperialism and conquest of Philistia, Meunim, Moab, and Amalek (2 Kings 18:8; 1 Chron. 4:39–43) engendered Isaiah's expectation of a greater conquest to come: "They will swoop down on the Philistine hills to the west, together they will plunder the people of the east; they will conquer Edom and Moab, the Ammonites will be their subjects" (v. 14). Thus, Isaiah's initial hope was in Hezekiah. Unfortunately, he failed to measure up. However, the future Messiah will fulfill this prophecy.

Canonical Reading

Considered together, Isaiah 11:1–9 and 11:10–16 illustrate the dynamics of the prophet's original royal Davidic expectations pointing to a near realization only partially realized and then a complete fulfillment later in an escalated pattern. In 11:1–9, Isaiah voiced his early hope that once God had disciplined the sinful house of David at the hand of Assyria (10:1–34), Hezekiah would inaugurate a golden age of justice and perpetual peace. In partial fulfillment of his prediction, God did in fact rescue Jerusalem from Sennacherib in 701 BCE, thanks in no small part to Hezekiah's faith (36:1–37:38). Nevertheless, his alliance with Merodach-Baladan king of Babylon proved his undoing: rather than the means of deliverance from Assyria, it would be the cause of judgment in the form of the coming Babylonian exile (39:1–8).[51] As a result, Isaiah expounded on his early picture of imminent restoration of David's house. If the oracle would not be fulfilled in his day, he projected its fulfillment beyond the end of the Babylonian exile. In 11:10–16, he foresaw a coming king greater than Hezekiah, who would regather the exiles of Israel and Judah, creating a reunited Davidic kingdom and restoring its former glory. Thus, Isaiah 11:10–16 laid the foundation for eschatological messianism, which leads us to Isaiah's Servant Songs.

MESSIANIC TRAJECTORIES IN THE SERVANT SONGS

Isaiah portrays the Lord's ideal Servant in four oracles, popularly known as the Servant Songs (42:1–7; 49:1–13; 50:4–11; 52:13–53:12).[52] These texts are traditionally grouped together for three reasons: the ideal Servant's identity is anonymous;[53] the ideal Servant obeys Yahweh;[54] and the ideal Servant fulfills his calling despite suffering and so eventually is exalted by God.[55]

---

51. In 721 BCE, Merodach-Baladan threw off Assyrian control and declared himself king of Babylon (721–710). In 710, however, the Assyrian king Sargon II (721–705) forced Merodach-Baladan to flee Babylon. When the Assyrian king Sennacherib (705–686) assumed the throne in 705, Merodach-Baladan instigated a revolt, only to be defeated in 703. When he learned that Sennacherib was unable to subdue Jerusalem in 701, Merodach-Baladan sent an envoy to meet this great king. See Jean-Jacques Glassner, "Assyria Chronicles" in *Mesopotamian Chronicles*. Writings from the Ancient World (Atlanta: Society of Biblical Literature, 2004), 194–97, 204–5, 259 n. 4, 260 nn. 21, 25.

52. A select sampling of sources for further reading: Randall Heskett, *Messianism within the Scriptural Scroll of Isaiah* (New York: T&T Clark, 2007); F. Duane Lindsey, *The Servant Songs: A Study in Isaiah* (Chicago: Moody Press, 1985); Tryggve N. D. Mettinger, *A Farewell to the Servant Songs: A Critical Examination of an Exegetical Axiom* (Lund: C. W. K. Gleerup, 1983); Francis Landy, "The Construction of the Subject and the Symbolic Order: A Reading of the Last Three Suffering Servant Songs," in *Among the Prophets: Language, Image, and Structure in the Prophetic Writings* (ed. David J. A. Clines; Sheffield: JSOT Press, 1993); Hans M. Barstad, "The Future of the 'Servant Songs': Some Reflections on the Relationship of Biblical Scholarship to Its Own Tradition," in *Barr Festscrift* (Oxford: Clarendon Press, 1994), 261–70; H. H. Rowley, "The Servant of the Lord in the Light of Three Decades of Criticism," in *The Servant of the Lord, and Other Essays on the Old Testament* (Oxford: Basil Blackwell, 1952).

53. In contrast to other passages in Isaiah in which "Israel" is identified as God's Servant (41:8, 9; 43:10; 44:1, 2, 21; 48:20; 49:3), the ideal Servant is anonymous in three of the four Servant Songs (42:1; 49:5, 6; 50:10; 52:13; 53:11).

54. While Israel failed to live up to its calling as the Lord's Servant due to sin (42:19, "My servant is blind, my messenger is truly deaf! My covenant partner, the servant of the LORD, is blind!"), the Lord's ideal Servant obeys Yahweh and fulfills his calling despite unjust suffering (42:4; 49:7–8; 50:4–11; 52:13; 53:12).

55. The Servant Songs share common themes: God calls the Servant as light to the nations by establishing justice on earth (42:1–4, 6–7; 49:5–6); the Servant fulfills his calling despite suffering (42:4; 49:4, 7–8; 50:6–9; 52:14–53:10); he is God's agent in the second exodus (42:7; 49:8–13); God exalts him over all earthly kings (49:7; 52:13–15).

Contextual Reading of the Servant Songs

All four Songs highlight the Servant's suffering (42:4; 49:4, 7–8; 50:5–9; 52:14; 53:3–11). The first Song (42:1–7) highlights his refusal to give in to discouragement; he perseveres despite opposition and fulfills his calling. In the second Song (49:1–13), the Servant laments that his path is not smooth, yet he endures since God reveals his suffering will bring redemption, not just to Israel but to all nations. The third Song (50:4–11) describes the unjust corporeal punishment he suffers from those who treat him as a false prophet: his back is scourged, his beard torn from his cheeks and his face spat upon.[56] The final Song (52:13–53:12) describes the nature of his suffering and pivotal role it would play in God's redemptive program.[57] Our discussion of the Servant Songs will focus on the nature of the Servant's suffering and ultimate exaltation by God.

The Nature of the Servant's Suffering

The nature of the Servant's suffering is clearly unjust. In fact, his plight mirrors Job's plight in many ways.[58] They both suffer unjustly, onlookers misinterpret their suffering as divinely deserved punishment for sin, and the community is appalled and shuns them.[59] Both must rely on God alone to vindicate their innocence, death seems certain, and it appears they would suffer the fate of the wicked.[60] Yet God rescues his suffering servant from death and exonerates him (Isa. 49:8; 53:10–11; Job 42:7–17). Both graciously intercede for their accusers (53:12b; Job 42:10). God rewards both by exalting them in the eyes of their contemporaries (Isa. 52:13; 53:12, 15; Job 42:9–12), blessing

---

56. Corporeal punishment in ancient Israel involved flogging the back (Exod. 21:20; Deut. 25:2–3; Prov. 10:13; 19:29; 23:13, 14; 26:3), or striking the cheek (1 Kings 22:24; Mic. 5:1; Ps. 3:7; Job 16:10; Lam. 3:30; 2 Chron. 18:23). Christians see this as prophetic of the Roman scourging of Jesus (Matt. 27:26; Mark 15:15; Luke 23:33; John 19:1–3). However, Israel is figuratively pictured as being struck on the cheek and beaten on the back when Zion was destroyed and her citizens taken into exile (Isa. 51:23; Lam. 3:30).

57. See Bernd Janowski, Peter Stuhlmacher, and Daniel P. Bailey, eds., *The Suffering Servant: Isaiah 53 in Jewish and Christian Sources* (Grand Rapids: Eerdmans, 2004); Henning Graf Reventhlow, "Basic Issues in the Interpretation of Isaiah 53," in *Jesus and the Suffering Servant* (Harrisburg, PA: Trinity Press International, 1998), 23–38.

58. J. C. Bastiaens, "Language of Suffering in Job 16–19 and in the Suffering Servant Passages of Deutero-Isaiah," in *Studies in the Book of Isaiah: Festschrift Willem A. M. Beuken* (ed. Willem A. M. Beuken, J. van Ruiten, and M. Vervenne; Louvain: Leuven University Press, 1997).

59. Unjust suffering (Isa. 50:6; 53:9; Job 6:24–30; 9:1–10:17; 19:6; 27:1–6; 34:5); misinterpretation (Isa. 53:4–6; Job 4:17; 9:2; 11:2; 15:14; 22:3; 25:4; 32:2; 34:5; 35:2; 36:7); shunned (Isa. 53:1–3; Job 6:14–21; 12:4; 16:10; 17:2–9; 19:1–6, 13–22; 30:1–15);

60. Divine vindication (Isa. 49:4; 50:7–9; Job 6:29; 8:3; 9:15, 20; 10:15; 12:4; 13:18; 16:18–22; 17:8; 19:23–29; 27:5, 6; 31:6, 35); death seems certain (Isa. 53:7–9; Job 17:1, 10–16; cf. 3:20–26; 6:8–13); and it appears they would suffer the fate of the wicked (Isa. 53:9; Job 16:11).

each with numerous offspring (Isa. 53:10b; Job 42:13–15) and long life (Isa. 53:10b; Job 42:16–17). Yet for all these similarities, the Servant's suffering and reward would outstrip that of Job. For his suffering would play the pivotal role in God's program of redemption of all people (Isa. 42:1–4; 49:5–8; 53:5, 6, 12); and God would bestow on him unprecedented worldwide honor (Isa. 49:7; 52:13; 53:12).

In What Way Would the Servant Bear the Sin of Others?
Does the Servant suffer vicariously on behalf of others or unjustly as the consequence of being a member of a nation requiring punishment? One set of passages depicts him suffering on account of the sins of others: "for (מִן) our transgressions . . . for (מִן) our iniquities . . . for (מִן) the transgression of his people" (53:5, 8). When prefixed to terms for sin elsewhere, the term highlighted above depicts an innocent party unjustly suffering as a consequence of God's punishment of the sin of others, e.g., Jeremiah 12:4, "The animals and birds die on account of the evil of the inhabitants of this land!" (cf. Isa. 57:1; Lam. 4:13; Mic. 7:13). There are no clear examples elsewhere in which an innocent party suffers vicariously to atone the sin of others. It is the unprecedented use of this idea that makes this text so suitable for its eventual use of Jesus.

According to 53:11, the Servant will bear the people's sins: "He will bear their iniquities."[61] When used literally, the verb "bear, carry" (סָבַל) depicts the subject carrying a heavy load on its shoulder. For instance, Isaiah uses the term to describe God carrying his people (46:4) and later of people carrying heavy load (46:7)(cp. Gen. 49:15; Ps. 144:14). It is used of carrying sin elsewhere only in Lamentations 5:7, where an innocent generation suffers the consequences of punishment of the previous generation's sins: "Our fathers sinned and are no more, yet we bear their iniquities" (RSV); "our ancestors sinned and are now dead, so we are left to bear their punishment" (NET).

In Isaiah 53:12, the meaning of the expression, "He bore the sin of many," is also open. Used with terms for sin, the verb "to bear" (נָשָׂא) has a broad range of meanings.[62] The closest parallels to 53:12 describe innocent

---

61. For the exegetical ambiguity in v. 11, see Anthony Gelston, "Knowledge, Humiliation, or Suffering: A Lexical, Textual, and Exegetical Problem in Isaiah 53," in *Of Prophets' Visions and the Wisdom of Sages: Essays in Honour of R. Norman Whybray on His Seventieth Birthday* (ed. R. N. Whybray, Heather A. McKay, and David J. A. Clines; Sheffield: JSOT Press, 1993).

62. The term is used as follows: (1) person bearing his own sin, that is, being held accountable for his actions (Lev. 5:1, 17); (2) a person suffering the punishment of his sin (Gen. 4:13; Num. 14:34); (3) a person incurring the guilt of someone else's sin (Lev. 19:17); (4) a person suffering the effects of punishment of the sin of others (Num. 14:33; Ezek. 4:4–6); (5) a person unjustly suffering punishment for the sin of others (Ezek. 18:19–20); (6) God taking away the guilt of the people's sin, that is, forgiving their sin (Gen. 18:24, 26; 50:17); (7) the scape goat symbolically carrying away the sin of Israel into the desert

persons suffering the effects of God's punishment of the sins of others: "Your sons will wander in the wilderness for forty years and suffer for your unfaith-fulness" (Num. 14:33); "the son shall suffer for the iniquity of his father" (Ezek. 18:19–20); "You shall bear their iniquity" (Ezek. 4:4–6). However, there are also two passages in which the term is used in a Levitical sense of removing the sins of the nation (Lev. 10:17; 16:22). While Isaiah 53:12 may be understood in terms of unjust suffering or vicarious suffering, it is impos-sible to determine the original meaning simply on the basis of the contextual reading. So while this expression does not demand an atoning sacrifice, nei-ther does it prohibit this.[63] It is in this open expression that we find another case of divinely inspired messianic mystery.

The Nature of the Servant's Sacrifice

The precise meaning of 53:10b is discussed since it is beset with numerous uncertainties. The verse has been rendered in four different ways: (1) Yahweh offers the Servant as a sacrifice: "if You make his soul an offering for sin" (KJV); (2) the Servant offers a traditional sin-offering: "if he himself makes an offering for sin" (NET note); (3) the Servant makes restitution: "if he himself makes restitution" (JPS); (4) passive sense: "once restitution is made" (NET).[64] This diversity of translations highlights the issues of the verse.

The first question we need to ask is simply this: Did Isaiah mean "resti-tution" (Num. 5:7–8; BDB 79.3) or "guilt offering" (Lev. 5:6, 7, 15; BDB 79.4)? Both are viable options. The latter is more likely since a subsequent statement explains 53:10b: "He bore (אָשָׁם) the sin of many" (53:12). When the term "guilt offering" (אָשָׁם) and expression "bear sin" (נָשָׂא הֵטְא) appear together elsewhere, the former refers to a guilt offering, which one presents for sin whose responsibility he assumes (e.g., Lev. 5:17, 18).

Assuming a guilt offering is in view, the meaning of 53:10b remains enig-matic since the syntax can be taken in two ways: (1) the Servant presents a tra-ditional guilt offering on behalf of the sins of the people: "If he himself makes a guilt-offering . . ." (2) God treats the suffering/death of the Servant as a guilt offering on behalf of the sins of the people: "If you treat his soul as a guilt-offering . . ."[65] Both options are valid and contextually viable. The first views

---

(Lev. 16:22); (8) the priests symbolically removing the sins of Israel by eating meat of the sin offering (Lev. 10:17).

63. Bruce R. Reichenbach, "By His Stripes We Are Healed," *JETS* 41 (1998): 551–60.

64. The NET Bible translation follows the BHS editors who suggest emending the MT reading תָּשִׂים (hiphil) to תֻּשַׂם (qal passive): "If [an offering/restitution] is made . . ." Our discussion assumes the MT reading is original.

65. The first approach takes the verb תָּשִׂים as third feminine singular, the feminine singular term נַפְשׁוֹ ("his soul") as the subject of the verb, and the noun אָשָׁם ("guilt-offering") as the direct object: "If he himself makes a guilt offering . . ." The second approach takes the verb תָּשִׂים as second masculine singular, the feminine singular term נַפְשׁוֹ ("his soul")

the Servant presenting a traditional guilt offering on the altar in his ministry of intercession on behalf of those who unjustly mistreated/accused him. This finds support from one approach to verse 12: "He bore responsibility for the sins of the many and made intercession on behalf of the transgressors." In the second view, God treats the Servant's suffering as having atoning value. This finds support from an alternate approach to verse 12: "He bore the sins of the many and intervened on behalf of the transgressors." Since this line is fraught with such ambiguity, it is easy to understand how the original readers would not necessarily have read 53:10 as predicting the Servant would suffer vicariously to atone for sin by a substitutionary death. Yet it also is easy to see the language and imagery allows for the messianic potential of an atoning sacrifice.[66] What the uncertainty shows is that such a connection can exist, especially if the uniqueness of the overall expression is appreciated.

Would the Servant Actually Suffer Death?
Isaiah 52:13–53:12 pictures the Servant in danger of violent premature death, yet it is not clear from a contextual reading whether he actually dies. There are five significant contextual statements that may lead us to believe the language and imagery suggests his death. Yet they do not demand it because it may simply picture the servant's life is in danger of death.

First, the terminology in 53:5 may be understood as a fatal or non-fatal assault. The verb "wound [someone]" (חלל) refers to an assault that may be fatal (Isa. 51:9; Ezek. 32:26) or non-fatal (Ps. 77:10[9]; Prov. 26:10; Ezek. 28:9). The parallel verb, "bruise, crush" (דָּכָא), likewise refers to physical assault, whether fatal (Job 6:9; Ps. 89:10) or non-fatal (Ps. 143:3; Lam. 3:34). While the Servant's life is placed in danger, it is not clear whether or not he dies.

Second, the statement, "He was cut off from the land of the living" (53:8), seems to depict the Servant's death. The verb, "cut off" (כָּרַת), often refers to suffering a violent death (Gen. 9:11; Lev. 26:22). Yet when Jeremiah

---

as the direct object, and the noun אָשָׁם ("guilt offering") as an adverbial accusative of respect: "If You make/treat his soul as a guilt-offering . . ."
66. For example, see Antti Laato, "Isaiah 53 and the Biblical Exegesis of Justin Martyr," in *Rewritten Bible Reconsidered: Proceedings of the Conference in Karkku, Finland, August 24–26 2006* (ed. Antti Laato and J. van Ruiten; Winona Lake: Eisenbrauns, 2008); Angela Russell Christman, "Selections from Theodoret of Cyrus's Commentary on Isaiah," in *The Theological Interpretation of Scripture: Classic and Contemporary Readings* (ed. Stephen E. Fowl; Malden, MA: Blackwell, 1997); E. Robert Ekblad, "God Is Not to Blame: The Servant's Atoning Suffering according to the LXX of Isaiah 53," in *Stricken by God? Nonviolent Identification and the Victory of Christ* (ed. Brad Jersak and Michael Hardin; Grand Rapids: Eerdmans, 2007); J. Alan Groves, "Atonement in Isaiah 53," in *The Glory of the Atonement: Biblical, Historical, and Practical Perspectives: Essays in Honor of Roger Nicole* (ed. Roger E. Nicole, Charles E. Hill, and Frank A. James; Downers Grove: InterVarsity, 2004).

laments, "I have been cut off!" (Lam. 3:54), he had not actually died, but feared death was certain: "I am about to die!" (NET). To be cut off from the land of the living may refer to a violent death (Job 27:8; Pss. 88:5; 109:13; Zech. 13:8), or be in a life-threatening situation (Pss. 31:22; 88:5[6]; Lam. 3:54; Ezek. 37:11).[67] Both biblical and ancient Near Eastern literature often depicts the plight of someone in danger of death as being as good as dead. For the ancient Israelite, death was not a static state into which he entered when his body expired, but a dynamic power that threatened to cut him off from the realm of the living.

Third, the statement, "they prepared his grave" (53:9), certainly suggests the Servant already had died. However, a stereotypical feature in biblical and ancient Near Eastern literature is the just sufferer lamenting death seemed so certain that his grave had already been prepared. Job laments his death seemed so certain that his grave was ready for him: "the grave awaits me!" (Job 17:1, NET). Likewise, ancient Near Eastern texts often refer to people preparing a grave for someone whose death seemed certain, even though the sufferer eventually recovered.[68]

Fourth, 53:10 depicts God afflicting the Servant with physical malady, but it is not clear whether it is fatal or non-fatal. The verb "become ill" (חָלָה) depicts someone falling sick with fatal illness. For instance, the term is used to describe Jacob's condition just before he dies of old age (Gen. 48:1), Abijah's fatal illness (1 Kings 14:1, 5), Ahab's fatal illness from a battle wound (1 Kings 22:34), Elisha's terminal illness (2 Kings 13:14), and Hezekiah's near fatal illness, one which he survives (2 Kings 20:1, 12). Yet it is also used to describe non-fatal illnesses like that of King Asa's foot disease (1 Kings 15:23) and of King Ben Hadad of Syria who is ill but later recovers (2 Kings 8:7, 19).

Finally, 53:12b is unclear whether the Servant's life was merely in jeopardy or actually forfeited. Although traditionally rendered, "He poured out his soul to death" (KJV, RSV), this expression literally means, "He exposed his

---

67. Other examples also exist. An ancient Israelite suffering a life-threatening plight may describe himself as laid in the dust of death (Ps. 22:15), drawing near the gates of Sheol (Pss. 88:3[4]; 107:18), being dragged down to Sheol by its cords (2 Sam. 22:5–6; Pss. 18:4–5[5–6]; 116:3), descending to Sheol (Pss. 9:13; 22:15; Lam. 3:55), residing in the depths of the Pit (Ps. 88:3, 6), or shut in Sheol (Ps. 88:8[9]; Jon. 2:6).

68. For example, death seemed so certain for Shubshi-meshre-Shakkan that his family already had dug his grave and made funeral arrangements: "My grave was waiting and my funerary paraphernalia ready; before I died, lamentation for me was finished" (*COS* 1.153). Yet he was restored to health: "The tomb he had prepared for him was set up for a feast . . . Marduk can restore to life from the grave" (*COS* 1.153). In another text, a righteous sufferer: "My family gathered round to bend over me before my time; my next of kin stood by ready for the wake . . . until the Lord raised my head and brought me back to life from the dead" (*COS* 1.152). He describes his deliverance from certain death thus: "He snatched me from the jaws of death . . . he wrested the shovel from the digger of my grave" (*COS* 1.152).

soul to death" (הֶעֱרָה לַמָּוֶת נַפְשׁוֹ). In its only use elsewhere, it does not mean to experience death, but for one's life to be in jeopardy of death: "do not expose me (אַל־תְּעַר נַפְשִׁי) to danger!" (Ps. 141:8, NET).

Thus, none of the five statements describing the Suffering Servant's plight in Isaiah 53:12 demands his premature death because the language and imagery is fraught with ambiguity. Yet when considered together, the plight of the Servant seems so bleak that it is difficult to read this passage without assuming that he dies. The only reason his death is not clear is that 53:10–11 describes God providing life and blessings to him after he had suffered, while 52:13 and 52:15 portray God exalting him after he suffered (cf. 49:8–9). Thus, we are left with two options. First, God would rescue the Servant from premature death after he suffered a life-threatening plight. Second, God would rescue the Servant from the power of death after he had physically died. Nonetheless, the weight of the likelihood is that the Servant dies. If the comparison to a sacrifice is made (53:10b), then a death seems even more likely. Yet a human sacrifice would have been unthinkable, given God's rejection elsewhere of human sacrifice as a pagan practice. So while the sacrificial death of the Messiah was present in the divinely designed wording of our passage, it would have been unthinkable to its original readers. This explains why no one in the first century was expecting the Messiah to die a propitiatory death. But this is precisely what God did in Jesus the Messiah.

In What Way Would the Servant's Life Be Restored?

According to Isaiah 53:10b, the Servant would be rewarded by God for his suffering with the enjoyment of life: "He will see [his] seed and prolong [his] days." The idiom, "to see one's seed," means one lives a long life to see his children and grandchildren (Gen. 33:5; 48:11; 50:23; Ps. 128:6; Isa. 29:23). However, the idiom elsewhere always takes the pronoun, "see *his/your* seed," which does not appear in 53:10. Although it might simply be assumed, one wonders why it is omitted here. If we view his experience as parallel to Job, we would assume his life was spared and he lived to see his grandchildren (Job 42:16). Yet the omission of this pronoun allows for and points to a messianic potential: the Servant would live beyond the grave to see the redeemed "seed."

According to 53:10b, the Servant would experience life after suffering: "He will prolong [his] days" (53:10b). The idiom, "prolong one's days," means to enjoy longevity of physical life (Exod. 20:12; Prov. 28:16). After Job suffered, God restored him to health and he lived a long full life (Job 42:16–17).[69] Nevertheless, 53:10b differs from the standard idiom, since it does not explicitly say the Servant's own days would be prolonged, but

---

69. An Akkadian text reads: "The years and days you were filled with misery are over. Were you not ordered to live, you could not have lasted the whole of this grievous illness . . . I will see to it that you have long life!" (*COS* 1.151).

literally reads, "He will prolong days." Here again, we can see how the original contextual reading is puzzling, yet loaded with messianic potential. If read in the light of the standard idiom, 53:10b would suggest God rescued the Servant from premature death then extended his life. Yet the departure from the standard idiom allows another reading: the Servant did die, but he experienced life beyond the grave, and provided eternal life to those on whose behalf he suffered. Again, in a context where an offering is in view, a death also seems the more likely sense, given the fact that Jesus did indeed die and rise from the dead.

According to 53:11, the Servant is restored to life after he suffers: "after the travail of his soul, he will see light."[70] The expression, "see light," literally refers to seeing the sun (Job 31:26; 37:21; cf. Deut. 4:19). Since the living see the sun, to see the light is idiomatic for being rescued from death (Isa. 9:2[1]) or having one's life sustained (Ps. 36:9, "In your light we see light," cf. NET, "You are the one who sustains life"). The term "light" is often figurative for life (Job 3:20; 33:30; Ps. 56:14). The related idiom, "those who see the sun," refers to the living (Eccl. 7:11; cf. Ps. 58:8[9]; Eccl. 6:5; 11:7); those who die "never again see the light" (Ps. 49:19; cf. Job 3:16). Thus, the precise meaning of 53:11a is unclear. On the one hand, it could mean the Servant would be rescued from the threat of death: God would sustain his life. Yet it is equally plausible that after the Servant died, he would again see light: God would raise him from the dead. As before, we opt for the latter in light of the full combination of images and in the light of the historical event of the resurrection of Messiah Jesus.

In What Way Would the Servant Be Exalted?

The last two Servant Songs reveal that God would exalt the Servant as a reward for his successful completion of his calling in the face of suffering (49:7; 52:13; 53:11–12). Initially, the Servant would be despised by the Gentile nations, but one day all rulers would be subjugated to him: "Kings will see him and rise in respect; princes will bow down" (49:7). This portrait clearly carries royal connotations. Then as now, it was standard protocol to stand in the presence of special people out of respect.[71] The act of prostrating oneself

---

70. The Masoretic Text (Codex Leningradis, ca. 1008 CE) reads, מֵעֲמַל נַפְשׁוֹ יִרְאֶה, "after the travail of his soul, he will see," which is awkward as it lacks an object. The two much earlier Isaiah manuscripts from Qumran (ca. 100 BCE) preserve the reading, מעמל נפשו יראה אור, "after the travail of his soul, he will see *light*." This early textual tradition is reflected in the Septuagint. The similarity of יראה אור may have led to accidental omission of the second word by a copyist. Thus, the Dead Sea Scrolls preserve the original.

71. Lot stands before two angelic beings and bows down with his face (Gen. 19:1), Abraham stands and bows before the local people, Hethites (Gen. 23:7), people are to stand in the presence of the aged and the elder (Lev. 19:32), Abigail stands and bows her face to David (1 Sam. 25:41), King Solomon stands and bows before Bethsheba (1 Kings 2:19),

on the ground was conventional protocol in the presence of a king.[72] Since the Servant would rule over restored Israel, Isaiah pictures the kings of all nations bowing before Israel as well (Isa. 45:14; 49:23; 60:14). Some suggest the Servant is Israel; however, if we view the book of Isaiah as a whole, it is more consistent to view the nations bowing to Israel as a result of the exaltation of the Servant. For Israel, where there is a nation, there is a king, especially if one treats Isaiah as a unit. The royal hope clearly was expressed in the early portion of the book.

The Servant's exaltation is also described in the fourth Song: "He will be elevated, lifted high, greatly exalted!" (52:13). The term "elevate" (רוּם) is used elsewhere of God elevating a person by enthroning him (Ps. 89:19[20]; cf. Num. 24:7). The term "lift up" (נָשָׂא) is used of political leaders in positions of authority (Isa. 2:12–14). As a result of his faithfulness, God would exalt the Servant over all the kings of the earth (49:8–9; 52:12, 15; cf. 53:15). Elsewhere in the book of Isaiah, both terms describe God's heavenly throne (Isa. 6:1; 57:15). Thus, this language allows a messianic potential: God would elevate him to his own heavenly throne.

The Identity of the Servant

We now come to the most vexing question yet: "Who was the Suffering Servant?" There is no consensus among interpreters who consider this. On the basis of clues in the book of Isaiah in general and Isaiah 40–66 in particular, the Servant has been identified with the following candidates: (1) corporate national Israel, (2) the righteous remnant of Israel, (3) the prophet Isaiah or another prophet such as Jeremiah, (4) the Israelite king in exile, or (5) the ideal Davidic king/the Messiah.[73]

This array of options is due to the fact that the term "servant" (עֶבֶד) has a wide range of forms and potential referents in the book of Isaiah. It occurs thirty-three times in three singular and four plural forms: "the servant of

---

Mordecai does not stand and bow before Haman (Esth. 5:9) and young men stand and old men remained standing when Job secured his seat in the public square (Job 29:8).

72. David bows his face to the ground before King Saul (1 Sam. 24:8). Mephibosheth, Joab, Absalom, Ziba, Ahimaaz, Araunah, Bethsheba, and Nathan bow their face to the ground before King David (2 Sam. 9:6; 14:22, 33; 16:4; 24:20; 1 Kings 1:16, 23, 31). And Adonijah bows his face to the ground before Solomon (1 Kings 1:53).

73. R. N. Whybray, *Thanksgiving for a Liberated Prophet*, JSOTS 4 (Sheffield: University of Sheffield, 1978); David J. A. Clines, *I, He, We, and They: A Literary Approach to Isaiah 53* (Sheffield: JSOT Press, 1976); Fredrik Hägglund, *Isaiah 53 in the Light of Homecoming after Exile* (Tübingen: Mohr Siebeck, 2008); Joseph Alobaidi, ed., *The Messiah in Isaiah 53: The Commentaries of Saadia Gaon, Salmon ben Yeruham, and Yefer ben Eli on Isaiah 52:13–53:12* (New York: Peter Lang, 1998); Antti Laato, *The Servant of YHWH and Cyrus: A Reinterpretation of the Exilic Messianic Programme in Isaiah 40–55*, ConBOT 35 (Stockholm: Almqvist & Wiksell, 1992); Robert R. Ellis, "The Remarkable Suffering Servant of Isaiah 40–55," *SWJT* 34 (1991): 20–30.

Yahweh," "his servant," "my servant," "the servants of Yahweh," "his servants," "your servants," and "my servants." In most cases, the servant's identity is made explicit by an accompanying statement or made clear from the context. The plural expressions designate corporate national Israel (54:17; 56:6; 63:17; 65:8, 9, 13, 14, 15; 66:14). Three singular expressions designate an individual: "my servant David" (37:35); "my servant Eliakim" (22:20); "my servant Isaiah" (20:3; cf. 44:26). Eight singular expressions are collective for Israel: "Israel my servant" (41:8, 9; 44:1, 2, 21; 48:20; 49:3). This leaves six cases in which the singular title is not explicitly identified (42:1; 49:5, 6; 50:10; 52:13; 53:11). In two cases, the anonymous titles, "His servant" (49:5) and "my servant" (49:6), occur in an oracle in which the singular, "Israel my servant" (49:3), appears previously. The other four anonymous titles, "my servant" (42:1; 52:13; 53:11) and "His servant" (50:10), occur in oracles in which his identity is not explicitly stated. The attentive reader will realize that all six of these anonymous singular expressions appear in the four identified Servant Songs (42:1–7; 49:1–13; 50:4–11; 52:13–53:12).

Enigmatic Identity of the Suffering Servant in 49:1–13
The threefold use of the term in 49:1–13 is peculiar. It is the only oracle in which the title is marked in one case (49:3, 'my servant Israel'), but unmarked in two others (49:5, 'his servant,' and 49:6, 'my servant'). Ordinarily, we would equate the unmarked uses with the initial marked use. Yet this is an unusual case since three features in 49:5–8 may suggest that Isaiah distinguished the Suffering Servant in 49:5–8 from Israel as God's Servant in 49:3.[74]

First, the Suffering Servant's identity is unclear since Isaiah 49:5–6 may be interpreted in two different ways: (1) God created/called the Suffering Servant to bring Israel to repentance, implying the Suffering Servant is distinct from Israel: "He formed me from birth to be his Servant *to restore* (לְהָשִׁיב) Jacob to himself and regather Israel . . . he said, 'Is it too insignificant for you to be my servant *to reestablish* (לְהָקִים) the tribes of Jacob and *to restore* (לְהָשִׁיב) the remnant of Israel?'" (2) God created/called the Suffering Servant by bringing Israel to repentance, implying the Servant is Israel: "He formed me from birth to be his Servant *by restoring* (לְשׁוֹבֵב) Jacob and regathering Israel to himself . . . he said, 'Is it too insignificant that you should be my servant *by reestablishing* (לְהָקִים) the tribes of Jacob and *by restoring* (לְהָשִׁיב) the remnant of Israel?'" In terms of Hebrew grammar, both are valid options. So the Servant's identity in 49:5–6 is not clear from a purely exegetical level.

Second, the Suffering Servant's identity is unclear since 49:7 may be interpreted in two dramatically different ways: (1) the Servant is abhorred by

---

74. Christopher Seitz, "'You Are My Servant, You Are the Israel in Whom I Will Be Glorified': The Servant Songs and the Effect of Literary Context in Isaiah," *CTJ* 39 (2004): 117–34; Peter Wilcox, "The Servant Songs in Deutero-Isaiah," *JSOT* 42 (1988): 79–102.

the nation and subservient to rulers: "the despised one, *the one abhorred by the nation* (מְתָעֵב גּוֹי), the servant of rulers," which distinguishes the Servant from the nation; (2) the Servant is the nation abhorred by the Gentile rulers: "the despised one, *the abhorred nation* (מְתָעֵב גּוֹי), the servant of rulers," which identifies the Servant as the nation. Since both options are viable, the identity of the Suffering Servant is enigmatic when considered from a purely contextual perspective.

Third, the Suffering Servant's identity is unclear as his calling in 49:8 may be interpreted in two dramatically different ways: (1) God called the Servant to become a covenant-keeping nation: "I will make you a covenant people" (NJPS); (2) God called the Servant to function as mediator of a new covenant with the nation: "I will make you a covenant for the people" (NIV, TNIV, ESV), "I will make you a covenant to the people" (RSV), "I will give you as a covenant to the people" (CEV), "I will make you a covenant mediator for the people" (NET, NIVR). The first pictures God transforming the disobedient nation into an obedient covenant-keeping people (cf. 56:4, 6). The second views the Servant as an individual, who would mediate a new covenant between Yahweh and Israel (cf. 54:10; 55:3; 59:21; 61:8).[75] Once again, it is impossible from a purely contextual perspective to determine the precise identity of the Servant.

Although the relationship of the Suffering Servant to Israel in Isaiah 49:5–8 is unclear, it is much more clear in 49:9–13. Yahweh portrays the Servant as a second Moses who will play the pivotal role in the "second exodus" (49:8–13; cf. 42:7). Just as Moses orchestrated the rescue of the Hebrews from slavery in Egypt (pictured as a prison), the Servant would function as God's agent to free captives from the darkness of their prisons (42:7; 49:9). Elsewhere Isaiah describes the Babylonian exile as a prison (Isa. 3:24; 10:4; 14:17; 49:24, 25; 61:1). Yet while Cyrus king of Persia would function as God's anointed in issuing the decree to allow the Jewish exiles to return from Babylonian exile (Isa. 44:28–45:4), the Servant would orchestrate a greater "second exodus" of the nation of Israel (42:7; 49:9–13; cf. 49:14–50:3; 50:10–52:12; 54:1–17). This suggests that the identity of the Servant is narrowing as we proceed. What Israel was, the servant as the embodiment of the people became. By the time we get to Isaiah 53, the identity appears to narrow to an individual who suffers for the people.

Canonical Reading of the Servant Songs
Although the precise identity of the Servant could appear uncertain when considered from a near contextual perspective of the Servant Songs themselves, a canonical reading of the Servant Songs, especially when the book

---

75. R. E. Clements, "Isaiah 53 and the Restoration of Israel," in *Jesus and the Suffering Servant* (Harrisburg, PA: Trinity Press International, 1998), 39–54.

of Isaiah as a whole is considered, shows us how we should read the text itself. When the Servant Songs are connected to the rest of Isaiah, one notices dramatic similarities between the Servant and the ideal Davidic king in 11:1–16.[76] Like the ideal Davidic king of 11:1–9, the Servant is endowed with the divine spirit (42:1; cf. 11:2) to establish justice (42:3–4; cf. 11:3–5). Like the ideal Davidic king of 11:10–16, the Servant will play the pivotal role in the "second exodus" in God's eschatological work of redemption (42:7; 49:9–13).[77] Moreover, the Servant and the ideal Davidic king are both depicted through the image of a "shoot" (שֹׁרֶשׁ) sprouting up from the ground (11:10; 53:2). So we conclude the Servant and the ideal Davidic king in 11:1–16 are one and the same.[78]

When viewed from a canonical perspective and even within the book of Isaiah, it is clear that the Servant Songs also reflect royal Davidic conventions. Just as God called David's dynasty to promote social justice (Pss. 45:4, 6–7; 72:1–4, 12–14; Jer. 21:12; 22:3, 13, 15; Ezek. 45:9), God called the Servant to promulgate social justice (42:1–4). In fact, the Servant's calling to promote social justice (42:1–4) and issue decrees to liberate prisoners (42:7) pictures him along the lines of ideal ancient Near Eastern kings like Hammurabi.[79] Just as David established social justice in ancient Israel (2 Sam. 8:15), the Servant would succeed in doing the same (42:4). By establishing justice, Isaiah's portrait of the Servant corresponds to Jeremiah's picture of the coming Davidic Branch and Ezekiel's vision of the Davidic Shepherd, who will establish justice (Jer. 23:5; 33:15; Ezek. 37:24). Just as the royal psalms depict all kings one day bowing down and serving the Davidic king (Pss. 2:10; 72:11), Isaiah predicts all kings will bow down before the Servant (49:7; 52:13, 15). Furthermore, the expression, "He will succeed" (53:12) (הִשְׂכִּיל) often refers to the success of a nation's leader (Josh. 1:7–8) or its king (1 Kings 2:3; 2 Kings 18:7). This recalls David's success (1 Sam. 18:5, 14, 15). Jeremiah

---

76. Richard Schultz, "The King in the Book of Isaiah," in *The Lord's Anointed: Interpretation of Old Testament Messianic Texts* (ed. Philip Satterthwaite, Richard Hess, and Gordon Wenham; Grand Rapids: Baker, 1995), 158

77. For the Servant pictured as a Second Moses, see Gordon Hugenberger, "The Servant of the Lord in the 'Servant Songs' of Isaiah: A Second Moses Figure," in *The Lord's Anointed: Interpretation of Old Testament Messianic Texts* (ed. Richard S. Hess, Gordon J. Wenham, and Philip E. Satterthwaite; Grand Rapids: Baker, 1995), 105-40.

78. Robert B. Chisholm Jr., "The Christological Fulfillment of Isaiah's Servant Songs" *BSac* 163 (2006): 387-404; H. H. Rowley, "The Suffering Servant and the Davidic Messiah," in *The Servant of the Lord, and Other Essays on the Old Testament* (Oxford: Basil Blackwell, 1952); Stanley Porter, "Introduction: The Messiah in the Old and New Testaments," in *The Messiah in the Old and New Testaments* (ed. Stanley Porter; Grand Rapids: Eerdmans, 2007), 1–12.

79. Shalom Paul, "Deutero-Isaiah and the Cuneiform Royal Inscriptions," *JAOS* 88 (1968):182; Moshe Weinfeld, *Social Justice in Ancient Israel and in the Ancient Near East* (Jerusalem: Magnes, 1995), 47–52, 60–61, 141.

predicted the coming new "David" would succeed in his calling: "I will raise up for them a righteous Branch for David; he will rule over them successfully (וְהִשְׂכִּיל)" (Jer. 23:5; cf. 3:15). While the Servant would succeed in fulfilling his calling, Isaiah laments Israel lacked all spiritual understanding, which prevented the nation from succeeding in its calling as Yahweh's servant (Isa. 44:18; cf. 42:18–19; 43:8; 44:18; 59:10).[80] Finally, the term "servant" is often a royal title in ancient Near Eastern literature.[81] It also functions this way in the Hebrew Bible where people like David, Nebuchadnezzar, the ideal Davidic king, and the Branch are called "My servant."[82] If the Servant, who is depicted as a royal figure in the Servant Songs, is not the ideal Davidic king of Isaiah 11:1–16, then who is he?

Finally, Isaiah's portrait of the Suffering Servant bears striking similarities to Zechariah's later picture of the Suffering Shepherd (Zech. 11:4–17; 13:7; cf. 12:10). According to Zechariah 11:4–17, the people would wrongly reject the Good Shepherd, leading to his execution in 13:7–9. However, Zechariah 13:7 pictures the unjust death of the Good Shepherd as a pivotal event in God's redemptive plan for Israel. Like the Good Shepherd of Zechariah, the Suffering Servant would be rejected by his people but play a key role in God's plan of deliverance. So even if it was initially unclear that the Suffering Servant in Isaiah 53 would be an individual suffering on behalf of the nation Israel, this is clearer by the time we get to Zechariah's portrait of the unjust suffering and death of the Good Shepherd. All of this points to a figure in the Servant who should be tied to the king. The royal Servant would suffer death first, then be exalted.

CONCLUSION

The contribution of Isaiah to the progressive revelation of the Messiah cannot be overestimated. Like Nathan (2 Sam. 7:8-16), he spoke of an unending Davidic kingdom; like Amos, Hosea, and Micah, he spoke of a new David to come. However, Isaiah's portrait of this future ideal Davidic king ruling over an everlasting kingdom transcended previous conceptions. The visions of 11:1–9 and 11:10–16 placed his reign in the eschatological future. The oracle in 9:1–6, celebrating his birth and enthronement, portrayed him as God's representative in terms that far exceeded ancient Near Eastern conventional language.

---

80. Mark A. Christian, "The Servants in the Songs," *STRev* 49 (2006): 365–76.
81. The Akkadian term "servant" is a royal title: M.-J. Seux, *Epithetes Royales Akkadiennes et Sumeriennes. Ouvrage publie avec le concours du Centre National de la Recherche Scientifique* (Paris: Letouzey et Ane, 1967), 360–63.
82. "My servant David" (2 Sam. 3:18; 7:5, 8; 1 Kings 11:13, 32, 34, 36, 38; 14:8; 2 Kings 19:34; 20:6; Isa. 37:35; Jer. 33:21, 22, 26; Ps. 89:3, 20; 1 Chron. 17:4, 7;); "My servant Nebuchadnezzar" (Jer. 25:9; 27:6; 43:10). Cf. also the messianic titles, "My servant David" (Ezek. 34:23–24; 37:24–25), "My servant the Branch" (Zech. 3:8).

Isaiah also spoke of the Suffering Servant as an individual who must be distinguished from the collective designations of the nation, plural references to the prophets, and singular references to various individuals such as Isaiah himself. The Servant would play the key role in God's program of redemption of Israel as well as all other nations, functioning as the mediator of the new covenant. Yet his pivotal place in God's purposes would not be understood by the nation. Isaiah predicted that he would be rejected, his life placed in jeopardy and perhaps even dying before God would rescue him from the grave and reward him. Being exalted by God, he would be elevated over all earthly kings. It is here that his royal position becomes most clear, providing strong links to Isaiah's other oracles of the ideal Davidic king.

Thus, when both sets of prophecies are read together, we have the ideal Servant who suffers first and then is exalted by God to universal prominence over all earthly kings. His surprising royal position fits nicely with Isaiah's other portraits of the ideal Davidic king who as the earthly representative of God reigns over an everlasting kingdom. The prophets Jeremiah, Ezekiel, Daniel, and Zechariah will continue to develop God's revelation of this ideal figure to come.

CHAPTER SIX

MESSIANIC TRAJECTORIES IN JEREMIAH, EZEKIEL, AND DANIEL

In a seeming, surprising challenge to God's promise of an enduring dynasty (2 Sam. 7:10–16), the events of 605–586 BCE saw the destruction of Jerusalem, razing of the temple and carrying away of the last surviving Davidic ruler into exile. Yet Yahweh had warned repeatedly that the privilege of promise to David had its responsibilities, ones that involved obedience to God.[1] What did the destruction of Zion and dismantling of the royal throne mean for the future of David's dynasty? Confronted by these historical realities, three prophets—Jeremiah, Ezekiel, Daniel—revealed that judgment was not God's last word since God had made an irrevocable promise to David. The promise would stand. Each foresaw a coming day when Yahweh would deliver his people and restore the kingdom through a divinely chosen servant. Yet since they each offer a different piece of the same puzzle, each envisioned a distinctive feature of the promise to come. While they share many features in common, we nevertheless find each makes his own contribution to future expectations.

MESSIANIC TRAJECTORIES IN JEREMIAH

The prophetic career of Jeremiah began in 627 BCE (the thirteenth year of Josiah's reign), continued through the fall of Jerusalem in 586 BCE (during

---

1. In Nathan's oracle, God promised to discipline David's son if he sinned (2 Sam. 7:14). Subsequent passages state that the uninterrupted continuation of the dynasty in any individual generation depended on obedience (1 Kings 2:3–4; 3:3, 14; 6:12; 8:25a, 26; 9:4-5a, 6–9; 11:4, 6, 33, 38; 14:8; 15:3, 11; 2 Kings 14:3; 16:2; 18:3; 2 Chron. 6:16; 7:17–18; 28:7; Ps. 132:12). Yet in spite of human sin, God would fulfill his irrevocable promise of an eternal throne upon which one of David's sons would always sit (2 Sam. 7:10–13, 15–16; 1 Kings 8:25b; 9:5b; Pss. 132:11; Jer. 33:17, 26).

Zedekiah's reign) and ended some time in the early exilic period.[2] Jeremiah had called Judah and Jerusalem to repent in the hope of avoiding judgment. When repentance was not forthcoming, God judged the nation by destroying the temple, dismantling the Davidic throne and sending the people into exile. Yet Jeremiah revealed that if the people would repent, God would restore the exiles to the land, the Levites to the altar, and the Davidic line to the throne.

Although Jeremiah clung to God's promise of an everlasting Davidic dynasty (33:14–26), he emphasized that survival of the house of David in any individual generation depended upon obedience (17:19–27; 22:1–23:4). With the exception of Josiah, the Davidic kings in his day were evil (1:18; 2:26; 15:4; 19:4, 13; 22:2–3, 13; 24:8; 32:32; 44:9, 17, 21). Jeremiah announced that God would remove the Davidites from the throne and send the dynasty into exile (4:9; 13:13, 18; 17:19–24; 19:3; 20:5; 21:7, 11–14; 22:6, 10–11, 13, 18, 24, 28–30; 25:18). Thus, none of the immediate descendants of Jehoiakim and Jehoiachin would occupy the throne (22:24–30; 36:30)

> **A Day of Devastation**
>
> In 586 BCE, Jerusalem was destroyed, the Temple razed, the final group of Judeans taken into Babylon exile, and the Davidic dynasty dismantled.
>
> From 605 BCE when Daniel was first deported to Babylon, to 597 BCE when Ezekiel and Jehoiachin were deported, to 586 BCE when the third and final deportation occurred, Jeremiah prophesied in Judah about God's punishment as well as God's restoration.

Nevertheless, Jeremiah revealed that God one day would restore David's dynasty. Although God would punish the wicked "shepherds" (kings) of Judah, whose evil had led to the scattering of his flock (Jer. 10:21; 23:1–2; 50:6), he would replace them with faithful leaders, once he regathered the exiles from Babylon (Jer. 3:15; 23:3–4). Like David, the ideal shepherd, they would have the heart and skill to watch over his flock: "I will give you shepherds who will be faithful to me" (3:15); "I will install shepherds over them who will care for them" (23:4). As the plural "shepherds" suggests, Jeremiah envisioned the restored leadership that included the return of a royal dynasty. He also predicted the coming of a new "David" (30:9, 21) and a "righteous branch for David" (23:5). Expressed in the singular, it is easy for us to see the messianic potential of this kind of language. Yet Jeremiah also associated the coming "branch" (23:5–6) with a collective image (33:14–26). He prophesied a restoration of the structure of the nation and called them to ethical righteousness and faithfulness. He did so appealing to the structures currently associated with the nation. Jeremiah (human author) called for the future ethical restoration of David's throne as a reversal of the

---

2. For a chronological placement of Jeremiah among the kings, deportations, and fall of Judah, see page 71.

Babylonian exile using the picture of a reconstitution of the preexilic social and political institutions, while God (divine author) used this backdrop to picture the eschatological Messiah he had in mind all along. We focus attention on Jeremiah 23:1–8 and 33:14–26, two parallel passages that best epitomize this messianic mystery.

Contextual Reading of Jeremiah 23:1–8

The prediction of the righteous branch to come in Jeremiah 23:1–8 can only be fully appreciated in the light of its literary context, where it concludes a series of oracles concerning the house of David (21:1—23:8). As the central section of the book of Jeremiah, this cycle of oracles laid main blame for the Babylonian disaster at the door of the royal house, but predicted its restoration following the exile through a righteous branch of David. The oracles are arranged symmetrically to contrast the imminent judgment and coming restoration of the Davidic throne.

> A God's Rejection of Unrighteous Zedekiah: Coming Exile of Jerusalem (21:1–10)
>> B God Demanded Righteousness from the Davidic Dynasty (21:11–22:7)
>> B' God Denounced Wickedness of Post-Josianic Davidic Kings (22:8–30)
> A' God's Provision of Righteous Branch: Coming Exodus from Babylon (23:1–8)

The opening oracle announced Jerusalem's exile and God's rejection of Zedekiah, who was unable to live up to his name, "Yahweh is my righteousness" (21:1–10). The closing oracle predicted the restoration of the Babylonian exiles and God's provision of a righteous branch, under whose rule Judah would go by the name, "Yahweh is our righteousness" (23:1–8). The middle oracles indicted the post-Josianic kings of failing to promote righteousness and justice (21:11–22:7) and announced judgment of each of these individual kings (22:8–30). Thus, 23:1–8 was a fitting conclusion to this cycle of oracles concerning the house of David, since it predicted a future second exodus that would reverse the imminent Babylonian exile, and also envisioned a coming righteous branch who would replace the current unrighteous Davidic kings.

Jeremiah 23:1–8 consists of four stanzas, which develop related themes. In verses 1–2, the prophet denounced the unrighteous "shepherds," that is, the post-Josianic kings of 21:1–22:30, who had brought about the scattering of God's flock. In verses 3–4, Jeremiah predicted God would regather his people from Babylonian exile and provide good "shepherds," whose competent leadership would prevent the flock from being scattered again (cf. Jer.

30:15). In verses 5–6, he envisioned the coming of a righteous "branch" for David, whose rule of moral righteousness and social justice would transform Judah/Jerusalem into a covenant-keeping community. In verses 7–8, Jeremiah depicted the future restoration of the exiles from Babylon as a second exodus, which would inaugurate this new age of deliverance and blessing.

The Good Shepherds and the Regathered Flock (23:1–4)
Jeremiah 23:1–8 concluded the cycle of 21:1–23:8 dealing with Davidic kingship. After indicting the four post-Josianic kings in 21:1–22:30, Jeremiah pronounced judgment on these wicked shepherds in 23:1–2. In 22:12, he denounced these kings as evil shepherds for failing to care for the sheep by upholding moral righteousness and social justice (21:11–22:7). Although he held them responsible for God's flock being scattered in exile (23:1–2), the prophet foresaw that God would restore the remnant of his flock from exile and provide competent shepherds to care for God's sheep by providing moral righteousness and social justice (23:3–4) (cf. Jer. 3:15).

Since the wicked "shepherds" in 23:1–2 referred to the last rulers of the house of David, the good "shepherds" in 23:3–4, by way of analogy, referred to godly Davidites or those allied to them. Jeremiah seemed to express a hope that the deliverance of a postexilic period Judah would be led by a restored Davidic dynasty. Jeremiah did not explicitly designate these Davidites as kings, but the term "shepherd" was a common royal metaphor in biblical and ancient Near Eastern texts. Jeremiah may have preferred the term "shepherds" over "kings" to reveal that the future leadership would represent a fundamental break from the exploitative tyranny of the wicked post-Josianic kings. It might also suggest that those associated with the king would share in the rule to come in a way that moved the focus beyond just the king. Transformation was necessary to ensure the coming shepherds would care for the nation by upholding righteousness and providing justice, the fundamental dynastic duty (21:11–22:7). The term also would have evoked the image of David, the ideal shepherd-king, who epitomized the moral standards his royal descendants were called to emulate (Ps. 78:70–72; Ezek. 34:23; 37:24).

The Righteous Branch and the Second Exodus (23:5–8)
In verses 5–6, Jeremiah envisioned the coming of a royal figure, upon whom he conferred the title, "righteous branch." This moniker was a conventional title in Northwest Semitic royal inscriptions designating the rightful heir to the throne: "legitimate scion." Seen in the context of Jeremiah 21:1–23:4, which indicted the four post-Josianic kings, this designation conveyed that he alone, unlike his unrighteous predecessors, would be the legitimate heir of David's throne. His rule would be divinely sanctioned since he would fulfill the dynastic duty by upholding moral righteousness and providing social

justice like Josiah. Thus, Jeremiah pictured him as a Josiah *redivivus*—not a bodily resurrected Josiah, but the moral embodiment of the last Davidic king to uphold the dynastic standard of promoting moral righteousness and social justice.

Many interpret the branch as exclusively prophetic of the Messiah who will reign forever in his own person over eschatological Jerusalem. Considered from an initial contextual perspective, however, the reign of the righteous branch is closely associated with Jeremiah's depiction of the coming age of restoration following the Babylonian exile. Just as the good shepherds would begin to care for God's flock once God would regather them from exile in Babylon (vv. 1–4), the reign of the branch over restored Jerusalem (vv. 5–6) would include a second exodus, in which God would return the exiles from "the land of the north," Jeremiah's stereotypical name for Babylon (vv. 7–8). The parallelism between the good shepherds (vv. 3–4) and the righteous branch (vv. 5–6), as well as the return from Babylonian exile (vv. 1–2) and the Second Exodus (vv. 7–8), is reinforced by the symmetrical arrangement of this oracle:

> A The Wicked Shepherds Had Scattered God's Flock into Babylonian Exile (vv. 1–2)
>> B The Good Shepherds Would Care for God's Flock Regathered from Exile (vv. 3–4)
>> B' The Righteous Branch Will Reign over Restored Judah/Jerusalem (vv. 5–6)
> A' The Lord Will Restore the Exiles in a Glorious Second Exodus (vv. 7–8)

The Lord Will Restore the Exiles in a Glorious Second Exodus (vv. 7–8)

The opening and closing stanzas create a reversal: God had scattered his flock in the Babylonian exile (vv. 1–2), but would restore his people in the second exodus (vv. 7–8). The two middle stanzas mirror images: just as God would provide good shepherds to lead his regathered flock (vv. 3–4), he would provide a righteous branch to rule restored Judah (vv. 5–6).

The shepherds of verses 3–4 and the branch of verses 5–6 are closely linked by the parallelism of the opening line in each stanza: "I will raise up (וַהֲקִמֹתִי) a righteous branch for David to rule over them" (v. 5), clearly echoes, "I will raise up (וַהֲקִמֹתִי) shepherds over them to care for them" (v. 4). Yet while it is clear that the two are closely associated, the precise relationship between the plurality of the shepherds and singularity of the branch is ambivalent. Should we understand the branch in terms of a single individual—the eschatological Messiah—or as a collective for a restored Davidic dynasty equated with the good shepherds of verses 3–4? Or should we see one as encased in the other as it points to a more comprehensive deliverance?

What is key is that the identity of the branch in Jeremiah 23:5–6 is singular. Later in Jeremiah 33:14-26, Jeremiah pictures all this in simple restoration terms using the picture of the past regal and priestly structures that saw a line of kings to make the point. On the one hand, the line has the potential to be restored and therefore is called, when it returns, to be faithful. In the end, God's promise will be realized in one who would obey God and bring comprehensive deliverance. What the past line failed to do, the one to come would do. Jeremiah 33 ends with a warning about disobedience, but Jeremiah 31 had said the promise of a new era and deliverance would come to pass, being more sure than creation. The combination leads to a both-and reading of these texts, as well as to some development in how the wording comes to realization.

Inner-Biblical Interpretation in Jeremiah 33:14–26

While there is uncertainty about the identity of the branch in 23:5–6, Jeremiah 33:14–26 helps us see the complex relation between the promises. At first blush, Jeremiah 33:14–16 seems to restate 23:5–6, but on closer inspection this later passage develops the earlier oracle. Jeremiah 33:14–26 provides a picture for a key element of the meaning of the earlier oracle, the return of David's house with a call to be faithful this time around.

Jeremiah 33:14–26 unfolds in four steps. In 33:14–16, Jeremiah reaffirmed that Yahweh would fulfill his earlier promise in 23:5–6, expounding the original wording to clarify the way this could be fulfilled in the postexilic community after the return from Babylonian exile. For example, the original promise, "I will raise up a righteous branch" (23:5), which primarily carries a royal connotation, is reworded, "I will sprout up a branch of righteousness" (33:15), which adds a moral connotation, but without eliminating the original royal sense. In 33:17–18, Jeremiah explained this branch of righteousness would sprout up through a Davidic heir once again sitting on the throne and a Levitical descendant ministering in the temple. Since Jeremiah envisioned the possible full restoration of Jerusalem/Judah, this would demand reinstatement of the royal as well as priestly institutions, both of which should now promote the aforementioned righteousness. In 33:19–22, the prophet reaffirmed that God would fulfill his covenant promises by restoring the Davidic dynasty and a faithful priesthood by multiplying the descendants of David and Levi like the stars of the sky and sand of the seashore. In verses 23–24, Jeremiah refuted the popular misconception in his day that the Babylonian exile represented God's final rejection of the house of Israel and the house of Judah, since he would restore the house of David and the house of Levi. In spite of exilic evidence to the contrary, Jeremiah asserted that God would restore the house of Levi to the altar and the house of David to the throne.

Jeremiah 33:14–26 not only drew on 23:5–6, but on God's covenant promises to David and Abraham. The assertion, "David will never lack a successor on the throne of Israel" (Jer. 33:17), alluded to God's promise to David, "You will never lack a successor on the throne of Israel—if your sons watch their way by obeying Me" (1 Kings 2:4; 8:25; 9:4–5; 2 Chron. 6:16). The reassurance, "Just as I keep my covenant with day and night—that day and night always come at their appointed time—I will keep my covenant with my servant David that he always have a descendant on his throne" (Jer. 33:20–21), alluded to God's vow, "I have sworn by my holiness, I will not lie to David: his dynasty will endure forever, his throne as long as the sun before Me; like the moon it will remain forever, it will stand firm as long as the skies endure" (Ps. 89:35–37). The divine affirmation, "I will multiply the descendants of David like the stars in the sky that cannot be counted and the sand on the seashore that cannot be numbered" (Jer. 33:22), drew on the wording of God's oath to Abraham, "I will multiply your descendants like the stars in the sky and the sand on the seashore" (Gen. 13:16; 15:5; 22:17; 26:4; Exod. 32:13).

By alluding to God's promises to multiply Abraham's descendants like the stars and to perpetuate David's dynasty as long as day and night endure, Jeremiah 33:14–26 clearly discussed the promise of a branch for David in 23:5–6 in terms of the old, existing institutions, while not removing the presence of resolution in an individual king who was all the line hoped for. He also alluded to the promise already given in Jeremiah 31 of what the assured final deliverance would look like. The prophet foresaw a Davidic restoration that ultimately brings peace, righteousness, and deliverance, but there are steps in this process and periods of activity in view. Both the promise and the warning play key roles here in getting to the resolution of the prophecy.

Canonical Reading of Jeremiah 23:5–6 and 33:14–26

Many assume Jeremiah 23:5–6 was exclusively prophetic of the eschatological Messiah. Yet Jeremiah 33:14–26 makes an ethical call that uses the failed picture of the past to point to the future. He called for an ethical restoration of the Davidic dynasty to reign over restored Israel. In the end, one would be found: "the righteous branch." Jeremiah also warned of the consequences should those called kings not be godly. Judgment would come, but not at the ultimate expense of the promise to give deliverance through the Davidic line. In that contrastive culmination and choice is found the realization in Messiah Jesus who would meet the standard of righteousness.

Hermeneutics of Fulfillment

In partial fulfillment of Jeremiah 33:14–26, the Levitical priesthood was reinstated in the postexilic period, while the Davidic dynasty did not reappear on the throne. According to critical scholars, the non-fulfillment of the royal aspect of this oracle meant Jeremiah was nothing more than a wishful thinker. However, Jeremiah himself had warned that the dynasty's future involved repentance (Jer. 17:25; 22:2, 4). To be sure, he grounded his prediction of dynastic restoration in God's promise, "David will never lack a successor on the throne of Israel" (Jer. 33:17). Yet the original promise was a divinely granted privilege, which had responsibilities—"if your descendants watch their way by obeying me" (1 Kings 2:4; 8:25; 9:4–5; 2 Chron. 6:16). We may assume the ultimate restoration Jeremiah predicted looked to the hope of a righteous king, who, in fact, was lacking at that time. This is confirmed by the fact that the postexilic Zechariah declared the house of David would not be restored to its former position of prominence until it repented (Zech. 12:2—13:1).

We must also recognize that Jeremiah had only one piece of the puzzle. Since he had been an advisor to the last Davidic kings and knew of God's commitment to the Davidic line, it was only natural for him to have conceived for the future restoration of the Davidic throne in the light of a restored Davidic dynasty. As the rest of the Bible reveals, God would indeed restore David's throne, but through a single ideal Davidic king, Messiah Jesus. Moreover, God would extend his covenant promise to David to all believing descendants of Abraham (Jer. 33:22, 26; cf. Isa. 55:3), making them associates to the Davidic king like the stars in the sky.

Eschatological Interpretation and Messianic Potential

With the delay in the coming of the royal branch, Jeremiah 23:5–6 eventually came to be appropriately interpreted in the eschatological sense that Jeremiah had given it in terms of expressing comprehensive righteousness, awaiting its full realization in a singular righteous branch, Messiah Jesus. When read from a canonical perspective in the light of the postexilic realities, Jeremiah 23:5–6 came to be interpreted—and legitimately so—as prophetic of the eschatological Messiah. In fact, the exegetical thrust of the singular, "righteous branch," though pictured by Jeremiah 33:14–26 to permit the inclusion over time of a collective sense in light of the institution of the past, nevertheless culminated in a singular messianic potential. This kind of messianic realization represents a culminating significance, focusing the referent in light of the prophecy's language. It also fits within the continuity of the generic meaning of the original prophecy, by narrowing the focus from the line to the one in it who met the requirements of the promise. By doing so, it actually fulfills the ultimate intention of Yahweh to provide a righteous throne over restored Jerusalem/Judah.

Whereas Jeremiah 33:14–26 appeals to the ancient tradition of a dynasty, Jeremiah 23:5–6 is an example of the hermeneutical focusing of prophecy in ultimately pointing to a figure, which laid the foundation for the development of an eschatological Messiah. Having just one piece of the puzzle, Jeremiah foresaw the indescribable glories of the coming age of the new covenant through the lens of the structures of God's ancient covenants to David and Levi. Ezekiel will contribute yet another piece to our messianic puzzle.

MESSIANIC TRAJECTORIES IN EZEKIEL

Ezekiel, a Levitical priest, was carried away to Babylonia in 597 BCE, when the Babylonian king Nebuchadnezzar sent king Jehoiachin into exile.[3] Better known for his apocalyptic vision of the restoration of the temple in chapters 40–48, this cultic prophet had much to say about the future of the royal dynasty.[4] Ezekiel's approach to Davidic kingship is developed in three sets of passages.[5] The first set, dating from the late preexilic era prior to Jerusalem's fall, consisted of oracles of doom against the current occupants of David's throne (17:1–21; 19:1–9, 10–14; 21:25–27 [30–32]).[6] The second set, dating from the early exile after the dynasty was removed from the throne, consisted of oracles of hope for the dynasty (17:22–24; 29:21), epitomized by a coming David, who would shepherd God's flock regathered from exile and rule as prince over restored Judah/Israel (34:23–24; 37:24–25). The third set, dating from the latter part of the exile, consisted of apocalyptic visions of a prince and his future successors, who would primarily play a sacral role as patron and sponsor of the new temple, administering social justice and reversing the royal dynasty's past exploitation of the people (44:1–3; 45:7–9,

---

3. Although the biblical record mentions only Jehoiachin's deportation and subsequent release (*Captivity:* Jer. 22:24–30; 2 Kings 24:8-14; 2 Chron. 36:9–10; *Release:* Jer. 52:31–34; 2 Kings 25:27–30), Ezekiel's captivity in 597 BCE is mentioned in Josephus (*Ant* 10.6.3 § 98). For corresponding Mesopotamian Chronicles see *ANET* 203, fig 58; or Jean-Jacques Glassner, *Mesopotamian Chronicles*, Writings from the Ancient World (Atlanta: SBL, 2004), 229.

4. Scholars understand Ezekiel's royal/messianic expectations in three different ways. For example, Antti Laato, *Josiah and David Redivivus: The Historical Josiah and the Messianic Expectations of Exilic and Postexilic Times,* CBOT 33 (Stockholm: Almqvist & Wiksell, 1992), 154–64, represents a explicit direct prophetic approach that suggests Ezekiel envisioned the future eschatological Messiah ruling over a universal kingdom. J. J. M. Roberts, "The Old Testament Contribution to Messianic Expectations," in *The Messiah: Developments in Earliest Judaism and Christianity* (ed. James H. Charlesworth; Minneapolis: Fortress Press, 1992), 39-51, represents an approach that suggests Ezekiel envisioned only a restored Davidic dynasty, not the eschatological Messiah. Daniel I. Block, "Bringing Back David: Ezekiel's Messianic Hope," in *The Lord's Anointed: Interpretation of Old Testament Messianic Texts* (ed. Philip Satterthwaite, Richard Hess, and Gordon Wenham; Grand Rapids: Baker, 1995), 167–88, represents a mediating approach that suggests Ezekiel's oracles/visions ultimately find their fulfillment in the eschatological Messiah, but the prophet himself envisioned the future new covenant realities in terms of old covenant categories and therefore spoke in terms of a future restored Davidic dynasty.

5. Griphus Gakuru, *An Inner-Biblical Exegetical Study of the Davidic Covenant and the Dynastic Oracle*, Mellen Biblical Press Series vol. 58 (Lewiston, NY: Edwin Mellen Press, 2000), 195–205.

6. Panc C. Beentjes, "What a Lioness Was Your Mother: Reflections on Ezekiel 19," in *On Reading Prophetic Texts* (Leiden: Brill, 1996), 21–35; W. L. Moran, "Gen. 49,10 and Its Use in Ez 21,32," *Bib* 39 (1958): 405–25; Michael Fishbane, *Biblical Interpretation in Ancient Israel* (Oxford: Clarendon Press, 1985), 502.

16–25; 46:1–24; 48:21–22). We will focus on Ezekiel's oracles of the coming Davidic shepherd (34:22–24; 37:24–25) and his eschatological visions of the sacral Davidic prince (chs. 44–48).

Ezekiel 34:22–24 and 37:24–25

Ezekiel delivered two parallel predictions in 34:22–24 and 37:24–25, which both envision a new David, who would shepherd God's flock in the spirit of the dynasty's illustrious founder.[7] Both prophecies appear in longer oracles, which present common themes that unfold in the same order: Yahweh would restore the exiles to the land (34:1–10; 37:1–14); reunite Israel and Judah (34:11–12; 37:15–23); provide a Davidic prince to shepherd the once scattered flock (34:22–24; 37:24–25); and inaugurate a new covenant relationship with the new Israel (34:25–31; 37:26–28).

God's provision of the coming shepherd (34:23–24) is associated with his regathering of his flock, which was scattered among the nations in the Babylonian exile (34:11–22).[8] God would restore the repentant sheep of his flock to the mountains of Israel (34:11–13a) where they no longer would be prey of the foreign nations (34:22, 25–28), but would graze on lush pasture (34:13b–15). Once restored to their pasture in the land of Israel, the divine Shepherd would feed his sheep (34:13–16), an apt image for covenant blessings (34:25–31). The human agent through whom God would feed his sheep would be this Davidic prince (34:23–24). Ezekiel focused on the hoped-for figure as one who undershepherds the restored flock.

> **The Promise of a New Covenant**
>
> The prophets Jeremiah and Ezekiel predicted that God one day would inaugurate a new covenant with the House of Israel and the House of Judah. Jeremiah predicted God would write his Torah on the heart of his people through the new covenant (Jer. 31:31–34). Similarly, Ezekiel revealed that God would give his people a new heart through the new covenant (Ezek. 34:25–31; 37:26–28).

Ezekiel 34:11–12 and 37:15–23 envisioned reunification of Israel/Judah. Languishing in Babylonia, the prophet pictured the restoration of the nation when God would return the exiles to the land (37:21–22). Although the nation's division was caused by political problems, the two kingdoms remained separate due to spiritual separation. The Lord would ensure future unity by centering the people on the worship of Yahweh in a new covenant relationship (Ezek. 37:23). He would also reverse the antagonism between Israel and Judah

---

7. See Block, "Bringing Back David," 167–88; Daniel I. Block, *The Book of Ezekiel, Chapters 25-48*, NICOT (Grand Rapids: Eerdmans, 1998), 297–301; Robert B. Chisholm Jr., *Handbook on the Prophets* (Grand Rapids: Baker, 2002), 277–78; Leslie C. Allen, *Ezekiel 20–48*, WBC 29 (Word: Dallas, 1990), 158-63

8. W. H. Brownless, "Ezekiel's Poetic Indictment of the Shepherds," *HTR* 51 (1958):191-203.

by restoring a single king as a symbol of their new social unity (Ezek. 37:22, 24). The designation, David, portrays him as a David *redivivus*—not the resurrected son of Jesse, but the moral embodiment of the founder of the united kingdom (2 Sam. 5:1–5; 1 Kings 3:28).[9] Other texts also invoke this image, some using Josiah, showing it is not to be taken in the most literal sense.

Canonical Reading of Ezekiel 34:22–24 and 37:24–25

Although the return of the exiles in 538 BCE under Zerubbabel the Davidite was surely an act of God, this event certainly did not fulfill the full expectations of a glorious second exodus. Subsequent revelation would make it clear that the second exodus would be fulfilled in God's eschatological deliverance of his people through the agency of the Messiah. Thus, the restoration of the exiles under Zerubbabel the Davidite did not fulfill Ezekiel's prophecies of the second exodus and the coming ideal Davidic shepherd. Rather, the historical return of Zerubbabel and others merely pointed to a greater reality yet to come. When read in the light of the First Testament canon as a whole and viewed in the light of the historical realities of the postexilic period, the Christian can see the full messianic potential of Ezekiel's prophecies. As Bateman will show in part 2, the Jewish literature of the second temple period interpreted Ezekiel's image of the coming ideal Davidic shepherd in terms of the eschatological Messiah. Likewise, Bock will show in part 3 that the Second Testament proclaimed that Ezekiel's prophecies find fulfillment in Jesus the ideal Good Shepherd.

Contextual Reading of Ezekiel 44–48

Better known for its vision of the glorious eschatological new temple, Ezekiel 44–48 makes an important contribution to future Davidic expectations. While Ezekiel predicted a new David, who would shepherd God's regathered flock as prince over them (34:22–24; 37:24–25), he also envisioned a future prince who would function in a sacral role as the official patron sponsor of the new temple (44:1–3; 45:7–9, 16–25; 46:1–24; 48:21–22). While the prophet portrayed the new David of chapters 34 and 37 in traditional royal terms (ruling as king over Israel), he also envisioned this royal David as a cultic figure in chapters 44–48. Although these two sets of texts seemingly describe two distinct future expectations, both images would be brought together and unified in an unexpected way in the climatic revelation of Messiah Jesus.

Sacral Role of the Prince

In the preexilic period, the Davidic ruler as priest-king played an administrative role in organizing and financing the temple worship as its official sponsor

---

9. Allen, *Ezekiel 20–48*, 27–28, views this "David" not as the resurrected founder of the dynasty, nor of the eschatological Messiah, but as a moniker for a future Davidic heir who would restore the royal dynasty in the future era (postexilic period) as a David *redivivus*.

and patron (cf. Ps. 110:4). Ezekiel portrayed the eschatological prince in a similar way, but with an expanded role. To be sure, the Zadokite priests would continue to execute the daily ministrations at the altar with the high priest serving as the presiding official (43:22–24). Nevertheless, the prince would play an important role in cultic worship as its official sponsor and patron (45:22–25; 46:4–7, 13–15).[10] From the generous tract of land allotted to him, on which to graze animals and raise grain and olive trees, he would supply the animal and grain sacrifices to the temple to be offered on behalf of the people (45:16–17). Thus, he would be responsible to provide the burnt offering each Sabbath (46:4), but also to present the various offerings the people would bring (46:13–15).[11]

The traditional role of the preexilic king had been predominantly political and military, administering the affairs of state and leading the army into battle (Ps. 110:1–3, 5–7). This future prince, on the other hand, was also a cultic figure. While his earlier oracles of the new David explicitly presented him as "king" (Ezek. 37:22, 24), this term does not appear in these later visions. The eschatological prince in Ezekiel 44–48 is not identified as king. The avoidance of this term may have been intended to shift attention from the predominantly political and military role of the king in the preexilic period, effectively distancing him from his evil predecessors who sullied the reputation of Davidic kingship. As Ezekiel saw it, the future David primarily would operate in a cultic community of worship.[12]

Ezekiel 44–48 presents a fresh angle on the traditional royal expectations of the house of David. Ezekiel added a new focus moving from its main role of wielding political and military power to promoting worship of God.[13] We must not misconstrue this as anti-monarchic, but as a fresh revelatory development building from preexilic concepts of the monarchy.[14] This metamorphosis suggests an additional element in the role of leadership in the new

---

10. Block, *Ezekiel,* 679–80, notes, "As patron of the cult, the prince enjoys a privileged position, but he stands in the shadow of the priesthood, barred from the inner court and subject to clearly defined restrictions."

11. Block, *Ezekiel,* 659–60.

12. Gakuru, §6.3.1.3; Jon Levenson, *Theology of the Program of Restoration of Ezekiel 40–48,* Harvard Semitic Monographs 10 (Missoula: Scholars Press, 1976), 64, 75–101

13. Gakuru §6.3.1.3, notes: "For Ezekiel, it is when the people desist from political intrigue and war, and when the king and princes desist from abusing power and the cult that the nation performs its cultic duty as originally intended and discovers the true meaning and purpose of its calling. For Ezekiel, such is the ideal nation which Yahweh had intended for himself and from which he will never depart when he returns. The Davidic covenant was never . . . intended to create kings who were what they turned out to be. Rather, it was intended to make the worship of Yahweh stable, orderly and pure ..."

14. Walther Zimmerli, *Ezekiel* (Philadelphia: Westminster Press, 1983), 492.

covenant community. The chief duty of its leader was to seek to exalt God in worship and rule.[15]

Identity of the Prince

One of the enigmas in the book of Ezekiel is whether the Davidic prince of 34:22–24 and 37:25–26 should be identified with the sacral prince of chapters 44–48.[16] On the one hand, the repeated title "the prince" links him with the Davidic prince in chapters 34 and 37.[17] Since this title seems reminiscent of the formula, "my servant David will be prince" (34:24; 37:25), many identify the prince of chapters 44–48 with the Davidic shepherd in chapters 34 and 37. Although the text does not explicitly make this link, it is not only possible but quite likely.

Ezekiel 44–48 provides clues hinting at his Davidic ancestry. First, speaking proleptically, the prophet forewarned the prince and his future heirs to stop confiscating the land of the commoners, as their evil ancestors had done (45:8–9; 46:18).[18] This is a patent allusion to the wicked tendency of the royal dynasty to exploit the people in the preexilic period (Jer. 21:12; 22:3, 13–17; Ezek. 7:27; Mic. 3:1, 9). The point is important. It shows Ezekiel calling for a new era of righteousness, an ethical call for leadership to be moral. This is seen in the first words of the explanation of the vision (Ezek. 43:8–12). It is a full call to repentance and a morality that reaffirms God's standard for the future. Second, the prince would be responsible to ensure the land of the commoners not be illegally confiscated by the powerful rich (45:18; 48:22–24), to promote social justice and moral righteousness (45:9),

---

15. Block, *Ezekiel*, 670–77.
16. Levenson, *Theology of the Program of Restoration*, 57–73; Block, "Bringing Back David," 167–88; Chisholm, *Handbook on the Prophets*, 284.
17. The term "prince" (נָשִׂיא) appears nineteen times in Ezekiel: 44:3; 45:7–9, 16–17, 22; 46:2, 4, 8, 10, 12, 16–18; 48:21–22 (cp. with 34:24 and 37:25).
18. Block, *Ezekiel*, 654–55, writes: "The abrupt change from statistical legislation to accusation and exhortation here catches the reader by surprise. Yahweh opens by announcing an end to oppressive rule by the princes of Israel. The plural form *nesi'im* proves he is thinking not of the *nasi'* of the future, but of the haunting figures of kings of the past . . . they were guilty of confiscation of commoners' real estate (cf. 46:18) . . . In his vision of the future, however, Ezekiel consistently looks forward to righting all past wrongs. Here he declares that instead of confiscating the property of subjects, rulers are to protect the rights of all Israelites to their tribal allotments. The firmness of Yahweh's resolve to right past wrongs is reflected in v. 9. Yahweh was exasperated with the rulers of the past . . . Ezekiel's new order promises no utopia: the potential for exploitative rule still exists. In v. 9, Yahweh appeals to the [future?] princes directly, in the second person, to stop their abusive behavior, specified as violence, oppression, and expulsion of the people from their land. He calls for a new commitment to justice and righteousness, viz., the maintenance of Yahweh's covenant standards, especially the protection of the rights of the weak. To the cultic offenses of 44:6 have been added these mortal sins. Yahweh has had enough of both."

and to establish fair financial dealings (45:10–12). Of course, promotion of social justice and moral righteousness was the fundamental duty of the royal dynasty.[19] Moreover, the prophets repeatedly depict the ideal Davidic king to come as promoting righteousness and justice (Isa. 9:7; 16:5; 32:1; Jer. 23:5; 33:15). Third, the role of the prince as patron and sponsor of the new temple is consistent with Davidic kingship. Just as he would present offerings on behalf of the people on designated days of worship (46:4, 13–15), David and Solomon functioned as sacral kings, presenting sacrifices on behalf of Israel on important occasions (2 Sam. 6:13–14; 1 Kings 8:5).[20] Consequently, we may tentatively associate the Davidic prince of Ezekiel 34:24 and 37:25 with the sacral prince of chapters 44–48.[21] The prophet avoided any explicit reference to his royal status to emphasize his sacral role in this section (46:12–25). All mention of his Davidic lineage is suppressed in this concluding material to highlight fresh dimensions that would occur in the future within the new temple, priesthood, lay people, and even the dynasty of David.

Was Ezekiel 44–48 Exclusive Direct Prophecy of the Eschatological Messiah?

Many see the prince in Ezekiel 44–48 as exclusively prophetic of the eschatological Messiah. According to a popular approach, Ezekiel provided an architectural blueprint for the construction of the future millennial temple, whose cultic worship will be directed by the glorified Messiah, who himself will offer regular animal sacrifices in memorial of his once-for-all atoning sacrifice. Despite the widespread acceptance of this view, it is beset with obstacles, although there is a key element of truth in it. This reading needs some nuancing so the near term ethical call of the prophet is appreciated even as a fulfillment in the end is entailed.

An example of an insuperable difficulty in identifying the prince as exclusively prophetic of the Messiah is that he would not be impeccable—so full of perfection to be incapable of sin—but peccable—prone to sin as any mortal.[22] The prince would be required to provide a sin offering "on behalf of himself and all the people" (45:22), like the equally peccable Levitical high priests (Lev. 16:6, 11, 17, 24). Furthermore, Ezekiel forewarned the prince, whoever might occupy that office, to not confiscate lands assigned to the Israelite tribes, as had been the practice of their preexilic predecessors (45:9–12; 46:18). The temptation to exploit the poor apparently would be so great that Ezekiel foresaw God granting a generous land allotment to the prince as a safeguard to inhibit the prince and his dynasty from succumbing to his

---

19. Psalms 72:1–2; 89:14; 99:4; 122:5; 2 Samuel 8:15//1 Chronicles 18:14; 1 Kings 10:9//2 Chronicles 9:8; Jeremiah 22:3, 15. See Moshe Weinfeld, *Social Justice in Ancient Israel and in the Ancient Near East* (Minneapolis: Fortress Press, 1995), 55–56.
20. Chisholm, *Handbook on the Prophets*, 284.
21. Levenson, *Theology of the Program of Restoration*, 75–101.
22. Duguid, *Ezekiel and the Leaders of Israel*, 130.

hereditary inclination (45:7–8).[23] Sin also would continue to be a problem for the people as a whole. Otherwise, there would be no need for continual presentation of sin offerings, guilt offerings and burnt offerings "to make atonement" for sin (43:20, 26; 45:15, 17, 20).

Ezekiel framed the figure to come in human terms with potential to do well or poorly at points. The language is open going in two directions in a choice between good and evil. It set the standard of righteousness that a king was to meet as expressed in the ethical exhortation. It was framed to describe the ideals of kingship and the call to make right choices as opposed to being only an exclusively framed prediction. As such, it is an open-ended description, the ideals of which Jesus met as he took on the sacral role of kingship in terms of cult.

Therefore, Ezekiel's vision of the sacral prince represents a fresh stage in future royal expectations. On the one hand, his portrait of the coming prince constitutes a dramatic example of the progress of revelation from an emphasis on the traditional conceptions of a royal dynasty whose primary function had been political to this additional highlighting of a sacral dynasty whose role also would be priestly. On the other hand, Ezekiel did not yet focus on an immortal eschatological Messiah who would mediate the worship of God for all eternity in his own person.[24] He presented the Messiah in human terms, as a potentially faithful representative of a habitually sinful people who makes good choices in the face of options. Since God had given him only one piece of the puzzle, Ezekiel prophesied "in part" (1 Cor. 13:12). The full picture of the identity of this coming One would be revealed only by the bodily resurrection and heavenly ascension of Messiah Jesus.

Canonical Reading of Ezekiel 44–48

Perhaps the main hermeneutical challenge of Ezekiel 44–48 is the fact that the prophet envisioned the glorious temple and sacral prince as essential

---

23. Block, *Ezekiel*, 679–80, writes, "The realism of this portrait is remarkable . . . like the rulers of Israel in the past, he is vulnerable to temptations of self-aggrandizement and ever in danger of exploiting his office at the expense of his subjects."

24. Joachim Becker, *Messianic Expectations in the Old Testament* (Philadelphia: Fortress Press, 1980), 62–63, writes: "Undoubtedly, the Book of Ezekiel enshrines a monarchic expectation, but it must not be understood in a messianic sense . . . One should have no illusions about the status accorded the king in the book's expectations: he stands in the shadow of the theocracy and the privileged priesthood. His saving function is hardly recognizable . . . In Ezekiel 43–46 and 48, the king is a supernumerary of the hierocracy, subject to detailed regulation. He is mentioned without any messianic splendor, more for the sake of completeness. The fuller preexilic functions of the kingship are thoroughly dismantled. Several princes are mentioned in 45:8–9, and according to 46:16–18 the prince has sons and heirs. The monarchy is thus conceived in dynastic terms; despite the fantasy of the program in Ezekiel 40–48, it keeps its feet solidly on the ground."

elements of the coming age, whose inauguration he pictured as following the return of the exiles from Babylon. According to critical scholars, the failure of these visions to materialize immediately suggests Ezekiel was nothing more than a hopeful visionary. Yet the most casual reading of Ezekiel 40–48 reveals the suprahistorical nature of its genre, demanding a more sophisticated understanding.

Ezekiel's vision of the sacrifices at the temple in chapters 40–48 suggests fulfillment of his vision would transcend the culturally conditioned structures of the time. Details of how marvelous this period will be points to the transcendent nature of the hope, something most interpreters recognize in their discussion leading into debate about how the details work, a topic that is beyond the scope of this book.

Thus, we conclude that Ezekiel's predictions of the coming Davidic shepherd and sacral prince were contextualized on the model of the past. The coregent of God's rule in the preexilic period was embodied by the hereditary Davidic king, who played a sacral role (Ps. 110:4; Jer. 30:21). It was only natural for Ezekiel to anticipate the reinstitution of the line in the age to come (Ezek. 45:8; 46:16–18). His piece of the puzzle was the sacral dimension of the rule to come. Whereas Jeremiah laid the foundation for the future development of the indescribable glories of the eschatological Messiah, Ezekiel provided the sacral dimension of the Messiah's rule yet to come. Both built upon and expanded God's initial promise to David. Daniel will add yet another piece to our messianic puzzle.

MESSIANIC TRAJECTORIES IN DANIEL

Daniel's prophetic career began in 605 BCE, when Nebuchadnezzar deported him to Babylon. It ended in 536 BCE, the third year of Cyrus king of Persia (Dan. 10:1). The book of Daniel falls into two sections: (1) Diaspora narratives told in the third person (chs. 1–6), and (2) apocalyptic revelations recounted in the first person (chs. 7–12). Chapters 1–6 focus on the beginning of Gentile rule during the Babylonian and Persian periods, while chapters 7–12 focus on the end of Gentile rule at the close of the Greek period, culminating with the seven years of trouble and the eventual deliverance of God's faithful ones. In chapter 7, Daniel recounts a revelatory vision in which he saw a mysterious heavenly figure identified as "one like a son of man" (7:13–14).

Contextual Reading of Daniel 7:13–14

In chapter 7, Daniel received a revelatory dream featuring four beasts, which emerge from the chaotic sea (7:2–7), representing four Gentile empires (7:17). The dream highlights the fourth beast which had ten horns (7:7, 19), out of which a little horn with an arrogant mouth grew up (7:8, 20). This little horn would attack Israel/Jerusalem (7:21), then persecute the Jewish faithful for three and one-half years, but would be destroyed by God in judgment (7:11, 26–27). Then, the kingdom would be given to a mysterious heavenly figure, the "one like a son of man" (7:13–14), as well as to "the people of the holy ones of the Most High" (7:27).

One of the most enigmatic figures in the Hebrew Bible is the "one like a son of man," who is heavenly in origin and behavior (riding on clouds), but human in appearance.[25] In the climatic scene of Daniel's second apocalyptic vision (7:1–27), this mysterious character appears on the scene riding on the clouds, approaches the throne of the Ancient of Days, to whom he is escorted by an angel (7:13), then is given the eternal kingdom to rule over all earthly nations (7:14). Since the description of this heavenly figure is so brief, his identity is debated. Daniel was only told that he is associated with "the holy ones of the Most High" (v. 18), who are associated with "the people of the holy ones of the Most High" (v. 27).[26] From clues elsewhere, the former represent the angelic host (8:8), the latter the remnant of Israel (8:24).

When read by some from a purely historical/contextual perspective, this heavenly figure seems to be identified as an angel, either the angelic patron of Israel or representative of the angelic host. His transcendent heavenly portrait has veiled the identity of the figure, at least on a purely contextual exegetical level. Elsewhere in the book, the expression "one who looked like a man" refers to the "man" Gabriel (Dan. 8:15; 10:16), who is clearly an angel (9:21; cf. 10:5; 12:6). In chapter 7, the "one like a son of man" (7:13–14) is explicitly

---

25. The expression "son of man" consistently refers to a human as an individual or representative of humanity (e.g., Ps. 8:4; Job 16:21). As an individual in the created order, "man" is often the counterpart to "God," e.g., "You are a man and not God" (Ezek. 28:2; cf. Isa. 31:3.) In Daniel, singular "son of man" refers to a human: "O son of man" = "O human" (MT 8:17), and the plural "sons of man" refers to humans (Aram: 2:38; 5:21). The comparative singular "one like a son of man" = "one like a human" (Aram: 7:13), like the plural "one like the likeness of sons of man" = "one who looked human" (MT Dan. 10:16), refers to a heavenly figure who appears human. Dan. 10:16, identifies the "one like the likeness of sons of man" as the angel Gabriel. However the "one like a son of man" (7:13–14) is not only associated with angels (7:18), but rides the clouds like deity (Deut. 33:26; Ps. 68:4) and is described as a human. So he is heavenly in origin, but human in appearance. It is likely these last two traits explain why this title was Jesus' favorite way to refer to himself.

26. John J. Collins, *The Apocalyptic Vision of the Book of Daniel*, 116–17; idem, *The Scepter and the Star*, 158. The conferral of the kingdom is repeated three times: it is given to the "one like a son of man" (vv. 13–14), to "the holy ones of the Most High" (v. 17), and to "the people of the holy ones of the Most High" (v. 27). By way of analogy, the four beasts are interpreted as "four kings" (v. 17), yet the fourth beast is "a fourth kingdom" (v. 23). Thus a king can stand for a kingdom. So does the "one like a son of man" stand for "the holy ones of the Most High," who stand for "the people of the holy ones of the Most High"? Or are the three distinct but closely related? While all scholars agree that there is a parallels between the "one like a son of man" (vv. 13–14), "the holy ones of the Most High" (v. 17) and "the people of the holy ones of the Most High" (v. 27), opinions are divided as to what the parallels mean.

identified as representing "the holy ones of the Most High" (7:18), which refers to angels, often designated as "the holy *ones*."[27] While "the holy ones of the Most High" (7:18, 21–22, 25) are angelic, "the people of the holy ones of the Most High" (7:27) are human; the latter refers to Israel, the former to the angelic patron of Israel (8:24). While the little horn "waged war against the host of heaven" (8:8–14) in the heavenly realm, he "waged war against the people of the holy ones of the Most High" in the earthly realm (8:23–26). The victory of this angelic figure in the heavenly realm both effects and parallels the victory of the people of God in the earthly realm.[28]

Since Daniel 7–8 refer to the heavenly battle detailed in Daniel 10:12–11:1, the heavenly figure in 7:13 seems to some to represent the angelic host, perhaps Michael as the leader of that host.[29] He wages war against the little horn in the heavenly realm on behalf of Israel and receives the eternal kingdom on behalf of the host of angels and of Israel. Furthermore, Michael comes to the aid of the Jewish faithful during the seven years of terror under Antiochus IV (Dan. 12:1).

Nevertheless, it is important to recognize that Daniel stops short of actually identifying this heavenly figure as an angel or as symbolic for the angelic host. Furthermore, the description of the "one like a son of man" in Daniel 7:13–14 eclipses what seems appropriate for an angel, even Michael the archangel. The Most High God would bestow on him the rule over God's eternal kingdom; his reign over this kingdom will never cease. All peoples and nations will serve—if not worship—him (see Dan. 3:28 for another use of the same term, where it clearly means worship). He rides the clouds like deity (Deut. 33:26; Ps. 68:4). Furthermore, the beasts that precede are kingdoms headed up by regal dynasties themselves; so this vision is about rulership on earth. Angels never rule on earth on their own, but only serve God and empower human rulers. Therefore, identification of this figure as an angel is inadequate, since he is in a position ever more exalted than the angels.

Some identify the "one like a son of man" as the coming Davidic king.[30] Although Daniel does not identify this heavenly figure as a new David, several features are associated with future royal Davidic expectations. God will

---

27. See Psalms 16:3[4]; 89:5[6], 7[8]; Job 5:1; 15:15; Zechariah 14:5; Daniel 4:8–9, 17–18; 5:11; 8:24.

28. Thus, some identify the "one like a son of man" as a collective for the faithful remnant of Israel. For example, L. F. Hartman and A. A. DiLella, *The Book of Daniel*, AB 23 (Garden City, NY: Doubleday, 1978): 85–102.

29. John J. Collins, *The Apocalyptic Vision of the Book of Daniel*, HSM 16 (Missoula: Scholars Press, 1977), 123–52.

30. Rex Mason, "The Messiah in the Postexilic Old Testament Literature," in *King and Messiah in Israel and the Ancient Near East* (ed. John Day; Sheffield: JSOT Press), 338–64; A. J. Ferch, *The Son of Man in Daniel 7* (Berrein Springs: Andrews University, 1979), 4–12; G. R. Beasley-Murray, "The Interpretation of Daniel 7," *CBQ* 45 (1983): 44–58.

enthrone this figure (Dan. 7:13–14) in keeping with the divine enthronement of the Davidic kings (Pss. 45:6[7]; 110:1). He will rule over all nations (Dan. 7:13–14, cf. 27) in keeping with future Davidic expectations (Pss. 2:8–10; 72:8–11; 89:25; 110:1–2, 5–7; Isa. 9:7[6]). Yet this heavenly figure of Daniel 7:13–14, whoever he is, is not explicitly associated with future Davidic expectations, perhaps because of the emphasis on transcendent elements. In fact, nowhere does the book of Daniel mention or even allude to the Davidic covenant, Davidic kingship, or Davidic dynasty. Furthermore, there are differences in emphasis between prophetic expectations of a coming David and Daniel's vision of this coming figure. Whereas Daniel pictured the "one like a son of man" as a heavenly figure, the prophets pictured the coming Davidic king as earthly in origin, as the shoot of Jesse (Isa. 11:1, 10) and branch for David (Jer. 23:5; 33:15), whose ancestral roots go back to Bethlehem (Mic. 5:2). This heavenly figure comes on a cloud to the heavenly throne of God (Dan. 7:13), whereas the Davidic king was promised the earthly throne of David.[31] But there are links so that too much should not be made of the differences. The promised kingdom that would never fail in the canon looks to the completion of Davidic hope. The language of Micah 5:2 is open to roots for this figure from of old. The Second Testament appropriately will remove this dualism and confirm the intention of a tie between the Son of Man and Davidic hope.

Some suggest the "one like a son of man" is a hypostatization of the glory of Yahweh, or a heavenly divine b/Being with honors and powers normally predicated of God.[32] Indeed, several features in verses 13–14 associate him closely with deity. Just as God is worshipped, all nations and peoples will worship him (v. 14a). Just as the eternal kingdom belongs to God, the eternal kingdom is given to him (v. 14b). At the same time, several features distinguish him from the Ancient of Days. What has been God's from eternity past—kingship and worship—is now shared with this heavenly figure. This is a feature that has to be incorporated into how the figure is seen.

---

31. The historical Davidic king is promised an earthly throne (2 Sam. 7:13, 16; 1 Kings 2:4; 8:25; 9:5; Isa. 9:7[6]; Jer. 17:25; 22:2, 4; 33:17, 21; Pss. 89:29[30]; 122:5; 132:11–12). However, the divine invitation, "Sit down at my right hand" (Ps. 110:1) opens up the conceptual potential for a heavenly throne for the ultimate Davidic king.

32. Ferch, *The Son of Man in Daniel 7*, 4–12; Beasley-Murray, "The Interpretation of Daniel 7"; Sharon Pace Jeansonne, *The Old Greek Translation of Daniel 7–12*, CBQMS 19 (Washington DC: Catholic Biblical Association, 1988): 96–98. Sigmund Mowinkel, *He That Cometh* (Nashville: Abingdon 1954), suggests Daniel 7:13–14 is reminiscent of ancient Near Eastern mythological texts depicting a young deity inheriting the heavenly throne of an aged deity, e.g., Baal inheriting the throne of El in Ugaritic texts and Marduk inheriting the throne of Enlil in Mesopotamian texts. Mowinkel suggests this might hint at the deity of the "one like a son of man." But in the heavenly enthronement of Jesus, rather replacing the Ancient of Days, the Messiah sits down at "the right hand" of God (Eph. 1:20–22).

Lacking more precise identification, the most one may conclude is that this enigmatic figure is *sui generis*, that is, absolutely unique and in a class of his own within the canonical collection of Hebrew Scriptures.[33] His precise identity represented a fusion of human and divine elements, and it is the title Jesus preferred, precisely because of its comprehensiveness and uniqueness. The expectation this image generated was that this figure somehow would be associated with the culmination of the promises of deliverance. Later Jewish readings would reflect this emphasis in various ways (e.g., *1 En.* 37–71, where Enoch is the hope; and 4 Ezra 13 where the Messiah is portrayed this way). What was seen was that God would rule over his people through this heavenly regent. Daniel pictured an eschatological kingdom under the rule of an agent who has a combination of heavenly and human traits. Therefore, this text is directly prophetic.

Canonical Reading of Daniel 7:13–14

The complexity over the precise identification of Daniel's heavenly figure explains two features in early Jewish literature and Second Testament proclamation. First, although Daniel did not identity him as the Messiah, messianic concepts easily became attached to this character in second temple expectations (*1 En.* 37–71; 4 Ezra 13).

Second, Second Testament proclamation and events authenticating Jesus as the "son of man" were a divine interpretation of the imagery. God made transparent for those who would see the proper identification of Daniel's heavenly figure. Here was the heavenly-human combination Daniel described. In other words, our story about the Messiah and God's plan is both revelatory through the wording of texts and confirmed in history through its revelation in divine events culminating in Jesus that match those texts.

The mysterious heavenly figure of Daniel 7:13–14 is the closest Hebrew Scripture came to a revelation of the heavenly origin and divine nature of the eschatological Messiah. Daniel's image portrayed an individual who stands between God, the angelic host, and mankind. He is of heavenly origin, yet he looks human. He is distinct from the Most High, yet receives the honor normally reserved for God. He is distinct from humanity in authority, yet is associated with mankind and functions as patron of the faithful of Israel. His closest counterpart seems to be the angelic host, yet he is superior since he inherits the very throne of God and receives worship.

It is easy to see why the Greek (LXX) translators would equate him with the Most High; why early church fathers would see Trinitarian overtones in him. Why some Jewish interpreters would have reason to not equate him with God was related to their preconceptions about God. According to traditional

---

33. John Day, *God's Conflict with the Dragon and the Sea: Echoes of a Canaanite Myth in the Old Testament* (Cambridge: Cambridge University Press, 1985), 151–78.

Judaism, there could only be one God. This text however challenges that idea by introducing a power in heaven that shares things directly with God, including worship. This "son of man" shares authority with God with God's welcome—something both incarnation and ascension also establish. Daniel's description of this enigmatic figure was loaded with eschatological potential and meaning. It is easy to see why this heavenly figure is associated with the eschatological Messiah in later second temple literature (*1 En.* 37–71; 4 Ezra 13). He is the delivering figure of the end who would establish the kingdom of God.

CONCLUSION

The prophets Jeremiah, Ezekiel and Daniel each gave voice to a future expectation of one who was to come. Each foresaw a coming day when Yahweh would deliver his people and restore the kingdom through a divinely chosen servant. Since they each had a different piece of the same puzzle, each described distinct aspects of that coming. While they shared many features in common, we nevertheless find a complementary diversity in their future expectations. Jeremiah spoke of the righteousness the Davidic figure to come would bring. Ezekiel highlighted the sacral role the Davidic figure will have in the true worship of God. Daniel made it clear that this figure, associated with the kingdom which God will build, combines human and divine features and comes with authority. With these additions to the messianic puzzle pieces in place, one can also begin to sense where many earlier passages of promise ultimately were heading. The Messiah who is of the house of David also has features that indicate the presence of an inseparable identification with deity and the honoring of God as a result of forgiveness and deliverance obtained into a permanent new rule of God.

MESSIANIC TRAJECTORIES IN ZECHARIAH

Under the providence of God, Cyrus issued an edict in 538 BCE, allowing the Jewish people to return to Jerusalem to rebuild the temple (Ezra 1:1–14; 2 Chron. 36:22–23).[1] Once home, the postexilic community was under the leadership of two people: Zerubbabel, the Persian-appointed governor and grandson of Jehoiachin the last surviving Davidic king, and Joshua, the son of Jehozadak and successor to the Zadokite high priesthood (Ezra 1:5–2:70). The two soon restored the temple altar (Ezra 3:1–13), but foreign interference delayed the rebuilding of the temple for two decades (Ezra 4:1–24). In 520 BCE, Zerubbabel and Joshua resumed the temple with the encouragement of the prophets Haggai and Zechariah (Ezra 5:1–2; Hag. 1:1–15; 2:1–9). Haggai proclaimed that the successful completion of the temple would inaugurate a new era of blessing (2:6–9, 20–23). The completion and dedication of the temple in 516 BCE ushered in a new age of restoration for the postexilic community of Yehud (Ezra 6:12–15).

MESSIANIC TRAJECTORIES IN ZECHARIAH 1–8

Zechariah 1–8 addressed the future of the postexilic community. In 1:7–6:15, the prophet recounted a series of night visions that revealed God's future program. The visions highlighted the role Joshua the Zadokite high priest and Zerubbabel the Davidic governor would play in the building of the Temple and restoration of the community. The symmetrical arrangement of the eight visions highlights the pivotal role of Joshua and Zerubbabel in the unfolding of God's plan:

---

1. For corresponding Mesopotamian Chronicles see *ANET* 315–16. For the fall of Babylon see *ANET* 306-7; or Jean–Jacques Glassner, *Mesopotamian Chronicles*, Writings from the Ancient World (Atlanta: SBL, 2004), 235–37.

A 1:7–17 Yahweh will rebuild the second temple
 B 1:18–21 Yahweh will destroy the nations that scattered Judah
  C 2:1–13   Jerusalem will be repopulated with the
     exiles returning from Babylon
   **D 3:1–10   Joshua is cleansed/commissioned to preside
   over the temple until the branch comes**
   D' 4:1–15   Zerubbabel is empowered to complete the
      building of the Temple
  C' 5:1–11   Babylon will be repopulated with the sinners and sin
     of Judah
 B' 6:1–8 Yahweh will bring peace upon the earth
**A' 6:9–15 The branch—Joshua the high priest—will rebuild
the temple**

Two oracles in particular contribute to the progressive revelation of the royal expectations that provide a foundation for the eschatological Messiah: the consecration of Joshua the high priest as a sign of the coming branch (3:1–10); and the surprising coronation and designation of Joshua as the branch who would build the temple and sit on the throne, not as king but as priest (6:9–15).

> **Rebuilding the Temple**
>
> Although the foundation for the second temple was initially laid in 538 BCE (Ezra 3:8 13), temple construction was halted and did not resume until 520 BCE (Ezra 6:6–12; Hag. 1:1–2). Eventually, Haggai and Zechariah challenged the Jewish people to rebuild the temple. The second temple was completed and dedicated in 515 BCE (Ezra 6:15–18).

Zechariah 3:1–10
In 3:1–10, the prophet witnessed a scene in the heavenly temple involving earthly and heavenly characters: Joshua, the postexilic high priest; the angel of Yahweh and his counterpart; angelic and earthly priests who minister in the heavenly and earthly temples, respectively; and a mysterious figure called the branch, who was not present, but whose coming was announced.

Cleansing of Joshua the High Priest (3:1–5)
In his earlier night visions Zechariah witnessed the repopulation of Jerusalem and completion of the temple (1:7–2:13). Now, the prophet saw a heavenly scene in which Joshua, the successor to the Zadokite high priesthood, was cleansed and consecrated in anticipation of the restoration of temple worship. Zechariah witnessed Joshua's investiture as high priest in a purification ritual reminiscent of the consecration of Aaron (Exod. 25–Lev. 10). Joshua's filthy clothes, symbolic of sin, were removed and replaced with beautiful garments, symbolic of ritual purity, and a priestly turban placed on his head (cf. Lev. 8:6–9). The parallels between the ritual consecration

of Aaron and Joshua highlighted the continuity between the preexilic and postexilic priesthood. Yet the change in venue from the earthly to heavenly realm revealed the escalation in this new work of God to inaugurate the age of restoration.

Charge Given to Joshua the High Priest (3:6–10)

Just as Moses charged Aaron upon his installation as high priest (Lev. 8–10), the angel of Yahweh issued a threefold charge to Joshua the new high priest. In verses 6–7, the angel declared that if the high priest would fulfill his moral and cultic duties, God would grant him with great privileges. In verse 8, he announced that the restoration of the priestly institution functioned as a sign that God also would restore the royal institution through the coming branch (cf. Jer. 23:5–6; 33:14–26). In verses 9–10, Zechariah learned that the restoration of the priesthood in Joshua and the imminent arrival of the branch would inaugurate a new age of blessing. Since the sacrificial system had been disrupted for seventy years, God would atone the sins of his people on a single day, when the second temple would be dedicated and its sacrificial worship restored.

Duties and Privileges of the High Priest (3:6–7). If the high priest would obey Yahweh and fulfill his duties, he would be rewarded with a position of executive power over the temple: "If you walk in my walks and if you keep my charge, you will preside over my house and have charge over my courtyards" (v. 7a). Since this conditional promise carried a performative force, it effectively conferred on the high priest both his duties and his privileges in the same breath.

This bestowal of executive power over the temple to the high priest signaled a dramatic change. During the preexilic period, the Davidic kings, who functioned in the position of sacral kingship (cf. Ps. 110:4), exercised authority over the courtyards of the temple in erecting altars, or tearing them down. This executive authority was now transferred to Joshua the high priest. This unexpected announcement suggests an expanded role for the postexilic high priesthood, transferring to him tasks previously assigned to the preexilic king.

Whereas the Davidic king had been the leader of Israel during the preexilic period, the high priest would become the leader of the community throughout the second temple period. The elevation of the postexilic high priest was necessitated by the dismantling of Davidic rule from the time of the Babylonian exile forward. In effect, Zechariah 3:7 not only explains the elevation in the status of the high priest in the second temple period, it provided the original theological justification for this otherwise unexpected religio-sociological development. In the absence of a Davidic descendant sitting on the throne in Jerusalem, the traditional roles of the preexilic high priest and sacral king were combined in the person of the postexilic high priest. In effect, Joshua and his successors would function in a surrogate role for the missing king.

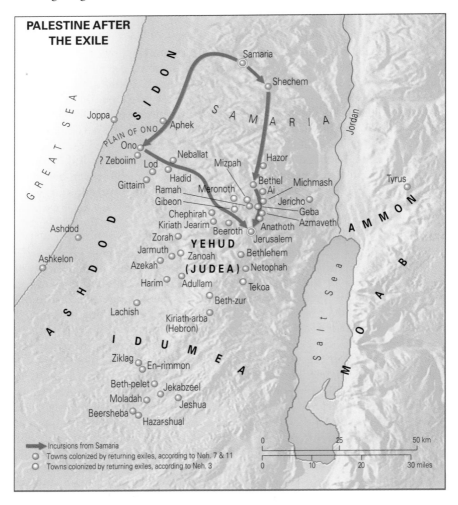

PALESTINE AFTER THE EXILE

The angel of Yahweh also proffered to the high priest entrée into the heavenly temple: "I will also give you access among these standing around you" (v. 7c). The designation, "these standing around you," is a tacit reference to the heavenly council mentioned in verses 1–5, while the term, "access," suggests the high priest in some mysterious way would journey back and forth, so to speak, between the earthly temple and the heavenly temple in the performance of his priestly duties. In the Hebrew Scriptures, the temple was conceived as sacred space mediating between heaven and earth.[2] When the high priest stepped into the Most Holy Place, representationally he entered into heaven, where God is enthroned on high with the ark of the covenant as the footstool of his feet. The service of the earthly temple mirrored the heavenly. The earthly temple and its human priesthood was a counterpart to the heavenly temple and its angelic priesthood. Thus, verse 7 conveys the pivotal role the high priest played in mediating between heaven and earth through his performance of sacrificial ritual at the temple.

High Priest as Portend of the Coming "Branch" (3:8). Zechariah learned that Joshua and his fellow priests were a portend (RSV: "men of good omen," NET: "symbols") of the coming branch. Yahweh's restoration of the priesthood guaranteed that he soon would bring upon the scene a mysterious figure designated as the "branch." This moniker occurs elsewhere only in Jeremiah 23:5–6 and 33:14–26, where God promised that once he had restored the people from Babylonian exile, he would raise up a righteous branch for David's throne and restore a Levitical high priest to the temple's altar. This pictured a day when all would be made right. The current arrangement of Zechariah would be temporary. By the symbolic cleansing and performative commissioning of Joshua the high priest (vv. 1–7), God had fulfilled the first part of his promise in Jeremiah 33:14–26. The consecration of the priesthood and imminent restoration of temple worship thus functioned as a sign guaranteeing that God also would fulfill the second and perhaps most important part of his promise: "I am about to bring the branch!"

The coming branch is given the traditional royal Davidic title, "my servant," depicting him as a second David, the servant of Yahweh *par excellence*. The combination, "my servant, the branch," recalls Jeremiah 33:14–26, where Yahweh promised to raise up "a righteous branch for David" (33:15), while thrice referring to the illustrious founder of the dynasty as "David, my servant" (33:21, 22, 26). The designation, "my servant," is also reminiscent of Ezekiel's favorite title of the ideal David to come, "my servant, David" (Ezek. 34:23–24; 37:24–25). It also echoes Isaiah's title for the Suffering Servant, "my servant" (Isa. 52:13; 53:11), a figure who would first suffer then be exalted over the kings of all nations, suggesting he would be recognized as a royal figure (Isa. 52:13). Thus, the traditional Davidic title, "my servant, the branch," suggests this one to come would be a royal figure after the pattern of

---

2. In his article on Psalm 15 entitled "The Worshipers Approach to God," Ronald E. Manahan discusses the concept and significance of "sacred space" for worship from Sumer to Greece and its relevance for understanding worship in ancient Israel. See *Authentic Worship: Hearing Scripture's Voice, Applying Its Truths* (ed. Herbert W. Bateman IV; Grand Rapids: Kregel, 2001), 55–77.

the renowned son of Jesse—a veritable David *redivivus*, who himself was the
pattern for the future renewal of righteous kingship.

Zechariah 6:9–15

Perhaps the most startling development in the book of Zechariah occurs in
the prophet's final night vision. In a revelatory dream, Yahweh instructed
him to coronate the branch, who would then take his throne and oversee the
completion of the temple. Much to the surprise of the reader—and undoubtedly initially to the prophet—he was not to coronate Zerubbabel the Davidic
scion, but Joshua the Zadokite high priest! It is difficult to exaggerate the significance of this development. It had a profound impact upon the structure
of leadership in the second temple community, to say nothing of its implications for the eschatological Messiah.

Zechariah's night vision unfolds in three acts. First, Yahweh instructed
him to make a crown and put it on Joshua's head (vv. 9–11). Then Zechariah
was to designate Joshua as the branch (v. 12), explaining that he would build
the temple, symbolically occupy David's throne as a priest, and thus unite the
royal and priestly branches of national leadership (v. 13). Once the temple
was finished, Zechariah was to deposit the crown as a memorial to those who
donated the material from which it was made—their contribution foreshadowing the participation of other exiles that would yet return to Zion to bring
about the completion of the temple (vv. 14–15).

Crowning of Joshua the High Priest (6:9–11). Yahweh instructed
Zechariah to make a crown from silver and gold donated by three Jews who
had returned from exile, and to set it on the head of Joshua the high priest.
The term "crown" (עֲטָרוֹת) designates the traditional emblem of royalty (Job
31:36), distinct from the priestly "turban" (צָנִיף), which previously had been
put on Joshua's head to wear when he ministered in the Temple (Zech. 3:5).
God's instruction to place this royal crown on Joshua, the son of Jehozadak
high priest, rather than Zerubbabel, the grandson of Jehoiachin the Davidic
descendant, comes as a surprise. Nothing in the preceding context prepared
the prophet or reader for this development.

Did the crowning of Joshua the high priest carry a performative, symbolic, or typological significance? If performative, the high priest was proclaimed king of the postexilic community in apparent contradiction to God's
promises of restoration of the throne to the house of David. If symbolic, the
high priest was designated the *de facto* political head of the community as
senior priest, but without publicly placing royal or monarchic aspirations
on him. If typological, this conferred the symbolic status of interim spiritual
and political ruler to the postexilic high priest until the yet future branch to
come would ascend the throne of David in the eschatological future. Thus,
the typological reading includes a symbolic dimension as well. The sense of

something temporary was suggested in the previous oracle, which allows this symbolic-typological combination to make sense. Just as the consecration of Joshua the high priest served the symbolic role of guaranteeing that God eventually would bring the royal branch to the temple (3:1–10), the symbolic crowning of Joshua may have conveyed that the high priest's rule over the temple was a prototype of the Davidic ruler still to come. The advantage of this reading is that we begin to see a combination of regal and priestly roles in the one to come.

Designation of Joshua as "Branch" (6:12). Yahweh instructed Zechariah to proclaim to Joshua the high priest, "Look, here is the man whose name is branch!" We may understand this in one of two ways. First, the designation of Joshua as the branch was actual, effectively transferring the traditional position of leadership from the Davidic king to the Levitical high priest—if not permanently, at least until the throne would be restored to the Davidic dynasty. Second, the designation of Joshua as the branch was symbolic, Joshua functioning as the typological surrogate for a future Davidic descendant to come, who one day would literally fulfill the prophecies of Jeremiah 23:5 and 33:15, "I will raise up a righteous branch for David."

In either case, the crowning of Joshua and designation as the branch is surprising for two reasons. First, Jeremiah 23:5 envisioned the coming branch in royal Davidic terms. Second, Zechariah 3:8 seemed to distinguish Joshua the high priest from the coming branch. So it is difficult to see how the crowning and designation of Joshua as the branch could represent a precise literal fulfillment of these prophecies. More likely, it represents some kind of essential, typological or already/not yet fulfillment. A precise literal fulfillment of Jeremiah 33:14–26 would demand the restoration of two individuals in the postexilic community, namely, a royal descendant of David to rule over the nation and a priestly descendant of Levi to minister before the altar. An essential fulfillment in the postexilic period would allow one individual to function in both roles. What might explain such an unexpected move?

Given the historical reality of the subjugation of the postexilic community of Yehud under Persian rule, it was impossible—politically speaking and on human terms—for a Davidite such as Zerubbabel to take the throne. God fulfilled his conditional promise to restore repentant Babylonian exiles to the land of Israel after seventy years (Jer. 25:11–12; 29:10; 2 Chron. 36:21; Ezra 1:1), but political subjugation of the Jewish people under Gentile rule would last longer than seventy years (Zech. 1:12; 7:5; cf. Dan. 9:24). Any attempt by a Davidite to ascend the throne would have been seen as an act of rebellion inviting reprisals from Persian authorities.[3]

---

3. See chapter 8 for a discussion of Persia's social-political conditions that contribute to what Bateman and others consider the dormancy of messianic expectations.

The crowning and designation of Joshua as the branch suggests the traditional role of the preexilic Davidic king as leader of the covenant community would be filled by the postexilic high priest during the interim that Yehud remained under Gentile rule. Joshua would function as the typological surrogate and functional equivalent of the royal branch. Once the community was delivered from Gentile rule, the way would open for the ultimate branch to ascend the throne. In the meantime, the existence of the high priest as ruler of the covenant community would function as a divine guarantee that the ultimate branch was yet to come. While Zechariah designated Joshua the high priest as the branch, his crowning pointed both typologically and prophetically forward to a royal Davidic figure that was not yet on the scene. Thus, when he would come, his rule would comprise more than previous Davidic kings.

The "already/not yet" identity of the branch is suggested by the juxtaposition of the initial declaration, "Look, here is the man [=Joshua] whose name is the branch!" (v. 12a), with the following prediction, "And he [=the branch] will sprout up from him [=Joshua]" (v. 12b). The seemingly contradictory statement—that Joshua is the branch, yet the branch one day will arise from Joshua—frames Joshua as both the present embodiment of the branch as well as the typological surrogate of the branch to come. Zechariah unequivocally identifies Joshua as the functional equivalent of the branch, yet indicates that the real branch to come would succeed the postexilic high priest as both the political and sacral ruler of the covenant community.

The prediction, "[the branch] will sprout up from him," is reminiscent of early prophetic traditions of a royal shoot who would sprout up from the root of Jesse (Isa. 11:1, 10). While Isaiah pictured a new David sprouting up from the ancestral roots of Jesse, Zechariah envisioned the branch sprouting from the priestly roots of Joshua. Whereas Isaiah predicted the coming king would descend from the genealogical line of David, Zechariah foresaw the coming branch as one day succeeding the high priest as the sacral ruler of the new covenant community.

The Branch Would Sit on the Throne As Priest (6:13). Zechariah declared that in his function as branch, Joshua would succeed in building the temple and sit on the throne as the embodiment of David for the postexilic community. While Zechariah previously commissioned Joshua and Zerubbabel to build the temple, the announcement that Joshua rather than Zerubbabel would sit upon the throne was something of a surprise. Nevertheless, it was in harmony with the preceding crowning of the high priest (vv. 10–11) and his designation as the branch (v. 12).

This declaration represents a dramatic revision of traditional preexilic royal Davidic expectations. God promised repeatedly that David would never lack a descendant sitting on his throne—provided his descendants obeyed

God from one generation to the next during the initial preexilic stage of ful-fillment.[4] When all the post-Josianic kings failed to fulfill this dynastic obliga-tion, God announced that none of their (immediate) descendants would sit on David's throne (Jer. 22:30; 36:30). Nevertheless, God promised to restore the dynasty so that David would never again lack a descendant sitting on his throne (Jer. 33:17, 21). Jeremiah had associated the restoration of a man sit-ting on the throne with a priest ministering before the altar (Jer. 33:14–26). While Jeremiah may have anticipated that these two offices would be fulfilled in two persons, the language was open. Zechariah revealed that the royal and priestly functions would be combined in one person. This was not altogether without precedent. After all, the occupant of the Davidic throne had func-tioned as a priestly king in the preexilic period (Ps. 110:4). In similar fashion, Joshua would function as a royal priest during the postexilic period.

The closing declaration in verse 13b, if rendered literally, may be trans-lated in one of three ways: "there will be a priest by his throne" (RSV, NET), "there will be a priest upon his throne" (KJV, NJPS) or "He will be a priest on his throne" (ASV, NIV). In the first case, the branch would sit upon his royal throne while Joshua high priest would stand at his side. In the second, Joshua the high priest would sit upon the royal throne of the branch. In the third, the branch would sit upon his royal throne in the person of Joshua the high priest. Interpreters debate between these options, however, the open-ness of the statement most likely reflects the complex relationship between the branch and Joshua. Whereas Joshua, the high priest, would function in the capacity of the branch as the ruler of the postexilic community, he also served as the typological surrogate for the royal branch to come. Joshua's consecration as high priest was a sign guaranteeing the coming of the branch (3:8). Thus, the role of the high priest as leader of the postexilic community foreshadowed the future rule of the branch to come.

Furthermore, Joshua's crowning was symbolic. In other words, the dec-laration that he would sit upon the throne was metaphorical. While Joshua would oversee the building of the temple, the royal palace, where the Davidic king traditionally sat upon his throne, would not be rebuilt during the postex-ilic period. Joshua would sit upon the throne of David in a metaphorical sense in his capacity as the ruler of Yehud. He would function in proxy of the future royal branch. In the absence of a Davidic heir on the dynastic throne of an independent kingdom, the hereditary office of high priest would function as the ruler—religious, political, and social—for the postexilic community, as long as it was under foreign rule. The leadership role of the high priest during

---

4. God promised David would never lack a descendant sitting upon his throne (1 Kings 2:4b; 8:25a; 9:5; Ps. 132:11; Jer. 33:17; 2 Chron. 6:16a; 7:18), provided his descendants obey God from one generation to the next (1 Kings 2:4a; 8:25b; 9:3–4, 6–8; Ps. 132:12; 2 Chron. 6:16b; 7:17, 19–20; cf. Jer. 17:24–25; 22:2–4); (cf. Ps. 89:27–52 [28–53]).

the second temple period would typologically represent the future Davidic Messiah to come. Thus, the continuing existence of the high priest as the interim ruler of the restored community would serve as a "portent" of God's promise to bring the branch.

Completion of the Temple (6:14–15). Zechariah's night vision closes with the declaration that those who were far off (the exiles still living in Babylon) would come to help those who were near (the exiles who had already returned) to build the temple. Yet this promise was related in the short term to the obedience of the postexilic community. Lest we minimize this concluding statement, the later oracles in Zechariah 9–14 were uttered in response to community's sin.

Canonical Reading of Zechariah 3:1–10 and 6:9–15

Zechariah 3:1–10 points to a symbol of the branch to come in the archetype of Joshua. The typological designation of Joshua the high priest as the surrogate of the royal branch to come played a pivotal role in God's progressive revelation about a future Messiah. The future royal expectation of the preexilic and exilic communities was the perpetuation of the Davidic dynasty one generation after another (1 Kings 2:4; 8:25; 9:3–8; Ps. 132:11–12; Jer. 17:25; 22:2, 4). While Jeremiah 23:5–6 predicted God would raise up a righteous branch of David, Jeremiah 33:14–26 related this not in terms of a single Davidic king who would reign for eternity, but as a dynasty of righteous Davidites who would rule one generation after another.

Yet Jeremiah 33:14–26, like Zechariah 3:1–10, also anticipated this royal branch would arrive on the scene shortly after the people returned from exile and the priesthood reconsecrated. Zechariah 6:9–15 revealed an unexpected program of "already/not yet" fulfillment. The "already" dimension was inaugurated in the ritual consecration and symbolic crowning of Joshua as the sacral ruler of the postexilic community. The "not yet" aspect was revealed in the typological role which the high priest would play as the surrogate for the royal Messiah to come.

Perhaps contrary to the expectations of the postexilic community, the royal branch did not, in fact, arrive on the scene in the imminent future. The oracles in Zechariah 9–14, which follow, addressed this enigma by appropriately connecting the prophet's original imminent expectation into a future eschatological hope. The promise of the approaching coming of the branch, "Look, I am about to bring the branch!" (Zech. 3:8), would be fulfilled in the future eschatological arrival of the Coming One: "Look, your King is coming!" (Zech. 9:9). This fresh eschatological development of future royal Davidic expectations in terms of priesthood was a critical factor in the development of later second temple expectations of the Messiah. Yet this was not simply a matter of the human development of religious thinking, but ultimately the result of the progress of revelation and divine design.

MESSIANIC TRAJECTORIES IN ZECHARIAH 9–14

Zechariah 9–14 consists of a collection of two sets of undated oracles in chapters 9–11 and 12–14, which develop the expectations of chapters 1–8 concerning the coming era following completion of the temple. These latter chapters build on the earlier future expectations, but develop a futuristic eschatology alongside the actualizing eschatology of the earlier visions.

Three passages played a crucial role in the development of future expectations: the royal entrance of the coming king into Jerusalem (9:9–10); the preservation and cleansing of the house of David (12:2–13:1); and the inauguration of the eschatological rule of Yahweh as King (14:9). Zechariah 9–14 associates the promise to David reaching its climax in the coming rule of Yahweh. The historical Davidic monarchy of the preexilic period would be related to the eschatological theocracy of Yahweh's universal rule over all nations (14:5, 9, 16, 17).

Zechariah 9–14 represents a dramatic development of earlier preexilic expectations of the future role of David's dynasty. God would preserve David's house and cleanse it from evil. It even would enjoy a prominent social position in the new community. Yet future fulfillment of the royal Davidic ideology would be affected by Yahweh himself who would rule as King of all the earth, fulfilling the dynastic ideals of moral righteousness and social justice, which the house of David consistently had failed to meet—not only in the preexilic but also in the postexilic eras. The solution to the failure of the house of David would not be left merely to humanity. This move opened the door for a transcendent figure to come whose rule would fulfill God's promise to David (showing how other earlier promises fit together). It also revealed Yahweh would rule.

Messianic Trajectories in Zechariah 9:9–10

Zechariah 9:1–17 is a prophetic hymn of the Divine warrior, which consists of two prose oracles (vv. 1–8, 11–17) framing a central poetic oracle (vv. 9–10). The opening and closing oracles depict God's rescue of Zion from foreign oppressors (vv. 1–8, 11–17). The central poem combines a hymn of praise and prophetic oracle, addressed to Zion and announcing the coming of Yahweh as King (vv. 9–10). By placing this poem in the center, this royal figure is presented as the linchpin whose arrival would inaugurate of a rule of peace and kingdom of universal proportions.

Contextual Reading

Zechariah 9:1–17 envisions the coming of the King in three successive acts. The Divine Warrior would march out against the traditional enemies of

Israel/Judah, starting in the north and moving south, exacting victory along the way (vv. 1–8). Then he would enter Zion as her citizens hail his triumphal entry by proclaiming his kingship and as the sign that their liberation from foreign oppression was at hand (vv. 9–10). The Divine Warrior would then defeat the foreign armies occupying the land, and then inaugurate a new age of universal peace (vv. 11–17). By way of analogy, the Allied Forces landed on Normandy Beach, France, on June 6, 1944, then advanced victoriously from north to south. On August 25, 1944, the 2nd Armored Division entered Paris in triumph, passing along the Champs Elysses and through the Arc de Triomphe. From Paris, the Allied Forces attacked the remaining German strongholds, eventually driving the enemy out of France by January 1945. Henceforth, total victory then was only a matter of time.

Victorious March of the Divine Warrior (9:1–8)
Verses 1–8 is a victory hymn of the Divine Warrior, which envisions Yahweh marching out against the traditional enemies of Israel, defeating them in battle, then moving into the land of Israel, where he would establish himself as ruler in his palace. Verses 1–7 trace Yahweh's itinerary, commencing in the north and moving south, concluding with his arrival outside Zion. While en route, he would overrun Aram (vv. 1–2a), Phoenicia (vv. 2b–4) and Philistia (vv. 2b–7). Upon arriving at his destination, Yahweh would encamp on the outskirts of Zion, like an army setting up camp at the end of a march, protecting the temple from foreign desecration (v. 8).

The Coming King's Royal Entrance into Zion (9:9)
While the preceding prose oracle closed with the divine warrior completing his march on the outskirts of Zion (vv. 1–8), this poetic oracle opened with a celebration of the victorious Yahweh entering Jerusalem as King (vv. 9–10). This oracle unfolded in four steps: celebration of the citizens of Zion at the approach of their King; entrance of the victorious King into Jerusalem mounted on a donkey; removal of weapons of war from Israel and establishment of peace with the nations; and inauguration of the universal reign of the King.

In the opening lines, the prophet plays the role of a herald who urges Zion to rejoice at the approach of her King.[5] The proclamation, "Rejoice greatly, O daughter Zion! Shout, O daughter Jerusalem! Look, your King is coming to you!" (Zech. 9:9), parallels God's earlier proclamation, "Sing out and be happy, O daughter Zion! Look, I am coming to settle in your midst!" (Zech. 2:10[14]). Both passages portray Yahweh coming to Zion, following his judgment of the recalcitrant nations and conversion

5. Other examples of the prophet heralding and urging Zion to rejoice at the approach of her King are evident in Isaiah 12:4–6; 54:1; Lamentations 4:21; Hosea 9:1; Joel 2:21–24; Zephaniah 3:14–15.

of repentant nations. There is one striking difference. While the former portrays the imminent coming of Yahweh to indwell the second temple that was currently under construction, the latter envisions the eschatological coming of the Divine Warrior to Zion itself to inaugurate his theocratic rule of universal peace. The imminent coming of Yahweh to indwell the temple (2:10[14]) foreshadowed his eschatological coming to rule the entire earth (cf. 14:5).

Some interpreters see a shift from Yahweh's march to Zion (vv. 1–8) to an eschatological Messiah entering Jerusalem in verses 9–10. As they see it, verses 9–10 do not envision the coming of the Divine Warrior into Jerusalem, but constitute direct prophecy about Jesus. However, the expression, "Look, [he] is coming!" occurs elsewhere in visions of God bringing eschatological salvation to Zion (Isa. 35:4; 40:10; 66:15; cf. 62:11; Mal. 3:1). Furthermore, the expectation of future kingship in chapters 9–14 is exclusively theocratic. Every use of the term "king" in future contexts is limited to Yahweh, who alone will rule all nations (14:9, 16, 17).

The prophet characterizes the coming King with terms and expressions fraught with open language. Verse 9b may be rendered in a way that depicts him as one who brings about justice through delivering Jerusalem: "He is just and bringing salvation" (KJV); however, it may also depict him as a military champion: "He is triumphant and victorious" (RSV).[6] Verse 9c may be nuanced in a way that depicts the coming one as a humble servant: "lowly and riding upon an ass" (KJV); or in a way that presents the coming King as triumphant: "victorious and riding upon an ass" (*HALOT* 854).[7] The context (vv. 1–8, 11–17) suggests the coming King is pictured as a victorious warrior who, having conquered his enemies, enters Jerusalem in triumph. However, in the progress of revelation, the actual arrival of the King in the person of Jesus the Messiah combines both of these images—the lowly servant and the victorious king.

In verse 9b, the prophet envisioned the King mounted on a purebred donkey. To picture a king riding on an ass may strike a modern reader as odd, but this was the stereotypical mount of royalty in the ancient Near East. A poetic text from Mari suggested it was more appropriate for a king to ride a

---

6. The adjective צַדִּיק has a range of meanings political: "legitimate" (NET); judicial: "vindicated" (NEB); moral: "just" (KJV); military: "triumphant" (RSV)." BDB 843.1a suggests צַדִּיק means "victorious" here. The related noun means "triumph" (Judg. 5:11; Isa. 45:25; 59:16; Ps. 98:2), "victory" (Isa. 41:2, 10; Ps. 48:10[11]). The term נוֹשָׁע occurs twice, referring to deliverance through victory in battle: "victorious" (Deut. 33:29; Ps. 33:16).

7. MT vocalizes the term as the adjective עָנִי which means: (1) "poor, needy," in financial sense, (2) "weak, powerless," in sociological sense, (3) "afflicted," as the pious afflicted by the wicked, (4) "lowly, humble," as meek and opposite arrogant. Others suggest the vocalization עָנֶה, as the adjective "triumphant, one who is conquers," derived from עָנה II "subjugate, defeat, conquer; cause to triumph, grant victory" (cf. *HALOT* 854).

donkey than a horse: "my lord should not ride a horse, let my lord ride in a chariot or a mule, and he will thereby honor his royal head." In the literature of Mari and Ugarit, the donkey also was the animal on which a deity may ride. In the Hebrew Scriptures, the purebred ass was the preferred mount of premonarchial chieftains (Judg. 5:10; 10:4; 12:14; 21:19–21; 1 Sam. 3:22) and monarchial era royalty (2 Sam. 13:29; 16:1–2; 18:9; 19:26[27]). This entrance of the King on a donkey is reminiscent of Solomon's entrance into Jerusalem, mounted on an ass, at the time of his royal coronation (1 Kings 1:33, 38, 44). It also alludes to Genesis 49:11, which envisions a royal figure whose mount was a purebred ass. In making this allusion, the referent is complex. Yahweh is coming but in a way connected to messianic hope. We need not choose between Yahweh's coming and the coming of King Messiah. They are wrapped up in each other.

The King's Universal Rule of Peace (9:10)
The coming King's entrance into Zion would inaugurate an age of universal peace. Yet this tranquility would be won through military triumph. Whereas the Divine Warrior had already defeated the traditional enemies of Israel during his campaign (vv. 1–8), his triumphant entrance in Jerusalem would be the first phase of his liberation of Israel/Judah from the foreign oppressors who were occupying its land (vv. 11–17). While the coming King would enter Zion on a purebred ass, the traditional mount of royalty, he would eradicate from Jerusalem/Ephraim every horse, the preferred mount for warfare. Elimination of the weapons of war would be wrought by forceful military intervention, not peaceful diplomatic means. Having defeated and disarmed all of his enemies, the King would inaugurate a reign of universal peace with all nations.

Canonical Reading of Zechariah 9:9–10
The contextual reading of Zechariah 9:1–10 tells us four things about Yahweh's future intervention associated with fulfilling his promises to David: he will come as a victorious warrior who has conquered his enemies and won over the repentant; he will enter Jerusalem as her long-awaited King; he will come as the virtual embodiment of the ideal David; and he will inaugurate a new age of peace. Naturally, this represents a dramatic development of the earlier traditional royal Davidic expectations of hope in an eschatological theocracy. How does this contribute to our canonical development of Messiah? Later authors of the second temple period would reflect upon and even develop this hope. Nathan's oracle had promised an enduring dynasty for David (2 Sam. 7:10–16), but whose initial perpetuity in any given generation during the preexilic period had been vouchsafed on faithfulness (e.g., 1 Kings. 2:4; 8:25; 9:3–8; Ps. 132:11–12; Jer. 17:24–25; 22:2–4). When Davidic rule was interrupted by the Babylonian exile, the prophets envisioned the future

eschatological restoration of David's dynasty through an ideal Davidic King.[8] Zechariah revealed that the ultimate eschatological fulfillment of these future royal expectations also would transpire through the theocratic rule of Yahweh (14:5, 9, 16, 17).

The total pervasiveness of the theocratic rule of Yahweh in Zechariah 9–14 causes some to argue that there is little room for a human Davidic king, but this is the wrong conclusion to draw. God will remain faithful to his earlier promise to David of an eternal throne, so we can be assured about the future role of the house of David and its relation to the eschatological kingship of Yahweh. So the emphasis on the theocratic rule of Yahweh in Zechariah 9–14 should not be misinterpreted as God abandoning his promise to restore Davidic rule in the future. God would work through the Davidic house in the end. We see something similar in the book of Ezekiel, in which chapters 34 and 37 envision the coming Davidic prince functioning in a royal role, while chapters 44–48 picture the coming Davidic prince in a decidedly sacral role. So it is not a matter of either/or but both/and. The future eschatological kingship of Yahweh as well as the kingship of the future eschatological Davidic king will be wrapped up in one another. Yahweh's presence and decisive work will be seen in the reign of the coming Davidic king.

Messianic Trajectories in Zechariah 12–14

Zechariah 12–14, the final collection of oracles in the book, consists of two prose oracles (12:2–13:6, 14:1–21), which picture Zion under siege by the nations, but celebrate God's rescue of his people, judgment of the nations and inauguration of the theocratic kingdom of Yahweh. The opening collection of prose oracles considers the future of the house of David in God's eschatological program (12:2–13:6). The closing collection of prose oracles picture the dawn of the theocratic kingdom in which Yahweh alone will rule as king over all nations (14:1–21). Bracketed between these prose oracles is the central poetic oracle, which depicts the enigmatic shepherd, who plays a crucial role in God's program of deliverance (13:7–9).

Contextual Reading of Zechariah 12:2–13:1

Zechariah 12:2–13:1 mentions "house of David" five times. Some interpreters assume mention of David's house reflects an expectation of restoration of the dynasty to the throne, or the future coming of the ultimate Davidic king. However, Zechariah 12:2–13:1 does not envision restoration of David's dynasty to the throne along lines of the past. David's house would play an

---

8. For previous discussions on the preexilic and exilic prophets that envisioned the restoration of David's dynasty see Amos 9:11–12 (see pp. 90–97); Micah 5:1–6 (see pp. 102–20); Isaiah 9:1–7; 11:1–9, 10–16 (see pp. 123–49); Jeremiah 23:5–6; 30:9; 33:14–26 (see pp. 167–75); Ezekiel 34:24–25; 37:25–26 (see pp. 175–84).

important role in the future age, but its place would be muted in comparison with its former prominence in the preexilic period. There would be something more to this ruler to come.

Future Status of the House of David (12:2–8)

This oracle envisions God's deliverance of Jerusalem from a future military attack by Gentile nations, but highlights the distinct roles of the Judahites, Jerusalemites, and Davidites as agents of God's triumph over of the nations. The prophet envisions a chain reaction among these three groups. The bravery of the common non-royal Jerusalemites would inspire the common rural Judahites to place their faith in Yahweh (v. 5). God then would empower the Judahites to achieve victory over the Gentiles (v. 6). By granting first blood to the non-royal ruralists, the pride of the urban citizens of Jerusalem and royal members of the house of David would be held in check: "Yahweh will give victory to the tents of Judah first, so that the glory of the house of David and the glory of the inhabitants of Jerusalem may not be exalted over the glory of Judah" (v. 7). During the preexilic period, the Jerusalemites and Davidites often were overwhelmed with arrogant pride over the common people of the land. By granting first victory to Judah, God would elevate the common folk to the same social status as the Jerusalemites and Davidites.

In the second phase of victory, God would shield Zion so that her weakest fighters would be like the mighty warrior David, and the Davidites would be like the presence of God mediated vis-à-vis the angel of Yahweh (v. 8). This dual reference to two groups in Zion—the feeblest of her citizens and more prominent Davidites—forms an *inclusio*, which describes the exalted state of all her inhabitants from lowliest to greatest. The glory of the lowly would be like that of the great (David), the glory of the great would be like that of the greatest (God). Nevertheless, the comparison of the glory of the house of David to the angel of Yahweh does not convey divine, royal, or messianic status to the dynasty. While the house of David would play a significant role in the future deliverance of Zion, the text describes a fresh angle on the restoration of the kingship and the coming of a future Davidic Messiah. Perhaps the point is that the victory would belong to the Lord. If so, a Davidite would be present, but it is not exclusively as a Davidite that his role would be realized but that God would provide the victory in a fresh way.

Although the house of David would play a role in the future eschatological deliverance of Zion, it would not function as the primary focus of Yahweh's blessing as it had in the past. Rather, it would share this honor with the ordinary citizens of Jerusalem as well as the common farmers of Judah. In essence, the traditional preexilic honor of the house of David as the agent of Yahweh would be democratized in the coming age. The house of David would be the head of the restored community, but all would share in the glory and benefits.

Future Repentance of the House of David (12:9–14)
Having described God's final deliverance of Jerusalem from the Gentile nations (12:2–8), the prophet next envisioned her repentance. Whereas God had poured out his wrath on Jerusalem as punishment for her sin, the prophet foresaw that he would pour out his pity on Jerusalem leading to repentance. The expression, "a spirit of pity," betokens God touching the hearts of his people so profoundly that they seek his mercy in genuine repentance (vv. 9–10).

Whereas 12:9–10 describes the depth of repentance, 12:11–14 describes its breadth. God's deliverance would move the heart of the people of Zion to repent. Repetition of the expression, "the house of David and the inhabitants of Jerusalem" (vv. 10, 14) forms an *inclusio*, conveying the entire community. The Davidites and Jerusalemites as a whole would repent of their guilt in the unjust slaying of God's servant, whom they wrongly had pierced

The people of Jerusalem and house of David would need God's forgiveness for their role in an unjust act. Yet the precise nature of their sin is unclear, since verse 10b may be translated in three ways: "they will look to *Me whom* they have pierced," "they will look to *Me concerning* the one whom they have pierced," or "they will look to *the one whom* they have pierced."

The verb "to pierce" (דָּקַר) refers to the violent act of thrusting a sword/ spear into a person, inflicting a fatal wound. Since it always refers to a physical wound elsewhere, most interpret this as the death of one of God's representatives. Others interpret it metaphorically in the sense that Yahweh was pierced by his people who wounded his heart. The Septuagint reflects this approach: "they will look to Me, whom they *mocked*." However, since 12:10–14 is filled with imagery and vocabulary associated with ancient Israelite practices of mourning for the dead, this strongly suggests that the physical death of an Israelite is in view.

The term "to pierce" (דָּקַר) occurs again in the following oracle (Zech. 13:3), describing loyal Israelites who will "pierce" false prophets (cf. Deut. 13:1–11). The juxtaposition of these oracles contrasts the people's illegitimate execution of one of God's true representatives in the past with the legitimate execution of false prophets in the future. This may suggest the one whom the people executed was the good shepherd of Zechariah 11:4–17, whom the people wrongly rejected, leading to his execution in 13:7–9. Several factors support this. First, the good shepherd meets opposition from the nation's leadership (11:4–14). Second, the rejection of the good shepherd is tantamount to rejecting Yahweh (11:13). Third, the good shepherd is killed (13:7–9). It is possible that the one who is "pierced" in 12:10 is the good shepherd of 11:4–17 and 13:7–9.

Future Cleansing of the House of David (13:1–6)
When the people of Jerusalem and house of David mourn the one whom they had pierced, the floodgates of divine mercy will be opened to them. God's absolution is conceived in terms of ritual cleansing from moral sin and ritual

uncleanness: "a fountain shall be opened . . . to cleanse them from sin and uncleanness" (13:1). The cultic instrument that would effect this cleansing is identified by the term "fountain," or "spring," which refers to a natural source of fresh water that flows out of the ground forming a stream or pool of water. The source of fresh water for Solomon's temple was the Gihon Spring with its natural opening on the southeast slope of Mount Zion. While the Gihon provided the fresh water for the ritual cleansing performed at Solomon's temple, Yahweh would provide the spiritual 'water' for the moral cleansing of the inhabitants of Jerusalem and the house of David in the coming age.

In the Israelite cult, ceremonial washing with fresh water was used in consecration rituals to cleanse the priests from earthly defilement, and in purification rituals to cleanse ordinary Israelites from earthly defilement of various kinds, including contact with a corpse. Thus, some understand Zechariah 13:1 as the ritual cleansing and divine forgiveness of the inhabitants of Jerusalem and house of David for their role in the death of "the one who had been pierced" in 12:10. Thus, the death of the one whom they had pierced is the reason for their *need* of divine cleansing. Their illegitimate shedding of his blood could only be cleansed by the "fountain" that Yahweh would open on Mount Zion (cf. 14:4, 8) to provide the spiritual waters of purification from their sin and defilement.

Canonical Reading

Zechariah 12:2–13:1 paints a sober picture of the role of the house of David in the future eschatological age, when it would be purged of its past guilt and moral failings. The house of David would take its place alongside every other family and group in the community in mourning and repentance for what they have done, and so would experience the mercy and forgiveness of God. The house of David would be present in the decisive period of restoration. Although the house of David would have a role in the renewed community, it would no longer be the isolated beneficiary of Yahweh's blessing. As Zechariah 11:4–17 and 13:7–9 suggests, the central agent in God's future deliverance of his people would be wrought by a mysterious figure depicted as a suffering shepherd. Yet the metaphorical designation, "shepherd," is reminiscent of the traditional Davidic motif. This suggests a relationship between the royal house of David and this enigmatic shepherd-like figure. All of this points to Jesus, as well as to a future for Israel, looking one day still to come for her repentance.

Zechariah 12:2–13:1 describes the future repentance and cleansing of the house of David, as well as the role it would play in the future deliverance of God's people. Zechariah 9–14 seems to reserve the future kingship for Yahweh himself (Zech. 9:9; 14:9, 10, 16, 17). This represents a dramatic shift of emphasis in God's progressive revelation of future royal expectations. On the one hand, Zechariah identifies the coming King, who would fulfill the traditional royal Davidic expectations, as none other than Yahweh himself. On the other hand, he hints at how the future kingship of Yahweh on earth was to be reconciled with traditional future royal Davidic expectations. Since the prophet had only one piece of the puzzle, he was left with a mystery concerning the future. Yet what he knew was important. A victorious shepherd would suffer at the hands of the people who must repent. That shepherd would represent the indisputable presence of Yahweh. The full key to this mystery would not be unlocked until the incarnation of the Son of God, who was fully human—fulfilling traditional royal Davidic future expectations—and fully God—fulfilling Zechariah's dramatic new vision of the future kingdom. Yet many of the elements are here in what God revealed to Zechariah.

CONCLUSION

Zechariah reveals continuity and discontinuity with God's promise to David, providing key insight into the future restoration of David's house. Zechariah 1–8 envisions the future coming of the Davidic branch (3:1–10; 6:9–15) and uses the typological picture of the sacred priest Joshua to remind the nation of a priestly dimension in the work to come. Zechariah 9–14 focuses on the future coming of Yahweh as the sole universal King of the eschatological kingdom, with allusions to the role of the restored house of David. Zechariah 9:9–10 points to the universal rule of the king. Zechariah 12:2–13:1 looks to a faithful Davidic rule having a strong association with Yahweh's presence even in the midst of suffering. God would be faithful to his promises to restore the Davidic throne; however, God's own rule and his own presence would be demonstrated in a new sense through the coming future Davidic king.

As the Hebrew canon came to a close, the future eschatological expectation of the postexilic community was fixed on the coming of Yahweh as universal King. Exactly how the royal house of David would fit with the future eschatological kingship of Yahweh was a mystery that was not yet explained. The later Jewish literature from the second temple period would continue to struggle with this tension. The Second Testament alone resolved this mystery: in the incarnation of the God-Man, we find the fulfillment of traditional royal Davidic expectations and expectations of the theocratic kingship of Yahweh. In Jesus, the two will become one.

THREE OBSTACLES TO OVERCOME, AND THEN ONE

The intent of *Jesus the Messiah: Tracing the Promises, Expectations, and Coming of Israel's King* is to make sense of Jesus' and the early church's messianic claim. Our goal is to trace the concept of messianism chronologically as it was introduced and developed in God's sacred writings we presently call "the Old Testament," reflected upon during the second temple period, and crystallized in the Second Testament (our New Testament). Johnston moved us through Hebrew Scriptures beginning with God's promise to Abraham about *kings* coming from his seed, to Jacob's blessing of *leadership* for Judah, to God's promise to David about *an enduring dynasty*, to God's promises to restore the Davidic dynasty after it was dismantled with the Babylonian exile. Having examined these numerous messianic trajectories in the First Testament, we now are ready to look at second temple reflections about Messiah. The goal is twofold: (1) to identify typical obstacles we need to overcome in order to trace the history of Messiah during the second temple period (ch. 8), and (2) to pick out, observe, and appreciate the multiple portraits of Messiah in second temple literature (chs. 9, 10, and 11).[1]

This chapter identifies three obstacles that challenge our ability in tracing the history of ideas about messianism during the second temple

---

1. Although I build upon my initial work, *Early Jewish Hermeneutics and Hebrews 1:5–13: The Impact of Early Jewish Exegesis on the Interpretation of a Significant New Testament Passage* (New York: Peter Lang, 1997) and a course I teach on second temple history and literature, I am indebted to several other works that helped further crystallize my recent thinking in this area: John J. Collins, *The Scepter and the Star: Messianism in Light of the Dead Sea Scrolls*, 2nd ed. (Grand Rapids: Eerdmans, 2010); James H. Charlesworth, Hermann Lichtenberger, and Gerbern S. Oegema, eds., *Qumran-Messianism* (Tübingen: Mohr Siebeck, 1998); Timo Eskola, *Messiah and the Throne* (Tübingen: Mohr Siebeck, 2001).

period: limited resources, blurred vision, and a lack of second temple historical and social sensitivities. The latter point is quite important because Jesus' audiences were a part of this period and likely thought in these historical and social terms, not just in terms that reflect their Hebrew Scriptures. Furthermore second temple texts indicate how the various pieces we saw in the canon were being put together in a variety of ways during this time. Finally they set a context to appreciate what the early church's handling of this material, including that of Jesus, was like. There is yet a fourth obstacle, which I will introduce at the close of this chapter.

LIMITED RESOURCES

It seems odd to suggest that there are limited second temple resources available to us that focus attention on eschatological messianic figures. You would think that over a 550-year period of time there would be an abundance of material on the subject. Yet there is not. The period began with the rebuilding of the temple in 515 BCE and ended with its destruction in 70 CE. Throughout the early and latter parts of the period, a vast amount of literature was written.

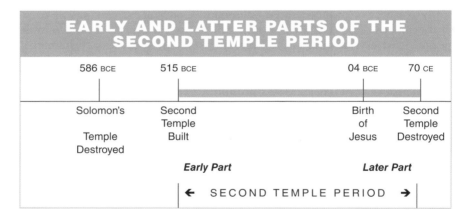

Literature written during the early part of the second temple period is consigned to canonical works: *historical* (Ezra, Nehemiah, Esther, and 1 & 2 Chronicles), *prophetic* (Haggai, Zechariah, and Malachi), and *poetic* (e.g., Ps. 148). Literature composed during the latter part of the period is more extensive and includes works that are non–canonical (apocrypha, pseudepigrapha, and Dead Sea Scrolls) and canonical (NT Gospels, Epistles, and Revelation). Naturally, what the non–canonical material has to say about Messiah is the focus of this portion of our book. Yet the available literature used to reconstruct a history concerning messianic expectations during the second temple period is limited.

OLD TESTAMENT APOCRYPHAL AND PSEUDEPIGRAPHAL DOCUMENTS

Old Testament apocryphal documents are Jewish religious writings that date from *circa* 300 BCE to 70 CE. Although at one time deemed as "hidden" secrets, today the Old Testament apocrypha is defined as a closed collection of either thirteen or sixteen works. They are

Additions to Esther	Additions to Daniel:
Baruch	Prayer of Azariah
Sirach	Bel and the Dragon
Tobit	Susana
Judith	Wisdom of Solomon
Letter of Jeremiah	1 Maccabees
3 Ezra (or 1 Esdras)*	2 Maccabees
4 Ezra (or 2 Esdras)*	3 Maccabees**
Prayer of Manasseh*	4 Maccabees**
	Psalm 151**

Old Testament pseudepigrapha documents are frequently described as second temple works that have been "falsely attributed" to another person. They tend to be written *circa* 250 to 200. For instance, the collection of psalms written *circa* 63 are "falsely attributed" to Solomon and thereby entitled the *Psalms of Solomon*.

Many people today recognize the Old Testament pseudepigrapha collection to consist of sixty-five works, and include most of the works marked with asterisks above as part of the pseudepigrapha collection. Thus, whether some words are more properly considered Apocryphal or Pseudepigraphal is a matter of some disagreement.

Prior to the discovery of the Dead Sea Scrolls, very little extra-biblical material addressed the coming of a royal Messiah figure. Even with the Scrolls, it seems that less than 6 percent of the extra-biblical literature actually speaks of an expected, royal Messiah figure. Old Testament apocryphal documents[2] and the Jewish author Josephus appear to ignore the issue. Furthermore, of the sixty-five Old Testament pseudepigrapha texts, there are only seven Jewish writings, four Christian writings, and two lengthy reworkings of earlier Jewish traditions that speak clearly of expected Messiah figures. And though the Dead Sea Scrolls have escalated our awareness of second temple messianism, of what remains of these documents only twenty fragments actually mention a regal Messiah. Thus anticipation of the restoration of David's dynasty appears to be absent from most

---

2. In 1546 the Council of Trent declared that the Roman Catholic Church intermingle ten Deuterocanonical books with the Old Testament, while three (*) were to be appended to the Second Testament. The Eastern Orthodox Churches and Russian Orthodox Churches, however, include three other works: 3 and 4 Maccabees, and Psalm 151 (**). See Michael D. Coogan, ed. *The New Oxford Annotated Apocrypha,* 3rd ed. (Oxford: Oxford University Press, 2001), 3–4.

of the extant literature written during the second temple period. The extrabiblical sources that specifically address the issue seem to be limited to the following documents presented in the chart on the regal messiah figure.[3]

DOCUMENTS THAT MENTION A REGAL MESSIAH FIGURE		
Pseudepigrapha Documents	**Dead Sea Scrolls**	
Jewish Texts	CD	(*Damascus Document*)
Psalms of Solomon	1QM	(*1QWar Scroll*)
1 Enoch: Dreams, Similitudes	1Q28	(*1QS = 1QRule of the Community*)
2 Baruch	1Q28a	(*1QS*ᵃ *= 1QRule of the Congregation*)
4 Ezra	1Q28b	(*1QS*ᵇ *= 1QRule of Blessings*)
3 Enoch	4Q161	(*4QpIsa*ᵃ *= 4QIsaiah Pesher*ᵃ)
Testament of the Twelve	4Q174	(*4QFlor = 4QFlorilegium*)
Patriarchs: T.Judah	4Q175	(*4QTest = 4QTestimonia*)
Jubilees	4Q246	(*4QpsDan ar = 4QAramaic Apocalypse*)
Christian Texts	4Q252	(*4QcommGen*ᵃ *= 4QCommentary on Genesis A*)
Odes of Solomon	4Q266	(*4QD*ᵃ *= 4QDamascus Document*ᵃ)
Apocalypse of Zephaniah	4Q285	(*4QSM = 4QSefer ha-Milhamah*)
Apocalypse of Elijah	4Q369	(*4QPEnosh = 4QPrayer of Enosh*)
Apocalypse of Sedrach	4Q376	(*4QapocrMoses*ᵇ *= 4QApocryphon of Moses*ᵇ)
Christian Editorial Reworks of Jewish Texts	4Q382	(*4QParaphrase of the Kings*)
	4Q423	(*4QInstructiong*)
Vision of Isaiah	4Q458	(*4QNarrative A*)
Testament of Adam	4Q496	(*4QM*ᶠ *= 4QWar Scroll*ᶠ)
	4Q521	(*4Qmessianic Apocalypse*)

---

3. Although it is difficult to pin down with regard to the date, province, and authorship of the *Testament of the Twelve Patriarchs*, the assumption here is that it along with the *Testament of Judah* are Jewish works with some Christian interpolations. For an opposing view see Kugler, *Testaments of the Twelve Patriarchs* (Sheffield, UK: Sheffield University Press, 2001).

Despite the limited sources, my goal in the subsequent chapters (chs. 9, 10, 11) is to isolate the multiple portraits of Messiah from the literature listed above. Like many other people familiar with both second temple *history and literature* (i.e., canonical and non–canonical), we too will come to recognize that there was no monolithic idea about a Jewish messianic figure but that there were multiple portraits present in the literature. Yet before revealing the various messianic portraits, we must admit that the twenty-first-century church's vision about the Messiah is somewhat blurred.

BLURRED VISION

My diagnosis of the cause of our blurred vision is essentially a twofold disorder: our familiarity with the Second Testament's teaching about Jesus and the early church's desire to distance herself from Judaism. First, our vision is naturally blurred because of our familiarity with the Second Testament and its teaching about Jesus. Our propensity is to read titles for Jesus like "Messiah" or "Christ," "son" or "son of God," "son of the Most High" or "son of man," back into history and literature, rather than allow terminology to develop as history unfolds. In other words, our tendency is to be anachronistic when looking at references about the Messiah. We typically read ancient literature through the lenses of the Second Testament and the post-resurrection of Jesus.[4] Thus our well-informed presuppositions about the Second Testament Messiah tend to blur our ability to distinguish, evaluate, and appreciate the competing messianic portrayals evident and developing in second temple literature.

Second, the church, during her formative years, distanced herself from Judaism, which also contributes to our lack of familiarity with second temple period expectations of Messiah. As converts and eventually leaders of the early church were coming more from a pagan rather than a Jewish influence, early church fathers composed discourses against Judaism. Virtually every major Christian writer of the first five centuries either composed a treatise in opposition to Judaism or made a comparison of Christianity and Judaism a dominant theme.[5] This is certainly evident in the Epistle of Barnabas and writings of Ignatius and Justin Martyr. This polemic against Judaism created a wedge between Christianity and Judaism which resulted in an even greater lack of familiarity with second temple period Messianic expectations. Instead of reading second temple period Jewish literature to better understand the

---

4. Even when studying the Gospels we tend to be anachronistic. For instance, I have argued elsewhere that most of the titles ascribed to Jesus throughout Mark's narrative story about Jesus and in Mark 1:1 serve only to present Jesus to be "the Christ" or the Hebrew equivalent "Messiah." Herbert W. Bateman IV, "Defining the Titles 'Christ' and 'Son of God' in Mark's Narrative Presentation of Jesus," *JETS* 50 (September 2007): 537–59.

5. Jaroslav Pelikan, *The Emergence of the Catholic Tradition (100–600)* in The Christian Tradition: A History of the Development of Doctrine (Chicago: University of Chicago Press, 1975), 12–27.

historical development of Messianic expectations, the early church fathers naturally set themselves in opposition to these Jewish expectations.

For instance, Justin Martyr, born of pagan parents around 100 CE and converted around 132 CE, was an influential Christian apologist from 152–165 CE. In his written discourse entitled *Dialogue with Trypho*, Justin widened the gap between Christianity and Judaism. As he debated a learned Jew, Trypho, Justin declared, "We are the true Israel," and thereby replaced the Jews as the chosen people of God with the church (*Dial.* 11.5).[6] Later in the same work, Justin confiscated Jewish Scriptures as belonging to the church (*Dial.* 29.2).

> I am positive I can persuade by these words even those of weak intellectual faculties, for the words which I use are not my own, nor are they embellished by human rhetoric, but they are the words as David sang them, as Isaias announced them as good news, as Zacharias proclaimed them, and as Moses wrote them. Aren't you acquainted with them, Trypho? You should be, for *they are contained in your Scriptures, or rather not yours, but ours.* For we believe and obey them, whereas you, though you read them, do not grasp their spirit.[7]

As Justin Martyr's dialogue continued, the learned Jew Trypho interrupted and raised an objection, namely that the Christological prophecies were not messianic, but rather they were references to historic kings in Israel. He continued by saying, "We Jews all expect that Christ will be a man of merely human origin, and that Elias will come to anoint him" (*Dial.* 49.1).

At which point, Justin employed the Old Testament as a Christological proof-text in order to establish that Jesus was the Messiah (*Dial.* 48–107). His rebuttal consisted of a simple prophecy—fulfillment scheme: (1) he stated an Old Testament prophecy, (2) he provided a short exposition, and (3) he summarized with a fulfillment report to confirm that Jesus was indeed the Messiah.[8] And

---

6. Murray points out that Justin Martyr was the first to make such an explicit claim in writing. Michele Murray, *Playing a Jewish Game: Gentile Christian Judaizing in the First and Second Centuries CE* (Waterloo, ON: Wilfrid Laurier University Press, 2004), 93. Another example is Tertullian. "For Tertullian," says Mason, "*Judaismus* ended in principle with the coming of Jesus and it survives only vestigially." He was responsible for "decoupling of the Judean people from its land and legitimacy" and made Judaism *"different in kind"* from Christian belief. Thus "Judaism was an unchanging, fossilized faith, not to be taken seriously or deserving proper attention." Steve Mason, *Josephus, Judea, and Christian Origins: Methods and Categories* (Peabody, MA: Hendrickson, 2009), 141–84 esp. 152–55.

7. Translated by Thomas B. Falls, *The Writings of Saint Justin Martyr* in The Fathers of the Church (Washington, DC: Catholic University Press, 1948), 165, 191. Emphasis is mine.

8. Oskar Skarsaune, *The Proof from Prophecy: A Study in Justin Martyr's Proof-Text Tradition: Text-Type, Provenance, Theological Profile* in Supplements to Novum Testamentum (Leiden: Brill, 1987), 191–227.

though Justin used the First Testament as a Christological proof-text and Trypho offered an overly generalized statement for "all Jews" about an expected Messiah figure, Johnston has pointed out that the Hebrew Scriptures did not offer a formal, explicitly direct, fully disclosed monolithic messianic concept. Rather, it moved in this direction progressively with bits and pieces that established patterns of divine activity in history that revealed what God was doing gradually.

Yet with the increasing availability of and growing interest in second temple literature, our understanding of first-century Judaism, with its customs and theological developments, appears to be regaining its Jewish roots, roots that were lost during the formative years of the Christian church. For instance, the variety of theological expectations, especially that of anticipated "messianic figures," had lost its diversity and its unique Jewish characteristics. And though our goal is to isolate messianic portraits chronologically as they proceeded out of the Hebrew Scriptures and then later reflected upon during the second temple period, our lack of historical and social sensitivities about second temple period expectations warrants an historical overview of the period.

LACK OF HISTORICAL AND SOCIAL SENSITIVITIES

As people living in the twenty-first century, we are sometimes ignorant of the historical and social events, influences, and opinions of those who lived during the second temple period. For instance, many followers of Jesus today seem to believe that every Jew yearned for the coming of "the Davidic Messiah." Yet that was not true. The extant literature of the period tells us differently. Thus the goal of this section is to reveal (1) the indifferences to messianism, (2) the dormancy of messianism, and (3) the evoking and inflaming of messianism during the second temple period. But first, a description of Judaism's historical and social setting warrants investigation.

Judaism's Social Setting

The destruction of Jerusalem's temple, the dismantling of David's dynasty, and the deportation of Judah's population in 586 BCE[9] not only disrupted God's chosen people and their way of life, it convincingly changed them. For

---

9. This is not to say that the territory of Judah was completely devoid of people. The book of Kings and its chronological reference to the reign of the kings does not end with Zedekiah (24:18–25:21), but rather includes Gedaliah's appointment as governor of the poor people who were allowed to remain in the land (25:22–26; cp. Jer. 52:15–16), and the eventual release of Jehoiachin in Babylon (25:27–30; cp. Jer. 52:31–34). See "Part 1, The Myth of the Empty Land Revisited" in *Judah and the Judeans in the Neo–Babylonian Period* (ed. Oded Lipschits and Joseph Blenkinsopp; Winona Lake: Eisenbrauns, 2003), 3–89. See Oded Lipschits, "Achaemenid Imperial Policy, Settlement Processes in Palestine, and the Status of Jerusalem in the Middle of the Fifth Century B.C.E." in *Judah and the Judeans in the Persian Period* (ed. Oded Lipschits and Manfred Oeming; Winona Lake: Eisenbrauns, 2006), 19–52.

instance, the insidious problem of idolatry, apparent during the first temple period (e.g., Isa. 44:6–22, Jer. 11:1–14, 25:1, 3, 81; Ezek. 8:1–3, 7–18, 12:1–6) was an adamantly opposed practice during second temple Judaism. Testimonies to this change are self-evident in at least two apocryphal works, the Letter of Jeremiah and Bel and the Dragon.

Bel and the Dragon and the Letter of Jeremiah were Jewish polemics against idolatry.[10] In Bel and the Dragon, written *circa* 200 BCE, Daniel faced life and death situations that challenged his personal piety and his Jewish faith in one God. Yet Daniel proved to the foreign king the fraudulent nature of the king's religion, namely that there is no supernatural reality behind the molten image of the idol named Bel. In the Letter of Jeremiah, however, written *circa* 300 BCE, the author was more direct. In this passionate and somewhat sarcastic sermon based on Jeremiah 10, the author depicted idols as helpless (vv. 8–16, 57–59), useless (vv. 17–23), lifeless (vv. 24–29), powerless (vv. 30–40a, 53–56), worthless (vv. 45–52), and empty show-offs (vv. 70–73). He described idol worshippers as foolish and shameful (vv. 40b–44). "Therefore" the author concluded, "one must not think that they are gods nor call them gods, for they are not able either to decide a case or to do good to men or women" (v. 64). "Better is the just person who has no idols" (v. 73b).

From these two apocryphal works at least two points can be made: (1) the gods of the nations, and by extension their priests, are frauds; and (2) the God of Israel is the only true deity.[11] It seems God finally convinced his chosen people of their need for change concerning the practice of idolatry. In fact, idolatry was a part of Judaism's litmus test for conversion. Gentiles desiring to convert to Judaism were expected to surrender all acts of idolatry and worship the one true God.[12] Thus idolatry during the second temple period was not to be tolerated and was the catalyst that ignited the Maccabean war (1 Macc. 1:41–43, 47, 54; 2:15–26). Nevertheless, it took Nebuchadnezzar's drastic destruction of Jerusalem in 586 BCE to produce change.

Compassionately, God's discipline of the nation in 586 BCE was not without national hope of restoration. Prophetic messages of discipline and doom, which were to be carried out by Nebuchadnezzar and the Chaldeans, were balanced with hope. More specifically, the hope of restoration comprised

---

10. For a more detailed discussion on Bel and the Dragon and the Letter of Jeremiah, see David deSilva, *Introducing the Apocrypha: Message, Context, and Significance* (Grand Rapids: Baker, 2001), 214–21, 237–43.

11. *Sirach* also addresses idolatry (unable to eat or feel: 30:19–20), as does the *Apocalypse of Abraham* (1:1–4; 25:1–6) and 4QPrayer of Nabonidus (4QPrNab *frags.* 1-8; unable to heal). This theme about idols being inanimate objects occurs in the Second Testament as well (1 Cor. 10:14–21; cf. Rom. 1:18–32, James 2:19, 1 John 5:21).

12. See Shaye J. D. Cohen, "Crossing the Boundary and Becoming a Jew," *HTR* 82 (1989): 13–33. I also address the issue in "Were The Opponents at Philippi Necessarily Jewish," *BSac* 155 (January–March 1998): 39–62.

of three items: a hope to *reestablish* God's people in the land, a hope to *rebuild* the temple, and a hope to *restore* David's dynasty, however vague the details.[13] God permitted Nebuchadnezzar to vanquish and thereby discipline his chosen people, but he did not allow them to become completely absorbed among the Babylonians (605–539 BCE). Nor did he permit them to become an extinct race among the Medes and Persians (536–331 BCE). The books of Daniel and the Additions to Daniel as well as Esther and the Additions to Esther serve as records of individual and national preservation.

Yet despite Isaiah and Jeremiah's statements of restoration, not everyone during the second temple period expected the reestablishment of David's dynasty in the same way. And despite the significant evidence from the Scrolls that indicates there are Jewish people looking for various Messiah figures, we ought not to conclude that every Jew anticipated the restoration of David's dynasty. This is particularly true of two well-known Jewish writers from the latter part of the second temple period. Josephus and Ben Sira never mention the restoration of the Davidic dynasty. In fact, both indicate that sin brought about the irrevocable end of the dynasty. Thus for some Jewish people there existed an indifference toward any kind of expectation of a Davidic messiah.

The Indifference to Messianism

Flavius Josephus

The first-century Jewish historian Josephus was born in 37 CE (*Life* 1 § 5), educated in all the Judean sects (*Life* 2 §§ 7–8, 12), honored with Roman citizenship (*Life* 76 § 423), and wrote several works at the close of the second temple period (*circa* 90–100 CE) before he died (*circa* 100 CE). On the one hand, two of his four works were written to dispel misinformation. Whereas *Antiquities* combatted the ridicule and misinformation that was characteristic of Roman portrayals of the Jews (*Ant* 1.1–2 §§ 1–6), *Life* combatted allegations against Josephus himself and his involvement in the war effort against Rome (*Life* 65 §§ 336–367). On the other hand, *Jewish Wars* was a rationale for the Jewish revolt of 66–70 CE (*War* 1.9–12), and *Against Apion* was a religious apologetic against a well-known Egyptian scholar, Apion (*Apion* 1.1 § 2; cp. 1.11 §§ 57–58). Apion had moved to Rome to teach rhetoric during the thirties of the first century and was an outspoken adversary of Jewish people.[14] All these works are important for understanding the Jewish people of the second temple period, yet none of them contains explicit information

---

13. Johnston identifies how and why the details are unclear in "Messianic Trajectories in Isaiah" (see specifically, Isaiah 9–11, pp. 135–56), "Messianic Trajectories in Jeremiah" (see specifically Jeremiah 23:1–8, 33:14–22; pp. 173–78) "Messianic Trajectories in Zechariah" (see specifically Zechariah 1–8, pp. 193–202).

14. For more information about Josephus and his writings see Steve Mason, *Josephus and the New Testament* (Peabody, MA: Hendrickson, 2nd ed., 1992); *idem, Josephus, Judea, and Christian Origins: Methods and Categories* (Peabody, MA: Hendrickson, 2009). For an

about Josephus's belief in an expected Davidite, nor do they anticipate a restoration of the Davidic dynasty. This is particularly true of the work entitled *Antiquities*. To begin with, Josephus believed the establishment of David as king and his dynasty was a tribute to the power of God.

> . . . so Boaz called the senate to witness, and bid the woman to loose his shoe and spit in his face, according to the law; and when this was done Boaz married Ruth, and they had a son within a year's time. Naomi was herself a nurse to this child; and by the advice of the women, called him Obed, as being to be brought up in order to be subservient to her in her old age, for Obed in the Hebrew dialect signifies a servant. The son of Obed was Jesse, and *David* was his son, *who was king*, and *left his dominions to his sons for one-and-twenty generations*. I was therefore obliged to relate this history of Ruth, because I had a mind to demonstrate the power of God, who, without difficulty, can raise those that are of ordinary parentage to dignity and splendor, to which he advanced *David, though he were born of such mean parents. (Ant 5.9.4 §§ 335–37, emphasis mine).*[15]

God raised David to power, despite his ordinary parentage, and his dynasty lasted for twenty-one generations. Yet as the story of David and his dynasty continued to unfold, the longevity of the dynasty, according to Josephus, was evidently conditional with no everlasting dimensions.[16]

> God appeared to Nathan that very night, and commanded him to say to David, that he took his purpose and his desires kindly, since nobody had before now taken it into their head to build him a temple, although upon his having such a notion he [God] would not permit him to build him that temple, because he had made many wars, and was defiled with the slaughter of his enemies; that, however, after his death, in his old age, and when he had lived a long life, there should be a temple built by a son of his, who should take the kingdom after him, and should be called Solomon, whom he promised to provide for, as a father provides for his son, by preserving the kingdom for his son a posterity, and delivering it to them; but that *he would still punish him if he sinned, with diseases and barrenness of land. (Ant 7.4.4 §§ 92–93; 8.4.6 §§ 125–29, emphasis mine)*

For Josephus, Solomon's success was dependent on obedience. It does not appear as though Josephus believed in any ever-lasting permanence of David's dynasty. This seems evident in his retelling of the dynasty's demise.

---

excellent abridged version of Josephus see Paul L. Maier's *Josephus: The Essential Works* (Grand Rapids: Kregel, 1988, 1994).

15. All translations from Josephus in this chapter are reproduced from Accordance.
16. H. W. Attridge, *The Interpretation of Biblical History in the Antiquitates Judaicae of Flavius Josephus*, HDR 7 (Missoula: Scholars Press, 1976), 78–83.

Now the city was taken on the ninth day of the fourth month, in the eleventh year of the reign of Zedekiah. They were indeed only generals of the king of Babylon, to whom Nebuchadnezzar committed the care of the siege, for he abode himself in the city of Riblah. (*Ant* 10.8.2 § 135)

And after this manner have the kings of David's race ended their lives, being in number twenty-one, until, the last king, who all together reigned five hundred and fourteen years, and six months, and ten days: of whom Saul, who was their first king, retained the government twenty years, though he was not of the same tribe with the rest. (*Ant* 10.8.4 § 143, emphasis mine)

Thus, the Davidic dynasty ended with Nebuchadnezzar's conquest of Jerusalem. Josephus gives no indication or hope of God restoring David's dynasty.[17] God's promise to David appears to be conditioned on the obedience of the Davidite. And though Josephus represented a late second temple perspective, the second well-known Jewish author, Ben Sira, writes nearly 150 years earlier.

Jesus ben Sira

Ben Sira, a scribe who lived and taught in Jerusalem before the Maccabean revolt of 167–164 BCE, wrote the apocryphal book entitled Sirach (also known as Ecclesiasticus or Wisdom of Jesus Ben Sira; see Sir. 50:27). "Ben Sira," according to deSilva, "was no reactionary, but he was definitely a conservative voice of the first and second century BCE, calling his pupils to seek their fortune, their honor, and their good name through the diligent observance of the demands of the God of Israel first and foremost."[18]

Based on the description of Simon II, a high priest in Jerusalem from 219–196 BCE mentioned in Sirach 50:1–24, the book was probably written sometime *circa* 180 BCE. Although Sirach is a book of wisdom teachings about proper speech, riches and poverty, honesty, diligence, choice of friends, sin and death, it is not totally proverbial. Sirach concludes with a hymn of praise about famous Jewish ancestors (41:1–49:16). Naturally, David was praised as one of Israel's great ancestors (47:2–11).[19] He was praised for his shepherding

---

17. For Josephus, according to Mason, the majority of monarchs are corrupt and decline into tyranny as evidenced in the destruction of the temple, the demise of the Hasmoneans, and the disastrous rule of Herod. The two greatest king tyrants of Judean history in Josephus's *Antiquities*, according to Mason, are Saul and Herod. Mason, *Josephus, Judea, and Christian Origins*, 194–208. Compare Per Bilde, *Flavius Josephus between Jerusalem and Rome: His Life, His Works, and Their Importance* (Sheffield: JSOT Press, 1988), 65-79.
18. deSilva, *Introducing the Apocrypha*, 153.
19. In a similar way, the apocryphal Psalm 151 recalls the life of David (11Q5 or 11QPsa). This poetic summary is based on 1 Samuel 16–17. It is narrated and written as if by David in the first person. Whereas Psalm 151:1–5 recounts how God chose David to be

skills (v. 2), his slaying of Goliath (vv. 4–7a), his defeating of the Philistines (vv. 7b), and his composing of psalms for God (vv. 8–10). At the close of this lengthy tribute to David, Ben Sira mused, "The LORD took away his sins and exalted his power (lit. "raised his horn") forever; he gave him a covenant of kingship and a glorious throne in Israel."[20] Yet the covenant appears to have been understood to be conditioned upon obedience because Ben Sira describes a permanent dismantling of the Davidic dynasty.

> Except for David and Hezekiah and Josiah, all of them were great sinners, for they abandoned the law of the Most High; the kings of Judah came to an end. They gave their power to others, and their glory to a foreign nation, who set fire to the chosen city of the sanctuary, and made its streets desolate, as Jeremiah had foretold. (Sir. 49:4–6, NRSV)

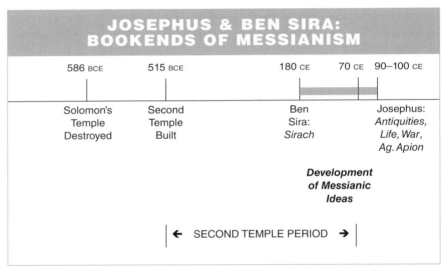

JOSEPHUS & BEN SIRA: BOOKENDS OF MESSIANISM

586 BCE	515 BCE	180 CE	70 CE	90–100 CE
Solomon's Temple Destroyed	Second Temple Built	Ben Sira: Sirach		Josephus: Antiquities, Life, War, Ag. Apion

Development of Messianic Ideas

← SECOND TEMPLE PERIOD →

According to Ben Sira, David's dynasty had ended, the power of the dynasty had been given to others, and the honor of the dynasty had been removed because of the great sins of the Davidic monarchs. Elsewhere Ben Sira emphasized that people have the power to choose to obey God. Each person, including

---

king of Israel (1 Sam. 16:4–13, 14–23), Psalm 151:6–7 recounts how David killed the Philistine Goliath in battle (1 Sam. 17:43, 51). Theological Lesson: The God of Israel can and does rescue his people from their sufferings in surprising ways. See Daniel J. Harrington, *Invitation to the Apocrypha* (Grand Rapids: Eerdmans, 1999), 170–72.

20. Alternative rendering: "The LORD forgave him his sins and exalted his strength (lit. "raised his horn") forever; he conferred on him the rights of royalty and established his throne in Israel." Translation by Patrick W. Skehan in *The Wisdom of Ben Sira*, AB (New York: Doubleday, 1987), 524.

kings, is responsible for his actions (15:11–17). The kings of the Davidic monarchy chose disobedience and thereby forfeited their right to rule. Only David, Hezekiah, and Josiah were deemed righteous. Ben Sira expressed no explicit hope of restoration of David's line. Thus as it was with Josephus, so it was with Ben Sira. Neither author seems to anticipate the restoration of the Davidic dynasty. The lack of expectation of a future Davidic Messiah was due to a belief that the longevity of the Davidic dynasty depended upon the obedience of the Davidite.[21] Together, these authors and their works serve as bookends for the literature studied in the following pages because messianic expectations flourished between the time Ben Sira and Josephus wrote their respective works.

Unfortunately the perspectives of Josephus and Ben Sira have been overshadowed by the highly publicized Dead Sea Scrolls that speak clearly of an anticipated Davidic Messiah. Yet "it is quite possible," according to John Collins, "that messianism was not a factor in the earliest formative stage of the Qumran community."[22] Perhaps this was because they believed obedience to their Teacher would influence God to respond accordingly. Regardless, this seldom-mentioned attitude of Josephus, Ben Sira, and perhaps even the initial founders of the Qumran community inform us that not everyone anticipated the restoration of David's dynasty. Thus it seems safe to say that many Jewish people of the second temple period did not express confident expectation of the coming of a Davidic Messiah. Yet why did First Testament messianic concepts, pregnant and ready to be developed, lay dormant and in mystery form for centuries? Or we might ask it this way: Why did they leave their messianic puzzle pieces boxed?

The Dormancy of Messianism

The political and social situations that induced and sanctioned the dormancy of messianic hope among the Jews may be attributed to both the Persian (539–331 BCE) and early Hellenistic imperialism over Judeans (332–164 BCE).[23] The Persians induced it, and the Jewish people sanctioned it during the Hellenistic period. In fact, it appears as though these two political and social situations factor into why the hope for the restoration of David's dynasty remained dormant like *embers* in smoldering ruins for most of the second temple period. Some might also add the Hasmoneans here, but their

---

21. Collins, *Scepter and the Star*, 40, writes, "For Sirach, the glory of David belongs to the past."
22. Collins, *Scepter and the Star*, 83. In fact, Collins argues "the evidence suggests that Messianism was virtually dormant from the early fifth to late second century BCE." ibid., 51.
23. I have selected 332 and 164 BCE for the following reasons. In 332 BCE, Alexander the Great defeated Gaza, the last obstacle to Egypt. Thus all the cities from Issus, including Jerusalem, to Egypt were his oyster. In 164 BCE, Judas "the Maccabee" cleansed the temple and restored a degree of religious freedom to Jerusalem. This is not to suggest that Hellenism ceased to exist in Judea after Judas cleansed the temple, but merely to identify a beginning for Hellenism in the geographical area and an eventual resistance against it, during which time their existed a sanctioning of messianic dormancy. More will be said below.

influence was a mixture of dominancy and a stirring that eventually inflamed the messianic issue. Therefore they are examined later in this chapter.

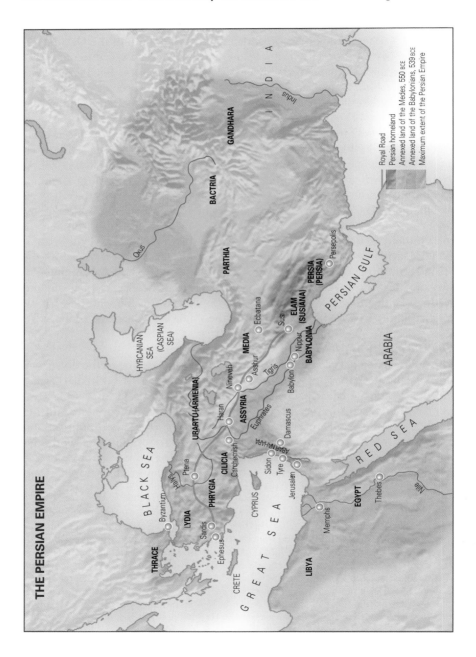

Inducing Messianic Dormancy
At least two factors contributed to *Persia's role in inducing messianic dormancy*: the Persian Empire's political and social structure and Judah's lack of economic and political importance. The first factor was a Persian socioethnic one. The Persian Empire established itself within the first fifty-three years of existence. Expansion began with Cyrus, conqueror of the Medes, Lydians, Babylonians, Bactrians, Parthians, and other people groups (539–530 BCE). It continued with his son, Cambyses, conqueror of Egypt (530–522 BCE), and it ended with Darius the Great, conqueror of Thrace (522–486 BCE). Persian imperialism extended from the Indus River in the East, to the Aegean Sea in the West, and the Nile River in the South. Thus, the Persian Empire spanned no fewer than twenty-three countries.[24]

Persian kings, however, retained and maintained the royal residences of the conquered states for themselves in that it was the Persian noble who was assigned to govern Persia's vast empire. Consequently, Ecbatana, Sardis, Bactra, Babylon, Susa, Saïs, and Memphis served as the empire's seats of power. Some, however, were reduced to the rank of a satrapal capital (like Memphis in Egypt) or subsatrapal capital (like Damascus in Syria), while others like Sardis in the west and Bactra in the east were deemed centers of Persian authority over wider regions. Still others, like Ecbatana, Babylon, and Susa were promoted to royal residences. "From the inception of the Empire," according to Briant, "it was this dominant socioethnic class that held power from the Indus to the Mediterranean and intended to keep it."[25]

This is not to say that local dynastic powers were non-existent in the Persian Empire. Persians recognized local dynasties, but their dynastic titles were relegated to that of governor.[26] Only those of Persian noble birth ruled and wielded royal power. Thus Persian imperialism, its political and social

---

24. Pierre Briant, *From Cyrus to Alexander: A History of the Persian Empire* (Winona Lake: Eisenbrauns, 2002), 172–83..

25. Briant, *From Cyrus to Alexander*, 352. See "The King's Men," 302–54. Of particular interest to the social and political scene in Persia see "The Seats of Power," 84–89; "The King and His Faithful: The Rationale of the System," 324–30; and "King and Satraps," 338–52. Cp. M. A. Danamayev, "Neo–Babylonian and Achaemenid State Administration in Mesopotamia" in *Judah and the Judeans in the Persian Period* (ed. Oded Lipschits and Manfred Oeming; Winona Lake: Eisenbrauns, 2006), 373–98.

26. Briant, *From Cyrus to Alexander*, 587. Cp. Lisbeth Fried, "The *'am ha'ares* in Ezra 4:4 and Persian Administration" in *Judah and the Judeans in the Persian Period* (ed. Oded Lipschits and Manfred Oeming; Winona Lake: Eisenbrauns, 2006), 123–45. This explains why Sheshbazzar and Zerubbabel, though dynastic heirs of David, are given the mere title of governor (Sheshbazzar: Ezra 1:8, 5:18; 1 Chron. 3:18; Zerubbabel: Ezra 4:1–3; Hag. 1:1; 2:2; 1 Esd. 5:4; 6:27–29). For more detailed discussions about the Davidic governors Sheshbazzar and Zerubbabel, see James C. VanderKam, *From Joshua to Caiaphas: High Priests after the Exile* (Minneapolis: Fortress, 2004), 1–23.

structure, a structure that dominated the Middle East for over two hundred years, induced messianic dormancy.

The second factor that induced messianic dormancy during the Persian period was Judah's lack of economic and political importance to Persia's aristocracy.[27] Situated in the mountain region, Judah's major city Jerusalem was not a major economic contributor to the Persian empire. Furthermore, Jerusalem was a distance from any major trade route. Finally, Jerusalem was not a major seat of political power. Judah's constituents were just one of many people groups within Persia's vast empire. Thus Scripture's presentation of Cyrus' edict, one that appears to stress Judah's importance to Persia (cp. Ezra 1:2–4; 2 Chron. 36:23; 1 Esd. 2:1–7), was an "optical illusion" because Judah was of no real *major* consequence to Persian nobility.

Evidence of this "optical illusion" endures on an ancient clay barrel. The inscription on the barrel recorded the edict issued by Cyrus early in his career as an imperialistic king.

> I resettled upon the command of Marduk, the great lord, all the gods of Sumer and Akkad whom Nabonidus has brought into Babylon to the anger of the lord of the gods, unharmed, in their former chapels, the places which make them happy. *May all the gods whom I have resettled in their sacred cities* ask daily Bel and Nebo for a long life for me and may they recommend me; to Marduk, my lord . . . .[28]

Cyrus' edict was the basis for all native populations, populations that were uprooted by the Babylonians, to return home and rebuild their temples. Everyone under Persian control was privy to Cyrus' policy.[29] What was recorded on Cyrus' Cylinder was analogous to what was done throughout his empire and was to benefit all people. Thus, like many other people groups, the first group of Jewish captives returned to rebuild their temple to their God.

---

27. See Oded Lipschits, "Achaemenid Imperial Policy, Settlement Processes in Palestine, and the Status of Jerusalem in the Middle of the Fifth Century BCE" in *Judah and the Judeans in the Persian Period* (ed. Oded Lipschits and Manfred Oeming; Winona Lake: Eisenbrauns, 2006), 19–52.
28. "Cyrus (557–529): Inscription on a Clay Barrel," translated by A. Leo Oppenheim in *ANET*, 208. Emphasis mine.
29. Although the proclamation of the cylinder relates specifically to Marduk and residents of Babylon, it could be concluded that the edict was directed only to Babylonians. See Amélie Kuhrt, "The Cyrus Cylinder and Achaemenid Imperial Policy," *JSOT* 25 (1983): 83–97. Yet VanderKam argues for an empire-wide policy that included three actions for other people groups: (1) rebuild the temple, (2) exiles return home, (3) take your temple vessels with you. VanderKam, *From Joshua to Caiaphas,* 3–4. For another discussion about the returnees see John Kessler's "Persia's Loyal Yahwists: Power Identity and Ethnicity in Achaemenid Yehud" in *Judah and the Judeans in the Persian Period* (ed. Oded Lipschits and Manfred Oeming; Winona Lake: Eisenbrauns, 2006), 91–121.

Further evidence of an "optical illusion" may be seen through Jerusalem's social problems. We know that Cyrus sent Sheshbazzar, leader, appointed governor, and perhaps even son of Jehoiachin (Ezra 1:8, 5:14; 1 Chron. 3:18; 1 Esd. 2:12), back to Judah with 42,360 people (Ezra 2:64). Under his leadership, the temple foundations are laid (Ezra 5:13–16). Thus those who returned to Jerusalem began to rebuild the temple around 538 BCE, but construction was halted in 530 BCE, while Cambyses was king, due to domestic squabbles. Yet the fact that these social problems were of no real consequence to Persian aristocracy evidences itself when no one hastened to ensure Jerusalem's temple was rebuilt once domestic disputes and obstacles arose among the Jewish people.

Squabbles among the Jews during the early part of the second temple period between the returnees (Zerubbabel and Jeshua) and those who had remained in the land (Rehum and Shimshai) were not unique to the empire (Ezra 4:1–24; 1 Esd. 2:16–30).[30] Judah's local jurisdictional squabbles were comparable to the tensions seen in Asia Minor between satraps where they continually disputed control over frontier territory.[31] Nevertheless, temple construction eventually resumed in 522 BCE and the temple was completed in 515 BCE while Darius the Great was king of Persia (Ezra 5:3–6:22; cp. 1 Esd. 3:1–4:61; 6:1–7:9). Thus, it took twenty-three years from the laying of the corner stone (538 BCE) till its completion (515 BCE) to rebuild the temple, a temple which initially took Solomon a mere seven years to build and was of far greater grandeur (cp. 1 Kings 6:38 with Hag. 2:3).

EARLY PERSIAN KINGS AND INFLUENCES DURING THE EARLY SECOND TEMPLE PERIOD

Persian King	Activities in Judah	Jewish Leaders
Cyrus the Great	Temple construction began	Sheshbazzar
Cambyses	Temple construction ceased	Squabbles: Returnees and Jewish remnants in the Land
Darius the Great	Temple construction resumed and completed	Haggai, Zechariah, Joshua, Zerubbabel
Xerxes	Edict issued on behalf of Jewish people	Esther and Mordecai
Artaxerxes	Establish the religious structure in Jerusalem and rebuild the walls of Jerusalem	Ezra and Nehemiah

---

30. Although these disputes may not have been unique to the empire, for the Jewish people they seem to have triggered the beginning of sectarianism in Jerusalem. See Albert I Baumgarten, *The Flourishing of Jewish Sects in the Maccabean Era: An Interpretation*, Supplements to the Journal for the Study of Judaism, volume 55 (New York: Brill, 1997), 5–28.
31. Briant, *From Cyrus to Alexander*, 587.

Consequently Persia's political and social structure as well as Judah's lack of real economic and political importance to the Persian aristocracy *induced messianic dormancy*. Yet like the stages in the life of a spring flower, Persia was an empire that (1) grew and blossomed quickly, (2) its growth ceased, and (3) eventually the flower faded away and the plant died. Thus the political and social stages of Persian imperialism may be described as (1) the quick growth of the empire (539–486 BCE), (2) the stagnation of the empire (486–423 BCE), and (3) the decline of the empire (423–331 BCE). The latter two stages prepared the way for Jerusalem to settle into a socio-religious temple city-state that ultimately sanctioned the messianic dormancy initially induced during the growth of Persian imperialism.

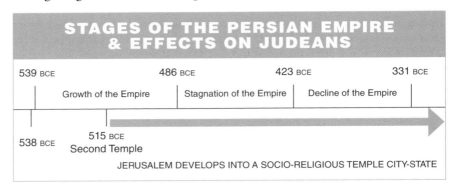

Sanctioning Messianic Dormancy

How did the Jewish people sanction messianic dormancy during the Hellenistic Period? At least three factors contribute to *the sanctioning of messianic dormancy*: (1) the liberations and conquests of Alexander the Great, (2) the subsequent squabbles over the division of Alexander's kingdom, and (3) the Maccabean success to impede Seleucid rulers who attempted to interfere with Jewish ways of life.

Alexander the Great. The first factor that prompted the sanctioning of messianic dormancy in Judea was Alexander the Great, whose focus of attention was the conquest of the Persian Empire. It was not the Jews of Judea. As with all historical figures, it helps to know why Alexander wanted to defeat the Persians and how he managed to emerge as the one to vanquish the Persians. The Persians and Greeks were at odds with one another for over two hundred years. At first, the Persians were the aggressors. Persian aggression began with Cyrus the Great, when he incorporated the Greek city-states of Smyrna, Sardis, Ephesus, Miletus, and others along the coast of Asia Minor into the empire (547–546 BCE). It continued with Darius the Great's attempt to defeat the Greeks at Marathon, but he was defeated (490 BCE). Yet he managed to expand into and control Thrace, the territory northeast of Macedonia. Persian aggression ended, however, with Xerxes (of Esther). Though victorious at Thermopylae (480 BCE), Xerxes was defeated at Salamis (480 BCE) and again at Plataea (479 BCE).[32] Thus Persian aggression against the Greeks ended. Nevertheless, Greek hatred for the Persians merely festered while they wrangled and waged war among themselves until Philip II managed to unify the Greek city-states against Persian imperialism.

City-state conflicts were unsettling realities among the Greeks for more than 120 years. Due to its ability to thwart Xerxes, Athens emerged first as the leader among the Greek city-states, ruled the Aegean Sea with confidence, and nurtured Greek civilization into its golden age (461–431 BCE). In time, however, Sparta became uneasy about Athenian confidence and control of the Aegean Sea. Uneasiness escalated into disputes, and these eventually erupted into war between the two city-states along with their respective allies in 411 BCE (typically referred to as the Peloponnesian War). When the dust settled, Sparta emerged victorious (404 BCE). Yet within thirty-five years another city-state, Thebes, usurped power away from Sparta (369 BCE). Similar power struggles continued until finally Philip II of Macedonia defeated the Thebean, Athenian, Corinthian, and other Greek troops at Chaeronea (7 August 338 BCE) and united the Greeks.

Philip II, a Macedonian noble educated in Thebes, maneuvered kingship over Macedonia in 359 BCE. He began his expansions in Thessaly and most of Thrace (he renamed an important Thracian city Philippi after himself) before

---

32. Briant, *From Cyrus to Alexander*, Cyrus: 35–37, Darius: 156–58, Xerxes: 529–33; Paul Cartledge, *Thermopylae: The Battle That Changed the World* (New York: Overlook Press, 2006).

moving into southern Greece. He used three techniques that were hallmarks of his success in pacifying the northern tribes of his territory and later the city-states of Greece: diplomacy, bribery, and military alliance. After his victory at Chaeronea, Philip appealed to the common hatred among the Greeks toward the Persians to inaugurate a "Common Peace" that unified the Greek city-states under one military commander. Philip of Macedonia was to be captain general of Greece's military forces. The intention of this federated force was to liberate the city-states along the coast of Asia Minor: Sardis, Ephesus, Miletus, and others. Philip, however, was assassinated in 336 BCE.[33] Enter Alexander the Great.

As we know, Alexander the Great—son of Philip II—led Greece into battle against the Persians. He was born in 356 BCE, educated by Aristotle in Athens, and nurtured to follow in his father's footsteps. At twenty years of age, Alexander assumed leadership over the Greek-city states and set out against Persia. After placing a wreath at the tomb of Achilles at Ilium (a pseudo-Troy), Alexander entered Asia Minor, defeated Darius III king of Persia at the Granicus River (spring 334 BCE), and liberated the Greek city-states of Sardis, Ephesus, Miletus, and others along the coast of Asia Minor.[34]

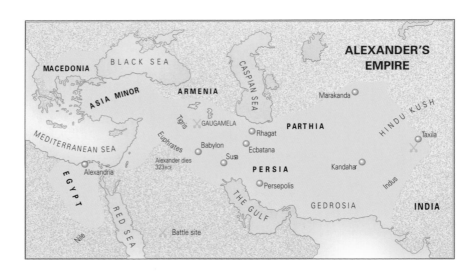

33. Miltiades B. Hatzopolulos and Louisa D. Loukopoulos, eds., *Philip of Macedon* (Athens: Ekdotike Athenon, 1992).
34. For an excellent biography of Alexander's conquests see Peter Green's *Alexander of Macedon, 356–323 B.C.: A Historical Biography* (Los Angeles: University of California Press, 1991).

Alexander, however, was no longer content with being a liberator. His military objectives shifted to that of conqueror of the Persian Empire and their king, Darius III. Once again, Alexander defeated Darius, this time at Issus (November 333 BCE). Although Darius and his pulverized army retreated eastward towards Media to regroup, Alexander advanced south, captured all Persian and Phoenicia ports (of particular importance, Tyre) along the Mediterranean Sea, and wintered in Egypt (332 BCE). In mid-April 331 BCE, Alexander headed north along the coastal road back to Tyre and eventually directed his forces east toward Gaugamela where Alexander once again encountered and defeated Darius for the last time in September 331 BCE. Unfortunately, after advancing on the richest cities of the Persian Empire (i.e., Babylon, Susa, Persepolis), securing Darius' corpse, and reaching the Indus River, Alexander returned to Babylon where he died at the age of thirty-three (323 BCE).[35]

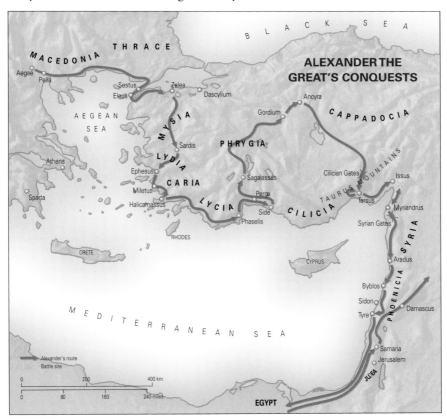

35. For more details about Alexander's kingdom expansion, see Green's *Alexander of Macedon, 356–323 B.C.*, 249. Compare Paul Cartledge's "Maps and Battle Plans" in *Alexander the Great* (New York: Overlook, 2004).

Due to Alexander's focus to liberate the Greek city-states along the coast of Asia Minor and conquer the Persian Empire, he never interfered with the affairs of Judea. This is not to say that Alexander had no contact with the Jewish people. On the one hand, Samaria resisted Alexander's forces and was destroyed and restructured as a Greek colony. On the other hand, Jerusalem submitted to Alexander and was granted legal, religious, and cultural rights, which they had under Persian rule.[36] Alexander was preoccupied with Darius, not Judea. Thus while Alexander was conquering and then attempting to transform the Greek and Persian cultures into one, the Jews of Judea continued to carry on as a Jewish temple city-state led by the High Priest, Jaddua. The lack of Greek interference in the socio-religious affairs of Judea prompted the sanctioning of messianic dormancy among Jewish people.

Squabbles over Alexander's Kingdom. The second factor that contributed to the sanctioning of messianic dormancy in Judea was the subsequent squabbles over Alexander's kingdom. Initially, regent rulers held together Alexander's vast kingdom (323–301 BCE). Alexander's generals, many who were Macedonian nobles, agreed (1) to divide the kingdom into provincial regions, (2) to govern those regions themselves as governors (or satraps), and (3) to remain united under regent rulers.[37] Yet twenty-two years of discontent, distrust, and disagreement between the regent rulers and provincial governors eventually resulted in war and a fourfold division of Alexander's kingdom. After defeating and deposing the third regent ruler Antigonus in 301 BCE, Alexander's kingdom was distributed among four Greek military leaders: Cassander claimed Macedonia and Greece, Lysimachus took possession of Asia Minor as far as Tarsus, Ptolemy was granted Egypt, and Seleucus obtained the remainder of Asia Minor to the Indus River, which included most of the territory of Syria.[38] Nevertheless, territorial discontent, distrust, and disagreement between regent rulers and provincial governors shifted to new issues, new skirmishes, and new

---

36. Josephus provides an account of Alexander meeting the High Priest Jaddua (*Ant* 11.8.5 §§ 329–39). Although probably embellished and disputed (see Cartledge, *Alexander the Great,* 265), VanderKam rightly argues that the record "rests upon some sort of historical foundation." VanderKam, *From Joshua to Caiaphas,* 67–85; cp. Green, *Alexander of Macedon,* 251, 540 n. 18.

37. R. Malcolm Errington, *A History of Macedonia* (Los Angeles: University of California Press, 1990), 115–29.

38. Errington, *History of Macedonia,* 130–147 (including the first paragraph under "2. After Ipsos"). By 280 BCE, three Greek dynasties remained: Ptolemaic in Egypt, Seleucid from Persia across Syria to Asia, and Antigonid controlling Macedonia. The Attalids of Pergamum overcame Greek rule in Asia Minor.

territorial boundary lines. This was particularly true between Seleucus and Ptolemy.

FIVE SYRIAN WARS	
First Syrian War (276–271 BCE)	Antiochus I wages war on Ptolemy II
Second Syrian War (260–255 BCE)	Antiochus I wages war on Ptolemy II
Third Syrian War (246–219 BCE)	Ptolemy III wages war on Seleucus II
Fourth Syrian War (219–217 BCE)	Antiochus III wages war on Ptolemy IV
Fifth Syrian War (202–198 BCE)	Antiochus III wages war on Ptolemy V

Territorial disputes between Seleucus and subsequent heirs (the Seleucids) and Ptolemy and subsequent heirs (the Ptolemies) erupted because Seleucus claimed territory occupied by Ptolemy, namely Judea, Samaria, Galilee, and other parts of southern Syria.[39] For over seventy years, the Seleucids battled the Ptolemies for control over Judea and southern Syria. After a series of five Syrian wars, Antiochus III of the Seleucids finally thwarted, defeated, and wrested control of southern Syria, Judea, Samaria, and Galilee away from the Ptolemies due to a decisive battle at Panion (198 BCE).

Obviously, the subsequent squabbles between Alexander's generals over Alexander's vast kingdom had little impact on the Jews of Judea. Alexander's generals were more concerned with positioning themselves for power than they were about the everyday affairs of Jerusalem. The Jewish people continued to carry on as a Jewish temple city-state led by a succession of high priests. After Jaddua, there was Onias I, Simon I (the Just),[40] Eleazar, Manasseh, Onias II, Simon II.[41] And though Judea came under a new Hellenistic régime, the century of Ptolemaic rule was not all that unpleasant. This is not to suggest that the Ptolemies never interfered in Jewish affairs (see

---

39. For a complete list of Seleucid and Ptolemaic rulers see Everett Ferguson, *Backgrounds of Early Christianity* (Grand Rapids: Eerdmans, second edition, 1993), 16–17.

40. Some have argued for Simon II to be "the Just." Yet VanderKam offers convincing evidence to the contrary. See James C. VanderKam, "Simon the Just: Simon I or Simon II?" in *Pomegranates and Golden Bells: Studies in Biblical, Jewish, and Near Eastern Ritual, Law, and Literature in Honor of Jacob Milgrom* (ed. D. Wright, D. N. Freedman, and A. Hurvitz; Winona Lake: Eisenbrauns, 1995), 303–18.

41. The chronology and completeness of our list of six High Priests during this period is disputed. For a discussion of theories about the missing names and a case for limiting and accepting the six names listed above see VanderKam in *From Joshua to Caiaphas*, 85–99. For a complete list of High Priests during the second temple period in chronological order see idem, 491–93, or see my chart in the appendix.

Jos *Ant* 12.3–6 §§ 172–86; Sir 50:1–24).[42] It is to say, however, that the Ptolemies allowed the Jews to exercise their socio-religious practices and embrace their ideals in Jerusalem with minimal interruption. Once again, these territorial disputes among the Greeks and the lack of interference by the Ptolemies contributed to Judea's sanctioning of messianic dormancy. Such pleasantry, however, did not exist for the Jewish people while under Seleucid control.

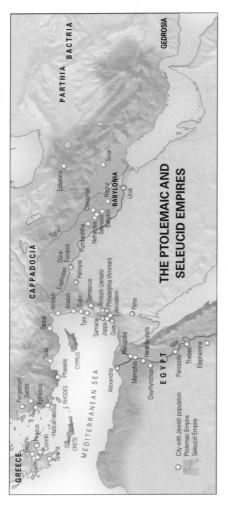

The Maccabees. The third factor that contributed to the sanctioning of messianic dormancy was the success of Judas Maccabee and his brothers as they impeded Seleucid rulers from imposing their Hellenistic ways on the Jewish inhabitants of Judea (1 & 2 Maccabees). At first, the Seleucids left the Jews alone for at least two reasons: the Jewish people in Jerusalem supported Antiochus III during the war against the Ptolemies (Jos. *Ant* 12.3.4 §§ 138–146),[43] and Antiochus' other aspirations. Mainland Greece appealed to Antiochus for military assistance against Rome. Yet Rome defeated him in Greece at Thermopylae (191 BCE) and again in Asia Minor at Magnesia (189 BCE). At Apamea, Antiochus signed a peace treaty that greatly affected the Seleucids (189 BCE). It forced Antiochus to cede Asia

---

42. Granted, 3 Maccabees speaks of Ptolemy IV Philopator (222–204 BCE) who levels many atrocities against the Jewish people. Yet 3 Maccabees is commonly described as a historical romance that seeks to encourage faithfulness to Jewish ideals in the midst of pagan persecution that displays clearly both anti-Jewish (2:28–30; 3:3–7) and anti-Gentile sentiments (4:16; 5:13; 6:9, 11). VanderKam contends that 3 Maccabees, written around the first century in Alexandria, "may reasonably be taken as reflecting what happened then," though placed historically during the time of Ptolemy IV. See *From Joshua to Caiaphas*, 183–85. See also deSilva, *Introduction to the Apocrypha*, 304–22.

43. For a critical evaluation of Josephus see VanderKam, *From Joshua to Caiaphas*, 185–88.

Minor to Rome, disarm most of his army, and pay a huge war debt, which would later burden his subsequent heirs.[44] And though the Seleucids maintained their right to rule and govern themselves, they were under the watchful eyes of Rome. Furthermore, the Seleucids were in desperate need of money in order to pay their war debt to Rome.

Nevertheless, subsequent heirs of Antiochus III redirected their energies to retain and control Judea. Of particular interest to us is Antiochus IV, who not only wished to retain and control Judea, but also wanted to convert the city of Jerusalem into a Greek city-state. The list of socio-religious atrocities against the Jews in Jerusalem began with Antiochus IV accepting money (a bribe) from Jason, the brother of Onias III, in order to secure the High Priesthood for himself. Jason then proceeded to transform Jerusalem from a Jewish temple-state into a Greek city-state complete with a council, citizen list, gymnasium, and new name, "the city of Antioch" (2 Macc. 4:7–17). Some Jews underwent surgery to mask their circumcision (1 Macc. 1:13–15, 2 Macc. 4:10–17), while others offered sacrifices to Hercules before participating in the quadrennial games at Tyre (2 Macc. 4:18–20).

The list of atrocities against the Jews lengthened when Antiochus accepted another bribe, this time from Menelaus. Unlike Jason, Menelaus was an unrelated member of the Oniad family of high priests. Thus, he was not of the High Priestly family who were appointed to govern the temple. Menelaus plundered the temple, stole money from the temple for Antiochus' war efforts in Egypt, and eventually changed the temple service from the worship of Yahweh to the worship of Zeus.[45]

The list of atrocities against the Jews was finalized when Antiochus IV prohibited all Jewish socio-religious practices in Jerusalem. Scriptures were destroyed. Sabbath observance and festivals were prohibited. Food laws were abolished. Circumcision was outlawed. Idol worship was mandated. And all those who failed to obey were put to death (1 Macc. 1:41–61; 2 Macc. 6:1–7:42).

First Maccabees, however, tells how one priest, Mattathias, along with his sons (particularly Judas, Jonathan, Simon) resisted

> **Desecration of the Second Temple**
>
> As part of his authorized religious persecution of the Jews (1 Macc. 1:41–61), Antiochus IV desecrated Jerusalem's second temple in 167 BCE by sacrificing a ritually unacceptable sacrifice, probably a swine, on the temple's altar of burnt offering and by calling it the temple of Olympian Zeus (2 Macc. 6:1–11; cp. Dan. 11:31).

---

44. Appian, *Roman History: The Syrian Wars* 7. 37–38. Concerning the treaty see also Polybius 21.16.1–17, 21.42.19–27; Diodorus 29. 10. 1; Livy 37. 44. 6–37, 41. 1. 1.

45. For more information about high priesthoods of Jason and Menelaus see VanderKam, *From Joshua to Caiaphas*, 197–226.

Antiochus and subsequent Seleucid rulers in order to restore Jewish socio-religious practices and ideals in Jerusalem. Although resistance began with Mattathias in 167 BCE (2:1–70), it was Judas, nicknamed "Maccabee" (the "hammer") who cleansed the temple and reestablished a degree of religious freedom in 164 BCE (4:36–61; 2 Macc. 10:1–9). After Judas died in battle, Jonathan assumed the lead. In time, he established some semblance of political control in 152 BCE (9:54–10:66). After Jonathan was killed, Simon assumed the lead. Eventually, Simon liberated Judea from Seleucid control in 143 BCE (12:49–13:42). Thus, "the yoke of the Gentiles was removed" (13:41). In fact, the Seleucid ruler Alexander Balas appointed Jonathan as high priest and made him "commander and chief magistrate" (στπατηγὸν καὶ μεριδάπχην) over Judea (10:18–20, 59–66). After Jonathan's death, another Seleucid ruler Demetrius II declared Simon as a "great high priest and chief magistrate" (ἀρχιέρεως μεγάλου καὶ στρατηγοῦ) over Judea (13:36–42). Even the Jews and their priests, according to the author of 1 Maccabees, "resolved that Simon should be their leader and high priest forever, until a trustworthy prophet should arise,

> . . . that he should be governor over them
> . . . that he should take care of the sanctuary and appointed officials
> . . . that he should be in charge of the sanctuary,
> . . . that the he should be obeyed by all,
> . . . that all contracts in the country should be written in his name,
> . . . that he should be clothed in purple and wear gold." (14:41–42, NRSV).

Naturally, Simon agreed to be "high priest, commander, and ethnarch" (ἀρχιερατεύειν . . . στρατηγὸς καὶ ἐθνάρχης) over the people of Judea (14:47).[46] Thus the military preoccupation of Antiochus III and the success of Judas and his brothers, *to a limited extent*, continued to sanction messianic dormancy.[47]

---

46. For more information about high priesthoods of Jonathan and Simon see VanderKam, *From Joshua to Caiaphas*, 251–85.

47. First Maccabees tells us that the Jews recognized that Simon was neither from the line of David nor from the line of Zadok; nevertheless, they declared him "king" and "priest" (cf. Ps. 110:1, 4) until "the Prophet" would arise in the future to straighten out this mess. Thus, 1 Maccabees suggests a certain future Davidic expectation that would be fulfilled in the future as a result of the work of the Prophet in setting things straight. In the meantime, the Hasmonean dynasty did the best that they could . . . in the absence of a legitimate Davidic king and Zadokite high priest (since Onias IV abandoned Jerusalem for Leontopolis in Egypt after Onias III, the last legitimate Zadokite priest, was assassinated under Menelaus).

In conclusion, First Testament messianic concepts, pregnant and ready to be developed, lay *dormant* and in *mystery* form for centuries during Persian and Grecian imperialistic control of Judea and her temple city-state, Jerusalem. While Persian imperialism may have initiated messianic dormancy due to factors of Persian socio-ethnicity, ultimately it was the Jewish people themselves who sanctioned messianic dormancy and permitted it to simmer during the rise of Greek imperialism. While world historical events took place around them, the people in Jerusalem appeared to settle into a pattern of contentment about exercising their socio-religious practices and embracing their ideals, ideals that excluded any anticipated restoration of David's dynasty. Yet the success of the Maccabees set off a chain of events that both *evoked* and eventually *inflamed* messianic speculations among the various groups of Jewish idealists (sectarians) in Judea.

Messianism Evoked and Inflamed

As suggested above, regal messianic speculations of a restored Davidic dynasty remain dormant as *embers* in a smoldering fire during most of the second temple period. Yet second temple ideologies about the restoration of David's dynasty are first *evoked* when dissatisfaction arise over the high priesthoods of Jonathan, Simon, and the subsequent royal priesthoods of Simon's heirs. However, it is the unsettling political involvement of Rome in Jewish affairs that eventually *inflame* eschatological messianism. We begin, however, with how the Hasmoneans *evoked messianism* in Judea.

Evoking Messianism

Whenever social and ideological shifts occur in a culture, inevitably someone is identified as the transitional figure. In our attempt to come to grips with the historical and social events, influences, and opinions of those who lived during the time when second temple messianism actually began, Jonathan and Simon appear to be the so-called "culprits" responsible for evoking the flames of eschatological messianism.

On the one hand, 1 Maccabees, written *circa* 100 BCE, presents Mattathias, Judas, Jonathan, and Simon as heroes, or a dynasty divinely appointed to fulfill God's purposes. In order to demonstrate that the dynasty stood in continuity with the heroes of Israel's past, the historiography of 1 Maccabees parallels that which was found in 1 and 2 Samuel and 1 and 2 Kings about David's dynasty. Thus Harrington speaks of 1 Maccabees as "dynastic history" because the major characters are portrayed as God's dynasty, the true Israel, who rid Judea of Seleucid oppression and explains how the Jewish high priesthood came to reside in this family.[48] Consequently,

---

48. Harrington, *Invitation to the Apocrypha*, 122–23. For a more detailed perspective, see "The 'History' that 1 Maccabees Crafts" in deSilva's *Introducing the Apocrypha*, 255–64.

the positive legacy of the Maccabean brothers was their ability to impede Seleucid rulers who attempted to interfere with the Jewish way of life. They obstructed Antiochus IV from accomplishing his list of religious atrocities against the Jewish people in Jerusalem and eventually circumvented Seleucid control over all of Judea.

On the other hand, the family of Jonathan and Simon were more accurately named Hasmonean, a name derived from the great-grandfather of Mattathias, Hashmon or Hashmonah.[49] As a family, they eventually emerged as a military monarchy over Judea, whose actions sparked numerous religious repercussions that eventually evoked a rise of messianism. Thus the Hasmoneans were a family of royal high priests, who descended from Mattathias, the father of Judas Maccabee. Yet what religious controversy did these non-Davidic Hasmoneans evoke as they restored the royal-priesthood? What was it that evoked a renewed interest in God's restoring David's dynasty?

First, Jonathan and Simon ignited a religious controversy when they accepted the high priesthood from Seleucid rulers. Although they fought and deposed Seleucid-appointed high priests Menelaus and Alcimus, Jonathan and Simon accepted appointments to the vacated high priesthood positions from Seleucid rulers. These appointments did not please numerous members of the Essene community. In their mind, this violated the Law. A group of Essenes responded to the Hasmonean social structure with the creation of a new social structure in the desert at Qumran and referred to Jonathan, Simon, and other members of the Hasmonean family as "wicked priests." A very well known Pesher text on Habakkuk from cave one of Qumran (1QpHab) reflects vividly how one segment of the Essene community[50] denounced Jonathan or perhaps Simon as an arrogant, lawless, rebel.[51]

---

49. Although 1 Maccabees does not mention the family name, Josephus (*Ant* 12.6.1 § 265) does mention Mattathias' kinship to be "the son of John, the son of Simon, the son of Asamoneus" (υἱὸς Ἰωάννου τοῦ Συμεῶος τοῦ Ἀσαμωναίου).

50. Evidence supporting that the Qumran community was a segment of the Essene sect is circumstantial, but it is substantial. See Josephus: *War* 2.8.119–61, *Antiquities* 18.1.18–22; Philo: *Every Good Man Is Free*, 72–91, *Hypothetica* 1–18; Pliny: *Natural History*, 5.17.4. For a more complete study see Geza Vermes and Martin D. Goodman, *The Essenes: According to Classical Sources* (Sheffield: JSOT Press, 1989); Philip R. Callaway, *The History of the Qumran Community: An Investigation* (Sheffield: JSOT Press, 1988), 63–87.

51. Jonathan, as argued by VanderKam, may be indeed the sole "wicked priest" mentioned in the Dead Sea Scroll 1QpHab 8:8–13 (*From Joshua to Caiaphas*, 267–70). Yet many throughout the years have speculated about the identity of the "wicked priest." See my overview in *Early Jewish Hermeneutics and Hebrews 1:5–13*, 84–86.

"And indeed, riches betray the arrogant man and he will not last; he who has made his throat as wide as Hades, and who, like Death, is never satisfied. All the Gentiles will flock to him, and all the peoples will gather to him. Look, all of them take up a taunt against him, and invent sayings about him, saying, You who grow large on what is not yours, how long will you burden yourself down with debts?" (Habakkuk 2:5–6) This refers to *the Wicked Priest* who had a reputation for reliability at the beginning of his term of service; but when he became ruler over Israel, *he became proud and forsook God* and *betrayed the commandments* for the sake of riches. He *amassed by force the riches of the lawless* who had *rebelled against God*, seizing the riches of the peoples, thus adding to the guilt of his crimes, and he *committed abhorrent deeds in every defiling impurity.* (1QpHab 8:3b-13a)[52]

HASMONEAN HIGH PRIESTS	
Jonathan	152–142 BCE
Simon	142–134 BCE
John Hyranus	134–104 BCE
Aristobulus I	104–103 BCE
Alexander Jannaeus	103–76 BCE
Hyrcanus II	76–67, 63–40 BCE
Aristobulus II	67–63 BCE
Antigonus	40–37 BCE

Second, subsequent heirs of Simon, John Hyrcanus, Aristobulus, and Alexander Jannaeus ignited religious controversy when they usurped the royal throne. Although John Hyrcanus could have employed the title, king, Josephus claimed that Aristobulus I was the first to have assumed the royal title, king (*Ant* 13.11.1 § 301). Thus, Aristobulus I added the title king to his title of high priest. VanderKam says, "The change in the Hasmonean ruler's title from a lesser one to that of king may have marked an important stage in the evolution of the Hasmonean state. It appears the roles of Aristobulus's predecessors differed from those of kings in little more than name, but

---

52. Translation comes from Accordance Software. Martin G. Abegg Jr., James E. Bowley, and Edward M. Cook are responsible for preparing the text and morphological analysis for electronic publication. Abegg's work with electronic data bases is extensive, having prepared the QUMRAN, MISH-T, SAMART-T, and BENSIRA-C/M Accordance modules for the study of ancient Hebrew Language and Literature.

they apparently refrained from adopting the title."[53] Clearly by the time of Alexander Jannaeus, Hasmoneans were deemed royal-priests.

These three Hasmonean "royal" priests expanded their kingdom, gradually, from the small geographical region of Judea to include Idumea, Samaria, the coastal strip, Carmel, Galilee, Perea, Gaulanitis (the Golan), and Moab. Within thirty-one years, Judea (as we know of it in the Second Testament) was created. Not since the time of Solomon had the nation of Israel been so large and unified under a single king-priest. Yet their apparent attempts to unify their kingdom by forcing Gentiles circumcision and obedience to Jewish law appear to have been more for political rather than religious reasons. Many regions, however, remained predominately Gentile.

Despite these fantastic advancements and territorial gains, Hasmonean rulers had an aversion to the Pharisees. Animosity between the Hasmoneans and Pharisees began with John Hyrcanus, but that animosity eventually escalates to mutual hatred with Alexander Jannaeus, who was known to have crucified large numbers of Jews, many of whom the Dead Sea Scroll 4QpNahum (4Q169) identified to be Pharisees.[54] Thus it is not surprising that the author of the *Psalms of Solomon*, perhaps a Pharisee,[55] denounced Hasmonean kings as those who usurped the Davidic throne by force and thereby tainted it.

> Those to whom you did not (make the) promise, they (the Hasmoneans) took away (from us) by force; and they did not glorify your honorable name. With pomp they set up a monarchy because of their arrogance; they

53. VanderKam, however, presents a problem with the claim as we find it in Josephus because Strabo contends that it was Alexander Jannaeus (16.2.40). *From Joshua to Caiaphas*, 313–15. Nevertheless, 4Q448 (4QApocrypha Psalm and Prayer) names Jannaeus as King Jonathan. See *From Joshua to Caiaphas*, 335–36.
54. Animosity began with John Hyrcanus, who broke socio-religious ties with the Pharisees (Jos *Ant* 13.10.5–6 §§ 288–296; VanderKam, *From Joshua to Caiaphas*, 297–304), and escalated to hatred with Alexander Genus, who crucified large numbers (perhaps 800) of Pharisees (cp. Jos *Ant* 8.13.5–14 §§ 372–383 with 4QpNah 1:1–9). For the historical ties between Josephus and 4QpNah see Callaway, *The History of the Qumran Community*, 164–68; VanderKam, *From Joshua to Caiaphas*, 319–30.
55. Some, like O'Dell, identify a Pharisee as the author. J. O'Dell, "The Religious Background of the Psalms of Solomon," *RevQ* 10 (1961): 241–57. Others, like Hann, argue for Essene authorship. R. R. Hann, "The Community of the Pious: The Social Setting of the Psalms of Solomon," *SR* 17 (1988): 169–89, esp. 184–89. Still others, like Rosen and Salvesen, search for parallels with Qumran sectarian literature. D. Rosen and A. Salvesen, "A Note on the Dead Sea Temple Scroll 56:15–18 and Psalm of Solomon 17:33," *JJS* 38 (1987): 99–101. Quite frankly, one may make a case that the work comes from a Jewish religious sect, but pinpointing what sect is difficult. See R. Wright "The Psalms of Solomon, The Pharisees, and the Essenes" in *1972 Proceedings* (ed. R. A. Kraft for the International Organization for Septuagint and Cognate Studies, 136–154; Missoula: Society of Biblical Literature, 1972).

despoiled the throne of David with arrogant shouting. (*Pss. Sol.* 17:5b-8; cp. 8:18–22)[56]

Obviously, the political and social unrest evident in second temple literature targeting the Hasmoneans was the first real hint of dissatisfaction that significantly evoked the flames of messianism among the Pharisees and the Essenes at Qumran. Whereas some literary works praised the Hasmonean dynasty, particularly 1 Maccabees, others like the *Psalms of Solomon* denounced the dynasty as illegitimate usurpers of royal power reserved for a Davidite. Thus, it is not surprising that the earliest literature that speaks of an expected "messiah figure" dates from after 150 BCE when Jonathan, the first Hasmonean, came to power. And though Hasmoneans evoked the flames of messianic expectation, Rome managed to create a full brush fire.

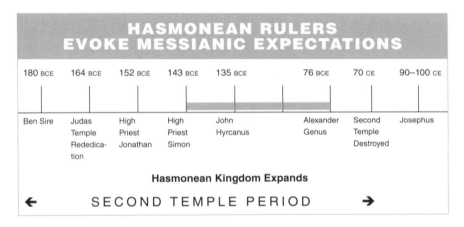

HASMONEAN RULERS EVOKE MESSIANIC EXPECTATIONS

180 BCE	164 BCE	152 BCE	143 BCE	135 BCE	76 BCE	70 CE	90–100 CE
Ben Sire	Judas Temple Rededica- tion	High Priest Jonathan	High Priest Simon	John Hyrcanus	Alexander Genus	Second Temple Destroyed	Josephus

Hasmonean Kingdom Expands

← SECOND TEMPLE PERIOD →

Inflaming Messianism
The flames of messianism soon erupted into a full brush fire when Rome, via the Roman general Pompey, arbitrated a dispute between the Hasmonean brothers John Hyrcanus II and Aristobulus II. Yet why would Rome arbitrate a dispute between two Hasmonean brothers in Judea? And why was Pompey called upon to settle it?

First, Rome arbitrated the dispute because they had a long-standing relationship with the Hasmoneans. According to 1 Maccabees and Josephus, the Hasmonean friendship and alliance with Rome began with Judas when he revolted against Antiochus IV (8:1–2a, 17–30). That relationship continued with Jonathan (12:1–18; cp. *Ant* 13.5.8 §§ 163–70) and was reaffirmed with

---

56. Translation by R. B. Wright, "Psalms of Solomon" in *The Old Testament Pseudepigrapha*, 2 vols. (ed. James H. Charlesworth; New York: Doubleday, 1985), 2:666.

Simon *circa* 138 BCE (15:10, 15–21; cp. 14:16–19, 40). Naturally subsequent Hasmoneans like John Hyrcanus maintained that friendship with Rome (*Ant* 13.9.2 §§ 259–66). Thus, 1 Maccabees emphasized the friendly relations

THE HASMONEAN KINGDOM

Independent Judea after Jonathan's campaigns, 142 BCE
Land conquered by Simon, 142-135 BCE
John Hyrcanus I, 128-104 BCE
Aristobulus I, 104-103 BCE
Alexander Jannaeus, 103-76 BCE
Boundary of Hasmonean kingdom, 76 BCE
Hellenistic city

between Rome and the Jews because they served Rome in monitoring Seleucid activities.

Later, when the Parthians in the east and Romans in the west were putting the squeeze on the Seleucids, the Hasmoneans experienced a period of peace (76–67 BCE). Salome Alexandria, the wife of Alexander Jannaeus, made peace with the Pharisees, ruled as queen, and positioned her son, John Hyrcanus II as high priest. Yet when Salome Alexandria died, her younger son, Aristobulus II, usurped control away from John Hyrcanus II, which erupted into civil war between the two with Pharisees siding with John Hyrcanus II and Sadducees siding with Aristobulus II. Thus the Jews appealed to an outside impartial source like Rome to resolve the dispute.

Second, Rome arbitrated the dispute, via Pompey, because Pompey was executing a military campaign in the region. In fact, Pompey, born in 106 BCE, spent most of his life on military campaigns and as a result was honored with three triumphal processions through the city of Rome. The first was in 81 BCE, the second in 71 BCE, and the third in 61 BCE.[57] The last triumph in 61 BCE is important to our discussion because it celebrated his suppression of piracy, his restoration of Rome's command of the sea, and his defeat of numerous regions and people groups in the east, one of which were the Jews who were listed among the many captives (Plu *Pompey* 45.1–2). After wresting control of the Sea from pirates, Pompey moved victoriously through Asia Minor toward Syria. When Pompey arrived in Damascus envoys from Syria, Egypt, and Judea courted him. Naturally the latter convoy was of most importance to this discussion.

Josephus tells us that the Judean convoy consisted of three delegations: the delegation representing John Hyrcanus II argued that Aristobulus II usurped control of the royal priest-

> **Jerusalem a Tributary of Rome**
>
> What began as a "Friendship and Alliance" between Judas Maccabee and Rome in 161 BCE (1 Macc 8:1–30), ended with intense Jewish resentment in 63 BCE (*Pss. Sol.* 17:11-17). Pompey, while settling a civil dispute between two Hasmonean leaders, conquered Jerusalem, desecrated the temple, and imposed a political solution on the country that benefited only Rome (Jos. *Ant* 14.4.1, 4 §§ 57, 69-79).

hood unlawfully; the delegation representing Aristobulus II argued that John Hyrcanus II was incompetent to rule; and the delegation representing the people desired the entire Hasmonean aristocracy be disbanded. And though Pompey listened, he postponed his decision (*Ant* 14.3.2–3 §§ 40–47). Aristobulus returned to Judea and made military preparations to resist Pompey in the event that the decision favored Hyrcanus (*Ant* 14.3.4 §§ 50–52). This act, however, did not sit well with Pompey. Aristobulus II was captured, Jerusalem was seized, and Judea was made a tributary of Rome (*Ant* 14.4.1, 4 §§ 57, 69–79). Needless

---

57. Robin Seager, *Pompey the Great: A Political Biography* (Oxford: Blackwell, 1979, 2002), 28–29, 36–37, 79–80.

to say, John Hyrcanus II was declared High Priest, but Judea's independence came to an end, and the High Priest became a vassal of Rome and subject to the Roman governor stationed in Syria (*Ant* 14.5. 4 § 91).

The responses to Pompey's intervention were varied. On the one hand, Josephus bemoaned the events due to the "sedition" between Hyrcanus and Aristobulus. This seems only natural because Josephus favored Hasmonean control.

> Now the occasions of *this misery* which came upon Jerusalem were Hyrcanus and Aristobulus, by raising a sedition one against the other; for now *we lost our liberty*, and *became subject to the Romans*, and were *deprived of that country* which we had gained by our arms from the Syrians, and were compelled to restore it to the Syrians. Moreover, the Romans exacted of us, in a little time, above ten thousand talents; and the royal authority, which was a dignity formerly bestowed on those that were high priests, by the right of their family, became the property of private men (*Ant* 14.4.5 §§ 77–78).

On the other hand, the author of the *Psalms of Solomon* appears to have praised the events as divine intervention whereby God's chosen agent, Pompey, "rewarded" the entire Hasmonean dynasty for their sins.

> Those to whom you did not (make the) promise, they (the Hasmoneans) took away (from us) by force; and they did not glorify your honorable name. With pomp they set up a monarchy because of their arrogance; they despoiled the throne of David with arrogant shouting. *But you, O God, overthrew them, and uprooted their descendants from the earth for there rose up against them a man* (Pompey) *alien to our race* (a Roman). *You rewarded them* (the Hasmoneans), *O God, according to their sins; it happened to them according to their actions* (17:5b-8).[58]

Yet unlike Josephus who was indifferent to the restoration of David's dynasty, the author of the *Psalms of Solomon* was not. The author pled for Yahweh's intervention. Based upon God's covenant with David, he wrote, "Lord, you chose David to be king over Israel, and you swore to him about his descendants forever, that his kingdom should not fail before you" (17:4). And though General Pompey was God's instrument to punish the Hasmoneans, neither Hasmonean nor Roman leadership was in keeping with God's promise to David. The author believed God promised David a kingdom—a kingdom that would not fail. His belief was based upon 2 Samuel 7:11b–16 and echoed in Psalm 89:3–4 (MT 89:4–5, LXX 88:4–5): "I swore to David

---

58. Translation by R. B. Wright, "Psalms of Solomon" in *The Old Testament Pseudepigrapha*, 2 vols. (ed. James H. Charlesworth; New York: Doubleday, 1985), 2:665.

my servant, I will establish your seed forever and build your throne to all generations." Thus the author cried out:

> See, Lord, and raise up for them their king, the son of David, to rule over your servant Israel in the time known to you, O God. Undergird him with the strength to destroy the unrighteous rulers, to purge Jerusalem from gentiles who trample her to destruction; in wisdom and in righteousness to drive out the sinners from the inheritance (Isa. 11:2b); to smash the arrogance of sinners like a potter's jar; to shatter all their substance with an iron rod (Ps. 2:9); to destroy the unlawful nations with the word of his mouth (Isa. 11:4); at his warning the nations will flee from his presence; and he will condemn sinners by the thoughts of their hearts (17:21–25).[59]

Consequently, the author's plea for divine intervention was based upon an expectation that God would raise up a Davidite who would purge Jerusalem of unwanted and unrighteous rulers and thereby restore David's dynasty. Yet this plea went unanswered until Jesus came. In the meantime the Jewish leaders in Jerusalem continued to court Roman political leaders.

ROMAN ALLIANCES WITH LOYAL JEWISH LEADERS

Roman Leaders	Jewish Leaders	Dates
Pompey	John Hyrcanus II (High Priest) Antipater (?procurator of Judea?)	63–48 BCE
Caesar	John Hyrcanus II (High Priest, ethnarch) Antipater (procurator of Judea) and his sons Phasael (Governor of Jerusalem) and Herod (Governor of Galilee)	48–44 BCE
Cassius	John Hyrcanus II (High Priest, ethnarch) Antipater (procurator of Judea, d. 43) and his sons Phasael (Governor of Jerusalem) and Herod (Governor of Galilee)	48–42 BCE
Mark Antony	John Hyrcanus II (High Priest, ethnarch until 40 BCE) Phasael and Herod (Tetrarchs of Judea until 40 BCE) Herod (designated King of Judea by Rome in 40 BCE)	42–31 BCE
Octavian (Augustus)	Herod (King of Judea)	31–4 BCE

According to Josephus, John Hyrcanus II, Antipater (Herod's father), and Herod continued to befriend the never-ending transitioning of political leaders in Rome. After Julius Caesar secured his political power in Rome and forced

---

59. Translation by R. B. Wright, "Psalms of Solomon" in *The Old Testament Pseudepigrapha*, 2 volumes (ed. James H. Charlesworth; New York: Doubleday, 1985), 2:667. Scripture insertions are mine but adapted from Collins, *The Scepter and the Star*, 54.

Pompey to flee to Egypt where he was murdered (48 BCE),[60] a new alliance was formed with Julius Caesar, which endured until 15th March 44 BCE (*Ant* 14.8.1–3 §§ 127–38; 14.10.1–2 §§ 189–95). With the death of Caesar, however, came a new alliance with Cassius (*Ant* 14.11.2–3 §§ 271–77). Yet Cassius' relationship with the Jewish leadership was short-lived because Octavian (future Caesar Augustus) and Mark Antony defeated Cassius in battle (42 BCE) and thereby avenged Julius Caesar's murder, which was provoked by Cassius and Brutus (*Ant* 14.11.1 § 270; 14.12.2 § 301). Naturally, another new alliance was formed, this time with Mark Antony (*Ant* 14.12.2–3 301–27). It was during this alliance that the Senate in Rome, along with Octavian and Antony's blessing, appointed Herod to be King over all of Judea (40 BCE; *Ant* 14.14.1, 3–4 §§ 370, 379–85). Herod's friendship with Rome remained strong, even after Octavian's subsequent dispute with Antony in Rome, defeat of Antonius at Actium (*Ant* 15.6.1 §161) and eventual death of Antony in Egypt (31 BCE).[61] For Herod made a new alliance with Octavian (*War* 1.1–2 §386–92). Subsequent heirs of Herod (sons: Archelaus, Antipas, Philip; grandson: Agrippa I; and great-grandson: Agrippa II) maintained friendship with Rome. Thus messianic expectations, which began with the Hasmonean dynasty, continued throughout the Herodian dynastic control of Judea (40 BCE-70 CE).

ROME'S INTERVENTIONS INFLAME MESSIANIC EXPECTATIONS

180 BCE	164 BCE	152 BCE	143 BCE		63 BCE	40 BCE	70 CE	90–100 CE
Ben Sira	Judas Temple Rededication	Jonathan	Simon	Hasmonean Rule	Pompey	Herod	Second	Josephus
					Rome's Intervention Inflames			

← S E C O N D   T E M P L E   P E R I O D →

CONCLUSION

When we began this chapter, we stated that four obstacles had to be overcome before we examined the various portraits of later second temple messianism

---

60. Seager, *Pompey the Great*, 168; Stacy Schiff, *Cleopatra: A Life* (New York: Little, Brown and Company, 2010), 12–14.

61. For a biography on Herod see Peter Richardson's *Herod: King of the Jews and Friend of the Romans* (New York: Columbia University Press, 1996). For a biography on one of Herod's sons, see Harold W. Hoehner's *Herod Antipas: A Contemporary of Jesus Christ* (Grand Rapids: Zondervan, 1980).

in the subsequent chapters. We have addressed three: limited resources, blurred vision, and a lack of second temple historical and social sensitivities. Hopefully we are a little more sensitized to these three issues.

First, I hope our sensitivities to second temple historical events are pricked enough to realize that historically the people of Jerusalem were of no real *major* consequence to Persian and Hellenistic imperialism. As world events transpired around them, the Jewish people were but one small part of many people groups absorbed by these great empires. This is not to say, however, that the aristocracies of these great world powers had no impact on the Jewish temple city-state. Obviously, the presence of Persian dominance initiated messianic dormancy in Jerusalem due to political and social structures, and the Jewish people themselves sanctioned it during the Hellenistic period because the Greek rulers were more concerned with positioning themselves for power and the Jews could do nothing to stop it. Yet this lack of significance enabled the Judeans to develop, exercise, and embrace their socio-religious practices and ideals with minimal interferences and with no restoration of David's dynasty in sight.

Therefore, it should not surprise us that not everyone during the second temple period anticipated the restoration of David's dynasty. For instance, neither Ben Sira nor Josephus expected a Messiah figure. Thus, second temple expectations about a Messiah figure are not ubiquitous. So, the respective works of Ben Sira and Josephus appear to serve as bookends for the development of messianic ideas because second temple ideologies about Messiah lay dormant until *evoked* by growing dissatisfactions with political and social movements in Jerusalem. Beginning in 152 BCE, the resurgence of messianism was ignited because of the internal religious dissatisfactions with the Hasmonean royal priesthood. Consequently second temple expectations about a Messiah figure did not exist in an unbroken time line or single tradition.

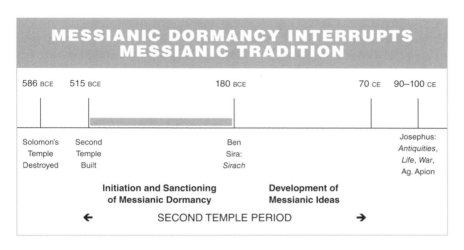

MESSIANIC DORMANCY INTERRUPTS MESSIANIC TRADITION

586 BCE	515 BCE		180 BCE		70 CE	90–100 CE
Solomon's Temple Destroyed	Second Temple Built		Ben Sira: *Sirach*			Josephus: *Antiquities, Life, War,* Ag. Apion
	Initiation and Sanctioning of Messianic Dormancy		Development of Messianic Ideas			
	←	SECOND TEMPLE PERIOD		→		

Second, I hope our sensitivities to second temple historical events are pricked enough to realize our familiarity with the Second Testament, particularly our understanding of Jesus, tends to blur our vision. Our vision is further blurred due to the chasm that developed between Jews and Christians, particularly as it pertained to the First Testament's presentation of historical figures in David's dynasty. Historically they were viewed as *only* a foreshadowing of Jesus. Yet as we work with extrabiblical literature, we need to allow the history of ideas about Judaism's messiahs to unfold naturally, particularly as those ideas and reflections were presented in literature written during the second temple's socio-historical context.

Finally I hope our sensitivities to second temple historical events are pricked enough to realize that our limited resources available for developing messianic profiles are restricted to the periods of the Hasmonean and Herodian dynasties that ruled over Judea for only *circa* two hundred years (152 BCE–70 CE) out of over five hundred years of second temple history (515 BCE–70 CE). Thus our limited resources tend to be dated accordingly.

Above all, the chapter should indicate how relevant all this historical activity and subsequent messianic reflection is for understanding the Roman world Jesus enters. This brings me to the fourth obstacle. Seldom is the literature and the subsequent mind-set of the people recording their anticipations about Messiah taken seriously. We tend to limit ourselves to the Hebrew Scriptures and the Second Testament alone. Thus, we are not sensitive to all that was being discussed during the second temple period. We sometimes do not appreciate the cultural, social, and theological setting Jesus confronted with when he ministered in Judea. Thus the literature of the second temple period and what it says about Messiah is important background for understanding what Jesus was up against when he began his ministry. Therefore, moving beyond the mere listing of the limited resources presented earlier in this chapter, the following chart isolates approximate times during the Hasmonean and Herodian dynastic periods in which messianic texts were written.[62] Although the dating at times may be speculative and in some cases elusive, it is helpful to disclose approximate time periods for when these messianic ideas emerged during the second temple period.

---

62. Compare Emanuel Tov, ed., *DJD*, vol. 39 The Texts from the Judaean Desert (Oxford: Clarendon Press, 2002), 352–75.

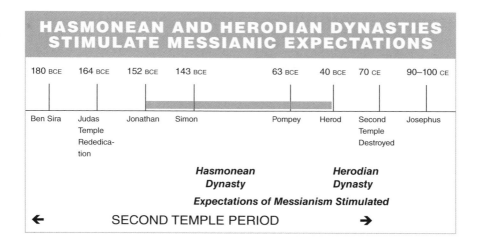

TIME PERIODS	CHRONOLOGICAL LISTING OF DOCUMENTS	SEQUENTIAL LISTING OF DOCUMENTS
Hasmonean Period (150–50 BCE)	**Early Hasmonean 150–125 BCE** *1 Enoch: Dreams* *Testament of the 12 Patriarchs: T.Judah* *Jubilees* **Mid-Hasmonean: 125–75 BCE** 1Q28 (1QS = *Community Rule*) 1Q28a (1QSa = 1Q*Rule of the Congregation*) 1Q28b (1QSb = 1Q*Rule of Blessings*) 4Q175 (4QTest = 4Q*Testimonia*) 4Q266 (4QDa = 4Q*Damascus Document*a) 4Q521 (4Q*messianic Apocalypse*) *1 Enoch: Similitudes* **Late-Hasmonean: 75–50 BCE** 4Q161 (4QpIsaa = 4Q*Isaiah Pesher*a) 4Q382 (4Q*Paraphrase of the Kings*) 4Q458 (4Q*Narrative A*) *Psalms of Solomon*	CD (*Cairo Document*) 1QM (1Q*War Scroll*) 1Q28 (1QS = *Community Rule*) 1Q28a (1QSa = 1Q*Rule of the Congregation*) 1Q28b (1QSb = 1Q*Rule of Blessings*) 4Q161 (4QpIsaa = 4Q*Isaiah Pesher*a) 4Q175 (4QTest = 4Q*Testimonia*) 4Q266 (4QDa = 4Q*Damascus Documenta*) 4Q382 (4Q*Paraphrase of the Kings*) 4Q458 (4Q*Narrative A*) 4Q521 (4Q*messianic Apocalypse*) *1 Enoch: Dreams* *1 Enoch: Similtudes* *Psalms of Solomon* *Testament of the 12 Patriarchs: T.Judah*

TIME PERIODS	CHRONOLOGICAL LISTING OF DOCUMENTS	SEQUENTIAL LISTING OF DOCUMENTS
Herodian Period (50 BCE to 100 CE)	Pre-Herodian 50–30 BCE 1QM (1QWar Scroll) 4Q246 (4QpsDan ar = 4QAramaic Apocalypse) 4Q376 (4QapocrMosesb = 4QApocryphon of Mosesb) 4Q496 (4QMf = 4QWar Scrollf) Early Herodian 30–1 BCE 4Q174 (4QFlor = 4QFlorilegium) 4Q252 (4QcommGena = 4QCommentary Genesis A) 4Q285 (4QSM = 4QSefer ha-Milhamah) Mid-Herodian 1–30 CE Late Herodian 30–68 CE 4Q369 (4QPEnosh = 4QPrayer of Enosh) 4Q423 (4QInstructiong[a]) Post Herodian 68–90 CE 4 Ezra 2 Baruch	4Q174 (4QFlor = 4QFlorilegium) 4Q246 (4QpsDan ar = 4QAramaic Apocalypse) 4Q252 (4QcommGena = 4QCommentary on Genesis A) 4Q285 (4QSM = 4QSefer ha-Milhamah) 4Q369 (4QPEnosh = 4QPrayer of Enosh) 4Q376 (4QapocrMosesb = 4QApocryphon of Moses[b]) 4Q423 (4QInstructiong) 4Q496 (4QMf = 4QWar Scrollf) Jewish Sibylline Oracles 4 Ezra 2 Baruch 3 Enoch (began during Maccabee era/final redaction 5th–6th century CE)

Naturally the First Testament's less than exclusively, direct pronouncements about Messiah, together with political and social events of the latter
part of the second temple period, namely the political and social upheaval
of the Hasmoneans and Herodians, eventually served to shape various messianic paradigms, which can be traced, though sketchily, in a small segment
of literature from around 150 BCE–70 CE. Consequently competing portraits
emerged about the future messiah, portraits we are now ready to explore.
Thus it is my hope that as we read through the next three chapters a fourth
obstacle may be eliminated, an obstacle that exists among many who study
the Second Testament (our New Testament), namely the lack of appreciation for the relevance of second temple literature in helping us appreciate the
reflections and contributions of first-century conceptual developments about
Messiah that emerge prior to the coming of Jesus and how those perspectives
factor into Jesus' message and ministry.

CHAPTER NINE

ANTICIPATIONS OF THE ONE CALLED MESSIAH

The epithet "Messiah" (מָשִׁיחַ) or "Christ" (χριστός) is just one of several designations in second temple literature used for royal Messiah figures. Naturally it is one of the most well known epithets used of Jesus in the Second Testament (our New Testament). The other is "Son" or "Son of God." Yet unlike the Second Testament, in which Jesus is the one and only Messiah, this chapter recognizes the multiplicity of expected messianic figures that existed before, during, and even after the time of Jesus' ministry. Thus, by isolating the term "messiah" (מָשִׁיחַ) in the First Testament and the following second temple Dead Sea Scrolls and Pseudepigrapha texts, we will piece together messianic portraits that emerged during in second temple literature as they were composed within their socio-political context.

MESSIAH IN OLD TESTAMENT, DEAD SEA SCROLLS, AND PSEUDEPIGRAPHA		
	Messiah, Anointed, Anointed One	Sequential Item Number and Composition Name: Abbreviated and Total Form
Old Testament Sources	1 Samuel 1 Kings 1 Chronicles Psalms Zechariah	
Dead Sea Scrolls	CD 1Q28 1Q28a 4Q252 4Q266 4Q382 4Q458 4Q521	CD (Cairo Damascus Document) 1Q28 (1QRule of the Community) 1Q28a (1QSa = 1QRule of the Congregation) 4Q252 (4QcommGen^a = 4QCommentary on Genesis A) 4Q266 (4QD^a = 4QDamascus Document^a) 4Q382 (4QParaphrase of the Kings) 4Q458 (4QNarrative A) 4Q521 (4QMessianic Apocalypse)
Pseudepigrapha Sources	Psalms of Solomon	

Unfortunately, not every manuscript that uses the term "messiah" will prove helpful. Fragmented manuscripts and interpretive uncertainties will blur some of our conclusions. Nevertheless, among the diversity of eschatological Messiah figures, the royal Messiah is the one most frequently profiled, though not exclusively, as a righteous person from the line of David who restores Davidic rule over his people. We begin with our need to recognize the multiplicity of expected messianic figures that prevailed during the time of Jesus' ministry.

PREVAILING MESSIANIC FIGURES

Simply defined, the Hebrew term "messiah" (מָשִׁיחַ) or the Greek equivalent term "Christ" (χριστός) means, "anointed" (with oil) or "Anointed One." In keeping with what Johnston told us about the term "messiah" (מָשִׁיחַ) in the First Testament, we know that prophets, priests, and kings were all "anointed" figures. The prophet Elijah anointed his successor, Elisha (1 Kings 19:15–16). Moses anointed Aaron as high priest (Exod. 40:13; cp. Lev. 7:36) and subsequent priests and high priests were to be anointed (Exod. 40:14–15, Lev. 16:32; cp. Sir. 45:15). Kings too were presented as anointed figures. Samuel anointed Saul (1 Sam. 10:1, 15:10) and David (1 Sam. 16:12–13; cp. Sir. 46:13), Nathan the prophet and Zadok the priest anointed Solomon (1 Kings 1:45, cp. 1 Chron. 29:22), and Elijah anointed Hazael over Syria and Jehu over Israel (1 Kings 19:15–16). Furthermore, it was not unusual for Israel's kings of history past to be called "the Lord's anointed" as in the case of David's reference of Saul (1 Sam. 26:9, 11, 23), the hymn writer's reference of David and his descendants (2 Sam. 22:51, Pss. 2:2, 18:50; cp. Lam. 4:20), and the psalmist's appeal to God for help on behalf of the Davidites (Pss. 84:9; 89:38, 51; 132:10, 17).

Therefore it should be of no surprise that the Dead Sea Scrolls and Jewish Pseudepigrapha documents use the term "messiah," "anointed," or "anointed one" to speak of either a prophet, priest, or king. Thus there are multiple types of messianic figures portrayed in second temple literature, which is self-evident in the following chart.[1]

---

1. Compare my list with Martin G. Abegg and Craig A. Evans, "Messianic Passages in the Dead Sea Scrolls" in *Qumran-Messianism* (ed. James H. Charlesworth, Hermann Lichtenberger, and Gerbern S. Oegema; Tübingen: Mohr Siebeck, 1998), 191–94. James H. Charlesworth, "Messianology in the Biblical Pseudepigrapha," in *Qumran-Messianism* (ed. James H. Charlesworth, Hermann Lichtenberger, and Gerbern S. Oegema; Tübingen: Mohr Siebeck, 1998), 21–22. For an English translation of the Old Testament Pseudepigrapha, see James H. Charlesworth, ed., *The Old Testament Pseudepigrapha*, 2 vols. (New York: Doubleday, 1985).

MULTIPLE MESSIAHS			
מָשִׁיחַ for Prophet	מָשִׁיחַ for Priest	χριστός or מָשִׁיחַ for King	χριστός or מָשִׁיחַ for Heavenly Figure or Apocalyptic Figure
CD 2:12	CD 12:23–3:1	CD 12:23–3:1	11QMelch 2.18
CD 5:2–6:1 (=4Q267 2:6 =	CD 14:19	CD 14:19 (= 4Q266	4Q171 1 10iv:25
6Q15 3:4)	(= 4Q266 f10i:12) CD	f10i:12)	(4QpPs^a.b = 4QPsalms
1QM 11:7–8	19:10–11	CD 19:10–11	Pesher ^a.b) Pesher on
4Q270 2ii:13–14	CD 20:1	CD 20:1	Psalm 37 (king = holy
4Q377 1ii:4–5 (of Moses)	1Q28 9.11	1Q28 9:11	spirit)
4Q521 1ii:1, 12–13	4Q375 1i:9	1Q28a 2:11–12	1 Enoch: Similitudes
4Q521 8:9 (messianic prophet)	4Q376 1i: 1	1Q28a 2:14–15	48:10
		1Q28a 2:20–21	1 Enoch: Similitudes 52:4
		4Q252 5:3–4	2 Baruch 29:3, 30:1
		4Q458 2ii:6	2 Baruch 39:7, 40:1
		4Q521 2ii:1; 12–13	2 Baruch 70:9, 72:2
		Psalms of Solomon	4 Ezra 7:28–29
		17:32	4 Ezra 11:37–12:34
		Psalms of Solomon	3 Enoch 45:5
		18 (title)	3 Enoch 48A:10
		Psalms of Solomon	
		18:5, 9	

Naturally the use of Messiah or Christ in these documents mirrors the First Testament's recognition of multiple messiahs or anointed ones,[2] but alongside this single similarity there are several differences. First, whereas in the First Testament "anointed" tends to be descriptive of an event, namely anointing a person for some specific service, in second temple literature it is more often a prescriptive title. Second, whereas in the First Testament, references to an "anointed one" speak of a physical and historical personality, second temple literature sometimes expands the usage to anticipate a heavenly or apocalyptic figure. Finally, whereas the First Testament uses the term to recall the anointing of a real living and breathing person alive at the time of the anointing, second temple literature employs the term to speak of both human and apocalyptic figures yet to come.

Obviously, it is beyond the scope of this work to develop a portrait or set of portraits for all four types of messiah figures. So attention will be primarily

---

2. This idea of multiple messiahs is not a new phenomenon. See *Judaisms and Their Messiahs at the Turn of the Christian Era* (ed. J. Neusner, W. S. Green, and E. Frerichs; Cambridge: Cambridge University Press, 1987). L. H. Schiffman, "Messianic Figures and Ideas in the Qumran Scrolls" in *Messiah: Development in Earliest Judaism and Christianity* (ed. J. H. Charlesworth; Philadelphia: Augsburg Fortress, 1992), 116–29.

though not exclusively on the epithet Messiah when used for a messianic king / royal Messiah. Thus we begin with the expectation of a co-ruling, royal Messiah with a messianic priest because they often appear together in Dead Sea Scrolls.

DIARCHY: MESSIAH KING AND MESSIAH PRIEST

Because an expected diarchy is so well known, whenever the concept of Messiah is addressed today, people anticipate a discussion about two Messiahs. Belief in binary messianism, a "Messiah king" and a "Messiah priest," occurs most clearly in three Dead Sea Scrolls: CD (*Cairo Damascus Document*), 1Q28 (*Rule of the Community*), and 1Q28a (*Rule of the Congregation*). As we focus attention on the regal Messiah, we shall see that his functions are at best blurred together with the priestly Messiah and that binary messianism permeates the scrolls discovered in the nearby caves that surrounded the ruins of Qumran. But we must first begin with what prompted this belief in two Messiah figures.

Two factors may explain this second temple diarchy. First, the *Rule of the Community* and the *Rule of the Congregation* appear to express a sectarian community's disapproval of the non-Davidic Hasmoneans, who are combining two separate offices of anointed king and anointed high priest into a single office. Thus these two mid-Hasmonean documents (125–75 BCE) may evidence the community's explicit disapproval of the emerging royal priesthoods of John Hyrcanus, Aristobulus, and/or Alexander Jannaeus (see ch. 8, 241–43).

Second, disapproval over the Hasmoneans may have been fueled and supported biblically by Zechariah. As is evident from Johnston's presentation in chapter 7, the prophet Zechariah begins his ministry in 520 BCE. It is believed that he was born a Jewish refugee in Babylonia (Zech. 1:1, 7; cp. Neh. 12:10–16) and returned to Jerusalem *circa* 539 BCE under the leadership of Zerubbabel and Joshua (Neh. 12:4) to rebuild the temple (2 Chron. 36:21–23; Ezra 1:1–4; 6:3–5). Although the foundation was laid in 536 BCE (Ezra 3:8–13), temple construction halted and did not resume until 520 BCE (Ezra 6:6–12; Hag. 1:1–2). In time, however, the second temple was completed and dedicated *circa* 515 BCE (Ezra 6:15–18). Zechariah's ministry, then, was clearly with the returned exiles in Jerusalem (4:8–10, 6:10, 14; 7:2–3, 9; Neh. 12:12, 16). As a prophet, he envisioned what appears to be an uncharted and an innovative form of leadership for the reconstitution of Jewish community life and its recently reconstructed temple.

Unlike preexile times, Zechariah appears to have envisioned two thrones with two occupants (Zech. 6:9–14).[3] Both the Davidite, who is called the

---

3. James C. VanderKam, *From Joshua to Caiaphas: High Priests after the Exile* (Minneapolis: Fortress, 2004), 438–42. Yet Johnston differs here. He suggests that there was only one (not two) crowns. He does not see two different individuals sitting on two thrones and wearing two crowns simultaneously. Rather, he sees two individuals sharing one crown

branch, as well as Joshua the high priest, was given a crown, they sat on their respective thrones, and they appear to rule in a harmonious manner. Nevertheless the branch is someone who is yet to come to build the temple, to bear royal honor, and to rule Israel. Thus the branch was a futuristic person from David's line because during the time of Zechariah, local dynasties had no political clout in Persia's socio-political system of government.

Yet the simultaneous anointing of a king and a priest is not unprecedented in Israel's history. Solomon and Zadok were also anointed during a single ceremony (1 Chron. 29:22; cp. 1 Kings 1:45). Furthermore God promised that he would bless the house of Israel and the house of Aaron (Pss. 115:12, vv. 9–10; 135:19). Perhaps these biblical presentations also contributed to the scroll's presentation of a diarchy. Naturally the position of high priest was firmly established during the period of messianic dormancy (515–150 BCE). Yet Zechariah's innovative form of twin leadership appears to allow for the concept of two anointed eschatological Messiah figures, which then is echoed within three documents: CD, 1Q28, 1Q28a.

CD (Cairo Damascus Document)

The *Cairo Damascus Document* makes four references about a Messiah King and Messiah Priest (12:23–13:1; 14:19; 19:10–11; 20:1). From them we learn that the future coming of these two Messiah figures serves first and foremost as the beginning of the messianic age, but also as an incentive for community members to obey community rules and to warn of impending consequences for any community backslider in the pre-messianic age.

The document consists of two medieval manuscripts (abbrev. MS): MS A and MS B. They were not found among the Dead Sea Scrolls but rather in Cairo, Egypt. Furthermore, they were first published in 1910, long before the first scrolls were discovered in 1947.[4] Yet today, CD is treated as one of "the foundational works of the Qumran community" due to the discoveries of Cave 4 in 1952.[5] Among the hundreds of fragmented texts discovered in Cave 4, archeologists found several fragments that had corresponding concepts, similar language, and shared details with the medieval document, which we refer to as CD. Thus not only did the fragments confirm CD's relationship with some of the fragments found in caves near the ruins of Qumran, several Cave 4 fragments were labeled *4QDamascus Document* (4QDa–h=4Q266–

---

and one throne in succession. Thus Joshua effectively functioned as a typological forerunner for the eschatological branch to come. See his more complete discussion, 187–96.

4. Whereas MS A is a tenth-century medieval manuscript, MS B is dated to the twelfth century. Solomon Schechter was the first to publish the *Cairo Damascus Document*, but he entitled it *Fragments of a Zadokite Work* (Cambridge: Cambridge University Press, 1910).

5. Joseph M. Baumgarten, "Damascus Document" in *Encyclopedia of the Dead Sea Scrolls*, 2 vols. (ed. Lawrence H. Schiffman and James C. VanderKam; Oxford: Oxford University Press, 2000), 166–70.

273).[6] Subsequently the fragment 4Q266 (4QDa) is frequently noted along-side CD citations. In fact, today the medieval text is considered a reliable copy of these fragmented texts.

The *Cairo Damascus Document* is typically divided into two major sections: "The Admonition," and "The Law and Communal Rules." "The Admonition" reviews Israelite history by focusing on Israel's past and future punishment as well as God's gracious salvation of Israel's "remnant" (1:1–10; also referred to as "a sure house in Israel" in 3:19, "the House of Judah" in 4:11, and "those who entered the new covenant in the land of Damascus" in 6:19, cp. 6:5, 7:19).[7] The first two references to dual messianism occur at the close of "the Admonition," where the text speaks of God's future punishment of wicked backsliders.[8]

> [19:7]When the oracle of the prophet Zechariah comes true, O sword, be lively and smite [8]My shepherd and the man loyal to me so says God. If you strike down the shepherd, the flock will scatter. [9]Then I will turn my power against the little ones (Zechariah 13:7). But those who give heed to God are the poor of the flock (Zechariah 11:7): [10]*they will escape in the time of punishment*, but **all the rest will be handed over to the sword when the Messiah of** [11]**Aaron and of Israel comes**, just as it happened during the time of the first punishment, as [12]Ezekiel said, Make a mark on the foreheads of those who moan and lament, (Ezekiel 9:4) [13]but the rest were given to the sword that makes retaliation for covenant violations. *And such is the verdict on all members of* [14]*His covenant who do not hold firm to these laws: they are condemned to destruction by Belial.* (19:7–14, emphasis mine)

> *So there is one fate for everyone who rejects the commandments of God* [19:33]and abandons them to follow their own willful heart. *So it is with all the men who entered the new covenant* [34]in the land of Damascus, *but then turned back and traitorously turned away from the fountain of living water.* [35]They shall not be reckoned among the council of the people, and their names shall not be written in their book from the day [20:1]the Beloved Teacher dies **until the Messiah from Aaron and from Israel appears**. Such is the fate

---

6. Actually, the title *4QDamascus Document* represents several fragments. They are labeled alphabetically and assigned numbers as well. 4QDa = 4Q266, 4QDb = 4Q267, 4QDc = 4Q268, 4QDd = 4Q269, 4QDe = 4Q270, 4QDf = 4Q271, 4QDg = 4Q272, 4QDh = 4Q273.

7. Joseph M. Baumgarten and Daniel R. Schwartz, "Damascus Document" in *The Dead Sea Scrolls*, vol. 2: Damascus Document, War Scroll, and Related Documents (ed. James H. Charlesworth; Tübingen: Mohr Siebeck, 1995), 4–9.

8. The translation comes from Accordance Software. Martin G. Abegg Jr., James E. Bowley, and Edward M. Cook are responsible for preparing the text and morphological analysis for electronic publication. Abegg's work with electronic data bases is extensive, having prepared the QUMRAN, MISH-T, SAMAR-T, and BENSIRA-C/M Accordance modules for the study of ancient Hebrew Language and Literature.

for all [2]who join the company of the men of holy perfection and then become sick of obeying virtuous rules. (19:32–20:2, emphasis mine)

These two citations, directed to a sectarian group of people who occupied nearby Qumran, served as a warning for all to obey: "Fellow Qumranians, hold firm to our community regulations" (my dynamic equivalent; 19:14, 32). The future fate for those who rejected God's commands or left the community was threefold: they will be handed over to the sword when the diarchy appears (19:10), all backsliders will forever relinquish community membership privileges (19:35), and they can expect a destructive form of condemnation (19:14). Thus the future coming of two Messiahs served first as an incentive for community members to obey community rules and second to warn of impending consequences for any community backslider in this present age.[9]

The next two references about dual messianism occur in the second major section of the *Cairo Damascus Document*. The document elaborates on biblical law as well as communal rules about the purity of the temple and its city (11:19–12:2), prescribes treatment of transgressors and Gentiles (12:2–11a), discusses dietary laws (12:11b–15a), impurity rules (12:15b–22a), communal rules (12:22b–14:19), a penal code for infractions of communal discipline (14:20–22), and a set of oaths of those wishing to enter the covenant community of Qumran (15:1–15a). It is while handling the communal rules (12:22b–14:19) and penal code for community infractions (14:20–22) that the second set of references to binary messianism appears.[10]

These are the rules [12:21]for the sage to live by with all that is living, according to the regulation for every occasion. If [22]the seed of Israel lives according to this law, they shall never know condemnation. This is the rule [23]camps, who live by these rules in the era of wickedness, **until the appearance of the Messiah of Aaron** [13:1]**and of Israel** (12:21–13:1)

CD 14:17–19	4QDa = 4Q266 f10i:10–13
This is the exposition for those who live in the camps, [and these are the fundamental rules of . . .] [14:18][the assem]bly. And this is the exposition of the regulations by which [they shall be governed in the age of [19]wickedness **until the appearance of the Messi]ah of Aaron and of Israel**, so that their iniquity may be atoned for. (emphasis mine)	This is the exposition [f10i:11][for those who live in the camps, and th]ese are the fundamental rules of the assembly. And this is the exposition of [f10i:12][the regulations by which] they [shall be gov]erned **until the appearance of the Messiah of Aaron and of Israel**, [f10i:13][so that their iniquity may be atoned for.

---

9. Collins suggests that this might be a reference to a single Messiah characterized by both functions as priest and king because Messiah is singular. This argument might apply to CD 12:12–13:1 as well. See John J. Collins, *The Scepter and the Star: Messianism in Light of the Dead Sea Scrolls,* 2nd ed. (Grand Rapids: Eerdmans, 2010), 79-87. However, most understand these passages to speak of a binary messianism.

10. The translation comes from Accordance Software (italic mine) as well as the scripture citation and insertion "interpreter of." Martin G. Abegg Jr., James E. Bowley, and Edward M. Cook are responsible for preparing the text and morphological analysis for electronic publication.

These three references speak of the importance for community members to obey community rules in the present age in order to prevent a future condemnation (12:22), and so that the Messiahs, when they come, might make atonement for sins (14:19). Thus community rules and regulations were to be obeyed *until* these two Messiahs appeared and apparently assumed their respective religious and political leadership roles.

In summary, it seems the Cairo Document's portrait of these two Messiahs involve a threefold and shared function: to condemn the disobedient, to punish apostates, and to atone for sin. Yet ultimately the expectation of these two Messiahs serves to deter apostasy in the community and define *the end* of one time period (i.e., pre-messianic age) and *the start* of another (i.e., messianic age). Nothing in the context, however, warrants these Messiahs to be angelic or divine figures. They are human personalities, who together shoulder future religious and political responsibilities and in essence corule over the community. Nothing, at this point however, seems to indicate explicitly a Davidic regal figure. Perhaps there was an implied connection with Zechariah that might warrant speculation about an expected royal figure from the line of David who would rule alongside a priestly Messiah. Further support will be discussed later when we examine the epithet "prince." In the meantime the appearance of the title Messiah in 1Q28 warrants our attention.

1Q28 (1QS = Rule of the Community)

Officially entitled *Rule of the Community*, 1Q28 is sometimes referred to as *The Manual of Discipline*. It is one of three separate works that make up a single scroll discovered in 1947, published in 1951, and enshrined in 1955.[11] Following 1Q28, the scroll also contains the *Rule of the Congregation* (1Q28a) and the *Rule of Blessings* (1Q28b). Although only one copy survives for both the *Rule of the Congregation* (1Q28a) and the *Rule of Blessings* (1Q28b), subsequent copies of 1Q28 have been found in Cave 4 (4QSa–j=4Q255–264).[12]

1Q28 defines the rules for the community during the pre-messianic age by describing the ritual ceremony for entering the covenant community (1:16–2:18), outlining the annual renewal ceremony, denunciations, and

---

11. Sukenik discovered the scroll. M. Burrows, J. C. Trevor, and W. H. Brownlee published the work in *The Dead Sea Scrolls of Saint Mark's Monastery* (New Haven, 1951). The manuscript was enshrined at the Shrine of the Book in Israel. See Yigael Yadin, *The Message of the Scrolls* (New York: Simon and Schuster, 1957).

12. Of the ten fragments from Cave 4, only three appear to have enough text to be deemed of value. They are 4QS^b = 4Q256 and 4QS^d = 4Q258 from *circa* 25 BCE, and 4QS^e = 4Q259 from *circa* 100 BCE. See Elisha Qimron and James H. Charlesworth, "Cave IV Fragments" in *The Dead Sea Scrolls*, vol. 1: Rule of the Community and Related Documents (ed. James H. Charlesworth; Tübingen: Mohr Siebeck, 1995), 52–103.

atonement practices (2:19–3:12), providing an exposition of the community's dualistic beliefs (3:13–4:26), supplying rules for life in the community and precepts for punishment (5:1–7:25), issuing a charter for the new congregation (8:1–10:8), and closing with a hymn of praise (10:9–11:22).[13] It is within the charter for the new congregation where binary messianism is mentioned.

> At that time the men [9:6]of the Yahad shall withdraw, the holy house of Aaron uniting as a Holy of Holies, and the synagogue of Israel as those who walk blamelessly. [7]The sons of Aaron alone shall have authority in judicial and financial matters. They shall decide on governing precepts for the men of the Yahad [8]and on money matters for the holy men who walk blamelessly. Their wealth is not to be admixed with that of rebellious men, who [9]have failed to cleanse their path by separating from perversity and walking blamelessly. They shall deviate from none of the teachings of the Law, whereby they would walk [10]in their willful heart completely. They shall govern themselves using the original precepts by which the men of the Yahad began to be instructed, [11]doing so **until there come the Prophet and the Messiahs of Aaron and Israel**. (9:6–11)[14]

Obviously very little is said about the expected coming of the Messiahs of Aaron and Israel. Yet while this particular community (=*Yahad*)[15] waits, the Aaronic priests (perhaps of Qumran) carry out religious, judicial, and financial responsibilities.[16] Nevertheless, what can be said about both Messiahs is that both appear to be human figures whose appearance once again marks *the end* of the pre-messianic age. And though information about the Messiah of Israel is sparse, a subsequent document 1Q28a expects him to usher in and preside over the banquet meals during the messianic age.

---

13. Michael A. Knibb, "Damascus Document" in *Encyclopedia of the Dead Sea Scrolls* (ed. Lawrence H. Schiffman and James C. VanderKam; Oxford: Oxford University Press, 2000), 793–97. Compare Elisha Qimron and James H. Charlesworth, "Rules of the Community" in *The Dead Sea Scrolls*, vol. 1: Rule of the Community and Related Documents (ed. James H. Charlesworth; Tübingen: Mohr Siebeck, 1995), 1–51.
14. The translation comes from Accordance Software (italic mine) as well as the scripture citation and insertion "interpreter of." Martin G. Abegg Jr., James E. Bowley, and Edward M. Cook are responsible for preparing the text and morphological analysis for electronic publication.
15. The term *Yhad* is a self-designation for the people of Qumran that means "unity." Thus 1QS is a constitution of charter for the *Yhad*, which Abegg contends is not so unusual when compared with charters from elsewhere in the contemporary Greco-Roman world. See Abegg, *The Dead Sea Scrolls*, 123.
16. 4Q541 (4QAaron A) may serve as a warning to a descendant of Levi not to afflict the poor and defenseless. References to crucifixion might serve as a condemnation and warning against Alexander Jannaeus' behavior and an exhortation that descendants of Levi should not practice such things. Collins, *The Scepter and the Star*, 123–26.

1Q28a (1QSa = Rule of the Congregation)

The *Rule of the Congregation* (1Q28a) presents life in the community as an enactment or "a messianic mirror image" of things yet to come. The community appears to live life as though the messianic age has already arrived, though it was yet to come. Thus, what they believed about the future is to affect the way they live in the present. After its introduction (1:1–6), the *Rule of the Congregation* addresses the stages of life of the sectarian (1:6–9), the disqualification of service due to age (1:19–22), the tasks of the Levitical order (1:22–25), the specific duties of the council of the community (1:25–27), a list of people included and excluded from the community (1:27–2:10), and closes with the convocation and future messianic banquet (2:11–22).[17] It is at the end of this work that the term "Messiah" occurs three times.

> [2:11]The procedure for the [mee]ting of the men of reputation [when they are called] to the banquet held by the Council of the Yahad, **when [God] has fa[th]ered (?)** [12]**the Messiah among them**: [the Priest,] as head of the entire congregation of Israel, shall enter first, trailed by all [13][his] brot[hers, the Sons of] Aaron, those priests [appointed] to the banquet of the men of reputation. They are to sit [14]be[fore him] by rank. **Then the [Mess]iah of Israel may en[ter,]** and the heads [15]of the th[ousands of Israel] are to sit before him by rank, as determined by [each man's comm]ission in their camps and campaigns. Last, all [16]the heads of [the con]gregation's cl[ans,] together with [their] wis[e and knowledgeable men,] shall sit before them by [17]rank. [When] they gather [at the] communal [tab]le, [having set out bread and w]ine so the communal table is set [18][for eating] and [the] wine (poured) for drinking, none [may re]ach for the first portion [19]of the bread or [the wine] before the Priest. For [he] shall [bl]ess the first portion of the bread [20]and the wine, [reac]hing for the bread first. Afterw[ard] **the Messiah of Israel** [shall re]ach [21]for the bread. [Finally,] ea[ch] (member of) the whole congregation of the Yahad [shall give a bl]essing, [in descending order of] rank. This procedure shall govern [22]every me[al], provided at least ten me[n are ga]thered together.[18]

Thus while describing a future banquet, the Messiah of Israel enters the banquet hall after a priest (perhaps the Messiah of Aaron; 2:11–13), presides over the community as they appear to sit in some military formation (2:14–17),

---

17. Lawrence H. Schiffman, "Rule of the Congregation" in *Encyclopedia of the Dead Sea Scrolls* (ed. Lawrence H. Schiffman and James C. VanderKam; Oxford: Oxford University Press, 2000), 797–99. Compare Elisha Qimron and James H. Charlesworth, "Rules of the Community" in *The Dead Sea Scrolls*, vol. 1: Rule of the Community and Related Documents (ed. James H. Charlesworth; Tübingen: Mohr Siebeck, 1995), 1–5.

18. The translation comes from Accordance Software (italic mine) as well as the scripture citation and insertion "interpreter of." Martin G. Abegg Jr., James E. Bowley, and Edward M. Cook are responsible for preparing the text and morphological analysis for electronic publication.

and signals when to eat (2:17–20). Consequently, the Messiah of Israel once again appears to be a human figure; here however he presides over and administers instructions during a military banquet. Nevertheless, it is the priestly Messiah who appears to be "the head of the entire congregation" (2:12).

Summation

The dissatisfaction over the socio-political activities of the non-Davidic Hasmoneans appears to evoke a renewed interest in God's restoration of the high priest's rule as an office to be separated from kingship. Thus CD, 1Q28, and 1Q28a appear to speak of two messianic figures that seem to co-rule together and share similar religious responsibilities. Furthermore, it appears that diarchy stands opposed to the Hasmonean royal priesthood and echoes Zechariah 6:1–14 whereby a Levitical priest and a Davidite are crowned, sit upon their respective thrones, and rule together. Couple this with Solomon's and Zadok's simultaneous anointment (1 Chron. 29:22; cp. 1 Kings 1:45) and God's promise to bless the house of Israel and the house of Aaron (Ps. 115:12, vv. 9–10; 135:19), this idea of a diarchy was in keeping with an historical pattern. And if the *Testament of Judah* speaks messianically, then a similar perspective exists in the *Testament of the Twelve Patriarchs: Judah 21:1–4.*

> [1]And now, children, love Levi so that you may endure. Do not be arrogant toward him or you will be wholly destroyed. [2]To me [Judah] God has given the kingship and to him, the priesthood; and he has subjected the kingship to the priesthood. [3]To me he gave earthly matters and to Levi, heavenly matters. [4]As heaven is superior to the earth, so is God's priesthood superior to the kingdom on earth . . .[19]

Although the expected diarchy may have some scriptural basis in 1 Chronicles, 1 Kings, the Psalms, and Zechariah,[20] there are at least two differences. First, in 1 Chronicles and 1 Kings, king Solomon and the high priest Zadok do not share power equally. Solomon presides over Zadok. Yet Zechariah presents, though obscurely, two Messiahs co-ruling equally, which the Dead Sea Scrolls appears to echo at times (CD 14:19; 19:10, 14, 32, 35). Nevertheless there is evidence elsewhere indicating that the priestly Messiah presided over the royal Messiah (1Q28a 2:12; *TJudah* 21:2–4; cp. 4Q161 3:24–25). However, the exact relationship between the two Messiahs appears to be shrouded in mystery. Second, in 1 Chronicles and 1 Kings, King Solomon alone was enthroned

---

19. Translation by H. C. Kee, "Testament of the Twelve Patriarchs" in *The Old Testament Pseudepigrapha*, 2 vols. (ed. James H. Charlesworth; New York: Doubleday, 1985), 1:800.
20. One might also appeal to Zechariah's vision of the two "sons of oil" (4:14; cf. 4Q254 4:2). Thus Zechariah 3:3, 4:14, and 6:1–14 may have influenced the writers of CD and the expected diarchy of both priest and king.

and governed the kingdom, while the high priest Zadok served in the temple. Yet in Zechariah, the high priest Joshua was viewed as a surrogate ruler until the Davidic branch arrived. Thus the manuscripts CD, 1Q28, 1Q28a present two human Messiah figures both of whom appear to execute religious leadership roles equally and simultaneously. Together they were to signal the *end* of one time period and *begin* another. Thus, we might summarize our results about the regal Messiah in the following manner.

PORTRAYALS OF THE DIARCHY

OT Sources	Primary Passage: Zechariah 3:8, 6:1–14 Secondary: 1 Chronicles 29:22 1 Kings 1:45 Psalm 115:9–10, 11 Psalm 135:19
Dead Sea Scrolls	CD 12:23–3:1 CD 14:19 (4Q266 f10i:12) CD 19:10–11 CD 20:1 1Q28 9.11 1Q28a
Pseudepigrapha Sources	*Testament of the Twelve Patriarchs: T.Judah*
Various Elements	The royal messiah is David's scion The royal messiah is a human personality The royal messiah is a co-ruler over Israel
Various Functions	He ushers in the messianic age He shares religious leadership roles (implied) He accedes to the priestly messiah He condemns those who disobey God's commands He condemns apostates who left the community He makes atonement for sin He presides over future military banquet meals

Dating of Manuscripts	Mid- Hasmonean: 125–75 BCE
	  1Q28 (1QS = *Community Rule*)
	  4Q266 (4QDa = *4QDamascus Document*[a])
	Political Situation: Hasmonean Rule
	  John Hyrcanus I (135–104 BCE)
	  Aristobulus I (104–103 BCE)
	  Alexander Jannaeus (103–76 BCE)

MONARCHY: MESSIAH KING

The well-publicized profile of a dual messiahship ought not to overshadow the possible profile of a royal Messiah who rules alone. Five texts appear to use the term to speak of a single royal Messiah figure: 4Q252, 4Q382, 4Q458, 4Q521, and the *Psalms of Solomon*. Yet the fragmentary evidence of two Dead Sea Scrolls as well as the interpretive uncertainties tied to a third are not clear support for a single eschatological regal messianic figure. Nevertheless, that is not the case for 4Q252 and the *Psalms of Solomon*. We begin, however, with the less certain texts from Qumran and work toward the *Psalms of Solomon*.

4Q382 (4Q Paraphrase of the Kings)[21]

Of the four documents listed above, 4Q382 is of little value to our discussion and hardly worth mentioning. Yet it does contain the epithet Messiah and thereby included in Messiah text lists.[22] 4Q382 consists of 154 papyrus fragments from the late Hasmonean period (75–50 BCE) when John Hyrcanus II and Aristobulus II were generating civil unrest while arguing over leadership of Judea (see ch. 8, 244–25). Many of these extremely fragmented papyri are limited to isolated words or letters, which is also the case with 4Q382 16:2. In fact our fragment consists of four lines. And though the ink is deemed very poor, the mention of a Messiah of Israel (מְשִׁיחַ יִשְׂרָאֵל) appears to exist.[23] Due to its fragmentation, however, we can only assume that if we had the complete manuscript, the mention of a Messiah of Aaron might also appear, we can only assume the Messiah of Israel is human, and we can only assume the similar roles of those already revealed in CD, 1Q28 and 1Q28a. Thus the poor condition of the manuscript and multiplicity of assumptions devalue 4Q382 for our discussion here.

4Q458 (4Q Narrative A)[24]

In a similar vein, 4Q458 (*4Q Narrative A*) is of dubious value because it too is sketchy with nineteen fragments. Of the nineteen fragments, only two are of any real importance in that they contribute a little something to our discussion. To begin with, 4Q458 may have been composed during the late Hasmonean period (75–50 BCE), once again while civil war between John Hyrcanus II and Aristobulus II was in process (67–63 BCE). Thus, it was

---

21. The analyzed transcriptions of 4Q382 = *4Qpap paraKings et al., 4QpapTehillot Avot* are presented by Saul M. Olyan in *Qumran Cave 4.VIII* (DJD 13; Oxford: Clarendon Press, 1994), 363–416.
22. Abegg and Evans, "Messianic Passages in the Dead Sea Scrolls," 191–94, 203.
23. Olyan, "*4Qpap paraKings et al.,*" 373.
24. The analyzed transcriptions of 4Q458 = *4Q Narrative* are presented by Erik Larson in *Qumran Cave 4.XXVI* (DJD 36; Oxford: Clarendon Press, 2000), 353–65. Robert Eisenman and Michael Wise, *The Dead Sea Scrolls Uncovered* (Shaftesbury, 1992), 46–50. The symbols [. . .] indicate that portions of the text are missing in the manuscript.

a text composed during a period of political and religious uncertainties in Jerusalem, Samaria, and Galilee, which may have heightened the desire for a messianic figure to arrive on the scene and settle the issue of Jewish rulership.

Furthermore, 4Q458 speaks ever so briefly of an anointed Messiah figure. We read, "and he destroyed him and his army [. . .] and it swallowed up all the uncircumcised [. . .] and he will count him righteous and he will go against [. . .] anointed with the oil of kingship of [. . . .]" (2ii 3–6). "Both the imagery and the extent of the defeat inflicted," says Larson, "suggest the final battle between the forces of good and evil, supporting the notion that the anointed one is none other than the Messiah."[25] The previous mentioned scene of conflict and war in the document strengthens Larson's argument (see frg 1:5–10). Thus, in 4Q458 the Anointed One is clearly a regal Messiah who was painted as one who would be both a victorious warrior and a righteous person. He would destroy the uncircumcised and lead in righteousness.

Although the manuscript's brevity prevents us from saying too much, we can suggest the portrait of messianic military leader parallels 1Q28a where the Messiah of Israel presides over a military banquet. Nevertheless, as it was with 4Q382, to exclude the possibility of a binary messianism would be presumptuous at best. Another questionable text is 4Q521. Yet unlike 4Q382 and 4Q458, the questionability of 4Q521 is not because of its fragmentation but because of the uncertain identity of "anointed one."

4Q521 (4QMessianic Apocalypse)[26]

Although 4Q521 is commonly spoken of as *4QMessianic Apocalypse*, its alias title is *On Resurrection*. Like CD, 1Q28, and 1Q28a, it too is a mid-Hasmonean text (125–75 BCE) written while either John Hyrcanus, Aristobulus, or Alexander Jannaeus was in power (see ch. 8, pp. 241–43). Unlike CD, 1Q28, and 1Q28a, however, 4Q521 is not necessarily a product of those who lived at Qumran. Rather it may have been hidden in the caves along with other works like *1 Enoch*, *Jubilees*, and Tobit. Regardless of its origin, 4Q521 consists of sixteen fragments, yet several fragments may be placed into two groups with clearly identifiable themes. Whereas the first group (fragments 2ii + 4) focuses attention on the theme of messianic blessings during the future eschaton (2:1–14), the second group (fragments 7:1–8 + 5ii:7–16) directs our attention to the theme of final judgment by way of reviewing God's creative power (2:1–3) as well as by way

---

25. Larson in *Qumran Cave 4.XXVI*, 354. Larson also points out that the phrase "anointed with the oil of gladness" is not found in the Bible or elsewhere in the scrolls. The closest parallel, however, occurs in Psalm 45:7. Thus a conceptual link to royal psalm to a Davidic referent exists.

26. The analyzed transcriptions of 4Q521 = *4Q Messianic Apocalypse* are presented by Émile Peuch in *Qumran Cave 4.XVIII* (DJD 25; Oxford: Clarendon Press, 1998), 1–38. See also Tabor and Michael Wise, "'On Resurrection' and the Synoptic Gospel Tradition: A Preliminary Study," *JSP* 10 (1992): 15–61.

of describing the destiny of the cursed (they die) versus the blessed (they will be resurrected; 2:4–6).

Naturally the first group of fragments about messianic blessings is of importance to our discussion because they reveal the miraculous marvels performed during the eschatological age once the LORD's Messiahs or Messiah has appeared. To begin with, the author of 4Q521 evidences dependence on Psalm 146 (cp. lines 1–8). His dependence, however, deviates from the psalm in that rather than God a Messiah figure is the referent. For 4Q521 reads, "For the heavens and the earth shall listen to his Anointed One" (or "Messiah"). Thus, it appears the "Anointed One" is God's agent and not God himself through whom he seeks out the pious, hovers over the poor, and renews the faithful (f2ii:5–6). God honors the pious, sets prisoners free, heals the blind, and lifts people up through an eschatological Messiah figure (f2ii:7–8).

Furthermore, the author of 4Q521 is also dependent on Isaiah 61:1, for we read in 4Q521 that ". . . the Lord will perform marvelous acts such as have not existed, just as he said, for he will heal the badly wounded and will make the dead live (or "revive the dead"), and will proclaim good news to the poor . . . and enrich the hungry" (f2ii:12–13).[27] Unlike in Isaiah where the prophet Isaiah himself is the anointed one, here in 4Q251 it seems that the referent points forward to an eschatological anointed figure.

Obviously some people of the first century believed the heavens and the earth would listen to the LORD's Messiah. Whether it is the LORD himself or the LORD through his messianic agent, it appears as though the resurrection of the dead, the healing of the critically wounded, and the sending of the good news to the afflicted would occur during the messianic age via a Messiah figure. These activities could support an expected royal Messiah figure (Matt. 11:2–5; cp. 11QApPsa),[28] as well as an eschatological prophetic Messiah figure like Elijah (cp. 1 Kings 17:17–24; Sir. 48:3; Mark 8:28).[29] It seems reasonable to suspect that an eschatological royal Messiah figure could be an agent of the LORD, and thereby capable of activities similar to that of a prophet (f2ii:1, 12–13).[30] Yet the identity is dubious at best, perhaps because

27. Translation by Florentino García Martínez and Eibert J. C. Tigchelaar, *The Dead Sea Scrolls: Study Edition*, vol. 2 (4Q274–11Q31) (Grand Rapids: Eerdmans, 1998), 1045. For a variation see Michael Wise, Martin Abegg, and Edward Cook, *The Dead Sea Scrolls* (New York: HarperSan Francisco, 1996), 420–21.

28. Likewise in Mark 1:14–8:21, Jesus appears to be "the Christ" because he is a superior miracle worker and thus Peter acknowledges, "You are the Christ." Herbert W. Bateman IV, "Defining the Titles 'Christ' and 'Son of God' in Mark's Narrative Presentation of Jesus," *JETS* 50 (September 2007): 537–59.

29. See Collins, *Scepter and the Star*, 117– 22; John J. Collins, "Jesus, Messianism, and the Dead Sea Scrolls," in *Qumran–Messianism* (ed. James H. Charlesworth, Hermann Lichtenberger, and Gerbern S. Oegema; Tübingen: Mohr Siebeck, 1998), 112–19.

30. Peuch, *Qumran Cave 4.XVIII*, 1–2; idem., "Une apocalypse messianique (4Q521)," *RevQ* 15 (1992): 497.

there was an accepted mystery about the type of Messiah yet to come. Will he be a prophetic Messiah? Will he be a royal Messiah? Will he be a combination of both prophetic and royal whereby a combination of two roles is evident in one person as Josephus' portrayal of John Hyrcanus: high priest and prophet (*Ant* 13.10.7 § 299)? Unfortunately due to 4Q521's fragmentation, we may never know. Nevertheless, whoever this expected Messiah is, he appears to be human with future expectations of resurrection, "the blessed will be resurrected" (f2:4–6). However, unlike the 4Q382, 4Q458, and 4Q521, our next manuscript 4Q252 (*4Q Commentary on Genesis A*) is much more helpful.

4Q252 (4Q Commentary on Genesis A) [31]

Composed sometime during the disquieting reign of Herod the Great (30–4 BCE), 4Q252 (4Q*commGen*[a]), comprised of six fragments, comments on selected passages from Genesis 6 to 49. The surviving portions of the manuscript ponder four personalities in Genesis: Noah (1:1–2:8), Abraham (2:8–10), Amalek (4:1–3), and Jacob (4:3–6). The text sometimes deals with chronology, such as the chronology of the flood story (1:3–2:5) or of Abraham's life (2:8–10). It sometimes attempts to resolve problems like the object of Noah's curse (2:5–8) or the identification of the 120 years of Genesis 6:3 and their location within Noah's life (1:1–3). Other times it provides an explanation of a passage, which is the case for Jacob's blessing in Genesis 49:10 (5:1–5). Consequently the first part of the document appears to address Israel's past, while the latter part of the document looks forward to Israel's future, particularly as that future entails the coming of a royal Messiah. Thus, it is the latter part of 4Q252 (5:1–5) that concerns us here, for we read

> [5:1] *A ruler shall [no]t depart from the tribe of Judah* when Israel has dominion. [2][And] the one who sits on the throne of David [shall never] be cut off, because the "ruler's staff" is the covenant of the kingdom, [3][and the thous]ands of Israel are "the standards," **until the Righteous Messiah, the Branch of David, has come** (Genesis 49:10). [4]**For to him and to his seed the covenant of the kingdom of his people has been given for the eternal generations**, because [5]he has kept [. . . Interpreter of] the Law with the men of the Yahad.[32]

---

31. Initial analyzed transcriptions of 4Q252 (*4Q Commentary on Genesis A*) are edited by George Brooke in *Qumran Cave 4.XVII* (DJD 22; Oxford: Clarendon Press, 1968), 185–207. See also Gerbern S. Oegema, "Tradition-Historical Stueies on 4Q252" in *Qumran–Messianism* (ed. James H. Charlesworth, Hermann Lichtenberger, and Gerbern S. Oegema; Tübingen: Mohr Siebeck, 1998), 154–74.

32. The translation comes from Accordance Software (italic mine) as well as the scripture citation and insertion "interpreter of." Martin G. Abegg Jr., James E. Bowley, and Edward M. Cook are responsible for preparing the text and morphological analysis for electronic publication.

Of Genesis 49:10, only the first part of the verse is actually quoted: "The scepter shall not depart from Judah." The rest of 4Q252 5:2–5 represents the simple sense or an allusion to Jacob's blessing to Judah that also appears in Jeremiah 33:14–17. Five points seem relevant here. First, an attribute of this forthcoming Messiah is clearly his righteousness. Second, the author equates Messiah of righteousness with the branch of David, a point we will discuss more fully in the next chapter. For now, he is an undeniable Davidite. Third, God's covenant with David and his offspring are presented as an enduring one, in contrast to Ben Sirach and Josephus, who both viewed the covenant as having been terminated. Thus for this author, there is an unending Davidic promise and future restoration of David's dynasty. Fourth, this forthcoming messianic offspring of David may be one who interprets the Law along with other men of Judah. Finally, there is no mention of another Messiah figure. This last point raises the issue of authorship and community association.

Is 4Q252 a Qumran sectarian manuscript? Because this fragmentary document lacks a beginning and an ending, it is possible that discussions about a messianic diarchy are forever missing. Yet the presentation and its method of interaction with scripture may betray 4Q252 to be a non-sectarian text and thereby open considerations for a single ruling regal Messiah figure. There is no hint of diarchy here in this portion of the text. Furthermore, it seems the methods of interpretation used in 4Q252 differs from the other texts found in the nearby caves of Qumran. For instance there is no clear scriptural quote followed by an interpretation as in Pesher texts. There is no clear statement indicating that scripture is even being cited. Perhaps the document became part of the Dead Sea Scroll collection found in the caves surrounding Qumran in much the same way as 4Q521, Tobit, *1 Enoch*, and other texts were.

Regardless of how 4Q252 became part of the collection of Dead Sea Scrolls found near Qumran, its contents seem to support a single ruling Davidic Messiah. But whether or not other portions missing from 4Q252 might have discussed a priestly messianic figure, we can say this about the regal figure: he is one who will rule in righteousness, who will interpret the Law, and whose human offspring will perpetuate David's dynasty. One text, however, that was not discovered in the surrounding caves of Qumran, but speaks unquestionably of a single ruling Messiah figure, is the *Psalms of Solomon*.

Psalms of Solomon

Composed during the first century (*circa* 70–45 BCE) some time after the time of Pompey's invasion of Jerusalem (63 BCE), the *Psalms of Solomon* appears to be the most significant non–Qumranian work written during a period of time when competing forms of Jewish nationalism were emerging in Judea.[33]

---

33. See chapter 8, pp. 239–43; for authorship of the *Psalms of Solomon* see p. 243 n.56.

The Hasmonean dynasty was crumbling because of family disputes over who would rule Judea. Both John Hyrcanus II (backed by Antipater and the Pharisees) and his brother Aristobulus II (backed by the Sadducees) looked to Rome (Pompey) to resolve their differences. Delay led to Aristobulus's hostile response, Pompey's defeat of Jerusalem, and Rome's securing Judea for herself.[34] Thus, Wright labels the *Psalms of Solomon* as "literature of crisis."[35] It is a riveting text that begins with discontentment over Hasmonean hierarchy and Pompey's presence, but appears to climax with great expectations for God to fulfill his covenant made with David many centuries ago.

The *Psalms of Solomon* consists of eighteen psalms that acknowledge several theological themes. Among them are divine kingship (2:30, 32; 5:19; 17:1, 34, 46), life after death in a bodily resurrection (2:31, 3:12), and God's covenant relationship with Abraham (9:9; 18:3) and David. In fact, the author's ultimate plea for Yahweh's intervention is based upon the Davidic covenant of promise. The author of *Psalms of Solomon* 17:4 implores: "Lord, you chose David to be king over Israel, and you swore to him about his descendants forever, that his kingdom should not fail before you." God's sworn oath is a guarantee—a guarantee that Yahweh will fulfill his covenantal promise to David. Thus the future Messiah figure will be a Davidite. As the seventeenth and eighteenth psalms close the *Psalms of Solomon*, they provide an extensive plea and picture for a Davidic Messiah unlike any of the Dead Sea Scrolls. Yet the term "messiah" occurs only in the last two chapters.

The combination of two terms "Lord" and "Messiah" clearly profiles the expected royal Davidite as "the Lord Messiah" (17:32, 18 heading; 18:7). More specifically, he is portrayed as "a righteous king" who will be "taught by God" (17:32). In the broader context of 17:26–32, this "Lord Messiah" gathers a holy people whom he will lead in righteousness, will not tolerate unrighteousness, will judge unrighteousness, will excommunicate all unrighteous people, and will extend his righteous rule over all people groups. There will be no unrighteousness among the people he governs (17:26–27, 30, 32). In the context of 18:1–9, the Lord Messiah's reign is an appointed one yet to come but when it comes the Lord Messiah's rule will be stern and righteous (18:6–8). There is no evidence of a priestly Messiah. Like 4Q252, this royal Davidite reigns alone and is righteous. There is no evidence of this royal Messiah being a victorious warrior, but other parallel references to this expected Messiah figure via the use of the epithet "Son," which we will examine shortly, does support a victorious royal warrior.

---

34. The historical descriptions in *Psalms of Solomon* 2, 8, 17 appear to parallel Josephus, *Wars* 1.6.1–1.7.7 § 120–58 concerning Pompey's attack on Jerusalem.

35. R. B. Wright, "Psalms of Solomon" in *The Old Testament Pseudepigrapha*, 2 vols. (ed. James H. Charlesworth; New York: Doubleday, 1985), 2:643.

Summation

At this point, only two documents support a single ruling Messiah figure: Q252 and without any question the *Psalms of Solomon*. The fragmentation of 4Q382 and 4Q458 as well as the dubious interpretation of 4Q521 blur our ability to present a well-focused regal messianic portrait. Nevertheless the following chart summarizes what we can say about the various elements and functions of the eschatological Messianic figures presented in 4Q252, 4Q382, 4Q458, 4Q521, and *Psalms of Solomon*.

PORTRAYALS OF MESSIAH	
Old Testament Sources	Primary: 2 Samuel 7
Dead Sea Scrolls	4Q252 (non-Qumran text) 4Q382 (fragmented) 4Q458 (fragmented) 4Q521 (? interpretation)
Pseudepigrapha Sources	*Psalms of Solomon*
Various Elements	The royal messiah is David's scion The royal messiah is a human personality The royal messiah is a righteous leader The royal messiah is a ruler over Israel
Various Functions	He rules in righteousness He judges in righteousness He is taught by God

Socio-Political Context of Manuscripts	Mid-Hasmonean: 125–75 BCE
	    4Q521 (*4QMessianic Apocalypse*)
	
	    Hasmonean Rule: Priest-King Office
	        John Hyrcanus I (preamble), Aristobulus I, Alexander Jannaeus
	Late-Hasmonean: 75–50 BCE
	    4Q382 (*4QParaphrase of the Kings*)
	    4Q458 (*4QNarrative A*)
	    Psalms of Solomon
	
	    Civil Unrest: Scuffle over Judea
	    John Hyrcanus II & Aristobulus II & Pompey's invasion
	Early Herodian 30–1 BCE
	    4Q252 (*4QcommGenA* = *4QCommentary Genesis A*)
	        Herod the Great: Consolidating and maintaining rule over Judea.

CONCLUSION

Of the twenty-one documents that cite the term "messiah," only nine may actually speak of a royal messianic figure. In keeping with Hebrew Scriptures, the term "messiah" refers to someone with an anointing from God and is not limited to a regal messiah figure, but rather takes into consideration other messianic possibilities: prophet, priest, king, and heavenly or apocalyptic figures. Thus it is of no surprise to find several eschatological Messiah figures presented in extra-biblical material.

From the nine documents that speak of a messianic king, not all the ancient texts have proven beneficial. Three Dead Sea Scrolls had limited significance due either to fragmentation (4Q382, 4Q458) or interpretive uncertainties (4Q521). The most helpful texts have been CD, 1Q28, 1Q28a, 4Q252, 4Q266, and the *Psalms of Solomon*. Four are extremely helpful for establishing a clear diarchy (CD, 1Q28, 1Q28a, 4Q266), and they appear to support something other than the return of the Davidic monarchy as in the days of King David. On the one hand, we might expect as much from authors who are members of a community of priests living at Qumran. On the other hand, sacred Scripture appears to leave open the possibility of shared leadership (e.g. Zech. 6:9–15). Yet the concept of a royal Messiah, who rules solo over Judea, appears unique in extant documents unique to and different from the many fragments found in the caves surrounding Qumran (*Pss. Sol.*, perhaps 4Q252).

Interestingly enough, however, five texts were written during the sociopolitical activities of the non-Davidic Hasmoneans, who had combined the separate offices of anointed king and anointed high priest into a single office (CD, 1Q28, 1Q28a, 4Q266, 4Q521). Thus while the Hasmoneans advocated a non-Davidic king-priest rulership, the expectation of both a Davidic Messiah and Levitical Messiah was anticipated by some Jewish people. Yet the roles of these messianic figures at times appear blurred. Other texts were written during the period of civil war between John Hyrcanus II and Aristobulus II, a civil war only to be squelched by the Roman general Pompey (4Q382, 4Q458, *Pss. Sol.*). Nevertheless all our documents were composed during periods of political dissatisfaction and / or unrest in the Hasmonean Kingdom. The diverse portraits of differing regal Messiahs appear to have at least two things in common. They are righteous people and victorious warriors who will correct the religious-political situation.

These were the worst of times in the Hasmonean Kingdom and the pressures of these times appear to have contributed to the subsequent portraits of diverse eschatological regal messianic figures. To summarize, we might say the following. First, the texts unanimously support a Jewish human king. Second, while most texts portray the royal Messiah as righteous (4Q458, *Pss. Sol.*), others appear to assume righteousness by way of his future condemnation of apostates and the unrighteous (CD, 1Q28, *Pss. Sol.*). Third, with uncertainty about the three questionable Dead Sea Scrolls, there is a split between texts that present a diarchy (CD, 1Q28, 1Q28a, 4Q266) and those that look to a single messianic figure (4Q458; *Pss. Sol.*). Fourth, only a few contexts portray the royal Messiah as a military leader (1Q28a, 4Q458). Yet as we shall see with the epithet "Prince" in these same manuscripts (CD, 1Q28, 4Q266), it becomes apparent that victorious warrior king Messiah figures are expected. Finally, some texts simply *imply* that the regal Messiah figures will be Davidic (CD, 1Q28, 1Q28a). Others, however, are more *explicit* (4Q252, *Pss. Sol.*). Nevertheless, as we consider the other epithets, it will become clear that the support for regal Davidic figures is constantly present.

CHAPTER TEN

ANTICIPATIONS OF THE ONE CALLED BRANCH AND PRINCE

Unlike chapter 9 where we examined an epithet that is applied regularly to Jesus throughout the Second Testament (our New Testament), here we isolate two epithets never used *explicitly* of Jesus: "the branch" and "the prince."[1] Yet both are unmistakable titles for the forthcoming royal Messiah in the First Testament as well as second temple literature. Whereas "the branch" occurs in three prophetic works within the Hebrew Scriptures and five second temple texts, references to "the prince" occur in ten extra-biblical texts and appear to allude back to the prophet Ezekiel. The chart, "Overview of Sources for the Branch," isolates those texts.

As we did in chapter 9, we will examine snippets from each text in order to piece together various elements and functions of the eschatological regal Messiah figure that reflects a second temple literary and socio-political context. In the end, we will observe that not only are the various portraits for "branch" and "prince" consistently and undisputedly about forthcoming Messiah figures who will come in righteousness and rule as David's human heir, but more predominately they portray Messiah as a victorious military leader who will not only restore David's dynasty but also reestablish an independent kingdom of Israel with no Gentile interference. We begin our exploration with the epithet "the branch."

---

1. Although Revelation 5:5 does not use the word "branch," it does make use of Isaiah 11 and branch imagery. Furthermore, there is some question whether Nazarene alludes to "branch" in Matthew 2:23. Some suggest there is a word play between the Hebrew word "branch" (*neser*) and Nazareth (*Nasrat*). Hagner points out that phonetically, the Hebrew of *Nasrat* (Nazareth) and *nesar* have the same middle consonant; that consonant is reflected in the ζ of the two words in either Ναζαρέτ or Ναζαρέο. Thus Matthew draws attention to Isaiah 7:14 by first alluding to Isaiah 11:1. See Donald Hagner, *Matthew 1–13*, WBC (Dallas: Word, 1993), 40–42.

OVERVIEW OF SOURCES FOR THE BRANCH

	Branch Shoot Root	Prince Chief Leader	Sequential Item Number And Composition Name: Abbreviated And Total Form	
Old Testament Sources	Isaiah Jeremiah Zechariah	Ezekiel		
Dead Sea Scrolls	4Q161 4Q174 4Q252 4Q285	CD 1Q28b 1QM 4Q161 4Q266 4Q285 4Q376 4Q423 4Q496	CD 1Q28b 1QM 4Q161 4Q174 4Q252 4Q266 4Q285 4Q376 4Q423 4Q496	(Cairo Damascus Document) (1QSb = 1QRule of Benedictions) (1QM = 1QWar Scroll) (4QpIsa^a = 4QIsaiah Pesher^a) (4QFlor = 4QFlorilegium) (4QcommGen^a = 4QCommentary on Genesis A) (4QD^a = 4QDamascus Document^a) (4QSM = 4QSefer ha-Milhamah) (4QapocrMoses^b = 4QApocryphon of Moses^b) (4QInstruction^g) (4QM^f = 4QWar Scroll^f)
Pseudepigrapha Sources	Testament of the Twelve Patriarchs: T.Judah	Jubilees		

THE BRANCH

As presented in previous chapters, three prophets offer lucid descriptions of a forthcoming "root," "shoot," and "branch": Isaiah, Jeremiah, and Zechariah. As Johnston pointed out in chapter 8, Zechariah built upon Jeremiah's prophecies. Whereas Zechariah set in motion early second temple period expectations about David's dynasty, Isaiah and Jeremiah portrayed events *before* Nebuchadnezzar dismantled the dynasty in 586 BCE. The following chart provides a visual chronology of these three prophets, the subsequent fall of northern Israel and then Judah, followed by the highlight era of the second temple period.

As Johnston discussed in chapter 5, the prophet Isaiah began his ministry *circa* 740 BCE when Uzziah was king over Judah (1:1; 6:1) and ministered into the latter years of Hezekiah's reign, which ended in 686 BCE (1:1; 39:1–8). In Isaiah's day, people were threatened by Assyria, an empire that was beginning to expand westward. In fact, Isaiah and the kings of Judah watched as northern Israel fell to the Assyrian kings: Tiglath-pileser in 732 BCE (2 Kings 15:17–29; cp. *ANET* 194), Shalmaneser V and Sargon II in 722 BCE (2 Kings 17:1–6; 18:9–12; cp. *ANET* 195–96). Yet God spared Jerusalem from Sennacherib's assault in 701 BCE because king Hezekiah of Judah heeded Isaiah's warnings (cp. Isa. 20:1–6 with 2 Kings 19:32–34; Isa. 37:14–21, 33–37; see also *ANET* 199–200).

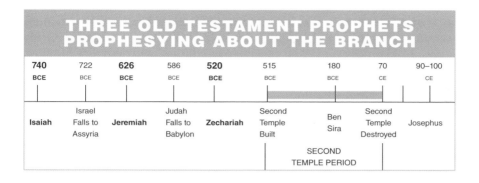

740	722	626	586	520	515	180	70	90–100
BCE	BCE	BCE	BCE	BCE	BCE	BCE	CE	CE
Isaiah	Israel Falls to Assyria	Jeremiah	Judah Falls to Babylon	Zechariah	Second Temple Built	Ben Sira	Second Temple Destroyed	Josephus
						SECOND TEMPLE PERIOD		

On the other hand, the prophet Jeremiah began his preaching ministry in 626 BCE when Josiah was king (1:2) and continued until the fall of southern Judah in 586 BCE (7:2; 22:1; 27:1–2; 32:1). Unlike the historical setting of Isaiah, in Jeremiah's time Babylon was the nation expanding north, defeating Assyria, and then moving west, subduing nations like Judah. Jeremiah was a prophet of exceptional fortitude who spoke frankly to both God (12:1; 15:10–18; 20:7) and the leaders of Judah (5:1–15; 13:1–14; 23:1–4; 22:13–19). He preached relentlessly against the sin of idolatry, the need for repentance, and a future for the nation of Israel. Although Jeremiah gave little attention to the details of the future of David's dynasty, it is clear that the forthcoming Davidic king would not be like Jehoiachin and Zedekiah, namely unrighteous and disobedient.

Unlike Zechariah, an early second temple canonical work, later second temple extra-biblical texts do not limit their allusions to Jeremiah's prophecy but include Isaiah's version. Like Zechariah, however, four Dead Sea Scrolls (4Q161, 4Q285, 4Q252, and 4Q174) and one pseudepigrapha text (the *Testament of Judah*) reflect, interpret, and reapply references about the branch. As we shall see, the portrayals of "the branch" are consistently Davidic heirs, regal Messiah figures, and victorious warriors. We begin with two scrolls that quote the prophet Isaiah, 4Q161 and 4Q285.

4Q161 (4QpIsa^a = 4QIsaiah Pesher^a)[2]

Five commentaries on the book of Isaiah were found in cave four in the nearby ruins of Qumran. All were extremely fragmented but painstakingly pieced together. 4Q161 is one of those five commentaries. Although initially referred

---

2. John M. Allegro edited the initial analyzed transcriptions of 4Q161 or "Commentary on Isaiah (A)" in *Qumran Cave 4.I* (DJD 5; Oxford: Clarendon Press, 1968), 11–13. More recent analyzed transcriptions of 4Q161 are presented by Maurya P. Horgan, "Isaiah Pesher 4 (4Q161=4QpIsa^a)" in *Hebrew, Aramaic, and Greek Texts with English Translations*, vol. 6b (DDS, ed. James H. Charlesworth; Louisville: Westminster John Knox, 2002), 83–97.

to as *4QCommentary on Isaiah*ᵃ (4QcommIsaᵃ) its eschatological predictions warrant the more recent label *4QIsaiah Pesher*ᵃ (4QpIsaᵃ).[3] Composed during a time of Hasmonean civil strife and Israel's future uncertain (75–50 BCE), 4Q161 is comprised of ten fragments and preserves quotations from and commentary on Isaiah 10:22–11:5.

> **Pesher**
>
> The term *"pesher"* is a loan word from Aramaic, which literally means "interpretation." Pesher texts (upper case "P") evidence a pesher interpretive process (lower case "p"). The pesher process is unique to the first-century Qumran community. The process is an eschatological revelation of the First Testament prophets. Thus Pesher texts like 4Q161 and many others reveal first century eschatological interpretations of prophetic Scriptures, which are portrayed as divinely guided works of interpretation.

The first thirty-five chapters of Isaiah were written against the background of Assyrian aggression and emphasized the need for God's people to hear and believe God. Chapters 1–12 spoke of divine judgment (3:1–4:1; 5:8–30; 9:8–10:4) and the future restoration of the Jewish nation (4:2–6; 8:19–9:7; 10:20–34; 11:1–16). The reference to the branch in Isaiah 11:1–5 rests between the author's discussion about God's deliverance of a Jewish remnant (10:20–34) and the Davidite who will rule over that remnant (11:10–16). We read in Isaiah 11:1–5:

1A shoot will grow out of Jesse's root stock, a bud will sprout from his roots. 2The Lord's spirit will rest on him—a spirit that gives extraordinary wisdom, a spirit that provides the ability to execute plans, a spirit that produces absolute loyalty to the Lord. 3He will take delight in obeying the Lord. He will not judge by mere appearances, or make decisions on the basis of hearsay. 4He will treat the poor fairly, and make right decisions for the downtrodden of the earth. He will strike the earth with the rod of his mouth, and order the wicked to be executed. 5Justice will be like a belt around his waist, integrity will be like a belt around his hips. (NET)

Clearly, Isaiah's presentation of "the shoot of Jesse" and "the sprout" indicates a descendant of David without naming him. Nevertheless, God's spirit guides and directs him. He has a healthy respect for God. He judges all situations with righteousness. And, he is a victorious warrior, capable of defeating

---

3. For my selected discussion about Pesher texts and pesher method see *Early Jewish Hermeneutics and Hebrews 1:5–13: The Impact of Early Jewish Exegesis on the Interpretation of a Significant New Testament Passage* (New York: Peter Lang, 1997), 79–116. For a comprehensive study, see James H. Charlesworth, *The Pesharim and Qumran History: Chaos or Consensus?* (Grand Rapids: Eerdmans, 2002)

the wicked. Thus, it seems only natural that the author of 4Q161 would quote Isaiah 11:1–5 to speak of a forthcoming regal Messiah, and would do so in keeping with Isaiah's literary presentation, though those who are a problem for God's people (i.e., "the wicked") apparently differ for the author of 4Q161.

4Q161 begins with Isaiah 10:22–23, which addresses the deliverance of God's remnant (f1i:20–f7iii:9). We will return to this portion of 4Q161 later when we discuss the epithet of "the prince." In the meantime, the focus of our discussion here will be on a subsequent quotation from Isaiah 11:1–5, which addresses the forthcoming Davidic branch, followed by an interpretation (ff7–10iii:11–25). We read in 4Q161,

Quotation

3:11["A rod will grow from] Jesse's stock, a sprout [will bloom] from his [roots;] upon him wi[ll rest] the spirit of 12[the Lord: a spirit of] wisdom and insight, a spirit of good coun[sel and strength], a spirit of true know[ledge] 13[and reverence for the Lord, he will delight in reverence for] the Lord. [He will not judge only] by what [his eyes] see, 14[he will not decide only by what his ears hear;] but he will rule [the weak by justice, and give decisions] 15[in integrity to the humble of the land. He will punish the land with the mace of his words, by his lips' breath alone] 16[he will slay the wicked. 'Justice' will be the sash around] his waist, 'Tr[uth' the sash around his hips."] (Isaiah 11:1–5). 17[(vacat)]

Interpretation

18[*This saying refers to the Branch of*] *David, who will appear in the las[t days,* ...] 19[...] his enemies; and *God will support him with [a spirit of]* strength [...] 20[... and *God will give him] a glorious throne,* [a sacred] crown, and elegant garments. 21[... He will put a] scepter in his hand, and *he will rule over all the G[enti]les,* even Magog 22[and his army ... all] the peoples his sword will control. As for the verse that says, "He will not 23[judge only by what his eyes see,] he will not decide only by what his ears hear," this means that 24[he will be advised *by the Zadokite priests,*] and as they instruct him, *so shall he rule, and at their command* 25[he shall render decisions; and always] one of the prominent priests shall go out with him, in whose hand shall be the garments of [....]4 [emphasis mine]

---

4. The translation is from Michael Wise, Martin Abegg Jr., and Edward Cook, *The Dead Sea Scrolls: A New Translation* (New York: HarperCollins, 1996), 210–11. For another translation see Florentino García Martínez and Eibert J. C. Tigchelaar, *The Dead Sea Scrolls Study Edition,* vol. 1 (Grand Rapids: Eerdmans, 1997), 317.

Although 4Q161 is clearly fragmented,[5] the quotation from Isaiah 11:1–5 is unmistakable. Remaining faithful to the prophet's statement, the author of 4Q161 makes it clear that the branch is a Davidite (3:11). And the author's straightforward interpretation that follows maintains that perspective: "[This saying refers to the branch of] David, who will appear in the las[t days]" (3:18).[6]

Building upon Isaiah's unnamed referent, the subsequent interpretation of Isaiah 11:1–5 builds upon Isaiah's portrait of the sprout and even heightens that picture. 4Q161's interpretation of the branch of David restates clearly that he will be endowed with God's spirit and that he will rule the nations ("his sword will control"). Yet the author appears to heighten Isaiah's presentation when he places a great deal of emphasis on his royal authority coming from God. As it is the case in First Testament usage, "throne" and "scepter" remain symbols for authority. Furthermore, the eschatological Davidite will judge and render decisions according the advice of Zadokite priests. Thus, this document presents us with a portrait of a regal Messiah's rule over a Jewish kingdom as well as the Gentile nations with priestly assistance. Needless to say, 4Q161 provides us with an uncomplicated portrait concerning the branch. Our next document, which debuted in controversy, does not.

4Q285 (4QSM = 4QSefer ha-Milhamah)[7]

Comprised of ten fragments, 4Q285 was initially deemed the "Dying Messiah" and the "Pierced Messiah" text. At first, it was argued that the portrait painted in 4Q285 was of an expected Davidic Messiah who would be put to death. However, the ambiguity within the text demanded reconsideration. As it turned out, the one who is killed was not the Davidic Messiah. The victorious warrior from "Jesse's stock" is the one who condemns and puts to death the leader of the Kittim (that is, the Romans).[8] Another copy of this work was discovered in cave eleven (11Q14). Thus both documents prove helpful in our constructing this document's portrait for the regal messianic

---

5. The [ ] with inserted clauses and phrases indicate the suggestions of Dead Sea Scroll scholars who work with, translate, and are well acquainted with the manuscripts. The [. . .] indicate gaps too damaged to make suggestions.

6. By using the term "Branch" here of Isaiah 11:1-6, 4Q161 is linking the "Branch" of Jeremiah 23:5-6 with the "Sprout" of Isaiah 11:1-6.

7. For the analyzed transcriptions of 4Q285 see Philip Alexander and Geza Vermes, "285. 4QSefer ha-Milhamah" in *Qumran Cave 4.XXVI* (DJD 36; Oxford: Clarendon Press, 2000), 228–46.

8. For discussions of 4Q285 see Geza Vermes, "The Oxford Forum for Qumran Research Seminar on the Rule of War from Cave 4 (4Q285)," *JJS* 43 (1992): 85–90; Markus Bockmuehl, "A 'Slain Messiah' in 4Q Serekh Milhamah (4Q285)?" *TynBull* 43 (1992): 155–69; and Martin G. Abegg Jr., "Messianic Hope and 4Q285: A Reassessment," *JBL* 113/1 (1994): 81–91.

branch. Furthermore, like 4Q161, the author of 4Q285 was true to Isaiah's literary context, yet he ignored Isaiah's historical situation in his reapplication of the text.

4Q285 describes a final victorious battle of Israel and has the dubious distinction as having two additional names: "4QEschatological War" (Vermes) or "The War of the Messiah" (Wise, Abegg, Cook). In fact, 4Q285 narrates a final battle scene, led by the prince of the congregation, a battle that begins on the mountains of Israel but ends at the Mediterranean Sea (f4:1–10). It records the pronounced blessings of the high priest after the final victory over the Kittim (f8:1–12; 4Q14 f1 2:2–15), and it provides the high priest's orders for burying the dead and cleansing the land (f10:5–6). Yet important to this discussion is fragment 5:1–6, which begins with a citation from "Isaiah the prophet."

> [. . . just as it is written in the book of] Isaiah the prophet, "And [the thickets of the forest] shall be cut down ²[with an ax, and Lebanon with its majestic trees w]ill fall. *A shoot shall come out from the stump of Jesse* ³[and a branch shall grow out of his roots"* (Isaiah 10:34–Isaiah 11:1). *This is the]* *Branch of David.* Then [all forces of Belial] shall be judged, ⁴[and the king of the Kittim shall stand for judgment] and *the prince of the community* [*sic*]—the Bra[nch of David]—*will have him put to death.* ⁵[Then all Israel shall come out with timbrel]s and dancers, and the [High] Priest shall order ⁶[them to cleanse their bodies from the guilty blood of the c]orpse[s of] the Kittim.⁹ [emphasis mine]

4Q285 describes a final eschatological war and is discussed below with the *War Scroll.* In the meantime, the author of 4Q285 cites two verses from Isaiah: Isaiah 10:34 and 11:1. Whereas initially Isaiah 10:34 referred to the defeat of the Assyrians of Isaiah's day, here "the thickets of the forest that will be cut down" have been reapplied to the Kittim or the Roman empire.¹⁰ Furthermore the prospective Davidic Messiah in Isaiah 11:1,

---

9. The translation is from Wise, Abegg, and Cook, *The Dead Sea Scrolls,* 293. For another translation see García Martínez and Tigchelaar, *The Dead Sea Scrolls Study Edition,* vol. 2, 643. Although rendered fragment 5, in *Qumran Cave 4.XXVI* (DJD 36) it is fragment 7 (pg 239). Yet in the latter two translations, the prince and high priest condemn the king of the Kittim for war crimes and order the sentence of death.

10. The term "Kittim" may refer to western nations in general (Jer. 2:10), the western region of Greece (1 Macc. 1:1), all the coastlands and maritime countries of the Mediterranean (Jos *Ant* 1. 6. 1 § 128), or the western region of Rome which prevented Antiochus IV from entering Egypt (Dan. 11:30; see J. A. Goldstein, *I Maccabees,* AB [New York: Doubleday, 1976], 191–92, 45). Some suggest Kittim to reference the Seleucids (H. H. Rowley, "The Kittim and the Dead Sea Scrolls," *PEQ* 89 [1956–1957]: 92–109; C. Rabin, "Alexander Jannaeus and the Pharisees," *JJS* 7 [1956]: 3–11). However, most people believe that when Kittim occurs in later second temple literature like Qumran

who leads this campaign, is an expected warrior Messiah who will not only condemn but will also put to death the leader of the Kittim, which seems to echo verse 4 of Isaiah where the future offspring of David will "kill the wicked." Finally, references to a shoot from Jesse, the branch of David, and prince are synonymous designations for the same person, which is an important point to remember as we move to discuss the title "prince." But for now, note that they are presented as one and the same victorious Davidic warrior. These connections are made on the basis of pattern. What was Assyria in Isaiah is now Rome. Although Isaiah may have hoped that Hezekiah would be the one to rid Israel of her enemy, namely Assyria, Johnston noted in chapter 5 that the openness of Isaiah's prophecy was projected to a forthcoming regal Davidite, which 4Q285 portrays to be a regal Davidite still to come.

Testament of Judah

Recorded in the book of Genesis are appropriate blessings pronounced by Jacob to the twelve tribes of Israel just prior to Jacob's death (49:28–29). Johnston pointed out in chapter 1 that these blessings are arranged in the birth order of Jacob's sons. The *Testaments of the Twelve Patriarchs*, of which the *Testament of Judah* is the fourth, builds upon Genesis 49. And though it *does not* follow the same order, it purports to be the words of the twelve patriarchs to their sons, which are both ethical and predictive.[11] Moving beyond the Christianized portions within the *Testaments of the Twelve Patriarchs*, the exact date of the composition appears elusive. Yet it seems reasonable to suggest that the document was initially composed during the early Hasmonean period when the non-Davidic royal-priests of John Hyrcanus, Aristobulus, and Alexander Jannaeus were expanding the Hasmonean Kingdom's borders (*circa* 150–125 BCE).[12] Central for this discussion is the testaments of Levi and Judah because while addressing Israel's future they speak of Judah as king (*T. Jud.* 1:6; 24:1–6) and Levi as his superior (*T. Levi* 18:1–11). The latter point was mentioned above in our conclusion for "Anticipation of the One

Pesher texts and the War Scroll, it refers to Rome. C. J. Detaye, "Le Cadre Historique du Midrash d'Habacuc," *ETL* (1954): 323–43, esp. 323–30. Vermes, *Discovery in the Judean Desert* (New York: Desclee, 1956), 79–85. *EncJud*, 1971 ed., s.v. "Kittim"; *ISBE*, 1986 ed., s.v., "Kittim"; *EDSS*, 2000 ed., s.v. "Kittim."

11. Johnston points out that the order of Jacob's pronouncements in Genesis 49 is largely based on birth. Yet in the *T. 12 Patr.*, the *T. Zeb.* is placed before *T. Iss.*, and the *T. Naph.* is placed before *T. Gad* rather than after *T. Ash.* Compare the chart in chapter 1 (p. 8). Yet like Genesis 49, the blessings of Judah and Joseph do not stand out in the literary structure.

12. For a traditional discussion about dating the text see H. C. Kee's "Testament of the Twelve Patriarchs" in *The Old Testament Pseudepigrapha*, 2 vols. (ed. James H. Charlesworth; New York: Doubleday, 1985), 1:777–78. For a more recent discussion see R. S. Kugler, *Testaments of the Twelve Patriarchs* (Sheffield, 2001).

Called Messiah" (pp. 281–82). Here, however, we focus attention on the *Testament of Judah* 24 where we read

> ¹And after this there shall arise for you a Star from Jacob (Num. 24:17) in peace: And a man shall arise from posterity like the Sun of righteousness, walking with the sons of men in gentleness and righteousness, and in him will be found no sin. ²And the heavens will be opened upon him to pour out the spirit as a blessing of the Holy Father (Isa. 11:2).

> ⁴This is the *Shoot of God* (Isa. 11:1) Most High; this is the fountain for the life of all humanity. ⁵Then he will illumine the scepter of my kingdom, and *from your root will arise the Shoot*, ⁶and through it will arise the rod of righteousness for the nations, to judge and to save all that call on the Lord.¹³ [emphasis mine]

In this document, the "Star from Jacob" and "the Shoot" (or "branch") are one in the same person, a Davidic scion. The author portrays him as a righteous man, a man in whom no sin will be found. He is a man filled with God's spirit "as a blessing" from God and seems to be reminiscent of God's spirit coming upon David (1 Sam. 16:12–13). Finally, he is a man who will rule the nations in righteousness as he judges and saves those who call upon God. The idea that God would save all who call upon him, Gentiles included, was spoken of as early as Solomon's dedication of the first temple (1 Kings 8:41–43). Thus, there may be an anticipation and hope for a regal Messiah who would be in keeping with David and Solomon.

In conclusion, 4Q161, 4Q285 and the *Testament of Judah* refer to "the shoot" (or "sprout") from Isaiah 11:1–5 in a similar manner. The shoot symbol in these texts portrays human personalities yet to come from the line of David. Yet only 4Q161 and 4Q285 speak collectively of the shoot as victorious warriors in the final battle between good and evil. Furthermore, only 4Q161 and the *Testament of Judah* portray the shoot to be individuals who are divinely empowered and whose individual reigns will extend over both God's people and the nations. Unique to 4Q161 is the presentation of the branch readily advised by Zadokite priests. Unique to the *Testament of Judah* is the fact that the shoot is righteous, he is a judge, and he is in some way a savior. Nevertheless 4Q161, 4Q285 and the *Testament of Judah* reflect upon and reapply Isaiah to point to a new historical situation, their own. In a similar way, 4Q252 and 4Q174 echo "the branch" citations in Jeremiah.

---

13. The translation is by Kee, "Testament of the Twelve Patriarchs," 1:801.

4Q252 (4QcommGena = 4QCommentary on Genesis A)[14]

As we mentioned in the previous chapter, the six fragments of 4Q252 were composed sometime during the reign of Herod the Great (30–4 BCE). After pondering three personalities in Genesis: Noah (1:1–2:8), Abraham (2:8–10), Amalek (4:1–3), the author addresses Jacob (4:3–6). Needless to say, the explanation of Jacob's blessing in Genesis 49:10 (5:1–5) is important here because it appears to echo Jeremiah's reference to the branch of which there are two: Jeremiah 23:5–6 and 33:14–18. Johnston makes it clear that the literary contexts for both passages point to the prediction of judgment and restoration of David's dynasty. The first reference, Jeremiah 23:5–6, came immediately *after* Jeremiah announced the exile of Judah's king Jehoiachin (or Jeconiah) in 597 BCE (Jer. 22:24–30). Thus in chapter 23, Jeremiah anticipated another Davidic scion to succeed Jehoiachin. We read that

> [5]The days are surely coming, says the LORD, when **I will raise up for David a righteous Branch**, and he shall reign as king and deal wisely, and shall execute justice and righteousness in the land. [6]In his days Judah will be saved and Israel will live in safety. And this is the name by which he will be called: "The LORD is our righteousness." (23:5–6, emphasis mine)

The second reference came *before* Jeremiah's pronouncement of doom and final overthrow of Judah's king Zedekiah in 586 BCE (34:1–7). Obviously Jeremiah was not presenting a chronological account of events. In this passage he urged repeatedly for Zedekiah to surrender (21:1–10; 34:1–5, 17–22; 37:3–10, 16–17; 38:14–23), but not without a promise about a future Davidite. Jeremiah reiterated his understanding about a forthcoming David in chapter 33 when he writes

> [14]The days are surely coming, says the LORD, when *I will fulfill the promise I made to the house of Israel and the house of Judah*. [15]In those days and at that time **I will cause a righteous Branch to spring up for David**; and he shall execute justice and righteousness in the land. [16]In those days Judah will be saved and Jerusalem will live in safety. And this is the name by which it will be called: "The LORD is our righteousness." [17]For thus says the LORD: **David shall never lack a man to sit on the throne of the house of Israel** [18]and the levitical priests shall never lack a man in my presence to offer

---

14. For the analyzed transcriptions of 4Q252 see "252.Commentary on Genesis A" by George Brooke in *Qumran Cave 4.XVII* (DJD 22; Oxford: Clarendon Press, 1996), 185–207. Compare Gerbern S. Oegema, "Tradition-Historical Studies on 4Q252" in *Qumran–Messianism* (ed. James H. Charlesworth, Hermann Lichtenberger, and Gerbern S. Oegema; Tübingen: Mohr Siebeck, 1998), 154–74.

burnt offerings, to make grain offerings, and to make sacrifices for all time (33:14–18, emphasis mine)

Thus while discussing new leadership over a regathered nation of Israel (23:1–8) and again while reaffirming God's covenant with David, Israel, and Levi (33:14–22), Jeremiah spoke about the coming of a righteous branch of David who would restore the Davidic dynasty and the kingdom of Israel. Unlike Isaiah where the branch's rescue mission appeared limited to the captive remnant of northern Israel, in Jeremiah the mission expanded to involve the southern kingdom of Judah. Thus 4Q252's reflection on Jeremiah is on the anticipation of restoration of David's dynasty. Judgment has come on the dynasty, where is the restoration?

The author of 4Q252, like Jeremiah, anticipated the coming of a Davidic branch to restore Israel's kingdom, but the author reinforced his belief by first citing Jeremiah 33:14–17. Furthermore, 4Q252 links two First Testament citations together due to conceptual similarities. The piecing together of passages from different sacred texts based upon conceptual similarities is a common and significant element in the process of reflection and interpretation during the second temple period.[15] Thus 4Q252 began by quoting the first part of Genesis 49:10, then quickly presented the simple sense of Jacob's blessing to Judah through Jeremiah 33:14–17. We read

> [5:1] *A ruler shall [no]t depart from the tribe of Judah* when Israel has dominion. [2][And] the one who sits on the throne of David [shall never] be cut off, because the "ruler's staff" is the covenant of the kingdom, [3][and the thous] ands of Israel are "the standards," until *the Righteous Messiah, the Branch of David, has come* (Genesis 49:10). [4]For to him and to his seed the covenant of the kingdom of his people has been given for the eternal generations, because [5]he has kept [… Interpreter of] the Law with the men of the Yahad.[16] [emphasis mine](4Q252 5:1–5)

Unlike the first part of 4Q252, which addressed historical personalities of the past, this passage anticipated Israel's future. Particular attention is given to an expected Messiah figure. Several points seem relevant here. First, the branch of David, in keeping with Hebrew Scripture, comes from the tribe of Judah. Second, the branch of David is a Messiah of righteousness. Thus he

---

15. Numerous examples could be given here, but we limit our examples to 4Q174 and 4Q175, which will be discussed later in this chapter.
16. The translation is from Wise, Abegg, and Cook, *The Dead Sea Scrolls*, 277. For other translations see García Martínez and Tigchelaar, *The Dead Sea Scrolls*, 1:505; and Brooke, "252.Commentary on Genesis A," 205–6.

himself is righteous. Third, God's covenant with David and his offspring are presented as permanent, which contrasts Ben Sira and Josephus (see p. 219). Thus the portrait painted here is one that pictures the Davidite as human and as having future descendants who would be his royal successors (cf. Ps. 45:16). Furthermore, this forthcoming offspring of David may even be an interpreter of the Law along with other men of Judah. Yet this presentation of the branch as a possible interpreter of the law appears to contradict messianic portrayals in 4Q174. Quite often these messianic figures are composite pictures or reflections in various passages and ideas from different places that ultimately inform an author's view. Thus a more synthetic type of reading is often at work in these texts, even when only a single passage is actually cited, which is quite clear in 4Q174.

> **Midrash**
>
> The term *"midrash"* comes from the Hebrew term *darash* which means "to search," "to seek," "to examine," "to investigate." Yet the term *"midrash"* identifies both a type of literary work (upper case "M") and a process (lower case "m"). Although most Midrash are Rabbinic works dated second century CE and later, 4Q174 and 4Q175 appear to be prototypes of later Rabbinic works.

4Q174 (4QFlor = 4QFlorilegium)[17]

Consisting of twenty-six fragments, 4Q174 is an early Herodian text composed sometime during the reign of Herod the Great (40–4 BCE). Unlike 4Q161, which is a Pesher text, many consider 4Q174 to be a Midrash because of the manner in which it strings together so many quotations from Hebrew Scriptures.[18] This text belongs undeniably to a sectarian community because it reflects many views found in other texts that have been identified as sectarian (e.g., 1QM. 1QS). For instance, 4Q174 speaks of two Messiahs: a regal Messiah of David and a teaching Messiah (probably a priestly Messiah of Aaron). Throughout 4Q174, biblical passages are woven together that the community's theological beliefs about an eschatological sanctuary and two forthcoming Messiahs. Exodus 15:17c–18 and Deuteronomy 23:3–4 focus on issues surrounding the Lord's sanctuary and the people of the sanctuary while 2 Samuel 7:10b, 11, 12b, 13b–14a and Amos 9:11 focus on the Davidic Messiah, the branch. When these passages from the Hebrew Scriptures are

---

17. Initial analyzed transcriptions of 4Q174 (4QFlor = *4QFlorilegium*) are edited by John M. Allegro in *Qumran Cave 4 – I* (DJD 5; Oxford: Clarendon Press, 1968), 53–57. More recently the analyzed transcriptions of 4Q174 have been presented by Jacob Milgrom, "Florilegium: A Midrash on 2 Samuel and Psalm 1–2 (4Q174 = 4QFlor)" in *The Dead Sea Scrolls*, vol 6b (ed. James H. Charlesworth; Tübingen: Mohr Siebeck, 2002), 248–63.

18. For my discussion about Midrash texts and midrash process, see *Early Jewish Hermeneutics and Hebrews 1:5–13*, 45–77. For a more complete discussion see Jacob Neusner, *Judaism and the Interpretation of Scripture: Introduction to the Rabbinic Midrash* (Peabody, MA: Hendrickson, 2004).

united, they form a theological statement about the sectarian community's belief in a forthcoming human Davidic king, who will one day come and rule over his eschatological sanctuary. We read

> [3:2][I appointed judges] over my people Israel" (2 Samuel 7:10–11a). This "place" is the house that [they shall build for him] in the Last Days, as it is written in the book of [3][Moses: "A temple of] the Lord are you to prepare with your hands; the Lord will reign forever and ever" (Exodus 15:17). This passage describes the temple that no [man with a] permanent [fleshly defect] shall enter, [4]nor Ammonite, Moabite, bastard, foreigner or alien, forevermore (Deuteronomy 23:3–4). Surely his holiness [5]shall be rev[eal]ed there; eternal glory shall ever be apparent there. Strangers shall not again defile it, as they formerly defiled [6]the Temp[le of I]srael through their sins. To that end he has commanded that they build him a Temple of Adam, and that in it they sacrifice to him [7]proper sacrifices. As for what he said to David, "I [will give] you [rest] from all your enemies" (2 Samuel 7:11b), this passage means that *he will give them rest from [al]l* [8]*the children of Belial*, who cause them to stumble, seeking to destroy the[m by means of] their [wickedness.] They became party to the plan of Belial in order to cause the S[ons of] [9]Li[ght] to stumble. They plotted wicked schemes against them, [so that they might fall pr]ey to Belial through guilty error. [10]"Moreover the Lord decl[ares] to you that he will make you a house," and that "**I will raise up your offspring after you**, and establish the throne of his kingdom [11][fore]ver. **I will be a father to him, and he will be my son**" (2 Samuel 7:11c, 12b, 13b–14a). **This passage refers to the Shoot of David**, *who is to arise with* [12]*the Interpreter of the Law*, and *who will [arise] in Zi[on in the La]st Days*, as it is written, "And I shall raise up the booth of David that is fallen" (Amos 9:11). This passage describes the fallen Branch of [13]David, [w]hom he shall raise up to deliver Israel.[19] (4Q174 3:2–13)

It is clear that God will provide peace (i.e., "rest") from the enemies of this forthcoming Davidic scion. These enemies are deemed the children of Belial, a name we have seen previously in CD and 4Q285. The forthcoming Davidite will have a special or unique relationship with God. He is human and will have offspring to carry on a never-ending Davidic dynasty. He will arise alongside an interpreter of the Law, a priestly Messiah figure. Finally, God will raise up this Davidic branch to deliver the nation of Israel. Thus he is a victorious warrior.

---

19. The translation is from Wise, Abegg, and Cook, *The Dead Sea Scrolls*, 227–28. For other translations see García Martínez and Tigchelaar, *The Dead Sea Scrolls*, 353–54. For the exegesis of 4Q174 see George J. Brooke, *Exegesis at Qumran: 4QFlorilegium in Its Jewish Context* (Sheffield: JSOT Press, 1985).

Summation

God promised, through Isaiah and Jeremiah, to "raise up for David a branch of righteousness." And though the exact referents for the branch may vary between Isaiah and Jeremiah, their ambiguity or difference in emphasis made them worthy of further reflection during the latter part of the second temple period (75–4 BCE). Thus based on Isaiah and Jeremiah, five Dead Sea Scrolls appeal to, reflect upon, and paint varying portraits of Davidic scions who will arise during the last days (4Q161, 4Q174) to restore David's dynasty. Most portraits appear to reveal their respective Messiahs as victorious warriors over Israel's enemies (4Q161, 4Q174, 4Q285), rulers over a restored kingdom of Israel as well as Gentile nations (4Q161, 4Q174, *T. Jud.*), and able to judge righteously (4Q161, 4Q285, *TJud*). Yet there are differences. One empowers their Messiah with God's spirit (4Q161), another has him guided by Zadokite priests (4Q161), and another appears to paint him as an interpreter of the Law (4Q252). Two portraits clearly reveal offspring that will ensure the endurance of David's restored dynasty (4Q174, 4Q252). The following chart summarizes various elements of these future Messiah figures and the numerous functions of the branch of David.

PORTRAYALS OF THE BRANCH	
Old Testament Sources	Primary Passages: Isaiah 11:1–5 Jeremiah 23:5–6; 33:14–15 Zechariah 3:8, 6:12–14 Secondary Links Genesis 49:10 Numbers 24:17 2 Samuel 7:10–14 Amos 9:11
Dead Sea Scrolls	4Q161 7–10iii:22 4Q174 1–3i:11–13 4Q252 5:3–4 4Q285 5:3–4 (cp. 4Q11)
Pseudepigrapha Sources	*Testament of the Twelve Patriarchs: T.Judah 24:4*
Various Elements	The branch is a Davidic scion The branch is a human personality The branch is a victorious military leader The branch is a ruler The branch is righteous The branch is divinely empowered The branch is an interpreter of the Law

Various Functions	The branch ushers in a new time period The branch reestablishes David's dynastic rule The branch rules Gentile nations The branch rules with priestly assistance The branch leads military campaigns The branch delivers Israel from the Romans The branch condemns and kills wicked leaders The branch has offspring that succeed him

Dating of Manuscripts	Early Hasmonean 150–125 BCE
	Testament of the 12 Patriarchs: T.Judah
	
	Late-Hasmonean: 75–50 BCE
	4Q161 (*4QpIsaᵃ = 4QIsaiah Pesherᵃ*)
	
	Early Herodian 30–1 BCE
	4Q174 (*4QFlor = 4QFlorilegium*)
	4Q252 (*4QcommGenᵃ = 4QCommentary Genesis A*)
	4Q285 (*4QSM = 4QSefer ha-Milhamah*)
	
	Political Situation:
	1. Expansion of the Hasmonean Royal-Priests:
	  Early Hasmonean 150–125 BCE
	2. Transition from Hasmonean to Herodian Rule:
	  Late Hasmonean & Early Herodian
	  Hasmonean Civil War (67–63 BCE)
	  Hyrcanus II (63–43 BCE)
	  Herod (37–4 BCE)

PRINCE OF THE CONGREGATION

As it was with the branch, First Testament references about a prince that are reflected upon later during the second temple period lead to expanded interpretations about him in second temple literature. As we know from Johnston's discussion in chapter 6, the epithet "prince" is used predominately, though not exclusively, by the prophet Ezekiel. According to Josephus, king Nebuchadnezzar carried off Ezekiel to Babylon. Although just a boy at the time, Ezekiel was deported along with king Jehoiachin of Judah and some three thousand other Jews to Babylon in 597 BCE (*Ant* 10.6.3 § 98). Like Jeremiah, his contemporary and counterpart in Jerusalem, Ezekiel spoke of the restoration of David's dynasty. While writing in Babylonian captivity, Ezekiel provided among other things a message of hope concerning the future restoration of David's dynasty. Yet unlike Jeremiah, Ezekiel never used the symbol of branch but rather favored the epithet "the prince" for the Davidic king. Whereas prince Zedekiah would be carried off into exile to die (12:12–14), another Davidic prince would arise to shepherd and feed God's people (34:23–24), unite and rule over God's people in the land (37:24–25), and provide temple sacrifices for God's people (45:17, 22–25; 46:12–15). Thus according to Ezekiel, the future united kingdom was guaranteed a shepherd, that is a Davidic prince, one that God would "appoint" to be over the congregation. As we will see, later second temple texts built upon Ezekiel hope, but they said much more because of another passage in the book of Numbers.

In Numbers 27:16–17 we read, "Let the Lord, the God of the spirits of all humankind, appoint a man over the community, who will go out before them, and who will come in before them, and who will lead them out, and who will bring them in, so that the community of the Lord may not be like sheep that have no shepherd" (NET). Due to the conceptually parallel ideas, one second temple author links both passages together to profile "the prince" (Ezekiel) to be the man "over the community" (Numbers). He is God's "appointed" human personality, a shepherd, more specifically a person from the line of David who will restore David's dynasty.

Nevertheless, there are ten portraits of the prince presented in later second temple literature. With few exceptions, CD, 1Q28b, 1QM, 4Q161, 4Q266, 4Q285, 4Q376, 4Q423, 4Q496, and *Jubilees* present portraits that paint him to be a military messianic figure. And though most of the extra-biblical literature presents the prince in a military context, none do so as clearly as 1QM and 4Q376. Yet 4Q423 (*4QInstruction^g*).

4Q423 (*4QInstruction^g*)[20]

Among the numerous manuscripts from Cave 4 there is a group of seven manuscripts that contain ethical teachings to be instilled by an "instructor" in his disciples. They are called *Instructions^a-g* or *Sapiential Works A^a-g* (4Q415–418, 423).[21] Ultimately they appear to be instructions for a disciple so that he might persevere in doing good and thereby avert the impending and eternal punishment that awaits the sinner on judgment day.[22]

The proverbial-like content of these manuscripts resembles that of Ben Sira's apocrypha work, Sirach, which was written around 180 BCE. Yet our particular fragmented manuscript *4QInstruction^g* may have been composed while Herod the Great's grandson, Agrippa I, ruled in Israel (37–44 CE). Thus *4QInstruction^g* was written sometime during the late Herodian period (30–68 CE) and perhaps shortly after the resurrection of Jesus (Acts 12:1–19, Jos *Ant* 19.8.2 §§ 343–52).

4QInstruction^g has an agricultural theme, which served to remind a disciple that God provides the crops, warns against pride when God yields a

---

20. For the analyzed transcriptions of 4Q423 see "423. 4QInstruction^g (*Mûsar leMevîn^g*)" by Torleif Elgvin in *Qumran Cave 4.XXIV* (DJD 34; Oxford: Clarendon, 1999), 505–33.

21. For a complete discussion of *Instructions^a-g* or *Sapiential Works A^a-g* (4Q415–418, 423) see *Qumran Cave 4.XXIV* (DJD 34; Oxford: Clarendon, 1999).

22. Émile Puech, "Resurrection: The Bible and Qumran" in *The Bible and the Dead Sea Scrolls: The Princeton Symposium on the Dead Sea Scrolls*, 3 vols. (ed. James H. Charlesworth; Waco, TX: Baylor University Press, 2006), 3:265–68.

hefty harvest, and commands the set times for harvesting to be commemorated.[23] At one point, the sage appears to compare the disciple with a farmer, who knows how to plant crops properly without intermingling them as prescribed in the law. This procedure is, as you might expect, in keeping with an ancient scriptural text, Leviticus 19:19 (4Q418 f103; 4Q423 ff2–4). Employing the same metaphor, the instructor then cautioned his disciples against offending God's ordained authorities, as Korah had done in his rebellion against Moses (see Num. 16:1–33). It is at this point that 4Q423 5:1–5 refers to the "prince" or "leader."

> [5:1]watch yourself lest [. . .] [. . .] the judgment passed on Korah, and because he has opened your ear [5:2][to the secret of the way things are . . . the he]ad of the clans [...] and ***the prince*** (sic) ***of your people*** [5:3][. . .] He has assigned the inheritance of all those who exercise authority and the purpose of every thing that is done is in his power, and he [has ...] the actions of [...] [5:4][... judging] all of them in truth, and he has appointed duties to fathers and sons to [. . .] with all the native-born and spoken [5:5][. . . for] those who till the soil he has appointed the summer festivals and the gathering of your crops at the proper time.[24]

The passage evokes the need to identify the author's referent. Does the context reference the prophetic leader Moses from Israel's past? Does it speak of contemporary leaders of the community? Or does the context anticipate an eschatological Davidic prince whose functions will parallel those of Moses? For the sake of our discussion, fragment five of 4Q423 may reference, though ambiguously, an eschatological Davidic prince for two reasons: the overall emphasis of *Instructions*[a–g] on the future and the text's reasoning with the disciples: "because he has opened your ear to the secret of the way things are . . . and *the prince of your people*."[25] Thus perhaps, for the sake of this chapter, the prince is an eschatological Davidic leader, though the other two options are possible.

Yet equally questionable is the referent "He" in 4Q423 5:3–5. Is it a reference to God only? Or is it a reference to God working through the prince? If the latter is correct, then God, through his appointed prince,

---

23. Elgvin presents the instructions as they were for a farmer, while others appear to argue that they are teachings of a sage for his disciples. Compare Elgvin, "4QInstruction," 505 with Wise, Abegg, and Cook, *The Dead Sea Scrolls,* 378.

24. The translation is from Wise, Abegg, and Cook, *The Dead Sea Scrolls,* 389. For other translations see García Martínez and Tigchelaar, *The Dead Sea Scrolls,* 2:889; and Elgvin, "4QInstruction[g]", 518–19.

25. Although Evans has in the past argued for Moses (s.v. "Prince of the Congregation" in *EDSS*, 2:693), he more recently views the referent to be messianic ("Are the 'Son' Texts at Qumran Messianic?," 136).

assigns inheritances, judges the actions of people in truth, appoints people to perform certain responsibilities, and appoints times for festival celebrations. Jewish theology readily acknowledges that God appoints servant-leaders to carry out his predestined plans (i.e., Nebuchadnezzar in Jer. 25:8–12; Cyrus in Isa. 44:28–45:7; Sir. 10:4–5; Jos *War* 2.8.7 § 140), and often appeals to historical rebellions of Israel's past as a warning to obey God's directives (Num. 14:1–9, 32:6–14; Ezek. 20; Sir. 47:23–24, 48:15). Consequently 4Q423 does not portray the prince to be a military leader, but rather presents a debatable reference to an eschatological Davidic prince who will carry out God's preordained plans and thereby functions like a human national or political leader. The *War Scroll* (1QM), however, paints the prince as Israel's military leader.

1QM (1QM = 1QWar Scroll)

The *War Scroll* reflects a sectarian rendition of a war that will end all wars. Ultimately it is a war between good and evil, which involves both human and angelic beings (1:10–11; 7:16; 12:1; 15:14). And though 1QM might be a late Hasmonean to early Herodian document (*circa* 75–30 BCE) written just before the Roman Senate appointed Herod the Great ruler over Judea, Samaria, and Galilee (40 BCE), 1QM is about an eschatological war between "the sons of light" (those whose paternal father is God)[26] and "the sons of darkness" (those whose paternal father is Belial).[27] It is, as Abegg claims, Qumran's version of the Battle of Armageddon.[28]

The contents of the *War Scroll* strike me as a chaplain's military service manual that provides regulations for preparing and executing the war, which involves battle trumpets (2:15–3:11), banners (3:12–5:2), and operational matters (5:3–9:16); prayers and blessings to be recited during the different phases of the war (9:17–15:3), a description of the sequence of the war

---

26. Whether "the sons of light" refers to all of Israel (twelve tribes) or only or only some of them (Levi, Judah, and Benjamin), they are a faithful remnant (1:1–3; 2:18; 3:13–17; 11:6–13; 12:1–5, 13–16; 13:7–13; 15:11; 17:7–8; 19:5–8). A multitude of angels who dwell with God in the heavens (12:1; cp. 4QM1v-vi: 1:1) are presented as battling alongside of "the sons of light" (1:10–11; 7:6; 12:1; 15:14; cp. 4QM 1i, ii, iii: 1, 3) as well as their commander, Michael, Gabriel, Sariels, and Raphael (9:15–16).

27. "The sons of darkness" refers to the army loyal to Belial (1:1, 5; 3:6, 9; 4:2; 15:2; 16:11) and the enemies are the Kittim (1:2, 4, 6, 9, 12; 11:11; 15:2; 16:3–6, 9; 17:12, 14, 15; 18:2, 4: 19:10). Belial is a satanic being who stands against God's people (1QS iii 13–iv. 26). He is the "prince" of the kingdom of wickedness (1QM xvii. 5–6). He reigns over his satanic forces and his reign is one of injustice (1QS i. 16–18; iv. 19–20). Likewise, people (like the Kittim; see n. 9) who are not part of this sectarian community are perceived as people part of Belial's kingdom (*Jub.* 14.31–33; 1QM xiii. 10–13). See *Encyclopedia of the Dead Sea Scrolls*, 2000 ed., s.v. "Demons."

28. Wise, Abegg, and Cook, *The Dead Sea Scrolls,* 150.

against the enemy (i.e., the Kittim; 15:4–18:8), and a prescribed ceremony of thanksgiving after victory (18:10–19:14).[29]

It is within the section of regulations where we encounter the title prince. His name is to be displayed on both banners (1QM 3:15b-16; 4Q496 10:4) and shields (1QM 5:1). In fact, just before the author addresses operational matters for battle, we read in the *War Scroll*, "and on the sh[ie]ld of the Prince of the Whole Congregation they shall write his name, the names 'Israel,' 'Levi,' and 'Aaron,' and the names of the twelve tribes of Israel according to their order of birth, [2]and the names of the twelve chiefs of their tribes" (5:1–2).[30] Thus 1QM paints the prince to be a person whose name is displayed before all people in this final confrontation between good and evil. However, 4Q376 paints the prince as one who receives divine direction as he enters into battle.

4Q376 (3QapocrMosesb = 4QApocryphon of Moses[b])[31]

Consisting essentially of one fragment, 4Q376 appears to be a manuscript with close if not exact parallels with 4Q29 (*Liturgy of the Three Tongues of Fire*), which together provide us with a divinatory or testing process through the high priest's use of two stones (cp. Exod. 28:9–12; Jos *Ant* 3.214–215). Clearly, the first half of 4Q376 speaks of an anointed high priest receiving direction by way of two stones (i:1–ii:3). Yet particular significance to this discussion comes from the second half of the fragment (iii:1b-3) where we read: "And if 'the Prince' of the whole congregation is in the camp or i[f ...] his enemy and Israel is with him, or if they march on a city to besiege it, or in respect to any matter which [...] "to the Prince" [...] the field is distant (?)."[32] It appears that based upon the judgment of the high priest, the prince is to execute his military engagements.

Although 4Q376 reflects handwriting that transitions between the late Hasmonean (75–50 BCE) and early Herodian (30–1 BCE) periods, Josephus dates the disuse of such stones around the time of John Hyrcanus (134–104 BCE; *Ant* 3.8.9 § 214–18). If composed by those who copied manuscripts at

---

29. The outline is a combination of two sources: (1) Jean Duhaime, "War Scroll (1QM; 1Q33; 4Q491–496 = 4QM1–6; 4Q497)" in *Damascus Document, War Scroll, and Related Documents* (DDS, ed. James H. Charlesworth; Louisville: Westminster John Knox, 1995), 80. (2) Wise, Abegg, and Cook, *The Dead Sea Scrolls*, 151.

30. The translation is from Wise, Abegg, and Cook, *The Dead Sea Scrolls*, 155. For other translations see García Martínez and Tigchelaar, *The Dead Sea Scrolls*, 1:119–21; and Duhaime, "War Scroll (1QM; 1Q33; 4Q491–496 = 4QM1–6; 4Q497)," 80ff.

31. The analyzed transcriptions of 4Q376 (4QapocrMoses[b] = 4QApocryphon of Moses[b]) are edited by John Strugnell in *Qumran Cave 4.XIV* (DJD 5; Oxford: Clarendon Press, 1995), 121–36.

32. The translation is a variation from Strugnell, 4Q376 (4QapocrMoses[b] = 4QApocryphon of Moses[b]), 127. For another translation see García Martínez and Tigchelaar, *The Dead Sea Scrolls*, 2:743.

nearby Qumran, 4Q376 would appear to suit the sectarians' perception that prophecy was present among them, which is evidenced in Pesher texts (e.g., 1QpHab 7:1–5; 1QS 9:18–20). Regardless of the manuscript's presentation of the priestly messiah's use of divination, it seems this military Messiah figure parallels the one in 1QM.

In conclusion, the battles mentioned in 1QM, 4Q376, and 4Q496 cannot be proven dogmatically to be one and the same, though they appear to be the same battle headed by an eschatological prince. The prince portrayed in each document is the central figure. In two documents, his name appears to be displayed on both shields and banners for war (1QM, 4Q496). The other leaves his name to be a mystery (cp. 1QM 11:6). At least one document portrays the prince receiving advice or divine guidance from a priestly Messiah (4Q376). Perhaps this priestly Messiah's activity and presence provides some concord between 4Q376 and 1Q28a. Regardless, other functions of these military princes appear "top secret" except in the following texts.

Unlike 1QM, 4Q376, and 4Q423, the remaining five Dead Sea Scrolls (CD, 1Q28b, 4Q161, 4Q266, and 4Q285) paint the prince clearly as a Davidic heir due to their explicit connections with the historical figure of Jacob and the symbols of "shoot" or "branch," "star," and "scepter." Of particular significance are the scriptural appeals to Genesis 49, Numbers 24, Isaiah 11, and Amos 9 in *Cairo Damascus Document* (CD), *4QDamascus Document*^a (4Q266), and *4QSefer ha-Milhamah* (4Q285) because they heighten and expand Ezekiel's initial conceptual understanding for the title. Nevertheless, like 1QM, 4Q376, and 4Q496, these three texts (CD, 4Q266, and 4Q285) present three portraits of future Davidic military heroes, whose activities exceed those of a military leader. We begin with CD and 4Q266.

CD (Cairo Damascus Document) and 4Q266
Once again, 4Q266 parallels the *Cairo Damascus Document* and together they contain an identical reference about the prince (7:20; cp. 4Q266 f3iii22). As stated earlier, the *Damascus Document* may be divided into two major sections: "The Admonition," and "The Law and Communal Rules." Our citation concerning the prince occurs in the admonitions to the community, specifically as those admonitions concern God's future punishment of all those who reject God's laws.

To begin with, these authors believed that God would reestablish David's fallen dynasty (7:16). Naturally, the symbol of "the star" from Jacob (7:19) linked with God's promise to "re-erect the fallen tent of David" (7:16) anticipates the restoration of David's dynasty (cp. *T. Jud.* 24:1). Furthermore the compound symbols of "the star" from Jacob (7:19) with the coming of "a staff" expects the restoration of the nation of Israel. Thus in context, the prince is painted as a human personality from the line of David who re-establishes ("re-erects") David's dynasty (7:16, 19). He is both a ruler over the nation of Israel (7:20a) and a military leader who battles the "sons of Sheth" (7:20b). Yet he would not be a military jarhead. It seems he would be an interpreter of the law. 4Q285 paints a similar portrait of the forthcoming prince.

MESSIAH AS INTERPRETER OF THE LAW

CD (Cairo Damascus Document)	4Q266 (4QD^a = 4QDamascus Document^a)[33]
The books of Law are the tents of 7:16 the king, as it says I will re-erect the fallen tent of David (Amos 9:11). The king is 7:17 <Leader of> the nation and the "foundation of your images" is the books of the prophets 7:18 whose words Israel despised.	
The star is the interpreter of the Law 7:19 who comes to Damascus, as it is written, A star has left Jacob, a staff has risen 7:20 from Israel (Numbers 24:17). **The latter is the leader of the whole nation; when he appears, he will shatter** 7:21 all the sons of Sheth (Numbers 24:17). [emphasis mine]	The star] is the interpr[eter of the] Law f3iii:20 who comes to] Damascus, as it is written, [A star has left [Jacob,] f3iii:21 [a staf] f [has risen] from Israel (Numbers 24:17). **The latter i[s] the Leader of [the who]le [nation; when he appears,]** f3iii:22 **[he will shatter]** all the sons of Sheth (Numbers 24:17). Th[ey escaped in] f3iii:23 the first [period of God's judgment,] but those who held back [were handed over] to the sword. [emphasis mine]

4Q285 (4QSM = 4QSefer ha-Milhamah)[34]

As discussed above, 4Q285 was initially deemed the "Dying Messiah" and the "Pierced Messiah" text. Yet the death is not about the forthcoming Davidic Messiah, but rather about a Messiah who puts to death the leader of the Kittim (that is, the Romans). Furthermore, we identified the document's portrait of a messianic figure while discussing the epithet "branch." The portion of the text examined below begins with a citation from Ezekiel.

> 4:2 ***Prin]ce of the congregation*** and all Is[rael . . .] 3[. . . concerning that which wa]s written[in the book of Ezekiel the prophet, "And I will strike

---

33. The analyzed transcriptions of 4Q266 = 4QD^a are presented by Joseph M. Baumgarten in *Qumran Cave 4.XIII* (DJD 18; Oxford: Clarendon Press, 1996), 23–93. Translation is by Baumgarten, 43–45.

34. For discussions of 4Q285 (4QSM=4QSefer ha-Milhamah) see Geza Vermes, "The Oxford Forum for Qumran Research Seminar on the Rule of War from Cave 4 (4Q285)," *JJS* 43 (1992): 85–90; Markus Bockmuehl, "A 'Slain Messiah' in 4Q Serekh Milhamah (4Q285)?" *TynBull* 43 (1992): 155–69; Martin G. Abegg, "Messianic Hope and 4Q285: A Reassessment," *JBL* 113/1 (1994): 81–91.

your bow from your left hand] ⁴[and bring down your arrows from your right. You shall fall] upon the mountains of [Israel you and all your troops and the peoples that are with you" (Ezekiel 39:3–4). . . .] ⁵[. . . the] Kittim [. . .] ⁶[. . . ***the P]rince of the Congregation*** to the[Mediterranean] Sea[. . .] ⁷[. . . And they shall flee] from Israel at that time[. . .] ⁸[. . . And the High Priest] shall stand before them and they shall arrange themselves against them[in battle array . . .] ⁹[. . .] and they shall return back to the land at that time[. . .] ¹⁰[. . .] then they shall bring him before the ***Prince of[the congregation*** . . . (4Q285 4:2–10)

The picture painted is one of victory. The prince stands as a victorious warrior over the vanquished Romans (4:5). Roman legends are presented in the background as fleeing from his military forces (4:7), and Rome's leader is brought before the prince (4:10). Immediately following this fragment is the one we examined above that describes the fate of this leader at the hands of the prince: "and the king of the Kittim shall stand for judgment and the prince of the community—the branch of David—will have him put to death" (7:4). Thus 4Q285 paints a portrait of a victorious warrior messianic that combines two First Testament images: the branch (Isaiah, Jeremiah) and the prince (Ezekiel). They are one in the same person in 4Q285. He is a Davidite who not only defeats the Romans he condemns and puts to death their leader. He then proceeds to reign in righteousness in fulfillment of Isaiah 11. And like 4Q285, 4Q161 is yet another manuscript that connects the prince with the branch.

4Q161 (4QpIsaa = 4QIsaiah Peshera)[35]

As mentioned previously, 4Q161 is one of five extremely fragmented commentaries on the book of Isaiah found in the caves surrounding Qumran. It was composed during a period of socio-political uncertainty in Judea (75–50 BCE). Having examined the quotation from Isaiah 11:1–5 about the Davidic branch (ff7–10iii:11–25), we now address the passage that speaks of the prince. The document begins with Isaiah 10:22–23, which addresses the deliverance of God's remnant (f1i:20–f7iii:9).

After God inaugurated a series of Assyrian deportations of the northern Israel, Isaiah believed a remnant of Israel would survive God's judgment. He believed a branch, a righteous Davidic ruler would not only rescue that remnant but that he would defeat Israel's enemy, reunite the nation of Israel, and rule over the kingdom of Israel. According to Johnston, this Davidic shoot (Isa. 11:1) should be identified with the Davidic branch (Jer. 23:5; cf. Zech. 3:8; 6:9-15). 4Q161 is like Jeremiah in that it builds upon Isaiah's anticipation of a branch, yet interprets Isaiah with greater force.

---

35. The analyzed transcriptions of 4Q161 (4QpIsaᵃ = *4QIsaiah Pesher*ᵃ) are presented by John M. Allegro in *Qumran Cave 4.I* (DJD 5; Oxford: Clarendon Press, 1968), 11–13.

"Therefore, t[hus say]s the L[ord God] ²:¹⁰[of Hosts, Don't be afraid, my people liv]ing in Zio[n, of Assyria, of the r]od [he beats you with, of the staff he raises] ²:¹¹[against you as Egypt did; for] very soon [now my anger will be spent, my wrath against] ²:¹²their [corruption.] Then [the Lord of Hosts] will st[ir up a Lash, as when Midian was defeated at the Cliff of] ²:¹³[Or]eb; his own S[taff he will raise over the sea as he did against Egypt. On that day] ²:¹⁴[his] burden will drop [from your shoulder, his yoke from your neck-the yoke will break because the neck will be so fat!"] (Isaiah 10:24–27). ²:¹⁵[This refers to . . .] ²:¹⁶[. . .] when they return from the "wilderness of the Gen[tiles" (cf. Ezek. 20:35) [. . .] ²:¹⁷. . . *the Staff is the Leader of the Nation*, and afterward he will remove [the yoke] from them . . . [emphasis mine] (4Q161 2:9–17) ³⁶

This text paints a picture of hope despite the threat of foreign conquest (Isa. 10:24–27), followed by a picture of judgment (Ezek. 20:35), but it concludes with the God raising "the Staff" to defeat the enemies of Israel. The "staff" is a symbol for a Davidic ruler mentioned previously (cp. CD 7:19, 4Q161 3:11, 4Q252 5:2). Whereas in Isaiah the enemy is Assyria and in Ezekiel the enemy is Babylon, in 4Q161 they are the Gentiles who are defined later in the text as "the Kittim" (or Rome). Whereas in Isaiah the hope rests in a future branch of David and in Ezekiel in a future prince of David, 4Q161 refers to this future hope as "the Staff" as the leader of the Jewish nation. Thus this portrait is clearly of the one who removes "the yoke" of Roman interference in Israel. We saw this kind of pattern appeal to shift an enemy's identification before; as God worked then, he works now. We have also seen an equating of symbols for a future messianic figure as well in 4Q285 and in our next text 1Q28b.

1Q28b (1QSb = 1QRule of Benedictions)

As mentioned in chapter 9, 1Q28 consists of three individual works: *Rule of the Community* (1Q28), *Rule of the Congregation* (1Q28a) and *Rule of Blessings* (1Q28b). The work that demands our attention is 1Q28b, for it reveals a series of blessings reserved for the messianic age and recited by a forthcoming "instructor." These blessings were to be directed to (1) the general membership (1:1–7), (2) the priestly Messiah (2:1–3:21), (3) the priests of the community (3:22–5:19), and finally (4) the military Messiah (5:20–29). It is within the final set of blessings that we have the most explicit passage whereby the prince is painted as a royal military Messiah.

---

36. The translation is from Wise, Abegg, and Cook, *The Dead Sea Scrolls*, 209. For other translations see García Martínez and Tigchelaar, *The Dead Sea Scrolls*, 1:315; and Allegro, "Commentary on Isaiah (A)", 12–13.

²⁰(Words of blessing) belonging to the Instructor, by which to bless *the Prince of the Congregation* whom [God chose . . .] ²¹[. . .] And he shall renew for him the Covenant of the [Ass]ociation, so as *to establish the kingdom of his people forev[er,] [that "with righteousness* he may *judge the poor,]* ²² [and] *decide with equity for [the me]ek* of the earth," (Isaiah 11:4) *walk before him blameless* in all the ways of [his heart,] ²³and establish his covenant as holy [in] distress for those who seek H[im. May] the Lord li[ft] you up to an eternal height, a mighty tower in a wall ²⁴securely set on high! Thus may you be r[ighteous] by the might of your [mouth,] *lay waste the earth* with your rod! With the breath of your lips ²⁵may you *kill the wicked!*" (Isaiah 11:4, modified) *May he give [you "a spirit of coun] sel and eternal might* [rest upon you], the spirit of knowledge and the fear of God" (Isaiah 11:2). May "righteousness ²⁶be the belt [around your waist, and faithful]ness the belt around your loins" (Isaiah 11:5). May he "make your horns iron and your hoofs bronze!" (Micah 4:13). ²⁷*May you gore like a bu[ll . . . May you trample the nati]ons like mud in the streets! For God has established you as "the scepter"* (Numbers 24:17; Genesis 49:10) ²⁸over the rulers; bef[ore you peoples shall bow down, and all nat]ions shall serve you. he shall make you mighty by his holy name, ²⁹so that you shall be as a li[on among the beasts of the forest;] your [sword will devour] prey, with none to resc[ue.] (1Q28b 5:20–29, emphasis mine)[37]

The presence of the prince of the congregation as a royal Messiah is evident in the clause: "For God has established you as 'the scepter' over the rulers" (5:27). Yet the functions of this royal military Messiah are based upon Isaiah 11 and linked with Genesis 49 and Numbers 24. Although called the branch in Isaiah, here in 1Q28 he is the royal prince. The portrait is one of explicit expectation: to establish the kingdom, in righteousness judge the poor, decide equity for the meek, lay waste the earth, and kill the wicked. Furthermore the author petitions God to provide a spirit of counsel, might, and knowledge. With the merging of passages from Hebrew Scriptures there is the synonymous use of epithets. Although our next text, *Jubilees*, is not considered a sectarian composition, copies of the book were found in the caves near the ruins of Qumran.

Jubilees

The book of Jubilees retells the stories found in Genesis and early parts of Exodus as though they were divine revelations to Moses while on Mount Sinai (1:1–29). Considered to be composed around 161–140 BCE when Judas Maccabee led a revolt against Antiochus IV for religious freedom (see ch. 8,

---

37. The translation is a variation of Wise, Abegg, and Cook, *The Dead Sea Scrolls,* 149–50. For another translation see García Martínez and Tigchelaar, *The Dead Sea Scrolls,* 1:107–8.

pp. 237–39),[38] at least fourteen copies of the book were found at Qumran.[39] Thus the book of Jubilees appears to have been a popular work and perhaps an important text.

Jubilees divides nicely into six units: Introduction (ch 1), Creation and Adam stories (chs. 2–4), Noah stories (chs. 5–10), Abraham stories (chs. 11–23), Jacob and his family (chs. 24–25), and Moses stories (46–50).[40] Naturally, the unit of *Jubilees* that interests us here are the stories about Jacob and his family. Of particular value are the blessings of Jacob given to Judah (of Gen. 49:8–12). Thus *Jubilees'* account of Jacob's blessing says,

> [18]And to Judah he said, "May the Lord give you might and strength to tread upon all who hate you. ***Be a prince***, *you and one of your sons for the sons of Jacob*; may your name and the name of your son be one which travels and goes about in all the lands and cities. Then *may the nations fear before your face*, and all of the nations tremble, and every nation trembles. [19]And with you will be the help of Jacob and *with you will be found the salvation of Israel.* [20]And *on the day when you sit on your righteous throne of honor, their will be great peace for all the seed of the beloved's sons.* Whoever blesses you will be blessed, and all who hate you and afflict you and curse you will be uprooted and destroyed from the earth and they shall be cursed. (31:18–20; emphasis mine)[41]

Obviously, the prince is from Jacob's tribe and presented as one who will rule over the nation of Israel. He will be feared among the nations, save Israel, and create peace.

Summation

It appears that the title prince is generally spoken of an expected Davidite. Out of nine extra-biblical documents, only one had any major interpretive uncertainties, 4Q423. Several documents share similar snippets that paint their portraits of a forthcoming Davidic prince to be a victorious military leader (1QM, 4Q161, 4Q174, 4Q285, 4Q376, *Jub.*). But others emphasize

---

38. For a detailed discussion on dating see O. S. Wintermute, "Jubilees" in *The Old Testament Pseudepigrapha*, 2 vols. (ed. James H. Charlesworth; New York: Doubleday, 1985), 2:43–44.
39. VanderKam lists fifteen documents: 1Q17, 1Q18, 2Q19, 2Q20, 3Q5, 4Q216, 4Q217 (?), 4Q218, 4Q219, 4Q220, 4Q221, 4Q222, 4Q223–224, 11Q12. For further discussion see James C. VanderKam, "Jubilees, Book of" in *Encyclopedia of the Dead Sea Scrolls*, 2 vols. (ed. Lawrence H. Schiffman and James C. VanderKam; Oxford: Oxford University Press, 2000), 1:435.
40. The outline is adapted from Wintermute's outline, "Jubilees," 2:35. My one alteration concerns the Abraham stories. Rather than two units: Abraham stories (chs. 11–23:8) and a Digression on Abraham's death (chs. 23:9–32), I present one.
41. The translation is by Wintermute, "Jubilees," 2:116–17.

in their portraits this victory to be over the Romans (4Q161, 4Q285, cp. CD, 4Q266). Two portraits highlight his restoration of the Davidic dynasty (CD, 4Q266). While some portraits emphasize a prince ruling over the nation of Israel (CD, 4Q266, 4Q161, *Jub.*), two include a Davidic prince ruling over the nations (4Q161, 4Q174). Yet the prince is portrayed in two portraits to be more than a military jarhead; he is also capable of interpreting the law (CD, 4Q266). The following chart features the various descriptions and functions highlighted in each of the numerous portraits that attempt to capture the eschatological prince of David.

PORTRAITS OF THE PRINCE

OT Source	Primary:
	   Ezekiel 34:23–24, 37:24–25, 39:3–4, 46:12–15
	
	Secondary:
	   Genesis 49
	   Numbers 27:16–17
	   Isaiah 11
	   Amos 9

Dead Sea Scrolls	CD 7:19b-20 (4Q266) 1Q28b 5:20–28 1QM 5:1 4Q161 2–6:ii:19 4Q266 f3iii:21 (CD) 4Q285 4:2, 6; 5:4; 6:2 (4Q11) 4Q376 f1iii:1, 3 (11Q29) 1QM 3:15 (4Q496) 4Q423 f5:2 (4Q418a 3) 4Q496 f10:3–4 (1QM)
Pseudepigrapha Reference	*Jubilees* 31:18 (cp. vv. 11–15)
Various Elements	The prince is a Davidic scion The prince is a human personality The prince is a victorious military leader The prince is a political ruler The prince is a leader over Israel The prince is an interpreter of the Law
Functions	The prince reestablishes David's dynastic rule The prince has offspring that succeed him The prince accepts advice from the priestly messiah The prince leads military campaigns The prince delivers Israel from the Romans The prince condemns and kills wicked leaders

Dating of Manuscripts	Mid- Hasmonean: 125–75 BCE
	  1Q28b (*1QRule of Blessing*)
	  4Q266 (*4QDamascus Document*[a])
	
	Late-Hasmonean: 75–50 BCE
	  4Q161 (4QpIsa[a] = *4QIsaiah Pesher*[a])
	
	Transition to Herodian: 50–30 BCE
	  4Q376 (*4QApocryphon of Moses*[b])
	  4Q496 (*4QWar Scroll*[f])
	
	Early Herodian 30–1 BCE
	  4Q285 (*4QSefer ha-Milhamah*)
	
	Late Herodian 30–68 CE
	  4Q423 (*4QInstruction*[g])
	
	Political Situation: Hasmonean Rule
	  John Hyrcanus I (135–104 BCE)
	  Aristobulus I (104–103 BCE)
	  Alexander Jannaeus (103–76 BCE)

CONCLUSION

Thirteen documents cite the undisputed epithets "branch" and "prince" for an expected royal messiah figure (see the chart, page 300). Five documents specify the branch, nine specify the prince, and two specify both (4Q161, 4Q285). As it was for the First Testament prophets, so it was for second temple authors, the titles were interchangeable. On the one hand, Isaiah spoke of the "shoot/sprout," Jeremiah and Zechariah spoke of the "branch," but the Dead Sea Scroll texts typically put these together using Jeremiah's title of the "branch" when discussing Isaiah 11:1–6. On the other hand, Ezekiel favored the epithet "the prince" to speak of a forthcoming Davidic scion. Thus the portraits of the branch and the prince have overlapping features.

Historically, four texts were written during the socio-political activities of the non-Davidic Hasmoneans, who controversially had combined the separate offices of anointed king and anointed high priest into a single office (CD, 1Q28b, 4Q266, *TJud*). Yet most of our extra-biblical sources were written during the distressful period of civil war between John Hyrcanus II and Aristobulus II, a civil war only to be squelched by the Roman general Pompey (4Q161, 4Q174, 4Q252, 4Q282) and the subsequent years of transition to Herod's reign (4Q376, 4Q496). These latter two periods of time reek with political uncertainty and dissatisfaction over Israel's leadership. Perhaps this is the reason why the branch and the prince are profiled as the one who is a righteous and victorious warrior who will correct the situation or one like it.

Regardless of the precise historical reason, these second temple sources present clearly and unanimously the branch and the prince to be a human personality from David's lineage who restores David's dynasty. The portrayals often overlap in their presentation of him as a forthcoming military leader

(1QM, 4Q174, 4Q285, 4Q376), who defeats the Romans and Belial (CD, 4Q174, 4Q285) and even puts Rome's military leaders to death (4Q285) during the last days (4Q161, 4Q174). Some portraits include his restoration of David's dynasty (CD, 4Q266), others expand and/or emphasize his restoration of the Jewish nation (CD, 4Q161, 4Q266). Some portraits include his offspring, which enables the dynasty to be never ending (4Q174, 4Q252). Naturally, many present him as one who presides as a victorious ruler of nations (4Q161, 4Q174), a judge of peoples (4Q161, 4Q285, 4Q423, *TJud*), and even as one who saves (*TJud*). He is not, however, without assistance. Sometimes they paint him as one who is divinely empowered with God's spirit (4Q161, *TJud*), other times he is seen to have divine authority (4Q161), and other times he is advised by Zadokite priests (4Q161). Finally, it appears as though he is both righteous (4Q252, *TJud*) and an able interpreter of the law (CD, 4Q252, 4Q266).

As with the previous epithet, the functions of the branch and prince are variously presented in their relationship to Law and to a priestly figure. For example, sometimes he himself appears as an interpreter of the law (CD, 252) and other times he arises alongside an interpreter of the law (4Q174). Furthermore it is generally conceded that in CD and 4Q266 the Messiah of Israel and the prince are two epithets for the same eschatological figure.[42] Yet unlike CD and 4Q266 where the functions of the Messiah of Israel appear to be merged with the Messiah of Aaron (14:19; 19:10, 14, 35), here the prince's duties are clearly military (cp. 1Q28a 2:11–22).

---

42. Craig A. Evans, "Messiah" in *Encyclopedia of the Dead Sea Scrolls*, 2 volumes (ed. Lawrence H. Schiffman and James C. VanderKam; Oxford: University Press, 2000), 1:541.

CHAPTER ELEVEN

ANTICIPATIONS OF THE ONE CALLED SON

The epithet "son" for messianic figures occurs in various forms: "son," "firstborn," "son of God," and "son of man." The ones most familiar and commonly ascribed to Jesus are "Son of God" and "Son of Man." For twenty-first-century readers of the Second Testament (our New Testament), the mention of the phrase "Son of God" generally triggers a theological presupposition about Jesus, his deity. Yet prior to the time of Jesus, all four designations were applied to numerous referents, none of which would have been considered a preexistent person of the godhead. For instance, in both the sacred Hebrew writings and later reflections in second temple literature, "son of God" is used to reference angelic heavenly beings.[1] In biblical and non-biblical writings variations of "son" could reference one's honored status or special relationship with God: God's chosen people (Exod. 4:22, Hosea 11:1, Jer. 31:9), God's righteous people (Wis. 2:18; 5:5), or even Adam (Luke 3:38). This is particularly true of David's heir, Solomon. In 2 Samuel 7, David's forthcoming son would be heralded as God's "son" (echoed in Ps. 2), and in Psalm 89 the expected ideal Davidite is called God's "firstborn son."

Generally, the title "son" focused attention on the relational or honored status of Israel's king with Yahweh and not the ontological existence of the king as God or one who was part of the godhead (cp. Deut. 6:4). Furthermore the developed belief in the transcendent nature of God during the second temple period would have prevented Jewish people to conceive of God living among them as an eschatological Messiah figure. Nevertheless, second temple reflections of Should this be capitalized?scripture and longings for a messianic "son" appear to heighten the mysteries surrounding an anticipated messianic figure. This is evident in at least seven second temple texts: 1Q28a, 4Q174,

---

1. In the Hebrew text, "sons of God" (בְּנֵי הָאֱלֹהִים) speaks of angelic beings (Gen. 6:4; cp. *1 En.* 6:1–2; Job 1:6, 2:1). In the LXX: Deuteronomy 32:43, Psalms 29:1, 89:6.

4Q246, 4Q369, *Psalms of Solomon, 1 Enoch,* and *4 Ezra.* Reflections upon the First Testament's concept of "son," "son of God," "firstborn son," and "son of man" in these texts will disclose a spectrum of second temple portraits unlike those evident in the previous two chapters. Some will remain the same, but others will be heightened and more ambiguous. We begin our discussion with 4Q174 and 4Q246, which base their profile upon 2 Samuel 7.

4Q174 (4QFLOR = *4QFLORILEGIUM*)[2]

As you may recall from our discussions on "the branch," 4Q174 is an early Herodian text composed sometime during the reign of Herod the Great (40–4 BCE). This undeniable sectarian text anticipated two Messiahs: a regal Messiah of David and a teaching Messiah. Furthermore, it describes an eschatological sanctuary to be built during the last days. Although we have seen this text in the previous chapter, we present 4Q174 3:2–13 again so that we might emphasize the title "son" in context.

> 3:2[I appointed judges] over my people Israel" (2 Samuel 7:10–11a). This "place" is the house that [they shall build for him] in the Last Days, as it is written in the book of 3[Moses: "A temple of] the Lord are you to prepare with your hands; the Lord will reign forever and ever" (Exodus 15:17). This passage describes the temple that no [man with a] permanent [fleshly defect] shall enter, 4nor Ammonite, Moabite, bastard, foreigner or alien, forevermore. Surely his holiness 5shall be rev[eal]ed there; eternal glory shall ever be apparent there. Strangers shall not again defile it, as they formerly defiled 6the Temp[le of I]srael through their sins. To that end he has commanded that they build him a Temple of Adam, and that in it they sacrifice to him 7proper sacrifices. As for what he said to David, "I [will give] you [rest] from all your enemies" (2 Samuel 7:11b), this passage means that he will give them rest from [al]l 8the children of Belial, who cause them to stumble, seeking to destroy the[m by means of] their [wickedness.] They became party to the plan of Belial in order to cause the S[ons of 9Li[ght] to stumble. They plotted wicked schemes against them, [so that they might fall pr]ey to Belial through guilty error. 10"Moreover the Lord decl[ares] to you that he will make you a house," and that "*I will raise up your offspring after you,* and establish the throne of his kingdom 11[fore]ver. *I will be a father to him, and he will be my son*" (2 Samuel 7:11c, 12b, 13b-14a). *This passage refers to the Shoot of David,* who is to arise with 12the Interpreter

---

2. Initial analyzed transcriptions of 4Q174 (4QFlor = *4QFlorilegium*) are edited by John M. Allegro in *Qumran Cave 4. I* (DJD 5; Oxford: Clarendon Press, 1968), 53–57. More recently, Jocab Milgrom, "Florilegium: A Midrash on 2 Samuel and Psalm 1–2 (4Q174 = 4QFlor)" in *The Dead Sea Scrolls,* vol. 6b (ed. James H. Charlesworth; Tübingen: Mohr Siebeck, 2002), 248–63.

of the Law, and who will [arise] in Zi[on in the La]st Days, as it is written, "And *I shall raise up the booth of David* that is fallen" (Amos 9:11). This passage describes the fallen Branch of [13]David, [w]hom he shall raise up to deliver Israel.[3]

The author does not differentiate between "son," "the shoot," and "the booth of David." As it was in the Hebrew Scriptures, this forthcoming son of David will have a unique relationship with God (2 Sam. 7). Contextually, son of David is linked with "the shoot of David" (Jer. 33:20–21). The booth of David (Amos 9), however, appears to refer to the restoration of David's dynasty. So the son or shoot is portrayed to be a human personality whose offspring will carry on a never-ending Davidic dynasty. He is also a victorious warrior who delivers the nation of Israel from her enemies. His relationship with God will be a special or unique relationship and God will provide for him peace (i.e., "rest") from all his enemies. Yet he would arise alongside an interpreter of the Law, a priestly Messiah figure. Once again it is important to note that the two separate topics about the sanctuary and the Davidic king in the Hebrew Scriptures are united in 4Q174 to form a theological statement about a sectarian community's belief in a forthcoming royal son of God, who will come during the last days and rule over a sanctuary or community of people.

4Q246 (4QPSDAN AR = *4QARAMAIC APOCALYPSE*)4

The Dead Sea Scroll 4Q246, sometimes known as the "son of God" text, was first acquired in 1958, lectured on at Harvard University in 1972, and eventually published in 1992. The delayed publication of this two-column fragmented manuscript generated an aura of mystery and divergent discussions, but 4Q246 eventually transformed our understanding of the first-century Jewish use of the title "son of God." As such it is one of the texts that demonstrate why the Dead Sea Scrolls are important and how they changed the way New Testament studies looks at Jewish backgrounds to Jesus.

Composed just prior to the Roman Senate's appointment of Herod the Great to be ruler over Judea, Samaria, and Galilee (previously the Hasmonean Kingdom), which had been overrun by the Parthians (40 BCE), 4Q246 begins with the vision whereby a seer appears to be falling before the throne of a

---

3. The translation comes from Accordance Software. Martin G. Abegg Jr., James E. Bowley, and Edward M. Cook are responsible for preparing the text and morphological analysis for electronic publication. Abegg's work with electronic data bases is extensive, having prepared the QUMRAN, MISH-T, SAMAR-T, and BENSIRA-C/M Accordance modules for the study of ancient Hebrew Language and Literature.

4. The analyzed transcriptions of 4Q246 (4QpsDan ar = *4QAramaic Apocalypse*) are edited by Émile Puech in *Qumran Cave 4.XVII* (DJD 22; Oxford: Clarendon Press, 1996), 165–84.

king (1:1–2). The explanation that follows (1:3–2:9) anticipates violent wars and speaks of someone who will be "hailed as son of God" and "they will call him son of the Most High" (2:1). Most of what remains of this fragmented manuscript is the interpretation of the vision. In the middle of this extensive interpretation, the designation "son of God" is equated with "son of the Most High." Thus we read

> [2:1]*He will be called* **son of God**, and *they will call him* "**son of the Most High**."* Like the sparks [2]that you saw, so will their kingdom be; they will rule several years [3]over the earth and crush everything; a people will crush aonther people and a province another province. [4][*vacat*] until the people of God arise and make everyone rest from the sword. [5]**His kingdom will be an eternal kingdom** and all his ways will be in truth. **He will judge [6]the earth** with truth and **everyone will make peace**. The sword will be removed from the earth [7]and **all cities will pay him homage**. The great God will be his strength. [8]He will wage war for him; he will place the nations in his hand and [9]he will cast them down before him. His rule will be an eternal rule and none of the abysses . . . (4Q246 2:1–9)[5]

Previous usage of the phrase "son of God" in the Hebrew Scriptures allow for various referents. It might be used in a negative historical sense to speak of Antiochus IV Epiphanes whose name gives the notion of a human king being God manifest.[6] Yet many view the reference positively as either an eschatological angelic ruler,[7] or an eschatological Jewish Messiah.[8] Unfortunately, determining to whom the referent refers is difficult to determine.

In 4Q246 1:1, the opening situation involves a vision and a royal court scene similar to that of Daniel 7:1–3 (cp. 4Q246 2:1–36). In fact, the wording in 4Q246 2:5 and 6 seems to correspond with Daniel 7:27 and 7:14 respectively. These conceptual links between 4Q246 and Daniel 7 have generated two ways of describing the "son of God" figure. On the one hand, if the "son of God" is connected with the little horn of Daniel 7:8 and 25, then he is a negative eschatological villain, perhaps Antiochus IV or his alleged son

5. The translation is a modified translation from Florentino García Martínez and Eibert J. C. Tigchelaar, *The Dead Sea Scrolls Study Edition*, vol. 1 (Grand Rapids: Eerdmans, 1997), 495. For another translation see Michael Wise, Martin Abegg, and Edward Cook, *The Dead Sea Scrolls: A New Translation* (New York: HarperSanFrancisco, 1996), 269–270.
6. Wise, Abegg, and Cook, *The Dead Sea Scrolls*, 268–270.
7. Florentino Garcia Martinez, "The Eschatological Figure of 4Q246," in *Qumran and Apocalyptic: Studies on the Aramaic Texts from Qumran* (Leiden: Brill, 1992), 162–79.
8. John J. Collins, *The Scepter and the Star: The Messianism in Light of the Dead Sea Scrolls*, second ed. (Grand Rapids: Eerdmans, 2010), 171-90. Johannes Zimmermann, "Observations on 4Q246–The 'Son of God'" in *Qumran–Messianism* (ed. James H. Charlesworth, Hermann Lichtenberger, and Gerbern S. Oegema; Tübingen: Mohr Siebeck, 1998), 135–53.

Alexander Balas. On the other hand, if the "son of God" is connected with "one like the son of man" in Daniel 7:13, then he is a positive eschatological hero, a future Davidite. In either case, the son is portrayed as an eschatological figure. Johnston's study in chapter 6 shows how complex this image is with its mixture of transcendent and earthly event features, as well as its individual or corporate elements. So how one attempts to make connections between the figure in 4Q246 and the Daniel 7 figure is important.

Yet despite these seeming similarities with Daniel 7, there are at least three weak links. First, in 4Q246, it is the people who trample other people (2:3), whereas in Daniel 7 it is the fourth beast. Second, in 4Q246, it is the "great God" who fights (2:7–8), whereas in Daniel 7:21 it is the little horn who wages war on God's people. Finally, in 4Q246, there is no mention of "one like a son of man," whereas in Daniel he is a key figure. Thus the conceptual links between 4Q246 and Daniel 7 appear unsubstantial.[9] So we ask ourselves, is there another possibility?

Moving beyond the questionable dependence of 4Q246 on Daniel 7, the conceptual and verbal links to 2 Samuel 7 appear most significant. In fact, Evans argues the similar wording in 2 Samuel 7:11b–17, 4Q246, and Luke 1:32–35 appears to support a triple parallel.[10]

COMPARISON OF 2 SAMUEL 7, 4Q246, AND LUKE 1

2 Samuel 7:9–17	4Q246 2:1, 5	Luke 1:32–33
I will make for you a great name (7:9)		He will be great (1:32)
he shall be a son to me (i.e., God, 7:14)	they will call him 'son of the Most High' (2:1)	And will be called the Son of the Most High (1:32)
I will establish the throne of his kingdom forever (7:13)		And the Lord God will give him the throne of his father David (1:32) He will reign over the house of Jacob forever, (1:33)
Your house and your kingdom shall be made sure forever (7:16)	his kingdom will be an everlasting kingdom. (2:5)	And his kingdom will be an everlasting kingdom. (1:33)

9. See Loren T. Stuckenbruck, "Formation and Re-Formation of Daniel" in *The Bible and the Dead Sea Scrolls*, vol. 1: Scripture and the Scrolls (ed. James H. Charlesworth; Waco, TX: Baylor University Press, 2006), 117–20.
10. Craig A. Evans, "Are the 'Son' Texts at Qumran Messianic? Reflections on 4Q369 and Related Scrolls" in *Qumran–Messianism* (ed. James H. Charlesworth, Hermann Lichtenberger, and Gerbern S. Oegema; Tübingen: Mohr Siebeck, 1998), 141–43.

The triple parallel between 2 Samuel 7, 4Q246, and Luke 1 supports a common tradition, namely that "son of God" and "son of the Most High" anticipate an earthly messianic king. Likewise Collins, after demonstrating the lack of similarity with Daniel 7 and highlighting the connection with Luke 1, concludes that, "4Q246 is most plausibly interpreted as referring to a Jewish Messiah."[11]

Thus the portrait painted of this forthcoming Davidic scion in 4Q246 is quite clear. He is a Jewish man, a Davidic Warrior-Messiah who is expected to make peace on earth (2:6), people everywhere will pay homage to him (2:7), and his kingdom will endure for a long period of time. Unlike the previous references to a messianic figure, there is no evidence of a diarchy here. He appears to be a lone messianic figure of Davidic origin who will have a unique relationship with God because of his description as son of the Most High, which parallels "son of God."[12]

1Q28A (1QSA = *1QRULE OF THE CONGREGATION*)

Needless to say, the reappearance of 1Q28a reinforces the significance of the text for this discussion. Previously, while discussing the epithet "Messiah," we learned that the closing segment of this manuscript profiled the Messiah to be a warrior that would appear in the last days, preside over the community, signal when to eat during a military banquet, and corule with a priestly Messiah (see "1Q28a [1QSa = Rule of the Congregation])," p.262). Here we want to focus attention on an allusion to the term "son" from Psalm 2. Not surprising, the allusion occurs within the convocation and description of the future messianic banquet where the term "Messiah" occurs two times (2:11–15).[13] Once again we read,

> [2:11]The procedure for the [mee]ting of the men of reputation [when they are called] to the banquet held by the Council of the Yahad, **when [God] has fa[th]ered (?)** [12]**the Messiah among them**: [the Priest,] as head of the entire congregation of Israel, shall enter first, trailed by all [13][his] brot[hers, the Sons of] Aaron, those priests [appointed] to the banquet of the men of reputation. They are to sit [14]be[fore him] by rank. **Then the [Mess]iah of Israel may en[ter,]** and the heads [15]of the th[ousands of Israel] are to

---

11. Adela Yarbro Collins and John J. Collins, *King and Messiah as Son of God: Divine, Human, and Angelic Figures in Biblical and Related Literature* (Grand Rapids: Eerdmans, 2008), 65–73.

12. Marin Hengel, *Studies in Early Christology* (Edinburgh: T & T Clark, 1995).

13. Lawrence H. Schiffman, "Rule of the Congregation " in *Encyclopedia of the Dead Sea Scrolls* (ed. Lawrence H. Schiffman and James C. VanderKam; Oxford: Oxford University Press, 2000), 797–99. Compare Elisha Qimron and James H. Charlesworth, "Rules of the Community" in *The Dead Sea Scrolls*, vol. 1: Rule of the Community and Related Documents (ed. James H. Charlesworth; Tübingen: Mohr Siebeck, 1995), 1–5.

sit before him by rank, as determined by [each man's comm]ission in their camps and campaigns.[14]

The portrait presented here is of a Messiah figure to be "fathered" (metaphorical "begotten") of God and echoes the language of Psalm 2:7. Despite the need for Dead Sea Scroll scholars to restore the term "fathered" in the manuscript above, it seems a general agreement exists that the phrase parallels Psalm 2:2, 7 and thus the concept conveyed is that the anticipated Messiah is a "begotten son."[15] In other words, the forthcoming Messiah figure, like the kings during the heyday of David's dynasty, is not only a military leader but also has a special relationship with God. He is God's "son." It is not that he is divine, but rather this intimate relationship with God provides the king significant status as God's viceregent.[16] Thus the forthcoming Davidic scion is thereby considered God's regal son. However, our next text, 4Q369, is a bit different because it echoes Psalm 89, a royal psalm whose religious and social setting occurs either during the Babylonian exile (after 586 BCE) or sometime during the early second temple period (after 515 BCE).

4Q369 (4QPrayer of Enosh)[17]

Unlike the three manuscripts discussed above, the basis for 4Q369 is Genesis and yet has conceptual links to Psalm 89. Consisting of ten fragments of poor quality and numerous gaps, 4Q369 appears to have been a narrative about the patriarchs, arranged genealogically, and interrupted by brief prayers. This late Herodian manuscript, from around the time Jesus was crucified (30–68 CE), opens with a speculative prayer supposedly offered by Enosh at a time when people began to worship shortly after the beginning of civilization (Gen. 4:26; cp. *Jub.* 4). In fact, the manuscript's name, *Prayer of Enosh*, was

---

14. The translation comes from Accordance Software. Martin G. Abegg Jr., James E. Bowley, and Edward M. Cook are responsible for preparing the text and morphological analysis for electronic publication. Abegg's work with electronic data bases is extensive, having prepared the QUMRAN, MISH-T, SAMAR-T, and BENSIRA-C/M Accordance modules for the study of ancient Hebrew Language and Literature.
15. Evans, "Are the 'Son' Texts at Qumran Messianic?", 138–40.
16. Collins rightly emphasizes the ambiguity inherent in the term "begotten" to suggest that something more than relational may be intended here. Although the king of Israel was not divine in the sense of the Most High God, the statement "'begotten' by God is a statement about *a nature and status conferred on him*, not just about a tutorial relationship." But Collins seems to push the ambiguity of the term "begotten" too far in that he seems to understand "a nature and status conferred on him" to mean that the Davidite embraced the idea that he was in some sense divine (p. 204). Collins and Collins, *King and Messiah as Son of God*, 22–24, 204.
17. The analyzed transcriptions of 4Q369 (*4QPrayer of Enosh*) are edited by Harold Attridge and John Strugnell in *Qumran Cave 4.VIII* (DJD 13; Oxford: Clarendon Press, 1994), 353–62.

initially suggested due to the prayer uttered by Enosh in the text.[18] Yet the manuscript contains a fairly well preserved section about God's firstborn son who has been deemed a messianic Davidic figure. Thus we read

"And you made him **a firstborn son** to you [. . .] [7]like him for **a prince and ruler** in all your earthly land [. . . [8] . . . the] cr[own of the] heavens and the glory of the clouds [you] have set [on him . . . [9] . . .] and the angel of your peace among his assembly. And h[e . . . [10]gave] to him righteous statutes, **as a father to [his s]on** [. . . [11] . . .] his love your soul cleaves to for [ever. [12]. . .] because by them [you established] your glory [. . .]" (4Q369 2.6–12)[19]

Despite the lack of specificity about the prince's identity, the individual is generally conceded to be an eschatological messianic figure.[20] Furthermore, the term "son," which is linked to "firstborn" and "as a father to his son," echoes parallel concepts in Psalm 89:26–27, "He will cry to me, 'you are my Father, my God . . . I also shall make him *my* firstborn'" (cp. 4Q236). By now, the language of this post-exilic psalm has become standard for a royal Davidite, and thereby enables us to conclude that the titles firstborn, prince, and son have become synonymous expressions for Israel's king (2 Sam. 7, Ps. 2, Ezek. 34, 37, 39). Thus conceptually implicit in 4Q236 is the anticipation of a Davidic scion that will appear as God's ruler (line 7), who will govern according to God's righteous statutes (lines 7, 10), and who will have an intimate relationship with God (lines 6, 10), which are all in keeping with Psalm 89. Furthermore, he will have descendants who will carry on the dynasty: "to his seed for their generations an eternal possession" (line 4), which mirrors the portrait of Messiah in *Psalms of Solomon*.

PSALMS OF SOLOMON

By now, the *Psalms of Solomon* should be a familiar text. The author's displeasure over Hasmonean hierarchy and Pompey's presence is unmistakable as too is the book's climax, which expresses the author's desire for God to restore David's dynasty. So far we have focused attention on the title Messiah and his profile as the expected "Lord Messiah" (17:32, 18 heading; 18:7; see

---

18. The name *4QPrayer of Enosh* was derived by Attridge and Strugnell, *Qumran Cave 4.VIII*, 353.
19. I modified the translation from Johannes Zimmermann, "Observations on 4Q246—The 'Son of God'" in *Qumran-Messianism* (ed. James H. Charlesworth, Hermann Lichtenberger, and Gerbern S. Oegema; Tübingen: Mohr Siebeck, 1998), 175–90. Compare Florentino García Martínez and Eibert J. C. Tigchelaar, *The Dead Sea Scrolls: Study Edition*, vol. 2 (Grand Rapids: Eerdmans, 1997), 731.
20. Evans, "Are the 'Son' Texts at Qumran Messianic?", 135–53. For additional support, see Zimmermann, "Observations on 4Q246," 175–90.

page 270). Yet here we want to feature a significant section of the psalm that profiles the son.

> See, Lord, and raise up for them their king, **the son of David, to rule over your servant Israel in the time known to you**, O God. Undergird him with the strength to destroy the unrighteous rulers, to purge Jerusalem from gentiles who trample her to destruction; in wisdom and in righteousness to drive out the sinners from the inheritance (Isa. 11:2b); to smash the arrogance of sinners like a potter's jar; to shatter all their substance with an iron rod (Ps. 2:9); to destroy the unlawful nations with the word of his mouth (Isa. 11:4); at his warning the nations will flee from his presence; and he will condemn sinners by the thoughts of their hearts (17:21–25).

> **He will gather a holy people whom he will lead in righteousness**; and he will judge the tribes of the people that have been made holy by the Lord their God. He will not tolerate unrighteousness (even) to pause among them, and any person who knows wickedness shall not live with them (17:26–27).

> **And he will have gentile nations serving him under his yoke**, and he will glorify the Lord in (a place) prominent (above) the whole earth. And he will purge Jerusalem (and make it) holy as it was even from the beginning, (for) nations to come (Isa. 2:2) from the ends of the earth to see his glory, to bring gifts to her children who had been driven out, and to see the glory of the Lord with which God has glorified her. And he will be a righteous king over them, taught by God (Jer. 23:5). There will be no unrighteousness among them in his days (Jer. 23:5), for all shall be holy, **and their king shall be Lord Messiah** (17:30–32).[21]

The portrait of the "son" differs in the *Psalms of Solomon* from those evident in previous texts. The emphasis is not on the son's intimate or unique relationship with God as God's chosen king. Rather, he is explicitly the son of David, a physical descendant of David. Furthermore, an unmistakable connection exists between the "Messiah" and "son of David" titles (cp. 1Q28a). Thus the references to "Messiah" and "son of David" are two ways of speaking about the same person. Portrayed as a military leader, he purges Jerusalem of Gentile control and presence. In fact, this son of David will be given prominence among Gentile rulers and nations. He generates a desire for nations to come to Jerusalem bearing gifts to the people of Jerusalem, serving him as Jerusalem's king, and seeing the glory of God (cp. 1 Kings 8:41–43). And

---

21. Translation by R. B. Wright, "Psalms of Solomon" in *The Old Testament Pseudepigrapha*, 2 vols. (ed. James H. Charlesworth; New York: Doubleday, 1985), 2:667. Scripture insertions are mine but adapted from Collins, *The Scepter and the Star*, 54.

though the details are obscure it is clear that this author anticipates the son of David, the Lord Messiah, to be a physical ruler of David who will condemn sinners and rule in righteousness.

So far, the designations "son," "son of God," and "firstborn" were employed in second temple texts to anticipate a human regal figure from the line of David. The various portrayals of these messianic "sons" evidence no super human abilities or traits, no characteristics of a divine, and no indication that he is a heavenly or apocalyptic figure. Yet *1 Enoch* paints a portrait unlike any other, for the picture of messiah in *1 Enoch* exceeds the dimension of a man.

1 ENOCH

Concerning the history of theological development within Judaism, *1 Enoch* has been deemed "the most important pseudepigraph of the first two centuries."[22] Today, as it is studied in conjunction with the Dead Sea Scrolls, *1 Enoch* continues to contribute to our developing comprehension of second temple theological reflections. A compilation of several works from various time periods, *1 Enoch* is typically divided into five units: the introduction (1–36), the book of parables (37–71), the book of astrological reckonings (72–82), the book of dreams or visions (82–90), and the letter of Enoch (91–108). Of these, the *book of parables* is most significant to this chapter because it expands the concept of the "son of man" in Daniel 7.

Unfortunately, the *book of parables* (37–71) was not found among the many fragments in the nearby caves of Qumran. Naturally, this has caused the book to be suspect for the discussion of Jewish messianism. The looming question is why were the parables excluded? Perhaps it was because they were a late addition. The allusion to the Parthians in *1 Enoch* 56:5–7 suggests, however, that they were written after the beginning of Herod's reign (40 BCE) when the Parthians invaded Galilee, Samaria, and Judea.[23] Furthermore, the silence of Jerusalem's destruction may suggest a pre-70 CE date.[24] Thus they may have been composed sometime between 40 BCE and 70 CE. Now if other texts from that same time period (e.g., *Pss. Sol.* dated *circa* 63 BCE) were not found among the Dead Sea Scrolls, perhaps it was because their Teacher of Righteous was more important to the sectarian community than Enoch, "so

---

22. R. H. Charles, "The Book of Enoch," in *The Apocrypha and Pseudepigrapha of the Old Testament in English*, 2 vols. (Oxford: Clarendon, 1913), 2:163. Similarly, Nickelsburg echoes Charles when he muses that *1 Enoch* is "arguably the most important text in the corpus of Jewish literature from the Hellenistic and Roman periods." George W. E. Nickelsburg, *1 Enoch* (Minneapolis: Fortress, 2001), 1.

23. M. A. Knibb, "The Date of the Parables of Enoch: A Critical Review," *NTS* 25 (1979): 345–59.

24. Suter, *Tradition and Composition in the Parables of Enoch* (Missoula: Scholars Press, 1979), 29–32. Naturally, Suter presupposes a direct connection between the fragments found in the caves that surround the ruins of Qumran.

the Qumranians would not welcome the parables where Enoch is the key eschatological figure."[25] Unlike Daniel 7:15–27 where the identity of the "one like a son of man" is left a mystery, the parables are explicit in their identity of the "son of man": he is Enoch.

> Then the angel came to me [Enoch] and greeted me and said to me, "You, son of man, who art born in righteousness and upon whom righteousness has dwelt, the righteousness of the Antecedent of time will not forsake you (71:14).[26]

One Enoch 71:14 is significant for another reason. It's difficult to argue that Christians produced these parables when the Second Testament clearly presents Jesus to be the Son of Man, not Enoch. "It is hardly conceivable," according to Collins, "that a Christian author would have written about a figure called 'Son of Man' without identifying him explicitly as Jesus."[27]

Whatever the reason for its exclusion from the fragments discovered in the caves surrounding Qumran, one should not dismiss the "son of man" discussions and its contributing reflections to second temple Jewish eschatological expectation and messianism. Clearly we have not recovered every possible text that was hidden in the Dead Sea region. Furthermore, these finds are only a part of what circulated in this key period of second temple Judaism. With that in mind, we now direct attention to the parables of *1 Enoch* 38–71.

The *book of parables* consists of three parables (38–44; 45–57; 58–69) and an epilogue (70–71). Four types of material make up the unit: (1) a series of journeys, (2) narratives of Noah and the flood, (3) events leading to the judgments, and (4) judgment allusions. Yet the theme of judgment resonates throughout the book. Of particular significance is the transformation of Daniel's "one like the son of man" into a more than human eschatological figure.[28] In Daniel 7, the fourth kingdom would be given to a mysterious heavenly figure, the "one like a son of man" (7:13–14) as well

---

25. Darrell L. Bock, "The Parables of Enoch: Early Judaism, Jesus, and Christian Origins" (ed. James H. Charlesworth and Darrell L. Bock; London: T&T Clark, forthcoming). The debate and uncertainty over the date of the *Parables of Enoch* (1 Enoch 37–71) is staggering. Nevertheless Bock does an excellent job tracing the dating debate.

26. The Son of Man is identified as Enoch in six recent translations coming from 1978–2004 (Knibb, Fusella, Isaac, Black, Olsen, Nickelsburg-VanderKam). This translation is by E. Isaac, "1 (Ethiopic Apocalypse of) Enoch" in *The Old Testament Pseudepigrapha*, vol. 1 (ed. James Charlesworth; Garden City, NY: Doubleday, 1983), 50.

27. John J. Collins, *King and Messiah as Son of God*, 87. Similar sentiments are made by Knibb, "The Date of the Parables of Enoch," 350.

28. For a more thorough overview, see Adela Yarbo Collins, "The Origin of the Designation of Jesus as 'Son of Man'" *HTR* 80 (1987): 391–407; reprinted in *Cosmology and Eschatology in Jewish and Christian Apocalypticism* (Leiden: Brill, 1996), 139–58; summarized in *King and Messiah as Son of God*, 156–73.

as to "the people of the holy ones of the Most High" (7:27). He is heavenly both in origin and behavior (riding on clouds), but unmistakably human in appearance. He is a seemingly mix of humanity and transcendence, a person shrouded in mystery, which seems to be a thematic presentation of God who seems to conceal the ambiguity of eschatological events in Daniel (cp. 7:28; 8:27). Yet *1 Enoch*'s reflection reshapes Daniel's portrayal of "the one like the son of man" that paints a distinctively unique portrait of a key eschatological agent.

First, Daniel's "son of man" is an undefined yet distinct figure from God. *One Enoch*, however, identifies the "son of man" to be the "messiah." Three terms are used synonymously in *1 Enoch*: messiah, son of man, and elect or chosen one.[29] Nevertheless like Daniel, the frequently referenced "Lord of the Spirits" (God) is distinguished from messiah (48:10), son of man (46:3), and the elect or chosen one (49:2). Thus these epithets do not refer to God but serve as references for another person other than God. Of insurmountable importance here is the link between son of man and Messiah. Revealing this principle eschatological figure is seen as the key anointed agent during the era of deliverance.

Second, Daniel's "son of man" is a heavenly figure described as "one who looks like the son of man" (Dan. 7:13). Likewise, *1 Enoch* says, "there was with him [God] another individual, whose face was like that of a human being. His countenance was full of grace like that of one among the holy angels" (46:1). As it was with Daniel, we ponder whether the "son of man" is an angelic figure or not. If the heavenly figure in 11QMechizedek (11Q13) is angelic, then perhaps the "son of man" is as well. But even the identity of the heavenly figure in 11Q13 is unclear. Regardless, it is clear that the "son of man" in *1 Enoch* is a preexistent heavenly figure of sorts. Or he is, at the least, a transcendent figure. He was given a name "the Before Time" (48:2). Yet the epilogue, though not without its own set of difficulties, reveals the "son of man" to be Enoch (71:14).[30] So whoever this individual is, whether Enoch or some other heavenly figure, he is to be esteemed along with the Lord of the Spirits. *One Enoch* 71:14 declares he is "born for righteousness" and that righteousness dwells on him. "All those who dwell upon the earth shall fall and *pay homage* before him" (48:5a; cp. 52:4 "messiah") as well as "glorify, bless, and sing the name of the Lord of the Spirits [God]" (48:5b).[31] Thus the son of man became "the Chosen One" who was concealed in the presence of

---

29. See messiah (48:10; 52:4), son of man (46:3–4; 48:2; 62:5, 7, 8, 14; 63:11; 69:27, 29; 70:1; 71:17), and elect one or chosen one (40:6; 45:3, 4, 5; 49:2, 4; 51:3, 4; 52:6, 9; 53:6; 55:4, 8, 10; 62:1).

30. See Collins, *King and Messiah as Son of God*, 91–93. John J. Collins, "The Son of Man in First-Century Judaism," *NTS* 38 (1992): 448–66.

31. Is the translation of "worship" in 48:5 to be understood as "pay homage" to because of his position as a sovereign who judges?

the Lord of the Spirits [namely God] prior to the creation of the world (48:6). Unfortunately, the Lord of the Spirits and his Messiah were denied their due respect (48:10; cp. Ps. 2:1–2).

Third, Daniel's "son of man" was presented a kingdom (7:13–14) after the Ancient of Days judged the Gentile nations (7:9–11, 26–27). Yet Daniel's picture is reinterpreted in *1 Enoch* when the "son of man" is presented to be both a sovereign and a judge. Unlike the son of man in the book of Daniel, the son of man in the book of Parables is a heavenly figure who sits noticeably on the throne of glory on the day of judgment and is looked upon by people, officials, political leaders, and angelic beings.

> On that day, my *Elect One shall sit on the seat of glory* and make a selection of (or "he will try") their [angelic beings] deeds . . . (45:3)

> . . . says the Lord of Spirits, "Kings, potentates, dwellers upon the earth: you would have to see *my Elect One, how he sits in the throne of glory* and judges Azaz'el and all his company [angelic beings], and his army, in the name of the Lord of the Spirits" (55:4).

> The [Lord of the Spirits] placed the *Elect One on the throne of glory*; and he shall judge all the works of the holy ones in heaven above, weighing in balance their deeds (61:8).

> Thus the Lord commanded the kings, the governors, the height officials, and landlords and said, "Open your eyes and *lift up your eyebrows—if you are able to recognize the Elect One!* The Lord of the Spirits has sat down on the throne of his glory, and the spirit of righteousness has been poured out upon him. The word of his mouth will do the sinners in; and all oppressors shall be eliminated from before his face. On the day of judgment, all the kings, the governors, the high officials and the land lords shall see and recognize him . . . and pain shall seize them *when they see that Son of Man sitting on the throne of his glory* (62:1–5, emphasis mine).

> Thenceforth nothing that is corruptible shall be found; for that *Son of Man has appeared and has seated himself upon he throne of his glory*; and all evil shall disappear from before his face . . . and he shall be strong before the Lord of the Spirits (69:29, emphasis mine).[32]

The portrait appears breathtaking. Literally seated next to God, positioned as a sovereign, is the son of man. As a sovereign, he also has authority

---

32. Translations are by Isaac, "1 Enoch," 34, 38, 42-43, 49.

apparently equal with God's and yet different. Although the Lord of the Spirits has given the "son of man" authority to judge, he does not judge sinners; that is still reserved for God (62:2; cp. Dan. 7:11, 26–27). The extent to which the son of man exercises eschatological judgment appears limited to judging the righteous and angelic beings. Nevertheless, the added function of an eschatological judge paints a non-ambiguous picture of shared authority with God as God's right hand man. So how does this picture of the Messiah differ from most others?

First and foremost he is a heavenly Messiah figure who appears not to have had an earthly career. This aspect of an eschatological heavenly Messiah is unlike all of those portraits presented previously. Missing is the image of a victorious, powerful, human warrior king. Second, God declares he is "before time," suggesting his preexistent status. And yet, third, he remains a heavenly figure who is less than God. This heavenly Messiah figure is visually differentiated from God in that he is *like* the son of man with characteristics of an angel. Fourth, he is conceived for righteousness and appears to be the embodiment of righteousness. Fifth, the Messiah shares unmistaken authority with God in that he participates alongside God in the future judgment as a sovereign. Finally, the epithets son of man and Messiah are synonymous terms. This synonymous usage will reemerge at the trial of Jesus when he answers: "Are you the Christ, the Son of the Blessed One?" Like *1 Enoch*, Jesus makes it quite clear that Messiah and son of man are one and the same person. He answers the question of his messiahship with "I am," then continues, "and you will see *the Son of Man sitting at the right hand* of the Power and *coming with the clouds of heaven.*" It is important to restate, however, that this picture of Messiah in *1 Enoch* is distinct from the other portraits when Enoch's picture is placed alongside the others. For as we will see, *4 Ezra*'s reflections of Daniel 7 replicate the portraits of a human figure.

4 EZRA

It may be reasonable to question the legitimate contribution that *4 Ezra* makes to our discussion. Composed sometime after the destruction of the temple (70 CE), this apocalyptic text, written by a Jew in Judea, wrestles with why God delivered the Jewish people into the hands of their enemies. Thus unlike our previous documents, *4 Ezra* is a post-Herodian text (70–90 CE). The angst about the Jewish situation is not the same as that presented in the *Psalms of Solomon* and our Dead Sea Scrolls. It is worse. The second temple now stands in ruin.

The nation has experienced unprecedented socio-political and religious turmoil at the hands of the Romans. Although the author provides no explanation as to why God allowed this catastrophe to occur, he finds solace in the fact that there will be final retribution in the afterlife. Yet Reddish points out that "the major focus is not on the judgment, rewards, and punishments in the afterlife but on the final battles between the messiah and the wicked."[33]

The book opens with a divine call, directed to a man of priestly descent, whose name is Ezra (*4 Ezra* 1:1–3). After rebuking the Jewish people (1:4–2:32), Ezra turns to the Gentiles (2:33–41) and is privy to a series of seven visions. Three are summarized below.

1. The first opens like a lament over the circumstances of the Jewish people, moves to inquiries about the forthcoming new age, and ends with an assurance that the end of the age is near (3:1–5:20).

2. Ezra begins his second vision by issuing a complaint about God's abandonment of his chosen people to the Gentiles, but again God assures Ezra that the inauguration of a new age is at hand and he is privy to a list of signs marking the end of the age (5:21–6:34).

3. The lengthy third vision advances among other things God's creation, the expected messianic kingdom, discussions about the final judgment, the future state of the righteous and the wicked, an exhortation directed to Ezra to stop brooding, and a restatement about the signs that will mark the end of the age (6:35–9:25).

While these first three visions are dialogues between Ezra and the angel Uriel concerning the justice of God, the last of these three visions speaks directly of a future messianic kingdom, one that will be established on earth, ruled over by a Messiah figure, and will endure for four hundred years before eternal judgments begin.[34] Yet the turning point in the book occurs in visions four, five, and six, because the city of Zion finds encouragement in its future restoration, the

> **Apocalyptic and Apocalypse**
>
> "Apocalyptic" generally speaks of some sort of disclosure of heavenly secrets in a visionary format that are revealed to a seer for the benefit of a religious community that is experiencing suffering and thereby perceives itself as being victimized.
>
> "Apocalypse" generally speaks of a genre that conveys the idea that the world is about to end in a cataclysmic manner, when all wrongs will be righted, and all just people will be resurrected and rewarded in a blessed heavenly existence.

---

33. Mitchell G. Reddish, *Apocalyptic Literature: A Reader* (Nashville: Abingdon Press, 1990), 61.
34. For another overview see Bruce M. Metzger, "The Fourth Book of Ezra" in *The Old Testament Pseudepigrapha*, 2 vols. (ed. James H. Charlesworth; New York: Doubleday, 1985), 1:516–18.

Messiah's vanquishing of the Roman Empire, and the long-awaited rise of the son of God is that of a military victory who destroys God's enemies.

4.　Opening with a woman in mourning, the fourth vision describes the woman's transformation into a glorious city, which is eventually identified to be the heavenly Zion in the day of salvation (9:26–10:59).

5.　The fifth vision is an allegory illustrating the future of the Roman Empire, represented by the eagle, which will be punished eventually by God's messiah (11:1–12:39).

6.　In the sixth vision, Ezra sees something like a man coming out of the sea; an innumerable multitude of men come to make war on him, yet he annihilates his enemies with a stream of flaming fire from his mouth (13:1–13).

The last vision is a divine directive about ninety-four books that had been revealed to him.

7.　The final vision is one of Ezra being commissioned to make public the twenty-four Hebrew canonical books and the other seventy esoteric books were to be reserved for only the wise (14:1–48).

The third (6:35–9:25), fifth (11:1–12:39), and sixth visions about the messiah and his kingdom are important here. To begin with, the third vision makes explicit mention of the coming of God's son, the Messiah.

> [26]For behold, *the time will come*, when the signs which I have foretold to you will come to pass . . . [28]**for my son the Messiah shall be revealed** *with those who are with him, and those who remain shall rejoice four hundred years.* [29]And *after these* **years my son the Messiah shall die**, *and all who draw human breath.* [30]And the world shall be turned back to primeval silence for seven days, as it was at the first beginnings; so that no one shall be left. [31]And after seven days the world, which is not awake, shall be roused, and that which is corruptible shall perish. [32]And the earth shall give up those who are asleep in it . . . [33]and the Most High shall be reveled upon the seat of judgment . . . [36]then the pit of torment shall appear, and opposite it shall be the place of rest . . . (7:26–36, emphasis mine)[35]

As we have seen in previous Dead Sea Scrolls (CD, 1Q28, 4Q161, 4Q266), the Messiah remains as a figure yet to be revealed. Yet when God's

---

35. The translation is by Metzger, "The Fourth Book of Ezra," 1:537–38.

son, the Messiah, comes he will rule for four hundred years and will not experience death until after his four-hundred-year reign, at which point he will die. Thus, God's son is an extraordinary human personality. *2 Baruch*, another pseudepigraphal work written a short time after *4 Ezra*, describes this messianic period as a time of plenty (29:4–7; 73:2–74:4).[36] At this point, however, there is no indication that he is a descendant of David. At the close of his four-hundred-year reign, the Most High will sit on his judgment seat, the pit of torment will appear, as well as "the place of rest" (i.e., Kingdom of God; cp. Heb. 4:1–13).

Our next text from *4 Ezra* is a portion taken from the fifth vision about an eagle and a lion (11:1–12:39). Whereas the first portion of this vision is presented in an allegorical format (11:1–12:3), the latter portion is a request and an interpretation of that allegory (12:4–39), a snippet of which is presented below.

> He said to me, "This is the interpretation of this vision which you have seen: The eagle which you saw coming up from the sea is the fourth kingdom which appeared in a vision to your brother Daniel.
>
> And as for the lion that you saw rousing up out of the forest and roaring and speaking to the eagle and reproving him for his unrighteousness, and as for all his words that you have heard, **this is the Messiah whom the Most High has kept until the end of days**, *who will arise from the posterity of David*, and will come and speak to the Romans [sic]; he will denounce them for their ungodliness and for their wickedness, and will cast up before them their contemptuous dealings. For first he will set them living before his judgment seat, and when he has reproved them, then he will destroy them. But he will deliver in mercy the remnant of my people, . . . and make them joyful until the end comes . . . (12:10–11, 31–34; emphasis mine)[37]

Naturally, the entire fifth vision can be likened to Daniel's vision of the four beasts (Dan. 7:1–14). Here in *4 Ezra*, however, the Messiah, symbolized by the lion, destroys the Roman Empire, symbolized by the great eagle. The Messiah, who is from David's family, not only destroys the Romans, he delivers a remnant of Israel. The Messiah is presented as one whom the Most High has kept until "the end of days" (cp. *4 Ezra* 7:28). And though

---

36. Like *4 Ezra*, *2 Baruch* is concerned about Rome's destruction of Jerusalem. Like *4 Ezra*, *2 Baruch* is structured around seven visions and thereby an apocalypse. Like *4 Ezra*, *2 Baruch* speaks of the coming of the anointed one as a royal warrior (39:7–40:2; 70:9; 72:2), as a judge and / or destroyer of nations (39:7–8; 40:1; 72:2). For further reading see A. F. J. Klijn, "2 (Syriac Apocalypse of) Baruch" in *The Old Testament Pseudepigrapha*, 2 vols. (ed. James H. Charlesworth; New York: Doubleday, 1985), 1:615–52.

37. The translation is by Metzger, "The Fourth Book of Ezra," 1:550.

no explicit mention of son occurs, "from the posterity of David" parallels the phrase "son of David" in *Psalms of Solomon* 17:21 above. In both cases, the Messiah is clearly a human descendant of David.

Our last citation is a portion taken from the sixth vision about a "son of man." Once again the vision about the son of man (13:1–13) is followed by a request and an interpretation (13:14–58). It is an interpretation of the sixth vision about the man from the sea who is called God's son (13:32).

> This is the interpretation of the vision: *As for your seeing a man come up from the heart of the sea*, this is he *whom the Most High has been keeping for many ages*, who will himself deliver his creation; and he will direct those who are left.

> Behold the days are coming when the Most High will deliver those who are on the earth. . . . *my son will be revealed, whom you saw as a man coming up from the sea.*

> He will stand on the top of Mount Zion. And Zion will come and be made manifest to all people, prepared and built, as you saw the mountain carved out without hands. And **he, my Son, will reprove the assembled nation for their ungodliness**, . . . and will reproach them to their face with their evil thoughts and with the torments with which they are to be tortured. (selections from 13:25–26, 29, 32, 35–38; emphasis mine)[38]

Although similar to the son of man in Daniel 7:13–14, there are at least two differences. First, in Daniel the son of man has a royal role as ruler over God's eschatological kingdom. There is no link to David or indication that he is a messiah figure. Yet in *4 Ezra* the primary role of the son of man is a military one, which parallels the profile of the Messiah in *4 Ezra* 12. Thus it seems "son of man" and "my son the Messiah" are one and the same person, who is a royal warrior as an heir apparent of David. The second difference is that in Daniel the son of man seems to be a heavenly figure, while in *4 Ezra* he is clearly human. Thus, 4 Ezra's reflections are obviously different from *1 Enoch* 37–71.

In summary then, *4 Ezra* profiles the son, God's Messiah, son of man, to be a person from David's family who will come at the end of days as a royal warrior. He will set things right in Israel. He will defeat the Romans, rule over a remnant of Israel, rule over an earthly kingdom for four hundred years, and eventually rule God's eschatological kingdom.

---

38. The translation is by Metzger, "The Fourth Book of Ezra," 1:552.

Summation

The title son with its numerous variations were found in four Dead Sea Scrolls (1Q28a, 4Q174, 4Q246, 4Q369) and three (four if we include *2 Bar.*) other texts (*Pss. Sol., 1 En., 4 Ezra*). The isolated snippets from these texts served to broaden our perspective about second temple Jewish expectations about the Messiah. These passages about a son continue to reveal him to be a descendant of David (1Q28a, 4Q174, 4Q246, *Pss. Sol., 4 Ezra*) who will appear in the last days (1Q28a, 4Q174, *4 Ezra*) as a victorious royal warrior (1Q28a, 4Q174, 4Q246, *Pss. Sol., 4 Ezra*). Unlike 4Q174 and 4Q369, however, *4 Ezra* presents this Davidic descendant dying without heirs. He is the last of David's family to rule before God's final judgment. Nevertheless, they all present him as a ruler over a future Israel, and most present him as having a special or unique relationship with God, the Most High (1Q28a, 4Q174, 4Q246, 4Q369). The following chart serves as an overall summary of the elements attributed to this figure across this literature.

PORTRAYALS OF THE SON	
OT Sources	Primary References: 2 Samuel 7 Psalm 2 Psalm 89 Daniel 7 Secondary References: 1 Chronicles 17 Jeremiah 33
Dead Sea Scrolls	4Q174 3:1–11 4Q246 2:1–9 1Q28a 2:11–15 4Q369 2:6–12
Pseudepigrapha Reference	*Psalms of Solomon* 17:21–33 *1 Enoch* 71 *4 Ezra* 7:28–29; 11:32, 37, 52; 14:9
Various Elements	The son is a Davidic scion The son is a human personality The son is a victorious military leader The son is a ruler, a sovereign The son is righteous The son is a heavenly figure who looks like a man

Various Functions	The son ushers in a new time period The son reestablishes David's dynastic rule The son rules Gentile nations The son rules with priestly assistance The son leads military campaigns The son delivers Israel from the Romans The son condemns and kills wicked leaders The son has offspring that succeed him The son is an interpreter of the Law The son judges people and angels in the future

Dating of Manuscripts	Late Hasmonean: 75–50 BCE
	   Psalms of Solomon
	
	Pre-Herodian 50–30 BCE
	   4Q246 (4QpsDan ar = *4QAramaic Apocalypse*)
	
	Early Herodian 30–1 bce
	   4Q174 (4QFlor = *4QFlorilegium*)
	   1 Enoch 71 (perhaps best placed here)
	
	Late Herodian 30–68 CE
	   4Q369 (4QPEnosh = *4QPrayer of Enosh*)
	
	Post Herodian 68–90 CE
	   4 Ezra (*2 Baruch*)
	
	Political Situation: Transition from Hasmonean Rule
	Herod (37–4 BCE)
	Herod's Heirs (4 BCE– CE)
	Herod's Grand/Great sons (30–68 CE)

CONCLUSION

The apostle Paul writes, "When the appropriate time had come, God sent out his Son, born of a woman, born under the law, to redeem those who were under the law, so that we may be adopted as sons with full rights" (Gal. 4:4). Speaking historically, that appropriate time was during the end of king Herod's reign. At nearly seventy years of age, Herod was severely sick and ready to die. Many in Jewish leadership, because of their increasing dissatisfaction with Herod's socio-political agendas, longed for the eschatological Messiah.

As we conclude "Expectations of Israel's King," hopefully our historical overview has shown clearly that God sent Jesus into a historical period of time when attitudes about the restoration of David's dynasty were diverse. Some people had forgotten God's promise and their beliefs about any restoration were in a state of dormancy, a dormancy that was initially induced when Persia controlled Judea, yet later sanctioned by the Jewish leadership during the early years of Grecian domination. Others, however, were indifferent to the promise. After five hundred years of non-Davidic rule, authors like Ben Sira and Josephus revealed their disbelief in the promise of a forthcoming

Davidic scion. David's dynasty was a past historical event with no future. Still others were zealous for a restoration not only of David's dynasty but also the kingdom of Israel. Their discontent with the socio-political situations in Israel sparked and inflamed their hearts for a mighty Davidite to come and set things right. Thus when Jesus was born in that little town of Bethlehem, a variety of attitudes about the restoration of David's dynasty existed among the Jews of Judea.

We focused attention on texts written by people who believed in the restoration of David's dynasty. The authors referred to this expected Davidite in one of four ways: Messiah, branch, prince, and son and their variations.

VARIOUS REGAL KING REFERENCES

	Messiah, Anointed, Anointed One	Branch, Shoot, Root	Prince, Chief, Leader	Son, Son of God, Firstborn, Son of Man
Old Testament Sources	1 Samuel 1 Kings 1 Chronicles Psalms Zechariah	Isaiah Jeremiah Zechariah	Ezekiel	2 Samuel 7 Psalm 2 Psalm 89 Daniel 7
Dead Sea Scrolls	CD 1Q28 1Q28a 4Q252 4Q266 4Q382 4Q458 4Q521	4Q161 4Q174 4Q252 4Q285	CD 1Q28b 1QM 4Q161 4Q266 4Q285 4Q376 4Q423 4Q496	1Q28a 4Q174 4Q246 4Q369
Pseudepigrapha Sources	*Psalms of Solomon*	*Testament of the Twelve Patriarchs: T.Judah*	*Jubilees*	*Psalms of Solomon 1 Enoch 4 Ezra*

Unfortunately, the extra-biblical literature on the subject was limited because it was only after disconcerting socio-political situations of the Hasmoneans that people renewed any hope in God's restoration of David's dynasty. This hope resonates clearly in six Dead Sea Scrolls (1Q28, 1Q28a, 1Q28b, 4Q175, 4Q266, 4Q521) composed while the dynastic family of non-Davidic royal priests, the Hasmoneans, was in power (125–75 BCE). Jewish hope escalates in seven other texts (4Q161, 4Q382, 4Q458, *Pss. Sol.*, 1QM, 4Q246, 4Q376) composed when Rome was intruding in Jewish affairs (75–30 BCE), and continues in four other texts (4Q174, 4Q252, 4Q285, *1 En.*) composed during Herod's rule over Judea (30–1 BCE). Thus most of our extra-biblical material that anticipated a regal Messiah figure was written within a period of 125 years (125 BCE and 1 BCE). These are highlighted in the shaded portion of the two charts below.

Furthermore, through the snippets of the texts examined we discovered that the multiple uses of Messiah in the First Testament were mirrored in extra-biblical material. For instance, in isolating the "Messiah" epithet, second temple literature spoke clearly of at least four messianic figures: Messiah prophet, Messiah priest, Messiah king, and heavenly Messiah. Thus a range of competing messianic figures emerged. Nevertheless we focused on an expected royal Messiah. Typically, the individual portraits painted often shared several features: his humanity (lineage), his authority (leadership), and his relationship with God (chosen).

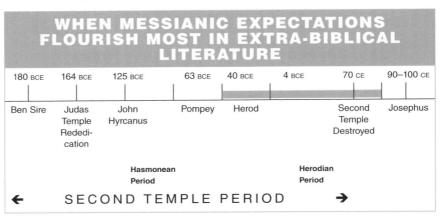

Despite the seemingly nice package presented above, it was also clear that at least one text presents the Messiah as an eschatological heavenly figure who is human-like with characteristics of an angelic being, and who is given divine authority to judge (*1 En.*; cp. 11QMelch). Thus some of the messianic portraits are consistent, some contradictory, some ambiguous, and at least one totally different.

Parallel Portrait Elements
There are at least three features painted consistently in second temple literature about the regal eschatological Messiah. First, he is most often human. Excluding 4Q382, 4Q423, and 4Q496 because of interpretive uncertainties, fifteen texts anticipate a human personality, four of which expected the royal Messiah to have offspring. Only *1 Enoch* presents us with a heavenly figure (perhaps 11QMelch is another).

Second, most portraits present the Messiah as a descendant of David, a Davidic scion. A variety of avenues were employed to make this connection.

Sometimes it was by direct citations from Hebrew Scriptures (Gen. 49; 2 Sam. 7; Pss. 2, 89; Isa. 11; Jer. 33; Zech. 6; Ezek. 37, 45). Other times there were conceptual links to Davidic symbols (star of Jacob, scepter of Judah) or appellations (Jesse's stock, son of Jacob). Yet the Messiah's place of birth is never mentioned. Rather, the snippets we studied revealed a synonymous interchange of epithets, as the chart below shows. People clearly anticipated a regal figure from David's family and referred to him with interchangeable epithets.

The final common and unwavering element in most of these portraits is that the Messiah would be a royal warrior, a military leader. Banners serve as visual signs announcing his leadership. There is nothing secret about his arrival. Thus we can say with some degree of certainty that people who anticipated a regal Messiah expected him to be a sort of take-charge military

		Hasmonean Period				Herodian Period			
		Early 150–125 BCE	Mid 125–75 BCE	Late 75–50 BCE	Pre 50–30 BCE	Early 30–1 BCE	Mid 1–30 CE	Late 30–68 CE	Post 68–135 CE
HUMANITY (lineage)	Davidic Scion	Jubilees, TJudah	1Q28, 1Q28a, 4Q266=CD	4Q161, Pss Sol	1QM, 4Q246, 4Q376	4Q174, 4Q252, 4Q285		4Q369	4 Ezra, 2 Baruch
	Human	Jubilees, TJudah	1Q28, 1Q28a, 1Q28b, 4Q266=CD, 4Q521	4Q161, 4Q382 (UK), 4Q458, Pss Sol	1QM, 4Q246, 4Q376	4Q174, 4Q252, 4Q285		4Q369, 4Q423 (UK)	4 Ezra, 2 Baruch
	Offspring			Pss Sol		4Q174, 4Q252		4Q369	
AUTHORITY (Leadership)	Military Leader	Jubilees, TJudah	1Q28a, 1Q28b, 4Q266=CD	4Q161, 4Q382, 4Q458, Pss Sol	1QM, 4Q246, 4Q376	4Q174, 4Q285			4 Ezra, 2 Baruch
	Political Leader	Jubilees, TJudah	4Q266=CD, 4Q521	4Q161, 4Q382 (UK), Pss Sol	4Q246	4Q174		4Q369, 4Q423	4 Ezra, 2 Baruch
	Righteous Leader/Judge	Jubilees, TJudah	1Q28, 1Q28b, 4Q266=CD	4Q161, 4Q458, Pss Sol		4Q252, 4Q285, 1 Enoch		4Q369, 4Q423	4 Ezra, 2 Baruch
	Endowed with God's Spirit	TJudah	1Q28b	4Q161		4Q174			
RELATIONSHIP WITH GOD (Chosen)	Unique Relationship with God		1Q28a	Pss. Sol.	4Q246	4Q174		4Q369	
	Interpreter of the Law	Jubilees, TJudah	4Q266=CD			4Q252			4 Ezra, 2 Baruch

man who would be extremely successful in ridding Israel of her enemies. He is, in fact, a victorious royal warrior in all his military pursuits, particularly as they concern the thwarting of Rome and restoring David's dynasty and the kingdom of Israel (cp. 1QM, *Pss. Sol.*).

Certainly these elements are found in the First Testament, particularly as they appear to be foundational of both the branch and prince mentioned in Isaiah, Jeremiah, and Ezekiel. Yet equally grounded in Should this be capitalized?scripture is one debated and contradictory element.

EPITHETS FOR THE EXPECTED REGAL KING

Epithet	Messiah	Branch	Prince	Son
Messiah	CD 1Q28 1Q28a 4Q252 4Q266 4Q382 4Q458 4Q521 *Pss. Sol.*	4Q252	CD 1Q28 1Q28b 4Q266	4Q174 *Pss. Sol.* *4 Ezra*
Branch	4Q252	4Q161 4Q174 4Q252 4Q285 *TJud*	4Q161 4Q285	4Q174
Prince	CD 1Q28 1Q28b 4Q266	4Q161 4Q285	CD 1Q28b 1QM 4Q161 4Q266 4Q285 4Q376 4Q423 4Q496 *Jubilees*	4Q369
Son	4Q174 *Pss. Sol.* *4 Ezra*	4Q174	4Q369	4Q174 4Q246 1Q28a 4Q369 *Pss. Sol.* *4 Ezra*

A Debated Element: The Structure of Final Leadership

The foremost contradiction is between the anticipation of a political and religious diarchy as opposed to a Davidic monarchy. Six documents endorse a diarchy (CD, 1Q28, 1Q28a, 4Q174, 4Q266, *T. Jud.*). Seemingly the vague allusion to the crowning of the high priest and future branch of David in Zechariah supports the idea of a diarchy. Furthermore, the historical reality of the high priest ruling over the second temple for some five hundred years would suggest God's endorsement of a royal high priest. Yet it seems three texts anticipate a Davidic monarchy (4Q246, 4Q252, *Pss. Sol.*, perhaps 4Q521). Naturally these texts are non-sectarian, though two were found among the Dead Sea Scrolls. Certainly Jeremiah and Isaiah support the reestablishment of the monarchy. Yet it is difficult to determine how extensively the belief in a diarchy was during the time of Jesus. Nevertheless, discontent over the Levitical dynasty of the Hasmoneans sparked and inflamed a desire for a return to some sort of diarchy.

Some Inconsistent Features

There are at least three ambiguities surrounding this eschatological Messiah figure. First and foremost concerns his coming. Although people anticipated a royal warrior from David's family, no one knows the time of his coming. The literature speaks mystically of his coming during "the last days" (CD, 1Q28, 4Q161, 4Q266, *4 Ezra*). It is clear that whenever he comes he will be very visible when he ushers in a new time period. Yet when will that period begin? When God? When will you send him? When will this new era begin? These questions are never answered.

Second and equally mystical is the name of this person. Although people anticipate a son of David, the diverse epithets keep the reader guessing. The quest to know the identity of the branch, the prince, the Messiah, or the son remained unanswered. Though it seems his name would be eventually plastered on shields and banners (1QM, cp. 4Q496), the use of cryptic epithets keep people wondering.

Third, the functions of this royal warring Messiah appear obscured by his diarchic relationship with the royal priest. Earlier works (CD, 1Q28, and 4Q266) present a co-leadership between a Messiah king and Messiah priest. They share in the leadership and judgment of the disobedient and apostates from the community. They also join together in atoning for sins in ways familiar to the Law. Later texts present the prospective Davidic Messiah to be a warrior who is guided by a royal priest (4Q376). He judges and rules under the advisement of Zadokite priests. In fact, the religious Messiah appears superior to the political Messiah (1Q28a, *T. Jud.*). Yet *1 Enoch* presents him reigning and judging at the right hand of God. Finally, he is portrayed as an interpreter of the law and yet an interpreter of the law emerges alongside the royal Davidite (4Q174). Perhaps the regal Messiah will function apart from the Levitical priesthood. How will the relationship between a Messiah king and a Messiah priest work? The uncertainties and ambiguities in these portrayals exist because the Hebrew Scriptures lacked an explicit, fully-disclosed, monolithic "messianic concept." Many questions about the Messiah remained a mystery throughout the second temple period.

Furthermore, there are several puzzle pieces about Messiah that remain missing. Although most of the portraits point to a powerful and victorious messianic figure, missing is a Messiah who silences people from announcing his coming. Missing is the concept of a suffering Messiah. Missing is a Messiah whose kingdom and rule extends over the seen and unseen of all creation. Missing is a resurrected Messiah who returns to consummate an already inaugurated kingdom. Missing is a Messiah miraculously born of a virgin in Bethlehem. Missing is a Messiah who is a divine Davidic regal priest. Yet with the coming of the historical Jesus, God turns over several significant pieces of his messianic puzzle, puzzle pieces that people were unable to see let alone link together based upon their own preconceived understanding of the Hebrew Scriptures. Having set the conceptual and theological atmosphere surrounding the eschatological Messiah into which Jesus was born, we are now ready to address "The Coming of Israel's King" and the unifying of this portrait into a cohesive whole through the revelation that came in Jesus.

CHAPTER TWELVE

MESSIAH CONFESSED: REVELATION AND THE CATHOLIC EPISTLES

As we begin part three, the political influences of the Assyrians, Babylonians, Persians, and Grecian Empires no longer factor as Israel's enemies. Rome now dominates the world scene. Caesar Augustus has established peace and significant stability in the region that affects the Mediterranean world for years to come. It is at this time that a major transition in redemption history is about to occur. The age of promise and expectation has passed and the age of fulfillment is before us as we examine the Second Testament and address the coming of Israel's King.

It might seem odd, but the issue of Jesus as the Messiah in the Second Testament has been controversial, at least as far as tracing the root of the idea back to Jesus himself goes. The goal of these chapters is to trace the theme of Jesus the Messiah in the Second Testament as well as connect that hope to the studies emerging from the Hebrew Scriptures and second temple Jewish texts. There is no doubt that Second Testament texts confessed Jesus as the Messiah or Christ; that is, the promised, sent, and anointed one of God, plays a major role in Second Testament texts. The term "Christ" functions as a constant designation for Jesus, almost like a family name, whether it still retains its titular force or not.[1]

---

1. For the argument against Christ being merely a "name" for Jesus without titular force, see Craig Blomberg, "Messiah in the New Testament," in *Israel's Messiah in the Bible and the Dead Sea Scrolls* (ed. Richard S. Hess and M. Daniel Carroll R.; Grand Rapids: Baker Academic, 2003), 111–50. William Klein responds in the same pages, arguing that some uses are merely the use of a name with no titular force. This is a debate we shall not enter into in this essay. Suffice it to say that a substantial number of the uses, as we shall see, go beyond the mere use of a name. Blomberg's essay is a good reminder that there is content in most of the New Testament uses of the term. As we shall see, the term "Christ" is more than a label or title. The Christ does things.

HISTORICAL EVENTS OF THE SECOND TESTAMENT

First Emperors of the Roman Empire[1]	Jewish Rulers and Major Conflicts with Rome	Transition in Redemption History The Age of Fulfillment
Julio-Claudian Dynasty	Herodian Dynasty	Davidic Dynasty Restored (already \ not yet)
Augustus (31 BCE–4 CE)	Herod the Great (40–4 BCE)	Jesus' Birth (late 5 \ early 4 BCE)
	Archelaus: Judea (4 BCE–6 CE)	
Tiberius (14–37)	Philip: Northeast Galilee (4 BCE–37 CE)	Jesus' Death & Resurrection (33 CE)[2]
Caligula (37–41)	Antipas: Galilee & Perea (4 BCE–39 CE)	**Second Testament Testimonies**[3]
Claudius (41–54)	Agrippa I (37–44)	James & Galatians (mid–late 40s)
		1 & 2 Thessalonians (early 50s)
Nero (54–68)	Agrippa II (50–92??)	1 & 2 Corinthians, Romans (mid–late 50s)
		Colossians, Philemon, Ephesians, Philippians (early 60s)
		Mark, Matthew, Luke-Acts (late 50s –late 60s)
Roman Civil War (68–69)	**Jewish Wars against Rome (66–73)**	1 & 2 Timothy, Titus, Hebrews, 1 Peter, 2 Peter, Jude (mid –late 60s)
Flavian Dynasty		
Vespasian (69–79)		
Titus (79–81)		
Domitian (81–96)		John, Johannine Letters, Revelation (mid 80s–mid 90s)

Regardless, it is clear from the 529 or so uses of the term "Christ" in the Second Testament that the term is an important one for the Second Testament.[3] It is one of the most basic ways to refer to Jesus. An overview of statistics helps us

---

2. For dating of the birth and death of Jesus, see Harold Hoehner, *Chronological Aspects of the Life of Christ* (Grand Rapids: Zondervan, 1977); Ben Witherington III, "The Birth of Jesus" in *Dictionary of Jesus and the Gospels* (ed. J. B. Green and S. McKnight; Downers Grove: InterVarsity, 1997), 60–74.

3. The exact number of uses depends on how one sees certain text critical problems. A search of the Second Testament by Accordance using the Nestle-Aland 27th edition of the Greek

to appreciate just how pervasive the term is in the Second Testament. From Accordance search we see the following distribution of uses of *Christos*:

USES OF *CHRISTOS* IN THE SECOND TESTAMENT					
Gospels and Acts		**Pauline Epistles**		**General Epistles**	
Matthew	16	Romans	65	Hebrews	12
Mark	7	1 Corinthians	64	James	2
Luke	12	2 Corinthians	47	1 Peter	22
John	19	Galatians	38	2 Peter	8
Acts	25	Ephesians	46	1 John	8
		Philippians	37	2 John 3	3
		Colossians	25	3 John	0
		1 Thessalonians	10	Jude	6
		2 Thessalonians	10	Revelation	7
		1 Timothy	15		
		2 Timothy	13		
		Titus	4		
		Philemon	8		

It is significant that fully 382 of the 529 uses are from the Pauline Epistles. This represents 72.2 percent of the total uses of this term. The only book not to use the term is 3 John. Add to this the uses by all the Epistles and apocalyptic literature and the total is 438 of the 529 uses or 82.8 percent. Considering this is about 40 percent of the Second Testament, the use of the term "Christ" is far more prevalent in the non-narrative sections of the Second Testament, even though it is prevalent in all its parts. This is a good reason to work backwards, namely to start with Messiah confessed in the Epistles and Revelation and move to the Gospels. There are other important reasons for working backwards.

1. It allows us to work from the least controversial texts to the more controversial texts. This means we make fewer assumptions as we proceed.

2. It allows us to work backwards to sort out the roots of the potential source of such usage.

New Testament yields 529 uses. Blomberg uses the number 531. Depending on how one resolves text critical issues in certain texts, the number of uses will be in this range.

3. While the non-Gospels are explicit about the messianic connection and show no hesitation to use the title openly, the Gospels reflect for the most part a more implicit usage. Why this is needs careful development and having seen how forthright the non-Gospels are helps us to really appreciate the difference in the Gospels' presentation once we get there.

4. The ethical and associative thrust that is developed by the epistolary texts brings a fresh emphasis to the use of the title. Seeing this emphasis as we start our comparison juxtaposes it to the Hebrew Scripture and second temple texts we have already surveyed, making the contrast starker.

5. It allows us to end with one of the most important issues, whether Jesus' teaching led into the early church confession of Jesus as the Christ. So we end with a look at the case for the historical authenticity of these texts as central to the ultimate confession we see so explicitly elsewhere.

These number of uses of the term "Christ" (Greek term for Messiah) raise the question of the relationship of this hope to the variety of expressions that accompanied either the Messiah or the age of the eschaton of deliverance for which Judaism longed. What our survey shall show is a synthesis and linking together of ideas that often were treated more distinctly or separately in the Jewish texts we have already surveyed in either the Hebrew Scripture or second temple period. This synthesis allowed Christians to claim that an era of fulfillment had been reached and unify the biblical portrait of promise. This synthesis permitted many fresh ideas to be connected to the setting forth of the Messiah, as the term has become a magnet for all types of eschatological ideas in the new Jesus community. It is as if the hope of traditional texts has worked as a collection point to which many additional and related ideas have become attached. In other words, as God's messianic puzzle was gradually coming into focus, pieces that seemed unrelated are now being reconsidered and connected to God's messianic portrait of promise. Perhaps another way of saying it is that some texts became pillars or beams off of which other ideas could build. The result is a scope of description for Messiah that far expands what was said in the distinct categories of the earlier usage of these texts. This synthesis is more like a grand fusion of ideas, some previously attached to Christ, others to the eschaton in general, and others growing out of the fresh associations the revelatory events in Jesus also produced. The completely fresh combination in this grand fusion are: the theme of messianic suffering (Isa. 53; Ps. 118), the splitting of the messianic package into two comings because suffering precedes glory (Dan. 7:13–14, Ps. 110:1), and the appeal to a priesthood according to the order of Melchizedek where a king-priest becomes the emphasis in contrast to the Dead Sea Scroll's diarchy (Pss. 2:7, 110:4). The description of the Christ in the Second Testament becomes an overwhelming deluge of associations and ideas because this title has become a core title around which Jesus is affirmed. In fact, in many texts this connection is simply assumed and not argued for at all. This is why many of the texts about the Christ we examine do not appeal to earlier texts but merely develop the portrait of Jesus as Christ. Many ideas connect to passages from the Hebrew Scripture and/or its second temple reflection, but are not really explained in terms of those connections. Often it is the mere presence of eschatological realization that makes the association. Many other ideas, which we also want to trace, grow out of the experience with Jesus the Messiah himself. In this latter sense, Jesus is the Word John's Gospel preached.

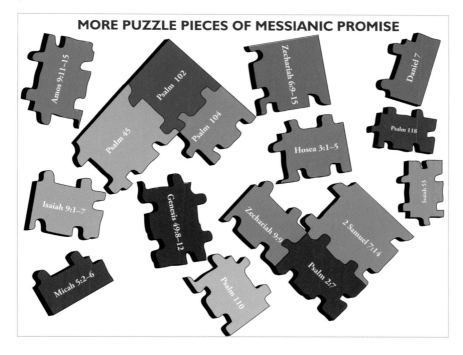

MORE PUZZLE PIECES OF MESSIANIC PROMISE

The goal of Part 3, "The Coming of Israel's King," is threefold: (1) to trace the usage of *Christ* in the Second Testament, (2) to see if a case can be made for the roots of this usage in Jesus himself (christological fulfillment), and (3) to point out in a few key places how explicit texts from the earlier Testament are used messianically. Again, unlike the historical and literary sequence followed in previous chapters, we work backwards, in a sense from the evidence of the Epistles and Revelation to that of the Gospels and the ministry of Jesus.

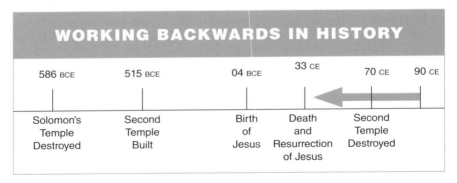

We do this because the least controversial points come in the epistolary and apocalyptic material; for here we get the direct testimony of the authors of those works as to what they believed. In the Gospels the evangelists mediate the portrayal of the story of Jesus so that getting to his view has been a matter of much more debate and discussion. By working backwards, we go from ideas that have a larger consensus back to those that are more disputed. So Part 3 of our book divides in four parts: (1) Messiah Confessed: Revelation and the Catholic Epistles, (2) Messiah Confessed: Pauline Epistles, (3) Messiah Preached: Acts, and (4) Messiah Veiled and Presented: Gospels and Historical Jesus Questions. It seems appropriate to begin with the earliest confessions of Jesus that are found in non-Pauline writings.

MESSIAH CONFESSED: REVELATION AND THE CATHOLIC EPISTLES

As we begin our look at the coming of Israel's king in Revelation and the Catholic Epistles, it is significant that the title "messiah" comes from a Jewish context, as the other essays in this volume so visibly demonstrate. By the time we get to the Catholic Epistles and Revelation, the outlines of what Christ meant for Christians by the end of the first century have become clear, as its "confessional" use illustrates. These Epistles and Revelation date from the mid-forties to the nineties. In saying this, we take an early date for James. If James is later, as some place him, then the span of these books is the sixties to the nineties. By the time of the later Catholic Epistles and Revelation in the nineties, the general lines of emphasis about the Christ are well established as we will show by working through every use of the term "Christ" in Revelation and in the Catholic Epistles. We shall also see that certain themes are shared between books and authors. Again we work mostly backwards with this material.

Revelation

The book of Revelation is considered by many to have been written during the time of Domitian, the last of the Flavian emperors of Rome. It is an apocalyptic text. This means that it uses the symbolism of dualism (good versus evil) and a behind-the-scenes perspective revealing a heavenly, transcendent point of view about what is to come. This dualism is the dominant imagery and is a part of apocalyptic where the heavenly perspective of good and evil interact in battle. To say the text uses imagery does not mean the book is non-referential. The symbols portray and describe spiritual realities as well as what is to come. Jesus' appearances and the various visions open up this heavenly perspective, working as commentary on what God is doing.

Confession of "Christ" in Revelation

Revelation is a book that presents Jesus as the exalted Christ, the heavenly king, who rules over God's kingdom as a result of his sacrifice. When we turn our attention to John's apocalyptic portrayal of Jesus, we see that John uses the term "Christ" in clusters at the start and finish of the book. Of the seven uses, three come in the first five verses and two come in Revelation 20. In Revelation 1:1, 2, and 5, it is Jesus Christ who is the source of John's revelatory experience. This Jesus is portrayed as an exalted heavenly figure who sits with God in heaven (Rev. 4–5). The Christ sits over an eternal kingdom (Rev. 11:15). That kingdom operates with authority that comes from the Christ (Rev. 12:10). One day, the saints shall rule with Christ for a thousand years as priests of God and Christ who have avoided the second death (Rev. 20:4, 6). Clearly in the apocalypse, this title is a regal one that also has exalted heavenly overtones. Jesus is a transcendent king, not merely an earthy one.

Two sets of these texts are very revealing: Revelation 1:5–8 and the heavenly scene of Revelation 4–5. The introduction of Jesus in Revelation 1:5 places the title in a context where Jesus is declared also to be "Ruler over

> **Domitian: The Last of the Flavian Emperors**
>
> Domitian was the second son of Vespasian, the founder of the Flavian dynasty after Nero's downfall and suicide (June 68). **Vespasian's** reign lasted nearly ten years (July 69–June 79). His first son **Titus** succeeded him in June 79, but the premature and sudden death of Titus in September 81 escalated **Domitian** to power. He was an autocrat unlike both his father and brother. Domitian was hostile to Christians and persecuted them (Eusebius, *Hist. Eccl.* 3.18.4). To the delight of the Senate, a number of his personal staff stabbed him to death on September 18, 96. It was during the periods of Vespasian, Titus, and Domitian that **Josephus** wrote and even established a personal residence within the emperor's house.

the kings of the earth." In addition, it is Jesus who brings people into the kingdom, exerting an authority from heaven in light of his work that elevates his delivered children into membership in the heavenly rule (vv. 5–6). This probably allows Jesus to be called the Alpha and the Omega, the Almighty (v. 8). It is this position that allows Jesus to write to the individual churches in Revelation 1–3. He writes to them as their exalted ruler. In the context (v. 7) are cited three texts from the Hebrew Scripture, Daniel 7:13, Zechariah 12:10, and a variation on the wording of Genesis 12:3. Each of these texts are important as eschatological texts. Daniel 7 is tied to the title Son of Man, Jesus' favorite self-designation and the one he used to refer to his own eschatological activity. Zechariah 12 also looks to an eschatological figure who has been rejected. Genesis 12 is part of the Abrahamic promise but here rather than blessing there is accountability for how Jesus was treated. Here the rejection puzzle piece affects the reading. That rejection image is seen in the fact Jesus is seen as a lamb in Revelation 4–5. Normally lambs do not sit on thrones, nor is a lamb seen as powerful. The image points to his sacrifice as one rejected, but his presence on a throne points to his power and capability that came as God vindicated him. In the end, Jesus is rejected by many but vindicated by God so his authority to rule is shown to come from God's work on his behalf. Revelation 4–5 will develop this idea. These texts are read prophetically in Revelation 1 as fitting into the decisive eschatological period. This is what permits them to be seen as messianic in their application to Jesus. Association with the eschaton, which belonged to the original context in the Hebrew Scripture, is the hermeneutical key to their prophetic use here.

In the heavenly scene in Revelation 4–5, Jesus serves and rules as a lamb worthy to open the book that reveals what is ahead. He sits on a heavenly throne as the conquering Lion of the tribe of Judah, the root of Jesse that has brought victory (Rev. 5:5). The Davidic link is a messianic association that recalls the entire development of the promise from the First Testament through the second temple period. The Judah link reaches back to themes introduced in Genesis 49, while the Davidic hope grows out of the promise of a Davidic line in 2 Samuel 7 and expressed in graphic fullness in non-biblical texts like *Psalms of Solomon* 17–18. What was expressed in First Testament and second temple texts in mostly earthly terms now has a heavenly aura about it in Revelation. It is the Davidic link that allows Revelation 4–5 to be included as a messianic text, even though the term "Christ" does not appear in this scene. This observation serves as a reminder that sometimes we can have a concept without having a particular term present. That this connection should be made is what Revelation 11:15 and 12:10 indicate, where the term does appear with Jesus in this heavenly role. The picture of the Lion who is the Lamb adds one more central idea to the image—exaltation has come as a result of sacrifice (Rev. 5:9). It is the Lamb's blood that has purchased this new status for God's children from every nation, making them priests and members of the kingdom. This repeats what we saw in terms of the associations in Revelation 1, suffering precedes exaltation in the portrait.

Christological Fulfillment in Revelation

How does this portrait fit with the variety of earlier or extant Jewish expectations? The transcendent and authoritative nature of the victorious figure is similar to what we see in a variety of Jewish texts: Daniel 7, *1 Enoch* 37–71 with its portrait of the Son of Man, as well as *4 Ezra*.[4] Yet there are also key differences. With Daniel 7, there is a tension between the individual and the corporate image, since in 7:27 the Son of Man is associated with God's people as a whole. I would want to argue that this corporate conclusion in Daniel 7 does not exclude an individual dimension to this authority, since what comes is the kingdom of God replacing flawed earthly dynasties. Nevertheless, the exclusive individual emphasis draws on one side of the Danielic picture. With *1 Enoch*, the Son of Man figure is identified as Enoch in chapters 70–71. So here we do have an individual portrait, but one that points to an ancient luminary. The tension between the identification of Enoch and the idea of pre-existence in *1 Enoch* 46 has always been a problem in the reading of *1 Enoch*. A completely transcendent figure that is Alpha and Omega in Revelation gives a fresh take on how this combination can work. Transcendence is again the difference from *4 Ezra*. The messianic figure who is a militaristic Son of Man reflects a human figure in *4 Ezra*. This stands in contrast to Revelation, with an exalted figure who has heavenly traits as well as human ones and who has both suffered and wielded power. Jesus in Revelation is a powerful figure who brings victory on earth, but the shadow of his suffering is something *4 Ezra* does not appeal to in his portrait. In sum, it is the fusion of images and the unique exaltation of Jesus that makes the messianic picture of him different from other Jewish eschatological claims.

In conclusion, the confession of Jesus as the Christ in this last book of the Second Testament reflects a high view of Jesus who rules over the kingdom of God with shared authority from the Father. In Revelation Messiah is regal and heavenly in thrust, reflecting the impact of a Jesus raised to the throne room of God. However, this exaltation is not disinterested in Jesus' earthly work. In fact, this position is made possible because of what the Lamb Christ did in giving himself so that others might be brought to God. The triumph of the Christ in Revelation is both the result of the exalting work of God and the sacrifice of the Lion-Lamb.

---

4. For Johnston's discussion on Daniel 7, see chapter 6 (pp. 182–87). For Bateman's discussion on *1 Enoch* and *4 Ezra*, see chapter 11 (pp. 304–12).

Catholic Epistles

Typically, eight books make up the Catholic or General Epistles: Hebrews, James, 1 Peter, 2 Peter, 1 John, 2 John, 3 John, and Jude. Although these works make up less than 10 percent of the Second Testament, their unique perspectives about early church issues, like the presentations of Jesus as the Messiah with specific appeals to a series of texts from promises of the former era (Heb. 1:1–2), make valuable contributions to our awareness of the early church. The book of Hebrews makes distinct contributions because of its highly developed theological and christological commentary based on earlier texts. The other books also have much to offer by showing that merely using the name of Jesus does not express a true embrace of him. The Johannine texts are important here. And while they are not uniform in their manner of presenting this material, these letters have much to offer us in terms of understanding the portrait of Jesus as the Christ.[5]

Johannine Epistles

Confession of "Christ" in Johannine Epistles. Three letters make up the Johannine Epistles. It is clear from 1, 2, and 3 John that Jesus is confessed as the truly human Christ whose teachings are to be heeded. The third epistle addresses the obligation of the church to support God's servants teaching and preaching the gospel (3 John 8). The first and second epistle address important christological themes. What are people to believe about Jesus? What teachings about Jesus should be embraced? Who is it that actually has a relationship with God? How does one determine whether a person is "in" or "out" of the community? How does one "remain" in a right relationship with God? All three letters were probably written toward the end of the first century when Domitian was emperor of Rome. At the center of all these questions is the person of Jesus and the author's use of the term "Christ."

The three uses of 2 John point to a Jesus who teaches and is confessed. Verse 7 speaks of false teachers who do not confess Jesus *as* the Christ coming in the flesh while verse 9 notes that those who do not remain in the teaching about Jesus do not have God. It is Jesus as the promised anointed one who is highlighted here. He is seen as a ruler who also teaches and is to be obeyed. Verse 3 has the term in a greeting of blessing, as the request is that grace, mercy, and peace come to believers from God and from Jesus, the Christ, the Son of the Father. For John, Jesus as the Christ is a source of teaching and blessing, sharing authority from the Father and calling his people to faithfulness and obedience.

---

5. For a presentation where the theme of promise is fulfilled in Jesus as Christ in the Catholic Epistles see Herbert W. Bateman IV, "Theology of the General Letters" in *Interpreting the General Letters*, Kregel Exegetical Handbook Series (Grand Rapids: Kregel, forthcoming).

Perhaps the idea of a Messiah who purges and makes his people holy, a key theme of the second temple period is at play here, because the Johannine letters focus on an authentic righteousness that comes from those truly associated with Jesus, the Messiah. However, there is no explicit citation of texts in this short letter.

Similar in thrust is 1 John. Fellowship involves us with the Father and his Son, Jesus Christ (1:3). Jesus is the comforter from the Father whose work makes him our advocate when we sin (2:1–2). Such a theme parallels what we saw in Revelation 1:7 and Revelation 4–5 and the work of the Lion-Lamb. It is Jesus' work that clears the way for God's people and permits him to work on their behalf. To deny that Jesus is the Christ is to tell the lie and be the antichrist (2:22). This remark indicates how central the confession of Jesus as Messiah was for the church. By the nineties when this letter was written such a confession is regarded as a reflection of fundamental faith.

However, there is an ethical dimension to this role as well. In urging that believers follow the commandment to love, John notes that the command is to believe on the name of "His Son Jesus Christ" and love one another (3:23). The command of the Son who also is Christ has ethical implications for our relationship to other believers. Everyone who confesses that Jesus Christ has come in the flesh has come from God and reflects the presence of God's Spirit (4:2). Those who believe that Jesus is the Christ are born of God (5:1). These ideas show that people who embrace the Christ have come into a new family with those who share the new birth. This truth underscores the moral imperative to love the brother, a true spiritual family relative.

Jesus Christ has come both in terms of water and the blood, probably an allusion to his real human presence (5:6). To be in the Son (that is, to be related to Jesus) is to be in the truth. So three ideas dominate the use of the term Christ in 1 John: (1) it is tied to his Sonship to God (fully four of the eight uses in this epistle), (2) it is a term of core confession, an idea to be appreciated as a result of the work and testimony of the Spirit, and (3) the Christ shares authority from God and is to be loved and obeyed. Jesus is both fully human and yet was sent from God as Son and Christ to be "the word of life." In all of this, no Hebrew Scripture texts are cited explicitly.

Christological Fulfillment in Johannine Epistles. This portrait of Jesus, especially in his work in the context of his genuine humanity, stands in contrast to the more earthly-political-militaristic portrait of other Jewish texts. The role of Jesus is as one who clears the way for righteousness, not in a conquering victory, but through a spiritual provision and advocacy on behalf of God's people. This example also provides an ethical basis for the exhortations of the book. Where in works like *Psalms of Solomon* or *4 Ezra* the messianic figure purges by military power and judgment, here Jesus purges by provision of a way of forgiveness, exercising a different kind of power. Where vindication of the saints is stressed as the holy city is purged in these Jewish texts, John focuses on how the activity of the one who is the Christ works *for and in* those who are vindicated. Although John does not lack a sense of Jesus' authority, the scope and emphasis in this exercise of authority differs.

Jude

Confession of "Christ" in Jude. This work conceptually is a twin to 2 Peter. Written perhaps between 60–65 while Nero was emperor of Rome, it treats the threat of false teachers destined for condemnation (5–10, 14–16), false teachers who are living ungodly lives (11–13), and makes an appeal to hold fast to the faith till the end (17–23).[6] Concerning Jesus as the Christ, Jude emphasizes him to be the Lord who shares authority with God and is confessed as the mediator of salvation.

This letter has six uses of the term "Christ" in verses 1, 4, 17, 21. The first two are part of his greeting where he makes it clear that Jude is a servant of Jesus Christ writing to those who are being kept for Jesus Christ (v. 1). This idea reappears at the end of the epistle where we are said to await the mercy of our Lord Jesus Christ, an allusion to surviving judgment (v. 21). The idea of being kept fits nicely with the apocalyptic theme of the letter. The warning is about those ungodly people who deny our "only Lord and Master, Jesus Christ" (v. 4). Less significant is the use in verse 17 where it is the predictions of the apostles of the Lord Jesus Christ that Jude wants his audience to recall. The epistle ends with praise to the God, our Savior through Jesus Christ our Lord. God is praised for being able to keep us from falling and present believers blameless. Again in this letter the Christ shares authority and is a confessed mediator of salvation. Fully four of the uses in this letter come with the title Lord juxtaposed. Such linkage of titles and images, united in Jesus, is part of how the church describes Jesus' comprehensive fulfillment of promise.

Christological Fulfillment in Jude. There is no explicit appeal to past concepts of Messiah in terms of First Testament passages here. Rather we have a filling out of what the judgment in the end looks like. The roots of this idea are tied to ideas from apocalyptic imagery tied to Jesus as judge. The ideas do fit the portrait of authority that are tied to the deliverance that comes with the redeeming figure of the eschaton in the Jewish expectation.

---

6. For the preference of an early date over claims the letter is pseudonymous, see Wilder, Charles, and Easley, *Faithful to the End*, 211–15. Significant to me is the lack of ecclesiastical terminology that one might expect from a letter written later.

Petrine Epistles

Confession of "Christ" in 2 Peter. Like the book of Revelation, 2 Peter is apocalyptic. Perhaps written around the time of Nero, it seems to be addressed to Gentile Christians who, according to the author, "received a faith as precious as ours" (1:1), where "ours" may speak specifically of Gentile Christians. Whoever the recipients are, it is an epistle of warning (3:17–18) clearly driven by concerns about spiritual growth (1:3–21), false teaching (2:1–22), and the end (3:16).[7]

Like Jude, it is the Lordship of the Christ that is stressed. Fully 6 of 8 uses juxtapose Lord and Christ with the expression, "Lord Jesus Christ" (1:8, 11, 14, 16; 2:20; 3:18). The Lord Christ is known and makes known (1:8; 2:20; 3:18), has an eternal kingdom (1:11), reveals to Peter that he will die soon (1:14), and is the one who has come with power and who is not a myth (1:16).

Savior also appears with Christ four times (1:1, 11; 2:20; 3:18). So all the apocalyptic references of this section of the Second Testament highlight the authority Christ has. Peter is an apostle of Jesus Christ (1:1). In fact, in the rest of the Second Testament we never get the description "an apostle of Jesus." Where Jesus is mentioned, so is the term Christ. The point is the authority of the one commissioning. This

> **Nero, the Last of the Julio-Claudian Dynasty**
>
> Nero was an only child of the great-grand-daughter of Augustus, Julia Agrippina. Later when he married the daughter of Claudius, Octavia, these two facts helped serve to secure his succession to Claudius. Once Claudius died in October 54, the Senate was quick to confer power to Nero. Throughout his reign he struggled with dynastic rivals and popularity with people of property. The latter was accentuated 19 June 64. For nine days a fire consumed three of fourteen sections of the city of Rome. Only four were untouched by the blaze. Nero redirected blame on an unpopular group of people called Christians who had recently refused to join pagan ceremonies. They were both crucified and used as living torches to light Nero's races in the Vatican Circus (Tac *Ann*. 15:44; Suet. *Nero* 16.2). He would eventually take the life of Paul (*circa*) and Peter (*circa*).

---

7. For this dating, see Wilder, Charles, and Easley, *Faithful to the End*, 125–45. Among many New Testament scholars, this book is commonly dated later and not tied to Peter. For such a date, see Richard Bauckham, *Jude, 2 Peter*, WBC (Waco: Word, 1983), 134–35. Key to such a view is accepting pseudonymity for such works, a position more problematic than is often noted. For a rejection of the idea that the church accepted such cases of authorship, see E. E. Ellis, "Pseudonymity and Canonicity of the New Testament Documents," *Worship. Theology, and Ministry in the Early Church* (ed. W. J. Wilkins and T. Paige; JSNTSup 87; Sheffield: Sheffield Academic Press, 1992), 212–24; T. L. Wilder, "Pseudonymity and the New Testament," *Interpreting the New Testament: Essays on Method and Issues* (ed. D. A. Black and D. S. Dockery; Nashville: Broadman and Holman, 2001), 296–335.

picture of the authority of the Lord Christ is something 2 Peter shares with Jude and Revelation. This is part of what one confesses when one says the Jesus Christ is Lord. In fact, he is "our God and Savior Jesus Christ," one of the few Second Testament texts that directly asserts that Jesus is God. (1 Pet. 1:1).

Christological Fulfillment in 2 Peter. This kind of authoritative, judging, eschatological hope resonates well in the Judaism of the second temple period, but the portrait of Jesus as Messiah is more comprehensive and more transcendent in how tightly Jesus is linked to deity. Second Peter is like Jude in how it develops this messianic, eschatological and apocalyptic expectation from the base of Jewish hope.

Confession of "Christ" in 1 Peter. Written to a mixed group of Jews and Gentile Christians "scattered throughout Pontus, Galatia, Cappadocia, Asia, and Bithynia" (1:1), this epistle was probably written around 64 or 65 just before Peter was martyred at the hands of Nero.[8] The letter is an exhortation (5:12) to be steadfast in holiness (1:13–2:3), in submission (2:13–3:22), and in living for God (2:4–12; 4:1–5:11) even if in the midst of suffering. The epistle emphasizes that Jesus is the predicted model in suffering but will be coming in glory.

As evident throughout the epistle, Peter loves the term "Christ," using it twenty-two times in a brief five chapters, thirteen times simply as Christ, eight times as Jesus Christ, and once as Lord Jesus Christ. The first passage points to the honor that will come to Jesus Christ when salvation is completed at his coming (1:7), a gift of grace that comes with the revelation of Jesus Christ (1:13). On the other end of the temporal spectrum is the time when the prophets by the Spirit of Christ predicted the sufferings of the Christ (1:11). This text speaks of a prophetic link between what the prophets taught and what has taken place in Christ. This text does not mean that all these texts are exclusively or directly prophetic. They simply affirm that when one sees the portrait as a whole what one sees is what Jesus did. The prophets were looking for such a figure and comprehensive deliverance. They did not know the time or individual. How this works prophetically has to be traced because the text does not tell us that much detail as a summary text and because one has to

---

8. Some challenge Peter being the author here. For this discussion see L. Goppelt, *A Commentary on 1 Peter*, trans. John Alsup (Grand Rapids: Eerdmans, 1993), 373–78. Goppelt defends the traditional connections made here. For a contrastive view that sees a pseudonymous reference, Norbert Brox, *Der Erste Petrusbrief. Evangelisch-Katholischer Kommentar zum Neuen Testament* XXI (Zürich: Neukirchen-Vluyn, 1979), 246–48. A careful argument for Petrine authorship appears in Karen Jobes, *1 Peter,* BECNT (Grand Rapids: Baker, 2005), 5–41.

appreciate the variety of ways prophecy works in an ancient understanding, something else we have tried to trace.

The salvation Jesus brought was rooted in a ransom provided by the blood of Christ, who suffered like a lamb without blemish (1:19). Believers are living stones in a temple to God who are to offer spiritual sacrifices to God through Jesus Christ (2:5).

First Peter 2:5 introduces an important context for appeal to prophetic texts. That appeal is rooted in texts from Isaiah 28:16, Psalm 118:22 (=117:22 LXX); and Isaiah 8:14 (vv. 6–8). Psalm 118 will be an important text in Jesus' use in the Synoptic Gospels. It will be treated more fully in our discussion of Christ in the Gospels. The Psalm is used in a typological-prophetic manner, since the original Psalm is about the king, rejected by some, leading the people into worship. So Jesus fits into this portrait of one rejected whom God exalts. Once again we see texts related to suffering and rejection that come to the fore in the messianic presentation of Jesus. Isaiah 8 is used similarly. The sign child is tied to judgment associated with Assyria (Isa. 8:7). Here the prediction is even Israel will stumble over the Lord and his ways, but he will be a sanctuary to those who trust in him. Peter's use makes a christological application of all of this, moving in a typological-prophetic direction. Just as was the past experience of Israel when kings rejected God's way, so Jesus is rejected by the people but reflects the way of God. Isaiah 28 is similar to Isaiah 8. Ephraim has made a treaty Isaiah calls a covenant with Sheol (v. 15). The cornerstone God has placed in his coming actions will result in judgment for those who made this move of unfaithfulness. Peter's emphasis is not on the judgment to come, but on the vindication of the stone laid and how it benefits those who trust what God has done. This usage also is typological-prophetic. This kind of prophetic fulfillment argues that the past has a pattern of activity that events tied to Jesus replicates. This is why this type of fulfillment is called pattern fulfillment. God designs the pattern of the near event and the realization in Christ. One mirrors or patterns the other event. The prophetic element is seen in the mirror of the divine design.

Christ's suffering also leaves us with an example (2:21) to be followed (4:1). In fact, when we suffer in Christ, we should rejoice and realize that we are blessed (4:13–14) because we are called to eternal glory in Christ (5:10). Believers are called to always reverence Christ as Lord (3:15). When believers are reviled for their good behavior in Christ, those who revile are put to shame (3:16). It is as Christ that Jesus died for sins once for all (3:18). Baptism, the appeal to God for a good conscience, saves through the resurrection of Jesus Christ (3:21). Believers are to act in the use of their gifts from God in a way that God is glorified in everything through Jesus Christ (4:11). Peter himself is a witness of Christ's sufferings (5:1). Finally, Peter offers peace to all who are in Christ (5:14).

In sum, it is clear that Christ is a title for Peter that looks to his predicted suffering and glory. The model of the suffering and glorified Jesus moves from God revealing the Christ in his suffering for us to bringing us, his children, into eternal glory. The role of the Christ as a mediator also receives attention. Jesus serves as the mediator of a ransom and the one through whom blessing comes.[9]

A closer look at key texts reveals these themes. First Peter 1:10–13 shows that the predicted activity involves two key periods: the sufferings appointed for the Christ and his coming glory. Christ's return completes the gift of grace promised long ago. In 1:18–21, it is the precious blood of the Lamb through which Christ provides salvation. This act especially leads to the glory God gave the Christ.

In 2:4–10, we get Peter's first explicit use of the Hebrew Bible to portray Christ's work of suffering-rejection and exaltation.[10] Appealing to language from Psalm 118, Jesus Christ is called a precious cornerstone. The rejected one is now exalted, the first stone in a sacred temple God is building. As already noted, the use of the Psalm takes a text picturing the reception of an embattled king at the temple and uses it to picture in pattern (typology) how God receives another opposed king, the Messiah. The stumbling stone is now an exalted stone. This passage from Psalm 118 serves as one of the key messianic texts for the Christ's suffering. It appears often through the Second Testament and is tied to Jesus' own usage, something we shall consider later.

A second suffering text appears in 2:22–25. Here it is the suffering Servant imagery of Isaiah 53 that is the key point of appeal. Jesus died as a rejected innocent.[11] He suffered in silence. He bore our sins and brought healing by doing so. Here is a presentation of the core work of Jesus as the Christ. Such work cleared the way for forming God's people. By responding to Jesus' work, they have "turned back to the Shepherd and Guardian of their souls." This idea is summarized later in a doctrinal summary where Christ suffered once for sin, the just for the unjust (3:18). So the theme of Christ's suffering runs like a thread tying the letter together. This sacrificial manner of life drives believers to emulate Jesus' way of life (4:1–2), remembering that one day Jesus Christ will judge the living and the dead.

Both suffering and glory come together again in 4:13. The degree to which we share in the sufferings of Christ leads to rejoicing and gladness when Jesus returns in glory. Here is the core ethical message of the letter; it is rooted in the example of Jesus' work as the Christ. First Peter 5:10 summarizes the

---

9. Peter H. Davids, *The First Epistle of Peter*, NICNT (Grand Rapids: Eerdmans, 1990), 17–18.
10. For more detail, see Davids, *The First Epistle of Peter*, 85–86.
11. We have allusions to Isaiah 53:9 in verse 22, Isaiah 53:12 and 3 in verse 24, and Isaiah 53:6 in verse 25. For Johnston's discussion on Isaiah 53, see chapter 5 (pp. 154–61).

combination of ideas, "after you have suffered for a little while, the God of all grace who called you to his eternal glory in Christ will himself restore, confirm, strengthen, and establish you." The path of the Christ is suffering to glory.

Christological Fulfillment in 1 Peter. How does this fit with the Jewish expectations of the period? The centrality of the suffering as the key to messianic deliverance, leading the way to glory is unprecedented. However this original hope should be read (and there is much debate here as our earlier study of this text shows), the best we can tell Isaiah 53 was not read emphasizing the Messiah's suffering anywhere in Judaism, even though its language looks to personify this suffering around a single figure.[12] Other extant Jewish readings distinguish the suffering of God's people as the Servant from the triumphant notes struck concerning the eschatological figure drawn from the imagery of Isaiah 53 (e.g., the Targum on Isa. 53). This move represents one of the great differences between the claims of the early Christian movement and Judaism. This is one of the new notes of the Christian synthesis in its grand fusion of the messianic theme. The rejection emphasis we see here fits what we saw in Revelation and 1 John as well.

In conclusion, this Petrine epistle emphasizes the core of Jesus' work, suffering and then glory. The picture of victory is little different from other Jewish texts, where the eschatological deliverer, whether human or transcendent, is a figure of unquestioned and comprehensive authority. But the road taken to get there is distinct. For Peter, the great mystery and irony of eschatological and messianic hope is that the victory came through suffering and death.

James

Confession of "Christ" in James. This letter is a work of practical wisdom, whose closest parallel is Proverbs in the First Testament as well as apocryphal works like Sirach. Topics in James include prayer (5:13–18), temptation (1:2–18), discrimination (1:9–11; 2:3–7; 5:1–11), use of the tongue (3:1–18; 5:12), the unity of the community (4:11–12), as well as the tie between genuine faith and works (2:14–26). Being a book more of exhortation and practical proverbial teaching treating themes tied to Jesus' own teaching, the book of James has only two references to the Christ. James is a servant of the Lord Jesus

---

12. For comprehensive treatments of Isaiah 53, see William H. Bellinger Jr. and William R. Farmer, eds., *Jesus and the Suffering Servant: Isaiah 53 and Christian Origins* (Harrisburg, PA: Trinity Press International, 1998) and Bernd Janowski and Peter Stuhlmacher, eds. *The Suffering Servant: Isaiah 53 in Jewish and Christian Sources* (Grand Rapids: Eerdmans, 2004. Both studies indicate how early Judaism's use of Isaiah 53 did not have a clear suffering theme. For how Isaiah 53 works in the Second Testament, see *The Gospel According to Isaiah 53* (ed. Darrell L. Bock and Mitch Glaser; Grand Rapids: Kregel, 2012).

Christ (1:1) and notes that the faith of our Lord Jesus Christ is held without partiality for one's status (2:1). Even these two brief references show the note of authority tied to Jesus as believers are related to him as their Lord Christ as they exercise faith in him. However, no earlier texts are cited explicitly.

Christological Fulfillment in James. Due to the fact that James is more along the lines of wisdom literature, James' Christology is not very developed. Yet Jesus as the Christ has authority over church leaders (1:1) and the teachings of Jesus provide guidance for his followers (2:8, 5:12). As in second temple literature, the Messiah is presented as having authority over the community and his teachings are a guide to righteousness for that community. As in many of these Epistles, there is no direct use of older texts of hope, but the portrait implied assumes an authoritative role for Jesus that fits with such hope. It may well be assumed.

Hebrews

Confession of "Christ" in Hebrews. This letter is more like a sermon arguing for the superiority of Christianity over Judaism. Jesus is the promised exalted Christ, the regal priest according to the order of Melchizedek.[13] He is shown to be superior to the angels, to Moses, to Aaron, to sacrifices and to the temple. Psalm 110:1 and 4 dominate the presentation. The arrival of the New Covenant is emphasized. All this lays the basis for continuing to embrace Christ alone and maintain faith in him. The book is a commentary on how the Christian faith completes Jewish promise, rendering many elements of the former faith obsolescent. For the author of Hebrews, a move back to all the practices of Judaism for church members is a denial of Jesus, suggesting his work is not sufficient. For the author of this epistle, nothing could be more mistaken. Jesus' messianic work is a complete package for salvation, lacking nothing and needing nothing else. We examine some of the uses of the title in summary before looking to one of the key christological sections of the entire Second Testament in Hebrews 1. This epistle uses the term "Christ" strategically twelve times (3:6, 14; 5:5; 6:1; 9:11, 14, 24, 28; 10:10; 11:26; 13:8, 21).

The first two occurrences serve to identify Jesus' authority as the Christ and then to highlight the fact that believers have a partnership with Jesus as Christ. After laying the conceptual backdrop from promises out of the Jewish Scripture in Hebrews 1, the author tells us that Christ is faithful over God's house as Son. Unlike Moses who merely serves in God's house, Jesus

---

13. On the use of the Old Testament in Hebrews, see Wilder, Charles, and Easley, *Faithful to the End*, 40–42. Paul Ellingworth, *Commentary on Hebrews* (Grand Rapids: Eerdmans, 1993) has good technical discussions of the use of the Old Testament in this epistle.

is superior to Moses in that he has authority over it (3:6). Jesus serves as the high priest and apostle for our confession. Amazingly enough, all those who believe and continue to live by faith have a "partnership" in Christ (3:14).[14] Thus he is all we need to experience salvation.

The next two occurrences speak to expectations. Appealing to Psalm 2:7, the author of Hebrews first notes that Jesus did not elevate himself to the office of High Priest, but he was divinely put in charge to rule as king as well as to serve as high priest (5:5). The emphasis here is on divine vindication as seen in resurrection. This is precisely the emphasis we see coming out of the portrait of the Gospels–God raises Jesus and in the process shows him to be the Messiah.

The next expectation is directed to the Christian community. Followers of Jesus are to progress in their learning about the regal priest both intellectually and experientially. The elementary teaching about salvation is initially found in Christ. This is called the "doctrine of Christ," from which one is expected to move into maturity (6:1).

The next four occurrences of Christ (9:11, 14, 24, 28) serve to move us from looking at Jesus as king, to Christ as king-priest. In fact, Christ appeared as the high priest of the good things to come when he came to earth (9:11). It is his blood that purifies a conscience from dead works to serve the living God (9:14), a remark that is like what Peter said in his first epistle (1 Pet. 1:19; 3:20). With Christ's exaltation, he has entered into this new and superior priesthood. He is not in the temple on earth but now resides in heaven itself and in the heavenly sanctuary, having been offered only once to bear the sins of the many (Heb. 9:24, 28). The suffering and glory we saw in Revelation 4–5 and in 1 Peter is also present here. This remark about being offered once for sin is similar to Peter in describing Jesus' work for sin but adds to the picture the image of the exalted high priest mediating directly in God's presence.

---

14. The term "partnership" (μέτοχος, *metochos*) is an important term in Hebrews. The noun occurs five times in Hebrews (1:9; 3:1, 14; 6:4; 12:8). In Hebrews 3:1, it is used in connection with "holy brethren" and emphasizes the community's partnership with one another. Thus they share together in spiritual realities as sons of God (2:9, 13), as members of the same family (2:11), and as recipients who have common use of his riches (6:4; *TLNT*, 490). They are "fellow-Christians," namely partners with one another due to their call from God via Jesus, the Son (cp. 2:11–12). In Hebrews 6:4, the noun emphasizes a partnership with the Holy Spirit. In Hebrews 12:8, the noun emphasizes a partnership with God the Father as his children. Here in Hebrews 3:14, it emphasizes the community's partnership with Jesus: "We have become partners with Christ" (NRSV, NET) and thereby implies that the community takes part in activities and experiences with King Jesus. Adopted from Bateman's "Introducing the Warning Passages in Hebrew" in *Four Views on the Warning Passages in Hebrews* (ed. Herbert W. Bateman IV; Grand Rapids: Kregel, 2007), 48–49 n. 34; cp. 100 n. 34.

This move to a heavenly king-priest is made as a typological-pattern escalation of the hope as originally expressed in Psalm 110.[15] What was originally a metaphorical picture of the king's authority, as our earlier discussion showed, is now applied to a heavenly exalted figure with a meaning that presses language to the full. This kind of escalation is common in typological-prophetic fulfillment. The escalation points to an ultimate fulfillment in Jesus, as he fulfills the pattern in an extraordinary way. The earthly ideal king served as the model for a far more transcendent kingship, which God's acts had underwritten to indicate this proper association in this expanded sense.

The last occurrences are more like summary points (10:10; 11:26; 13:8, 21). The author of Hebrews reinforces the image with the note that believers are sanctified through the offering of the body of Jesus Christ once for all (10:10). Moses showed faith in suffering for the Christ rather than embracing the treasures of Egypt (11:26). The teaching and example of Jesus Christ is constant, as he is the same yesterday, today, and tomorrow (13:8). In fact, believers can experience the work of doing God's will and being pleasing to him through the equipping that comes through Jesus Christ (13:21). Here is the ethical implication of the teaching. For this author, the role of Jesus as the Christ is tied to his work of sacrifice and the exalted, mediatorial work as high priest. This heavenly position allows him to rule over God's house and God's people in conjunction with promises made long ago.

For the book of Hebrews, the key, sacred text concerning the promise is Psalm 110:1, 4. This text is so important that some have argued the book is a sermon based on Psalm 110. This royal psalm, which as we saw earlier, had originally summarized the hope for Israel's king. For the author of Hebrews, its fulfillment has now come in Jesus, the promised king. On the one hand, there is exaltation to God's very side. On the other, there is the eternal priesthood of the king-priest. Jesus belongs to a new priestly order, associated not with Aaron, but with another king-priest, Melchizedek.

Other promises add to this portrait, especially the litany of central eschatological texts cited in Hebrews 1.[16] Psalm 2:7 leads the way in showing that God has called this one, his Son. This Father-Son relationship also shows up at the end of the same citation string with the citation of 2 Samuel 7, which is the core kingship text for Israel. That messiah would be of the seed of David emerged from this promise. This text looked originally to a line of kings who represented

---

15. For this approach to Psalm 110, Herbert W. Bateman IV, "Psalm 110:1 and the New Testament," *BSac* 149 (1992): 438–53.

16. For a defense of the hermeneutics of pattern fulfillment discussed here, see Darrell L. Bock, "Single Meaning, Multiple Contexts and Referents: The New Testament's Legitimate, Accurate, and Multifaceted Use of the Old" in *Three Views on the New Testament Use of the Old* (ed. Kenneth Berding and Jonathan Lunde; Grand Rapids: Zondervan, 2008), 105–51. The idea of escalation in such texts is also treated in this article.

God and to whom they had a special relationship. But no one has the relationship of the Father to the Son as Jesus did, something the vindication of his resurrection affirms. The same hermeneutical, typological move that allowed Psalm 110 to take on a wider scope also takes place with Psalm 2 and 2 Samuel 7. Psalm 2 as a whole highlights the authority of the Son and the loyalty he is owed, an important point at the start of Hebrews as well, where perseverance is a major theme. Again messianic texts have an ethical implication.

Hebrews 1 roots the realization of promise in the juxtaposition of these texts, linking regal hope and Davidic imagery in central texts of the old hope. As we saw earlier, these passages have been presented and elaborated on across the centuries in Judaism up to the time of Jesus. What started out as a description of Israel's king is now applied in a complete sense to her present, permanent king. This new king was exalted by God to indicate the scope of the realized kingship now exercised from heaven as a result of resurrection and vindication. The way Messiah-Davidic hope and Sonship had come to be associated and connected shows that the claims of Hebrews are rooted in fundamental Jewish hopes, even though the argument of Hebrews is that the new way completes and transcends the old. A text like 4Q174 (4QFloriligium), already discussed earlier, shows how second temple Judaism also could juxtapose such texts. Their juxtaposition and association allowed for fresh associations in putting together what God is doing in and through his program involving Jesus.

In the middle of the citation string comes the appeal to Psalm 45, another royal Psalm. This text uses the occasion of a royal wedding to show a type of the total divine authority God gives to his Son. Once again typology is used hermeneutically to make the point and expand the meaning.[17] In tying the role of the now heavenly king with the creation, the extent of Jesus' authority is made complete. The exalted Jesus as Christ shares God's throne and can be addressed as God, because it is to the Son that the declaration is made of "Your throne O God is forever."[18] What was metaphor is now a fully realized relationship and realization. Metaphor has become reality. The ideal has become the realized. Again we have typological-prophetic escalation. One who represented God and carried his delegated authority (the king of Psalm 45) is the pattern for one who sits in God's presence and now bears direct, divine authority from heaven (Jesus).

---

17. In the original Psalm, the setting is the wedding of the king as the mention of a queen makes clear (Ps. 45:9–14). What is said of the king there is especially true of this special king in terms of his position before God. See Bock, "Single Meaning," 120.

18. For detailed discussion of the entire catena and the reading of this verse, Herbert W. Bateman IV, "Psalm 45:6–7 and Its Christological Contributions to Hebrews," *TJ* 22NS (2001): 3–21; idem. *Early Jewish Hermeneutics and Hebrews 1:5–13: The Impact of Early Jewish Exegesis on the Interpretation of a Significant New Testament Passage* (New York: Peter Lang, 1997).

In Hebrews 3–4, it is as faithful Son that the Christ presides over his house, his kingdom. Here it is the offer of rest as shalom that stands front and center. Psalm 95, again used as a pattern text, provides the commentary. The call is to enter the rest that God has provided through the faithful Son. It is a rest rooted in faith that the Son has done it all and has delivered comprehensively. The Psalm depicts the nation's Exodus experience as a picture of the rest Messiah now delivers, calling for a trust only in him. There is a consistency to how these texts are used in a typological-prophetic manner that shows how common this type of reading was.

In Hebrews 5–10, it is the Melchizedekian Christ who comes to the fore. For a second time Psalm 2:7 and Psalm 110 appear together, but here it is 110:4 that is the central text providing the key background. The picture is of a priest-king over a sacred house. The way into the sacred presence comes through suffering. Jesus is a different kind of high priest. He is a king, not merely a temple luminary, making him distinct from and superior to Aaron's line of priests. His kingship is eternal, giving it a duration that surpasses normal kingship. This difference in the sphere of his activity (in eternal kingship) is what makes the priesthood according to a distinct order from Melchizedek. This also allows the ministry of suffering in sacrifice to have an unending duration, permitting the offering for sin to be once for all.

Hebrews presents new emphases in the description of the Christ, but also has key overlaps with themes seen in other writings of this period. Christ's sufferings leading into glory is the key theme shared across these writings. Christ's work of suffering was a prerequisite for his glory. Suffering secured salvation; glory guarantees it.

Christological Fulfillments in Hebrews. Now how does this portrait compare with what we saw in earlier Jewish materials? In one sense, Jesus combines the offices of King and High Priest in ways that *could* evoke the image of the Hasmoneans, leading to criticism like that noted earlier in 1QpHab 8:3b-13a. The Essenes of Qumran clearly disliked what they saw as an abuse of the Law, which kept the high priest separate from the king. Hebrews answers this apparent problem in two key ways. First, the book begins with regal promises that in general met with a great deal of acceptance among Jews. Key to this portrait was the view of Psalm 110, which clearly is a psalm about a regal authority of some sort. This text described the honor the king was to receive and highlighted the unique relationship that king has to God as Son. Second, by appealing to Psalm 110:4, Hebrews points out that this priesthood is of a sort not covered by the example of the Aaronic priesthood. This is not a priest whose call is to supervise regular sacrifices of the temple. Rather his place is over the sacred house of God from heaven itself. It is a *regal* priesthood over a social entity distinct from the authority over an earthly temple that the Hasmoneans claimed. In this way, even though there is a priesthood combined with kingship, the combination belongs to a distinct priestly order. This claim is established through the citation of a sacred text from the worship book of Israel, the Psalter. So any idea that this claim is like that of the Hasmoneans falls to the side.[19] This fusion of kingship-priesthood is another fresh part of the grand fusion of messianic hope in the Second Testament. The Melchizedekian king-priesthood only appears explicitly in Hebrews and only is made as a theological point in Psalm 110 in the Hebrew Scripture. The use of Psalm 110 for Jesus, however, is one of the most common of associations with the messianic hope of Judaism. A close look at the roots of its key role awaits our discussion of the Gospels and Jesus' usage. What we have contended for in Hebrews is a typological-prophetic use. Kingship patterns in general apply to a greater degree to this unique kingship of Jesus.

The transcendent feature of this rule, rooted in the heavenly-earthly dualism that Hebrews emphasizes, also is a fresh emphasis in comparison to Jewish hope. Where Jewish hope tended to distinguish between either a transcendent hope in a Son of Man-like figure and a more earthly-grounded hope in a messianic figure, Hebrews pulls the two together. One sectarian solution, at least in some Dead Sea Scroll texts, solved the king-priest dilemma by distinguishing these two offices as well, with the hope of a ruling figure and a priestly messianic figure (CD 12:23–13:1; 14:19; 19:10–11; 20:1; 1QS 9:10–11; 1QS28a 2:11–22). Hebrews rejects this approach as well. What appeared ambiguous in the First Testament (Zech. 6) and remained unclear among the Dead Sea Scrolls is crystal clear in Hebrews, Jesus is God's divine royal priest. More than that, God's vindication showed that God had shown it to be so.

A second fresh feature is the way in which earthly metaphorical imagery has been pressed to its most comprehensive scope, now taking on relational, ethical depth as well as encompassing heaven and earth. This escalation in terms of heaven and earth develops directions already established in second temple hope, as the realization of the ideal is maximized to include everything God rules. Only a shalom that covers everything can guarantee realization that completes the promise. The ethical and associative thrust is highlighted to a significant degree in this letter, just as it will be in many other Second Testament texts.

CONCLUSION

The church's confession of Jesus as the Christ emphasizes his person, work, and authority. In a real sense four periods are focused upon: (1) the promises

---

19. The Hasmonean act to unite the Aaronic priesthood and kingship had no serious biblical precedent but was simply a reward for having rescued the nation and bringing the opportunity for theocracy to return to Israel (1 Macc. 14). The union of these offices was seen to be temporary which is why this practice counter to the Law was allowed. However, the community that went to Qumran found it unacceptable and argued it disqualified these rulers as being authentically faithful before God. See Bateman's discussion on "Messianism Evoked and Inflamed" in chapter 8 (p. 237).

about the Christ, especially his suffering, (2) the work of Christ in his ministry, primarily in suffering and for sin, and (3) the blessing Jesus mediates now so that believers are able to serve God with good works despite suffering, and (4) the glory to come after suffering when Jesus will usher in the eternal rule of God. It is the suffering and the glory of Christ the Catholic Epistles and Revelation highlight, suffering rooted in his offer for sin and glory that is a result of God exalting the Christ to God's very presence in heaven.

THE CHURCH'S CONFESSION

The Promises about the Christ

The Work of Christ in His Ministry

The Blessings Christ Mediates

The Glory of Christ After His Suffering

If we ask what texts are key to this understanding of Jesus, it is the covenant promises of God (see Heb. 1) and language like that of Psalm 2:7 and 110:1. In these texts God calls his chosen one Son and has him at his side. Hebrews and Peter point to such passages. The question where the promise of suffering in relation to sin comes from is harder to determine, but the emphasis on suffering then glory might evoke Isaiah 52:13–53:12, which has the same pattern and highlights the suffering of God's Servant. Isaiah 8 and 28 are also appealed to directly in 1 Peter. However, it is possible the author of Hebrews is simply extending the picture of sacrifice from the temple to the sacrifice of Jesus, since sacrifices in the temple often dealt with sin. There is another kind of suffering in Hebrews. It is suffering unjustly for simply being faithful to God. Here the history of the saints (Heb. 11) may be at work. Reading history this way has excellent precedent in the second temple period where God's people often suffer while being faithful (2 Macc. 7; 4 Macc. 8–18; Wis. 3–5). Psalm 118 with the exaltation of the rejected stone may have a key role to play here as well. First Peter is explicit in citing this text. The ideas of ransom, payment for sin, as well as the suffering-exaltation pattern fit here. So what is present is suffering related to sin (Isa. 53), but the persecution-rejection theme (Ps. 118; Isa. 8, 28) is probably at work when the theme is unjust suffering.

We also can compare this portrait to promise in the sacred Scriptures of the Jews and to expectation in the literature that expounded on such hope in the second temple period. Three ideas are key. (1) There is the total transcendence of the eschatological figure. This Jesus is the Alpha and Omega. He assumes a position at God's side that is without equal, despite his previous status as a human being. So he combines transcendence and equality with humanity in a way distinct from or at least more explicitly than most of these earlier texts. Only if we move into eschatological texts about figures not explicitly called messiah (such as in Dan. 7 or *1 En.* 39–71) do we come close to such a comprehensive authority. These Second Testament texts achieve a messianic emphasis by pulling together themes that earlier promise had either expressed separately in distinct images or that expectation had only partially combined. The move is perfectly legitimate given we are discussing the figure of eschatological deliverance. (2) We also see that the way of glory is taken through suffering. Jesus does possess comprehensive power and will exercise it, as hope had previously expressed both in the era of promise and in the reflection that took place in the era of expectation. However, the victory he brings comes through a denouement that other Jewish texts did not expect. (3) In Jesus, we see the early church combining ideas into a grand synthesis that other Jewish texts tended to either keep distinct or that existed in tension without a clear resolution of the seeming competing ideas. Perhaps this is best seen in the king-priesthood of Jesus in Hebrews. We also see this in a second combination, the way suffering works *for* the Servant who also is exalted. In this way a seeming dilemma from the older texts is resolved into a unified portrait. Yet despite these distinctions, there is enough that is parallel to indicate that the conceptualization is decidedly Jewish in its roots and development. That such Jewish roots are still present in these later Christian texts, when the early Christian faith is becoming more Gentile in makeup, is significant to note. Even as Christianity contended with Judaism in a book like Hebrews, it never lost its Jewish roots nor the claim that Jesus was the promised Christ who had come in realization of promise and expectation.

How did this work hermeneutically at this late stage? The most fundamental move was to bring together in a more unified manner themes that the entire Hebrew Scripture had raised in a more variegated way. Such readings used some of the configurations that the period of expectations had also contemplated. Other moves were fresh, as God's actions in Jesus were seen as revelatory of his promised Word read as a unified whole. The key point here is that the early church was not merely exegeting texts as individual, isolated lines of passages within individual books, but appealing to how these pieces fit into the larger world of the promises as a whole. The whole as the sum of related parts was most important. This meant that early Jewish texts of promise moved in certain directions later sacred texts were seen to pick up, develop, and explain. It was all God's single and singular story of promise. Some of these directions had already surfaced in expectations in specific segments that second temple Judaism had explored. Others were new. Yet all of it was rooted in the claim that what God had revealed, he had shown both in word and act, in Scripture and through Jesus. These two revelations reflected and refracted onto each other making each clearer, by revealing the promises and the patterns of divine activity and fulfillment.

In addition, with the combining of categories into a unified portrait came the appeal through expansive pattern fulfillment that kingship was comprehensive in its authority, occupying heaven and earth. Texts that originally had established kingship on the earth and used metaphors were now read so that the ideal was met and transcended to contain an authority coextensive with God's rule and presence. Only such an expanded authority could realize all that was being promised. The justification for this new reading was not only an appeal to a unified portrait of promise, but the acts of God vindicating Jesus, his claims and his authority, the greatest of which was his resurrection-exaltation to the very presence of God to share full divine authority.

A question to be raised is whether these later emphases are seen in other early Christian texts. How do Paul and the texts of the evangelists and Acts treat such themes? Is the remainder of Jewish themes in later texts evidence of earlier roots and of the persistence of Jewish themes in the synthesis that came with earlier Christianity? That is the fascinating question our further study of the theme of Messiah hopes to pursue in the survey of the remaining texts of this newly emerging first-century movement. The trajectories that began in the Jewish sacred texts of promise and reflected in the competing models of Jewish expectations emerged with Jesus' followers in ways that continued to associate the eschaton with Jewish concepts of hope. In the middle of that development stood the declaration that Jesus is the Christ of fulfillment. At least, that is what these later books of the Second Testament affirm.

MESSIAH CONFESSED: PAULINE EPISTLES

As we begin our look at the coming of Israel's king in Paul's Epistles, it is important to remember that the title Messiah emerges from a Jewish context. Initially it referred to a variety of specially commissioned figures of God (anointed priests, prophets, and kings) but later came to describe a specific eschatological figure (the Messiah). Yet the portraits expressing what that eschatological messianic figure was to look like and what he was to accomplish is expressed with some variety in both the sacred scriptures and later second temple texts. Consequently, the apostle Paul plays an important role in our understanding of Jesus as the Christ (Messiah) because he pieces together the messianic puzzle for us by means of confessions and declarations in Pauline texts. The fact that Paul uses confessional material means he is not innovating these claims. They come to him from the tradition of the church. So the confession he affirms predates him. He is by far the most prolific user of the title "the Christ." This term is a key title for the apostle. In saying this, I am disagreeing with the recent assessment of Magnus Zetterholm, who says:

> Even though Paul certainly believed that Jesus was the Messiah of Israel, we must conclude that he did not emphasize this aspect, and there can be little doubt that he presents it in a regal (?) way that differs significantly from the Gospels. In short, the messiahship of Jesus is in no way stressed in Paul's letters.[1]

Furthermore, Zetterholm's claim that this Pauline portrait represents a significant difference from the gospels is also overstated. The subordination of the title "Christ" to the idea of Lord is something Jesus' discussion of Psalm 110:1 in the Synoptics affirms (Matt. 21:41–44; Mark 12:35–37; Luke 20:41–44). I shall cover the details when we discuss this passage below. So Paul's emphasis is not different from but rather parallels that discussion.

For Paul, the concept of Lord is in some ways more comprehensive, but this is because Christ is a core title referring to Jesus. He is the Christ (Messiah).

---

1. Magnus Zetterholm, "Paul and the Missing Messiah" in *The Messiah in Early Judaism and Christianity* (ed. Magnus Zetterholm; Minneapolis: Fortress, 2007), 39.

MAJOR TRANSITIONS IN THE APOSTLE PAUL'S LIFE

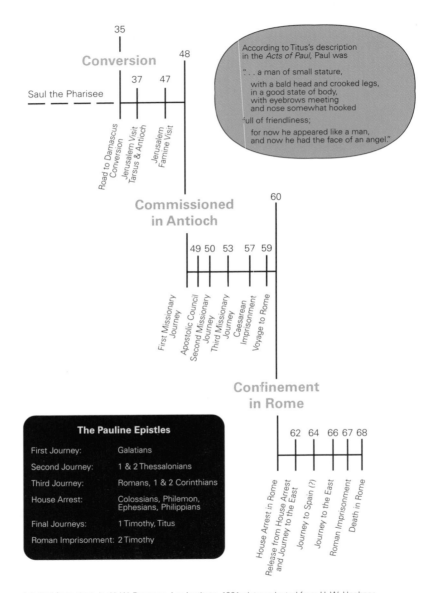

According to Titus's description in the *Acts of Paul*, Paul was

". . . a man of small stature,

with a bald head and crooked legs, in a good state of body, with eyebrows meeting and nose somewhat hooked

full of friendliness;

for now he appeared like a man, and now he had the face of an angel."

Conversion
35
48
37   47

Saul the Pharisee

Road to Damascus Conversion
Jerusalem Visit Tarsus & Antioch
Jerusalem Famine Visit

Commissioned in Antioch
60
49 50 53 57 59

First Missionary Journey
Apostolic Council
Second Missionary Journey
Third Missionary Journey
Caesarean Imprisonment
Voyage to Rome

Confinement in Rome
62 64 66 67 68

House Arrest in Rome
Release from House Arrest and Journey to the East
Journey to Spain (?)
Journey to the East
Roman Imprisonment
Death in Rome

The Pauline Epistles

First Journey:	Galatians
Second Journey:	1 & 2 Thessalonians
Third Journey:	Romans, 1 & 2 Corinthians
House Arrest:	Colossians, Philemon, Ephesians, Philippians
Final Journeys:	1 Timothy, Titus
Roman Imprisonment:	2 Timothy

Adapted from chart by H. W. Bateman, Lay Institute, 1991; dates adapted from H. W. Hoehner, "Chronology of the Apostolic Age," ThD dissertation, Dallas Theological Seminary, 1965.

Thus Paul's thirteen letters are of utmost importance to our discussion. They date from the fifties and sixties and may be divided into journey Epistles, house arrest Epistles, and Pastoral Epistles. And though it is beyond the scope of this work to provide a survey of Paul's life of ministry, we might summarize his life in three major movements: conversion, commission, and confinement. The point of this essay is to trace the extent to which Paul calls Jesus the Christ. The scope of these texts challenges Zetterholm's claim that Paul does not emphasize Jesus as the Christ. To show the depth of the Pauline references to the Christ we need to trace all the Pauline usage. We start with the Epistles written as he traveled.

JOURNEY EPISTLES

Paul wrote six Epistles while serving as a missionary. They are Galatians, 1 and 2 Thessalonians, 1 and 2 Corinthians, and Romans. For nine years Paul roamed throughout Asia Minor and Greece preaching Jesus, planting churches, and making disciples. His ministry often involved making the case for Jesus as the Christ in Jewish synagogues or in other settings where Jews were present. The book of Acts and Paul's letters testify to his activities throughout the Roman-controlled Mediterranean (Acts 13:5; 17:13, 17; 18:4, 19; 20:21; Rom. 1:16–17; 1 Cor. 9:20; 1 Thess. 2:2). Paul's Epistles may well indicate the type of arguments he made for Jesus as the promised Messiah.

First Journey: One Epistle, Galatians

Paul began the first of three missionary journeys around 48 CE and ended it around 49 CE. After establishing several churches in South Galatia, he wrote the epistle of Galatians for the people of Pisidian Antioch, Iconium, and Lystra-Derbe.[2] Thus *Galatians* is probably Paul's earliest letter and one of his most contentious. It addressed issues of Jew-Gentile relations in the new community at a point probably before a more comprehensive solution emerged.

Confessions of "Christ" in Galatians

Galatians addresses major issues in the Galatia community. Do Gentiles have to follow Judaism to be saved? How should Jewish believers relate to Gentiles in terms of the Law, especially in matters tied to table fellowship? The community of believers at Galatia is in danger of leaving behind the grace that saved them. Paul calls it turning to another gospel. He minces no words. As he corrects them, he uses the term "Christ" thirty-eight times.

---

2. For an overview of Paul's first missionary journey see John McRay, *Paul: His Life and Teaching* (Grand Rapids: Baker, 2003), 100–130; F. F. Bruce, *Paul: Apostle of the Heart Set Free* (Grand Rapids: Eerdmans, 1977; repr. 1986), 160–72.

At times, "Christ" is used as the basis of his authority. Paul opens the letter highlighting the fact that he is an apostle through Jesus Christ and God the Father (1:1). At other times, the term "Christ" is used as a common greeting of grace and peace through God our Father and the Lord Jesus Christ (1:3). What is of utmost importance is what is confessed and maintained about Jesus "the Christ."

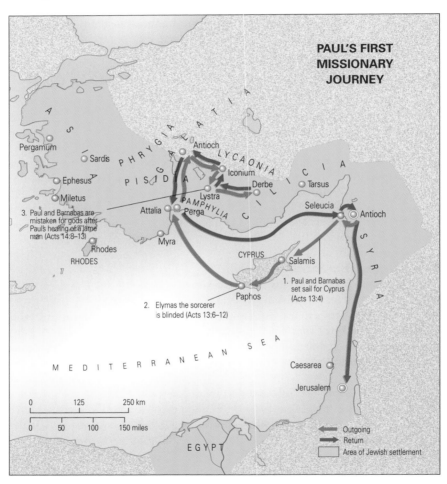

PAUL'S FIRST MISSIONARY JOURNEY

3. Paul and Barnabas are mistaken for gods after Paul's healing of a lame man (Acts 14:8–13)

2. Elymas the sorcerer is blinded (Acts 13:6–12)

1. Paul and Barnabas set sail for Cyprus (Acts 13:4)

The nature of the dispute about the gospel means that Paul opens the letter highlighting the fact that he is an apostle through Jesus Christ and God the Father (1:1). Paul also gives his common greeting of grace and peace through God our Father and the Lord Jesus Christ (1:3). He rebukes them for so quickly exchanging the one who called you in the grace of Christ for another gospel (1:6). The wording here is important for it is God, the one who called them, who is denied in this move. So Paul emphasizes the personal dimension of the gospel here with the link being the grace that comes in association with Christ. Those who are troubling them are perverting the gospel of Christ with their emphasis on works of the Law (1:7). He tells them that if he were seeking to please men he would not be a servant of Christ (1:10). The gospel he preaches is what he received by revelation from Jesus Christ (1:12). So Paul's work is rooted in the revelatory work of the Christ, something also suggested by his not being initially recognized by the Judean churches of Christ after Paul's long time away (1:22). These uses of "Christ" are rather straightforward; the Christ is at the center of the message and the call of Paul.

The problem began with false brethren who were spying out the freedom believers have in Christ Jesus (2:4). The key is the realization that we know that a person is not justified by works of the Law but through faith in Jesus Christ (2:16).[3] Just like Paul, those tied to his gospel have believed in Christ Jesus (2:16), in order to be justified by faith in Christ (2:16), and not by works of the Law. Paul focuses on the centrality of faith in Christ, mentioning the title three times in this one verse. It is Christ who is confessed in the church, because through this promised one God justifies by faith. It is this "Christ alone" gospel Paul defends in Galatians. If anything can show that Christ is an important title for Paul, it is this focus on the confession of faith in Jesus as the Christ.

Two more uses appear in the next verse. If in the attempt to be justified by Christ (2:17), believers are found to be sinners, then is Christ (2:17) the agent of sin? Paul asks this rhetorically. Of course not, he replies. Jesus is the one who overcomes sin, a point made by one of the most famous verses in Paul, where he notes that if he has been crucified in Christ (2:20), it is no longer he who lives but Christ (2:20) lives in him and the life he lives in the flesh he lives by faith in the Son of God. Here is Paul's detailed explanation of how Christ becomes incorporated with the believer and works through him by means of indwelling. Paul goes on to observe that if justification came by the Law, then Christ died to no purpose (2:21). So he rebukes them again and asks who has bewitched them before whose eyes Jesus Christ was publicly portrayed (preached and witnessed to) as crucified (3:1)? Christ's work in salvation and the relationship to him by faith are the central ideas in this part of Galatians. This sets up a discussion of the promise of the Spirit, a theme that will be a key link with how the Gospels present Jesus as the Christ.

---

3.   I do not accept a rendering of Christ's faithfulness in these verses as the point because such faithfulness is wrapped up in what the response of faith believes that Paul is highlighting as 3:2, 5–6 show.

In another tightly wound text, Paul begins with a declaration that Christ redeemed us from the curse of the Law, having become a curse for us (3:13). Paul notes that as a result in Christ Jesus the blessing of Abraham has come to the Gentiles, that those who respond might receive the Spirit of God. The Spirit is the incorporating gift of the Christ (3:14). This promise is rooted in the promise made to the singular seed of Abraham, that is, to the Christ (3:16). He goes on to explain that the Law locked all things under sin, as Scripture notes, so that what was promised to faith in Jesus Christ might be given to those who believe (3:22). So Christ redeems and gives the Spirit in line with promise that comes to those who believe.

So if Christ is the promise, then what about the Law? Does it have any remaining role? The Law was a pedagogue until Christ came (3:24). Now that faith has come, a pedagogue is no longer needed, because in Christ Jesus believers are all sons of God (3:26). For as many as were baptized into Christ (3:27) have put on Christ (3:27). Here identification with Christ is stressed as he is worn like clothes. We take the Christ with us everywhere and represent him everywhere. All believers are one in Christ Jesus (3:29), the language of incorporation. If one is Christ's, then one is also Abraham's seed, an heir according to promise (3:29). Again Jesus as the Christ is confessed as central to God's promise and it is Genesis 12 and the promise of a seed to Abraham that is key for Paul here. This promised seed that is the anointed one is a source of blessing for both Jew and Gentile, even as Genesis 12 promised that all the nations would be blessed through Abraham. Paul argues that the promise preceded the Law, so the Law was a kind of parenthesis in God's program until the promise was realized, tutoring humanity until the realization of promise came. In addition, relationship with God comes through an incorporated association with the promised one, something Law does not bring. This section of Galatians is a central one, so we shall return to it after our survey of uses of Christ.

Paul can commend the Galatians. He notes that when he was ill, they received him as if he were a special visitor, as if he were like an angel, even as if he were Christ Jesus (4:14). And Paul cares for them as he is in travail until Christ is formed in them (4:19).

Returning to the theme of grace and freedom, Paul notes that it was for freedom that Christ set believers free (5:1). Paul has in mind freedom from Law because of the presence of the Spirit in a call to love (3:14, 5:5–6). If the Galatians insist on being circumcised, Christ will be of no advantage (5:2). This severs one from Christ (5:4), making one justified by Law and not grace.

When Paul exhorts the Galatians to walk by the fruit of the spirit, he notes that those who belong to Christ Jesus have crucified the flesh with its passions and desires (5:24). That means living differently than the standards of the world, looking to restore one another from sin and bear one another's burdens in Christ (6:2).

Paul closes his letter noting that those who wish them to be circumcised want to make a good showing in the flesh and thus avoid being persecuted for the cross of Christ (6:12). In contrast, Paul wishes to glory only in the cross of our Lord Jesus Christ, by which the world has been crucified with respect to believers like Paul (6:14). With a standard salutation of the grace of the Lord Jesus Christ be with your spirit, Paul closes his letter.

Christological Fulfillment in Galatians

For Paul, the activity of the Christ in salvation, indwelling, and incorporation are at the core of Jesus' confessed work as Messiah. The new element here is the explicit citation of the promise to Abraham of a seed from Genesis. The Christ's relationship to the law also gets detailed treatment. The law was a pedagogue pointing to the Christ until he came, exposing sin and the need for a delivering promised one. Paul, in effect, gives the law a temporary role that served in God's plan until the promised Messiah came (Gal. 3:17–22). When Christ bore the curse of the law for us, he freed us and showed that justification was by grace, not by works of the law. The law as a pedagogue could be left behind. Grace and the indwelling Christ could become the means to guide the believer into the fruits of the Spirit. This death into new life accomplished a separation from the world that also could be likened to crucifixion.

The most central idea in Galatians connecting us to earlier sacred Jewish texts comes in Galatians 3. Here Paul plays with the singular-plural elements of the promised "seed," a promise originally made in Genesis 12:1–3.[4] In Genesis, the singular is highlighted as the promise applies to Isaac (not Ishmael) and to Jacob (not Esau). However, this singular route also has corporate elements, with descendants becoming as numerous as the sands of the sea when the promise is reiterated in Genesis and referenced to the entire nation of Israel (e.g., Gen. 22:17; 32:12; also compared to stars in the sky, Gen. 22:17). By the time we get to Exodus, the seed becomes a nation as it is liberated and travels to the promised land. Paul argues similarly that the seed is singular through the Christ in whom the promise resides (3:16) and extends to the multitude of sons made up of Jews and Gentiles who believe (Gal. 3:29). In this way, the Messiah's presence unifies the promise and people of God. This unification and incorporation applies to Jews and Gentiles. God's program has its victory in the reconciliation Messiah mediates.

Paul understands seed as being capable of a singular and a dual meaning from Galatians 3:29, where seed again becomes plural. In Romans 9:7–13, Paul makes the argument that not all sons of Israel are sons of promise. In that Romans text, Paul also recognizes that the promise comes through one to the many, much like the way he argues here, namely through Isaac and Jacob.

---

4. For Johnston's discussion on Genesis 12 and God's promise of singular seed, see chapter 1 (pp. 41–42).

So what we observe in Paul's usage is a theological reading of this Genesis 12 promise that not only deals with the promise of Genesis, but also with its narrative development into Exodus revealing a "one-into-many" pattern fulfillment.

What we see here in contrast to other Jewish texts is a more synthetic move. Paul is not reading the text in a common atomistic, rabbinic manner, but is reading theologically in light of the whole of the promise. The seed promise moves through one to many in Genesis. Paul reflects a common Jewish supposition about such a promise in reading a text in a one-to-many manner. This one-into-many idea seems to explain what Paul does with the seed promise about the Christ in Galatians. Yet another move by Paul is to associate the seed promise not to the nation of Israel, but to the community Jesus Christ forms, the new community. Here it is Paul's sense that the new figure and era have come; that is key to this reading. Such expectation also parallels some key elements of Jewish hope, where the decisive deliverer brings a new era (The hope of a new era in Dead Sea Scrolls 4Q174; 4Q175; *Pss. Sol.* 17–18).[5] The move leads into the idea of incorporation in Christ that is so central to Paul's teaching on the Christ in his letters. This is the community of Messiah. Those Christ delivers belong to Jesus and are incorporated in the Christ tied to the promise made to Abraham. That promise in Genesis 12, in turn, was God's answer to the dilemma of sin and the curse that Genesis 1–11 recounts. In this way, the "seed" of Abraham reaches back to the "seed" of the woman (See Appendix on Gen. 3:15).

Second Journey: Two Epistles, 1 and 2 Thessalonians
Paul's second missionary journey began around 50 CE, which ended later in 52 CE. After his return visit to the churches in South Galatia, Paul crossed the Hellespont into Greece, where he established churches in Philippi, Thessalonica, Berea, Athens, and Corinth.[6] While in Corinth, Paul wrote two Epistles, 1 and 2 Thessalonians. Together they describe the work of the Messiah yet to come and the call of Messiah to remain steadfast.

Confession of "Christ" in 1 Thessalonians
First Thessalonians emphasizes the community's incorporation in Christ and the one who is yet to gather his people. Along with Galatians, this is one of Paul's earliest letters. It contains ten uses of the term "Christ." The references are not as compact and so there is less interconnectedness between the references as in other Pauline letters.

---

5. For Bateman's discussions of 4Q174 see chapter 10 (pp. 278–79) and chapter 11 (pp. 296–97). For his discussions of *Psalms of Solomon* see chapter 9 (pp. 261–63) and chapter 11 (pp. 302–3).
6. For an overview of Paul's second missionary journey see McRay, Paul, 131–76; Bruce, *Paul,* 121–63.

It begins with a greeting to the church in God the Father and the Lord Jesus Christ (1:1). Paul is thankful for the Thessalonians' work of faith, labor of love, and endurance of hope in our Lord Jesus Christ (1:3). The theme of incorporation tied to the Christ, also noted in Galatians, appears here.

In the body of the letter, Paul observes that he did not make demands on them as he could have as an apostle of Christ (2:7). He came to them in gentleness. And he is pleased that they became imitators of the churches of God in Jesus Christ, which are in Judea (2:14). Timothy is a servant of Christ who was sent to them (3:2). The uses of Christ up to this point in the letter are simply uses of the title as a way of naming Jesus.

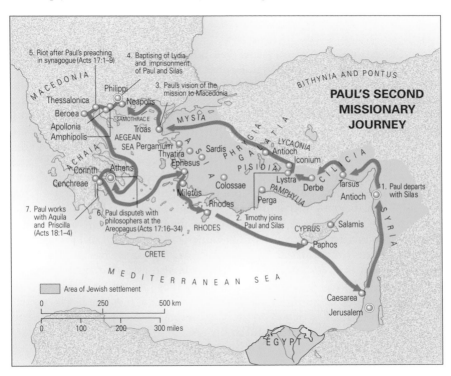

Later in his letter Paul discusses how the dead will be gathered. He notes that the dead in Christ will raise first and then those alive when the archangel calls will be caught up into the air together with the dead to meet the Lord (4:16). So Paul goes on to discuss salvation. He notes that believers are not destined for wrath but to obtain salvation through our Lord Jesus Christ (5:9). Paul exhorts them to be thankful for this is God's will in Christ Jesus (5:18). Paul closes the letter asking that the God of peace sanctify them so they may be kept sound at the coming of our Lord Jesus Christ (5:23) and that the grace of our Lord Jesus Christ be with them (5:28). These uses simply refer to the incorporation of believers in Jesus and the task of deliverance Jesus is yet to perform. There are no explicit appeals to texts from the Hebrew Scripture to explain the title in the letter.

Christological Fulfillment in 1 Thessalonians
This letter's use of the term "Christ" is less developed as many references simply are descriptions of those people who are in or are serving Christ. However, what is most emphasized is the role of the Christ in his completion of salvation in the future. The manner of the Christ's gathering at the end is a fresh detail. It comes through a word from the Lord (4:15).

Confession of "Christ" in 2 Thessalonians
Second Thessalonians focuses attention on the Christ to come and the ethical call of the Christ. This short letter also has ten uses of the term "Christ." Paul writes once again to the church of the Thessalonians in God our Father and the Lord Jesus Christ (1:1) with a greeting of grace and peace from God the Father and the Lord Jesus Christ (1:2). Paul prays that God may make them worthy of his call, fulfill every good resolve and work of faith by his power so that the name of the Lord Jesus may be glorified according to the grace of God and the Lord Jesus Christ (1:12). He then goes on to discuss the coming of our Lord Jesus Christ (2:1) as he tells them of the coming Antichrist. Paul gives thanks for them because God chose them from the beginning to be saved through the gospel so that they might obtain the glory of our Lord Jesus Christ.

As in 1 Thessalonians, Colossians, and Philippians, Paul looks to encourage through the future work of the Christ as he asks our Lord Jesus Christ to comfort the hearts of the Thessalonians with what he has just said and establish them in every good work (2:16). He also asks that their hearts be directed to the love of God and the steadfastness of Christ (3:5). This adds an ethical note to the exhortation. The call of the letter as a whole is to consider the future and what Christ will do for us. This reflection on the good future to come motivates us now to respond to his grace. He issues a command in the name of our Lord Jesus Christ that they stay away from those who are idle or those who do not follow the tradition received from Paul (3:6). Those who are idle are commanded and exhorted in the Lord Jesus Christ to do their work in quietness and to earn a living (3:12). The letter closes with a commendation to the grace of our Lord Jesus Christ (3:18). As with 1 Thessalonians, there is no explicit appeal to the Hebrew Scripture in explaining the Christ.

Christological Fulfillment in 2 Thessalonians
This letter does not have any significant development of the title. While covering what will come in the future work of the Christ, Paul also commands them how to live now in the name of Christ. The ethical implication

in knowing the Christ is that they represent him on earth, another idea tied to association or incorporation with Christ. The note of future hope in this letter parallels elements found in 1 Thessalonians, while also evoking the image of the Antichrist. These Antichrist themes are rooted in Daniel 9:24–27. There is no exposition of Daniel here, merely the appeal to a figure named there. Daniel is being read as a hope about the eschatological future, probably because of the way the Son of Man was already being understood within early Christianity. So here the portrait of the judging Christ is assumed as known.

Third Journey: Three Epistles: 1 and 2 Corinthians, Romans

Paul's third missionary journey began in the spring of 53 CE and ended around 57 CE. The focus of this third journey was to collect money from established churches to help relieve the stress of famine in Jerusalem.[7] The letters written during this journey are the most important Paul penned because these letters treat a variety of topics in defense of his apostolic role (1 and 2 Corinthians), as well as presenting the most unified statement Paul makes about his understanding of the gospel (Romans).

Confessions of "Christ" in 1 Corinthians

First Corinthians develops key Pauline ideas of incorporation. This association equips for a moral life and is rooted in the hope of resurrection. The term "Christ" appears sixty-four times in this letter.

Due to the fact that Paul addresses various problems and questions that the church in Corinth is facing, at times he uses the term "Christ" as his source of authority.[8] So his greeting highlights his role as an apostle of Jesus Christ (1:1).

Believers in Corinth are sanctified in Christ Jesus, a position they share with all who call upon the name of our Lord Jesus Christ (1:2). As is his custom, Paul greets his recipients with grace and peace from God our Father and the Lord Jesus Christ (1:3).

The Corinthians have been blessed with the grace of God given in Christ Jesus, something for which Paul is thankful (1:4). This is the result of the testimony about Christ being established in them (1:6). They have every gift they need as they await the return of our Lord Jesus Christ (1:7). It is this one who will establish them blameless in the day of our Lord Jesus Christ (1:8). This is because God is faithful when he called them into the fellowship with

---

7. For an overview of Paul's third journey see McRay, *Paul*, 177–222; Bruce, *Paul*, 286–324.
8. Sometimes Paul greets people and notes he is a slave of Jesus Christ. He notes believers as slaves in 1 Corinthians 7:22. But here and in 2 Corinthians 1:1, he highlights his role as apostle, someone commissioned directly by Jesus and serving him with that authority. Galatians 1:1 also has this note (Paul as slave is noted in Gal. 1:10). Also mentioning apostleship are the greetings in Romans (with slave), Ephesians, Colossians, 1 Timothy, 2 Timothy, and Titus (with slave).

his Son Jesus Christ our Lord. These appeals to the returning Christ and what he is to do remind us of the uses in the Thessalonian Epistles where what the Christ will do in the future matters and motivates.

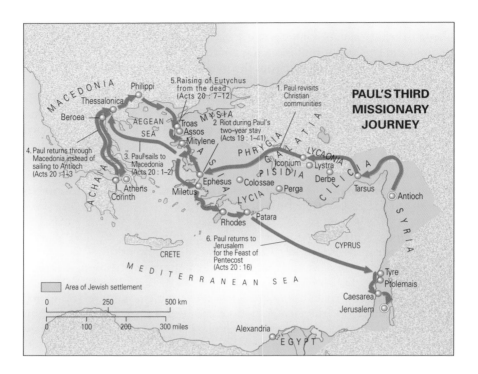

In the greeting to this letter, Paul highlights the solid and established position of the saints in Corinth and consistently mentions the Lordship of Jesus. Most of all, Paul tries to encourage the Corinthians to walk more faithfully. The ethical implications of Jesus' position gain more attention here as an outgrowth of the grace God has brought to the Corinthians. These ethical dimensions assume one appreciates the privilege of being connected to the Christ. One should strongly identify with Christ and that privilege taking on the responsibility to represent him well in our actions.

So Paul turns to exhortation and urges them through the name of our Lord Jesus Christ to not be divided (1:10). The church is split into parties, one of which claims Christ as their leader (1:12), but Paul asks if Christ is divided (1:13). Some are boasting about who baptized them, so Paul is grateful that Christ did not send him to baptize (1:17), but to proclaim the gospel. Paul's preaching did not use words of human wisdom so that the cross of Christ might not turn up empty in terms of its role in salvation (1:17).

The term "Christ" in this section looks to Jesus' presence and authority in the community, and Paul reviews his message noting that it is about Christ crucified (1:23), a message that shows Christ is the power and wisdom of God (1:24).[9] This is a message in contrast to the way the world operates, being an offense to Jews and foolishness to Gentiles. Nonetheless, as a result of it, they are incorporated in Christ Jesus, who is wisdom sent from God as well as righteousness, sanctification, and redemption (1:30). Fully one quarter of the uses of "Christ" appear in the first chapter of the letter as Paul lays the foundation for all he will say to them. In sum, Paul wishes to know nothing among them except Christ crucified (2:2). In the context, Paul appeals to the mystery of God now revealed through the Spirit in terms of what has taken place in Jesus (2:9). The crucifixion of the Lord of Glory and what that has yielded is the point. Here is a defense of the cross and the suffering it represents, as well as what it produces for those who embrace its truth by faith. So, as in many of the Epistles we have covered, the Christ in his suffering is important for understanding his work and also serves as a moral example for how to live.

The gift of the Spirit means that access is given to the mind of Christ (2:16), but the immaturity of the Corinthians means that he must speak to them as infants in Christ (3:1).[10]

He reminds the Corinthians that no foundation can be laid other than Jesus Christ (3:11). And using the picture of a holy temple, he again returns to incorporation language, noting that they are of Christ, just as Christ is of God (3:23). In thinking of the house and Paul's role, he sees himself as a servant of Christ, serving as a steward (4:1). The commitment of Paul and the apostles to Jesus has made them look as if they are fools for Christ's sake (4:10) in contrast to the "wisdom" in Christ of the Corinthians (4:10). Here Paul is rebuking the pride that has caused the Corinthians to think they know better than the apostle Paul. Paul can speak to them this way because although they have had many instructors in Christ (4:15), Paul is their father having birthed them in Christ (4:15). Paul's appeal to the title here focuses on its relational element as he appeals for allegiance to the Christ, pointing as well to the sacred nature of the community Christ built.

---

9. On the contrast in this passage between human wisdom and Christian wisdom, see David Garland, *1 Corinthians,* BECNT (Grand Rapids: Baker, 2003), 59–71. The cross in this text is not merely a reference to Jesus' death, but is seen as a hub from which all of salvation radiates, a kind of synecdoche of a part for the whole. In other words, the event of the cross opens the way to all of salvation. It is this "all" Paul preaches in the cross and its seeming shamefulness.

10. Note how the appeal to the Spirit is like Galatians, except here it is not so much the arrival of the new era or change in administration that is in view, but the ethical implications of what it means for the Christ to give the Spirit. The following discussion of the Spirit's presence creating a new, sacred temple in the community and in individuals goes the same direction.

As Paul turns to specific issues, the apostle underscores the role of Jesus Christ and his sacred connection to believers. In urging them to discipline a severely sinning brother guilty of incest, Paul reminds them that they should cleanse out the old leaven because Christ was sacrificed as a paschal lamb (5:7).[11] The sacred nature of the sacrifice and its implications for dealing with sin give the image an ethical thrust in calling for cleansing. In treating the issue of taking each other to pagan courts, he reminds them that they have been set apart by Jesus into a new community having been washed and justified in the name of the Lord Jesus Christ and in the Spirit of God (6:11). In turning to the idea that their body does not matter when it comes to holiness, he stresses that their bodies are members of Christ (6:15), so they should not take those bodies and make them members for immorality (6:15). Again it is the position and identity with Christ, along with the sacredness of his sacrifice, that is the ethical ground for these exhortations. Christ's work not only makes possible entry into the people of God, but the graciousness of the provision and the sacred nature of the association motivate a moral life.

In discussing the position of the slave and free man, Paul notes how a free man is a slave of Christ (7:22). As he turns to the question of meat offered to idols, he begins the discussion noting how Christians worship God the Father and one Lord Jesus Christ (8:6). It is here that there is a significant use of the Hebrew Scripture as Paul presents a confession built from the *Shema* and its confession of the one God (Deut. 6:4), but with one important difference. Paul's variation speaks into the world of polytheism and its many gods (6:5).

The text laid out in parallel structure in English is as follows:

But for us [there is] one God, the Father,
    From whom [are] all things and we for him,
And one Lord, Jesus Christ,
    Through whom [are] all things and we through him.

Here Paul presents *two* figures the church honors, God and the Lord Jesus Christ, both of whom are portrayed as Creator and both of whom are honored by those who believe. This creed is something Paul portrays as a confession by the church. The lines have the look of tradition, something Paul passed on and something the community confesses, something that predates Paul.

The key moves are seen in (1) how the titles God and Lord are distributed, (2) in who participates in the creation, and (3) that the context is a discussion of gods who are honored by people. This last point sets the context for

---

11.   On the imagery of leaven and sacrifice, Gordon Fee, *The First Epistle to the Corinthians* (Grand Rapids: Eerdmans, 1987), 216–18. Paul is urging them to become what they are, or better, become what God has made them into by his grace and the sacrifice of Jesus the Christ.

the first two points and makes the text a most significant declaration about the Christ. Both God and Lord in the context of being Creator look to describe who God is and what God does, since in Judaism only God creates (Isa. 44:24; 4 Ezra 3:4; Josephus, *Contra Apion* 2.192). The fact that "all things" are created through Jesus shows he is in the category of Creator, not creature. As Bauckham says, "No more equivocal way of including Jesus in the unique divine identity is conceivable, within the framework of second temple Jewish monotheism."[12] To show the connection to the *Shema*, one need only look at the LXX: "The Lord (*kurios*) our God (*ho theos*), the Lord (*kurios*), is one." In the LXX, God and Lord refer to the same figure. Paul's point is binitarian. There is one God and one Lord who participates in the creation as the Creator is Paul's point. Thus, this confession affirms a divine activity and status for Jesus as the Christ, appealing to language from Israel's confession of the one God in the process. Paul does not indicate in 1 Corinthians 8 how he got to this conclusion, but the work of God through Jesus, including especially the vindication of Jesus to God the Father's right hand is probably the key to the synthesis. At least 1 Corinthians 15 and the defense of resurrection are fundamental points in this direction.

The relationship to this exalted Christ has ethical implications when one thinks of eating meat offered to idols. When one leads a weak brother to act in a way that violates his conscience by eating meat offered to an idol in a temple, then one has destroyed a brother for whom Christ died (8:11). Such an act is a sin against Christ (8:13), again because the brother and Jesus are connected. Paul himself is an example of giving up rights as he makes every effort not to put an obstacle in the way of the gospel of Christ (9:12). Paul lives with those without the Law in conjunction with the law of Christ so that he might gain the lawless (9:21).[13] Here the Christ supplies a call to love that is to make one sensitive to others (Gal. 5:1–25).

Paul reviews the history of Israel and notes that Christ was the rock that supplied water to God's people in the desert (10:4; Exod. 17:6). Paul does not indicate how he makes the connection to Christ being the one who provided water here, but in doing so he substitutes Jesus as Christ for a role God would have been seen to have had by Jews reading this account. It is likely that for Paul Jesus was seen as the "public figure" who acts for God and represents his presence in the old era (John 1:18 may be a parallel idea). Next Paul urges them not to flirt with idolatry so that they put Christ to the test as Israel did in the past (10:9). Idols should be shunned, as participation in the Lord's Supper makes it clear that the cup that is shared is a participation in the blood

---

12. Richard J. Bauckham, *Jesus and the God of Israel: God Crucified and Other Essays on the New Testament's Christology of Divine Identity* (Grand Rapids: Eerdmans, 2008), 102.

13. This passage has significant implications for Acts 21, where Paul chooses to take a vow and show a connection to the Law. Some argue that Paul would never have done such a thing. The idea that Paul as one not under law lives under law to those under law says otherwise. For the discussion on Acts 21, see Darrell L. Bock, *Acts*, 643–44.

of Christ (10:16) and the bread is a sharing in the body of Christ (10:16), a declaration of allegiance not to be violated. In all of this they are to be imitators of Christ and his giving example, like Paul is (11:1). Christ's presence is the basis for fellowship and participation with him, as one affirms one's unity with him at the Supper. Once again an ethical awareness and sensitivity emerges from this sense of identity with the Christ.

In discussing the relationship of men and women, Paul notes a hierarchy in the program of God, where Christ is the head of every man (11:3) and God is the head of Christ (11:3). In turning to the discussion of gifts in the body, Paul notes that just as a human body is one but has many members, so is Christ (12:12) because the church at Corinth is the body of Christ (12:27). So the Christ equips and incorporates in such a way that all are bound together in one body and called to serve each other through the spiritual gifts Jesus provides.

When it comes to the teaching on the resurrection, it is Christ who died for our sins according to the Scriptures that is a core piece of the preached gospel (15:3).[14] Paul again appeals to a creedal tradition having been "passed on" here, showing this idea is not his alone. In a key series of linked comments, Paul highlights how central resurrection is by looking at the alternative that resurrection does not take place, a view that would be common among most Greeks, who generally did not believe that resurrection was possible. If this Christ is preached as one who was raised from the dead, then how can some deny that he was raised (15:12)? If there is no resurrection, then neither is Christ raised (15:13). But if Christ is not raised, then the apostolic preaching is null (15:14). The apostles become false witnesses for having testified that Christ is raised if in fact he is not (15:15). If the dead are not raised, then neither is Christ (15:16). If Christ is not raised, then the faith is in vain (15:17) and those who are asleep (i.e., dead) are destroyed (15:18). If in this life alone we have hoped in Christ, then we are the most pitied of all men, having believed in an empty hope (15:19). However, Christ is raised, the first fruits of those who sleep (5:20). In fact, it is in Christ all are made alive (15:22). There is an order to this: Christ was raised first (15:23), then those who are Christ's at his coming (15:23).

What is significant about this defense of resurrection and the gospel is that it is the title of the Christ that stands as the position from which Jesus performs his work of overcoming death. A function of the anointed one is to overcome death and bring life. Paul defends his own willingness to die for them through a pride he has in Jesus Christ (15:31). He does so in part because he knows that thanks can be given to God for the victory that comes through Jesus Christ (15:56).

A natural question to raise from chapter 15 is where did this scriptural hope come from. Paul does not cite any texts in detail, but three texts are at

---

14. On the background to this confessional piece of church tradition Paul cites here, Fee, *The First Epistle to the Corinthians*, 722–29.

work here. First, he clearly alludes to Psalm 110:1 as he speaks of the enemies being put under Jesus' feet in 15:25. Jesus at the right hand is a theme he shares with other letters (Rom. 8:34; Eph. 1:20; Col. 3:1). Second, Paul also alludes to Psalm 8:7 in 15:27, where he speaks of all things being put in subjection to the one who is representative man, since Psalm 8 is about the authority God gave to humanity over the creation. Here is a typological-prophetic reading of Psalm 8 where the escalation points to how Jesus uniquely realizes what people were created to be. Third, there is Paul's mocking use of Hosea 13:14 as it is linked with Isaiah 25:8. This move shows the reversal death has undergone in Christ. What in Hosea is a text pointing to fear of death has in Jesus Christ's resurrection become a text of hope where death is taunted. Jesus reverses a curse and turns it into a mere transition into new life. With a farewell, Paul closes the letter noting his love in Christ Jesus for them all (16:24).

Christological Fulfillment in 1 Corinthians
So in this letter a few new features appear, along with some standard uses. Standard uses involve the Christ whose story involves suffering and resurrection. This connects with themes we saw in Hebrews, 1 Peter, and Revelation. Nothing shows this as clearly as the way in which Psalms 8 and 110 are used in 1 Corinthians 15:20–28. Here Jesus' cosmic authority in the end is highlighted. He functions as both king (Ps. 110) and representative humanity, a second Adam (Ps. 8). [15] A variation on this emphasis comes in how Jesus is seen as wisdom. What Jews often attributed to the Law is now affirmed about Jesus (1 Cor. 1–4). This history of the Christ's authority growing out of the exaltation after his suffering stands at the core of the gospel and its preaching, something the apostles give witness to when they preach. This resurrection involved divine vindication of Jesus and showed by his exaltation to God's side who he truly was. This is why Jesus is confessed as the Christ. The theme of incorporation seen in Galatians reappears. But fresh emphases are placed on the position in Christ that salvation brings. As a result the believers' connectedness to Christ has ethical implications that this letter spells out in specific ways. It is a sacred connection to Christ that is not only confessed but that energizes the moral life. This association with the Christ and its precious, sacred nature lead to identification with Jesus and a sense of representing and reflecting him that calls believers to righteousness.

Confessions of "Christ" in 2 Corinthians
In a follow-up letter to Corinth where Paul defends his apostleship, there are forty-seven uses of the term "Christ." The thrust of 2 Corinthians is the community's connectedness to Christ as a new creation and their being called to suffer and to give.

---

15. On the use of Adam/Christ imagery, Garland, *First Corinthians*, 704–7.

Again as with 1 Corinthians, it is as an apostle of Jesus Christ that Paul writes (1:1) followed by his standard greeting of grace and peace from God our Father and the Lord Jesus Christ (1:2) and a frequent note of blessing given to the God and Father of our Lord Jesus Christ (1:3). Paul turns to suffering and notes that we share in the sufferings of Christ (1:5) just as through Christ we share in comfort (1:5). This theme of suffering is highlighted more in this Pauline book than any other of his Epistles.

Paul observes that in preaching the Son of God, Jesus Christ, they preached one who is the "yes" from God, the one in whom all God's promises are affirmed and realized (1:19). God is the one establishing them in Christ connecting them in a sacred relationship to the apostle (1:21).

It is clear that the letter is full of tension as Paul speaks of forgiving them in the presence of Christ (2:10) to keep Satan from gaining any advantage. Paul shares his anxiety as he preached the gospel of Christ (2:12) in Troas and then came to Macedonia looking for Titus. Paul gives thanks to God who always leads in triumph in Christ (2:14), as the fragrance of the knowledge of him is spread everywhere and as the apostles serve as the aroma of Christ in God to both the saved and perishing (2:15). Here the imagery has a mixture of Greco-Roman elements (with its picture of the victory parade that came with military success) and the Jewish picture of sacred sacrifice (as the aroma of God alludes to the sweet savor of the accepted sacrifice). The message they preach is not peddled, but is commissioned by God as they speak in Christ (2:17). The Corinthians themselves are a letter from Christ delivered by Paul's preaching (3:3). His confidence about their position comes through Christ toward God (3:4). As in Paul's other letters, what is central is the connectedness Christ produces. Again as elsewhere in Paul, a deep sense of connectedness to Christ functions as a core theology to motivate believers in their walk. Christology leads into ethics.

As Paul discusses the rejection of most Jews, he notes how only in Christ is the veil removed from a hardened mind (3:14).[16] The god of this world (Satan) has blinded the minds of unbelievers, so that they cannot see the light of the gospel of the glory of Christ (4:4). This is why Paul preaches not about himself but about Jesus Christ as Lord (4:5). It is the shining of light from the hearts that gives light of the knowledge of the glory of God in the face of Christ (4:6). Paul uses the common image of light shining in darkness and pointing to presence and life (Gen. 1:3; Isa. 9:1). So Paul lives by faith and aims to please God in all he does because he knows that one day all believers will appear before the judgment seat of Christ (5:10).

---

16. The imagery in 2 Corinthians 3 is difficult. For views, see the careful study by Scott Hafemann, *Suffering and Ministry in the Spirit: Paul's Defense of His Ministry in 2 Corinthians 2:14–3:3* (Grand Rapids: Eerdmans, 1990). Paul's point is that his ministry through the Spirit vindicates him, because the Spirit from the Christ represents the presence of God's new era, something that was intended to function more effectively than the Law could.

It is interesting to note that Paul's motivation for faithfulness in his letters has more to do with his allegiance and connectedness to Christ than to any thought about judgment or reward to come. God's future evaluation of our stewardship is a part of Paul's thinking, as the letters to Thessalonica and 1 Corinthians 3:11–15 show, but 2 Corinthians 5:10 is one of a few texts that has noted this judgment theme in contrast to the many texts that highlight a sacred connectedness to the Christ.

Paul again discusses his message and defends his gospel when he declares that the love of Christ drives them in their preaching knowing that one has died for all (5:14). There is discussion here whether Paul means our love for Christ or Christ's love for us that motivates. It may well be that Paul is thinking of all of this, since Christ's love for us generates the believer's love in response. However in discussing the sacrifice of Jesus, the starting point is clearly Jesus' act towards us. Paul notes that at one time he regarded Christ from a human point of view, but not any more (5:16). If anyone is in Christ, he is a new creation (5:17).[17]

Here again is the emphasis that is so Pauline. The work of Christ incorporates one into him and brings a new way of existence. All of this comes from God who reconciled us through Christ (5:18). In other words, in Christ, God was reconciling the world to himself (5:19). This makes Paul and those who share the gospel ambassadors for Christ as they deliver this message (5:20). The message is: We beg you on behalf of Christ, be reconciled to God (5:20). So in another tightly constructed Pauline passage we again see the central role of the Christ in the salvation message. It is the promised one of God who is preached as the means of reconciliation. Here is the heart of Paul's message in this epistle. At the core of the understanding of who Christ is are the events of what God has done through Jesus. His life and ministry were a revelation about the Promised One. In many cases, Jesus' activity explains him as the Christ versus citing texts from the Hebrew Scripture.

Again the connectedness to Jesus comes into play when Paul asks what Christ and Belial[18] have in common (6:15).[19] This is in the context of not being matched with unbelievers, that is, in sharing with their form of wor-

---

17. See also Galatians 6:14–16.
18. During the latter second temple period, a growing belief in demons emerged. Belial is the head of this demonic horde (1QS 2.19), he is the prince of the kingdom of wickedness (1QM 17.5–6), and his reign is one of injustice (1QS 4.19–20). Both demons and evil people make up his community (*Jub.* 14:31–33; 1QM 13.10–13). In fact, he ensnares people causing them to sin (e.g., *Jub.* 1:20; *1 En.* 69:6; *T.Reu.* 4:7). See *Anchor Bible Dictionary*, 1992 ed., "Belial"; *Encyclopedia of the Dead Sea Scrolls*, 2000 ed., s.v. "Demons." For a more technical study see R. M. M. Tuschling, *Angels and Orthodoxy*, Studies and Texts in Antiquity and Christianity (Tübingen: Mohr Siebeck, 2007).
19. On this passage and its use of the Old Testament, see William Webb, *Returning Home: New Covenant and Second Exodus as a Context for 2 Corinthians 6.14–7.1*, JSNTSup 85 (Sheffield: Sheffield Academic Press, 1993). Second exodus motifs are part of the themes of the new eschatological era into which the Christ is placed.

ship. In the catena of Hebrew Scripture texts that follow, both Isaiah 52:11 and 2 Samuel 7:8 are cited (vv. 17–18).[20] This is joined to a covenantal community text from Leviticus 26:11 (v. 16). Isaiah 52:11 is in a context that precedes the Servant Song where the Servant suffers before being exalted (Isa. 52:13–53:12). The call to holiness and deliverance fall side by side. Second Samuel 7 is the Davidic covenant text. What is interesting here is that the promise is democratized to apply not just to the Davidic line but to anyone connected to the line. Isaiah 55:3 does something similar. Paul is showing that incorporation in Christ brings covenantal benefits and a responsibility to live in holiness. Once again incorporation into Christ has ethical implications.

As Paul addresses giving, he looks to the example of Jesus, a theme recalling the Catholic Epistles. The grace of the Lord Jesus Christ was such, that though he was rich, he became poor for their sake (8:9), so that in his poverty they might become rich, an allusion to his taking on humanity and dying for them. The example of Christ's suffering and humiliation in taking on humanity is the ethical point of departure, just as we saw in 1 Peter. In noting the work of Titus as a messenger to the churches, Paul describes those churches as the glory of Christ (8:23). By giving, the ministry rendered will glorify God, as their obedience will acknowledge the gospel of Christ (9:13).

As Paul moves to close the letter, he exhorts them by the meekness and gentleness of Christ (10:1). The goal is to take every thought captive to obey Christ (10:5), a call to faithfulness and unity in the face of satanic opposition. He reminds them that if anyone is confident they are Christ's, as they indeed are Christ's, so are Paul and his group (10:7). He also reminds them that it was Paul's group that preached the gospel of Christ to them (10:14). So Paul betrothed them to Christ (11:2). Now he fears Satan is deceiving them and leading them astray in the sincere and pure devotion to Christ (11:3). He boasts that he was faithful in how he shared with them, something he can say as the truth of Christ is in him (11:10). He reacts against the false apostles and deceivers who disguise themselves as apostles of Christ (11:13). Paul sets forth his credentials versus the claims of his opponents in a necessary, but unflattering form of human boasting. So he is a servant of Christ just as they claim to be (11:23).[21] In his continued boasting to set forth his credentials, he notes a vision he experienced as a man in Christ fourteen years ago (12:2). But he does not like to boast but to stress his weakness that the power of Christ might rest on him (12:9). For Christ's sake he is content to

---

20. For Johnston's discussion of the servant songs in Isaiah, see chapter 5 (pp. 152–61). For Johnston's discussion of 2 Samuel 7, see chapter 2 (pp. 59–72).

21. Paul uses the word here for ministers in referring to servants of Christ. Part of his defense is that he is as much a called minster and bears the marks of representing the Christ as anyone. Linda L. Belleville, *2 Corinthians,* IVPNT (Downers Grove; InterVarsity, 1996), 288–91.

live in weakness (12:10). He is speaking in Christ and defending himself for their edification (12:19).

Paul closes the letter with a warning that they are seeking proof that Christ speaks in him (13:3). He calls on them to test themselves and see that Jesus Christ is in them, unless they fail the test (13:5). The connectedness that Paul continuously highlights is a product of the indwelling Christ being in them. This remark parallels his manner of speaking earlier in the letter when he discusses the Spirit's presence among them (2 Cor. 3:17–18; also 1 Cor. 3:17). So Paul closes his letter with a salutation asking for the grace of the Lord Jesus Christ, God's love, and the fellowship of the Spirit to be with them (13:14).

Christological Fulfillment in 2 Corinthians

In this letter we see how the incorporation of Christ continues to be a key Pauline theme. The centrality of the Christ in the message of reconciliation is also emphasized as a key idea in the preached gospel. Connectedness to Christ links Paul to the Corinthians, a link they should not let anyone seek to diminish nor tarnish. For Paul, Jesus as Christ is a powerful personal link and presence, not only for an individual's life but also for their relationship to others. This strong ethical dimension is to come into play as a way to work through conflict and differences. They are Christ's first. Jesus' own example in suffering and service should be the model they build their own responses around. Their allegiance to him should drive them to work together.

Paul does not engage in a great deal of christological explanation in this letter. The portrait of who the Christ is and what he does is largely assumed, fitting patterns tied to Jesus' position and suffering as key examples. A somewhat fresh note here is the picture of the Corinthians as a letter of Christ in 2 Corinthians 3. What Paul alludes to here is the presence of the Spirit. The language speaks of the Spirit written on the heart in fulfillment of New Covenant hope and promise. We saw this note about the Spirit in the epistle to the Galatians (Gal. 3), but in the Corinthian correspondence it has a fresh twist. Here we have language combining imagery from Jeremiah 31:33 (English) and Ezekiel 34:24–26. The Spirit is the incorporating link between Jesus' work and their position as people of God. Here is a key source for the relational emphasis we see in Paul. The Lord is called both the Spirit and the Spirit of the Lord here (2 Cor. 3:17–18). Their identity is that tightly associated. It is the Christ who sends this Spirit. This theme brings together two key eschatological ideas from Jewish hope, the work of righteousness that the Christ makes possible and the hope of a new eschatological era involving a change within the heart. In 2 Corinthians 4:4, this is called the "light of the glorious gospel of Christ." This linkage shows that often the way into christological discussion and development came from the recognition of the realization of eschatological hope in texts that in their original context did not directly invoke Messiah, but rather described the arrival of the new era with the promised deliverance. The ministry of Jesus made the linkage and showed the association.

The idea of the Spirit as a key element of the gospel Christ brings is a key Pauline theme. The Spirit energizes the new life of the new era. Here is yet another early Christian synthetic move on Jewish and second temple promise. There had been the hope of a Christ of a new era and of a work in the heart, even of a fresh presence of God's Spirit, but now the church claimed that the chosen one of God was directly responsible for all of it, even down to the giving of the Spirit. What comes together here is the nature of the special time, the eschatological era, with the figure responsible for making it happen: the Christ.

A second key collection of sacred text citations comes in 2 Corinthians 6:14–7:1. Here there is development of ideas about the sacred community and of messianic promises. In keeping with second temple usage of sacred texts, Paul strings together a collection of First Testament citations (Lev. 26; Isa. 52; 2 Sam. 7) so as to present a new community pictured as a sacred place and temple (2 Cor. 6:16), much as 1 Peter 2:4–10 presents. Paul begins with a citation from Leviticus 26:11–12. Yet he enhances the imagery from its original use. Leviticus speaks of God dwelling in the midst of his people. The Greek preposition ἐν in the phrase ἐν αὐτοῖς ("in them") can also have that meaning ("among" or "with"). However, Paul speaks here of God (as the Spirit) dwelling *in* his people, since he calls believers "the temple of the living God" in the previous clause. This is imagery he uses elsewhere in his writings of the corporate people of God (1 Cor. 3:16; Eph. 2:21–22 versus 1 Cor. 6:19 where an individual is in view). The following call to come out and be separate appeals to language from Isaiah 52:11 and reflects the ethical call of being holy, being set apart for righteousness.

The picture of God's people as sons and daughters reflects an extension of the Davidic promise of 2 Samuel 7 from the king alone to those incorporated in him, both male and female. All of them now are full family members with God as Father to all of them, not just to the king.[22] This extension of incorporation is something Paul most clearly and explicitly expresses in the Second Testament. The idea of intimacy involves a level of family intimacy that exceeds the language of the old era because of the gift of the Spirit. Christ as source of the sacred position of God's people and as building a sacred temple is something shared across various letters. So here we see developments of the expectation of the Christ, fresh application, and more widely used and common images of hope.

Confessions of "Christ" in Romans
In Romans, Paul identifies how it is that Jesus' work incorporates those who believe into life of the Spirit as they die to condemnation and the Law. This

---

22. For a more complete discussion of this passage see Bock, "Single Meaning,," 140–46.

key Pauline letter has the most uses of the term "Christ" in Paul, but its concentration is not as great as in some of the smaller Pauline letters, such as Philemon, Philippians, and Ephesians in terms of use per thousand words.[23]

Paul introduces himself as the bondservant of Jesus Christ in 1:1 and notes that the Son of God was marked out by God as such when God raised Jesus Christ our Lord from the dead (1:4).[24] Those in the church are called "in" Jesus Christ (1:6). This is an important expression for Paul. It and others like it speak of people placed corporately in Christ. So this reference is another example of the incorporation language so central to Paul's presentation of the believer's self understanding and identity. These references highlight a relational dimension to one's connection to Jesus that comes as a result of faith. They also indicate a representational feature of this relationship that calls for allegiance to Christ by faithfully representing the one to whom the believer is indebted and associated. In addition in this set of references we see a juxtaposition of Jesus as promised Christ and as God's Son. The descent from David is a key element that shows up here for a messianic dimension to this juxtaposition. So here we are connected to a promise that runs as far back as 2 Samuel 7 in terms of how it was understood by many Jews in the first century. This Davidic hope appears in texts like *Psalms of Solomon* 17–18 and some of the Dead Sea Scrolls appealing to the hope of the Davidic line (4QFlor), but there is a less militaristic flavor to Paul's use than in those texts. The spiritual incorporation Paul speaks of here seems to be his contribution to this hope.

In a standard Pauline greeting, grace and peace come from God our Father and the Lord Jesus Christ (1:7). It is through Jesus Christ that Paul gives thanks for the Romans and the testimony of their faith (1:8). With this flurry of references, Paul concludes his use of the materials in the introduction of his letter. The distinctive thing about these uses is the highlight on the relational dimension of Jesus as Christ. A person is corporately placed into

---

23. Accordance traces this and notes that Philemon has a "hit rate" of 20.73 words per thousand, while Philippians (19.33) and Ephesians (16.50) come next. Romans is 7.85. The lowest rate in Paul is for Titus at 5.16. As a comparison, in the Catholic materials and Revelation, the most intense use appears in 1 Peter with a rate of 11.26, while Revelation is the lowest at 0.63. Interestingly the Pauline rates are very high in comparison with the narrative sections of the Second Testament, where the rates are far lower: Matthew (0.75), Mark (0.53), Luke (0.53), John (1.04), and Acts (1.20).

24. Romans 1:2–4 is a doctrinal summary about Jesus that could well reflect early church tradition about him as the balanced lines in the verses suggest; Thomas Schreiner, *Romans*, BECNT (Grand Rapids: Baker, 1998), 38–45. Peter Sthulmacher, *Paul's Letter to the Romans: A Commentary*, NTL (Louisville: Westminster/John Knox, 1994), says these verses "contain the history of Christ told in the Gospels in short form" (p. 19). The term "marked out" literally means "horizoned." It points to a display or a making clear of something.

Christ as a result of faith. Called through him, one shares identity with him and benefits from him.

The theme of authority for Jesus Christ appears next in 2:16, where people and their secrets will be judged by Christ Jesus.[25] The flipping of the names from their usual order (i.e., from Jesus Christ to Christ Jesus) may or may not be significant, but in some texts where Christ Jesus occurs in Paul, it is Jesus in actions related to his return that are in view. It is almost as if the term in this order means the "Anointed King" Jesus. However, as we shall see, the flipping of the names also appears in contexts where Jesus' current work is in view.

A central idea in Romans is that justification comes apart from the law. Here we revisit a theme, but with more detail, that we saw in Galatians 2–4. One is justified through faith in Jesus Christ (3:22). The reversal of the normal name pattern appears again when Paul speaks of the redemption that comes in Christ Jesus (3:24). Here is a text where Jesus' past work is reflected in the midst of the reversal of the names. The peace that believers possess comes through our Lord Jesus Christ (5:1). What is interesting is that in the exposition of this idea in Romans 5:1–11, the term appears by itself twice. It is Christ who died for the ungodly (5:6), and Christ who died for sinners (5:8). Reconciliation comes through Jesus Christ (5:11), just as its product, peace, did. When Paul contrasts Adam and Jesus in 5:12–21, it is in the one man Jesus Christ that the gift of grace comes (5:15), while grace and the gift of righteousness reign to eternal life though Jesus Christ our Lord (5:17, 21). In this section on the key theme of salvation, it is Jesus' corporate and mediating roles as Christ that are key. Also important is how suffering and resurrection are linked here. Death provides forgiveness, while resurrection provides life. His suffering to his exaltation leads to our reconciliation (5:10–11).

Several uses cluster in Romans 6. Believers were baptized into Christ Jesus (6:3). Just as Christ was raised from the dead, so we too are raised in newness of life when we come to him as baptism pictures (6:4). In other words, if we have died together with Christ, so we also shall be raised in him (6:8), knowing that Christ was raised from the dead no longer to die having shown that death does not reign over him (6:9). Thus we are dead to sin and alive to God in Christ Jesus (6:11). Again in combination, it is the flipped version of the names that are in view as Jesus does his work as the Christ. This emphasis on the provision of new life will set up the discussion of the availability of the indwelling Spirit in Romans 8, a true sign that the new era has come through what the Christ has done.[26]

---

25. This theme echoes what we shall see in Acts 10:40–42 and 17:30–31. Jesus serves as the judge of the living and the dead.
26. Schreiner, *Romans*, 302–3 has a nice chart of how the argument in 6:1–14 works. As a result of the work of Christ, one is now alive to the power of God in Christ Jesus. Sin can be and is overcome.

When it comes to the Law, believers have died to the Law through the body of Jesus Christ so that we now belong to another, namely, to him (7:4). The deliverance Jesus brings is highlighted in that thanksgiving can come to God through Jesus Christ our Lord because he has delivered us from the body of sin, as Romans 8 will elaborate.

Fully ten of the uses in this letter appear in Romans 8. Paul is setting forth and confessing how central Jesus' work as Christ is. In none of these uses, except the last, does the additional description of Jesus as Lord appear. Jesus does his mediating work as the Christ, the one who is anointed over the kingdom blessing of God. That exalted role gives Jesus complete authority. So there is no condemnation in Christ Jesus (8:1), for the law of the Spirit of life is in Christ Jesus (8:2).[27] It is the Spirit of God that dwells in God's children (8:9), for if Christ indwells someone, then the human spirit is alive because of righteousness and the gift it provides (8:10). The one who raised Jesus Christ from the dead will also give life to the bodies of those in whom his Spirit dwells (8:11). If we are God's children, then we are coheirs with Christ in God's promises (8:17). It is Christ, the one who was raised to God's right hand (Ps. 110:1), who intercedes for us so no one can bring a charge against us (8:34). No one can separate us from the love of Christ (8:35) or from the love of God in Christ Jesus our Lord (8:39). No chapter in the Second Testament so eloquently describes Jesus Christ's saving and securing work. At the root of the picture of what exaltation achieves is the invocation of Psalm 110:1, as Jesus sits at God's right hand and intercedes for us.[28] Clearly this is a central text, whose implications move in many directions, both in terms of pointing to life and reconciliation, as well as to the ongoing ministry of intercession Jesus exercises for us.

When Paul turns to his love of the Jewish people, he says that he speaks the truth in Christ that his grief for the Jewish people is great (9:1). He would be willing himself to become an anathema from Christ for the sake of his brothers (9:3). This is because the promise of the Christ, among other blessings, belongs to them (9:5).

However, the obstacle is how Jews view the law and their failure to appreciate what God had done in Christ, what Paul calls the stumbling stone (9:32–33). Here Paul cites imagery from Isaiah 8:14 and 28:16. We saw this text cited in 1 Peter 2:6 and discussed it there. Paul uses this text in the same way here. Jesus is a stone over which the nation stumbled, but that is precious and exalted by God. In addition, what many Jews do not realize and accept is

---

27. As Stuhlmacher, *Paul's Letter to the Romans*, stresses (pp. 117–18) this chapter contrasts the debilitating effect of the Law on our flesh (Rom. 7) with the liberating and empowering capability that comes the Spirit (Rom. 8). Here is the power of the gospel of Christ Paul described in Romans 1:16.
28. For Johnston's discussion of Psalm 110, see chapter 3 (pp. 89–98).

that Christ is the goal or termination (*telos*) of the law (10:4).[29] If the later allusion to Jeremiah 31 in Romans 11:27 is in play, then Christ's death opened up a new era and a new covenant. This is what has been missed, how suffering and sacrifice clear the way for the new era. This also explains why so many Second Testament texts on the Christ treat his suffering. It is key to securing the arrival of the new era.

A citation from Deuteronomy 30:12 becomes the focus next as Paul asserts that the word of faith is not so far away that one must ascend to heaven to find it or descend into the abyss to get it. To do this is either to bring Christ down from heaven or to bring Christ up from the dead (10:6–7).[30] Paul's point in referring to the Christ here argues that to suggest that the word of faith is far away undoes Jesus' death and exaltation. The idea that the word of faith is far away suggests that the confession of him as Lord saving is not accessible. So he reminds them that the word of faith is near. It is not hard to find or grasp. Paul can use a text that was about the law to refer to Christ because of what he says about the Law both here and in general. The law points to Christ as *telos* (Rom. 10:4). So what is said of the law can be said of Jesus. In Galatians 3–4, Paul noted the law was brought in alongside of promise as a pedagogue. In other words, the law leads to the new era and the promise of a seed. So again what is said of the revelation of the law can also be said of the Christ to whom it points.

It is preaching about Christ that leads to saving faith (10:17). Again, the central role of Jesus as the Christ is what Paul highlights in the use of the term. The difference between Romans 1–8 and 9–11 is that in the earlier chapters it is the individual experience that is the focus, while in 9–11 it is the corporate status of Jews and Gentiles.

A final citation appears in Romans 11:26–27. The eschatological work of the Deliverer is noted in the exposition that follows as Paul cites Isaiah 59:20 alongside of Jeremiah 31:33. What allows this link? It may be that the reference to the Spirit among the people in Isaiah 59:21 also points to placing the law on the heart and the promise of the Spirit of the new era from Jeremiah 31, as well as texts like Ezekiel 34–36. In Isaiah the protector appears to be the God of Israel. Paul now specifies the forgiveness is rooted in the One

---

29. The meaning of the term *telos* is disputed in this verse and can mean either goal or termination. It is hard to be sure which is meant. For us, what is important is that Christ and the promise tied to him is central to how the law has become less relevant now that Christ has come. The Jewish failure to appreciate this relationship between the law and the Christ is one of the great obstacles to salvation. For a discussion of this term's meaning and the themes of this book, see Douglas Moo, *The Epistle to the Romans*, NICNT (Grand Rapids: Eerdmans, 1996).

30. I discuss the hermeneutics of how this citation of Deuteronomy works in "Single Meaning," 132–40. We are again revisiting themes treated in Galatians, but now with more detailed argument from Paul.

through whom God worked. This text is part of what Messiah will do one day for Israel. In this context, Israel must be ethnic Israel, since they are Paul's concern in these chapters and stand in contrast to the responsive Gentiles. One day Messiah will complete his promise and deliver the nation to whom the promise was originally made.

We see a new emphasis here in Romans 7–10, already introduced in Romans 3:20–31. It is how Jesus relates to the law. There is no longer an accuser against us. Even something as holy as the law cannot lead to our condemnation when one is allied to the Christ. Non-condemnation is a central feature of what the work of Christ accomplishes. In Romans 5:1, Paul refers to the result as peace with God. What 2 Corinthians referred to as reconciliation, Paul portrays here as a legal action that means there is no break between God and the child he created. The one reestablishing this secure bond is the Christ. Peace and reconciliation are the result (Rom. 5:1, 11). In addition, we can think of this individually or corporately as Jew and Gentile. Anyone, Jew or Gentile, who confesses Jesus as Lord in his work as Christ benefits (Rom. 10:5–13).

As Paul turns to apply his teaching, he begins by returning to the incorporation that comes in salvation. Believers comprise one body in Christ (12:5). Because of this identification, believers are to put on the Lord Christ Jesus and make no provision for the flesh (13:14). So Paul affirms the ethical implication of being a representative of Christ, of belonging to him and his community through incorporation.

The Christ is both example and authority for living. Christ died and lived again that he might be Lord of both the living and the dead (14:9), so whether we live or die we are the Lord's. In the verses that follow there is the appeal to the judgment seat of God and that every knee will bow to the Lord and give praise to God (14:10–12). This is laid out with ambiguity as to whether the Father or Lord Jesus is meant. The context speaking of the Christ as Lord of the living and the dead usually suggests Jesus' role in the judgment (Acts 10:42–43). The background to the language of bowing the knee comes from Isaiah 45, one of the strongest monotheistic chapters of the Hebrew Scripture. This Isaiah text will reappear in Philippians 2, where it clearly refers to Jesus. So it appears we have another example of where texts that refer to the God of Israel are applied to the work of the Christ. The relationship of the Son and Father in a kingdom rule context is so close the change can be made, even while keeping a touch of ambiguity in how it is done. Here the future is a motivation for how we act now. We have a stewardship before Christ for which we are accountable.

So the pursuit of righteousness, peace, and joy are the calling of those who serve Christ (14:18). This yields acceptance from God and approval by people. Christ modeled sensitivity to others, because he did not come to please himself but bore reproach for the sake of others (15:3). Here Psalm 69:9 (= 68:10 LXX) is cited with the remark about bearing the reproaches of others. Here is a psalm about the righteous sufferer and the application is typological-prophetic, since this Psalm is not just about Jesus' righteous suffering. So a person is to appreciate the Christ's example and to live in harmony. This is in accord with Christ Jesus (15:5), with the result that the God and Father of our Lord Jesus Christ is glorified (15:6). So believers are to welcome each other as Christ has welcomed them (15:7). Christ himself became a servant to the circumcised and showed the example (15:8). In the emphasis on model, Paul echoes 1 Peter.[31]

In a catena of texts arguing that the Hebrew Scripture looked forward to a day when Gentiles would be blessed, one of the texts cited is Isaiah 11:10. Here is a text that was about the Davidic line and the hope that one day the root of Jesse would rule Gentiles and give them hope. The Hebrew text speaks of Gentiles seeking guidance here, while the LXX speaks of hope. So here again, Jesus being of the line and promise of David is used prophetically. This links us back to Romans 1:2–4; the Christ is of the seed of David. Here the deliverance of the eschatological era and the person come together.

In some personal remarks, Paul notes that he is a minister of Christ Jesus (15:16), so that in Christ Jesus he is proud of his work (15:17). The only thing of which he speaks is what Christ has brought about through him (15:18). So he preaches the gospel of Christ and especially desires to do so where Christ has not been named (15:19–20). Paul desires to come to them one day in the fullness of the blessing of Christ (15:29). He appeals to them by our Lord Jesus Christ and by the love of the Spirit to pray for his protection and service to the saints (15:30). So the incorporation Paul affirms is connected to what he does in ministry. Jesus as the Christ impacts how we live and how we serve. What is stressed in Paul's teaching is how comprehensively Christ represents a worldview, not only does he have authority over life, but being in him impacts how we even see life and engage in it.

His colleagues share in this connectedness to the Christ. So Prisca and Aquila are fellow workers in Christ Jesus (16:3). Epaenetus was the first convert in Asia in Christ (16:5). Andronicus and Junias were in Christ before Paul was (16:7). Urbanus is a fellow worker in Christ (16:9). Apelles is approved in Christ (16:10). All the churches of Christ send greeting (16:16). So Christ as the head of the body produces a connectedness between all believers, regardless of their location. Finally, Paul warns about opponents who bring division in opposition to this doctrine, noting that such persons do not serve our Lord Christ (16:18).

As Paul closes the letter, he commends the Roman believers to the grace of our Lord Jesus Christ (16:20). In the final doxology, he asks God to

---

31. Schreiner, *Romans*, 747–49, mentions the Old Testament roots here of Psalm 69, because of the appeal to Psalm 69:9. He notes these comments are a commentary on the strong helping the weak from Romans 14:15.

strengthen them according to the gospel and preaching of Jesus Christ and notes that the disclosure of the gospel leads to obedience of faith, a cause for everlasting praise to the only wise God through Jesus Christ (16:25, 27). In this text, Paul also notes how some of these connections were mysteries now made clear. In other words, they were implicit in the Scriptures of old but now have been made evident by what God has shown in Jesus. Here is how Paul says it in a word of praise to God: "Now to him who is able to strengthen you according to my gospel and the proclamation of Jesus Christ, according to the revelation of the mystery that had been kept secret for long ages, but now is disclosed, and through the prophetic scriptures has been made known to all the nations, according to the command of the eternal God, to bring about the obedience of faith—to the only wise God, through Jesus Christ, be glory forever! Amen." Here we see the combination we have argued for in this book. There are the prophetic Scriptures of old and there is the ministry of Christ. Together they make clear in a progressive revelation of the mystery what God's program about the Christ involved. The mystery is now revealed and made clear through what God has done and through what the Scriptures taught.

So Romans highlights the work of Christ Jesus. Only briefly is he noted as judge. This letter concentrates on the work of salvation as Jesus brings redemption, reconciliation, and peace. Paul stresses connectedness to Christ. We share in the benefits of his death and resurrection. We are incorporated into the Christ and his body, the church. It is this note of incorporation that dominates Paul's discussion of the work of the Christ Jesus in Romans.

Christological Fulfillment in Romans

When we compare this portrait with earlier expectations about the Christ, we see that the Christ figure for Paul is more than one who does things for God and his people, as these earlier texts hoped for and proclaimed. Rather, Christ is the hub around which divine activity, salvation, and life's perspectives rotate.[32] He is not just a key who unlocks salvation; he is the center around which salvation revolves and to which salvation is permanently and inseparably connected. So Romans gives us exposition of older passages, texts like Isaiah 8:14, 11:10, 28:16, 45:18; 59:20; Psalm 69:10, 110:1; and Jeremiah 31:33. They often are not merely cited alone, but in combination with other ideas. Many are familiar texts cited elsewhere. We see a combination of texts about the time of deliverance and texts about the Davidic hope or a righteous sufferer. Some are directly prophetic (Jer. 31; Isa. 11:10 about the ultimate reach of Davidic hope), while others are typological-prophetic (Ps. 69; 110:1; 8:14; 28:16). Some that in the Hebrew Scripture looked to what God would

---

32. Whereas in 1 Corinthians, it is the cross that serves as the hub of these descriptions, in Romans it is Jesus as the Christ that is front and center.

do now discuss what Jesus did or will do as the deliverer (Isa. 45:18; 59:20). We see a synthesizing and development of these ideas about deliverance and the Messiah, especially in a direction that highlights the ethical implications of what it means to be a part of the new community the Christ has formed. Where texts or ideas are present, it is things like Jesus' Davidic roots that are set forth (Rom. 1:2–4) or his role in opening up salvation to the nations (15:12). What the gospels will call discipleship is what Paul covers through the results of incorporation into Christ.

House Arrest Epistles: Ephesians, Colossians, Philemon, Philippians

Ephesians, Colossians, Philemon, and Philippians are commonly referred to as the "Prison Epistles" or "The Captivity Epistles" because Paul writes as a prisoner in all of them.[33] Yet in reality Paul is under house arrest in Rome. Thus perhaps a better designation is "House Arrest Epistles." Regardless of how we label these four Epistles, they were written while Paul was in confinement. Here we will see fresh lines of development in how incorporation into the Christ impacts those who have embraced Jesus as the promised center of divine activity.

Confessions of "Christ" in Ephesians

Ephesians concerns itself with Gentile incorporation and reconciliation as those who were far away are brought near and equipped with blessing. This epistle highlights the church as Jew and Gentile through Christ's peace having a role in God's program.[34] Amazingly there are forty-six uses of the term "Christ" in this very short epistle. Paul writes as an apostle of Christ Jesus (1:1) to those who are faithful in Christ Jesus (1:1) with his standard greeting of grace and peace from God our Father and the Lord Jesus Christ (1:2). As with 2 Corinthians, Paul opens with a blessing to the God and Father of our Lord Jesus Christ (1:3) who has blessed believers with every spiritual blessing in the heavenlies in Christ (1:3). In the program of God, believers

---

33. Paul calls himself "the prisoner of Christ Jesus" (Eph. 3:1), and all four letters contain explicit references to his imprisonment (Col. 4:3, 18; Philem. 10, 13, 22, 23; Eph. 3:1; 4:1; 6:20; Phil. 1:7, 13). Second Timothy, although written while Paul was in prison, is not included in the prison Epistles because the severity of the confinement indicates that it was a different imprisonment and is written to an individual, not a church community. See David Capes, Rodney Reeves, and E. Randolph Richards, *Rediscovering Paul: An Introduction to His World, Letters, and Theology* (Downers Grove: InterVarsity, 2007), 201–35.

34. For a comprehensive treatment of this book, see Harold Hoehner, *Ephesians: An Exegetical Commentary* (Grand Rapids: Baker, 2002). His treatment includes a defense of Pauline authorship for this letter. A more popular version of his work in "Ephesians" is in *Ephesians, Philippians, 1–2 Thessalonians, Colossians, Philemon*, CBC 16 (ed. Philip W. Comfort; Carol Stream: Tyndale House, 2008). Another solid commentary is by Peter O'Brien, *The Letter to the Ephesians*, NIGTC (Grand Rapids: Eerdmans, 1999).

were predestined into adoption through Jesus Christ (1:5), part of a divine program to sum up all things in Christ (1:10). Those who were the first to hope in Christ have been appointed to live to the praise of his glory (1:12). In this introduction, Paul sets forth the theme of promised and divinely planned blessing that comes in Christ, a plan that predates creation. The fresh element here is connecting the work of the Christ to the pre-Creation, a planned program of God.[35]

Paul's prayer is that the God of our Lord Jesus Christ might give the Ephesians a spirit of wisdom and revelation, a work that is the extension of God's Spirit in them (1:17). He wants them to know the hope, riches, and especially the power God has given them. This power is like that which God worked in Jesus Christ in the resurrection and exaltation of Jesus to God's side, when God seated Jesus above all authority and gave him as head over the church (1:20).[36] Once again the backdrop for this idea is the language of Psalm 110:1 and the emphasis is on the authority of Jesus as a heavenly ruling figure. The vindication of God has led into the rule of Jesus and incorporation of people into his community. The power Paul prays about is also seen in how God took believers out of their sin and made them alive together with Christ (2:5). He seated them together in the heavenlies in Christ Jesus (2:6). This emphasis on what takes place together is another way to highlight the corporate aspect and connection the Christ provides. Christ has produced a new community. The goal is to show the riches of his grace in Christ Jesus (2:7). Believers are God's workmanship in Christ Jesus, created in Christ Jesus for good works (2:10). In many ways, Ephesians 2:8–10 summarizes the theme of Christ's work in the book. As is common in Paul, it is incorporation into Christ and solidarity with him that is highlighted. Once again, the ethical implications are spelled out in the issue of how the goal of the plan in Christ was to grace people with an ability to please God through their works, which do not save but reflect salvation.

Paul turns next to how Gentiles were incorporated into Christ, for there was a time when they were without Christ (2:12). But now in Christ Jesus, those who were far off have now been brought near (2:13) through the blood of Christ (2:13). The peace that comes from the Messiah's work is not just between a person and God, but between groups. This ethical dimension of Jesus' work was revolutionary in a context where Jews and Gentiles had been enemies, with the issues between them intensified since the Maccabean War and Judea's fall to Pompey and Rome. This ethical union in the church

---

35. This theme will also be picked up in the Gospel of Luke and Acts, where Jesus' activity is part of the plan of God and what "must" take place in God's salvation program.
36. This emphasis on power points to themes already seen in Romans, especially 1:16 and chapters 6–8.

receives a heightened emphasis in Ephesians in comparison to his other letters.[37] In the language about being brought near we have an allusion to Isaiah 57:19. In fact, God has built a sacred temple of people, that is, his church with Jesus Christ as the cornerstone (2:20). The image of the temple is like 1 Peter, and to a lesser extent, Hebrews with Jesus pictured as operating over a house.

As Paul reviews his own ministry as a bondservant of Christ (3:1), he discusses his own insight and understanding about the mystery of Christ (3:4). Again the mystery was revealed in Christ, opening the door for connecting pieces of what Scripture had taught. Now that Christ had come and had ministered with God acting through him, these connections should be seen and appreciated as part of God's program. What has now been made clear is that Gentiles are coheirs, fellow members of his body and copartakers in the promise in Christ Jesus through the gospel (3:6). To Paul was given the task of proclaiming to Gentiles the unsearchable riches of Christ (3:8). The revelation of this program to the powers in heaven fulfills the eternal purpose God has realized in Christ Jesus our Lord (3:11). So Paul prays for the Ephesians that Christ might dwell in their hearts (3:17) so they might come to apprehend the scope of Christ (3:19). Christ is to live actively in them so God can be praised for his work. So to the one whom works this power in them be glory in the church and in Christ Jesus forever (3:21).

In the church, God has given gifts according to the measure of the gift of Christ (4:7). Here Paul cites Psalm 68:18 (=67:19 LXX). This text speaks of the victory associated with the Exodus that Paul now applies to the second exodus God brought through Jesus.[38] This is yet another typological-prophetic use of the text where the Exodus models what messianic salvation also looks like. What the victory of Jesus allowed was for gifts of blessing to come out of the victory. With the power of opponents removed and new power made available (as Paul prayed about in Eph. 1 and 3), gifts can now be exercised for mutual benefit of the body. Christ's work again leads into practical application. These gifted roles exist for the edification of the body of Christ (4:12) as all attain the unity of the faith and the knowledge of the Son to the measure of the fullness of Christ (4:13). By living the truth in love, the church grows into the head, into Christ (4:15).

---

37. Once again this theme overlaps with Luke–Acts, where Jesus' suggestion of including Gentiles in blessing meets with hostility from some Jews. Not only that but the same move by Paul makes for the same reaction (Luke 4:16–30; Acts 13:44–51; 21:27–36); Hoehner, *Ephesians*, 56–58.

38. For a detailed consideration of this text, its background, and use of the Old Testament, see W. Hall Harris, *The Descent of Christ: Ephesians 4:7–11 and Traditional Hebrew Imagery*. Arbeiten zur Literatur und Geschichte des hellenistischen Judentums (Leiden: Brill, 1996).

In a series of exhortations, Paul notes that believers are to be kind and tenderhearted and forgiving as God in Christ was forgiving (4:32). They are to walk in love as Christ (5:1). They should live differently from the world knowing that the immoral do not have an inheritance in the kingdom of Christ (5:5). It is Christ the example that is prominent here. People are called to awake from the dark so Christ can shine on them (5:14).[39] They are to be thankful in the name of the Lord Jesus Christ (5:20) and be subject to each other out of reverence for Christ (5:21). Here the appeal is to the Christ as an ethical example and source for ethical living. This we have also seen in other Epistles, especially in Paul (1, 2 Thessalonians; 1 Corinthians; Romans) and Peter (1 Peter— Christ as model).

Christ is the example of the relationship in the home as the husband is the head of the wife as Christ is the head of the church (5:23). As the church is subject to Christ (5:24), so is the wife to be to the husband. Husbands are to love their wives as Christ loved the church and gave himself up for her (5:25). Husbands are to nourish and cherish their wives as Christ does the church (5:29). The mystery of the one flesh in marriage is rooted itself in the mystery of the one flesh of Christ and the church (5:32). So also slaves are to serve as to Christ (6:5) and as servants of Christ (6:6). Paul closes his letter with a salutation of grace to all who love our lord Jesus Christ (6:24).

Christological Fulfillment in Ephesians

In Ephesians Paul again points to union with Christ as the ground for action and understanding, while also showing how the example of Christ is a model for our own walk. The doctrinal roots again appeal to imagery from Psalm 110:1, now stated in terms of the results that come from Jesus' exaltation to the heavenlies. This is but a variation on a common theme. This focus on the exalted status of Jesus is central to this entire book. It is from here Jesus exalts those who belong to him. From heaven, he equips them as the appeal to Psalm 68 draws on the Exodus as a pattern fulfillment of the victory of Jesus as a second exodus experience. A third key text is the eschatological promise of bringing near those who were far away. Here it is the idea of Gentile inclusion that is emphasized as part of Jesus' corporate work. This imagery comes from an eschatological section of Isaiah (52:7). It elaborates themes that reach back to Isaiah 2:2–4. The text also is close to another one Paul cited in Romans 11 (Isa. 52:11). Some Jewish sacred texts anticipated a blessing to come for the Gentiles; Paul declares it is fulfilled. So here we have

---

39. It is debated whether 5:7–14 is a call to unbelievers to come into the light through the example believers provide (O'Brien, *Epistle to the Ephesians*, 372–74) or is addressed to believers not to be unduly influenced by the world (Hoehner, *Ephesians*, 103–6). It is hard to be sure, but in general believers are of the light and so would not need to come into it in Paul's thinking. So we prefer the view of O'Brien here.

a synthesis we have seen elsewhere in parts, linking Christology, the gifts of ecclesiology, and eschatology. What the letter emphasizes is how love and unity in the body should be the result of these messianic benefits.

Confessions of "Christ" in Colossians

Colossians is very much a sister epistle to Ephesians, except it also responds to a threat that involves an excessive preoccupation with aesthetic practice as a way of gaining a special spiritual status and position.[40] Its message is simple: Christ is our only source for life. Nothing needs to be added to what he provides. One need only draw upon what he makes available. Paul is contending with the idea that there exists a kind of advanced spirituality that comes from a rigorous pursuit of aesthetic concerns or drawing on additional transcendent powers. Christ alone has given all we need for spiritual maturity.[41] This epistle with its focus on Christology has twenty-five uses of the term "Christ." Paul writes as an apostle of Christ Jesus (1:1) to the saints and faithful brethren in Christ (1:2). Paul is grateful always giving thanks to God the Father of our Lord Jesus Christ for the testimony of the Colossians (1:3) and the report of their faith in Christ Jesus (1:4). They responded to the truth as they heard it from Epaphras, a faithful minister of Christ (1:7).

Paul notes that he rejoices in his sufferings for they fill up what was lacking in Christ's afflictions for the sake of his body (1:24). The idea here is that Christ's work of suffering itself leads into others journeying on the same path. Sharing in Jesus' suffering is a part of the goal of his work that needs completing. There may even be the idea that there is a set amount of messianic suffering, so the more Paul suffers the more that quota is being used up, bringing us nearer to Jesus' return.[42] This labor on behalf of Gentiles is part of a mystery, which is Christ indwelling Gentiles, the hope of glory (1:27). This point about mystery and Gentile incorporation is like Ephesians 3. The goal is to present every person mature in Christ (1:28). Paul's labor is for the saints. The benefits of Christ's work should encourage them because their hearts are knit together in love and they possess all the riches of an assured understanding and knowledge that comes from this divine mystery in Christ

---

40. Among solid treatments of Colossians are Peter O'Brien, *Colossians, Philemon*, WBC (Waco: Word, 1982) and Ben Witherington III, *The Letters to Philemon, the Colossians, and the Ephesians: A Socio-Rhetorical Commentary on the Captivity Epistles* (Grand Rapids: Eerdmans, 2007).

41. More debated and unclear is whether what Paul is fighting is a kind of Jewish mysticism that called for discipline in gaining spiritual access to heaven in an experience (so O'Brien in his commentary) or a syncretistic influence of Jewish and Hellenistic influences emphasizing dealing with spirits and astrology (so Clinton E. Arnold, *The Colossian Syncretism*, WUNT 2.77 (Tübingen: Mohr/Siebeck, 1995). It is still not clear which of these options is best, although I still slightly prefer the Jewish mysticism option. What is evident is that Paul sees the alternative as deflecting focus on what Christ has provided.

42. Witherington, *The Letters to Philemon, the Colossians, and the Ephesians*, 144–45.

(2:2). Paul rejoices to see their good order and the firmness of their faith in Christ (2:5). Christ's work of suffering is the root of incorporation and blessing. This theme has been present in most of the Pauline Epistles.

Christ is a standard of truth for their faith and its ground. So as they received Christ Jesus as Lord (2:6), so they should live in him, giving him the same honorable place in their heart from moment to moment. They should shun philosophy and empty deceit that is according to human tradition and the spirits of this world and not according to Christ (2:8). They have been circumcised with a circumcision without hands, putting off the body of flesh in the circumcision of Christ (2:11). No one should pass judgment over them with regard to food, drink, festival, new moon, or Sabbath; for these are only a shadow of what is to come and the substance belongs to Christ (2:17).[43] If they have died with Christ to the elemental spirits of the world (2:20), then they should not allow anyone to have them submit to regulations with regard to food that is a reflection of human teaching. If they have been raised with Christ (3:1), they should seek the heavenly things, that is, those attributes Paul goes on to describe in verses 8–17. This can be done because their lives are hidden with Christ in God (3:3). When Christ who is their life appears (3:4), then they shall appear with him in glory.

So in this series of exhortations, the connection to Christ is seen as the key to all blessing; nothing else or no one else is needed. The suggestion from the teachers that the work of the Christ is not enough is answered by an appreciation of the comprehensive results Jesus' work achieves. Here it is a combination of incorporation and the future work of Christ that is confessed and that is key to keeping one's focus right. While pursuing the things of heaven and the character God seeks to give, the peace of Christ is to rule in one's heart (3:15) and the word of Christ is to dwell richly in them (3:16).

Slaves are urged to obey their masters and fear God, knowing that the reward comes from the Lord Christ they are serving (3:24). Paul asks for prayer that a door for the word may be opened to declare the mystery of Christ (4:3). Epaphras, a servant of Christ Jesus, sends them greeting (4:12), completing the references to Christ in Colossians.

So in this letter we see a combination of incorporation and identification with Jesus' future work as a key motivator for the believer's walk. The confession of Jesus as the Christ is not a matter of mere knowledge or placing Jesus in the correct dogmatic or titular slot. It reflects a confession that is taken into the inner part of the believer by faith and that continually works

---

43. This is the verse that points to a Jewish backdrop for what is taking place. The key studies making the case for such background is F. O. Francis, "Humility and Angel Worship," in F. O. Francis and W. A. Meeks, *Conflict at Colossae* (Missoula: Scholars Press, 1975), 197–207 and A. T. Lincoln, *Paradise Now and Not Yet* (Cambridge: Cambridge University Press, 1981), 110–34.

itself out in motivating the believer. The Jesus follower's identity is now fully connected to Jesus the Christ through a sacred binding that comes by faith and through the Spirit of God. In sum, Christ confessed leads to the believer being transformed as the example of Christ and obedience to him leads into a new way of living.

Christological Fulfillment in Colossians
Again the christological core in Colossians is found in an appeal to Psalm 110:1 imagery that explains Jesus' exaltation and heavenly session. This heavenly role applies the language of that text in the most comprehensive sense. In doing so, an "earthly" category is revealed to truly possess a transcendent scope. This represents "high" Christology as Jesus shares position with God and administers blessing from God the Father's very presence. This move is like the one we saw in Hebrews and Peter.[44] We shall see elements of it in Acts in a speech like the one in Acts 2. It is also like 1 Corinthians 15:20–28, only now it is Jesus' present authority that is highlighted versus that in the future. Although the image of the Son of Man in *1 Enoch* is close to such imagery, the unbroken connection between the work of Jesus and his position by the Father is stated in a unique way because of the greater comprehensive scope of blessing and mediation here. Whereas the Son of Man in *1 Enoch* primarily judges at the end, here Jesus is a source of blessing within current history as well.

Confessions of "Christ" in Philemon
Philemon is a letter that emphasizes how identification with Christ elevates anyone who confesses him and is tied to him.[45] Interestingly, this short letter has more references per word than any other Pauline letter in its eight uses. Paul writes as a chained one of Jesus Christ (v. 1) and gives a greeting of grace and peace from God the Father and the Lord Jesus Christ (v. 3). He prays that the fellowship of faith might promote the knowledge of all the good that is ours in Christ (v. 6). As we shall see, this means practical, ethical knowledge. In Christ, Paul commands Philemon to do what is required of him with respect to Onesimus, his slave (v. 8), yet Paul as a prisoner of Christ Jesus (v. 9) also appeals to Philemon. In asking Philemon to be gracious to the slave Paul asks that Philemon refresh Paul's heart in Christ (v. 20). Greetings come from Epaphras, a fellow prisoner in Christ Jesus (v. 23). He closes the letter with a commendation of that the grace of the Lord Jesus Christ be with your spirit (v. 25).

Christological Fulfillment in Philemon
This letter simply shows the consistent link between Jesus and those who minister for him. This link gives an ethical basis for ignoring not only social

---

44. See chapter 12 for Petrine epistles (pp. 332–36) and for Hebrews (pp. 337–42).
45. For Philemon, see Witherington, *The Letters to Philemon, the Colossians, and the Ephesians.*

status but for being gracious to a brother in Christ who also serves in the new community. This ethical, relational development is something we also saw in the Corinthian Epistles. Actually, it is a dominant messianic theme in almost all of Paul's letters. There is an advantage and a benefit to being associated with Messiah.

Confession of "Christ" in Philippians

Philippians is about joy for the work Jesus as Christ is bringing to completion.[46] In this short epistle about fellowship and partnership, Paul uses the term "Christ" thirty-seven times. Paul and Timothy as servants of Christ (1:1) greet all the saints in Christ (1:1) with a commendation of grace and peace from God the Father and the Lord Jesus Christ (1:2). Paul writes confidently that the God who began a good work in them will work to complete it until the day of Jesus Christ (1:6).[47] It is right for Paul to feel this way because he loves them with the affection of Christ Jesus (1:8). His hope is that they will be made pure and blameless for the day of Christ (1:10), filled with the fruit of righteousness that comes through Jesus Christ (1:11) to the glory of God. In this introduction we see a highlighting of the Christ's progressive saving work extending into the future in a way that is more pronounced than the other Pauline Epistles we have treated so far. Incorporation with the Christ and his provision is very much a work in progress that will come to fruition in the end. This is why promise is both already realized and with yet still more to come.

As Paul considers his ministry, he notes that his chains in Christ are evident to all as he writes from prison (1:13). He observes that Jesus is preached with different motives, as some preach Christ from envy and rivalry, while others do it from good will (1:15). Some preach Christ out of partisanship in the hopes of hurting Paul (1:17). All Paul cares about, however, is that Christ is proclaimed. In this, Paul rejoices (1:18). He also knows how their prayers and the help of the Spirit of Jesus Christ will bring about his deliverance (1:19). He desires the Christ be honored in his body (1:20). For Paul to live is Christ, and so dying would be gain (1:21). He desires to depart and be with Christ (1:23). But remaining behind with them will be ample cause for glory in Christ Jesus (1:26). Paul runs everything in his ministry through the lens of what serves Christ best.

---

46. For this work, the commentary by F. F. Bruce, *Philippians,* NIBCNT (Peabody, MA: Hendrickson, 1989) is still excellent, as are the treatments by Peter O'Brien, *The Epistle to the Philippians* (Grand Rapids: Eerdmans, 1991) and Gerald Hawthorne, *Philippians,* WBC (Waco: Word, 1983).

47. Philip Comfort, "Philippians," in *Ephesians, Philippians, 1–2 Thessalonians, Colossians, Philemon,* CBC 16 (ed. Philip Comfort; Carol Stream: Tyndale House, 2008), 156–57. He notes how it is common to offer a prayer to the gods in opening a letter in the Hellenistic world. Paul often follows this custom and praises God in the process.

So Paul exhorts them to love in a manner worthy of the gospel of Christ (1:27). They should not be frightened of opponents, because to them it has been granted no only to believe but to suffer for the sake of Christ (1:29). He notes that if there is any encouragement in Christ, any love, any fellowship of the Spirit, any affection and sympathy, then they are to complete Paul's joy by being of the same mind and having the same love (2:1). They are to have the same mind as was in Christ Jesus (2:5), when he took on humanity and death on behalf of others.[48] The result of his work is that one day every tongue will confess that Jesus Christ is Lord to the glory of God (2:11).

The passage where Christ is set forth as an example also has some of the highest Christology anywhere in Paul's letters. Philippians 2:6–11 is likely a hymn of the early church. So Paul reaches into the worship of the community to set forth an example of Jesus' service and humility in taking up both the human condition and death. Here the example of suffering and exaltation gets its most lyrical presentation in the Second Testament. The Hebrew Scripture is not cited in the hymn but is alluded to. One allusion is clear, while the other is debated.

The debated point is whether there is Adamic background from Genesis 1–3 in the hymn or not.[49] The alternative is to see pre-existence as the point with the hymn operating in a kind of reverse parabola in that Jesus comes from heaven to earth and then returns up to heaven in the end. I prefer the interpretation as pointing to divine pre-existence, in part because emptying to become a person of Philippians 2:7 does not make sense if an Adamic background is present at the start of the hymn. One can appeal to the attempt to gain the tree of life as reflecting this effort to grab onto deity for Adam, and thus appeal to Genesis 3, for the "one made in the form of God." However the idea of emptying points in the direction of a pre-existent state in heaven with humanity being taken on as an act of humbling. Our exposition assumes this larger christological backdrop, but the point I will make about the use of Isaiah works no matter which background is operating in the hymn. And the ethical point that Jesus did not play on status works regardless of whether one sees Adamic background as present or not.

Clearer than the rightfully, much debated point about whether Adamic background is present or not is how the hymn ends in verses 10–11. This is an important point of the hymn—where Jesus ends up. The twin themes of every knee bowing and every tongue confessing has precedent from the Hebrew Scripture. This text was used in Romans 14, but it appears here in a

---

48. In all likelihood, Philippians 2:6–11 is a famous early church hymn. See Ralph Martin, *Carmen Christi: Philippians ii:5–11 in Recent Interpretation and in the Setting of Early Christian Worship* (Cambridge: Cambridge University Press, 1967).

49. For a defense of Adamic Christology being present here, James D. G. Dunn, *Christology in the Making*. 2nd ed. (Grand Rapids: Eerdmans, 1996 [1989]), 114–21.

context where its usage is clearer than the ambiguous reference there. Again we need a full context from the Hebrew Scripture to get the force of the point. In Isaiah 45:20–25, God is calling all to account for denying the Creator and choosing to engage in idolatry rather than give God the honor due to him. So he calls the nations to court and says this:

> [20]Gather together and come! Approach together, you refugees from the nations! Those who carry wooden idols know nothing, those who pray to a god that cannot deliver. [21]Tell me! Present the evidence! Let them consult with one another! Who predicted this in the past? Who announced it beforehand? Was it not I, the LORD? I have no peer, there is no God but me, a God who vindicates and delivers; there is none but me. [22]Turn to me so you can be delivered, all you who live in the earth's remote regions! For I am God, and I have no peer. [23]I solemnly make this oath– what I say is true and reliable: 'Surely every knee will bow to me, every tongue will solemnly affirm; [24]they will say about me, "Yes, the LORD is a powerful deliverer."'" All who are angry at him will cower before him. [25]All the descendants of Israel will be vindicated by the LORD and will boast in him. (Isa. 45:20–25 NET)

This text is one of the clearest declarations of God's uniqueness and sovereignty in the Hebrew Bible. God declares that allegiance will be uniquely his one day. There is no other God, nor is there any other savior or judge. The indication of this divine position is the fact that one day everyone will acknowledge this.

Every knee will bow and every tongue will confess that God is the Lord a powerful deliverer. The name given above every name is that which affirms the sovereignty of the creator God over those whom he rules. There is no other place to go. There is no other one to whom to turn. One day all creation will know and affirm this. That is Isaiah's teaching.

Now Paul was a rabbi. He surely knows this background as he cites this hymn with its intentional allusion to Isaiah 45. However, in the Philippian hymn the bowing of the knee and the confessing of the tongue include giving such honor to the Lord Jesus. His work of emptying and death is so in conjunction with the Father and so rooted in a heavenly origin that the honor due the God of Israel will come to be given to the one through whom God worked. Once again we see the that substituting Jesus in the place of the God of Israel is made, justified by the calling and activity of Jesus at God's behest. Note how the hymn makes it clear that God is the one gifting Jesus with this name and role. Jesus does not act nor does he claim to act independently of the Father. But they are like a double helix in a piece of DNA, a package deal, operating as an inseparable team to deliver and save with a mighty hand stretched out ironically through the death of a frail human who once had been in the presence of God and who afterward was vindicated back to that original position. To see and speak of one is inevitably to speak and see the other. This is "high" Christology indeed, and the point is made for an ethical outcome. Despite having this position, Jesus served and emptied himself in incarnation and death. The example of Jesus is humility and service. One thinks of Jesus' own teaching here as possible background (Mark 10:35–45). Paul says this is the mind of Christ Jesus. The scriptural point argues that the exaltation of Jesus shows his person and authority. The role is not a claim of Jesus, but comes from an act of God. This text shows why the emphasis on resurrection is about divine vindication, as well as indicating that this act of God decisively reveals who Jesus is. This hymn explains what Romans 1:2–4 speaks of as a marking out as Son of God through resurrection or a "horizoning" pointing to this role.

Once again, it is Christ the example that is a key model for behavior. This is the second key theme we have seen regularly in Paul with incorporation in the Christ as the first. The two themes also go together. Christ's work and association with him is both the source and inspiration for ethical behavior.

Paul exhorts them to be blameless and not grumble so that he might be proud of them in the day of Christ (2:16). Paul notes that others may not look after the interests of Jesus Christ (2:21), but Timothy, who he will send to them, does. Another commendable laborer is Epaphroditus, who almost died for the work of Christ (2:30).

In this key exhortative section, Paul makes it clear that Christ is everything and his own accomplishments are nothing. Those of the true circumcision worship God in spirit and glory in Jesus Christ (3:3). Whatever Paul's earthly credentials, he counts them all as nothing for the sake of Christ (3:7). He counts all things as loss for the worth of knowing Christ Jesus as his Lord (3:8). In fact, he counts all things as human waste in order to gain Christ (3:8) and be found in him having a righteousness through faith in Christ (3:9).[50] This is how he can know the power of the resurrection. Here we see a union Paul has with Christ that comes from Paul's appreciation and response to God's grace through the promised one. This is reminiscent of language we saw in Galatians 2:20. Paul wishes to achieve the full experience of resurrection and presses on to that goal because Christ Jesus has made Paul his own (3:12). So Paul presses on for the prize of the upward call of God in Christ Jesus (3:14). Others are enemies of the cross of Christ (3:18), but the citizenship Paul shares with believers is in heaven from where a Savior, the Lord Jesus Christ will come (3:20). Again we see a stress on what Christ

---

50. Although many translations soften the term σκύβαλα to mean "rubbish" (NASB, NRSV, NIV), Paul's shocking appeal to "human dung" or "human excrement" (σκύβαλα) in Philippians 3:8 shows how much Paul's view of his past accomplishments under the law changed.

will provide on his return as an emphasis of this letter. Moreover what the Christ provides takes care of everything. There is no need to appeal to any other source of provision, especially personal achievement or relationship to provisions of the law.

Paul exhorts them to pray and notes that the peace of God will guard their hearts and minds in Christ Jesus (4:7). As Paul closes his letter, he expresses confidence that God will supply their every need according to his riches in Christ Jesus (4:19). He tells them to greet every saint in Christ Jesus (4:21) and commends them to the grace of the Lord Jesus Christ (4:23).

Christological Fulfillment in Philippians
In this letter three themes dominate. One is the impact and motivation that the future work of the Christ has on our life today. To be prepared for the Day of Christ motivates Paul. This is like how the reality of resurrection was said to motivate in 1 Corinthians and fits with the exhortations in the Thessalonian letters. Second is the example of Christ as a model for behavior. This is similar to appreciating what it means to be associated with Messiah that we saw in 2 Corinthians 6:7. Third is the sense of intense, present identification and representation Paul has with Christ. This also motivates his every action. This is like what we see in Philemon. So in this letter the ethical dimensions of Jesus as the Christ stand out. However, none of these three themes is really new. What we have here is a combination, even triangulation, of themes previously we used in pairs.

Beyond this we see a clear presentation of the exalted status of Jesus. Using Isaiah 45 and a text about God's unique authority in the context of defending monotheism, the Messiah is now seen as exalted Lord by God's act, sharing in this position and authority. These interpretive moves are possible because of what God has shown Jesus to be and the position God has given to Jesus in exalting him. What God has done in Christ is an act of revelation showing who Jesus is and how pieces of the scriptural puzzle come together.

Pastoral Epistles: 1, 2 Timothy, Titus
After his release from house arrest in Rome (*circa* 62), Paul does some extensive travel that involves visiting church plants as well as perhaps traveling to Spain. It is during these travels that he writes Titus and 1 Timothy.[51] Later, while imprisoned in Rome awaiting execution (*circa* 68) he writes 2 Timothy. Titus, along with 1 and 2 Timothy, are generally referred to as the "Pastoral Epistles."[52] These Epistles are distinct from the rest of Paul's letters because

---

51. For discussions about Paul's later journeys see McRay, *Paul*, 223–60; Bruce, *Paul*, 441–55.
52. For a defense of the Pauline authorship of these letters, Philip Towner, *1–2 Timothy & Titus*, IVPNT (Downers Grove: InterVarsity, 1994, 13–35, esp. 30–35. Also solid in treating the book is William D. Mounce, *The Pastoral Epistles* (Nashville: Thomas Nelson,

the instructions are communicated to a church indirectly (i.e., they are given to Timothy or Titus, who in turn are to pass them on to the churches they pastor). Furthermore these Epistles contain instructions and admonitions for certain offices (elders and deacons) in the Christian congregation. Thus they provide by far the most detail we get anywhere in the Second Testament as to the structure of the early church. Yet what they say about it is rather minimal in terms of church forms or issues of style of worship. Far more important than how church is to be done or the forms of services are the qualifications of those who minister and the unity they are to have around the core teaching of the faith. Finally these letters provide a kind of "pastoral counseling" between Paul and two of his closest associates in the ministry.

Confessions of "Christ" in 1 Timothy

First Timothy presents both doctrinal summaries of Christ's work for sinners and a call to teach trust in Jesus, the Christ. The first epistle was written to Timothy while he was ministering to the churches in Ephesus. It has fifteen uses of the term "Christ." Paul the apostle of Christ Jesus (1:1) writes by command of God our Savior and Christ Jesus our hope (1:1). The standard greeting involves grace, mercy, and peace from God the Father and Christ Jesus our Lord (1:2).

Paul is grateful to Christ Jesus that he has given Paul strength and appointed him to serve (1:12). It was the grace of the Lord that overflowed for him with the faith and love that are in Christ Jesus (1:14) when Paul was saved. It is a sure thing that Christ Jesus came into the world to save sinners (1:15). In Paul, Jesus Christ has displayed in the foremost of sinners (that is, in Paul) his perfect patience for an example to those who were to believe (1:16). In speaking of prayer, Paul notes that there is one God and one mediator between God and humanity, the person Jesus Christ (2:5). The doctrinal summaries of 1:15 and 2:5 give the core of what the church confessed about Jesus' work.[53] These texts, with their emphasis on Christ's saving work for those who are unworthy, match not only what we have seen in the Pauline letters (especially Rom. 5:6–8), but also what Revelation and 1 Peter say about the Christ. Paul sees himself as a prime example of one who was not worthy of such an act as the Christ performed on his behalf.

As he discusses deacons, Paul observes how those who serve in this manner gain good standing and great confidence in the faith, which is in Christ Jesus (3:13). For Timothy to teach what Paul is writing to him will

---

2000). Another excellent discussion of these books is by I. H. Marshall, *The Pastoral Epistles*, ICC (London: T&T Clark, 1999).

53. Doctrinal summaries abound in Timothy and appear in 1 Timothy 3:1 and 4:9 as well as in 2 Timothy 2:11 and Titus 3:8; Towner, *1–2 Timothy and Titus*, 55, note on 1:15. These texts point to teaching that circulated in the church and that taught core orthodox doctrine. Marshall, *The Pastoral Epistles*, 326–30, has an excursus on these passages and the formula of the trustworthy sayings.

show him to be a good minister of Jesus Christ (4:6). Paul advises against putting younger women on the widows' roll for fear that they might come to have desire against Christ and seek to marry (5:11). The suggestion is that rather than trust Christ for their well-being, they will seek and find a husband. Paul charges Timothy to keep these rules in the presence of God, Christ Jesus, and the angels (5:21). This kind of charge in Christ's name we saw in 2 Thessalonians. After giving advice on how to teach slaves and masters, Paul says that if anyone teaches otherwise or does not accord with the sound words of our Lord Jesus Christ that accord to godliness, then he is puffed up and knows nothing (6:3). Again Paul issues a charge to Timothy in the presence of God and Christ Jesus (6:13). This Christ was the one making the good confession before Pilate, and so Timothy should work to keep the commandment unstained until the appearing of our Lord Jesus Christ (6:14). There are no explicit Hebrew Scripture texts about the Christ in this letter. Everything taught is a development of the idea that Jesus is the Christ.[54]

Christological Fulfillment in 1 Timothy
In this letter the distinctive features are the doctrinal summaries involving Jesus as one who died for sinners and as the one mediator. Here is the core past work of Jesus presented in a fresh way through a doctrinal summary that assumes the suffering-glory model of Christian messianism. Also new are the solemn individual commands Paul issues in the name of Christ to Timothy indicating standards by which to run the church. This builds on the relational, ethical associations that Paul likes to highlight as an implication of being in Christ. This relational emphasis was something we see consistently in his letters. The Timothy material is written in such a way that the content of the work of Jesus is assumed as known. This is not surprising since Timothy was a companion of Paul and is a minister of the gospel.

Confessions of "Christ" in Titus
The message in the epistle to Titus is somewhat similar to that of 1 Timothy. It emphasizes that Christ's work is the basis of doctrinal summaries and is a call to a godly life. This short epistle has only four uses of the term, the smallest amount in any letter of Paul. He writes as an apostle of Jesus Christ (1:1) and gives a greeting of grace and peace from God the Father and Christ Jesus our Savior (1:4). The other two remarks appear in the epistle's body as part of doctrinal declarations. They reflect the teaching emphasis of this

---

54. There is a reference in 1 Timothy 6:15 about the only Sovereign, the King of kings and Lord of lords that looks as if it could be about Jesus Christ. But a check of the contextual development shows this title refers to God the Father who no man has ever seen or can see because he dwells in unapproachable light. Interestingly, this very title of King of kings and Lord of lords is applied to Jesus in Revelation 19:16, while its reverse Lord of lords and King of kings appears in Revelation 17:14.

letter to a fellow minister. One is about how grace has instructed us to live in a godly manner until the coming of our great God and savior, Jesus Christ, the one who gave himself to redeem believers from all iniquity and purify for himself a people who are zealous for good deeds (2:14). Here is an explicit text where Jesus is called God by Paul.[55] The other doctrinal declaration speaks about how God our Savior appeared to save us by his mercy and by the washing and regeneration of the Holy Spirit, which he poured out richly on us through Jesus Christ our Savior. So we are justified by grace and become heirs of eternal life (3:6). This second text not only shows Jesus' work as Christ as key to salvation, it also provides a wonderful summary of what the gospel provides. The provision of the Spirit is why Paul called the gospel the power of God in Romans 1:16–17, as the work of the Christ in Romans 8 showed. Thus the Pastorals summarize ideas in Paul's other letters.

Christological Fulfillment in Titus

So the Christ does the work of salvation and grace through his work to redeem and his gifting unto life through the Spirit, two central components of salvation for Paul. Again we see doctrinal summaries putting the core theology together and building off of key elements in what it means to be connected to Messiah.

Confessions of "Christ" in 2 Timothy

This follow-up epistle to Timothy is intended to prepare Timothy to share in the sufferings of Jesus as well as to provide some doctrinal summaries to be taught. In this epistle, Paul uses the term "Christ" thirteen times. Paul writes as an apostle of Christ Jesus (1:1) by the will of God according to the promise of life in Christ Jesus (1:1). He greets him with grace, mercy, and peace from God the Father and Christ Jesus our Lord (1:2).

Paul calls for sharing in suffering for the gospel in the context of God's power. Thus God saved them and called them to a holy calling by virtue of his purpose and grace, which he gave in Christ Jesus ages ago (1:9). This God was made evident in the appearing of our Savior Christ Jesus who abolished death and brought life and immortality through the gospel (1:10). This exhortation has the force of a doctrinal summary, but it also serves an ethical purpose. So Paul exhorts Timothy to follow the pattern of sound words he has heard from Paul. These words are also a part of the faith and love that are in Christ Jesus (1:13). In other words, Timothy is to be strong in the grace that is in Jesus

---

55. Marshall, *The Pastoral Epistles*, 272–82, works through the interpretive options on the phrase "great God and savior" and shows how the most likely sense treats the pair as one and refers to Jesus. Key here is the one article referring to both God and savior. For a more thorough discussion about this grammatical construction, see Daniel B. Wallace, *Granville Sharp's Canon and Its Kin: Semantics and Significance in Studies in Biblical Greek* (New York: Peter Lang, 2009).

Christ (2:1). Here we have received a calling residing in Christ and received virtues effective for life in faith, love, and grace. This emphasis looks like the heavenly things of Colossians, which also described effective virtues. Timothy is to share in suffering as a good soldier in Christ Jesus (2:3).

In another doctrinal summary, Paul recalls that one is to remember Jesus Christ, risen from the dead, descended from David as preached in Paul's gospel (2:8), a gospel for which Paul also suffers. Any idea that Jesus was not a real human being is precluded by what Paul says here. Incarnation, suffering, and resurrection are all affirmed here.[56] Paul endures everything for the sake of the elect that they may obtain salvation in Christ Jesus with its eternal glory (2:10). In fact, all who desire to live a godly life in Christ Jesus will be persecuted (3:12). So Timothy should continue in what he has learned from the sacred writings, which are able to instruct for salvation through faith in Jesus Christ (3:15). Paul also charges Timothy in the presence of God and Christ Jesus that Timothy should preach this word, which Paul calls the word (4:1).

Encouragement for Timothy to be strong comes from Christ the example, as the one who suffers and calls to suffering. This is like 1 Peter and several of Paul's other Epistles.

Christological Fulfillment in 2 Timothy
The distinctive feature of the Pastorals' portrayal of the Christ is the presence of the term in a variety of doctrinal summaries about the work of Jesus as the Christ. Second Timothy fits this pattern of usage. This feature suggests a formalizing of the teaching in short synopses that are designed to help teach those in the church. These summaries remind them of some of the faith's most central teaching. Christ's work and its ethical implications that reflect this core doctrine are what is to be passed onto church members. To live a life of virtue in the midst of being ready to suffer is the emphasis in this teaching. Jesus the Christ as an example, even in suffering, is something we have seen in many of the epistles in the Second Testament. Jesus' works for sin as Savior and as the source of grace are also highlighted. In terms of where this emphasis fits with earlier expressions in Paul, there is little new here, because by this time Paul's letters had already set forth a full portrait of the Christ, something he had surely already taught Timothy and Titus.

CONCLUSION

The use of "Christ" in Paul contains certain emphases that his 382 uses reflect. Jesus Christ and Christ Jesus alternate in ways that prohibit any point being made of the difference. The most important idea is how believers are incorporated into Christ and share in their identity with him. Key topics include Christ's indwelling, the church as the body of Christ, how believers

---

56. Towner, *1–2 Timothy and Titus*, 175.

are to put on Christ, how Christ is Paul's life, and how believers have been crucified, raised, and baptized with Christ. Central also is how Jesus has given the Spirit. In all of these themes, the key point is the solidarity that Christ has with his believers, how he has made them truly his people.

The basic work Christ performs appears in various doctrinal summaries. Jesus as Christ suffers on behalf of his people, dies for the sake of his people, or offers himself on the cross on behalf of the sin of his people. This work is sometimes mentioned as a part of God's plan.

When it comes to how Paul connects to past expectations, those associations require comparing concepts and emphases because Hebrew Scripture texts are cited in only a small selection of the Christ references. Although explicit ties to Scripture are rare, Psalm 110:1 imagery and the promise to Abraham are the two most common themes besides the general portrait of the Suffering Servant figure of Isaiah 52:13–53:12. The descent from David also appears here and there to underscore a Son of David, messianic connection, as for example when Isaiah 11:10 is appealed to in Romans 15:12. These themes are most often put to ethical use, as a ground for exhorting that believers follow the example of Christ as a means of reflecting faithfulness to his grace, his work and the position to which he has given us. This ethical dimension of the role of the Christ seems to be a fresh emphasis in comparison with older text of promise and expectation, which simply looked to the victory, vindication, or righteousness the promised one would bring. There had been the belief that the delivering figure at the end would bring victory and a purging of the people, but the idea that he would be an ethical model to follow was less common. What had been called for in the past was continued loyalty to God in the hope that the coming one might appear. Such a view was the premise of the sectarian community of Qumran and the call to follow the law of the Pharisees. Repentance and loyalty to that which marked out Jews as Jews was the way to prepare for the eschaton.

We also see some texts that point to righteous suffering, such as Psalm 69. Also eschatological texts appear in several places, texts such as Jeremiah 31. Several texts are typological-prophetic (Ps. 69; 110:1; 8:14; 28:16). Previous events pattern what salvation looks like, those events include the Exodus (Ps. 69) and the later exilic judgments of Israel (Isa. 8 and 28). Other texts that had looked to what God would do now discuss what Jesus did or will do as the deliverer (Isa. 45:18; 59:20). Isaiah 45 is the most outstanding example of this move, as in Philippians 2 every knee will bow to Jesus Christ as Lord. Another key use was of the *Shema* in 1 Corinthians 8:4–6. Here the confession of the one God of Israel has turned into a binitarian confession of the Father as God and Jesus as Lord, with both functioning as Creator. These substitution texts are rooted in what the resurrection-exaltation of Jesus shows, the vindication of God and the demonstration of Jesus as sharing complete heavenly authority.

So Christians came to take a different route in presenting the Messiah. They highlight not military power, but spiritual gifting and a rule from heaven among those allied to the raised Messiah.[57] The appeal to Christ's power to judge is left for what is to come in his return to judge. These early Christians appealed to what God had done in and through Jesus alongside the Hebrew Scripture and claim the two aligned. God's work through the Christ would deal with sin from the inside out and through a deliverer whose suffering would be the means to cleansing and the release of the new life found in God's Spirit. In addition, there was added a call for loyalty to God and Christ that is reflected in the imitation of the Christ's way of living, especially in his suffering and service. There is also some appeal to the future goal of salvation and appearing before him blameless on the Day of Christ as a basis of an ethical appeal, but this is not as emphasized as one might expect. The theme of personal loyalty and connectedness to Christ and gratitude for his work seems to be much more of an emphasis as a motivation. In many ways a trip through these uses leads to a review of the whole scope of Pauline teaching as they are woven into the full fabric of his writing.

When it comes to the explicit hermeneutical use of texts from Judaism and the Hebrew Scripture, there is little different here when it comes to teaching about the Christ from other early Christians. As with the Catholic Epistles, we see frequent appeals to texts that point to patterns of escalated realization. This is true of Psalm 110 and the Pauline themes of resurrection-exaltation tied to it in texts like Isaiah 8 and 28 or Psalm 68. Paul simply presents a greater array of texts that work in these areas and in the case of the seed, highlights Jesus as the seed. Texts that look at rejection and suffering are also common with Isaiah 52 and 53 leading the way here. What is interesting here is that some texts fall just outside the famous Servant passage of Isaiah 52:13–53:12, by using Isaiah 52:7 and 11. We also see cases of more direct prophetic appeal, especially in texts dealing with eschatological contexts such as Jeremiah 31:33 or Isaiah 11:10. In other words, there is no one hermeneutical means by which the texts of the Hebrew Scripture are used to make messianic points. Do these patterns of reading go back even further and connect even wider? Do they parallel the Gospels, Acts, and even perhaps the Jesus they present? That is the question for our next two chapters.

---

57. For Bateman's concluding discussions about the expected Messiah figure, see chapter 11 (pp. 314–20).

THE MESSIAH PREACHED AND VEILED

We have seen in the Epistles and Revelation how the early church often used the title "Christ" and how it served as a ground of explicit confession and exhortation to a proper way of life. Whether one highlights Christ's example, his saving work, or Jesus' incorporating work, the point is that identification of Jesus as "the Christ" and loyalty to him is central to encouraging a faithful walk.[1] In the early church as important as Christ's teaching and work is, Jesus' goal is that believers work out their salvation in a way that honors God's grace.

We now work backwards from Acts to the Gospels, from a very direct proclamation of Jesus as Messiah in Acts, to more veiled presentations of this key figure and role in Matthew, Mark, and Luke. The Gospels and Acts were

---

1. Briant suggests this concept of identification and loyalty to a king has its beginnings with one's personal relationship with Persian regal figures. He says, "All of the characteristics attributed to the king's men are wrapped up in a single word: 'faithfulness' (*pistis*)." Numerous examples are given to validate his claim. In fact, Briant muses, "it is generally believed that the Classical vocabulary (*pistis/fides*) renders a Persian concept" and not a Greek one. This sort of dynastic loyalty to the Persian king emphasized "a one-to-one relationship" that connected people to the king rather than one's family or a noble's bloodline. Pierre Briant, *From Cyrus to Alexander: A History of the Persian Empire*, trans. Peter T. Daniels (Winona Lake: Eisenbrauns, 2002), 324–26. Alexander the Great later applies this Persian concept of ruling after he conquers the Persian Empire (331 BCE). Errington points out that "institutional loyalty of the old kind (Macedonia nobility) was no longer sufficient" and that "only loyalty to the person of the king would count." R. Malcolm Errington, *A History of Macedonia* (Berkeley: University of California Press, 1990), 114. So there was background in the culture for this kind of loyalty. Add to that the covenant context in Judaism of relating to God and you have yet another, even more crucial influence on how the relationship to God, his plan, and his kingdom were seen. Through these means, both people out of a Greco-Roman and Jewish context could appreciate these exhortations to loyalty. The incarnation intensifies all of this. So in a far more profound way, identification, loyalty, faithfulness (*pistis*) to Jesus, the Christ, is expected.

designed to be read as full accounts, each in their own right, even as they seek to tell us about Jesus and his followers. The main obstacle raised about Jesus in the Gospels and Acts is this: many in Israel have rejected a promise originally intended for them. These accounts reveal the central role that Jesus has as the one who announces and brings the new era.

The Gospels have a close genre parallel in the ancient world, what was called the *bios* or ancient biography.[2] They are not, however, exhaustive "womb to tomb" presentations about a person's life. Rather than focusing on physical description, tracing psychological thinking and describing personal development like modern biographies, *bios* highlights the key events that surround a person, his deeds, and his teaching that are useful for learning lessons in life. That is very much what the Gospels do. The key characters are Jesus and God, as Jesus carries out God's plan.

Acts belongs to a different kind of genre. It is a *legitimization* document: its goal is to explain and legitimize the early church and its roots. This was necessary because in the ancient world what counted in religion was its age and time-tested quality. Since Christianity was new, it needed to explain how it could be new and still be of merit. The answer was that although the form of the emerging movement from Jesus was new, the faith itself was old, rooted in promises and commitments God made to Israel long ago. In fact, the new movement did not seek to make itself into a new entity. Rather, it was moved in a new direction when official Judaism rejected and expelled it from the synagogue, with the result that (in accord with God's plan, as Acts clarifies) the gospel was taken to the Gentiles. As a result, a new group of people had gathered around Jesus, what the people in Antioch called Christians (Acts 11:26). Acts tells this story showing how God's promise of God expanded as far as Rome, the capital of the world.

Thus these works combine history and application. So how is Jesus Christ seen in documents that were written somewhere near the fall of Jerusalem in 70 CE?[3]

---

2. Richard Burridge, *What Are the Gospels: A Comparison with Greco-Roman Biography,* 2nd ed. (Grand Rapids: Eerdmans, 2004). This is an update of work originally done in 1992.
3. The standard dates many conservatives use for the gospels run from Mark in the late fifties to late sixties, to Matthew and Luke being written in the sixties. John is most often put in the nineties, although a few argue for a date in the sixties. Acts is placed anywhere from 62 CE until the Fall. However, many will place the Synoptic Gospels and Acts after 70, between 70–100 CE. Regardless these are first-century documents and our earliest and best sources about Jesus and the early church. The date of Acts is closely related to that of the first volume to which it is associated, the Gospel of Luke. D. A. Carson and Douglas Moo, *An Introduction to the New Testament*, 2nd ed. (Grand Rapids: Zondervan, 2005), 77–330, for discussion from a conservative perspective, while Raymond E. Brown, *An Introduction to the New Testament* (New York: Doubleday, 1997), 99–382, nicely surveys the broader discussion of these issues.

MESSIAH PREACHED IN ACTS

Like ancient Greek historians, Luke orders history geographically, region by region, rather than chronologically. On the one hand, Luke's Gospel orders events about Jesus, his words and deeds, beginning in Galilee, then moves to Samaria, and ends in Judea and Jerusalem. Acts, on the other hand, orders events from Jerusalem to the world. The latter presents the spread of the message about Jesus from Jerusalem (2:1–8:3), to Judea and Samaria (8:4–12:25), and throughout the Roman Empire to Rome (13:1–28:31). The book is about the Christ of the kerygma.[4] He was unjustly rejected and so was a righteous sufferer. Yet God exalted him to the throne of heaven to demonstrate that Jesus was the Christ. Jesus is now ministering from God's side, offering forgiveness and the gift of the Spirit for life to those who come to him by faith. That faith can be described as repenting or turning as well. Naturally Acts portrays Peter, Stephen, Philip, and especially Paul as central messengers in spreading the Gospel about Jesus, who is the Christ. Thus in Acts we see Christ preached and we get a sense of the mission Jesus generated.

So the burden of Acts is to legitimize the church, that is, to show how even though it is a new entity; it is a movement tied to promises made by God long ago.[5] This is important because in the ancient world to be a new religion meant less credibility than one with ancient roots. Acts explains how the rejection of the promise by many Jews is not evidence that God is judging the church. Neither is the inclusion of Gentiles in a formerly Jewish movement a violation of the program of God. No, God knew of the rejection of Jesus and his early followers. He also had always planned to include the nations. Rooted in the promise of the Jewish Scripture, this new movement is quite old, and at its center is the promised anointed agent around whom the arrival of the promise rotates, the exalted Lord who is the Messiah, Jesus. So where incorporation and ethics drives Paul's portrait of Messiah, promise and realization drive the picture in Acts.

---

4. The term *kerygma* (noun: κήρυγμα; verb: κηρύσσω) means a public declaration, preaching, or message preached. It is the most commonly used term for preaching (Matt. 12:41; Luke 11:32). Other nouns used are "the gospel" (*euangelion*: Matt. 4:23; Mark 14:9; Acts 15:7), "the word" (*logos*: Acts 2:41, 4:4, 10:44, 20:7), "report" (*akoē*: Matt. 4:24; Mark 1:28; John 12:38), and "teaching" (*didachē*: Matt. 7:28–29; Acts 2:42; 5:28; 13:12; 2 John 9).

5. My work, *Acts, BECNT* (Grand Rapids: Baker, 2007), attempts to show this point in some detail, including how what became the church started out making its appeal directly in the synagogues as a realization of Jewish promise and hope. There are many fine treatments of Acts. Excellent treatments of this book include I. H. Marshall, *The Acts of the Apostles: An Introduction and Commentary* (Grand Rapids: Eerdmans, 1980) and Ben Witherington III, *The Acts of the Apostles: A Socio-Rhetorical Commentary* (Grand Rapids: Eerdmans 1998). For the theology of Luke-Acts, Darrell L. Bock, *A Theology of Luke-Acts* (Grand Rapids: Zondervan, 2012).

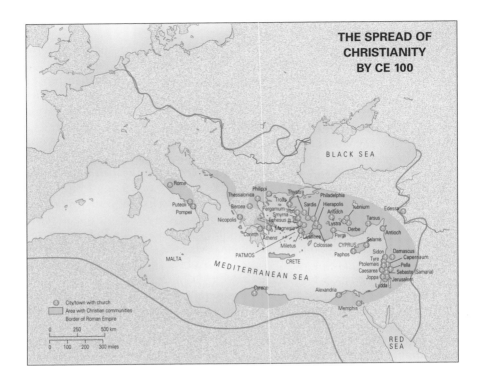

The term "Christ" appears twenty-five times in the Book of Acts. These occurrences appear in Peter's *speech* of Pentecost (ch. 2), Peter's healing of the lame man and subsequent *explanations* (chs. 3–4), Philip's and Saul's *preaching* in Samaria and Damascus (chs. 8–9), Peter's visit to Cornelius and subsequent *report* to Jewish believers in Jerusalem (10:1–11:17), Paul's *preaching* among the Gentiles (11:19–18:31), and Paul's *defense* before Roman authorities (24–26).

Peter's Speech at Pentecost

The term "Christ" first appears in the context of Peter's important speech at Pentecost in Acts 2. It occurs three times. Here we get a sense of the biblical backdrop for the use of the term in the early church. This speech is often said to reflect the *kerygma* or preaching of the early church.[6] The person of Jesus as the fulfillment of God's promise stands as the theme of the speech. Peter links together four passages from the Hebrew Scriptures to declare that Israel should know that God has made Jesus Lord and Christ, the very Jesus the

---

6. C. H. Dodd, *The Apostolic Preaching and Its Development* (London: Hodder & Stoughton, 1936).

leaders crucified (2:36). The four passages are Joel 2:21 (promised distribution of the Spirit and calling on the Lord to be saved), Psalm 16 (to present the promise of immediate bodily resurrection of the Messiah), Psalm 132:11 (to note the promise of a descendant of David on the throne), and Psalm 110:1 (the promise that one day David's Lord would sit at the right hand of God). The weaving together of such texts takes place as Peter explains the resurrection and exaltation of Jesus as well as the coming of the Holy Spirit. In fact, many key words are repeated in the exposition that uses the Jewish method of *gezerah shewa* to link passages and ideas together.[7] So we get the repetition of "poured out" (Acts 2:17, 18, 32), "Lord" (Acts 2:21, 34, 36), "wonders" (Acts 2:19, 2:22), "flesh" (Acts 2:26, 31), "corruption" (Acts 2:27, 31), "Hades" (Acts 2:27, 31), "right hand" (Acts 2:33, 34), and set/sit (Acts 2:30, 34). These link words appear in both the texts that use the Hebrew Scripture and in the explanation of the events. The links tie the passages into a unified portrait, making the synthesis and showing exactly how the passages are being understood in terms of the events of Jesus' life. This is a means of putting the puzzle pieces together into a coherent picture.

In particular, one linkage is especially important. The allusion to Psalm 132:11 with its roots in 2 Samuel 7 points to God foreseeing, through the prophet David's utterance, the resurrection of the Christ (2:31), which leads to the exaltation of Jesus through the vindication of God to God's right hand, where Psalm 110:1 is the key text. The proper response to this message is being baptized in the name of Jesus Christ for the forgiveness of sins (2:38). Now authority for forgiveness comes from God through Jesus and is not associated with regular sacrifices. Now forgiveness, a right of God to grant, comes through the name of Jesus, the One who is Lord and Christ.

The key to this speech is the "synthetic" reading of the promise we have seen before. However, only in Hebrews 1 do we get a similar string of texts to present Jesus. Peter is putting the portrait of the Messiah together for his audience. Here the arrival of the Spirit in the era of the eschaton is combined with the hope of God's total deliverance through the Messiah now made possible by resurrection. Peter argues that the gift of the Spirit is tied to the resurrection-exaltation of Jesus. Psalm 110:1, another central passage throughout the Second Testament as well as in this speech, ties all of this together by explaining that Jesus mediates the blessing of the Spirit from God's right hand. All of

---

7. Longenecker defines *gezerah shewa* as a "verbal analogy for one verse to another; where the same words are applied to two separate cases, it follows that the same consideration apple to both." Thus a single word can link together two passages from the Hebrew Scriptures even though they may be from two different books. Elsewhere, Longenecker argues that authors of the Second Testament "shared in the Jewish presuppositions of corporate solidarity and redemptive correspondences in history, and all used such widespread Hillilian exegetical principles as . . . gezerah shawah." Richard N. Longenecker, *Biblical Exegesis in the Apostolic Period* (Grand Rapids: Eerdmans, 1999), 20, 189.

this is part of an old promise made to David that his line would be part of the blessing, something many Hebrew Scriptures promise and second temple Jewish expectation held as possible, as our earlier study showed. The citation of Psalm 132 alludes to 2 Samuel 7 and reflects the popular first-century reading of the promise as referring to the ultimate hope of a single triumphant deliverer.[8] These trajectories are rooted in promises from the Hebrew Scripture. Peter is claiming that one who puts these Scriptures together properly will see that Jesus is the realization of what God promised. He also is arguing that God showed Jesus to be this key figure by vindicating him in resurrection. Text and revelatory event belong together. They each point to the other.

The key to this synthetic reading is the clear transcendent dimension with which the promise is read. God acts and reveals in doing so. Resurrection looks to the life hereafter. Spirit bestowal comes from above. The location of enthronement is at God's side in heaven. What often had been seen as being a promise carried out in earthly terms now is clearly set forth in more comprehensive transcendent terms. This is done by a pattern-escalation hermeneutic. Promises are a parallel to the way things were done in the past but with a "plus" that shows Jesus is unique. It is the transcendent dimension set with God's action that supplies the "plus," the escalation.[9] This way to read the promise was very Jewish. As salvation was often seen as reflecting things God had done in the past, so that salvation is like a "new creation" or a "new exodus." Judgment to come would be like judgments of the past called "the Day of the Lord." Note how in this Acts 2 speech the Day of the Lord is invoked in verse 20. Joel 2 was an eschatological text, looking to the day of decisive deliverance and a provision of the Spirit for all people. This text is directly prophetic but has built within it the image of the Day of the Lord which was a typological or pattern event built off of the example of the locust plague Joel also describes. Psalm 16 speaks of protection for the Psalmist. There is no greater protection than preventing the decay of death. Peter makes it clear that ultimately this Psalm cannot be about David, since he is in the grave. The "plus" factor of such extensive protection from death began with Jesus, making him unique. So although David as psalmist in his cry for protection is the basis of the pattern, the ultimate prophetic fulfillment is Jesus who completes the pattern, for protection is unique to Jesus. Psalm 110:1 works off of a similar pattern. Here what was said of the Israel's king as God's representative and out of the hope that one day the ideals of kingship would be realized

---

8. This idea of a triumphant deliverer is clearly evident in second temple literature and identified in Bateman's conclusion for the term "Messiah" (p. 271), the terms "branch" and "prince" (p. 301), the summation for the son (page 322), and the concluding statements for all titles (p. 323). I have worked through the speech in detail in Bock, *Acts*, 108–37.

9. This is the hermeneutic discussed in Darrell L. Bock, "Single Meaning, Multiple Contexts and Referents," in *Three Views of the New Testament Use of the Old Testament* (ed. Kenneth Berding and Jonathan Lunde; Grand Rapids: Zondervan, 2008), 118–20.

are now said to have met their match in what God has done with Jesus. The key difference in these examples is that the parallel at the end is greater and more comprehensive than what went before. In this way, the hopes of old were declared to be the prophetic fulfillments of the present, even as they are rooted in patterns of lesser activity in the past.

Peter's Healing of the Lame Man and Subsequent Explanations

In Acts 3, Peter heals a lame man in the name of Jesus Christ (3:6). In his explanation of the healing and its significance, Peter notes how God foretold by all the prophets that his Christ should suffer, something Jesus has fulfilled (3:18). This Christ God has sent, attesting through divine acts to the one appointed for them. That Christ is Jesus (3:20). Once again, Acts 3 shows the "synthesis" approach. There is a general appeal to what "Scripture" teaches about Jesus' suffering and the idea of a return. The promise is tied to texts in the Torah, the only place in Acts that develops promise strictly from this most fundamental part of the Hebrew Scripture. Jesus is presented as a Mosaic-like Prophet, as Peter appeals to Deuteronomy 18. This is a leader-prophet, a role closer to a regal-like figure, the messianic prototype, than anyone else in the Torah.[10] The generic appeal to the prophets starting from Samuel also alludes to the promise of the Davidic line. This remark is then combined with the promise made to Abraham and the promise of blessing to the world through the posterity of Abraham. So here we have the case made for Jesus from the Abrahamic and Davidic promises, while also appealing to the work of Moses. In many ways, this is the ultimate synthetic combination. These speeches are putting pieces of the puzzle together and show a unified portrait.

A further explanation of this healing occurs in Acts 4 and repeats the claim that it is in the name of Jesus Christ of Nazareth that this man is standing (4:10). Jesus is the one that the Jewish leaders crucified but that God raised from the dead. Jesus is the one rejected yet exalted cornerstone, language from Psalm 118:22. Acts 4 looks to the pattern of the king leading the nation in worship as one sent by God. The king comes before God in thanks for God's work on behalf of the nation in the face of a threat and the rejection by some. Psalm 118 plays a key role in explaining Jesus in the gospels,

---

10. Although vague, 4Q521 presents the Lord's messiah to be one who would heal and send the good news to the afflicted via either a regal or prophetic messianic figure. Josephus speaks of John Hyrcanus as a political figure, a high priest and prophet (*Ant* 13.10.7 § 299). So the concept of a leader-prophet already existed and could be at work here. See Bateman's initial discussion in chapter 9 (p. 268). Of course the prototype for the category was Moses himself and the way he as a leader of the people confronted Pharaoh through the power of God. What a prophet like Moses does is lead the people and perform works of deliverance that also have judgment implications for those who reject them. Thus the call to obey this prophet like Moses in Acts 3:23. Hyrcanus lacked the power element that Moses so consistently displayed.

as we shall see. Two points exist here. The first is that the rejected stone has become exalted. This point appeared in 1 Peter 2:4–11. The second is that rejection points to suffering. In context, the Psalm makes the point that the rejected leader still comes in the name of the Lord. The idea from Acts 3 that heaven holds Jesus for a time also points to the completion of the promise while alluding to Jesus' exalted place at God's side. The pattern of rejection followed by divine exaltation is evoked. That exaltation gives Jesus a position from which there is authority still to be exercised. When some Jews might have objected that Jesus had not yet evidenced the power of a full victory, the reply was that this exercise of judgment authority is what is left to do when he returns.[11] Thus the transcendent element of the promise is also a part of this synthesis of promise texts surrounding the activity of the Messiah that also points to future work. Jesus as Christ blesses now by giving the Spirit (Acts 2), but he also will judge in the future (Acts 3). The key to the divine testimony is the move God makes taking Jesus from human rejection to divine exaltation.

Acts sets forth through its preaching the scriptural justification for the claim that Jesus is the Christ. The appeal to Scripture clusters in ways not seen in the epistolary treatments where such a backdrop may well be assumed. Messages like these indicate to us what the content of messianic teaching was that filled the church, especially as it engaged in mission to both Jew and Gentile.

In the latter part of Acts 4, we get the use of Psalm 2:1 as a backdrop for the fact that the kings of the earth and the rulers of Israel have gathered and conspired to oppose the Lord and his Christ (4:26).[12] This is part of the promised rejection and suffering. The one who comes to redeem is rejected by many he came to serve. This raises the possibility that Acts sees suffering as not only pointing to suffering for sin but the suffering of an undeserved

---

11. Many Jews who reject Jesus today do so in the claim that a rejected Messiah who has exercised no judging power to bring justice and righteousness to earth is not a Messiah at all. The Christian reply is that there is power to forgive sin and give the Spirit now (Acts 2) and there is the judgment yet to come (Acts 3). Behind the Christian claim stands the vindication of God in resurrection-ascension to God's right hand. This is why Psalm 110:1 is such an important text.

12. The hermeneutics of how Psalm 2 is used is one of the central examples in my "Single Meaning," 125–32. A text that would have been read throughout its past as being in defense of Israel now challenges the nation because her leaders have rejected Jesus. The hermeneutical key to the Psalm is its address to those who oppose God and his anointed. In the Midrash on Psalm 2 in later Judaism, this psalm was read as being about periods throughout Israel's history. Such conspiracies of opposition took place in the time of Pharaoh, Sisera, Nebuchadnezzar, and even will take place through Gog and Magog (among several examples raised in the exposition of the Midrash). What is a little surprising is that this text is now read so that Israel is on the side of those who oppose God. The hermeneutical key is that the anointed has been opposed by them, bringing them into the application of the psalm.

rejection, an unjust suffering. In fact, often in Acts, this is what is being emphasized about Jesus' suffering. It was unjust (so also in the use of Isaiah 53 in Acts 8:32–33).

So the apostles were found daily in the temple teaching and proclaiming the good news that the Christ is Jesus (5:42). The way this is worded is important. There is a portrait of Christ that Jesus fits and unifies. Jesus is the realization of the proclaimed and planned promise of God about the Christ. With this first cluster of references in Acts 2–4, there is a long break before we meet another use of the term.

Philip's and Saul's Preaching in Samaria and Damascus

The next time we see the term "Christ" comes as Philip goes out to proclaim the good news in Samaria, preaching the Christ to them (8:5). Many Samaritans came to faith when Philip proclaimed the kingdom of God and the name of Jesus Christ (8:12). Acts has a second emphasis besides the detailed use of Scripture to explain the Christ. It is the emphasis on the name of Jesus Christ, a reference to his presence and power.[13]

In the latter part of Acts 8, we get an allusion to Isaiah 53 and the suffering of unjust rejection and judgment (vv. 32–33), but Acts 8:26–40 does not refer to the Christ. Still the passage is framed by preaching Jesus as the Christ in the previous and following scenes in Acts 8 and 9, so the passage is likely relevant to this portrayal, especially when this dimension of unjust suffering appears in Acts 3–4.

In Acts 9, Saul is like Philip, for Paul also preached in Damascus confounding the Jews by proving that "this one is the Christ." This is another reference to Jesus fitting the portrait of the promised one (9:22). The name is appealed to again when Jesus Christ heals Aeneas as Peter proclaims (9:34). The picture of Jesus as the authoritative Christ who heals also echoes the way Jesus will be seen in the Gospels. This combination of the Christ who heals looks to be another possible product of synthesis. Josephus has a picture of Solomon as son of David who has power and wisdom to deal with Satan and exorcism.[14] This kind of conceptual background could be at work here.

---

13. This emphasis starts with the exhortation to call on the name of the Lord in Acts 2:22, but in such a way that the Lord Christ is invoked at baptism as the linkage of v. 22 to Acts 2:34, 36, and 38 shows.
14. Josephus, *Antiquities* 8.2.1-5 §§ 41-48 points to such a view and Jewish tradition, although it does not use any titles to make the point. Furthermore, 4Q11 (11QApPsa) 2:2–9 reads: "Solomon, and he will invoke . . . the spirits and the demons, . . . These are the demons, and the Prince of Animosity . . . who . . . the abyss . . . the great . . . his people . . . cure." The translation is from Florentino García Martínez and Eibert J. C. Tigchelaar, *The Dead Sea Scrolls: Study Edition*, vol. 2 (4Q274–11Q31) (Grand Rapids: Eerdmans, 1998), 1201. For further discussion of first-century perspective of Solomon and other extrabiblical sources see Dennis C. Duling, "Solomon, Exorcism, and the Son of David"

Peter's Visit to Cornelius and Subsequent Report to Jewish Believers in Jerusalem

The ministry of Jesus Christ is proclaimed as one through whom God preached peace (10:36). This speech also calls Jesus Lord of all, a title that also points to authority. Peter commanded Cornelius and his household to be baptized in the name of Jesus Christ. He made this call after the Spirit came upon them (10:48). Later Peter explained that these Gentiles had received the same gift from God that God gave to the Jewish believers when they believed in the Lord Jesus Christ (11:17). The reference to Jewish believers looks back to Acts 2. So how could Peter prevent the Gentiles from being baptized when God had given them the repentance unto life? This linkage of the work of the Christ and the Spirit is another "synthetic" theme of the new era. Peter recognized its significance immediately. God providing his Spirit to Gentiles with the presence of the Christ is a key proof of that period's opening up to include Gentiles. God only gives his Spirit to those who had been cleansed, so they must be forgiven and accepted by God. This specific synthetic move pulls together a key event of the eschatological era, the presence of the deliverer, with essential evidence that someone belongs to God, namely the marking of people with God's Spirit (Acts 1:4–5, 2:1–4; cp. Luke 3:16, 24:49). Messianic hope and new covenant promise (Jer. 31:31–33) combine here.[15] What Jeremiah described as taking place only in Israel now also includes Gentiles. Once again promise escalates. This is another theme we shall see in the gospels, but we already saw this idea in Paul as he emphasized the Spirit as the key to the presence of the new era promise in Galatians 3. The giving of the Spirit reflects a core idea of what the Messiah does that indicates salvation is part of the early Christian teaching. John the Baptist as the forerunner will declare that the one to come will baptize with the Spirit. There is yet another significant break in the use of the term Christ after Acts 11. In line with the concerns of Acts, the term returns in discussion of the issue of Gentile salvation and Paul's ministry and mission to them.

Paul's Preaching among the Gentiles

Judas Barnabas and Silas are sent with Barnabas and Paul as men who have dedicated their souls for the sake of Christ to communicate the results of the council in Jerusalem (15:26). The allusion of souls dedicated to Christ parallels Paul's teaching of incorporation of Jesus and the representation of Jesus by those associated with him. These ministers serve the Christ who sits over the

---

HTR 68 (1975): 235–52. See also Michael Wise, Martin Abegg, and Edward Cook, *The Dead Sea Scrolls: A New Translation* (New York: HarperCollins, 1996), 453.

15. A similar juxtaposition of Davidic hope and covenant promise was present in Romans 11:26–27, only there the deliverer text from Isaiah 59 had its roots in the work of God now applied to Jesus. In Acts, no texts are cited, only the acts of God are juxtaposed.

new community. Another passage in Acts 13, speaks of Paul and Barnabas as "servants" of the Lord, showing an overlap of taking on the Servant role Jesus had.[16] However in Acts 13, the Christ is not explicitly invoked, although the promise of a seed from David is. This certainly points in a messianic direction (Acts 13:22–23). In fact this speech in verse 25 alludes back to Luke 3:15–17 where John the Baptist taught that the way to know Messiah had come is when he baptizes with the Spirit. The allusion surfaces as John portrays himself as not worthy to untie the thong of the sandal of the One to come. There is an implicit messianic allusion here. So the passage, even though the idea of Savior is the key title there, does overlap with Acts 15:26 more than an initial look might suggest.

Paul exorcizes a demon from a slave girl in Philippi by calling on the demon of divination to come out of her in the name of Jesus Christ (16:18). This use looks to the authority of the Christ, much like that attached to works of healing back in Acts 9:34.

In a pattern like earlier uses, Paul proclaims from the Scriptures in the synagogue that the Christ must suffer and rise from the dead (17:3) and that "this Jesus, whom I proclaim to you is the Christ" (17:3). Similar is the preaching in Corinth, as this kind of expression becomes a pattern and formula in Acts. Also Paul testifies to the Jews that the Christ was Jesus (18:5). In Ephesus, it is Apollos who powerfully confuted the Jews in public demonstrating by the Scriptures that the Christ was Jesus (18:28). Once again, all these scenes use a generic appeal to what Scripture teaches and do not cite specific texts. A narrative reading of Acts shows from the other earlier speeches which texts stand behind such an appeal. Yet another break in usage takes us to Paul's defense speeches in Acts 24.

Paul's Defense before Roman Authorities

Acts ends with several of Paul's defense speeches before Roman authorities. Paul is before the governor Felix and Drusilla, who hear Paul speak on faith in Christ Jesus (24:24). In a later examination Paul proclaims that he is saying nothing but what the prophets and also Moses say. These sacred texts proclaim that the Christ must suffer and that by being the first to rise from the dead, he comes to proclaim light both to the people and the Gentiles (26:23). This remark has an allusion to Isaiah 49:6, a servant text actually cited, as we just noted, in Acts 13:47, where it appealed to the activity of Barnabas and Paul as representatives of Jesus' work. The book ends with Paul in custody in

---

16. In Acts 13:47, Isaiah 49:6, part of the Servant songs, is cited and applied to Paul and Barnabas, not to Jesus. They are now the light to the Gentiles, bringing salvation to the ends of the earth (Acts 1:8). These two servants identify with and extend the work of Jesus. Appeal to the pattern of the Servant's work and the extension of Jesus' presence through his followers is at work here.

Rome yet able to teach the things concerning the Lord Jesus Christ boldly and openly (28:31). These final uses are also generic in force.

So the threefold stress in Acts involves (1) generic claims that the Scriptures teach about the suffering, resurrection, and distribution of the Spirit by the Christ, (2) that this Christ is Jesus, since he has done these things, and (3) that evidence that God is working through Jesus is shown in what is done through the name of Jesus Christ and as well as in the vindication through the resurrection-ascension that God performed.

Christological Fulfillment in Acts

We have seen that the appeal to promise in Acts brings together a variety of promise themes. Some of these promises were previously attached to the Messiah, while other expectations were more descriptive of the end time period without being explicitly tied to the Messiah in the Hebrew Scripture or second temple texts.

Acts ties the Messiah to four themes or events that were more descriptive of the end time period. The first is the coming of the Spirit. Here Joel 2:28–32 is explicitly mentioned, as is the proclamation of John the Baptist (Acts 1:5, 11:17–18). In the background is the hope of God bringing his Spirit to his people (Jer. 31:31–33; Ezek. 34:24–26).[17]

The second and third themes are suffering and resurrection. Suffering in Acts has to do as much with the rejection of the Promised One and the injustice tied to it as it does with his work in relationship to sin (compare Acts 8:32–35 with Acts 20:28). Resurrection is tied to texts like Psalm 110:1. The passage is associated with the promise of exaltation. Acts also uses for this theme the word of confidence coming from Psalm 16. This confidence reflects a pattern fulfillment and is pushed to its most comprehensive scope. So we likely move from an original context where delivery from death for a regal figure becomes escalated to a resurrection for the one

> **Resurrection to Exaltation of Jesus**
>
> Prior to his exaltation, the Gospels speak of numerous resurrection appearances of Jesus (Matt. 28:9–10, 16–17; Luke 24:13–44; John 20:11–29). Likewise Paul points out that Jesus appeared to more than five hundred people (1 Cor. 15:6). It is only after these resurrection appearances that Jesus is then taken up into heaven (Luke 24:50–53, Acts 1:1–11) where his earthly ministry ends and his exaltation as regal-priest begins as he sits, rules, and ministers at the right hand of God (Heb. 1:3).

---

17. Although 4Q161 and *T. Jud.* portray the eschatological messiah to have God's spirit, neither text appears to present the messiah as one who pours God's Spirit on his people (see pp. 269-72, 288-89). Jon Levison traces the role of the Spirit in Judaism in the second temple Judaism in *The Holy Spirit in First Century Judaism* (Leuven: Brill, 2002). Putting these ideas together is part of the fresh synthesis Jesus and the church offered to Jewish promise.

promised to bring the promise. These developed elements underscore also a transcendent element to this promise.

Finally, the power Jesus possesses as the Christ emerges from the transcendent position God gives to the Christ in resurrection. So healing and exorcism can take place in his name. Such abilities are not limited to the eschatological messiah (4Q251) but are presented in Acts as something to be passed on to those who follow him. This theme reflects a description of the new era in the older Hebrew Scripture texts more than being descriptions of explicit messianic activity. However, the roots of this connection are not made explicit in Acts. Rather, they are affirmed in the Gospels when John the Baptist asks Jesus about whether he is the One to come. Jesus answers by pointing to what the promises of Isaiah show about the period of salvation (Isa. 29:18; 35:5–6; 42:18; 26:19; 61:1). Those passages point to the kind of thing Jesus is doing (Luke 7:22–23) and thus the nature of the time as the promised era of deliverance. Now that one understands the new era is present, one can also appreciate that the key figure of that era is also present. Thus, Jesus answers the question indirectly but affirmatively. He is the One to come.[18] Since Luke is the prequel to Acts, the student of Acts knows of this theme.

In sum, Acts gives us new themes and much more synthesis than we saw in the epistolary material. It works explicitly with passages, where most of the epistles simply alluded to promises. These texts represent a combination of both fresh and similar kinds of associations from what we saw in the Jewish second temple era. The portrait of Messiah in Acts draws on a wide array of older promises, some going back explicitly to messianic hope and other tied to hopes about the new era in general. Pulling these texts together gives us a more complete picture of who Messiah is. Event and text work together here to make this happen.

MESSIAH VEILED AND PRESENTED IN THE GOSPELS

The roots of claims like those in Acts can be seen in the Gospels, which use the term "Christ" fifty-four times between them. Some of these uses are theoretical, discussing what the Christ is to be like without naming Jesus as that figure. These uses are like generic uses in Acts, except in Acts texts describing the Christ, are then said to connect to Jesus. Other texts are more enigmatic, reflecting a care, almost restraint, with which the presentation of Messiah is set forth in the Gospels. This enigmatic use is probably present to prevent a misunderstanding of what the term means when it is applied to Jesus. It also

---

18. For how all of this worked itself out in term of the use of the Old Testament in Acts, see Darrell L. Bock, *Proclamation from Prophecy and Pattern: Lucan Old Testament Christology*, JSNTSup 14 (Sheffield: Sheffield Academic Press, 1987) and Mark Strauss, *The Davidic Messiah in Luke-Acts*, JSNTSup 110 (Sheffield: Sheffield Academic Press, 1995).

prevents misunderstanding about how Jesus is using the term versus how the confession could be taken, given the fluidity of Jewish belief about the figure of the new era. The period of expectation in the second temple era reflected on the texts of the Hebrew Scripture and presented a wide variety of messianic options as our earlier study of this period showed. It meant that without careful explanation the term "messiah" could be misunderstood.[19] We proceed in the likely written order of the Gospels, with Mark first and John last.

Another feature of this material is how the concept of Messiah is tied to other imagery, especially categories like Son of Man, Son of God, or the idea of the Christ suffering. We shall begin to trace these links. One of the key features in these texts is how concepts are brought together out of a context drawing on both the Hebrew Scripture and out of reflections that we see in second temple Judaism.[20]

Veiling and Presentation of "Christ" in Mark

The Gospel of Mark is about unjust suffering as a model for discipleship and exaltation. It appears to raise two important questions about Jesus. The first question is simply this: Who is this man? Naturally, Jesus is the Messiah, the central figure of the new era but in a way that requires qualification and explanation (8:27–33). Part of that qualification is seen in the second question Mark pursues. What kind of Messiah is he? As the narrative unfolds Jesus is obviously a suffering Messiah (8:31, 9:31, 10:33–34, 15:21–38). This suffering Messiah is one of the most emphasized elements of the early church's claims about Jesus, alongside the sense of exaltation given to Jesus. The portrait of suffering combines elements of Isaiah 52:13–53:12 with Psalm 118 and Psalm 2. It is the element that the Gospels indicate was the most difficult for Jesus' followers to grasp about his claims. This was because in Jewish thinking the messiah was a strictly powerful and victorious figure, no matter in what form he appeared.[21] This point was demonstrated in our own overview of these texts, especially when we remember that Isaiah 53 was not read as being about

---

19. Exactly how this may have worked and how Jesus chose to handle such a variety of expectations is a topic of our next chapter when we look at Jesus and the idea of Messiah.

20. Adela Yarbo Collins has an article entitled "The Messiah as Son of God in the Synoptic Gospels," in *The Messiah in Early Judaism and Christianity* (ed. Magnus Zetterholm; Minneapolis: Fortress, 2007), 21–32, that discusses this linkage as it relates to the ambiguous Son of God title. She argues on primarily narrative grounds that Mark is more ambiguous in his use of the title, while Matthew and Luke have a stronger sense of Son of God because of their stress on the unique form of Jesus' birth, a point to be noted. However, within the revelation of how the term is presented in Jesus' ministry these Gospels run fairly parallel in force.

21. Human messianic figures that are both powerful and victorious are presented in texts like 1QM, 4Q161, 4Q174, 4Q285, 4Q458. Cosmic messianic figures that are both powerful and victorious are presented in texts like 11QMelch.

messiah when suffering was described there. Rather, suffering was read as applying to the nation.[22]

This stream of suffering, whether for sin or because of injustice and rejection, is also a theme we have seen in the epistolary material as having a major role, as well as being the base from which ethical exhortation comes. This kind of deep seeded location across the tradition suggests it is an old theme. Of all the Gospels Mark highlights this idea the most.[23] Suffering is the focus of much of Mark's presentation of Jesus. It is seen in the prediction of Jesus' death and his teaching on discipleship when it comes to bearing the cross, which is about bearing up with rejection like that Jesus faced.

Psalm 118

Psalm 118 is a thanksgiving song for military victory of the king. Cast in the form of a processional cultic entrance liturgy, the psalmist approaches the temple gates (vv. 5–19) and enters the temple courtyard (vv. 20–28), where he presents a thank offering (v. 27).

The identity of the central speaker is unclear, but likely he is the Davidic king returning from battle to acknowledge God's hand in delivering him from certain death and granting him triumph (vv. 5–19).

The presiding priest calls the assembled worshippers to praise God (vv. 2–4), the Davidic king recounts God's deliverance (vv. 5–19) and the community responds in antiphonal praise (vv. 20–27).

To exemplify this remarkable turn of events, they quote a proverbial statement, "The stone the builders rejected has become the cornerstone" (v. 22).

When his enemies threatened to defeat him, the Davidic king was like a stone discarded by the temple builders as useless; however, since God brought about his stunning victory, it is now clear that he plays an important role like the cornerstone of the temple.

The worshipping community greets his entrance into the temple with the proclamation, "Blessed is the one who comes in the name of Yahweh!" (v. 26).

Although this faithful worshipper was rejected by others (his enemies on the battlefield), he is ultimately recognized as the earthly representative of the true God, whose deliverance vindicated him.

---

22. See the Targum to Isaiah 53, where any suffering in the passages is attached to Israel not to the individual figure of the Servant, despite the wording of the Hebrew text. On Isaiah 53 and all the issues tied to it in the Hebrew Scriptures, Judaism, and the Second Testament, see Darrell L. Bock and Mitch Glaser, eds., *The Gospel according to Isaiah 53* (Grand Rapids: Kregel, 2012).

23. Solid commentaries on Mark include William Lane, *The Gospel according to Mark* (Grand Rapids: Eerdmans, 1974), Robert Guelich, *Mark 1:1–8:26,* WBC (Dallas: Word, 1989), Craig Evans, *Mark 8:27–16:20* (Nashville: Thomas Nelson, 2001); R. T. France, *The Gospel of Mark* (Grand Rapids: Eerdmans, 2002); and Robert Stein, *Mark* (Grand Rapids: Baker, 2008).

Mark's Use of "Christ" as a Heading

Mark only uses the term "Christ" seven times, but the first use is more as a narrative heading for the gospel.[24] Mark begins the gospel of Jesus Christ with the story of John the Baptist (1:1). In the synoptic gospels, John is the forerunner to Jesus, performing a baptism that prepares people for the coming of God's deliverance in Messiah. John the Baptist also announces that the Messiah will bring the Spirit in baptism, a way to picture life in the new era, in a manner that his use of water symbolizes. So again we have pattern and escalation in the way in which promise is connected to fulfillment. John baptizes with water to picture cleansing. Jesus washes with the Spirit to give life. Of course, John is drawing not so much on messianic promises here as on general expectations tied to the new era and combining them with messianic deliverance. This is part of the synthesis we have been discussing throughout this study.

Given that more skeptical critics often argue that the Gospels project back into its materials later teaching that only the early church held, this restrained use by Mark about what the Christ will bring (not yet identified as Jesus) is amazing. This restrained usage and the not so common presence of the title in gospel passages have led some to speak of a messianic secret or to argue that Jesus really did not present himself as messiah. This is a question to which we shall return in the next chapter after our survey of texts from the Gospels. What this restrained use does show is that the term was handled with care by this evangelist, reflecting as well the careful manner with which the early church described Jesus' treatment of the claim.[25]

Mark's Use of "Christ" as Confession

A full eight chapters pass before the term shows up in the narrative. It is Peter's confession at Caesarea Philippi that Jesus is the Christ. This is the first

---

24. Bateman observes that with the exception of Mark 1:1 and 9:1, Χριστός always has the definite article, ὁ ("the Christ": 8:29; 12:35; 13:21; 14:61; 15:32), which points Jesus out to be "the Christ" or "the Messiah" *par excellence*. Furthermore, he argues that the term Χριστός is only one of several ways Mark refers to Jesus as the hoped- for anointed one. Herbert W. Bateman IV, "Defining the Titles 'Christ' and 'Son of God' in Mark's Narrative Presentation of Jesus," *JETS* 50 (Sept. 2007): 537–59.

25. This "secret" argues that the identification of Jesus as the Messiah is a product of the early church, not something Jesus affirmed. But the restrained manner of how Mark handles this issue in light of the explicit emphasis throughout the early Christian materials we have already surveyed suggests that the restrained manner of disclosure is not the early church reading back into Jesus, but the church recording with care how Jesus handled this potentially ambiguous title, given the variety of Jewish expectation tied to the idea. One of the advantages of tracing this teaching backwards is that the contrast between the explicitness of early church proclamation and the care of how the Gospels handle the idea becomes obvious. On this point, the Gospels reflect an earlier perspective to the issue of how to talk about Messiah.

explicit use in the narrative (8:29). This confession is shared with Matthew and Luke. Jesus will carefully frame this confession around the idea of coming suffering as the story proceeds. The way he also forbids the disciples to discuss this term upon its confession (8:30) shows there is both a recognition of its appropriateness, and yet a hesitation that some may not understand exactly how Jesus accepts the term's use.[26] It is this suffering element attached to Jesus' understanding of the entire concept that seems to drive this hesitation to make the term a public one at this point, given the exchange between Peter and Jesus in the next scene (Mark 8:31–33). Jesus has much to teach the disciples before they use the term widely. By the last week of Jesus' ministry such hesitation in his self-portrayal disappears.

The paucity of references until this point also raises the question of how Peter came to confess this. As we shall see, it is not so much by what Jesus said or the titles he gave himself that caused Peter to come to this view, but what Jesus did. When activity tied to the end is associated with Jesus' actions then an understanding emerges that he must be the delivering figure of the new era. However, that is a story for the next chapter of our study.

Early Messianic Pretenders

Messianic expectations written during the latter part of the second temple period triggered messianic aspirations. During Jesus' early childhood (4 BCE to 6 CE), several messianic pretenders announced their messiahship, took up arms, but were defeated by Rome. For instance, just after Herod's death in 4 CE, while baby Jesus was still in Egypt with Mary and Joseph (see Matt. 2:13–23), Josephus tells of a shepherd named Athronges. He set himself up as king, placed a diadem on his head, organized a governing council, and slew a great number of Romans. Within short period of time, however, Rome along with Herod's son, Archelaus, defeated Athronges (*Ant* 17.10.7 § 278–284; *War* 2.4.3 § 60–64).

Another messianic pretender emerged when Jesus was around twelve years old. Judas the Galilean, considered by Josephus as the founder of a "fourth philosophical sect" (*War* 2.8.1 § 118–19), rebelled against Rome to reestablish a free nation. He and his followers were a group of religious Jews who resurrected the ideology of freedom that existed during the time of the Maccabees. Thus in 6 CE, Judas' intention for plundering an armory in Sepphoris was to fulfill his own ambitious desire for "royal honor" (βασιλείου τιμᾶς; *Ant* 17.10.5 § 271–72; Acts 5:37). Other self-seeking messianic pretenders would follow. So Jesus was very careful in how he explained and framed his messiahship.

---

26. Josephus tells us of another historical figure who acted out on his messianic aspirations. His name was Simon and his actions took place while Jesus was still a child. He was a former slave of King Herod who "dared to place a diadem on his head (διάδημά τε ἐτόλμησε περιθέσθαι). After being proclaimed king by a group of followers (αὐτὸς βασιλεὺς αναγγελθείς), he raised an army and torched the Herodian palace in Jericho and several other royal palaces. Unfortunately, he would eventually be caught by Roman officials and lose his head in Perea (Josephus *Ant* 17.10.5 § 271-272.; *War* 2.56).

Mark's Use of "Christ" by Jesus

Jesus promises in private teaching to his disciples that whoever gives one of his disciples a cup of water to drink because they bear the name of Christ will gain a reward (9:41). This remark is only in Mark, although similar ideas come in the other Gospels when the idea is set forth that to do something to one of Jesus' disciples or for them is to do it to Jesus (Matt. 25:37–40). The idea of association with Jesus and representation of him is tied to such a teaching. It may have fueled Paul's understanding of incorporation in the Christ.

In public teaching, Jesus raises a theoretical question about Messiah in 12:35. He asks how the scribes can call the Christ the Son of David, when a Psalm by David calls him David's Lord. The Psalm is Psalm 110:1. There is an implied answer to the dilemma built on an idiom where not x but y means not so much x as y. (So God desires mercy [x] not sacrifice [y] means he desires mercy [x] more than sacrifice [y].) The point of the idiom is that Lord is the Christ's key title more than Son of David.[27] This text also appears in Matthew and Luke. This passage is the introduction of the central Psalm 110 text into the mix of passages the church appealed to present Jesus. It is one of the most important passages regularly used to claim Jesus as the Christ. What is interesting here is that the text's first use is part of the theoretical discussion about how to see the Messiah. More than Son of David, Messiah is to be Lord and is intimately associated with God's presence and God's ruling authority as pictured by the image of the right hand. Jesus is not called the Christ here. The discussion is theoretical and the key role of seating at the right hand is not the key point here. Only the key titles matter. This Psalm 110 text becomes a central passage for justifying the transcendent aspect of the messianic role when the right hand becomes the point. This transcendence serves with the suffering idea as the second of the two most basic things said about Messiah in the early church.

Behind the question Jesus raises about why David called his promised one Lord is the idea that usually in this culture the younger serves and gives honor to the elder in the family. So how can the reverse be the case here? The answer is that in this case the position of Messiah transcends the normal human order, because of the unique position this figure has next to God. So now not just the elder but even the progenitor of the promise gives honor to the one who will realize it. This text is being read as a pattern escalated fulfillment, in that the king of Israel also represented God's authority, only now

---

27. Stein, *Mark*, 569 argues that the idea here is not to deny Jesus is the Messiah. He notes how Jesus accepted the cry of Bartimaeus to him as Son of David in Mark 10:47–48. So, the call to David's coming kingdom, as Jesus enters Jerusalem, is also seen as positive by Mark (11:10).

that authority is going to extend directly from God's very presence and the Lordship he will possess will be total.

When someone says that the Christ is here or there, the disciples are not to believe it (13:21). This private remark to the disciples is also a part of Matthew and is a part of the Olivet Discourse. Only Jesus brings the full messianic hope with his return. As the rest of the discourse shows, the deliverer's coming in judgment will be obvious when it takes place.

Mark's Concluding Use of "Christ"

In Mark 14:61 Jesus is asked by the high priest if he is the Christ the son of the Blessed One. Jesus' reply in terms of Psalm 110:1 and Daniel 7:13 leads to the Jewish leaders asserting to Roman authorities that Jesus independently claimed to be king. That was the political charge that emerged from this exchange. In religious terms, the Jewish leadership understood the response as blasphemy because Jesus made a claim to share glory with the God of Israel. This was seen as a violation of the command to only give honor to God and the belief that God's presence is so glorious he shares honor and his throne with no one. Since they did not accept Jesus' claims, they perceived the remarks to be an offense to God. Of course, the question was, could Jesus actually be who he was claiming to be here? This crucial query is shared by Matthew and Luke. In all of the synoptic gospels this exchange bears significant theological and christological weight.[28]

The final Marcan use involves Jesus being taunted by those looking at his crucifixion. They say to those around him, "let the Christ, the King of Israel, come down from the cross, that we may see and believe" (15:32). Witherington rightly recognizes that "the idea of a 'crucified anointed one of God' would have been seen as an oxymoron, since it was believed that crucifixion was a sign that a person was cursed, not anointed by God."[29] The use of "Christ" in this context is unique to Mark. It also is highly ironic in Mark's use, because what the taunters think is not taking place, namely, a vindication of Jesus, actually will take place, making salvation possible.

---

28. I have written a full monograph on this text and its background in Jewish thinking. *Blasphemy and Exaltation in Judaism: The Charge against Jesus in Mark 14:53–65*, Biblical Studies Library (Grand Rapids: Baker, 2000). The original version of this work appeared in 1998 from WUNT and Mohr Siebeck in Germany. There I defend the idea that this material can be viewed as authentically rooted in what took place at the examination of Jesus. This reply is crucial because in it is the implicit indication from Jesus that God will vindicate the Son of Man (i.e., Jesus) and that such an act will restore Jesus to his rightful place at God's side. From there, Jesus will do the rest of the work God has called him to do, including participation one day in the final judgment.

29. Ben Witherington III, *New Testament History: A Narrative Account* (Grand Rapids: Baker, 2001), 140, 155. The idea of cursing comes from Deuteronomy 21:23.

Christological Fulfillment in Mark

So in Mark, except at his trial before the Jewish leaders, Jesus does not attach himself explicitly in public to the idea of Messiah. He works more implicitly in Mark. He asks questions in public about the Christ, accepts the call of others to him as Son of David (as with Bartimaeus), allows himself to be proclaimed king as he enters into Jerusalem, and tells a story about a son being slain by tenants as he appeals to Psalm 118:22 and its picture of a rejected one exalted by God. This Psalm 118 text is one Peter uses as well (Acts 4:11; 1 Peter 2:7). Psalm 118 also appears in the entry scene as Jesus is proclaimed as coming in the name of the Lord. It is verse 26 that is cited from the Psalm. So this kingship text became an important text for affirming the rejection of Messiah as well as his acceptance by God. We have already noted how this text is used in a typological-prophetic way in discussing its use in Peter.

In private Jesus accepts to a degree Peter's confession of him as Messiah, but Mark does not highlight Jesus' preaching about himself as Messiah.[30] What he does highlight about Jesus, "the Christ," is this: he came to suffer and give is life as a ransom for many (10:45). In Mark 10:45, Jesus does this as Son of Man. Although the concept of one person making the ultimate sacrifice, giving his life for the restoration of Israel, was prevalent at this time, it was not a concept connected with the anticipated Messiah.[31] This was a newly emphasized piece of information that was to complete God's messianic puzzle. What Mark does is not highlight the use of title, but rather a series of functions Jesus performs. These functions reflect and bring deliverance. In so doing, Jesus possesses an authority like that of God. So Jesus forgives, sins (2:1–12), rules about the Sabbath as son of man (2:23–28), calms the seas (4:35–41), changes sacred liturgy about the Exodus to point to a new

---

30. Bateman has argued, however, that the designations of "son of God," "son of David," "son of the Most High," "son of the Blessed One" are synonymous epithets for Christ. "Defining the Titles 'Christ' and 'Son of God' in Mark's Narrative Presentation of Jesus," *JETS* 50 (Sept. 2007): 537–59.

31. Several examples may be given here. One is of Eleazar, a Jewish priest being goaded by Greeks to eat cooked meat before him and merely pretend as though it were pork. Four Maccabees 6:24–29 tells us: "When they saw that he was so courageous in the face of the afflictions, and that he had not been changed by their compassion, the guards brought him to the fire. There they burned him with maliciously contrived instruments, threw him down, and poured stinking liquids into his nostrils. When he was now burned to his very bones and about to expire, he lifted up his eyes to God and said, 'You know, O God, that though I might have saved myself, I am dying in burning torments for the sake of the law. Be merciful to your people, and let our punishment suffice for them. Make my blood their purification, and take my life in exchange for theirs.'" See also 2 Maccabees 7:37–38; 1QS 5:5–6, 9:3–4.

deliverance (14:22–24), and claims God will place him at the divine right hand (14:62).[32]

Veiling and Presentation of "Christ" in Matthew

The Gospel of Matthew combines narrative and discourse to provide the reader with both the life and teachings of Jesus.[33] The Gospel is built around five key discourses (Matt. 5–7; 10; 13; 18; 24–25) with scenes of action coming in between these units. As the narrative unfolds, Matthew uses the term "Christ" sixteen times. It serves as the foundational confession for the church of her singular teacher with divinely sent authority who was rejected by the world.

Matthew's Introduction of the "Christ"

Matthew leaves no doubt about Jesus as the Christ. He opens his Gospel with a genealogy of Jesus Christ, son of David, son of Abraham (1:1). He notes at its end that Jesus the one called the Christ was born of Mary (1:16), while also noting that fourteen generations stretch respectively from Abraham to David, from David to the exile and from the exile in Babylon until the Christ (1:17), possibly a numerological reference to the name David, for the consonants in that name in Hebrew add up to fourteen.

David = דָּוִד			
English \ Hebrew Consonants with Numerical Value			Total DVD Value
D = ד	V = ו	D = ד	
4	6	4	14
4 (D) + 6 (V) + 4 (D) = 14 (Generations)			

---

32. This key idea of how Jesus is presented in the Gospels and how his relationship to God is developed will be a major concern of our next chapter. I have developed this focus on activity as a key to the opening up of christological awareness in *Jesus according to Scripture* (Grand Rapids: Baker, 2002), especially in the concluding section of the book.

33. Key commentaries on Matthew are David Turner, *Matthew*, BECNT (Grand Rapids: Baker, 2008), John Nolland, *The Gospel of Matthew* (Grand Rapids: Eerdmans, 2005), Michael Wilkins, *Matthew: From Biblical Text to Contemporary Life* (Grand Rapids: Zondervan, 2003), and Craig Keener, *A Commentary on the Gospel of Matthew* (Grand Rapids: Eerdmans, 1999).

These genealogical references of Jesus are unique to Matthew. Jesus is a figure who is tied to Israel's promises through both David and Abraham.

After this introduction by the evangelist there again is a long pause before the title shows up in the narrative. In a Matthean narrative aside the evangelist notes that John the Baptist, while in prison, heard of the work of Christ and so sends messengers to ask if Jesus is the one to come or should they expect another (11:2). The text is important because it shows that Jesus highlighted the work in the new era more than the confession. It also indicates that promise of the new era's presence shares in importance in identifying who Jesus is and what is going on. This is shown in Jesus' reply using a series of works that point to the promised time of salvation from Isaiah (Isa. 28:19; 35:5 LXX; 42:18; 26:19; 61:1).[34] So Jesus' answer to the messianic question is yes, but it is shown by what Jesus does, not so much by what he claims.[35] This teaching is shared with Luke. It reflects a synthesis that shows up in preaching in Acts, the combining of descriptions of the era with passages about promised figures.

Matthew's Use of "Christ" as Confession

At Caesarea Philippi Peter confesses Jesus as the Christ the son of the living God (16:16). In Matthew's version, this private confession gets a ringing endorsement by Jesus in this private teaching context. Jesus declares that God has revealed this to Peter. This explicit endorsement is only in Matthew. But then Jesus commands them not to tell anyone he is the Christ (16:20). In this call to temporary silence Matthew echoes Mark. This call to wait to go public is likely because the people would not understand the type of Messiah Jesus will be in light of the variety of portraits in second temple Judaism that emphasize the Messiah as a powerful figure. In addition, Jesus had not yet underscored the necessity of Messiah's suffering, something Jesus now starts to do after the confession.[36] The remark unique to Matthew in this context is the emphasis on the divine work of opening the person to understand and appreciate such teaching. Also unique is that this confession makes Peter into an example of how Jesus will build his church.[37] In fact, among the Gospels, the term church appears only in Matthew, showing up three times total (here and in Matthew 18).

---

34. This list is very much like one that appears in 4Q521. For Bateman's discussion of 4Q521 see chapter 9 (p. 266).

35. Nolland, *The Gospel of Matthew*, p. 452, speaks of implicit Christology here.

36. The authenticity of this confession is supported by the event that follows. Jesus rebukes Peter as representing Satan, when the disciple suggests the Son of Man will not suffer. It is very unlikely the church would have invented such a rebuke to Peter.

37. The point here is that Jesus can work with anyone who sees that Jesus is the commissioned anointed one, a figure who is uniquely at the center of God's program.

Later Messianic Pretenders

After Jesus assumes his heavenly role as exalted Messiah, three messianic pretenders presented themselves during the rise of the early church. After the death of Herod Agrippa I (grandson of Herod the Great), Theudas, a magician and self-proclaimed prophet (προφήτες γὰρ ἔλεγεν εἶναι), gathered a large number of followers at the Jordan River and crossed over into Judea. Taking no chances numerous people were killed and Theudas was beheaded at the command of the Roman Governor, Fadus (Josephus, *Ant* 20.5.1 § 97–98; cp. Acts 5:36).

The second messianic pretender came from Egypt. He too claimed to be a prophet (προφήτες εἶναι λέγων). He gathered a following on the Mount of Olives and promised that he would destroy the walls of Jerusalem with but a command from his mouth. The Roman governor, Felix, sent troops against the group, but the Egyptian escaped (Josephus, *Ant* 20.8.6 §169–72; *War* 2.13.5 § 61–63; cp. Acts 21:37–38).

The third pretender arose during the second century. His name was Simon bar Kosiba or Bar Kokhba. He lead a massive revolt against Rome in 132–135 BCE. His efforts resulted in the minting of coins and a short-lived independent state. Rabbinic material recognizes Bar Kosiba to be the Messiah and refers to him as "ruler," "prince," and "son of the star." One Rabbi even declares, "This is the King Messiah" (Jerusalem Talmud: Ta'an. 4.68d). Rome eventually squelched the revolt, captured Jerusalem, and changed Judea's name to Palestine.

As in Mark, Matthew notes the healing by the Son of David (Matt. 20:29–34) and Jesus entering Jerusalem as King (Matt. 21:1–11).[38] In Matthew's version of the entry, he shows the crowd citing Psalm 118:26, a text already used elsewhere. He also uniquely cites Zechariah 9:9 as fulfilled, although the other Synoptics describe the humble entry on a donkey. As Jesus draws near to Jerusalem, he exercises less care about the association with messianic themes in his public acts. This is because he is moving toward forcing a response to his ministry in Jerusalem.

Matthew's Use of "Christ" by Jesus

The next reference, already discussed in the above section on Mark, is the public, theoretical discussion of the Christ as Son of David and Lord from Psalm 110:1 (22:42). In a text unique to Matthew and in a private teaching context, Jesus tells the disciples not to be masters of anyone for there is only one master for disciples, the Christ (23:10). This use pictures the authority of the Christ and shows the structure of the new era where the only one to follow is the Christ. Unlike Judaism, where one had a choice of rabbis to follow, as well as a variety of traditions, Jesus makes it clear that at its core,

---

38. On the significance of Jesus' entry into Jerusalem as a historical event, see Brent Kinman, "Jesus Royal Entry into Jerusalem," in Darrell L. Bock and Robert L. Webb, *Key Events in the Life of the Historical Jesus*. WUNT 247 (Tübingen: Mohr Siebeck, 2009), 383–427. Now also available in a paperback through Eerdmans (Grand Rapids, 2010).

the new community has one teacher and one example, the Christ. Paul clearly follows this idea when he calls the church to imitate him even as he follows the Christ (1 Cor. 11:1).

Next Jesus warns the disciples in private teaching not to be deceived in the future when many go out proclaiming themselves to be the Christ (24:5).[39] Neither are they to believe it when someone says that the Christ is here or there, a remark already discussed in the section on Mark (24:23).

Matthew's Use of "Christ" by Others

The high priest's question about whether Jesus is the Christ, the Son of God is the next reference (26:63), a text also already treated in the discussion of Mark. As in Mark, the reply draws on the combination of Psalm 110:1 and Daniel 7:13, combining imagery of the Christ with that of the Son of Man. Earthly hope and transcendent expectation are combined into one synthetic portrait. It is important to appreciate that the title Son of Man is always on Jesus' lips in the Gospels. Jesus prefers to refer to himself as this human-transcendent figure that is related to God's kingdom not made with hands. One of the early church's key synthetic moves surrounding the messianic portrait, namely, that the deliverer is both heavenly and human comes from this text's influence. Daniel 7 is used in a directly prophetic manner. Linking the cosmic delivery figure as the key figure of the eschaton also allowed a potential link to Messiah, opening up ways to synthesize the portrait of Messiah. Psalm 110:1 allows the cosmic picture of Daniel 7 to become associated with a divine exaltation in the language of Psalm 110:1.[40] In this way kingship, messianism, and Son of man can be linked.

Those holding Jesus mock him in using the title. Jesus is blindfolded and asked to prophesy as the Christ by identifying who is striking him (26:68). Although this scene is in the other Gospels, the term "Christ" in it appears only in Matthew. The incident pictures the unjust, sometimes callous, rejection of the Christ.

Pilate offers a choice between Barabbas and Jesus, the one called the Christ (27:17). The term's appearance here is also unique to Matthew. It is important, because Pilate presents Jesus as one who makes a regal claim, one that Rome did not grant. Thus this scene summarizes the political issue that swirled around Jesus as he was brought to Pilate.

When the crowd selects Barabbas, Pilate asks what he should do with Jesus the one called Christ (27:22). The crowd asks that he be crucified. This final use of the term is also unique to Matthew. The scene suggests that Pilate

---

39. For more on Bar-Kokhba see Yigael Yadin, *Bar-Kokhba* (London: Weidenfeld and Nicolson, 1978). Aaron Oppenheimer, "Bar Kokhba Revolt" in *Encyclopedia of the Dead Sea Scrolls*, 2 vols. (ed. Lawrence H. Schiffman and James C. VanderKam; Oxford: Oxford University Press, 2000), 1:80–83.

40. For Johnston's discussion of Psalm 110, see chapter 3 (pp. 89–98); and for Daniel 7, see chapter 6 (pp. 182–87).

framed the issue of Jesus in terms of his claim to be another king, one Rome had not selected. Jesus' death as the "king of the Jews" is the reason Jesus is crucified according to the *titulus* Jesus bore with the cross. This placard explained why Rome was putting him to death. In the movement of the Gospel, Jesus is the rejected King God had sent. The Jewish leaders, the crowd in Jerusalem, and Rome reject him, despite all the reader of the Gospel knows Jesus had done.

Thus we see that Matthew has many unique passages that refer to the Christ, but no real additional confessions of the title by Jesus. Nonetheless, these additional references show that Matthew is much clearer about Jesus as the Christ than Mark is, at least in terms of the authority he was sent to exercise.

Christological Fulfillment in Matthew

One of the interesting features of Matthew is that when we approach the Sermon on the Mount, there is not a great emphasis on Jesus as the Christ. But this is somewhat misleading. The framing of the Gospel as a whole by the opening genealogy makes it clear that Jesus was birthed to be the promised one of David. Before we get to the Sermon in Matthew 4:12–17 as Jesus' ministry dawns, there is the allusion to Isaiah 8:23–9:1. This passage pictures Jesus' coming as the dawning of a great light upon both the nation (Zebulun and Naphtali) as well as on the land of the Gentiles (Galilee). As in many texts in the Gospels, Jesus is identified by the period he represents, since the Isaiah passage looks to God's decisive deliverance. So by the time we get to the Sermon, people from Israel and from the Gentiles areas, from Galilee to the Decapolis, come to hear him.

In the sermon Jesus gives a kind of "law" for the new era, interpreting the law of Moses and the tradition of the second temple period to point all along to an internal standard of righteousness. This standard is to exceed that of the scribes and Pharisees (5:20). When Jesus says that he will not remove one jot or tittle from the law, his point is illustrated and explained by the six antitheses that follow. In this call that the law seeks to examine the heart response, Jesus reveals the kind of messianic teacher he is, even to the point of claiming authority over how the law is seen. He also shows the righteousness he brings. Jesus will deliver a judgment of righteousness and purge sin, but he also will call for righteousness as the one over the kingdom. He shows an authority over the law and its understanding that does not cite other authorities as the rabbis did, but simply presents what God desires. Jesus has the feel of a leader-prophet like Moses, who brings a law with him. He brings a revitalized understanding of Torah.[41]

---

41. For an emphasis on this new Torah theme, see Terence L. Donaldson, *Jesus on the Mountain: A Study in Matthean Theology*, JSNTSup 8 (Sheffield: JSOT Press, 1985), 105–21.

This kind of teaching gets reinforced by the way Jesus handles issues like healing on the Sabbath and hand washing. Jesus' approach to questions surrounding purity and tradition stand in contrast to the manner in which some more scrupulous Jews kept the law. A truly new era was dawning, bringing new ways. In contrast to many Jewish expectations, where Messiah would reinforce the law in all its detail, Jesus reconfigured and deepened the emphasis to focus on the heart response before God.

Veiling and Presentation of "Christ" in Luke

The Gospel of Luke presents Jesus as the authoritative figure of the eschaton who brings God's salvation.[42] It opens with a lengthy literary preface (1:1–4) followed by an infancy narrative (1:5–2:52), preparations for ministry (3:1–4:13), Jesus' Galilean ministry (4:14–9:50), Jesus' journey to Jerusalem (9:51–19:44), ministry in Jerusalem (19:45–21:38), the passion narrative (22:1–23:49) and finally Jesus' resurrection appearances (23:50–24:52). There is more emphasis given to Jesus' teaching than in any of the other synoptic Gospels. Parables in particular receive an emphasis. Nonetheless there is an important balance between Jesus' teaching and action. Yet like the Gospel of Mark, Luke limits his use of the term "Christ" to twelve. Many of the twelveuses of the term Christ overlap with the other synoptics, but we begin with several usages of the term that are unique to Luke.

Luke's Unique Use of "Christ" in the Opening Chapters

As Luke begins his Gospel, he presents us with four unique usages of the term "Christ." The first appears in the angelic announcement of Jesus' birth to the shepherds, where they are told that a Savior who is Christ the Lord is born today in the city of David (2:10). The text combines the idea of deliverer (Savior) with that of the Christ, a concept introduced earlier in Luke 1:31–33 when Jesus is said to be destined for the throne of his father David as Son of God. So rule is in view here, messianic rule. These descriptions match emphases in these titles we saw in the Hebrew Scripture by focusing on the regal role. The term "Lord" reinforces that expectation and role. The Luke 1 passage has often been compared with a Dead Sea Scroll text (4Q246 2:1–9), a passage the expectations section treated. In that text the expectant figure is also called "Son of God" and "Son of the Most High." There also is discussion of the eternal kingdom and authority. The earlier discussion of this Dead Sea Scroll pointed to influence from 2 Samuel. In fact, this point of contact is one of the more fascinating among passages from the Gospels. It

---

42. Commentaries on Luke include my *Luke* 1:1–9:50 and *Luke 9:50–24:53,* BECNT (Grand Rapids: Baker, 1992, 1994), I. H. Marshall, *Commentary on Luke,* NIGTC (Grand Rapids: Eerdmans, 1978), and Joel Green, *The Gospel of Luke* (Grand Rapids: Eerdmans, 1997).

shows this kind of regal sonship idea about the Messiah had widely circulated among Jewish groups.[43]

Also unique to Luke is the narrative remark that Simeon had been told by God that he would not die until he saw the Christ of the Lord (2:26). These infancy texts open Luke up with a note that Messiah is present and stress the authority as well as the duration of that role for Jesus. In fact in the midst of this messianic opening in Luke's infancy section, the figures that surround Jesus and John the Baptist are pious Jews. Jesus' roots come out of a faithful Jewish belief.

> **Simeon's Confession**
>
> Luke presents the first confession of Jesus as the Messiah shortly after the birth of Jesus. The righteous and devout Simon, one who was looking for the restoration of Israel, says of Jesus, "Now according to your word, Sovereign Lord, permit your servant to depart in peace. For my eyes have seen your salvation that you have prepared in the presence of all peoples: a light, for revelation to the Gentiles, and for glory to your people Israel."

In another narrative remark unique to Luke, John the Baptist has important things to say about the Christ. This scene is in the other Synoptic gospels, but Luke frames it uniquely by making clear that John is responding to speculation about him being the Christ. Only in Luke is the context for John's declaration about the One to come after him given in a setting where people are asking specifically if John might be the Christ (3:15). This elaboration strengthens the connection between John and Jesus in terms of the contrast. It makes clear how one can identify Messiah's coming (and not just that of the new age as in Mark and Matthew). The key fact is that the Messiah will baptize with the Spirit. This is the sign of the Messiah's presence and a crucial indicator that the new era has come. Thus what Mark and Matthew imply, Luke makes explicit. Luke brings together a key new element of the new era (the provision of the Holy Spirit) with the person who is at the center of the new era (the Messiah). This Spirit-new era connection is something Paul (Gal. 3, Rom. 8) and Peter make much of as well (Acts 2).

Yet another uniquely Lukan narrative remark comes when the evangelist notes that Jesus commanded that exorcised demons be silent about him because they knew he was the Christ (4:41). This text, like the command to be silent in Matthew, shows that Jesus had some hesitation to loudly proclaim that he is Messiah, at least in most public contexts of his ministry until the final scenes near and in Jerusalem. The factors that led Jesus to tell the disciples to be silent also apply here to the demons' confession of him as the Christ. The title without any explanation will be misunderstood due primarily to the pervasive concept of military conqueror attached to an anticipated messianic

---

43. For example see Bateman's discussions about 4Q174 in chapter 10 (pp. 278–80) and 4Q174, 4Q246, 1Q28a, 4Q369, and *Psalms of Solomon* in chapter 11 (pp. 295–303).

figure (e.g., 1QM, 4Q161, 4Q174, 4Q285, 4Q458, *Pss. Sol.* 17–18) as well as other options for this figure that were circulating. Nevertheless, all these unique Lukan citations of Christ are stressing the authority the promised One possesses, which has some overlap with second temple expectations.[44]

Luke's Usage of "Christ" Similar to Other Gospel Writers
There are three occurrences where the use of Christ overlaps with the other Gospel writers. The first two usages evidence no difference. Peter's confession of Jesus as the Christ is the first. This remark is shared with Mark and Matthew (9:20). Luke's usage is very much along the lines of Mark's use. The next is the discussion of Psalm 110:1 and the Son of David versus Lord. This too is shared with the other synoptic gospels (20:41). Once again, the Lukan usage basically repeats what the other Gospels reflect.

The third overlapping occurrence with the other synoptics is the high priest's question about whether Jesus is the Christ (22:67). This usage is slightly different in Luke in that the reference to returning on the clouds from Daniel 7 is not present, only a session by the Son of Man at God's right hand. This focuses on the transcendent aspect of the messianic portrait as it is related to his exalted regal status.[45] The heavenly session is a key distinctive feature about Jesus as the Christ. The synthesis and simplification fits the emphasis on authority Luke has for the Christ. It fits with another uniquely Lucan feature, the presentation of an exaltation-ascension as a distinct event.

Luke does not use the title "Christ" in the scene of Jesus' entry into Jerusalem, but he is praised as the king who comes in the name of the Lord (Luke 19:38). This language is from Psalm 118:26, a text we have seen in many other contexts as well and whose use we have already treated in discussing it earlier use. This text also appears in Mark's account (Mark 11:9) and in Matthew (21:9).

Luke's Unique Use of "Christ" in the Closing Chapters
As Luke concludes his Gospel, four other unique usages of the term "Christ" appear. The first reference unique to Luke is the Jewish charge laid before Pilate that Jesus claims to be Christ a king (23:2). Here what we saw implied in the *titulus* and in the exchange with Pilate in Matthew and Mark is again made more explicit in the Jewish leaders' charges against Jesus. This Galilean claims to be a king of his own choosing apart from Rome. One of Pilate's

---

44. The idea of the new era representing the defeat of Satan can be seen in a Jewish text like *Testament of Moses* 10:1–2. So exorcisms point to a special time and figure; Bock, *Luke* 1:1–9:50, 439.

45. On why there is less of an allusion to Daniel 7 here than in Matthew and Mark, see the discussion in Darrell L. Bock, "Blasphemy and the Jewish Examination of Jesus," in *Key Events in the Life of the Historical Jesus: A Collaborative Exploration of Context and Coherence*, WUNT 247 (Tübingen: Mohr Siebeck, 2009), 638–52.

responsibilities as prefect is to protect Caesar's interests and authority. In effect, Pilate is challenged by the leaders to do his job by dealing with Jesus. This is made even more explicit in John's Gospel when the leaders say that if Pilate allows Jesus to go free he will show himself to be no friend of Caesar's (John 19:12).

In mocking, similar to but distinct from a text in Mark, Luke reports that some say that Jesus has saved others, so let him save himself, if this one is the Christ of God, the Elect One (23:35). Yet another mocker whom Luke describes with unique details is one of the thieves on the cross who also observes that this Jesus cannot be the Christ (23:39). He is rebuked by another thief, yet another unique Lukan detail. It is Jesus' role as the chosen anointed one of God that echoes through his passion in Luke, even on the lips of those who mock and reject him. The Passion section of Luke shows that the central dispute about Jesus at the end was his messianic claim.

Partly suggestive of this are allusions in a typological prophetic way to texts from the psalter to portray the unjust nature of Jesus' death or to show his faithfulness. All the Gospels make this point, but we discuss it here because at least six times in Luke 23 the declaration is made that Jesus is innocent even as he is headed to the cross. Here Psalm 22:19 points to the dividing of his garments. The offer of vinegar looks to Psalm 69:22. Jesus' cry entrusting himself to God is from Psalm 31:6. It comes in place of the more famous cry from Psalm 22 in Matthew and Mark about why has God forsaken him. All of these Psalms are about righteous suffering or reflect laments calling for God's justice. To these texts that appear in the Synoptics, John will add references to no bone being broken from Psalm 34:21 and a reference to the one pierced from Zechariah 12:10. Here are a cluster of texts designed to show that Jesus suffered a rejection common for one who is righteous and faithful before God. Of these texts, only Zechariah may have a more directly prophetic force. The others show Jesus as the righteous sufferer *par excellence*, the culmination in a pattern of suffering the righteous often face. These texts add to the collection of texts about the suffering of the one God has sent to represent righteousness as his anointed Christ.

Two final key and uniquely Lukan texts appear in postresurrection settings. On the Emmaus journey, Jesus rebukes his compatriots as being slow to believe all the prophets have written. Jesus stresses that it was necessary that the Christ should suffer and enter into glory as he expounded from Moses and the prophets (24:26). In a similar scene before the twelve and others gathered together, Jesus taught that it is written in the Scriptures that the Christ must suffer and rise from the dead and that repentance for the forgiveness of sins be proclaimed in his name beginning from Jerusalem (24:46). These generic appeals to Scripture anticipate what we also saw in Acts, the association of messianic themes with the teaching of the entirety of Scripture. This helps to explain and justify the synthetic reading Acts and the Gospels present.

Although there are not specific passages here, the ones already appealed to make the point for the one tracing Luke's narrative. Here we see why the name of Jesus Christ is emphasized in Acts, as well as why the Scripture becomes so important to the preaching there. It is these final emphases of suffering, resurrection, and preaching in his name that underscore Luke's portrayal of the title "Messiah." It is clear that for Luke by the time Jesus was crucified a key issue was the perception he claimed to be the Messiah and presented himself as such by what he did.

Christological Fulfillment in Luke

As with the earlier chapters, we see both fresh and parallel emphases here that we also saw in Acts. The idea of the unjust rejection of the Christ is a more emphasized theme, as is the way in which eschatological figures all unite in the eschatological work of the Christ, who also is Son of Man. This synthesis and wedding of earthly and transcendent hope is a key feature of the early community's presentation of Jesus as the Christ. The authority of this figure, the kingdom he rules over, and the emphasis on his delivering work has ample precedent in Jewish expectation. What the various portraits of Judaism often did was to locate such emphases in one portrait or another (the earthly versus the transcendent or the Messiah versus the Son of Man or deliverer or priest). The Gospels claim is that Jesus in his action and teaching brought these distinct hopes together into one unified concept and person.

Veiling and Presentation of "Christ" in John

Put the simplest way, John's Gospel presents God the Father sending the Christ, his Son, into the world.[46] This Gospel is distinct in many ways from Matthew, Mark, and Luke. It is dominated by dialogue discourses and a series of events, often called the seven signs. These miracles picture how what Jesus does brings a new era that completes Jewish hope and surpasses current practice (John 1–12). Jesus' summary acts and discourses as well as the Passion and Resurrection reveal that the glory of Jesus is found in his work of being "lifted up" by God through the cross. The "book of glory" completes the Gospel (John 13–21). More than 85 percent of this Gospel has unique material. So it should be of no surprise that most of the nineteen times the Gospel uses the term "Christ" are unique because of the lack of overlap John has with the other three Gospels. John clearly wrote with the intent to fill out the portrait of Jesus with a fresh perspective on him. That perspective is met right at the start when the infancy of Jesus is ignored and the story of John the Baptist

---

46. Key commentaries on John are those by Andreas Köstenberger, *John,* BECNT (Grand Rapids: Baker, 2004), Craig Keener, *The Gospel of John,* 2 vols. (Peabody, MA: Hendrickson, 2003), D. A. Carson, *The Gospel according to John* (Grand Rapids: Eerdmans, 1991), and Leon Morris, *The Gospel according to John,* NICNT (Grand Rapids: Eerdmans, 1971).

is delayed so that the evangelist John can explain that the Word who was God became flesh. John's Gospel tells the story of Jesus from heaven down.[47]

Seven Signs in John
Changes water into wine (2:1–11)
Heals a royal official's son (4:43–54)
Heals an invalid (5:1–15)
Feeds five thousand people (6:1–15)
Walks on water (6:16–24)
Heals a man born blind (9:1–41)
Raises Lazarus from the dead (11:1–44)

John's Use of "Christ" in the Prologue

John in his prologue contrasts the era of Moses with that of Jesus by noting that the law came through Moses, but grace and truth came through Jesus Christ (1:17). Jesus as the incarnate Christ brings a new era. John the Baptist is not the Christ (1:20), a remark close in force to a similar denial by John the Baptist in Luke 3. A similar remark comes in the question of why John baptizes if he is not the Christ (1:25). This question appears to suggest that John's water baptism pointed to a preparation for the arrival of salvation. This gospel's presentation is suggestive of a theme that Luke makes explicit in Luke 3:15–17. Andrew goes to Simon and announces, "we have found the Messiah (which means the Christ)" (1:41).[48] This unique, early confession in John indicates the understanding and hope that Jesus' earliest followers had. Apparently what they saw as a hope is confessed explicitly to Jesus later on in John 6:68–69 in John's equivalent to Caesarea Philippi. John the Baptist again repeats his denial that he is the Christ (3:28).

John's Use of "Christ" with the Samaritan Woman

The Samaritan woman and Jesus have a theoretical discussion about the Christ and where worship should occur. She remarks that she knows the Messiah the one called Christ is coming (4:25). This use of Messiah with the use in 1:41 are the two uses of the term in its Hebrew form in the Second Testament. Jesus discloses to her that he is that one. After her discussion with Jesus, she goes back into the town and notes that Jesus told her all that she ever did, leading her to ask if he might be the Christ (4:29). No detail is given here, only the title is used. All we are told is that Jesus as the Christ matches the one Judaism, and now Samaritans, had hoped for to deliver the people. The Samaritans had a hope about one to come who was a prophet like Moses, a leader-prophet. The idea that God will call for a worship of truth

---

47. The full elaboration of how John and the Synoptic interact between the earth-up and heaven-down portraits can be found in my *Jesus According to Scripture* (Grand Rapids: Baker, 2002).

48. On John's use of such confessions from disciples early in his material, see Köstenberger, *John*, 72.

and spirit matches the expectation of the Synoptics and the teaching of law focused on the heart that Jesus gave in Matthew 5–7 as reflective of God's call to righteousness.

John's Use of "Christ" When Jesus Faces Opposition

John 7 is loaded with speculation about whether Jesus is the Messiah. When Jesus faces opposition from the leaders, it is noted that he is speaking openly so the question becomes whether he might be the Christ (7:26). Yet there is a problem, for the people know that Jesus is from Nazareth, but the teaching is that no one will know where the Christ comes from (7:27). It is not clear where this idea about Messiah comes from, although it could be that the idea of a pre-existent or transcendent Messiah who lacks an origin, like that in Daniel or *1 Enoch*, could be alluded to here. Others in Jesus' audience are more open, as the question is raised whether the Christ could possibly do more signs that Jesus has done (7:31). Later in the chapter the dispute continues. Some are suggesting Jesus is the Christ (7:41), but others object whether the Christ can come from Galilee (7:41). Does not Scripture teach that the Christ is descended from David and comes from Bethlehem (7:42)? The allusion here is to Micah 5. The text as a Davidic hope was read as being prophetic about the coming messiah in the first century. The crowd is unaware of Jesus' birthplace as they speculate about this.

The debate here is about the origins of the end-time figure. Does he have no origin or have an earthly one? This question reflects the earthly-transcendent tension of various pictures in Jewish hope. The audience's view of the roots of Messiah as coming from Bethlehem differs from their remark in 7:27. The debate here about the origins of the Christ fits the Judaism of the period by thinking in either-or terms. The Messiah is transcendent or comes from Bethlehem. It also shows the variety of messianic views within Judaism are in play as people consider the options. The synthetic view of Jesus as Word and Christ, as transcendent and incarnate, makes the either-or into a both-and. It also is clear that the crowd does not realize Jesus was born in Bethlehem, so there is irony in their objection here for those who do know this.[49] The objection is an empty one on every count!

John's Use of "Christ" as a Confession

Three significant confessions occur in John's Gospel. First, confessing Jesus to be the Christ could mean removal from the synagogue as the parents of the healed blind man feared this consequence if they responded to Jesus' work positively (9:22). John's Gospel reflects a strong public perception that Jesus was understood as a messianic figure, even to the point of some Jewish communities reacting against it. Second, the Jews ask Jesus if he is the Christ

---

49. On this irony, see Carson, *The Gospel according to John*, 329–30.

(10:24). They want him to say it plainly. So John's Gospel shows that even though Jesus was not making a point of his being Messiah; the public was considering the idea. This fits the way the Synoptics portray Jesus' handling of the messianic title in public. Finally, Martha confesses Jesus to be the Christ, Son of God, he who is coming into the world (11:27). This confession nicely sums up the emphasis of this Gospel. Jesus is the Christ sent into the world by God from heaven. He brings God's promise, hope, and life. It, along with the scene involving the Samaritan woman, show that in spots Jesus did to some acknowledge who he was in a more private context.

John's Use of "Christ" in Jesus' Teaching

Jesus' teaching about the Son of Man being lifted up confuses the crowd who know that it is taught that the Christ will be around forever (12:34). Again this view of the Christ seems fueled by the picture of a transcendent Messiah, one of the views in Judaism some of the crowds in John's Gospel scenes appear to reflect on occasion (see John 7 discussion above). It is not clear which specific passage is in view or if the idea is that if the Messiah participates in the final judgment, then he is present through the end. If this final idea is present, then Son of Man texts might be in view like Daniel 7, *1 Enoch* 37–71 or *4 Ezra*.[50] One thing this view did not hold was that Messiah could suffer or be lifted up. This suffering element John plays off of with the expression "lifted up." The expression emphasizes how that suffering brings exaltation. This is certainly part of the fresh messianic synthesis the community has that has run through virtually all of our Second Testament texts—the theme of suffering leading into glory.

Jesus defines eternal life in his prayer for the disciples as knowing the only true God and the one who he has sent Jesus Christ (17:3). Here "eternal" life seems not only to be a description of life's duration, but its origin and quality: it is from above, from the one who is the source of everlasting life.

John's Use of "Christ" as Summary

Finally John summarizes noting that he has written his Gospel so that his readers might believe that Jesus is the Christ the Son of God. In believing they might have eternal life in his name. The note on the name is an interesting overlap with Luke and Acts. It is similar to the juxtaposition we discussed in Luke 1:32–33 and the allusion to ideas of the Son's authority that compare with the hope from 4Q246 (ch. 8, pp. 307–10).

Christological Fulfillment in John

The Gospel's use of the term "Christ" does show Jesus making selective public disclosures to specific individuals, but the bulk of the Gospel shows

---

50. For discussion of possible background, see Carson, *The Gospel according to John*, 445–46.

the controversy and questions that surrounded this public claim as well as showing Jesus' ambiguity to speaking directly about this title in public. Most of these passages show that a messianic hope was contemplated by some for Jesus, but that other details troubled some people about the claim. What this ambiguity by Jesus indicates is the topic of our final chapter on Jesus and the idea of Messiah.

CONCLUSION

In many ways the portrait of the term "Christ" in all the Gospels is quite restrained. It is a Messiah mostly veiled to the public in terms of explicit affirmation. Jesus reveals the nature of the times and his position far more by what he does than what he says. Most of the explicit remarks are in private settings or in narrative remarks that frame Jesus' ministry. Most such remarks do not actually come from within the events. There is a hesitation by Jesus to emphasize the term "Christ," at least in most public contexts. Only once as he approaches Jerusalem for the final time is this hesitation to present himself explicitly in public lifted. One element of this hesitation seems to be the point of potential confusion that the expectation of the Christ's suffering creates for an audience that did not anticipate such a feature for the Messiah. Our study of the era of promise revealed in the Hebrew Scriptures and reflections during the second temple period show the lack of such an expectation in terms of how messianic texts were read. The fact that Jesus emphasizes this theme privately to his disciples after the confession at Caesarea Philippi and that they struggle to understand how this could be true shows the point. The variety of views in Judaism also may have required that care be exercised so that a misunderstanding did not result.

Nonetheless, the pattern we have seen in other chapters also appears here. The synthesis of the hope brings together transcendent and earthly elements of the hope, as well as combining eschatological texts about the nature of the new era with texts about the delivering figure. A fresh feature of the portrait for the new community in terms of normal Jewish expectation is the unjust rejection and suffering theme that surrounds Jesus as the Christ. Another element of the combination that the Gospels introduce is how the Christ brings the Spirit of the new era. Here what comes with the new era is placed alongside the One who makes it happen. The nature of this anticipated deliverance draws both on existing Jewish expectations and titles, but also makes the scope of that deliverance touch all aspects of the creation. This is a direction which was rare in the contemplation of Messiah in Judaism. It appears only the transcendent elements of second temple hope reflected in texts like *1 Enoch* 37–71, although that text is influenced by the image of Daniel 7 with its Son of Man going directly into the heavenly presence of God.

Important texts are used in this material. Prominent are Psalm 110:1, Psalm 118, and Daniel 7:13. The issue of the promise to David and Abraham also appears. These are shown to be key texts in the way they were used by Paul and others in the Second Testament. The Gospels suggest many of these key texts were rooted in Jesus' own use or in events where they were raised in association with Jesus' activity. The juxtaposition of texts often brings together distinct topics and unites them into a more comprehensive synthesis of eschatological and messianic hope.

The most important observation we have is that in these materials are the beginning of a great synthesis from the claims about One being the Christ. What was a series of portraits of a variety of figures in the promise and expectations phase has been unified by the material in the Gospels and Acts. The ability to unify the hope and to claim God had acted to show it was so was at the core of the earliest Christian preaching that God had brought deliverance in Jesus the Christ. It means that the acts of Jesus are key to appreciating who he is and who he claimed to be. However, to take this final step we have to go back over our material more carefully. It also helps us with one other interesting feature of the Second Testament, that is, the contrast between the Gospels' lack of focus on this title and the obvious key role it plays in Acts, the Epistles and Revelation. We must pay careful attention to the actions of Jesus when looking at the Second Testament portrayal of the Christ. What does he do that gives indications about who Jesus saw himself to be? Did Jesus have a messianic self-understanding? Some people think we cannot get to the answer of this question, arguing that the Gospels are more a reflection of their time and the Christ of faith versus the Jesus of history. We do not see the difference as being that great, but it is a position that needs examination. The best way into this discussion is the debate surrounding the historical Jesus as Messiah. It is the central topic of this section's final chapter.

CHAPTER FIFTEEN

THE IDENTITY OF JESUS AS THE CHRIST IN HIS MINISTRY

We introduced this book with a question: Who is Jesus? Numerous contemporary responses were cited. Some argue that there is little to no continuity between Jesus' messiahship and the Hebrew Scripture (e.g., Crossan, Horsley, Sanders, Borg). They argue that the connections made are part of the early church's reading of theology back into those earlier texts and—in most cases—have little or no contact with Jesus' own teaching on the subject, since for many of these scholars Jesus had no messianic self-understanding. On the other end of the spectrum are those who see a great deal of connection between the Testaments in their affirmation and appeal to mostly directly predictive and prophetic texts about Messiah (e.g., Kaiser, Sailhamer). At the outset, it should be said this second approach has much more going for it than the first option. In several cases, the connections they make are there. The question is how these connections work and whether primarily direct prophecy is the key or whether the situation is more variegated.

Our approach has been to appreciate both the continuity and discontinuity about the concept of Messiah throughout Jewish history in both canonical and non-canonical works. Our focus has been on God's progressive revelation of his promise of Messiah as presented in the Hebrew Scriptures. We also have treated how this hope was reflected upon during the second temple period (sometimes well and sometimes poorly). That showed us that some ideas we see in the Second Testament were already at work in some of the earlier reflection on the Hebrew Scripture. Moreover, there was a variety of expectations about the Messiah in the time of Jesus because there were many distinct ideas about who this figure was, plus the failed efforts by some who claimed to be Messiah. Finally we considered how the Second Testament texts saw fulfillment in Jesus. We have argued for a mix of texts, some messianic, some regal, some eschatological, some about promise and some about the Spirit, all placed together in a grand synthesis in the new era.

We are now ready to answer our opening questions: Who is Jesus and was he significantly responsible for the emphases in the texts of the early Christian community, both by the actions of his ministry and his illumination of the messianic portrait in the Hebrew Scripture. This final chapter on the coming of the King considers the roots of the messianic confession in the early church. Do the roots for this confession go back to Jesus? How did Jesus present himself in ways like and unlike the expectations that had emerged about this figure during the latter part of the second temple period? In asking these questions we are attempting to show how one can corroborate that Jesus did make such claims beyond merely appealing to the theme's presence in the Second Testament. In considering these questions we see how history and interpretation work together to enlarge our understanding of biblical passages.

FOUR KEY POINTS ABOUT THE RECORD

As we turn to the historical Jesus, the Second Testament, and the question of Jesus as Messiah, certain key points need attention. First, we know that the name Christ was tied to Jesus early in the first century. Suetonius, a Roman historian who wrote biographies about twelve Roman emperors beginning with Julius Caesar, gives evidence that this name was used in Rome in the late 40s (*Claudias* 25.3–4). And followers of Jesus are called Christians in Antioch (Acts 11:26), some time between 35–40 CE. This incidental note in Acts, which has no reason to be a created detail by Luke, shows that the tie of followers to Jesus as the Christ was early.

Second, this connection to Christ also supports something that both the Gospels and Josephus tell us, namely, that the Jewish leaders and Pilate associated Jesus in some manner to being the Christ (*Ant* 18.3.3 §§ 63-64). That the Jewish leaders had a role in Jesus' death is something Josephus implies when he says that "the principal men among us" (τῶν πρώτων ἀνδρῶν παρ᾿ ἡμῖν) gave the suggestion to Pilate that Jesus be condemned. Now it might be possible that this messianic title was foisted upon Jesus by the leaders to get to a political charge, but the hard fact is that the deep resonance of the title at all levels of the Christian tradition makes this option less than likely. Why would the church accept a title for Jesus that he did not encourage them to give him, that had led to his disturbing death, and that could lead to charges of disloyalty to Rome for his followers?

Third, however, is the evidence in the Gospels themselves, which we have already traced. It shows Jesus' hesitation or at least qualification that he be tied publicly to the title of the Christ. Even when Peter confesses Jesus to be "the Christ" (ὁ χριστός; Mark 8:29), there are indications that this understanding had to be handled with care in public. Part of the reason is surely the misunderstanding such a confession might produce in light of the nature of Jesus' ministry, but what exactly this would have been must be explored by looking at key texts that could point to Jesus' being a messianic figure. The very indirect nature of these texts speak to their authenticity. If a messianic Jesus was a created concept by the church after the resurrection, it is likely the associations would have been more direct and less ambiguous, as we saw in Acts, the Epistles, and Revelation, where ambiguity is not a common characteristic of messianic claims at all.

Fourth, there is a counterbalancing observation. At the center of the gospel tradition at its various levels is the assertion that Jesus stands at the hub of the eschatological era. Even when a specific title for this role is not given, this central function given to Jesus in the context of decisive eschatological salvation and the promise of God would evoke messianic speculation about Jesus. This is a consistent and key part of the community's approach to the title. It is raised in one way or another in many Second Testament books. There is more to Jesus than his teaching about God; there is the program of God *he inaugurates and executes.*

No text shows this as clearly as John the Baptist's query from prison. Here John sends delegates to ask if Jesus was the One to come or should another be expected (Matt. 11:2–5 = Luke 7:18–23). This text, probably taken from Q, is important because it appears in a source that does not highlight Jesus' person and portrays John the Baptist as seeking to understand who Jesus is in a context where he also had been seen as a forerunner to him. This "embarrassing" presence of doubt on the part of the Baptist does not look like something the church would have invented, especially given the indirect affirmation the question generates. Jesus simply replies by pointing to what he is doing: the blind see (a healing without precedent from the Old Testament), the lame walk, lepers are cleansed, the deaf hear, the dead are raised, and the gospel is preached to them. Much of the language comes from phrases in Isaiah that describe activity of God's promised period of salvation (29:18—dead raised; 35:5—blind see, deaf hear, lame walk; 42:18—deaf and blind; 26:19—dead raised; 61:1—good news preached). Jesus is in the middle of all of this. This kind of reply raises the question whether it would be possible not to think of a messianic, delivering figure as being present, if God's decisive work of salvation has come. James Dunn, in a position not so unusual for many Second Testament scholars, thinks it is possible that Jesus saw himself as more than a prophet but whose activity was such that the disciples still attached him to messianic ideas even though Jesus avoided this description of himself.

A goal of this chapter is to challenge the view that Jesus' followers gave Jesus a title he refused to apply to himself. Our argument is that an examination of the key texts will show that Jesus did point followers in this direction, although he did so in ways that defined the term in very specific categories distinct from the various portraits of Messiah present in the second temple period.

Our four points are all key parts of the historical record about Jesus. Answering the question about how to see the historical development of the church's Christ confession requires a careful look at several key texts to understand the messianic trajectory and its varied configurations. The alternative explanation, like that from Dunn, also necessitates a studied inquiry into specific texts. In this chapter, we shall look at key texts to get at this question. And we shall also consider the case for historicity that one can make for what takes place in these passages. In many ways, even though this is the final chapter in our survey of Messiah from Judaism to Jesus, it is foundational to all we have already seen and a fitting climax to our study. The issues examined here form the hub of understanding how the variegated portraits of Judaism began to fuse into a single portrait for the early church.

KEY TEXTS AND EVENTS

Jesus' Preaching

The one text that gives us a glimpse of Jesus' preaching about his mission and role comes in his synagogue speech in Nazareth in Matthew 13:53–58, Mark 6:1–6a, and Luke 4:16–30. However, the key portion in these passages, giving the content of what was said, appears only in Luke in a setting likely moved forward in time to set the context for Jesus' Galilean ministry. Jesus cites Isaiah 61:1–2a and 58:6, declaring himself as the anointed one of these texts who has a dual role: proclaimer of God's time of deliverance and agent for the release it brings. He is anointed and preaches the gospel to the poor, proclaims release to the captives and sight for the blind, and sets at liberty those who are oppressed as he proclaims the acceptable year of the Lord.

The result is a side-by-side emphasis in terms of role. On the one hand, there is his role as prophet, as his later remarks in this text indicate. Those remarks point to a prophet lacking honor in his home and make comparisons to Elisha and Elijah. On the other hand, there is his role as eschatological deliverer. He brings the liberty he proclaims. This kind of role mixing or role juxtapositioning is common in passages where Jesus presents who he is. He comprehensively embodies the deliverance of God in what he says and does. Word, action, and being are united in this task. The eschatological time has brought the eschatological person. At the least, this text says this much.

The harder question is whether Luke 4 is explicitly messianic. The answer to this question is that it likely is. In making himself the key figure of the eschaton who delivers by setting free, Jesus is evoking a messianic expectation. When one places this text next to the events of Jesus' baptism with its divine voice connection to Psalm 2:7 and Isaiah 42:1, then a messianic connection is secure because the anointing Jesus describes in Luke 4 looks back to the baptism and its appeal to Psalm 2, a key psalm of Davidic promise. This baptismal event was one of the most important private experiences Jesus in the Synoptic Gospels. The baptismal calling is missional as well as christological, just as Luke 4 is.

What is important to note about Luke 4 is that Jesus sets these messianic claims within themes tied to the prophet and eschatological figure. So the presentation of Jesus as Messiah is veiled in that the claim is embedded with other claims.

Important to this understanding is what Isaiah 61 evoked to a first-century Jewish audience. Qumran attests to the passage's importance by describing the deliverance of God's true people in 1QH 18:14–15 while citing Isaiah 61. In another Dead Sea Scroll, the meek hear the message of God's mercy and salvation, language that recalls Matthew 5 and its beatitudes as well as this Lukan text. It is the poor, the *anawim*, who inherit the earth and delight in peace in 4Qp Ps. 37 (4Q171) ii 9–11. The poor are the focus of Jesus' mission in Luke 4. Finally, 11QMelch has Isaiah 61 woven into its entire exposition. In this text, the deliverer is Melchizedek who brings the year of Jubilee, the acceptable year of the Lord, and announces deliverance for the captives. This is a transcendent deliverer. What Jesus has done is to personalize and ground Isaiah 61 in an earthly figure. So here we have a glimpse of the synthesis evident in other Second Testament texts. In this case, the synthesis is associated with Jesus' own self-presentation, pointing to his self-understanding.

Jesus also has done something else relative to Judaism. By his juxtapositioning his declaration, Jesus frames and to a degree qualifies his messianic understanding. Jesus is not only Messiah. A Jewish expectation like that in Melchizedek fails to encapsulate all he is and does. Rather Jesus is more than Messiah, although the task of eschatological deliverance stands at the core of what Jesus is doing. He is the herald-prophet, who also is the deliverer of the eschaton. In other words, Jesus begins to bring the puzzle pieces together in Luke 4. Jesus' messianic preaching in Luke is "grooved" like the links in puzzle pieces to allow other concepts to be linked to it. This juxtapositioning feature is an aspect of mission presentation in the Gospels that occurs at all levels of the gospel tradition. It is so basic to the way the material consistently presents Jesus that it most likely goes back to one mind. This style of presentation looks to the method of the originating figure of the new movement. Jesus juxtapositions salvific events and questions about the coming one in response to John the Baptist in

> ### Jesus as Prophet
>
> Evidence of Jesus as prophet is threefold. Jesus *recognizes* himself to be a prophet when he says, "a prophet is not without honor, except in his hometown, and among his relatives, and in his own house" (Mark 6:4). Jesus *realizes* that others perceive him to be a prophet. The Samaritan woman muses, "Sir, I see that you are a prophet" (John 4:19; cp. Mark 8:27–28). Jesus *reacts* like a prophet when a disciple draws attention to the temple. Jesus predicts that "not one stone will be left on another" (Mark 13:2; cp. Matt. 24:1–2) and even weeps over the future destruction of Jerusalem (Luke 19:41–44). Yet Jesus is more than a prophet.

Matthew 11 and its parallels, so Luke 4 shows a similar linkage between prophet, eschaton, and the performing of the actual work of liberation. Jewish expectation may have wanted Jesus to be specifically either a prophet or a messiah. In this text, he presents himself as both, a two-for-one package of eschatological activity. However, Jesus is messiah in a way that already suggests that seeing him only in such terms risks not appreciating who he really is. This may well explain one reason why Jesus handles the title as ambiguously as he does later.

Peter's Confession at Caesarea Philippi

In Peter's confession at Caesarea Philippi there are features that appear only in one gospel, Matthew 16:13–20, combined with features that are a part of Mark 8:27–30 and Luke 9:18–21.

PETER'S CONFESSION AT CAESAREA PHILIPPI		
Mark 8:27-30	Matthew 16:13-20	Luke 9:18-21
27Then Jesus and his disciples went to the villages of Caesarea Philippi. On the way he asked his disciples, "Who do people say that I am?"	13When Jesus came to the area of Caesarea Philippi, he asked his disciples, "Who do people say that the Son of Man is?"	18Once when Jesus was praying by himself, and his disciples were nearby, he asked them, "Who do the crowds say that I am?"
28They said, "John the Baptist, others say Elijah, and still others, one of the prophets."	14They answered, "Some say John the Baptist, others Elijah, and others Jeremiah or one of the prophets."	19They answered, "John the Baptist; others say Elijah; and still others that one of the prophets of long ago has risen."
29He asked them, "But who do you say that I am?" Peter answered him, "You are the Christ."	15He said to them, "But who do you say that I am?" 16Simon Peter answered, "You are the Christ, the Son of the living God." 17And Jesus answered him, "You are blessed, Simon son of Jonah, because flesh and blood did not reveal this to you, but my Father in heaven! 18And I tell you that you are Peter, and on this rock I will build my church, and the gates of Hades will not overpower it. 19I will give you the keys of the kingdom of heaven. Whatever you bind on earth will have been bound in heaven, and whatever you release on earth will have been released in heaven."	20Then he said to them, "But who do you say that I am?" Peter answered, "The Christ of God."
30Then he warned them not to tell anyone about him.	20Then he instructed his disciples not to tell anyone that he was the Christ.	21But he forcefully commanded them not to tell this to anyone.

The clear affirmation of the messianic title is something Matthew presents in the most emphatic form among the synoptic Gospels, but the instruction not to say anything to anyone about the confession appears in all the Gospels. Why is there this difference in emphasis?

What we have already seen may well be a major clue. Messiah, or more particularly what the idea could evoke in people, is only a piece of the puzzle that explains who Jesus is and what his mission was. The term is so capable of generating misunderstanding that it must be accepted only in a qualified way. The term in its various uses in second temple Judaism almost demands fuller explanation in order to truly appreciate what the messianic role involves in terms of Jesus. But we are ahead of ourselves here. Let's take a closer look at this text, first in what all the accounts tell us and then in Matthew's own particular emphasis.

Matthew and Mark locate this event in the area of Caesarea Philippi. This was actually a Gentile city, full of pagan worship of multiple gods, numerous small temples, and Roman deities, as a visit to the current site in Israel will vividly attest. All versions have Jesus ask who the people think he is. All have a response in terms of prophets: John the Baptist (all), Elijah (all), the prophets (Matthew and Mark), and Jeremiah (Matthew). All versions have Jesus then ask who do the disciples say Jesus is. All responses point to the Christ, with Matthew adding the Son of the living God and Luke saying the Christ of God. Only Matthew has the long affirmation where Jesus speaks to Peter about the rock and notes that flesh and blood did not reveal this to him, but "my Father who is in heaven." Yet all the versions have Jesus tell them not to say anything about this to anyone.

Three features of this text are important: the basic contrast in the questions in the scene, Matthew's emphasis, and the command not to say anything publicly. First, *Matthew's text* is constructed around a contrast, and that is a key to the passage. Jesus asks questions that contrast what people think of Jesus with what the disciples think of him. The people see Jesus as some kind of prophet, but the disciples as Christ. This means that whatever else we say about this text, prophet is somehow an inferior or inadequate designation for Jesus; Messiah is superior.

Second, Matthew's emphasis tells us that Jesus clearly saw Peter's confession in a positive light, accepting it as an insight that God himself had given to Peter. The confession could hardly be more emphatically endorsed. It leads into a discussion of how it stands at the base of confession for the church Jesus will build. The more interesting question is whether the other Gospels are in agreement with this or as emphatic about it.

Luke places the entire ministry of Jesus in a messianic light by his introduction in the infancy narratives as well as his juxtaposition of Jesus' baptism with his synagogue speech. Luke also has a genealogy in his gospel, like Matthew, that goes through David. So his take is certainly positive as well.

Mark's point is more debated. However, this scene is the first use of the messianic title in the Gospel after the title's use in the Gospel's heading at Mark 1:1. There are no connections to David in Mark up to this point. The account of this scene in his gospel is very brief. There are the contrasting questions and then the command not to say anything to anyone about the confession. It can be said that Mark presents the issue with more ambiguity than the other Gospels. But does this mean that Mark somehow dissents from the use of this title? That seems quite unlikely. Mark 9:41 speaks of a cup given in the name of Christ. The evangelist also retains two key scriptural allusions to Messiah later in his Gospel, the discussion over what Psalm 110:1 means and the use of an allusion to that Psalm at the Jewish examination of Jesus. So this term is one he accepts. What Mark's portrayal represents, however, is a qualified kind of acceptance. This is where the command to silence becomes important.

So third, there is *the command not to say anything publicly*. It is Jesus' instruction for silence about the confession that tells us that Mark's emphasis fits what Jesus did and taught. In public, he tended to reveal who he was by his actions. The fact that Matthew has this word about silence as well, despite the intensity of Jesus' affirmation of Peter in that gospel, shows that this need for qualification of the term is something all the synoptic evangelists affirm. The key question is why there would be such a hesitation to make this messianic confession publicly.

Fortunately, one does not have to read long in any of the Synoptics to see the direction the answer goes. All of the Synoptics follow this scene with Jesus beginning his teaching that the Messiah must suffer, something Jewish expectation at the time did not teach. In fact, matching the unique emphasis of the affirmation is the emphatic way Matthew presents this scene as he has Jesus rebuke Peter with a "get behind me Satan" reply when Peter says such suffering cannot be (Mark 8:33 also has this remark, while Luke's version omits it). This juxtaposition is how Matthew indicates the ambiguity the term generated and the lack of emphasis given to it within Jesus' public ministry. Thus, the initial hesitation Jesus had about a public confession of Messiah during his ministry centered on the fact that the expectation of Messiah was a positive and powerful image in first-century Jewish expectation, no matter which particular form it took. The idea that this figure could suffer was not an element of that equation. Before Jesus could be widely seen to be the Christ, the disciples had to be clear that this was an element of Jesus' messianic task. We cannot stress this point too much.

The ambiguity around the term "Messiah" in some of the Synoptics is not a reflection of a retrojection of the term back into Jesus' ministry, but it is a reflection of the fullness of the Messiah's task in Jesus' own teaching. *Everyone around Jesus lacked this full portrait of glory and suffering. This difference in how the Messiah should be seen became a matter for instruction before the confession of Messiah could be properly understood, widely proclaimed, and embraced. To see Jesus as the Christ was foundational; he was not merely another teacher or prophet. Jesus as Messiah was the bearer of God's promised salvation, but that salvation would come at a messianic cost in suffering injustice and bearing sin that others at the time of Jesus' ministry did not yet realize had to be paid.*

What speaks for the historicity of Peter's confession is the united tradition of three gospel writers in affirming this confession and yet the very nuanced manner in which the messianic title is consistently handled. If a simple retrojection had taken place, reflective of the unqualified confession of the church to Jesus as the Christ (like what we see said so unambiguously in Acts, the Epistles, and Revelation), then one suspects this nuancing would be lacking. Even where Matthew is emphatic in embracing the title, the tensions tied to Jesus' handling of the term are not removed. There is something stubborn about the tension in the gospel tradition at this point that likely reflects the manner in which Jesus handled this title. At least this option is more likely than the idea that the church constructed a kind of post facto explanation of Jesus' work and teaching so it could confess a suffering but glorified Messiah that Jesus did not teach and that no one else held. Something about the manner in which Jesus handled this issue is most likely responsible for the way the Synoptics have handled the issue. These Gospels retain some note of tension about the confession of who the Christ is in the midst of Jesus' own ministry. In addition the rebuke of Peter in Matthew and Mark is too embarrassing a portrayal of a major church figure to have been created after the fact. Central to the tension is that the Messiah was not only to be a glorious figure as all had expected in a variety of forms but that the Messiah must also suffer for God's eschatological salvation to come. This contrastive emphasis is reflected as well in the occasional juxtaposition of messianic glory and suffering that appears consistently in the Second Testament (Luke 24:26; Acts 3:18–22; Phil. 2:6–11; 1 Pet. 4:13, 5:1).

Thus this scene at Caesarea Philippi and what follows it are crucial to appreciating why the Gospels do what they do with the term "Messiah." It is a key confessional term for those who follow Jesus, but only when properly appreciated as involving suffering as well as glory.

The Entry into Jerusalem

This event follows up on the pattern of the theme of the anticipated Messiah. It is one of the few events that is in all four Gospels (Matt. 21:1–17; Mark 11:1–11; Luke 19:28–40; John 12:12–19). Jesus coordinated this entry with the conscious choice to ride into Jerusalem in a self-conscious, public self-presentation. In fact, this portrayal is so messianic that many scholars have challenged it as not fitting Jesus. The key to the event is the juxtaposition of the arrival of a prominent figure and his entourage to the city with the processional that follows and his means of transportation—on a specific type of beast. The act was both provocative and yet so distinctive in its execution that a disjunction emerges that is key to understanding the act. Another key is that Jesus makes no attempt to stop the messianic declaration his disciples and the crowd generate as he enters.

The accounts agree on the regal acclaim Jesus received (Matt. 21:5; Mark 11:9–10; Luke 19:38; John 12:15). We previously discussed the use of Hebrew Scripture texts in the passage about the Jerusalem entry. Mark has a reference to the blessedness of the one who is to come and the approach of the kingdom of David. Luke shares the reference to the blessing of the one to come and has a note about peace in heaven and glory in the highest. Matthew has a similar two-fold note of blessedness for heaven and earth as the crowd sings "Hosanna in the Highest." Matthew also uniquely among the Synoptics adds an important narrative note explaining what took place. Matthew cites Zechariah 9:9, "Tell the daughter of Zion, Behold your king is coming to you, humble, mounted on an ass, and on a colt the foal of an ass." John shares this explanatory narrative note about Zechariah 9:9, while having the crowd call "Hosanna! Blessed is he who comes in the name of the Lord, even the king of Israel." Luke alone recounts an effort by the Jewish leaders to get Jesus to have the crowd stop their praise, something Jesus emphatically refuses to do. When one recalls that the church worked hard not to appear to be anti-seditious to Rome, the retention of this account, which does have that potential implication, reflects a stubbornness that argues this is an event that took place and made a deep impression.

The event itself recalls a regal entry in 1 Kings 1:33–40, where David's support of Solomon as his successor produces a public entry pointing to David's son as his chosen heir. A mule takes Solomon to Gihon to be anointed as king. Jehu has a similar kind of entry in 2 Kings 9:13. Both the processional and the King of David themes are invoked. It may well be that behind the Zechariah 9:9 image is the pattern set by this Davidic event. As Kinman notes, "The language employed immediately evokes memories of David because it addresses Jerusalem as the daughter of Zion—the city of David (2 Sam. 5:7, 9; 6:12, 16; 1 Chron. 15:1–3)."[1] These events point to the welcome of a king.

However, the welcome of a king is not necessarily the arrival of *the* Messiah. Some in the crowd could simply have seen it as the restoration of a regal hope or of the Davidic line. For an explicit messianic idea requires that one appreciates the action in the context of Jesus' ministry and possesses an understanding of that ministry. Some in the crowd probably did, while others likely did not. The disciples' and crowd's laying of the branches before the animal and the notes of praise suggest that the imagery of the event is only regal, although in hoping for deliverance it pushes in a messianic direction. Jesus and the disciples intended more, but many in the crowd may not have appreciated all that was happening. The perception emerged that the arrival was a hopeful one tied to the decisive arrival of the promise of a kingdom to David, something the crowd's notes of praise

---

1. Brent Kinman, "Jesus Royal Entry into Jerusalem," in *Key Events in the Life of the Historical Jesus* (ed. Darrell L. Bock and Robert L. Webb; Grand Rapids: Eerdmans, 2010), 401.

affirm. These notes of praise from Psalm 118 belong to the Hallel psalms (Pss. 113–118), sung at major festivals such as Unleavened Bread, Tabernacles, and Hannukah (*m Pesah* 5:7; *m Sukkah* 3:9). Mishnah, *Sukkah* 4:5 notes that crowds sang these psalms on the way to the temple during Tabernacles. When one recalls that the Synoptics frame this event with Jesus' healing of the blind man as Son of David, then regal implications are clear. Add to this the eschatological emphasis in Jesus' ministry that we have already noted, then the regal figure turns into a messianic one (Mark 10:46–52; Matt. 20:29–34; Luke 18:35–43). The entry also has the temple cleansing afterwards, an act that could evoke *Benediction* 14 (also called *Shemoneh Esreh* or *Amidah*, where the restoration of David and the cleansing of Jerusalem in the end are prayed for in this national prayer of Israel):

> "And to Jerusalem, thy city, return with mercy; and dwell in its midst as thou hast spoken; and build it soon in our days to be an everlasting building; and raise up quickly in its midst the throne of David. *Blessed art thou, Lord, who buildest Jerusalem.*"[2]

In sum, this entry is regal, and by implication given the nature of Jesus' preaching, it becomes eschatological and messianic. Jesus intended it as a public demonstration of who he was. As Jesus came to Jerusalem this final time, he was calling the nation to recognize her king. He made no effort to stop the public praise. Unlike earlier in his ministry, where he spoke of being king with hesitation, he was now ready to make his claim public and call the nation to make a choice. The journey to his death shows where the bulk of the nation's response ended up. That suffering was something he had also taught his disciples to expect, although it is clear that aspect of his message took the tragic events themselves to sink in.

The Christ at the Jewish Examination of Jesus and the Public Explanation of His Crucifixion

Jesus was crucified as a "King of the Jews." This is confirmed for us in two ways. First, the Gospels all report this as the point of the charge on the placard that accompanied Jesus to the cross. That placard is known as the *titulus*. Second, Josephus's remarks place the responsibility for this rejection at the hands of the Jewish leaders and Pilate (*Ant* 18.3.3 § 63-64). What this shows is that there was enough in Jesus' ministry to lead others to see him making regal claims. Jesus died as more than a prophetic figure.

What the Gospels show in their portrayal of the action leading into Jesus' death is a primarily a twofold movement in the Jewish and Roman

---

2. Translation from Emil Schurer, *The History of the Jewish People in the Age of Jesus Christ*, vol. II (ed. Geza Vermes, Fergus Millar, and Matthew Black; Edingburgh: T&T Clark, 1979), 458.

examinations of Jesus. The key events involve an examination before the Jewish leaders followed by Pilate's questioning. The examination by Pilate leads to the crucifixion based on charges that are largely political (Luke 23: 2–3), since only Pilate had the authority to crucify and a religious charge would be of no interest to him. This is in part why the charge shows up in regal form. A competing king to Caesar without being connected to the emperor's choice was something Pilate was responsible to stop. Pilate was also to keep the peace and make sure Rome got her taxes. According to Luke, the Jewish leaders present charges to Pilate that touch on all of these points, putting pressure on him to meet his responsibilities to Rome.

The Jewish examination is the key, because without it Jesus would not have been brought to Pilate. Here the discussion is both political and religious. Mark 14:53–64 covers this event. An initial effort to focus on a claim that Jesus would destroy the temple fails to get a collection of credible witnesses. So the discussion turns to the question about whether Jesus is the Christ, specifically "the Christ the son of the Blessed" as Mark puts it. The Jewish leadership asks a question about Jesus as Messiah. Jesus' reply gives them far more. He responds saying, "I am; and you will see the Son of man seated at the right hand of power [Ps. 110:1], and coming with the clouds of heaven [Dan. 7:13–14]." We have noted the two allusions to the Scriptures the Jews recognized in the reply. Jesus affirms the question and says more. Even the more indirect responses in Matthew and Luke to this question, that is, Matthew's "You have said so" (26:64) and Luke's "You say that I am" (22:70), represent qualified affirmations as well. Those Gospels are using an idiom. The idiom says it is as you ask but not quite with the sense that you mean. Jesus' reply and use of Scripture explain why the other two Gospels go the way they do.

The Jewish leaders saw Jesus' reply as blasphemous. In their view, this answer made him worthy of facing judgment for sedition before Pilate because he was making two claims simultaneously. In claiming a seat at God's right hand from Psalm 110:1, Jesus was appealing to a regal-Davidic psalm that pointed to kingship. In appealing to the imagery of Daniel 7 and riding the clouds, Jesus appealed to the picture of a transcendent ruler-judge who receives authority from God. In combining the two, Jesus was saying, I am the king and more than that, regardless of what happens now, God will give me a place at his side, In fact, I will be a ruler and judge, even over you. In other words, Jesus was saying I am not really on trial here; one day you will be subject to me. More than that, God will bring me to a place as Son of Man that means I am ruling from his side. Here Jesus claims that regardless of what is done, God will vindicate him. Beyond that, this vindication will result in a rule from the same throne as God's. Jesus makes a synthetic move here, bringing together and developing the portraits of promise and expectation into a unified, comprehensive picture.

Now the belief in Judaism was that God's glory was unique; so such a claim, although it was theoretically discussed with a figure like the Son of Man in works like *1 Enoch* 37–71, would have been heard as an affront to the unique glory of God coming from a humble Nazorean teacher of Judaism from the Galilean backwoods. This is why the leaders saw Jesus as blaspheming. They did not accept the claim and saw it as dishonoring God. The claim was worse than someone saying, I will go and live in the Holy of Holies in the temple, because Jesus had in mind God's very presence above, not the sacred locale where that presence was represented on earth. Jews had fought a war, the Maccabean War, to reclaim the honor of a desecrated temple.[3] Jesus' claims were more radical still.

The relevance of the Jewish examination for our topic is that again we get an affirmation from Jesus as the Messiah, this time in public. But once again we see this affirmation combined with other portraits, here with a transcendent Son of Man. What Jesus is doing here is showing, as he consistently has, that Messiah is at the base of who he is in his mission. However, there are other images to which Messiah attaches that are necessary in order to really understand who that Messiah is and what he is doing. Whereas with the confession by the disciples there was a need to appreciate that Messiah must suffer, here Jesus gives an open affirmation of total authority and vindication from God. What Jesus is doing with all of these scenes is to say, I am the Messiah, but that Messiah is also the Servant who suffers and the coming Son of Man who will rule and judge. In these synthetic links are the suffering-now-and glory-to-come pattern that shows up repeatedly in the Second Testament as a summary of Jesus' messianic career. The result is that Jesus as Messiah can suffer as the Epistles also proclaim, but one day he will return with fullness of glory and authority to judge. This also parallels what the rest of the Second Testament affirms and what the book of Revelation as a whole describes.

Thus this scene is a climactic one. Jesus goes fully public here as he faces his death. He proclaims the certainty of his vindication and authority even as the Jewish leaders try to bring his ministry to a halt by obtaining evidence for a political charge they can take to Pilate. Jesus' climactic confession ironically leads to his crucifixion. In a real sense, Jesus chose the cross by simply revealing who God would show him to be. Crucifixion for a political charge is what resulted, but it was not the end of the story the Jewish leaders had hoped it would be. The empty tomb followed and showed the divine vindication Jesus had anticipated for the Messiah. This vindication Jesus had announced to them. This claim of divine support and endorsement led to Jesus' death. The resultant resurrection was something God had done to set things straight

---

3. See Bateman's discussion of this event in chapter 8, "Three Obstacles to Overcome and Then One," 228–30.

and to show who Jesus was as God brought Jesus to sit at his side. In this, God showed Jesus to be more than a prophet and more than Messiah, at least as Messiah had been conceived of in most of second temple expectation. The synthesis showed Jesus to be Messiah, Servant, and exalted Son of Man in one unifying package that older revelation had set forth in distinct pieces.

THE HISTORICAL JESUS AS MESSIAH

We could elaborate on other scenes in Jesus' ministry that support the portrait of Jesus as Messiah, but the most important events are the ones we have treated. The case for the historicity of the events is strong. So we are gaining a glimpse of what Jesus did and taught as well as how others reacted to him. We see a Jesus who during most of his ministry was hesitant to publicly use the title "Messiah," not because of a question of whether that was who he was, but because of the great potential for a public misunderstanding of what that meant, given its varied and ambiguous use in Judaism.[4] Although Jesus conceived of a Messiah who would suffer and enter into glory, the public and the disciples originally held to a strictly glorious and authoritative Messiah. The disciples needed to have the suffering idea firmly in place before they could explain how Jesus saw his messianic role. The disciples and those who might be considering who Jesus was needed to appreciate this suffering feature. So Jesus spent much of his ministry teaching his disciples this messianic note of suffering, as well as the discipleship of cross-bearing that grew out of it. He waited to go public, excepting a few people here and there, until he entered Jerusalem.

To be sure, Jesus taught and acted in ways that declared his messianic functions, but often more with an emphasis on the time of salvation, the declaration of its presence, and the arrival of the eschaton as in Luke 4. In other words, Jesus publicly presented his messiahship through actions that pointed to the eschaton with him at its center. He preferred this manner of disclosure rather than emphatically using the messianic title himself in public teaching. In part, this was because the picture of Messiah in the first century was not clear, but was comprised of many disparate pieces. Jesus brought some of those pieces together into one image by what he did as much

> **The Suffering Messiah**
>
> A significant piece of the messianic puzzle, missing from the numerous expectations of messiah, was that of suffering. Jesus spent much of his ministry teaching people to grasp a simple truth: that though he was the Messiah, he was a suffering Messiah (e.g. Mark 8:31; 9:31; 10:33–34). Thus the emphasis of messiahship demonstrated work oriented to the future and not the present, whose kingdom was spiritual with yet a physical kingdom to come, and whose rule was both present and yet to come.

---

4. See Bateman's discussion in chapter 11, "Anticipations of the One Called Son," 314–20.

as by what he said. Those with ears to hear could see a messianic claim in what Jesus was doing and teaching. Those who were really paying attention could also see that this portrait of Messiah was far more encompassing than the normal Jewish expectation of the political deliverer or even the transcendent figure of Daniel and the books of Enoch. The missing piece was that the Messiah would suffer, opening the very door to glory through spiritual renewal, restoration, and forgiveness. More than being a political leader over other nations, Jesus was a spiritual leader on the way back to God. The Jewish portraits had expressed this largely earthly hope with rich variety. Jesus unified the pieces and showed there was far more to it than that.

CONCLUSION

Our survey is now complete. In the book of Revelation, "Christ" is a regal title that has exalted heavenly overtones. The confession of Jesus as the Christ in this last book of the Second Testament reflects a high view of Jesus who rules over God's kingdom with shared authority from the Father. It is clear that for the book of Revelation Messiah is regal and heavenly in thrust, reflecting the impact of a Jesus raised to the divine throne room and presence of God.

In the catholic Epistles the title "Christ," either used alone or as part of the naming of Jesus, points to four periods. First, there are the promises about the Christ, especially his suffering. Second, one can see Christ's work in ministry, primarily in unjust suffering and in dying for sin. Third, Jesus mediates blessing now so that believers are able to serve God and his will with good works that honor him. Finally, there is the glory to come when Jesus will bring God's eternal rule in total righteousness and shalom. The scriptural background for such usage included promises about the covenant, as Hebrews 1 showed. Key texts here are Psalm 2:7, Psalm 110, and ideas that sounded like Isaiah 52:13–53:12. The appeals are rooted in the patterns of God's work in the past now escalated to more comprehensive levels in Jesus.

The usage by Paul is dominated by the idea of incorporation into Christ. Through this union with Messiah, believers share in benefits and in a position Jesus provided through his death and resurrection. The result is that believers are said to be in Christ and the church is described as Christ's body. Various doctrinal summaries of Christ suffering for the sake of or on behalf of the sin of his people underscore the Christ's basic work. This work is sometimes mentioned as a part of God's plan. Although explicit ties to Scripture are rare, the imagery of Psalm 110:1 and the promise to Abraham are the two most common themes besides the general portrait of the Suffering Servant figure of Isaiah 52:13–53:12. The descent from David also appears here and there to underscore a messianic connection as a Son of David. These uses are most often put to ethical use, as a ground for exhorting that believers follow the example of Christ as a means of reflecting faithfulness to his grace, his work, and the position he has given us. There is a final emphasis in Paul that also has some Petrine parallels. That is an appeal to the future goal of salvation and appearing before him blameless on the Day of Christ. This glance towards the future also serves as a basis of an ethical appeal. In many ways a trip through these uses leads to a review of the whole scope of Pauline teaching as they are woven into the full fabric of his writing.

A threefold sequence about Messiah appears in Acts. (1) The Scriptures, properly understood as a whole, sets forth the Christ's suffering and resurrection, as well as Messiah's distribution of the Spirit. (2) This Christ portrait is what God showed Jesus to be. (3) The evidence that God is working through Jesus is shown in what is done through the name of Jesus Christ. Emphasis falls on the authority of the name and on the many Scriptures used to make the point. These scriptural texts include Joel 2:28–32; Psalm 110:1; Psalm 16:8–11; Psalm 132:11; Deuteronomy 18:15, 19; Genesis 22:18; Psalm 118:22; and Psalm 2:7. There also is the theme of Jesus' suffering and rejection, which involves injustice as well as provision for sin and forgiveness. Acts gives by far the most detail about explicit scriptural claims tied to the Christ.

As a whole the Gospels exhibit a more restrained use of the title with three themes dominating. First, there is the disciples' recognition that Jesus is more than a prophet; he is the Christ. Second, that confession is tempered, however, by Jesus' instruction that the disciples are not to declare this confession to anyone while Jesus teaches them about the necessity of Christ's suffering. Of the Synoptics, Matthew is the most explicit about Jesus accepting the title Christ. In the last week, however, Jesus goes more public with the claim and title. *However, the main way Jesus reveals his person and mission is not through claims but actions. These acts show him to be the central figure of the promised salvation of God, a point that displays his messianic role.* Probably the most important point is third. It is how Jesus juxtaposes the use of Messiah or messianic imagery with other images so that the term is like a "link piece" for him to which other concepts can be tied. This synthesis undergirds the later Second Testament uses and portraits of Messiah and eschatological hope. So links are made to Son of Man, Lord, eschatological Prophet, or Suffering Servant depending on the text in question. The eschatological era and its activity is central to these links. This linkage shows that although the Christ is a foundational title for Jesus, it is not so comprehensive that it can remain by itself until the full portrait of what it means has emerged. This key role is reinforced in John, who writes with this linkage in mind when he says that readers might believe that Jesus is the Christ, the Son of God, and that believing they might have life in his name.

This brought us to the question of the historical Jesus and the title. Jesus during most of his ministry was hesitant to use the title "Messiah" publicly. However, this was not because of a question of whether that was who he was. Rather he hesitated to work explicitly with this title in public because of the great potential for a public misunderstanding of what that affirmation meant. The plethora of options about Messiah that existed for Jews of the first century meant that Jesus had to exercise care in how he associated himself with the term. Messiah for Jesus was more than a military-political deliverer; he was distinct in that he would defeat Satan and bring a glorious righteousness. Messiah, as Jesus conceived of him, would also suffer and then enter into glory. This suffering-first-and-glory-to-come pattern was a unique feature in the Jesus' messianic understanding as compared with first-century Judaism and its varieties of messianism. Judaism's strictly glorious and authoritative Messiah, in whatever form it took, was missing an important key to the puzzle that anyone considering Jesus needed to appreciate. So Jesus spent much of his ministry teaching his disciples this note of suffering about the Messiah. He also waited to go public, with a few exceptions, until he entered Jerusalem a final time. To be sure Jesus taught and acted in ways that declared his messianic functions, but often more with an emphasis on the decisive time of salvation, or the declaration of eschaton's present arrival. Jesus presented himself as the central figure in the divine drama of promised salvation. The proper deduction left to those who paid attention was that this meant he was the anointed, promised One. Jesus' teaching went beyond the normal Jewish expectation of the political deliverer or even the transcendent figure of Daniel or the books of Enoch. The missing piece was that the suffering Messiah would open the very door to glory that the Jewish portraits expressed in such rich variety. Christ opened the door to glory because God would and did exalt him to a place at God's right hand. From here Jesus shares in divine presence and authority. In fact, this position indicated that Jesus Christ was more than a human deliverer. He was Lord with a fullness that equaled the authority of God.

The key texts that presented suffering were allusions to Isaiah 53 and especially Psalms that spoke of people's rejection but God's reception of Jesus, including Psalms about the righteous sufferer. Psalm 118 is particularly important here. The rejected stone is one God exalts and reflects one who comes in the Name of the Lord. The key texts for exaltation included not only this Psalm, but Psalm 110:1 and Daniel 7:13. In fact, Jesus being at God's right hand (Ps. 110:1) is a central confession of the early church. Of the many texts cited in the Second Testament, these are the most important and all were used by Jesus.

Thus, to call Jesus the Christ after his resurrection was to affirm all of this authority. Jesus as the Christ held in his hands the key to salvation and mediated those blessings to those who believed, incorporating them into himself. The Messiah could cleanse them from the stain of sin. He could purify them into his identity. He could raise them into the presence of God as citizens of the kingdom God had brought through the One who stood at the center of salvation. To confess Jesus as the Christ was to confess him as the Lord over salvation. Jesus is the promised anointed One who mediates the full blessing of God to those whose faith leads them to recognize the portrait. God showed Jesus to be this one when Jesus put all the pieces of the messianic puzzle together in one unified portrait. That image reflects promises, expectations, and realities God had revealed across time, showing Jesus to be the historic, long-awaited Messiah.

MESSIAH AND GENESIS 3:15

A "BOTH/AND" READING

We have saved discussion of Genesis 3:15 until now because—however it is understood—it is not an explicitly messianic text. This passage is often present in discussions about Jesus, seen as the first direct prophecy of Messiah and announcement of the gospel (the *Proto-Evangelion*). We consider the passage first in terms of its original historical, contextual meaning, then in terms of its fuller canonical significance in the light of the Second Testament, following the approach of the book as a whole.

There are two different views about this text. One argues it is the first hint of the gospel, since the seed of the woman will be victorious over the forces of evil the Serpent represents, namely, Satan. This reading sees the most direct messianic fulfillment. The second view argues there is no real hint of the gospel in the text. It is only about the introduction of conflict and the curse as a result of Eve's disobedience. This sees no real messianism nor messianic implication in the text by highlighting the near context and the curse. We suggest that there is an element of truth to both views. Set in its earliest frame, the text looks at the curse. However, seen in how the seed promise works from Genesis forward and how the reversal of the curse plays out in the fullness of Scripture, this text points to the gospel. The choice between the views should not be an either/or but a both/and. The most distinct feature of our approach is that it appreciates what the progress of revelation ultimately discloses about this text as the story unfolds.

GENESIS 3:15—THE LITMUS TEST

In many ways, Genesis 3:15 represents a litmus test to one's hermeneutical approach to the interpretation of messianic prophecy in the Hebrew Scriptures. Our approach to Genesis 3:15 gradually unpacks the verse vis-à-vis a threefold contextual-canonical, intertestamental, and apostolic lens. For the first portion, we consider the verse in its context in Genesis and the Torah. Then we examine how this passage is developed and its ultimate significance is unpacked in the frame of the larger biblical context of the canon.

Appendix

CONTEXTUAL READING: ORIGINAL EXEGETICAL MEANING

Our central initial question is, "What did the biblical narrator/author see and intend his original audience to understand?" We must distinguish what the Christian sees in Genesis 3:15 looking back (christological reading: ultimate messianic significance) from what the biblical narrator saw and intended his original audience to focus (contextual reading: original exegetical meaning). At either level of reading, we must recall that the canon is weaving together a larger story and gradually putting more pieces to the puzzle on the table as the story unfolds.

Admittedly, it is often difficult for the Christian reader to approach Genesis 3:15 with the same kind of literary innocence as its original audience. Yet in attempting to determine the original historical contextual meaning, this is precisely what we must attempt to unearth. We must be careful not to equate our own robust preunderstanding of where Genesis 3:15 eventually ends up with the literary/theological innocence of the original audience. To equate the two at the start is to over read Genesis 3:15 in the contextual step.

So we ask contextually, how does the book of Genesis and the Pentateuch as a whole present the Messiah on the basis of Genesis 3:15? Within the inspired texts of the First Testament are explicit connections to this "crush the head" promise made? Also, do the later books of the Hebrew Scriptures make a connection between Genesis 3 and the promise? When we ask these questions, we discover that neither the book of Genesis nor the entire Hebrew Scriptures as a whole speaks of the figure of the eschatological Messiah explicitly pictured as the coming "seed of the woman" who would "crush the head" of Satan. To be sure, the First Testament laid the foundation for the expectation of the eschatological Messiah; yet neither the rest of Genesis (leaving Genesis 3:15 aside) nor the Hebrew Scriptures connects Genesis 3:15 with the Messiah in terms of the woman's ultimate seed who would crush the head of Satan. This is nothing less than remarkable—if Genesis 3:15 was originally composed as direct prophecy. However, this dramatic silence is understandable—if our passage was not originally framed as only a direct and exclusive messianic prophecy.

Simply taking the rest of the book of Genesis into consideration, it is noteworthy that the covenant promises given by Yahweh to the patriarchs (Abraham, Isaac, Jacob) detail tremendous blessings, but the promise of the eschatological coming of the ultimate seed of the woman (along the lines of Genesis 3:15) is not one of them. Nowhere in the patriarchal narratives do we detect even the most subtle hint of this explicit idea. Taking the rest of the Pentateuch into account, we find not even the most vague allusion to Genesis 3:15. The conscious object of the faith of ancient Israel was not the expectation of the coming "head-crusher," but Yahweh alone as their Deliverer and Lord. This is not to deny that Genesis 3:15 has messianic potential, but it is to observe that its ultimate messianic import was only beginning to emerge at the time of Genesis's composition. The potential is seen in what Genesis and the First Testament do as a whole with the seed promise. Our point is that to see this, we need to trace and follow how these concepts develop.

Having distinguished a near contextual reading of Genesis 3:15 from later readings, we are ready to consider the passage and its central questions: What kind of oracle is Genesis 3:15? Who is the serpent and the seed of the serpent? Who is the seed of the woman? What is the nature of the conflict between the woman and the serpent, as well as the nature of the conflict between the woman's seed and the serpent?

Identity of the Serpent

Interpreters variously identify the serpent as (1) the personification of evil; (2) symbol of Satan; (3) a real snake whom Satan controlled/possessed enabling it to speak; or (4) a real snake which—perhaps like all animals in the Garden—could speak. Although the Second Testament interprets the serpent as Satan (2 Cor. 11:3; Rev. 12:9; 20:2), Genesis 3 does not explicitly make this identification, nor does any First Testament passage. In fact, the First Testament does not even clearly reveal the existence of Satan until much later (Job 1:6–12; 2:1–7; Zech. 3:1–2). The Second Testament will make the identification on the basis of appropriate canonical factors.

While the Second Testament ultimately identifies the serpent as Satan, the biblical narrator describes the serpent not as a supernatural demon, but as one of the animals of the field created by God (v. 1). The first curse leveled on him provides an explanation of the reason snakes slither on the ground (v. 14). The second curse focuses on the natural point of attack where snakes most naturally strike humans and humans most naturally strike snakes—at the head and upon the heel, respectively (v. 15). As a result, a number of ancient Jewish interpreters concluded that the serpent was simply a snake, albeit an unusual one. The fact that he talked may have been because snakes—or perhaps all animals—originally knew how to speak (*Jub.* 3:28; Philo, *On the Creation*, 156; Josephus, *Ant* 1.1.4 [1.50–51]).[1] This approach is reflected in an ancient Jewish interpretation of Genesis 3:14–15:

> [God] made the serpent, the cause of the deceit, press the earth with his belly and flank, having bitterly driven him out. He aroused a dire enmity between them [mankind and snakes]. The one guards his head to save it, the other his heel, for death is at hand in the proximity of men and malignant poisonous snakes. (*Sibylline Oracle* 1:59–64)

According to this approach, the fact that the snake was condemned to slither about on his belly (Gen. 3:14) merely implied that primeval snakes

---

1. James L. Kugel, *Traditions of the Bible: A Guide to the Bible As It Was at the Start of the Common Era* (Cambridge, MA: Harvard University Press, 1998), 98–100.

originally had legs. Also this approach down plays the supernatural identity of the serpent, since verse 1 presents the serpent as one of the "beasts of the field." As simple as this "animal" approach is, it seems to say too little.

The reader intuitively senses the serpent of Genesis 3 is no mere animal—at least nothing like any snake one encounters in the natural world! First, the serpent speaks—and even speaks the language of the woman. Second, the serpent is characterized as the most shrewd of all the beasts of the field (v. 1), exploiting the man's and woman's moral naivete (vv. 2–6). Third, this crafty agent presents himself not only as the antagonist of the narrative but the ultimate archetypal anti-theocratic figure.

Knowing later passages in the Second Testament (2 Cor. 11:3; Rev. 12:9; 20:2) identify the serpent with Satan, many Christian interpreters rightly conclude the ultimate agent of this temptation was the devil. Yet this identification is only explicit as a result of the progress of revelation. Since neither the biblical narrator of Genesis 3 nor his original audience was privy to these later passages, it is questionable whether either could or would have concluded that the serpent represented the chief demon whom Christians know as Satan. After all, the existence of Satan is only explicitly revealed for the first time in Job, and then only as the adversary, not tempter of the faithful (Job 1:6–12; 2:1–7). Here he asks permission to challenge the righteous Job, but he does not tempt directly. In fact, even the challenge to curse God and die comes from Job's wife (Job 2:9). When he appears later in the Hebrew Scriptures, again it is as adversary rather than tempter (Zech. 3:1–2; cf. 1 Chron. 21:1).

His role as tempter is not directly revealed until the Second Testament (Matt. 4:1, 3; Luke 4:13; 1 Cor. 7:5). More likely, the narrator and his original audience might have concluded the serpent represented personified evil or the embodiment of the temptation to rebel against God. In fact, many early Jewish and Christian interpreters viewed the serpent imagery in Genesis 3 as representing temptation.[2] However, when the Hebrew Scriptures later reveal Satan as archenemy of the faithful (Job 1:6–12; 2:1–7; Zech. 3:1–2), the theological and hermeneutical grid was provided for a more precise identification.

Genesis 3 certainly presents the serpent as the archetypal enemy of God and tempter of Adam and Eve. This pejorative characterization harmonizes with the stereotypical nature of the ubiquitous use of serpent symbolism in ancient Near Eastern literature. In biblical and ancient Near Eastern literature, the image of the serpent most often carries anti-theocratic connotations:

---

2. For example, Kugel, *Traditions of the Bible*, 98–100; Richard Henry Poplin and Gordon M. Weiner, *Jewish Christians and Christian Jews: From the Renaissance to the Enlightenment* (New York: Springer, 1994), 154 n. 22; John Smyth Carroll, *Prisoners of Hope: An Exposition of Dante's Purgatorio* (London: Hodder and Stoughton, 1906), 116; Henry Fanshawe Tozer, *An English Commentary on Dante's Divina commedia* (Oxford: Clarendon Press, 1901), 236; Glenn M. Davis, "Changing Senses in Genesis B," *PQ* 80 (2001): 113–31.

(1) the serpent was an object of worship in Canaanite fertility cults and Mesopotamian divination as the source of life and wisdom; (2) ancient Egyptian and Ugaritic mythology pictured the serpent as the personification of chaos; (3) in the Gilgamesh Epic, the protagonist found a plant which could give him immortality but lost out when a serpent stole the plant; and (4) the serpent was the archetypal unclean animal in Leviticus 11 and Deuteronomy 14. For these reasons, the serpent was an obvious candidate for an anti-God symbol. So culturally we understand why a serpent is present because of what it represents, but biblically and canonically we see there is more than a serpent. This is not an either/or choice, but a both/and matter, a point we will see in the passage again.

Identity of the Seed of the Woman

Interpreters variously identify Eve's "seed" (זֶרַע) as (1) her first offspring; (2) all her physical offspring; (3) all her spiritual offspring; or (4) her ultimate offspring—Messiah. In the Hebrew Scriptures, the term "seed" refers to a single descendant only ten times, always one's immediate child (Gen. 4:25). In most cases, it refers to (a) multiple children: 12 times, (b) multiple generations: 8 times; (c) future generations of multiple descendants: 132 times. The lexicons all classify its use in Genesis 3:15 as a collective for future multiple descendants (*BDB* 282.4b; *HALOT* 1:282.3a).

Although the conflict will involve the serpent's offspring (snakes) and the woman's offspring (humans), verse 15b depicts the conflict as between the serpent and the woman's offspring, reflecting the Hebrew concept of corporate solidarity.[3] Those who view this as only a prophecy of Christ's victory over Satan point to the singular form of the pronouns, verbs, and suffixes in verse 15b: "He (הוּא) will attack you (יְשׁוּפְךָ) on the head, but you (וְאַתָּה) will attack him (תְּשׁוּפֶנּוּ) on the heel." However, these singular terms may simply agree grammatically with the collective nouns "your offspring" (זַרְעֲךָ) and "her offspring" (זַרְעָהּ).[4] This ambiguity opens up the possibility that this passage is not only about conflict within the creation across time, but also that it

---

3. E.g., "Your offspring will be like the dust, and you [2ms] will spread out in all directions" (Gen. 28:14).

4. One ancient version (Aramaic Targum) and several modern translations (e.g., JPS, TEV, CEV, NET) take these singular forms in a collective sense: "They will attack you/your descendants on your heads, but you/your descendants will attack them on their heels." Other examples of singular pronouns and verbs used with collective singular antecedents appear in the Hebrew Scriptures (e.g., Gen. 16:10; 22:17; 24:60). Other examples of 2ms and 3ms pronouns used as a synecdoche for future descendants appear in the Old Testament (Gen. 28:13–14; 48:4, 19; Isa. 54:3). Elsewhere, a singular verb is used to match the singular term "seed," but the collective function is in view. For example, "Your descendants (lit. your seed) will possess the gate of their (lit. his) enemies" (Gen. 22:18), may be compared with, "May you. . . become the mother of thousands of ten thousands, and may your descendants (lit. your seed) possess the gate of their (lit. his) enemies "

applies to other humans—or an ideal singular descendant of the woman—as more of the story unfolds.

Nature of the Mutual Hostility

God decrees hostility between the woman and the serpent that would extend through all generations. The term "enmity" (אֵיבָה) refers to long-term hostility between mortal enemies (e.g., Num. 35:21–22; Ezek. 25:15; 35:5). Verse 15 envisions multi-generational conflict.[5] This multi-generational sense is conveyed by the expression, "between you and between the woman, between your offspring and between her offspring."[6] That there is ultimate eschatological triumph out of this conflict is not yet revealed, but comes later in the revelation of the full story line in the Second Testament.

The Hebrew grammatical structure of verse 15 indicates the stress on an ongoing mutually potentially fatal struggle between man and beast, not the defeat of either adversary. First, if the serpent's defeat was being portrayed, it is odd that the putative description of his destruction comes first. If he already had been fatally crushed by the woman's seed (v. 15ba), how could he yet bruise his heel (v. 15bb)? Second, the idea that the serpent only would deliver a crippling bite, but the seed would deliver a fatal blow does not represent the actual wording. The verb, שׁוּף "to strike, bruise" (*HALOT* 1446), is repeated in both lines: "He will *strike* (שׁוּף) you on the head, and you will *strike* (שׁוּף) him on the heel." This repetition of שׁוּף depicts a potentially fatal conflict with no victor. Just as humans would inflict fatal wounds by striking the heads of vipers, so also poisonous snakes would inflict fatal wounds by striking the heels of humans. Third, the different points of attack, "head" and "heel," need not suggest the human will gain the upper hand. In a primordial setting, the man's most natural attack would aim at the snake's head; and the snake would aim at a man's foot.[7] Fourth, the two verbs (imperfect forms of שׁוּף) function in an iterative sense, depicting repeated attacks between mankind and the serpent race.[8] Thus, a careful analysis of the near contextual emphasis in Genesis 3:15 does not result in a clear exclusive prophecy of Messiah's ultimate victory over Satan; rather, the divine judgment inaugurates the perpetual struggle between humanity and evil, personified in the serpent,

---

(Gen. 24:60). In several places, second and third person singular pronouns ("you" and "he") refer to future descendants (plural) (e.g., Gen. 28:13–14; 48:4, 19; Isa. 54:3).

5. For example, Franz Delitzsch, *The First Book of Moses* (reprint, Grand Rapids: Eerdmans, 1978), 100; Gordon Wenham, *Genesis 1–15*, WBC (Waco: Word, 1987), 79.

6. The tightest parallel is in the covenant-making oath uttered by Jonathan to David, "[May the LORD be] between you and between me, between my offspring and between your offspring forever" (1 Sam. 20:42).

7. Sigmund Mowinckel, *He That Cometh* (Oxford: Blackwell, 1956), 11.

8. Wenham, *Genesis 1–15*, 79.

the stereotypical figure of cosmic chaos. How that struggle is resolved comes later, giving this passage an even more profound message.

In noting how the messianic interpretation emerges more explicitly later is not to say a potential messianic meaning was absent initially. It simply indicates that the emergence of the solution to the conflict introduced here becomes more clear over time and then links back to this passage as a result of further revelation. For those who see a direct or exclusively, direct messianic prediction, this development can be difficult to see since the conclusion of where the passage is heading has already been made in their minds. We argue that it is made in part because of what the rest of Scripture shows about this promise. So it is there, but how it emerges is what is up for discussion.

CANONICAL READING: INNER-BIBLICAL DEVELOPMENT

The reading just presented is supported by how the rest of the First Testament handles this imagery. In the rest of the Hebrew Bible we find no hint of an explicit messianic interpretation of Genesis 3:15. Rather, the later inner-biblical development anticipates the future eschatological reversal of the curse presented in Genesis 3:15. It does so in part by adding a new line of discussion about a seed, that is, the seed from Abraham that passes through David and ultimately into a single figure of deliverance. It also does so through the general theme of eschatological deliverance that resolves and reverses the conflict portrayed in Genesis 3:15.

The only clear allusion to Genesis 3:14–19 in the First Testament occurs in Isaiah 65:17–25. It reverses all the curses of the Old Garden in the New Jerusalem: (1) men will no longer toil in vain (v. 23; cf. Gen. 3:17); (2) women will no longer give birth in pain to children borne to calamity (v. 23; cf. Gen. 3:16–17); (3) the woman's seed will be blessed, not cursed (v. 23; cf. Gen. 3:14–15); (4) serpents will no longer attack the woman's offspring but will be content to crawl on the ground (v. 25; cf. Gen. 3:14; also Isa. 11:8). Counterintuitive to an exclusively messianic expectation, the woman's "seed" (singular) is explicitly identified collectively as the redeemed people (plural) of God: "*they* (plural: הֵמָּה) will be the *seed* (collective singular: זֶרַע) blessed by Yahweh, along with *their descendants* (plural: וְצֶאֱצָאֵיהֶם)" (Isa. 65:23b). These factors suggest our contextual reading is the one Isaiah himself adopts. Isaiah does not identify the woman's seed as the eschatological Messiah; however, this does not mean he lacks a redeemer. Isaiah's implied agent of redemption is not the Messianic seed of the woman, but the Servant of Yahweh (Isa. 42:1–9; 49:1–13; 50:7–11; 52:13–53:12; 61:1–3), who also has regal characteristics (Isa. 9–11) as we argued in our chapter on Isaiah. This figure emerges in a full canonical understanding as an eschatological agent of deliverance who is messianic. So here is a point of connection, but it is not yet explicit in all its links within Isaiah. His connection is implicit as was the one in Genesis. While Isaiah envisions the eschatological reversal of the curse, we are not yet to the point where we have all the factors that went into seeing the full messianic dimension in Genesis 3:15.

MESSIANIC READING:
SECOND TEMPLE PERIOD JEWISH LITERATURE

The interpretation of Genesis 3 in general, and Genesis 3:15 in particular, was a topic of no little interest during the second temple period of Judaism. Three questions in particular were at the center of discussion: Who was the serpent? Who was the seed of the woman? What was the nature of the conflict between the serpent and her seed?

Identification of the Serpent

The overall interpretation of Genesis 3 is clearly tied to the identification of the serpent. Although the biblical narrator flatly asserted that the serpent was "more clever than any other beast of the field that the Lord God had made" (v. 1), this struck many Jewish interpreters as strange. After all, snakes are not particularly clever. While they can be dangerous to humans, they are hardly known for their intelligence. Furthermore, the snake seems to be more than merely a clever animal intent on leading the first humans astray. Also, it seemed unlikely to many Jewish interpreters that the judgment of Genesis 3:15 merely explained the natural repulsion that humans have toward snakes and the deadly threat that snakes pose. Moreover, how was this hostility between humans and snake greater than that between humans and other wild animals?

Many Jewish interpreters began to identify the snake as Satan (or his agent) or some other devil-like figure in disguise. This explained why this particular snake talked and was smarter than all other creatures and explained God's unusual judgment on the serpent in Genesis 3:15. Thus, God's pronouncement of judgment on the serpent was now interpreted as the inauguration of the perpetual spiritual conflict between Satan and all the physical descendants of the woman, that is, all humanity (e.g., *1 Enoch* 69:6; Apocalypse of Moses 16:4; 17:4; 4 Maccabees 18:7–8; *2 Enoch* 31:4–6; *3 Baruch* 4:8 [Slavonic]; 3 Baruch 9:7 [Greek]; Apocalypse of Sedrach 4:5; Testimony of Truth 47:3–6; Targum Pseudo-Jonathan Gen. 3:6; Wisdom 2:24; cf. Justin Martyr, *Dialogue with Trypho* 103).[9] This interpretive move was a natural one, given the kind of rebellion the snake had advocated.

Messianic Interpretation of Genesis 3:15 in the Versions

While Isaiah 65:17–25 reframed themes connected to Genesis 3:15 in terms of a future eschatological hope, later Jewish interpreters identified the agent of this eschatological redemption as Messiah. For example, Martin suggests the Septuagint rendered the passage in a manner reflecting a Messianic

---

9. Kugel, *Traditions of the Bible*, 98–100.

understanding: "I will put enmity between you and between the woman, between your seed and between her seed; *he* (αὐτόσ) will lay in wait for you on the head and you will lay in wait for *him* (αὐτοῦ) on the heel."[10]

The first clear Messianic interpretation of Genesis 3:15 occurs in the Aramaic translations (Targum Pseudo-Jonathan, Targum Neofiti, Fragmentary Targum, Targum Onkelos). All four Targums interpret this text as victory by the righteous descendants of the woman (faithful remnant of Israel) over Satan in the days of Messiah. For example:

> I will put enmity between you and the woman, and between your sons and her sons. It will come about that when her sons observe the Law and obey the commandments they will aim at you and strike you on your head and kill you. But when they forsake the commandments of the Law, you will aim and bite him on his heel and make him ill. For her sons there will be a remedy, but for you, O Serpent, there will not be a remedy, for they will make appeasement in the end in the day of King Messiah.[11]

It is important to note that although the Targums adopt a messianic interpretation, they do not identify the woman's seed as the Messiah, but as a collective for the woman's descendants. The Targum interprets the conflict between the woman's seed and the serpent as the perpetual battle between good and evil played out in history between Israel and Satan. When Israel obeys Torah, they triumph over the serpent; when Israel disobeys God, the serpent is allowed to afflict them. In the end time, the woman's seed (Israel) will be redeemed through the final atonement in time of the Messiah, pictured here as a royal rather than redemptive figure. The serpent will be defeated by the ultimate triumph of the redeemed remnant, whose eschatological righteousness (obedience to the Law) will crush the head of the serpent once and for all. So this reading is exploring possibilities for how the conflict of Genesis 3:15 is resolved, but there still is something missing. As with other areas we explored in the book, Christ and the revelation tied to him supply the missing pieces.

CHRISTOLOGICAL READING:
SECOND TESTAMENT FULFILLMENT

The Second Testament frequently mentions and alludes to various features of Genesis 3. Some passages refer to Satan as the "serpent," a patent allusion to the tempter in the garden (2 Cor. 11:3; Rev. 12:9, 14, 15; 20:2). Others refer to Satan's temptation and deception of Eve (2 Cor. 11:3; 1 Tim. 2:14),

---

10. R. A. Martin, "The Earliest Messianic Interpretation of Genesis 3:15," *JBL* 84 (1965): 425–27.
11. M. McNamara, *Targum Neofiti 1: Genesis, The Aramaic Bible 1A* (Edinburgh: T&T Clark, 1992), 61.

and the blatant sin and rebellion of Adam (Rom. 5:12–21; 1 Cor. 15:22; 1 Tim. 2:13–4). More central to the concerns of our study are the two passages whose language and imagery allude to Genesis 3:15 (Rom. 16:19–20; Rev. 12:17). In both cases, the serpent-seed conflict in Genesis 3:15 reflects the spiritual battle of Satan versus those who believe in Jesus Christ. In neither case is the seed of the woman in Genesis 3:15 interpreted as direct messianic prophecy of the incarnation of the Son of God or his triumph over the devil through his death and resurrection. The association shows that seed in Genesis 3:15 is seen in a corporate light.

This connection exists in part because of how the "seed" of Galatians 3:16, 29 and 4:4 are resolved in a singular/corporate move from Jesus to believers. The resolution of the conflict with Satan and his underlings (Gal. 4:3) in Galatians comes when God sent his Son, born of a woman with Jesus likely seen as a Second Adam, whose work can represent all humanity (e.g., Rom. 5:12–21). All of this makes Genesis 3:15 implicit but prophetic nonetheless. But other Second Testament texts make this more direct.

Allusion to Genesis 3:15 in Romans 16:19–20
Romans 16:19–20 adopts this corporate approach to the woman's seed: "I pray that you are wise to what is good and guileless as to what is evil, then the God of peace *will crush Satan under your feet*—the grace of our Lord Jesus Christ be with you" (Rom. 16:19–20, RSV). As in the Targums, the woman's seed is not Messiah, but the redeemed under whose feet the Serpent is crushed. Although Paul's interpretive approach is similar to that found in the Targums, there are several striking differences. Whereas the Targums only implicitly identify the serpent as Satan, Paul makes the identification explicit. While Targum Neofiti identifies the victorious seed of the woman as Israelites who obey the Torah, Paul identifies her triumphant offspring as Christians who receive God's grace through Jesus Christ. While Targum Neofiti depicts the serpent being crushed as the faithful of Israel obey the Torah, Paul depicts the serpent being crushed as those who believe in Jesus living in wisdom and without guile. The image of the faithful crushing Satan under their feet as they walk in wisdom and moral purity alludes both to the language of Genesis 3:15, but also to the themes of the pursuit of wisdom and the guile of the devil in the temptation narrative as a whole. Appearing as it does in Romans 16, it assumes that believers have access to the power and victory God had provided through Jesus, something that was the point of Romans 1–8 as a whole. God in Christ is the source of victory and the power believers now share (see John 12:31). In contrast to Adam and Eve who succumbed to the serpent's guile to seek wisdom through disobeying God's commandment, those who believe in Jesus Christ are rescued from the curse and are now empowered to crush the head of Satan as they live in true wisdom without guile.

Romans 16:19–20 reverses the imagery of Genesis 3:1–15. Rather than viewing Genesis 3:15 as a direct messianic prophecy fulfilled in Jesus Christ, Paul develops the original imagery to present a dramatic reversal of the ancient curse through the blessings of redemption. In other words, both curse and redemption are seen as being in the chapter. Of course, the person and work of Christ figures prominently in Paul's reversal of the old curse through the power of the new covenant since he closes his treatment with the benediction, "the grace of our Lord Jesus Christ be with you!" (v. 20). Nevertheless, Paul does not interpret Genesis 3:15 in terms of the *Proto-Evangelion*, for he identifies the "seed of the woman" who crushes Satan under its feet as a collective of the faithful who believe in Jesus Christ and live in moral purity through the Spirit. Still the key that allows this corporate reading in the Second Testament is the central role of Jesus and the attachment followers have to him. In this way, seed of the woman works in a singular-corporate manner as does the seed of Abraham in Galatians 3. What Jesus creates is a new humanity, redeemed and restored that the Second Testament argues is the seed. Jesus is key, but he is not alone in this role.

Allusion to Genesis 3:15 in Revelation 12:17

In the book of Revelation, John alludes to Genesis 3:15 in an apocalyptic vision that pictures the Satanic serpent/dragon engaged in conflict with the spiritual seed of the woman: "The dragon became enraged at the woman and went away to wage war on the remnant of her seed, that is, those who obey God's commandments and hold fast to the testimony about Jesus" (Rev. 12:17). John alludes to three features from Genesis 3:15.

First, John's depiction of Satan as a serpentine figure is consistent with the imagery of the serpent in Genesis 3. Although John uses the moniker, "the dragon," elsewhere in his book the terms "the dragon" and "the serpent" are interchangeable, both standing for Satan (Rev. 12:9; 20:2).[12]

Second, John pictures the dragon waging war against the seed of the woman. The precise identification of the woman in Revelation 12 is debated,

---

12. The description of Leviathan in Isaiah 27:1 as a "dragon" and "serpent" may be compared with two Ugaritic mythological texts that depict Baal smiting Leviathan, likewise described as dragon and serpent: "Was not the dragon vanquished and captured? I destroyed the wriggling serpent, the tyrant with seven heads!" (*CTA* 3 iii 38–39 in John C. Gibson, *Canaanite Myths and Legends* [Edinburgh: T&T Clark, 1978] 50); and "for all that you smote Leviathan the slippery serpent, [and] made an end of the wriggling serpent, the tyrant with seven heads" (*CTA* 5 i 1–3 in Gibson, *Canaanite Myths and Legends*, 68). These two Ugaritic myths depict Leviathan—the dragon and serpent—as the embodiment or personification of cosmic chaos. Isaiah demythologizes this imagery and reapplies it to depict Yahweh's eschatological victory over the power of cosmic chaos, which Christians traditionally identify as Satan. Similar apocalyptic imagery of four beasts emerging from the chaotic sea appears in Daniel 7. In the book of Revelation, John depicts Satan in 12:9 and 20:2 as both dragon and serpent—the embodiment of cosmic chaos, and in chapter 13 he pictures a satanic seven-headed dragon (cf. Isa. 27:1; Ps. 74:14) coming up from the sea.

but there is no question about the identity of "the remnant of her seed," since this collective group is identified by the appositional expression, "those who obey God's commandments and hold fast to the testimony about Jesus." John's picture of the serpent attacking the woman's seed is a patent allusion to Genesis 3:15. This is supported by the fact that the expression, "her seed" (τοῦ σπέρματος αὐτῆσ), appears in the Second Testament only in Revelation 12:17 and in the translated Hebrew Scriptures (LXX) only in Genesis 3:15.

While Revelation 12:17 alludes to Genesis 3:15, John's apocalyptic imagery does not represent the complete, future eschatological fulfillment of Genesis 3:15. The picture represents a theological extension of the original imagery. The original oracle of doom in Genesis 3:15 pictures the perpetual spiritual conflict between the serpent and all humanity (the future physical descendants of the woman). However, John narrows the referent to "the remnant of her seed," that is, the believing seed of the woman (the faithful) in distinction from her physical seed as a whole (all humanity). Furthermore, whereas the serpent in Genesis 3 is pictured in long-term spiritual conflict against all of the woman's future physical descendants, the dragon in Revelation 12 wages an unusually aggressive war against her spiritual descendants. Although many of the woman's spiritual seed would be martyred for their commitment to obey the commandments of God and holding fast to their faith in Jesus Christ (e.g., Rev. 13:7, 10; 14:12), their ultimate victory over the serpent would be wrought by God's intervention in judging the serpent and resurrecting them from the dead to reign with Christ (Rev. 20:1–6). Of course, the roots of the victory come as a result of the work of Jesus, as the praise in Revelation 4–5 makes clear and because as judge he will vindicate them in the end. So this text works in a similar way to Romans 16 moving from an assumption of Jesus' work to the power and enablement for success that believers have as a result of his work and their having drawn up it.

As was the case with Romans 16:19–20, John alludes to Genesis 3:15, but his reworking of this First Testament text does not produce merely the traditional *Proto-Evangelion*. It says even more. Both Paul and John present a theological reversal of the perpetual spiritual conflict between the serpent and the physical seed of the woman, depicting the spiritual seed of the woman (the faithful who believe in Jesus Christ and live in obedience to God) as engaged in conflict with Satan but ultimately triumphing over him through Christ's redemptive work and God's eschatological judgment. So while Genesis 3:15 originally portrayed the mess into which humanity was plunged as a result of the sin, the Second Testament presents a reversal and the solution to this problem, extending even beyond Jesus, while including him, to a corporate seed. Although the physical seed of the woman is engaged in a perpetual spiritual struggle against the serpent, her spiritual seed will eventually triumph through the person and work of Christ.

It might be something of a surprise to see that the Second Testament never explicitly interprets Genesis 3:15 along the lines of the traditional *Proto-Evangelion*. Nevertheless, the apostles Paul and John both utilize the original imagery of Genesis 3:15 to portray in dramatic reversal a victory that is the result of the redemptive work of Jesus Christ. In this use, Genesis 3:15 is seen prophetically through an implicit development that allows a "both/and" reading as discussing the curse and its ultimate resolution in an implicit prophecy fulfillment.

CHRISTOCENTERIC READING: THE PROTO-EVANGELION

The Christocentric interpretation of Genesis 3:15, known as the *Proto-Evangelion* enjoys a long tradition among Christian interpreters.[13] In this approach, the passage announces the Messiah's incarnation and eventual victory over Satan. Although the woman's initial offspring was Cain and Abel (Gen. 4:1–2), then the whole human race (Gen. 5:1–2), her ultimate descendant is the Messiah (Gal. 3:16; 4:4). The serpent is none other than Satan (Rom. 16:20; Rev. 12:9; 20:2). The serpent's seed are those in the kingdom of darkness, both demons and rebellious humans (John 8:44). Although the Serpent delivered a crippling blow to the woman's seed in his death on the cross, Jesus crushed Satan's head when he rose from the dead (1 Cor. 15:55–57; Col. 2:15) and destroys him in the future judgment (Rev. 12:7–9; 20:7–10).

The earliest known advocates of this view were the early church fathers, Justin (ca. 160 CE) and Irenaeus (ca. 180 CE).[14] This approach was articulated capably in the nineteenth century by Charles Briggs, Franz Delitzsch, and E. W. Hengstenberg.[15] It continues to find support among many contemporary Christian interpreters.[16]

---

13. For a succinct history of the interpretation of Genesis 3:15, see Jack P. Lewis, "The Woman's Seed (Gen. 3:15)," *JETS* 34 (1991): 299–319.

14. *Irenaeus, Adversus Haereses*, 5:21, Library of Christian Classics (Philadelphia: Westminster Press, 1953), 390–91. See Bateman's discussion concerning Justin Martyr in chapter 8 (pp. 211–13).

15. Charles A. Briggs, *Messianic Prophecy* (New York: Charles Scribner's Sons, 1886), 73; Franz Delitzsch, *Messianische Weissagungen* (1890), 23–28; E. W. Hengstenberg, *Christology of the Old Testament and a Commentary on the Messianic Prophecies* (reprint edition, Grand Rapids: Kregel, 1956), 1:14–30.

16. Walter C. Kaiser Jr., *Toward an Old Testament Theology* (Grand Rapids: Zondervan, 1978), 35–37, 77–79; idem, *The Messiah in the Old Testament* (Grand Rapids: Zondervan, 1995), 37–42; William Dyrness, *Themes in Old Testament Theology* (Downers Grove: InterVarsity, 1979), 116; T. Desmond Alexander, "Messianic Ideology in the Book of Genesis," in *The Lord's Anointed: Interpretation of Old Testament Messianic Texts* (ed. Philip E. Satterthwaite, Richard S. Hess, and Gordon J. Wenham; Grand Rapids: Baker, 1995), 19–39; idem, "Further Observations on the Term 'Seed' in Genesis," *TynBull* 48:2 (1997): 363–67; John Sailhamer, "The Messiah and the Hebrew Bible," *JETS* 44 (2001): 5–23; Daniel I. Block, "My Servant David: Ancient Israel's Vision of the Messiah," in *Israel's Messiah in the Bible and the Dead Sea Scrolls* (ed. Richard S. Hess and M. Daniel Carroll R.; Grand Rapids: Baker, 2003), 56 [17–56]; Ronald Bishop, "The Protoevangelium," *BI*

Some of its more capable advocates, such as Gordon Wenham and Victor Hamilton, appeal to *sensus plenior* to reconcile the original historical contextual meaning of Genesis 3:15 with its ultimate christological fulfillment.[17] Of course, this appeal to *sensus plenior* to reconcile the tension between the original contextual meaning and the ultimate christological fulfillment is the reason many scholars question the notion that Genesis 3:15 was the first *direct* prophecy of Christ in Scripture.[18] The problem with *sensus plenior* has been that it is a label that describes what is going on without explaining how it works. It is simply a "fuller meaning." Our appendix has tried to explain how the passage works as implicit fulfillment, explaining why we are among those who see a prophetic element in Genesis 3:15.

Nevertheless, this kind of christological reading of Genesis 3:15 seems to be a legitimate way to unpack God's plan of redemption since the Christian can see from the start where the rest of the Scriptures are heading. First, it affirms that the Son of God's incarnation and mission was to secure the redemption of the woman's faithful seed, the centerpiece of God's hidden plan of redemption from the beginning. Second, it harmonizes with the Second Testament proclamation that God's plan of redemption through the "seed" who was Messiah. This reading became clear in Jesus Christ through whom the full messianic significance of First Testament prophecy could now be understood, though blessing and seed where introduced as the solution as early as the promise of a seed to bless the world made to Abraham. Third, this kind of approach to Genesis 3:15 simply qualifies as a vivid example of gradually unpacking the full messianic significance out of texts within the Hebrew Scriptures, an unpacking that requires more than Genesis to be seen and appropriately moves us beyond the initial historical context.[19]

---

14 (Fall 1987): 28–29; Gilmore H. Guyot, "Messianism in the Book of Genesis," *CBQ* 13 (1951): 415–16 [415–21].

17. Gordon Wenham, *Genesis 1–15*, WBC (Waco: Word, 1987), 81; Victor Hamilton, *Genesis 1–17*, NICOT (Grand Rapids: Eerdmans, 1990), 200 n. 20, notes his dependence on W. S. LaSor, "Prophecy, Inspiration, and *Sensus Plenior*," *TynBull* 29 (1978): 56–57 [49–60].

18. For example, Hermann Gunkel, *Genesis* (reprint ed.; Göttingen: Vandenhoeck & Ruprecht, 1977), 21; John Skinner, *A Critical and Exegetical Commentary on Genesis* (Edinburgh: T&T Clark, 1930), 80–81; E. A. Speiser, *Genesis* (New York: Doubleday, 1969), 24; Gerhard von Rad, *Genesis* (London: SCM Press, 1972), 93; Bruce Vawter, *On Genesis: A New Reading* (Garden City, NY: Doubleday, 1977), 83–84; Claus Westermann, *Genesis 1–11* (London: SPCK, 1984), 260–61.

19. For discussion of the use of the Old Testament in the Second Testament, see Kenneth Berding and Jonathan Lunde, eds., *Three Views on the New Testament Use of the Old Testament* (Grand Rapids: Zondervan, 2008); Richard N. Longenecker, *Biblical Exegesis in the Apostolic Period*, 2nd ed. (Grand Rapids: Eerdmans, 1999); G. K. Beale, ed., *The Right Doctrine from the Wrong Texts? Essays on the Use of the Old Testament in the New* (Grand Rapids: Baker Academic, 1994).

INDEX OF CHARTS, ILLUSTRATIONS, MAPS, AND SIDEBARS

PERSON AND SUBJECT INDEX

ANCIENT SOURCES INDEX

SCRIPTURE INDEX

2:64	227	9:34	44
3:1–13	191	10:15	155
3:8–13	192, 256	11:2	155
4:1–3	225	12:4	155
4:1–24	191, 227	13:18	155
4:4	225	14:8	149
5:1–2	191	15:14	155
5:3–6:22	227	15:15	186
5:12	123	16:10	155
5:13–16	227	16:11	155
5:14	227	16:18–22	155
5:18	225	16–19	155
6:3–5	256	16:21	185
6:6–12	192, 256	17:1	155, 159
6:12–15	191	17:2–9	155
6:15–18	192, 256	17:8	155
		17:10–16	155
Nehemiah		19:1–6	155
2:6	86	19:6	155
3:7	62	19:13–22	155
9:7–8	40	19:23–29	155
9:28	54	21:9	44
12:4	256	22:3	155
12:10–16	256	25:4	155
12:12	256	27:1–6	155
12:16	256	27:5	155
		27:6	155
Esther		27:8	159
5:9	162	29:8	162
		30:1–15	155
Job		31:6	155
1:6	303	31:26	161
1:6–12	461, 462	31:35	155
1:21	125	31:36	196
2:1	303	32:2	155
2:1–7	461, 462	33:30	161
2:9	462	34:5	155
3:16	161	35:2	155
3:20	161	36:7	155
3:20–26	155	37:13	44
4:17	155	37:21	161
5:1	186	38:29	79
6:8–13	155	41:17	143
6:9	158	42:7–17	155
6:14–21	155	42:9–12	155
6:24–30	155	42:10	155
6:29	155	42:13–15	156
8:3	155	42:16	160
9:1–10:17	155	42:16–17	156, 160
9:15	155		
9:20	155		